T0212575

Lecture Notes in Computer Science   10266

Commenced Publication in 1973
Founding and Former Series Editors:
Gerhard Goos, Juris Hartmanis, and Jan van Leeuwen

Editorial Board

David Hutchison
  Lancaster University, Lancaster, UK
Takeo Kanade
  Carnegie Mellon University, Pittsburgh, PA, USA
Josef Kittler
  University of Surrey, Guildford, UK
Jon M. Kleinberg
  Cornell University, Ithaca, NY, USA
Friedemann Mattern
  ETH Zurich, Zurich, Switzerland
John C. Mitchell
  Stanford University, Stanford, CA, USA
Moni Naor
  Weizmann Institute of Science, Rehovot, Israel
C. Pandu Rangan
  Indian Institute of Technology, Madras, India
Bernhard Steffen
  TU Dortmund University, Dortmund, Germany
Demetri Terzopoulos
  University of California, Los Angeles, CA, USA
Doug Tygar
  University of California, Berkeley, CA, USA
Gerhard Weikum
  Max Planck Institute for Informatics, Saarbrücken, Germany

More information about this series at http://www.springer.com/series/7407

Julian M. Kunkel · Rio Yokota
Pavan Balaji · David Keyes (Eds.)

High Performance Computing

32nd International Conference, ISC High Performance 2017
Frankfurt, Germany, June 18–22, 2017
Proceedings

 Springer

Editors
Julian M. Kunkel
Deutsches Klimarechenzentrum (DKRZ)
Hamburg
Germany

Rio Yokota
Tokyo Institute of Technology
Tokyo
Japan

Pavan Balaji
Argonne National Laboratory
Argonne, IL
USA

David Keyes
KAUST
Thuwal
Saudi Arabia

ISSN 0302-9743   ISSN 1611-3349 (electronic)
Lecture Notes in Computer Science
ISBN 978-3-319-58666-3   ISBN 978-3-319-58667-0 (eBook)
DOI 10.1007/978-3-319-58667-0

Library of Congress Control Number: 2017939120

LNCS Sublibrary: SL1 – Theoretical Computer Science and General Issues

© Springer International Publishing AG 2017
This work is subject to copyright. All rights are reserved by the Publisher, whether the whole or part of the material is concerned, specifically the rights of translation, reprinting, reuse of illustrations, recitation, broadcasting, reproduction on microfilms or in any other physical way, and transmission or information storage and retrieval, electronic adaptation, computer software, or by similar or dissimilar methodology now known or hereafter developed.
The use of general descriptive names, registered names, trademarks, service marks, etc. in this publication does not imply, even in the absence of a specific statement, that such names are exempt from the relevant protective laws and regulations and therefore free for general use.
The publisher, the authors and the editors are safe to assume that the advice and information in this book are believed to be true and accurate at the date of publication. Neither the publisher nor the authors or the editors give a warranty, express or implied, with respect to the material contained herein or for any errors or omissions that may have been made. The publisher remains neutral with regard to jurisdictional claims in published maps and institutional affiliations.

Printed on acid-free paper

This Springer imprint is published by Springer Nature
The registered company is Springer International Publishing AG
The registered company address is: Gewerbestrasse 11, 6330 Cham, Switzerland

Preface

ISC High Performance, formerly known as the International Supercomputing Conference, was founded in 1986 as the Supercomputer Seminar. Originally organized by Hans Meuer, Professor of Computer Science at the University of Mannheim and former director of the computer center, the seminar brought together a group of 81 scientists and industrial partners who all shared an interest in high-performance computing (HPC). Since then the annual conference has become a major international event within the HPC community, and accompanying its growth in size over the years, the conference has moved from Mannheim via Heidelberg, Dresden, Hamburg, and Leipzig to Frankfurt. With over 3,000 attendees in 2016, we were happy to see that this steady growth of interest also turned ISC High Performance 2017 into a powerful and memorable event.

In 2007, we decided to strengthen the scientific part of the conference by presenting selected talks on relevant research results within the HPC field. These research paper sessions began as a separate day preceding the conference, where slides and accompanying papers were made available via the conference website. The research paper sessions have since evolved into an integral part of the conference, and this year the scientific presentations took place over a period of three days.

For the past several years, the ISC High Performance conference has presented an ISC-sponsored award to encourage outstanding research in HPC and to honor the overall best research paper submitted to the conference. Two years ago, this annual award was renamed as the Hans Meuer Award in memory of the late Dr. Hans Meuer, general chair of the ISC conference from 1986 through 2014, and co-founder of the TOP500 project. From all research papers submitted, the Research Papers Program Committee nominated the two papers with the highest review scores as finalists for the award and, based on the final presentations during the conference, elected the best paper.

For ISC High Performance 2017, the call for participation was issued in Fall 2016, inviting researchers and developers to submit the latest results of their work to the Program Committee. In all, 66 papers were submitted from authors all over the world. This year, too, a significant effort was made to improve the overall process. The Research Papers Program committee consisted of 52 members selected from several countries throughout the world. Furthermore, 23 external expert reviewers were invited from the community to help with paper reviews of specific topics. After initial reviews were in place, a rebuttal process was organized in which authors were given an opportunity to respond to reviewers' questions and help clarify issues the reviewers might have. To come to a final consensus on the papers to be accepted, we had a face-to-face meeting where each paper was discussed. Finally, the committee selected 22 papers for publication and for presentation in the research paper sessions.

We are pleased to announce that many fascinating topics in HPC are covered by the proceedings. The papers address the following issues in regards to the development of an environment for exascale supercomputers:

- Cost-efficient data centers
- Scalable applications
- Advancements in algorithms
- Scientific libraries
- Programming models
- Architectures
- Performance models and analysis
- Automatic performance optimization
- Parallel I/O
- Energy efficiency

We believe that this selection is highly appealing across a number of specializations. Two award committees selected papers considered to be of exceptional quality and worthy of special recognition:

- The Hans Meuer Award honors the overall best research paper submitted to the conference. The two finalists for this award were:
  "Designing Dynamic and Adaptive MPI Point-to-point Communication Protocols for Efficient Overlap of Computation and Communication" by Sourav Chakraborty, Hari Subramoni, and Dhabaleswar Panda.
  "An Overview of MPI Characteristics of Exascale Proxy Applications" by Benjamin Klenk and Holger Fröning.
- The Gauss Centre for Supercomputing sponsors the Gauss Award. This award is assigned to the most outstanding paper in the field of scalable supercomputing and went to:
  "Diagnosing Performance Variations in HPC Applications Using Machine Learning" by Ozan Tuncer, Emre Ates, Yijia Zhang, Ata Turk, Jim Brandt, Vitus J. Leung, and Manuel Egele.

We would like to express our gratitude to all our colleagues for submitting papers to the ISC scientific sessions, as well as to the members of the Program Committee for organizing this year's attractive program.

June 2016

Julian M. Kunkel
Rio Yokota
Pavan Balaji
David Keyes

Organization

Research Papers Program Committee

Research Paper Chair and Deputy Chair

Pavan Balaji   Argonne National Laboratory, USA
David Keyes   KAUST, Saudi Arabia

Architectures and Networks

Hans Eberle   NVIDIA, USA
Holger Fröning   University of Heidelberg, Germany
Pedro Garcia   University of Castilla-La Mancha, Spain
Wolfgang Karl   Karlsruhe Institute of Technology, Germany
Sébastien Rumley   Columbia University, USA
Federico Silla   Technical University of Valencia, Spain
Tor Skeie   Simula Labs and University of Oslo, Norway
Carsten Trinitis   TU München, Germany
Peter Ziegenhein   Institute of Cancer Research, UK

Applications and Algorithms

Ilkay Altintas   San Diego Supercomputing Center, USA
Yuefan Deng   Stony Brook University, USA
Vassil Dimitrov   University of Calgary, Canada
Jacek Kitowski   AGH University of Science and Technology, Poland
Scott Klasky   Oak Ridge National Laboratory, USA
Axel Klawonn   Universität zu Köln, Germany
Marek Michalewicz   ICM, University of Warsaw, Poland
Gabriel Noaje   HPE-SGI, Singapore
Lena Oden   Argonne National Laboratory, USA
Ulrich Rüde   Friedrich-Alexander University of Erlangen-Nuremberg,
                        Germany
Sven-Bodo Scholz   Heriot-Watt University Edinburgh, UK
Thomas Sterling   Indiana University, USA
Antonio Tumeo   Pacific Northwest National Laboratory, USA
Marian Vajtersic   University of Salzburg, Austria
Ana Lucia Varbanescu   University of Amsterdam, The Netherlands
Priya Vashishta   University of Southern California, USA

Data, Storage and Visualization

Thomas Bönisch   High Performance Computing Center Stuttgart, Germany
Mahdi Bohlouli   University of Siegen, Germany

Luc Bougé	ENS Rennes, France
André Brinkmann	Johannes Gutenberg-Universität Mainz, Germany
Matthieu Dorier	Argonne National Laboratory, USA
Steffen Frey	University of Stuttgart, Germany
Dean Hildebrand	IBM, USA
Hideyuki Kawashima	University of Tsukuba, Japan
Jay Lofstead	Sandia National Laboratory, USA
Kathryn Mohror	Lawrence Livermore National Laboratory, USA
Maria S. Perez	Universidad Politecnica de Madrid, Spain
Judy Qiu	Indiana University, USA
Shinji Sumimoto	Fujitsu, Japan
Ryousei Takano	AIST, Japan
Osamu Tatebe	University of Tsukuba, Japan

Programming Models and Systems Software

Abdelhalim Amer	Argonne National Laboratory, USA
Sunita Chandrasekaran	University of Delaware, USA
Adrian Jackson	EPCC, UK
Guido Juckeland	HZDR, Germany
Michael Klemm	Intel, Germany
Arthur Barney Maccabe	Oak Ridge National Laboratory, USA
Naoya Maruyama	RIKEN AICS, Japan
Simon McIntosh-Smith	University of Bristol, UK
C.J. Newburn	NVIDIA, USA
Will Sawyer	CSCS, Switzerland
Sangmin Seo	Argonne National Laboratory, USA
Martin Schulz	Lawrence Livermore National Laboratory, USA
Michela Taufer	University of Delaware, USA
Christian Terboven	RWTH Aachen University, Germany
Sandra Wienke	RWTH Aachen University, Germany

PHD Forum Program Committee

Florina Ciorba	University of Basel, Switzerland
Anshu Dubey	Argonne National Laboratory, USA
Anne Elster	Norwegian University of Science and Technology, Norway
Fernanda Foertter	Oak Ridge National Laboratory, USA
William Gropp	University of Illinois at Urbana-Champaign, USA (Chair)
Paul Kelly	Imperial College London, UK
Lois Curfman McInnes	Argonne National Laboratory, USA
Miriam Mehl	Universität Stuttgart, Germany
Kengo Nakajima	University of Tokyo, Japan
Boyana Norris	University of Oregon, USA
Amanda Randles	Duke University, USA

Olaf Schenk	Università della Svizzera Italiana, Switzerland
Ana Lucia Varbanescu	University of Amsterdam, The Netherlands
Richard Vuduc	Georgia Institute of Technology, USA
Gerhard Wellein	Friedrich-Alexander University Erlangen-Nuremberg, Germany (Deputy Chair)
Felix Wolf	Technische Universität Darmstadt, Germany
Roman Wyrzykowski	Czestochowa University of Technology, Poland

Research Posters Program Committee

Alvaro Aguilera	Technische Universität Dresden, Germany
Thomas Bönisch	High Performance Computing Center Stuttgart, Germany
Sunita Chandrasekaran	University of Delaware, USA
Andy Herdman	AWE, UK
Julian Kunkel	Deutsches Klimarechenzentrum, Germany
Simon McIntosh-Smith	University of Bristol, UK
Jaejin Lee	Seoul National University, South Korea
Marek Michalewicz	ICM, University of Warsaw, Poland
Matthias Müller	RWTH Aachen University, Germany (Deputy Chair)
Neil Stringfellow	iVEC, Australia
Jeffrey Vetter	Oak Ridge National Laboratory, USA (Chair)
Vladimir Voevodin	Moscow State University, Russia
Rich Vuduc	Georgia Institute of Technology, USA

Project Posters Program Committee

Alvaro Aguilera	Technische Universität Dresden, Germany
Yevhen Alforov	Deutsches Klimarechenzentrum, Germany
Eugen Betke	Deutsches Klimarechenzentrum, Germany
Ramaswamy Govindarajan	SERC, India
David Ham	Imperial College London, UK
Weicheng Huang	National Center for High-Performance Computing, Taiwan
Nabeeh Jumah	University of Hamburg, Germany
Oleksiy Koshulko	Glushkov Institute of Cybernetics of NASU, Russia
Michael Kuhn	University of Hamburg, Germany
Julian Kunkel	Deutsches Klimarechenzentrum, Germany (Chair)
Fang-Pang Lin	National Center for High-Performance Computing, Taiwan
Jakob Lüttgau	Deutsches Klimarechenzentrum, Germany
Anastasiia Novikova	University of Hamburg, Germany
Yuichi Tsujita	RIKEN AICS, Japan
Ying Qian	East China Normal University, China
Rio Yokota	Tokyo Institute of Technology, Japan

Tutorials Committee

Rosa M. Badia	Barcelona Supercomputing Center, Spain (Deputy Chair)
Pavan Balaji	Argonne National Laboratory, USA
James Dinan	Intel, USA
Adrian Jackson	EPCC, The University of Edinburgh, UK
Alice Koniges	Lawrence Berkeley National Laboratory, USA
Erwin Laure	Royal Institute of Technology, Sweden
Christian Perez	Inria, France
Enrique Quintana	Universidad Jaime I, Spain
Adrian Tate	Cray, USA
Michèle Weiland	EPCC, The University of Edinburgh, UK (Chair)

BoFs Committee

David Bader	Georgia Institute of Technology, USA
Toni Collis	EPCC, University of Edinburgh, UK
Dona Crawford	Lawrence Livermore National Laboratory, USA (Chair)
Ewa Deelman	University of Southern California, USA
Alba Dieguez Alonso	Technische Universität Berlin, Germany
Fernanda Foertter	Oak Ridge National Laboratory, USA
Horst Gietl	ISC Group, Germany
Gerard Gorman	Imperial College London, UK
Georg Hager	University Erlangen-Nuremberg, Germany (Deputy Chair)
Peter Kogge	University of Notre Dame, USA
Bernd Mohr	Jülich Supercomputing Centre, Germany
Kathryn Mohror	Lawrence Livermore National Laboratory, USA
Kengo Nakajima	University of Tokyo, Japan
Marie-Christine Sawley	Intel, France
Martin Schulz	Lawrence Livermore National Laboratory, USA
Happy Sithole	Centre for High Performance Computing, South Africa
Vladimir Voevodin	Moscow State University, Russia
Heike Walther	ISC Group, Germany
Jan Wender	science+computing, Germany
Andreas Wierse	SICOS BW, Germany
Roman Wyrzykowski	Czestochowa University of Technology, Poland

Workshop Committee

Rosa M. Badia	Barcelona Supercomputing Center, Spain
François Bodin	IRISA, France
Bronis R. de Supinski	Lawrence Livermore National Laboratory, USA
Jay Lofstead	Sandia National Laboratories, USA
Naoya Maruyama	RIKEN, Japan
Simon McIntosh-Smith	University of Bristol, UK
Bernd Mohr	Jülich Supercomputing Centre, Germany

Marie-Christine Sawley	Intel, France
Seetharami Seelam	IBM T.J. Watson Research Center, USA
John Shalf	Lawrence Berkeley National Laboratory, USA (Deputy Chair)
Michela Taufer	University of Delaware, USA (Chair)
Carsten Trinitis	Technische Universität München, Germany
Antonino Tumeo	Pacific Northwest National Laboratory, USA
Didem Unat	Koç Universitesi, Turkey
Rio Yokota	Tokyo Institute of Technology, Japan

Contents

Proxy Applications

Architecture and System Optimization

Energy-Aware Computing

Applications and Algorithms

Fully Resolved Simulations of Dune Formation in Riverbeds

Christoph Rettinger[1]([✉]) [iD], Christian Godenschwager[1] [iD], Sebastian Eibl[1] [iD], Tobias Preclik[1], Tobias Schruff[2] [iD], Roy Frings[2], and Ulrich Rüde[1] [iD]

[1] Chair for System Simulation, Friedrich-Alexander-Universität Erlangen-Nürnberg, Cauerstraße 11, 91058 Erlangen, Germany
christoph.rettinger@fau.de
[2] Institute of Hydraulic Engineering and Water Resources Management, RWTH Aachen University, Mies-van-der-Rohe-Straße 17, 52056 Aachen, Germany

Abstract. The formation and dynamics of dunes is an important phenomenon that occurs in many environmental systems, such as riverbeds. The physical interactions are complex and thus evaluating and quantifying the factors of influence is challenging. Simulation models can be used to conduct large scale parameter studies and allow a more detailed analysis of the system than laboratory experiments. Here, we present new coupled numerical models for sediment transport that are based on first principles. The lattice Boltzmann method is used in combination with a non-smooth granular dynamics model to simulate the fluid flow and the sediment particles. Numerical predictions of dune formation require a fully resolved modeling of the particulate flow which is only achieved by massively parallel simulations. For that purpose, the method employs advanced parallel grid refinement techniques and carefully designed compute kernels. The weak- and strong-scaling behavior is evaluated in detail and shows overall excellent parallel performance and efficiency.

Keywords: High performance computing · Computational fluid dynamics · Particulate flow · Fluid structure interaction · Dune formation · Lattice Boltzmann method · Granular dynamics · Grid refinement

1 Introduction

Sand dunes can be found in many different places on earth, for example in the great deserts of Kalahari, Gobi, Sahara, or at the seashore where sand dunes usually separate the sandy beaches from the hinterland. They are by no means static *topographic features* but their shape changes constantly due to the forces of wind. In fact, depending on their height and volume (some sand dunes have a height of more than 1,000 meters), constant and strong wind can move dunes some tens of meters per year [3]. Large sand dunes have also been found on planet Mars [21], Titan [32], and other planets where strong winds are able to *erode and transport* enormous amounts of sand on the planet surface. But besides wind there is also another universal power that is able to model the shape of planets, and that is *flowing water*.

© Springer International Publishing AG 2017
J.M. Kunkel et al. (Eds.): ISC High Performance 2017, LNCS 10266, pp. 3–21, 2017.
DOI: 10.1007/978-3-319-58667-0_1

Due to its high specific weight, flowing water is able to carry not only sand, but also boulders and gravel, collectively also referred to as *sediment* [7,36,46], for many kilometers; often the whole way from the source of a river to its mouth. On its way down along the path of the river or channel, the sediment grain size decreases, starting with large boulders and gravel at the source and ending up with small silt and clay grains at the mouth [13,15]. Somewhere in between, most sediment grains have the size of sand, which is defined to be in the range of 0.063-2.0 mm. If the major part of the sediment mixture is sand, the sediment transport can take place in form of sand dunes that move over the bed [25,28,44].

Those subaqueous dunes can become many meters high depending on the water depth and flow conditions [14,24] and thus act as obstacles to navigation, and their movement can be a threat to submarine structures. River engineers are interested in dunes because they play an important role in determining the sediment transport rate [44], but also because of their importance in quantifying the resistance of a channel to flowing water [41]. For example, predicting the depth of flow in a channel built with a given slope and designed to carry a given water discharge necessitates knowing the bed roughness.

For over one century, engineers have been conducting laboratory experiments on dunes and other bed forms [44,46]. Another famous method was (and still is!) observing and measuring bed form movement in natural flows [9,16,33]. Both methods come with their individual advantages and disadvantages. Despite significant progress in the past 25 years with regard to the understanding of the dynamics and kinematics of alluvial dunes, there are still some important areas where conventional methods have not been able to comprehensively shed light into the complex nature of dunes [6].

This is why engineers, geologists, sedimentologists, and other researchers are increasingly interested in applying high performance computing (HPC) methods to investigate sediment transport and dunes numerically [26,27]. Such approaches are especially helpful to drive the study of dune formation regarding four specific areas: (1) the influence of dune shape on flow turbulence and distribution of bed shear stress, (2) flow field modification resulting from bed form superimposition and amalgamation, (3) the scale and topology of dune-related turbulence and its interactions with sediment transport and the flow surface, and (4) the influence of oscillatory and combined flows, e.g., in marine environments, on dune formation. Simulations have several favorable features in comparison to laboratory experiments. Once set up and validated, they allow for large scale studies where single parameters can be adjusted with ease. By tracing the motion of single particles and analyzing the flow field within the sediment bed, a better insight into the physical processes can be obtained.

However, the challenges for a realistic simulation from first principles, i.e., without introducing empirical model assumptions, are numerous: On the one hand, a large enough setup has to be regarded containing several hundred thousand sediment grains. On the other hand, the developing flow structures have to be numerically fully resolved and this may require that each single sediment grain, their variation in size and shape, must be geometrically resolved. This, in turn, dictates an even finer resolution of the fluid flow, when its interaction with the individual particles must be accounted for. This kind of direct numerical simulation can only be tackled by a combination of efficient numerical algorithms together with the computing power of today's fastest super computers. To fully utilize their capabilities, we employ two coupled software frameworks that offer both, carefully tuned single-node performance and excellent scalability. The WALBERLA framework [18] has been developed for simulating complex flows with the lattice Boltzmann method and has been employed in various application scenarios, such as electron beam melting [2], solidification processes [5], or electro-kinetic flows [4,29]. The physics engine *pe* [23,38] is used to simulate granular dynamics. The flow over fully resolved porous structures has already been simulated in [11,12], however, assuming a fixed and immobile particle bed. The coupling algorithms for moving particles in a massively parallel setting are based on the methods developed in [19,20,40].

Following this work, we will here extend the functionality of WALBERLA and the coupling mechanism with the *pe*. We enable grid refinement for the coupled simulation to reduce computational burden in the computational fluid dynamics code. Additionally, we employ a hard contact solver in the granular dynamics code which eliminates particle overlaps and requires no fine temporal resolution of the contact dynamics. To analyze the central aspect of our parallelization strategy, i.e., the use of a co-partitioning between our two frameworks, we conduct a thorough performance study of this approach in the context of HPC and supercomputers. This extends the work reported in [26,27], where direct numerical simulations were used to study pattern formation of large sediment beds for the first time. We describe the physical background of the application in Sect. 2 which results in an experimental setup well suited for numerical simulations. The applied numerical methods are presented in Sects. 3.1–3.3. Details about their implementation and the parallelization strategy are given in Sect. 4. In Sect. 5, the outcome of a large scale simulation is discussed and both, weak and strong, scaling behaviors are reported. Section 6 concludes the paper with a summary of the main findings and an outlook of future research directions.

2   Physical Background

When studying bed forms produced by unidirectional (steady and uniform) flow of water over a sand bed in a laboratory experiment, it is common to use a flume setup like the one illustrated in Fig. 1. The flume has a rectangular cross section with a width of about one meter and is open at the top. The length of the flume is about a few tens of a meter. It is also possible to adjust the slope of the flume, which is why this kind of setup is called *tilting flume*. The sediment bed in our example consists of medium size sand (0.25–0.5 mm) and is planar at the beginning. The pump controls the mean flow velocity and the slope of the flume is adjusted to obtain a constant mean flow depth.

When continuously increasing the flow velocity for a given setup, different bed forms can be observed as depicted in Fig. 2. Besides dunes, ripples and antidunes

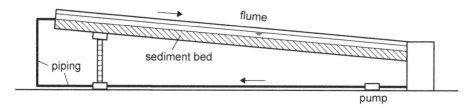

Fig. 1. Laboratory flume for studying bed forms produced by unidirectional flow.

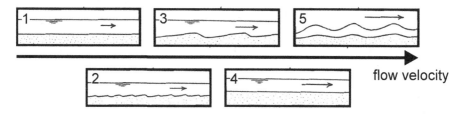

Fig. 2. Evolution of bed forms as a function of flow velocity at a given flow depth and bed material: (1) initial plane bed, (2) ripples, (3) dunes, (4), planar bed, and (5) antidunes.

are other types of bed forms that frequently occur in natural rivers and predicting their formation still remains a challenging task even at laboratory scales. The complexity mainly stems from the large number of influence factors. Apart from the mean flow rate, the sediment size and the flow depth will affect the transition and evolution of bed configurations. Other parameters are the density of the fluid and of the sediment grains, the fluid viscosity, and the gravitational acceleration.

When attempting to simulate such a setup numerically, however, the free flow surface imposes a degree of complexity to the system which can be avoided by slightly changing the setup. Figure 3 illustrates the alternative setup where the flow depth is doubled and the whole flume is covered with a solid plate, parallel to the mean plane of the bed. The flow structure in the lower half of the closed duct is nearly the same as in the original open-channel flow. The sediment

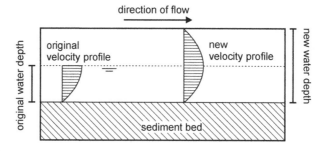

Fig. 3. Schematic setup of numerical flow simulation for the study of dune formation.

dynamics is thus expected to be similar as long as the effect of the free surface can be neglected. This is the case for all bed forms shown in Fig. 2 except for antidunes which necessitate the free surface. The advantage of a setup like this is that the slope of the channel does not need to be adjusted, as the water depth is fixed. This also has a positive effect on the behavior of the sediment bed, as we do not alter the angle at which gravity forces act on grains. From a simulation point of view, the stability is increased as large-scale eddies can now make their way across the center plane of the flow.

The foregoing setup can be used to study the transition between different bed configurations (ripples, dunes, etc.) or how dune height or length are affected by the several parameters (e.g., grain size, water depth, flow velocity, etc.) in numerical simulations.

3 Numerical Methods

3.1 Lattice Boltzmann Method

The lattice Boltzmann method (LBM) [8] is an alternative to conventional computational fluid dynamics (CFD) methods to simulate hydrodynamics, classically described by the Navier-Stokes equations. It originates from statistical mechanics and models the evolution of particle distribution functions (PDFs) on a Cartesian grid. Its high locality, as it requires direct neighbor access only, leads to an outstanding scaling behavior up to the full extent of current peta-scale supercomputers [18,22].

In this work, we apply the *D3Q19* lattice model [39] which features 19 PDFs f_q, $q \in \{0 \ldots 18\}$, where each is associated to a three-dimensional discrete lattice velocity c_q. The computational domain is discretized by cubic lattice cells with cell centers x. Written in a general form, the lattice Boltzmann equation is commonly subdivided into the *collision* step

$$\tilde{f}_q(x) = f_q(x) + \Omega_q(x) + S_q, \tag{1}$$

with the collision operator Ω_q and a source term S_q resulting in the post-collision values $\tilde{f}_q$. Succeeding, the *streaming* of the PDFs to their neighboring lattice cells

$$f'_q(x + c_q) = \tilde{f}_q(x) \tag{2}$$

is carried out to obtain the PDFs at the new time step f'_q.

The collision operator relaxes the PDFs towards their equilibrium values,

$$f_q^{\text{eq}}(\rho_f, u) = w_q \left(\rho_f + \rho_0 \left(3c_q \cdot u + \tfrac{9}{2}(c_q \cdot u)^2 - \tfrac{3}{2}u \cdot u \right) \right). \tag{3}$$

The macroscopic quantities, density $\rho_f = \rho_0 + \delta\rho_f$, with a mean density ρ_0 and a fluctuation $\delta\rho_f$, and fluid velocity u, are obtained as moments of the PDFs in each grid cell. The lattice weights w_q are stated in [39].

In particular, we make use of the TRT collision operator from [17] which splits the PDFs and their equilibrium values into symmetric and anti-symmetric parts:

$$f_q^{\pm} = \tfrac{1}{2}(f_q \pm f_{\bar{q}}), \quad f_q^{\mathrm{eq},\pm} = \tfrac{1}{2}(f_q^{\mathrm{eq}} \pm f_{\bar{q}}^{\mathrm{eq}}), \tag{4}$$

where $\bar{q}$ is the opposite lattice direction of q, such that $\boldsymbol{c}_{\bar{q}} = -\boldsymbol{c}_q$. The collision operator is then given as

$$\Omega_q^{\mathrm{TRT}}(\boldsymbol{x}) = -\tfrac{1}{\tau_+}\big(f_q^{+}(\boldsymbol{x}) - f_q^{\mathrm{eq},+}(\rho_f, \boldsymbol{u})\big) - \tfrac{1}{\tau_-}\big(f_q^{-}(\boldsymbol{x}) - f_q^{\mathrm{eq},-}(\rho_f, \boldsymbol{u})\big). \tag{5}$$

This model features two relaxation times $\tau_+, \tau_- \in (\tfrac{1}{2}; \infty)$, here related via $\left(\tfrac{1}{2} - \tau_+\right)\left(\tfrac{1}{2} - \tau_-\right) = \tfrac{3}{16}$ for improved accuracy [17]. The kinematic viscosity of the fluid can be obtained as $\nu = \tfrac{1}{3}(\tau_+ - \tfrac{1}{2})$.

To incorporate external forcing that can drive the flow, the source term

$$S_q = 3w_q\rho_0\big(\boldsymbol{c}_q - \boldsymbol{u} + 3(\boldsymbol{c}_q \cdot \boldsymbol{u})\boldsymbol{c}_q\big) \cdot \boldsymbol{a} \tag{6}$$

with the external fluid acceleration $\boldsymbol{a}$ has to be added to Eq. (1) [34].

Recently, LBM variants have been proposed that allow non-uniform grids to enable static and adaptive grid refinement. We employ the variant from [42] which adjusts the relaxation parameters on each grid level and executes twice the amount of LBM steps for each finer level.

3.2   Non-smooth Granular Dynamics

In contrast to the field of fluid dynamics, no equations exist that can accurately describe the bulk behavior of granular matter [35]. Thus, to simulate the response of the sediment bed to the fluid flow, we resolve individual grains including their geometric shape. Each particle is described by position $\boldsymbol{X}$, orientation $\boldsymbol{Q}$, translational and rotational velocity $\boldsymbol{V}$ and $\boldsymbol{W}$. The orientation is parameterized by a quaternion. We restrict ourselves to spherical particles meaning each shape can be simply described by its radius. Under the assumption of uniformly distributed mass, the density then determines the particle mass m and moment of inertia I. The Newton-Euler equations for rigid bodies describe the dynamics of the individual particles given forces $\boldsymbol{F}$ and torques $\boldsymbol{T}$. The contact model determines the forces and torques arising from contacts between the grains in addition to external forces and torques $\boldsymbol{F}^{\mathrm{ext}}$ and $\boldsymbol{T}^{\mathrm{ext}}$. With the intention to reproduce the stiffness of the collision micro-dynamics as accurately as possible we choose an inelastic hard contact model, where the particles would not overlap in an exact solution and thus leading to a better representation of the solid volume fraction than the commonly applied discrete element method (DEM). The hard contact model implies that velocity functions are discontinuous and position and orientation functions non-smooth. In order to get around resolving impulsive contact reactions in time, we discretize the continuous system by employing a time-stepping scheme, where we consider integrals of contact reactions $\boldsymbol{\lambda}$ over small time steps δt, which readily include the impulsive and non-impulsive contact reactions [43]. The contact model includes Coulomb friction with a coefficient of friction μ per contact. The time-stepping scheme is based on an integrator of order one resembling the semi-implicit Euler method. In each time step, the following non-linear system of equations is to be solved for each particle and contact, respectively:

$$X' = X + \delta t V' \tag{7}$$

$$Q' = (Q + \delta t M(Q)W') / \|Q + \delta t M(Q)W'\| \tag{8}$$

$$V' = V + \delta t m^{-1} F \tag{9}$$

$$W' = W + \delta t I^{-1} T \tag{10}$$

$$F = \sum_{\mathcal{C}_a} \lambda - \sum_{\mathcal{C}_b} \lambda + F^{\text{ext}} \tag{11}$$

$$T = \sum_{\mathcal{C}_a} (\hat{X} - X_a) \times \lambda - \sum_{\mathcal{C}_b} (\hat{X} - X_b) \times \lambda + T^{\text{ext}} \tag{12}$$

$$\delta V' = V'_a + W'_a \times (\hat{X} - X_a) - V'_b - W'_b \times (\hat{X} - X_b) \tag{13}$$

$$\lambda_n \geq 0 \quad \perp \quad \varepsilon \min(\xi,0)/\delta t + \max(\xi,0)/\delta t + \delta V'_n \geq 0 \tag{14}$$

$$\|\lambda_{to}\| \leq \mu \lambda_n \tag{15}$$

$$\|\delta V'_{to}\| \lambda_{to} = -\mu \delta V'_{to} , \tag{16}$$

where M is the quaternion matrix function, the subscript a (b) identifies the first (second) particle involved in each contact, $\mathcal{C}_a$ ($\mathcal{C}_b$) is the set of contacts whose first (second) particle involved in the contact corresponds to the particle in question, $\hat{X}$ is the point of contact, n is the contact normal pointing from particle b to particle a, and t and o extend the normal to an orthonormal contact frame spanning the tangential plane. ξ is the contact distance and $\varepsilon \in [0;1]$ the error reduction parameter. Equation (14) ensures that contact reactions are repulsive and no penetrations are allowed. The complementarity allows reactions to be non-zero if and only if the contact is closed. Equations (15) and (16) correspond to the conditions imposed by the Coulomb friction. Instead of including all potential collision pairs in the system, a prior contact detection algorithm selects a set of contacts that potentially become active in the current time step and thus reduces the number of constraints to the same order as the number of particles. More details and the extension to non-spherical contact problems can be found in [37, 38].

The system is solved using a blend of a weighted non-linear block Jacobi and a weighted non-linear block Gauss-Seidel with weighting factor $\omega \in (0;1]$. Whether the contact reaction approximation is chosen from the previous iterate or from the current iterate depends on whether the contact is owned by the local process or by a remote process. The parallelization details are described in Sect. 4. The contact constraints of each contact form a block in the relaxation scheme. Since the solver only efficiently removes local errors, the number of iterations is kept low and constant. In order to remove the global error we rely on the error correction term $\varepsilon \min(\xi,0)/\delta t$ in Eq. (14).

3.3   Fluid-Particle Interaction

To incorporate the fluid-solid coupling mechanism that transfers the momentum from the fluid to the particulate phase and vice versa, the LBM-specific

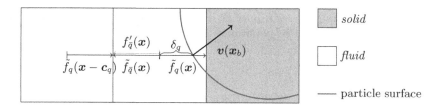

Fig. 4. Sketch of the particle mapping and the boundary treatment according to the CLI boundary scheme from Eq. (17).

momentum exchange method is applied which originates from [30] and was then extended in [1]. The main idea is to explicitly map the particle into the computational domain by marking cells with cell centers inside particles as *solid* in contrast to *fluid* cells.

Next to the particle surface, the fluid velocity has to match the particle velocity which is realized via boundary conditions. Here, we use the central linear interpolation (CLI) scheme from [17], given by

$$f'_{\bar{q}}(\boldsymbol{x}) = \tilde{f}_q(\boldsymbol{x}) + \frac{1-2\delta_q}{1+2\delta_q}\left(\tilde{f}_q(\boldsymbol{x} - \boldsymbol{c}_q) - \tilde{f}_{\bar{q}}(\boldsymbol{x})\right) - \frac{12\,w_q\rho_0}{1+2\delta_q}\boldsymbol{v}(\boldsymbol{x}_b)\cdot\boldsymbol{c}_q, \qquad (17)$$

where $\boldsymbol{v}(\boldsymbol{x}_b) = \boldsymbol{V} + \boldsymbol{W}\times(\boldsymbol{x}_b - \boldsymbol{X})$ is the particle velocity at the boundary location $\boldsymbol{x}_b$. The variable δ_q denotes the relative distance between the cell center and the exact surface position such that $\boldsymbol{x}_b = \boldsymbol{x} + \boldsymbol{c}_q\delta_q$. This increases the accuracy of the boundary treatment as subgrid information is used to improve the staircase approximation of the particle shape. A sketch of this boundary treatment is given in Fig. 4.

The momentum exchange idea is applied to obtain the cell local contribution to the hydrodynamic interaction force that acts on the submerged particles. This contribution is given as

$$\boldsymbol{F}_q(\boldsymbol{x}_b) = \left(\boldsymbol{c}_q - \boldsymbol{v}(\boldsymbol{x}_b)\right)\tilde{f}_q(\boldsymbol{x}) - \left(\boldsymbol{c}_{\bar{q}} - \boldsymbol{v}(\boldsymbol{x}_b)\right)f'_{\bar{q}}(\boldsymbol{x}) \qquad (18)$$

for a fluid-solid link q [30,45]. By summing up all contributions corresponding to a single particle, the hydrodynamic force $\boldsymbol{F}^{\mathrm{hyd}}$ and torque $\boldsymbol{T}^{\mathrm{hyd}}$ are obtained:

$$\boldsymbol{F}^{\mathrm{hyd}} = \sum \boldsymbol{F}_q(\boldsymbol{x}_b), \qquad (19)$$

$$\boldsymbol{T}^{\mathrm{hyd}} = \sum (\boldsymbol{x}_b - \boldsymbol{X}) \times \boldsymbol{F}_q(\boldsymbol{x}_b). \qquad (20)$$

These quantities, together with gravitational and buoyancy forces, represent the total external contributions, $\boldsymbol{F}^{\mathrm{ext}}$ and $\boldsymbol{T}^{\mathrm{ext}}$, which enter Eqs. (11) and (12).

Due to the explicit mapping, cells will change its state from *solid* to *fluid* as particles move across the grid. This requires the reconstruction of the PDF information before the simulation can continue. Here, we initialize the PDFs of such a converted cell with their equilibrium values, Eq. (3), based on a spatially averaged density and the local particle velocity.

Algorithm 1. Coupling algorithm for fluid-particle systems

---

for each coarse time step t **do**
    Map particle into fluid domain and reconstruct PDFs if necessary.
    for each LBM subcycle **do**
        Apply boundary conditions, Eq. (17).
        Perform LBM step, Eqs. (1) and (2) with TRT collision operator Eq. (5).
        Calculate hydrodynamic forces on particles, Eq. (18).
    end for
    Average forces on particles over LBM subcycles.
    Obtain total force and torque on particles, Eqs. (19) and (20).
    for each granular dynamics solver subcycle **do**
        Perform granular dynamics solver step, solving Eqs. (7)-(16).
    end for
end for

All these parts are carried out locally and thus work well in combination with the LBM in massively parallel setups [19,20,40]. Because of the explicit particle mapping, the grid can remain unchanged throughout the whole simulation which guarantees computational efficiency.

The complete algorithm for fully resolved simulations of fluid-particle systems is summarized in Algorithm 1. Besides the already mentioned parts, it features possible subcycling for LBM and the granular dynamics solver, i.e., these parts are carried out multiple times in one global time step. Using two LBM subcycles was proposed by [31] to damp oscillations in the hydrodynamic forces which are therefore averaged over the two subcycles. Subcycles for the granular dynamics integration can be necessary when applying solvers that require much smaller time step sizes than the LBM to accurately resolve the contacts between particles. Since our applied non-smooth granular dynamics solver uses internal iterations to achieve this goal, this subcycling is not needed in our case. We will refer to one iteration of Algorithm 1 as a 'coarse time step' to distinguish it from a single LBM time step inside the subcycling, which internally consists again of several subiterations because of the applied refinement strategy, see Sect. 3.1.

4   Implementation and Parallelization

All functionalities presented in Sect. 3 are implemented in the WALBERLA framework[1] which will be used for the reported simulations. WALBERLA is designed to facilitate the creation of portable, maintainable and robust HPC applications. However, its foremost design goals are outstanding performance and scalability to the full extent of current supercomputers. Only with both, a carefully tuned single-node performance and excellent scalability, the scarce and expensive compute hours on modern supercomputers can be used efficiently.

To adhere to these goals, WALBERLA performs the domain partitioning on the level of structured blocks of lattice cells. The concept of blocks allows the

---

[1] http://www.walberla.net.

design of efficient LBM kernels and communication schemes due to the structured layout of the lattice cells [18]. WALBERLA's domain partitioning also allows for a local adaption of the grid resolution to the requirements of the simulation. The implemented refinement strategy [42] is based on a forest of octrees: each block may be divided into eight sub-blocks, with the constraint that a neighboring block may only be off by one refinement level. This strategy preserves performance as the structured layout of the LBM cells persists.

The PDFs are stored on a block within a field of four dimensions: three spatial dimensions and one for the 19 PDF values per cell corresponding to the discretized lattice velocities. The communication at the block interfaces is done per *ghostlayer exchange*. This is required by the streaming step of the LBM, Eq. (2), which accesses the PDF values of the neighboring cells. The field's size is extended by one layer of ghost cells in each direction, which is filled with a copy of the PDFs from the neighboring blocks via MPI communication. For more details about WALBERLA's block layout, the reader is referred to [18,42].

The physics engine *pe*, that carries out the granular dynamics simulation, uses the same block domain decomposition as the fluid simulation in WALBERLA. Each particle is associated to exactly one block based on where the center of mass of the particle lies. All particle information like the state variables (position, orientation, velocities) and constants (mass, inertia matrix, shape) are stored on this block. The process this block belongs to is called parent process of the respective particle. The parent process is responsible for the time integration of each of its particles. If the center of mass of a particle leaves the block, the particle will be migrated to the new block.

In order to detect all contacts between the particles, each block additionally requires information about all particles intersecting with its bounding box. This is realized with the help of *shadow copies* of the intersecting particles and follows a similar concept as the previously described ghostlayers for the field data. Only the parent process integrates and moves the particles and thus has to update these particles' shadow copies on the intersecting blocks. This is implemented by a synchronization step after every time step. During this synchronization step also new shadow copies are instantiated as needed and old ones are deleted if no longer required.

The necessary communication between the shadow copies and the parent copy can be implemented as an efficient next neighbor communication if the following condition holds for all particles at all time steps:

$$r + ||\boldsymbol{V}||_2 \delta t + \gamma < l_{min} \tag{21}$$

with the bounding radius of the particle r (e.g., for spheres the radius, for boxes half the space diagonal), the particle velocity $\boldsymbol{V}$, a safety margin γ and the smallest diameter of the blocks l_{min}. This guarantees that the particles do not extend into the bounding box of the next neighbor block and that they will not reach this block during one single time step.

The treatment of the contacts is also distributed among the processes. The association of one contact to a process is delicate and out of scope of this paper [38]. During the resolution of the contacts an additional communication step is needed in every iteration of the solver (see Sect. 3.2) to collect all contributions to the final reaction from all shadow copies. This again involves a next neighbor communication. More details on the parallelization of the *pe* can be found in [38].

The applied coupling between the fluid and the particles, Sect. 3.3, uses the block data structures provided by LBM and the granular dynamics simulation. To obtain a consistent body mapping into the domain and to conserve the fine resolution, however, the particles have to remain on the same refinement level throughout the simulation. Thus, the area at which static grid refinement is applied has to be sufficiently large to ensure this condition.

5 Results

5.1 Compute Environment

All experiments are conducted on the petascale supercomputer SuperMUC located at the Leibniz Supercomputing Centre in Garching near Munich. We made use of the 18 thin node islands of SuperMUC phase 1, which consist of 512 nodes each. At most 8 islands are usable at the same time for a job during regular operations. Every node holds two Intel Xeon E5-2680 (Sandy Bridge-EP) eight-core processors and is equipped with 32 GiB of main memory. The interconnect within one island is a non-blocking tree network, while the islands are connected via a 4:1 pruned tree. We use IBM's MPI implementation for the interprocess communication.

5.2 Simulation Experiment Setup

The simulation of a realistic sediment bed and the subsequent dune formation under the effect of a fluid flow above it requires a careful setup of the initial state. This already begins with the generation of a sediment bed inside a horizontally periodic domain of size $L_x \times L_y \times L_z$. In our case, layers of spheres with diameter D and density ρ_s are continuously created at the top of the domain, equipped with random velocities. Affected by the gravitational field acting in negative z direction, the spheres settle and arrange at the bottom which is simulated by non-smooth granular dynamics described in Sect. 3.2. The simulation is terminated when the spheres are at rest. The thus generated flat bed features a solid volume fraction of around 0.63 which agrees well with findings for sphere packings created in this way [10]. Following [26], the average bed height h_s can be defined as that height at which the solid volume fraction averaged in both horizontal directions hits the threshold value of 0.1. This is then used as input for the actual coupled simulation where LBM is applied to simulate the fluid flow inside and above the bed, as explained in Sects. 3.1 and 3.3. The characteristic parameters of the setup are the bulk Reynolds number $Re_b = u_b h_f / \nu$, with the average velocity in streamwise direction u_b and the water depth h_f, and the Galileo number $Ga = u_g D / \nu$, with $u_g = ((\rho_s / \rho_f - 1)|\mathbf{g}|D)^{1/2}$ and the gravitational acceleration $\mathbf{g}$. In x, i.e., the streamwise, direction, the flow is

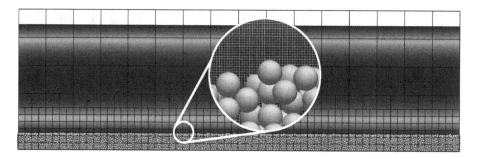

Fig. 5. Cross-sectional view of initial 3D simulation setup together with the block structure of the static grid refinement and a zoom to the fluid solid interface showing the grid cells.

driven via an external fluid force, Eq. (6), that results in a flow rate of $q_f = u_b h_f$. No-slip walls are applied in vertical direction z as boundary conditions. The flow velocity above the sediment bed, i.e., $h_s \leq z \leq h_s + h_f$, is initialized with the Poiseuille channel flow profile to yield the desired Re_b and which corresponds to the applied external fluid force. Three levels of static refinement are applied such that the sediment bed and an area of approximately the same height as the bed reside on the finest level. This allows for efficient simulations of the fluid flow in the large bulk area without losing accuracy in the vicinity of the bed. Since the static refinement poses some restrictions on the actual number of computational cells applied in each direction, i.e., it has to be multiples of the coarsest applied block size, the actual domain height L_z might be larger than $h_s + h_f$ but the difference is filled up with boundary cells. An example for the actual setup including the static refinement structure can be seen in Fig. 5 which coincides with the one depicted in Fig. 3.

5.3 Performance Analysis

We conduct strong- and weak-scaling experiments on SuperMUC to asses the efficiency and scalability of our implementation. We try to keep the benchmark problems as close to our production runs as possible, to generate information that helps steering the setup of our production runs towards a solid compromise of efficiency and performance. For all reported scaling results at least three measurements have been performed and the sample with the best performance has been chosen.

We ran three weak-scaling experiments with the block sizes 16^3, 32^3 and 64^3. We started each experiment with 6 nodes, i.e., 96 processes. The number of processes was chosen such that a refinement configuration close to the production runs could be achieved. This base element was then doubled in size by replicating it alternately in x- and y-direction for each successive run. The exact configuration of the base element is given in Table 1. The results of the weak-scaling experiments can be found in Fig. 6. The results show perfect linear scalability of

Table 1. Parameters of base element of weak-scaling domain. The base element is designed for 96 processes and is replicated in x- and y-direction to conduct weak-scaling experiments.

Block size	16^3	32^3	64^3
Domain size	$64 \times 64 \times 256$	$128 \times 128 \times 512$	$256 \times 256 \times 1024$
Initial avg. bed height	39	75	144
No. of LBM cells	417,792	3,342,336	26,738,688
No. of fluid cells	328,385	2,613,619	20,822,174
No. of particles	171	1,392	11,297
No. of blocks on level 0	2	2	2
No. of blocks on level 1	4	4	4
No. of blocks on level 2	96	96	96

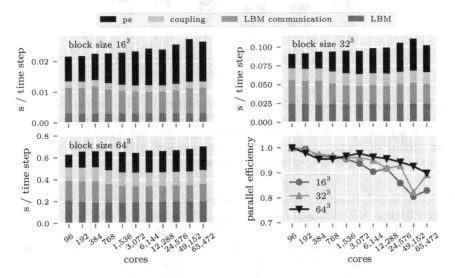

Fig. 6. Weak-scaling results. For each of the block sizes the required time per coarse time step is plotted. Each result is broken down in the four main subroutines of the simulation. On the bottom right the parallel efficiency of all runs is shown.

the LBM and coupling subroutines. The *pe* scales quite well, though not perfectly linear. The LBM communication captures not only the MPI communication but also any load imbalance that occurs due to the unequally distributed particles. In general we can see that the parallel efficiency at full scale is generally better with the larger 64^3 blocks (89.80 %) than with the 32^3 blocks (89.08 %) or 16^3 blocks (82.88 %). We assume this is due to the small message sizes at the smaller blocks which make the communication bound by latency instead of bandwidth.

The variations in execution time between the varying block sizes are clearly visible when comparing the weak-scaling runs. The differences in efficiency were

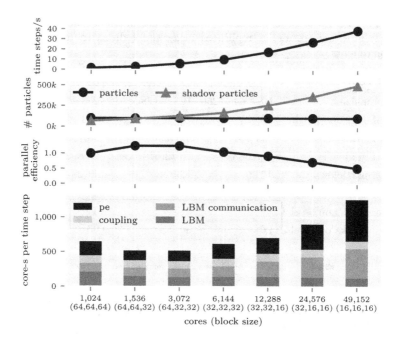

Fig. 7. Strong-scaling results of the simulation on SuperMUC. The *bottom* graph shows the amount of core seconds spent in each subroutine per coarse time step. Parallel efficiency is plotted on the *bottom center* graph. The *top center* graph illustrates the rising number of shadow particles as blocks get smaller. At the *top* the number of coarse time steps performed per second is visualized.

studied in detail during a strong-scaling experiment. The strong-scaling domain has size $2,048 \times 512 \times 512$ and consists of 213.91 M cells from which 160.50 M are fluid cells. It is spread over three refinement levels. In the special case of blocks of size 64^3 the domain consists of 301.99 M cells from which 248.58 M are fluid cells. Here, the domain is spread over two refinement levels.

The riverbed consists of 101,970 particles with a diameter of 10 and has an average height of 84. In Fig. 7, the efficiency of a fixed setup ran at different block sizes and number of cores can be seen. We measure the efficiency in the amount of core-seconds (core-s) we spend in each coarse time step. In general it becomes obvious that larger blocks offer better efficiency but less performance, which we measure in the number of coarse time steps computed per second. A slight anomaly can be seen at the largest block size of 64^3, where the efficiency drops compared to the next three smaller block sizes. This is due to the refinement setup and the requirement that neighboring blocks may not differ by more than one refinement level. Due to this restriction, the top layer cannot be coarsened twice but only once. Therefore more fluid cells are created and more core seconds have to be spent to update them. Another effect, that is well visible, is the *pe*'s quickly deteriorating efficiency with small block sizes. This corresponds well with the increasing amount of shadow particles that have to be updated in each of *pe*'s iterations. While at blocks of size 64^3 for each particle there are 0.68 shadow particles, at blocks of size 16^3 for each particle 4.85 shadow particles have to be updated on average.

Using the scaling runs as guideline we chose to use a block size of 32^3 for the production runs, as it is a good compromise between efficiency and performance.

5.4 Dune Formation Results

To study the evolution of the sediment bed surface, we use a domain size of $L_x/D \times L_y/D \times L_z/D = 409.6 \times 102.4 \times 64$ and $350{,}000$ spherical particles, generated as described in the previous section. This results in the sediment bed height $h_s/D = 7.5$. Blocks of size 32^3 are used and distributed to $24{,}576$ cores. The fluid height is set to $h_f/D = 50$. Regarding the characteristic parameters, $Re_b = 6022$, $Ga = 8.3$ and $\rho_s/\rho_f = 2.5$ is used. To fully resolve the particles, ten cells per diameter are applied. This setup features $864.02\,\mathrm{M}$ cells in total compared to $2{,}684.35\,\mathrm{M}$ if no refinement were used. The simulation is then started from the initialized Poiseuille velocity profile from Fig. 5. In Fig. 8, the temporal change of the bed surface is visualized. Initially, the structure is random as a result from the randomized flat bed generation. Next, the sediments with a slightly exposed position compared to their direct neighbors are carried away by the flow. They get transported over the sediment bed which now features a chaotic structure ($t^* = 53$). Afterwards, they begin to arrange such that they form spanwise clusters. Viewed from the top, these appear as dunes that move across the sediment bed ($t^* = 277$).

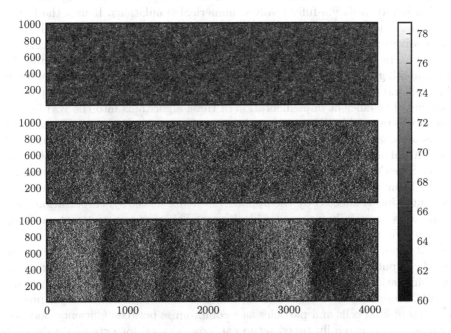

Fig. 8. Temporal evolution of the sediment bed at different non-dimensional times $t^* = t u_b / h_f$ (top: $t^* = 0$, center: $t^* = 53$, bottom: $t^* = 277$). The color depicts the local bed height when viewed from the top.

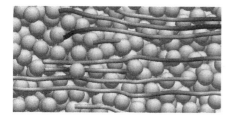 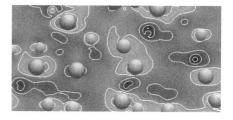

Fig. 9. Close-up top view of the riverbed and the flow properties. Left: Streamlines in the vicinity of the bed. Right: Wall shear stress distribution in a plane placed at the average bed height.

Furthermore, the simulation results allow a detailed analysis of the flow properties in the vicinity of the moving particles at the top of the bed. In Fig. 9, the velocity field is visualized with the help of stream lines to show the flow structures above and below the particles resulting from the flow from left to right. Additionally, the distribution of the wall shear stress at the position of the average bed height is given which exhibits complex pattern due to the interaction with the particles.

6   Conclusion

In this work, we presented a suitable and flexible approach to study dune formation in riverbeds via fully resolved numerical simulations. It uses the lattice Boltzmann method to represent the fluid dynamics which is especially well-suited for massively parallel simulations on supercomputers due to its strictly local data accesses. The interaction of the particles inside the sediment bed is described by non-smooth granular dynamics. The fact that momentum is transferred between the fluid and the solid phase and vice versa is used to establish the fluid-particle coupling. The efficient implementation of these algorithms into the WALBERLA framework in combination with static grid refinement techniques allowed us to simulate dune formation in systems with up to 864.02 M computational cells and 350, 000 spherical particles. We conducted strong- and weak-scaling benchmarks on the SuperMUC supercomputer that showed perfect linear scaling behavior for the LBM and the coupling subroutines. The performance of the granular dynamics simulation is affected by the applied block size as the synchronization overhead grows drastically for smaller block sizes. This shows an apparent challenge of such fully resolved coupled simulations: efficient particle simulations require several hundred particles per block which would then result in a too large number of computational cells per block. This, on the other hand, is undesired in the fluid simulation as it decreases the throughput in terms of time steps per second. Finally, these benchmarks allowed us to identify a suitable workload per process in terms of fluid cells and particles as a compromise between efficiency and performance. This carefully tuned setup can now be used for extensive validation against existing experimental data and ensures efficient usage of the valuable resources provided by the supercomputer. The physical focus of this work was on unidirectional non-oscillatory flow and spherical particles. However, the formation and dynamics of dunes is a complex physical phenomenon and depends on various physical parameters. Future work will thus investigate the influence of oscillatory and combined flows, different sediment shapes and size distributions on the system. Adaptive grid refinement for the coupling method and a synchronization strategy suitable for particles larger than one block will be added to the software framework to enable these studies. Such fully resolved simulations will then lead to a better understanding of the various physical mechanisms acting inside a riverbed.

Acknowledgments. The authors gratefully acknowledge the Gauss Centre for Supercomputing e.V. (www.gauss-centre.eu) for funding this project by providing computing time on the GCS Supercomputer SuperMUC at Leibniz Supercomputing Centre (LRZ, www.lrz.de).

References

1. Aidun, C.K., Lu, Y., Ding, E.J.: Direct analysis of particulate suspensions with inertia using the discrete Boltzmann equation. J. Fluid Mech. **373**, 287–311 (1998)
2. Ammer, R., Markl, M., Ljungblad, U., Körner, C., Rüde, U.: Simulating fast electron beam melting with a parallel thermal free surface lattice Boltzmann method. Comput. Math. Appl. **67**(2), 318–330 (2014). doi:10.1016/j.camwa.2013.10.001
3. Andreotti, B., Claudin, P., Douady, S.: Selection of dune shapes and velocities part 1: dynamics of sand, wind and barchans. Eur. Phy. J. B-Condens. Matter Complex Syst. **28**(3), 321–339 (2002). doi:10.1140/epjb/e2002-00236-4
4. Bartuschat, D., Rüde, U.: Parallel multiphysics simulations of charged particles in microfluidic flows. J. Comput. Sci. **8**, 1–19 (2015). doi:10.1016/j.jocs.2015.02.006
5. Bauer, M., Hötzer, J., Jainta, M., Steinmetz, P., Berghoff, M., Schornbaum, F., Godenschwager, C., Köstler, H., Nestler, B., Rüde, U.: Massively parallel phase-field simulations for ternary eutectic directional solidification. In: Proceedings of the International Conference for High Performance Computing, Networking, Storage and Analysis, SC 2015, pp. 8:1–8:12. ACM, New York (2015). doi:10.1145/2807591.2807662
6. Best, J.: The fluid dynamics of river dunes: a review and some future research directions. J. Geophys. Res.: Earth Surface **110**(F4) (2005). doi:10.1029/2004JF000218
7. Buffington, J.M., Montgomery, D.R.: A systematic analysis of eight decades of incipient motion studies, with special reference to gravel-bedded rivers. Water Resour. Res. **33**(8), 1993–2029 (1997). doi:10.1029/96WR03190
8. Chen, S., Doolen, G.D.: Lattice Boltzmann method for fluid flows. Annu. Rev. Fluid Mech. **30**(1), 329–364 (1998). doi:10.1146/annurev.fluid.30.1.329
9. Doucette, J.S.: Geometry and grain-size sorting of ripples on low-energy sandy beaches: field observations and model predictions. Sedimentology **49**(3), 483–503 (2002). doi:10.1046/j.1365-3091.2002.00456.x
10. Dullien, F.A.: Porous Media: Fluid Transport and Pore Structure. Academic Press, Cambridge (2012)
11. Fattahi, E., Waluga, C., Wohlmuth, B., Rüde, U.: Large scale lattice Boltzmann simulation for the coupling of free and porous media flow. In: Kozubek, T., Blaheta, R., Šístek, J., Rozložník, M., Čermák, M. (eds.) HPCSE 2015. LNCS, vol. 9611, pp. 1–18. Springer, Cham (2016). doi:10.1007/978-3-319-40361-8_1

12. Fattahi, E., Waluga, C., Wohlmuth, B., Rüde, U., Manhart, M., Helmig, R.: Lattice Boltzmann methods in porous media simulations: from laminar to turbulent flow. Comput. Fluids **140**, 247–259 (2016). doi:10.1016/j.compfluid.2016.10.007
13. Ferguson, R., Hoey, T., Wathen, S., Werritty, A.: Field evidence for rapid downstream fining of river gravels through selective transport. Geology **24**(2), 179–182 (1996)
14. Flemming, B.W.: Underwater sand dunes along the southeast African continental margin — Observations and implications. Marine Geol. **26**(3–4), 177–198 (1978). doi:10.1016/0025-3227(78)90059-2
15. Frings, R.M.: Downstream fining in large sand-bed rivers. Earth-Sci. Rev. **87**(1–2), 39–60 (2008). doi:10.1016/j.earscirev.2007.10.001
16. Frings, R.M., Kleinhans, M.G.: Complex variations in sediment transport at three large river bifurcations during discharge waves in the River Rhine. Sedimentology **55**(5), 1145–1171 (2008). doi:10.1111/j.1365-3091.2007.00940.x
17. Ginzburg, I., Verhaeghe, F., d'Humieres, D.: Two-relaxation-time lattice Boltzmann scheme: about parametrization, velocity, pressure and mixed boundary conditions. Commun. Comput. Phys. **3**(2), 427–478 (2008)
18. Godenschwager, C., Schornbaum, F., Bauer, M., Köstler, H., Rüde, U.: A framework for hybrid parallel flow simulations with a trillion cells in complex geometries. In: Proceedings of the International Conference on High Performance Computing, Networking, Storage and Analysis, SC 2013, pp. 35:1–35:12. ACM, New York (2013). doi:10.1145/2503210.2503273
19. Götz, J., Iglberger, K., Feichtinger, C., Donath, S., Rüde, U.: Coupling multibody dynamics and computational fluid dynamics on 8192 processor cores. Parallel Comput. **36**(2), 142–151 (2010). doi:10.1016/j.parco.2010.01.005
20. Götz, J., Iglberger, K., Stürmer, M., Rüde, U.: Direct numerical simulation of particulate flows on 294912 processor cores. In: Proceedings of the 2010 ACM/IEEE International Conference for High Performance Computing, Networking, Storage and Analysis, pp. 1–11. IEEE Computer Society (2010). doi:10.1109/SC.2010.20
21. Jackson, D., Bourke, M., Smyth, T.: The dune effect on sand-transporting winds on Mars. Nat. Commun. **6** (2015). doi:10.1038/ncomms9796
22. Hasert, M., Masilamani, K., Zimny, S., Klimach, H., Qi, J., Bernsdorf, J., Roller, S.: Complex fluid simulations with the parallel tree-based Lattice Boltzmann solver Musubi. J. Comput. Sci. **5**(5), 784–794 (2014). doi:10.1016/j.jocs.2013.11.001
23. Iglberger, K., Rüde, U.: Massively parallel granular flow simulations with nonspherical particles. Comput. Sci.-Res. Dev. **25**(1–2), 105–113 (2010). doi:10.1007/s00450-010-0114-4
24. Julien, P.Y., Klaassen, G.J.: Sand-dune geometry of large rivers during floods. J. Hydraul. Eng. **121**(9), 657–663 (1995). doi:10.1061/(ASCE)0733-9429(1995)121:9(657)
25. Kennedy, J.F.: The mechanics of dunes and antidunes in erodible-bed channels. J. Fluid Mech. **16**(04), 521–544 (2006). doi:10.1017/S0022112063000975
26. Kidanemariam, A.G., Uhlmann, M.: Direct numerical simulation of pattern formation in subaqueous sediment. J. Fluid Mech. **750** (2014). doi:10.1017/jfm.2014.284
27. Kidanemariam, A.G., Uhlmann, M.: Interface-resolved direct numerical simulation of the erosion of a sediment bed sheared by laminar channel flow. Int. J. Multiph. Flow **67**, 174–188 (2014). doi:10.1016/j.ijmultiphaseflow.2014.08.008
28. Kostaschuk, R.: Sediment transport mechanics and subaqueous dune morphology. In: River, Coastal and Estuarine Morphodynamics. Taylor & Francis (2010)

29. Kuron, M., Rempfer, G., Schornbaum, F., Bauer, M., Godenschwager, C., Holm, C., de Graaf, J.: Moving charged particles in lattice Boltzmann-based electrokinetics. J. Chem. Phys. **145**(21), 214102 (2016). doi:10.1063/1.4968596

30. Ladd, A.J.: Numerical simulations of particulate suspensions via a discretized Boltzmann equation. Part 1. Theoretical foundation. J. Fluid Mech. **271**, 285–309 (1994). doi:10.1017/S0022112094001771

31. Ladd, A.J.: Numerical simulations of particulate suspensions via a discretized Boltzmann equation. Part 2. Numerical results. J. Fluid Mech. **271**, 311–339 (1994). doi:10.1017/S0022112094001783

32. Lancaster, N.: Planetary science. Linear dunes on titan. Science **312**(5774), 702–703 (2006). doi:10.1126/science.1126292

33. Li, M.Z., Amos, C.L.: Sheet flow and large wave ripples under combined waves and currents: field observations, model predictions and effects on boundary layer dynamics. Cont. Shelf Res. **19**(5), 637–663 (1999). doi:10.1016/S0278-4343(98)00094-6

34. Luo, L.S.: Unified theory of lattice Boltzmann models for nonideal gases. Phys. Rev. Lett. **81**(8), 1618 (1998). doi:10.1103/PhysRevLett.81.1618

35. Mitarai, N., Nakanishi, H.: Granular flow: dry and wet. Eur. Phys. J. Spec. Top. **204**(1), 5–17 (2012). doi:10.1140/epjst/e2012-01548-8

36. Parker, G.: Surface-based bedload transport relation for gravel rivers. J. Hydraul. Res. **28**(4), 417–436 (1990). doi:10.1080/00221689009499058

37. Preclik, T.: Models and algorithms for ultrascale simulations of non-smooth granular dynamics. Ph.D. thesis, Friedrich-Alexander-Universität Erlangen-Nürnberg (2014)

38. Preclik, T., Rüde, U.: Ultrascale simulations of non-smooth granular dynamics. Comput. Part. Mech. **2**(2), 173–196 (2015). doi:10.1007/s40571-015-0047-6

39. Qian, Y.H., D'Humires, D., Lallemand, P.: Lattice BGK models for Navier-Stokes equation. EPL (Europhys. Lett.) **17**(6), 479 (1992)

40. Rettinger, C., Rüde, U.: Simulations of particle-laden flows with the Lattice Boltzmann method. PAMM **16**(1), 607–608 (2016). doi:10.1002/pamm.201610292

41. van Rijn, L.C.: Sediment transport, part III: bed forms and Alluvial Roughness. J. Hydraul. Eng. **110**(12), 1733–1754 (1984). doi:10.1061/(ASCE)0733-9429(1984)110:12(1733)

42. Schornbaum, F., Rüde, U.: Massively parallel algorithms for the lattice Boltzmann method on nonuniform grids. SIAM J. Sci. Comput. **38**(2), C96–C126 (2016). doi:10.1137/15M1035240

43. Studer, C.: Numerics of Unilateral Contacts and Friction: Modeling and Numerical Time Integration in Non-smooth Dynamics. Lecture Notes in Applied and Computational Mechanics, vol. 47. Springer, Heidelberg (2009)

44. Toyama, A., Shimizu, Y., Yamaguchi, S., Giri, S.: Study of sediment transport rate over dune-covered beds. In: River, Coastal and Estuarine Morphodynamics: RCEM 2007, Two Volume Set, pp. 591–597. CRC Press (2011)

45. Wen, B., Zhang, C., Tu, Y., Wang, C., Fang, H.: Galilean invariant fluid-solid interfacial dynamics in lattice Boltzmann simulations. J. Comput. Phys. **266**, 161–170 (2014). doi:10.1016/j.jcp.2014.02.018

46. Wilcock, P.R., Kenworthy, S.T., Crowe, J.C.: Experimental study of the transport of mixed sand and gravel. Water Resour. Res. **37**(12), 3349–3358 (2001). doi:10.1029/2001WR000683

Tile Low Rank Cholesky Factorization for Climate/Weather Modeling Applications on Manycore Architectures

Kadir Akbudak, Hatem Ltaief$^{(\boxtimes)}$, Aleksandr Mikhalev, and David Keyes

Extreme Computing Research Center, Division of Computer,
Electrical, and Mathematical Sciences and Engineering,
King Abdullah University of Science and Technology,
Thuwal, Kingdom of Saudi Arabia
{Kadir.Akbudak,Hatem.Ltaief,Aleksandr.Mikhalev,David.Keyes}@kaust.edu.sa

Abstract. Covariance matrices are ubiquitous in computational science and engineering. In particular, large covariance matrices arise from multivariate spatial data sets, for instance, in climate/weather modeling applications to improve prediction using statistical methods and spatial data. One of the most time-consuming computational steps consists in calculating the Cholesky factorization of the symmetric, positive-definite covariance matrix problem. The structure of such covariance matrices is also often data-sparse, in other words, effectively of low rank, though formally dense. While not typically globally of low rank, covariance matrices in which correlation decays with distance are nearly always hierarchically of low rank. While symmetry and positive definiteness should be, and nearly always are, exploited for performance purposes, exploiting low rank character in this context is very recent, and will be a key to solving these challenging problems at large-scale dimensions. The authors design a new and flexible tile row rank Cholesky factorization and propose a high performance implementation using OpenMP task-based programming model on various leading-edge manycore architectures. Performance comparisons and memory footprint saving on up to $200K \times 200K$ covariance matrix size show a gain of more than an order of magnitude for both metrics, against state-of-the-art open-source and vendor optimized numerical libraries, while preserving the numerical accuracy fidelity of the original model. This research represents an important milestone in enabling large-scale simulations for covariance-based scientific applications.

1 Introduction

The march toward exascale computing is well, underway with today's fastest systems capable of achieving near 100 PFlop/s in sustained peak performance on million of cores [22]. Technology scaling with incremental hardware evolution will most probably enable to cross the exascale barrier by 2021, as recently announced by the US Department of Energy. However, the current hardware roadmap development will not be able to get to exascale within a power budget of 20 MW that

© Springer International Publishing AG 2017
J.M. Kunkel et al. (Eds.): ISC High Performance 2017, LNCS 10266, pp. 22–40, 2017.
DOI: 10.1007/978-3-319-58667-0_2

many hardware architects and research agencies consider as a practical upper limit for such a system. Although, this power gap may be further reduced with advanced energy-efficient devices (e.g., hardware accelerators), algorithmic novelties around synchronization-reducing and communication-reducing concepts are paramount not only to ultimately design an exascale system at reasonable power levels, but also to ensure an efficient usage of the massively parallel underlying hardware.

Covariance matrices are ubiquitous in computational science and engineering. Large covariance matrices arise from multivariate spatial data sets, for instance, in seismic inversion to obtain estimates of uncertainty [11], in computational ground-based astronomy to enhance the observed image quality by filtering out the noise coming from the adaptive optics instrumentation and the atmospheric turbulence [21], or in climate/weather modeling to improve prediction using geospatial statistics approaches [24]. All the aforementioned scientific applications boil down to calculating the Cholesky factorization of a symmetric, positive-definite matrix problem, which turns out to be the most time consuming computational phase in their various respective simulations. The structure of these covariance matrices is often data-sparse, in other words, effectively of low rank, though apparently dense. The dense Cholesky allows to perform an exact factorization up to the machine precision while the low rank variant produces an approximation of the Cholesky factor up to a desired accuracy threshold. While not necessarily globally of low rank, covariance matrices in which correlation decays with distance are nearly always hierarchically of low rank. While symmetry and positive definiteness should be, and nearly always are, exploited for performance purposes, exploiting low rank character in this context is very recent, and will be a key to solving these challenging problems. Because these low rank approximations [14] operate on a lossy (but controllable) compressed representation of the original dense data structure, this directly translates into lower arithmetic complexities and memory footprint saving, which are key elements for reducing data movement and time to solution, while staying within the future exascale system power envelope.

Fully dense linear algebra approaches encounter high ($O(N^3)$) arithmetic complexity and the overhead of a large ($O(N^2)$) memory footprint where N is the number of objects to be correlated. This scaling is impractical when dealing with large data sets which, today, could usefully translate into covariance matrices with N in the billions. To tackle such problems, we study the numerical accuracy, the memory footprint and the performance of the tile low rank Cholesky factorization (TLR Cholesky) in the context of climate/weather modeling applications [24], by exploiting the data sparsity in the covariance matrix and relying on task-based programming model for asynchrony and dynamic load balancing. Experiments are conducted on Intel Xeon Haswell/Broadwell and Intel Xeon Phi Knights Landing. Results reported indicate up to an order of magnitude of memory saving as well as time to solution reduction on $200K \times 200K$ covariance matrix size, compared to the native dense Cholesky factorization, as implemented in the state-of-the-art high performance open-source and vendor software libraries. This emerging family of low rank matrix computations represents a breakthrough for the statistical computing community, for which the default use of high-level simulation software tool such as R [1] may often be limited in dimension scaling by expensive dense linear algebra kernels.

The remainder of the paper is organized as follows. Section 2 details related work. Section 3 highlights our contributions. Section 4 describes the climate/weather modeling simulation based on a geospatial statistics approach applied to the covariance matrix. We recall the state-of-the-art dense Cholesky factorization in Sect. 5, which is the most time-consuming phase of the application studied here. Section 6 outlines a new TLR Cholesky factorization, which additionally exploits the data sparsity of the dense covariance matrix. Numerical accuracy is provided in Sect. 7 and shows the flexible and robustness of the TLR matrix approximation for Cholesky factorization. Section 8 gives implementation details of the TLR Cholesky, which relies on the OpenMP task-based programming model for performance purposes. Section 9 presents the performance results and analysis and compares TLR Cholesky factorization against existing state-of-the-art implementations. We conclude in Sect. 10.

2   Related Work

Low rank matrix approximations under the rubric of hierarchical matrices or $\mathcal{H}$-matrices [14,17] have been extensively studied in the literature since the end of the 1990's, mainly from a theoretical perspective, with critical bounds derived on algorithmic complexities and memory footprint. Since then, many new data compression formats for $\mathcal{H}$-matrix approximation have emerged to cover a wide range of scientific applications such as finite and boundary element methods and Gaussian processes. These compression formats, e.g., hierarchically semi-separable (HSS), $\mathcal{H}^2$-matrix, hierarchically off-diagonal low-rank (HODLR), block low rank (BLR), are categorized depending on the data format structure (i.e., nested or non-nested basis) and the admissibility condition (i.e., standard/strong or weak). The former impacts both aforementioned bounds while the latter allows a fine-grained capture of the low rank structure of the matrix off-diagonal blocks.

Low rank matrix approximation relying on nested bases (i.e., $\mathcal{H}^2$-matrix [9, 10,15,16] and HSS [23]) provides the best theoretical bounds for algorithmic complexities and memory footprint for scientific problems which exhibit nested row and column basis. The latter are challenging to implement efficiently on manycore architectures due to synchronization points in the recursive tree. Data compression formats based on non-nested bases (i.e., $\mathcal{H}$-matrix [18,20], HODLR [3,6] and BLR [4]) have higher bounds but they are often capable of handling broader range of scientific applications than low rank data format with nested basis. In particular, BLR is probably the most straightforward low rank approximation format to implement because it does not rely on a recursive tree and adopts a flattened data structure instead, at the expense of showing the highest algorithmic complexity. BLR is currently under investigation in MUMPS [5] during the Schur complement involving frontal matrices [4].

This work presents the tile low rank (TLR) data format, which is similar to BLR, although it takes root from the well-known tile algorithms, as implemented in dense linear algebra libraries such as PLASMA [27]. Last but not least, this work aims at filling in the software gap by providing high performance TLR approximations for matrix operations, and therefore, minimizing the memory and complexity overhead of using dense matrix computations as the native approach.

3   Contributions

The contributions of the paper are fourfold. The authors (1) design a new and flexible tile low rank Cholesky factorization for dense covariance matrices, (2) provide a performance assessment on various leading-edge hardware architectures by looking at numerical accuracy, memory footprint and time to solution, (3) compare TLR Cholesky factorization against state-of-the-art vendor and open-source dense linear algebra libraries such as MKL [19] and PLASMA [27], respectively and (4) leverage performance of emerging architectures for climate/weather modeling applications.

4   Climate/Weather Modeling Applications

Large covariance matrices arise from multivariate spatial data sets in climate/weather modeling simulations to improve prediction using statistical methods and spatial data [24]. The crux of the modeling effort is to estimate a maximum likelihood objective function based on observations, as follows:

$$l(\theta) = -\frac{1}{2} Z^T \Sigma^{-1}(\theta) Z - \frac{1}{2} \log|\Sigma(\theta)|, \tag{1}$$

where θ is the vector of parameters to be tuned, Z a vector of observations, and Σ the covariance matrix, and where the vertical bars indicate a determinant. These matrices are symmetric, positive-definite and are based on covariances of presumed Gaussian processes. If we have only one Gaussian process, then the corresponding covariance matrix is simply scalar. In N-dimensional case, with N being the number of geographical locations to be correlated, we have N Gaussian processes, which leads to square N-by-N matrix. As is apparent from Eq. 1, the computational bottleneck of the maximum likelihood estimation is the calculation of the Cholesky factorization of the dense covariance matrix Σ, which is necessary to solve the linear system (i.e., forward and backward substitutions) as well as getting the logarithm of the covariance matrix determinant (i.e., product of the diagonal elements of the Cholesky factor). The dense Cholesky factorization, for instance, as implemented in the state-of-the-art simulation software R, requires $O(N^3)$ operations on $O(N^2)$ data. This is a prohibitive approach, given that N may be in the order of billions in readily contemplated applications. Alternative less expensive approximation approaches exist such as element thresholding, subsampling and iterative methods, however, these methods sacrifice the fidelity of the underlying statistical model.

The main idea consists in exploiting the data sparsity of the formally dense covariance matrix $\Sigma(\theta)$. This represents a cheaper computational algorithmic design, while still preserving the model fidelity up to a given accuracy. The resulting matrix is hierarchically of low rank and can be compressed using the tile low rank data format, which enables to better capture the low rankness structure of the off-diagonal blocks, thanks to its strong admissibility condition, as opposed to HODLR data format.

In this paper, we synthesize a set of covariance matrices as follows: given an N-by-N uniform grid of particles in unit square with exponential interaction $f(x, y) = e^{-\frac{|x-y|}{\beta}}$, we add random noise to coordinates of each particle and sort them in Morton order. So, if we have set of N^2 particles $\{X_i\}_{i=1}^{N^2}$, each element of the covariance matrix $\Sigma(\theta)$ can be defined as follows:

$$A_{ij} = e^{-\frac{r(X_i, X_j)}{\beta}}, \tag{2}$$

where $r(X_i, X_j)$ is a distance between particles X_i and X_j and β represents a covariance parameter, which measures the correlation between the Gaussian processes. Although the current kernel considered for the matrix generation is the Gaussian kernel, Matérn kernels, for instance, among other Gaussian processes kernels, can also be handled in the same manner. All in all, these kernels are asymptotically smooth, which lead to the possibility of low-rank approximations of different blocks of a matrix [25]. The ranks depend on how the clusterization of the spatial particles occurs, given the relative distance from one cluster to another. It is also noteworthy to mention that, in case of uniform distribution of N spatial points with N power of 2, Morton order space-filling curve may nearly be optimal.

5   State-of-the-Art Dense Cholesky Factorization

This section recalls the algorithmic evolution of the dense Cholesky factorization. The Cholesky factorization of an $N \times N$ real symmetric, positive-definite matrix A has the form $A = LL^T$, where L is an $N \times N$ real lower triangular matrix with positive diagonal elements.

5.1   Block Algorithms

Block algorithms, as implemented in LAPACK [7], emerged with cache-friendly hardware architectures in the late 1990's. The matrix computation is decomposed in two successive phases. The panel factorization consists in applying Level 2 BLAS transformations within a panel of the matrix only, followed by the update of the trailing submatrix, which accumulates all transformations from the current panel and applies them by means of Level 3 BLAS on the unreduced part of the matrix, as depicted in Fig. 1(a). The matrix computation algorithms proceed then on a smaller subset of the overall matrix as in Fig. 1(b), until the matrix is completely transformed, as seen in Fig. 1(c). Parallel performance is only exploited during the update of the trailing submatrix, during calls to compute-intensive multithreaded Level 3 BLAS, as provided for instance by vendor optimized BLAS implementations (e.g., Intel MKL [19]). Artifactual synchronization points in-between computational phases impede parallel performance, especially in presence of multicore architectures [2].

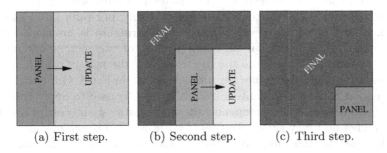

(a) First step.   (b) Second step.   (c) Third step.

Fig. 1. Block algorithms: LAPACK/MKL.

5.2 Tile Algorithms

Tile algorithms emerged with multicore architectures a decade ago. The dense matrix is broken into tiles, as seen in Fig. 2, where elements are contiguous in memory within each tile. Tile algorithms weaken the synchronization points revealed in block algorithms by bringing the parallelism in multithreaded BLAS to the fore. They create opportunities for asynchronous execution with potentials for look-ahead optimizations. The whole algorithm may be then represented as a directed acyclic graph, where nodes are computational tasks and edges define data dependencies between them. A dynamic runtime system is employed to schedule tasks across processing units, while ensuring data dependencies are not violated. PLASMA [27] and FLAME [13] represent the two state-of-the-art dense linear algebra libraries, which rely on tile algorithmic formulation.

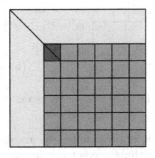

Fig. 2. Tile algorithms: PLASMA/FLAME.

6   The Tile Low Rank Cholesky Factorization

This section presents the tile low rank (TLR) approximation and Cholesky factorization.

The first phase is to create an approximation of each off-diagonal tile, typically by performing a singular value decomposition (SVD) and by keeping only the most significant singular values and their corresponding singular vectors, depending on the selected accuracy. The latter is a parameter, which is often application-specific. The diagonal tiles are typically full rank and cannot be approximated. The obtained off-diagonal data structure is no more a dense tile of contiguous elements but an outer product of two rectangular matrices $U_{ij} \times V_{ij}$ of size $nb \times k$, with nb the tile size and k the matrix rank (i.e., the k most significative singular values/vectors), as shown in Fig. 3. Our current TLR approximation offers two variants. Fixed ranks can be used to apply truncation across all off-diagonal tiles, independently of the data, at the cost of obtaining lower or higher accuracy across the tiles (see Fig. 3(a)). Though seemingly brute force, this may be the most cost-effective and per-iteration performant form of preconditioning for iterative solvers. The fixed accuracy variant permits to smoothly approximate the off-diagonal tiles depending on the accuracy needed by the application. This engenders variable ranks per tiles, as seen in Fig. 3(b), with an arbitrary illustration for six ranks (k_1 to k_6).

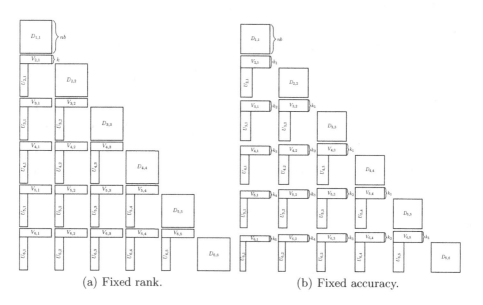

(a) Fixed rank.   (b) Fixed accuracy.

Fig. 3. Tile low rank matrix representation.

Once the dense matrix is approximated by means of tile low rank, a new family of linear algebra algorithms needs to be implemented to take into consideration the new compressed data layout. For the TLR Cholesky factorization, we reuse some of the ideas developed in the PLASMA library [27], although new monolithic kernels have to be designed. When using fixed rank k, all off-diagonal tiles of size nb are represented by a data structure of identical size, i.e., $nb \times k$. With fixed accuracy, the rank obtained may differ from one tile to another to maintain the expected accuracy threshold. Therefore, load imbalance issues may increase idle time and it is then paramount to rely on dynamic runtime systems in order to mitigate this overhead by ensuring all resources stay busy throughout the matrix computations.

7   Numerical Accuracy

This section aims at highlighting the robustness of the TLR compression and Cholesky factorization. We look first at synthetic covariance matrices and then at real geospatial covariance matrices from climate/weather modeling applications based on Gaussian processes.

7.1   Synthetic Matrices

Synthetic matrices are important to demonstrate the numerical robustness for new matrix algebra software. We create a template diagonal matrix S with three specific singular value decay rates (named as base 2, base 3, base 4), as depicted in Fig. 4. The singular values or diagonal elements of S in descending order follow these decay rates and reach close to machine precision in double precision arithmetic ($1e - 16$) for the first $53, 33$ and 26 singular values for base 2, base 3, and base 4, respectively. This matrix S is then multiplied on the left and right sides by orthogonal matrices to generate each data-sparse off-diagonal tiles.

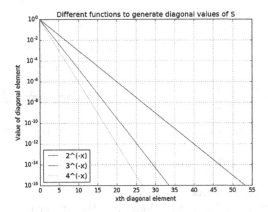

Fig. 4. Singular values decay rates and distribution of the template diagonal matrix.

Once all off-diagonal tiles have been generated, they can be compressed using an SVD. Extensive numerical experiments have been conducted on synthetic

covariance matrices to validate our TLR approach. The heat map Fig. 5 reports
the accuracy obtained for various fixed ranks and tile sizes (Fig. 5(a)) using
base 2 decay rate and the corresponding digit difference with the full dense
Cholesky factorization (Fig. 5(b)). The heat map Fig. 6 reports the accuracy
obtained for various fixed ranks and tile sizes (Fig. 6(a)) using base 3 decay rate
and the corresponding digit difference with the full dense Cholesky factorization
(Fig. 6(b)). The heat map Fig. 7 reports the accuracy obtained for various fixed
ranks and tile sizes (Fig. 7(a)) using base 4 decay rate and the corresponding
digit difference with the full dense Cholesky factorization (Fig. 7(b)). Indeed,
one can notice that double precision arithmetic (10^{-16}) is achieved from rank
truncations starting from $53, 33$ and 26 singular values for base 2, base 3, and
base 4, respectively.

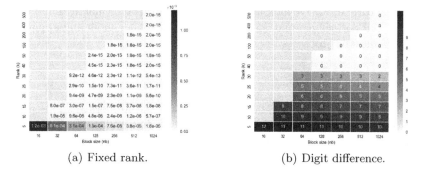

(a) Fixed rank.   (b) Digit difference.

Fig. 5. Singular value distribution base 2.

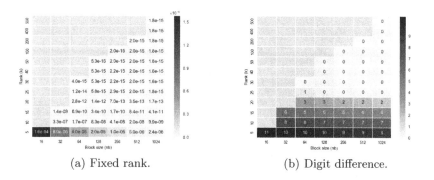

(a) Fixed rank.   (b) Digit difference.

Fig. 6. Singular value distribution base 3.

Figure 8 shows fixed accuracy instead, using base 3 decay rate, and reveals the
resulting rank with the following obvious rule: the higher the accuracy needed,
the higher the rank. Last but not least, the tile size nb parameter does not really
matter for these synthetic matrices in terms of numerical accuracy because the
template diagonal tile S is the same one used during data-sparse off-diagonal
tile generation. In fact, for the dense Cholesky factorization, the parameter nb

has an impact only on performance as it trades-off concurrency with sequential kernel performance. For tile low rank Cholesky factorization, nb has, in addition, a direct impact on the overall algorithmic complexity. For instance, for a given matrix size N, a large tile size nb would engender small memory footprint as well as number of floating-point operations at the price of a lower concurrency. On the contrary, if the large tile size nb would have been further decomposed into smaller ones, this would engender larger memory footprint as well as number of floating-point operations at the price of a higher concurrency.

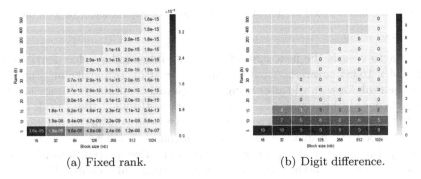

(a) Fixed rank. (b) Digit difference.

Fig. 7. Singular value distribution base 4.

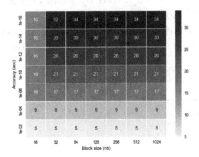

Fig. 8. Fixed accuracy for base 3.

7.2 Geospatial Statistics

The typical accuracy required for the studied climate/weather modeling application is 10^{-9}. Given this accuracy, Fig. 9 highlights the rank distributions for for 16384×16384 covariance matrix generated by Eq. 2 with $\beta = 0.1$ for $nb = 64, 128$ and 256: the whiter the picture is, the greater its data sparsity. The diagonal tiles are full ranks, regardless of the tile size, while the off-diagonal tiles are mostly data-sparse and can be approximated accordingly. In fact, perhaps the most striking feedback about this figure is that the majority of off-diagonal tiles can be dramatically approximated, while the initial matrix is completely dense.

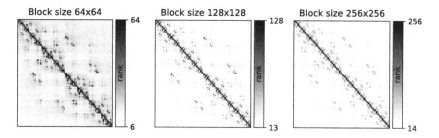

Fig. 9. Rank distributions for 16384×16384 covariance matrix using various tile sizes.

Figure 10 reveals the heat map of the rank and singular value distributions for 16384×16384 covariance matrix using $nb = 1024$. In particular, Fig. 10(a) shows the rank for each tile after using the application-specific accuracy of 10^{-9}. If dense linear algebra approaches were used, the bottom left tile of rank 17 with $U = 1024 \times 17$ and $V = 1024 \times 17$ would have been considered full rank and of size 1024×1024, instead. And this phenomenon is further exacerbated when looking at Fig. 10(b), which portrays the singular value distributions of selected off-diagonal tiles. While the singular values of the diagonal tiles are all significant, the singular values of off-diagonal tiles are actually characterized by an exponential decay, which has to be exploited for performance and storage purposes. Such characteristic may not be captured by weak admissible data compression formats, such as HODLR and HSS, due to nested dissection which operates only for diagonal blocks. The off-diagonal blocks may then necessitate larger rank to get compressed, which may have a non-negligible impact on performance and memory footprint.

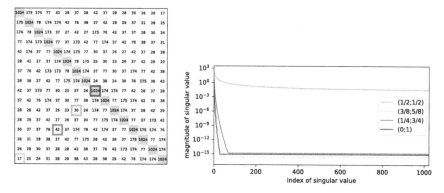

(a) Rank distributions.   (b) Singular values decay of marked tiles in Fig. 10(a).

Fig. 10. Rank and singular value distributions for a 16384×16384 covariance matrix using $nb = 1024$ with an accuracy threshold set to 10^{-9}.

8   High Performance Implementations

This section describes the high performance implementation of the TLR Cholesky factorization.

8.1   Numerical Kernels

The sequential TLR Cholesky algorithm can be expressed with the following four computational kernels:

HCORE_DPOTRF: The kernel performs the Cholesky factorization of a diagonal (lower triangular) tile. It is similar to LAPACK DPOTRF since the diagonal tiles are dense and full rank.

HCORE_DTRSM: The operation applies an update to an off-diagonal low-rank tile of the input matrix, resulting from factorization of the diagonal tile above it and overrides it with the final elements of the output matrix: $V_{(i,k)} = V_{(i,k)} \times D_{(k,k)}^{-1}$. The operation is a triangular solve.

HCORE_DSYRK: The kernel applies updates to a diagonal (lower triangular) tile of the input matrix, resulting from factorization of the low-rank tiles to the left of it: $D_{(j,j)} = D_{(j,j)} - (U_{(j,k)} \times V_{(j,k)}^T) \times (U_{(j,k)} \times V_{(j,k)}^T)^T$. The operation is a symmetric rank-k update.

HCORE_DGEMM: The operation applies updates to an off-diagonal low-rank tile of the input matrix, resulting from factorization of the low-rank tiles to the left of it. The operation involves two QR factorizations, one reduced SVD (with a rank truncation depending on the fixed rank and/or the fixed accuracy operation modes) and two matrix-matrix multiplications.

The most called computational kernel is HCORE_DGEMM and it also represents the one with highest arithmetic intensity. Once the sequential version of the code based on nested loops has been designed, we need to schedule the four aforementioned computational tasks on the underlying processing units.

8.2   Task-Based Programming Model

Task-based programming models have become methods of choice when targeting efficient parallel implementation, as they permit asynchronous thread executions after exposing fine-grained computational tasks. Static scheduling may be suboptimal here, especially in fixed accuracy mode, as this may result in load imbalance between tasks. Therefore, dynamic runtime systems are crucial to cope with the various tasks' workloads, besides handling dynamic frequency scaling of processors at runtime. Many dynamic runtime systems such as QUARK [26], StarPU [8], and OmpSs [12] exist for shared-memory systems. We use the task-based programming model and the dynamic runtime system, as implemented in OpenMP, for easy portability across hardware platforms. The TLR matrix generation and compression consist in generating the TLR matrix after performing an SVD using DGESVD on all off-diagonal tiles in an embarrassingly parallel

---

Algorithm 1. HiCMA_DPOTRF(HicmaLower, D, U, V, N, nb, rank, acc)

---

p = N / nb
for k = 1 to p **do**
  #pragma omp task depend(inout:D(k,k))
  hcore_dpotrf(HicmaLower, D(k,k), rank, acc)
  for i = k+1 to p **do**
    #pragma omp task depend(in:D(k,k)) depend(inout:U(i,k))
    hcore_dtrsm(V(i,k), D(k,k), rank, acc)
  end for
  for j = k+1 to p **do**
    #pragma omp task depend(in:U(j,k)) depend(in:V(j,k)) depend(inout:D(j,j))
    hcore_dsyrk(D(j,j), U(j,k), V(j,k), rank, acc)
    for i = j+1 to p **do**
      #pragma omp task
        depend(in:U(i,k)) depend(in:V(i,k))
        depend(in:U(j,k)) depend(in:V(j,k))
        depend(inout:U(i,j)) depend(inout:V(i,j))
      hcore_dgemm(U(i,k), V(i,k), U(j,k), V(j,k), U(i,j), V(i,j), rank, acc)
    end for
  end for
end for

---

fashion using the parallel for loops from OpenMP. The QR-based DGESVD is slower than the divide-and-conquer DGESDD but requires much less memory. Other SVD variants (e.g., randomized SVD) may directly generate the TLR data format without going to the dense representation. These variants may also overcome these performance issues but this is beyond the scope of this paper. Algorithm 1 shows the pseudo-code of the TLR Cholesky factorization for the lower triangular case. Each kernel call is annotated by pragmas describing the data directions from which the compiler is capable of tracking the data dependencies. Each kernel's API has extra parameters related to fixed rank and/or fixed accuracy, allowing an algorithmic flexibility for end-users. The TLR compression and Cholesky factorization is currently being packaged into the Hierarchical Computations on Manycore Architectures (HiCMA) library and will be released during 2017.

9 Performance Results and Analysis

This section presents the performance results and analysis of the TLR compression and Cholesky factorization in the context of a climate/weather modeling application based on geospatial statistics.

9.1 Environment Systems

We have ported our OpenMP-based TLR compression and Cholesky factorization to three systems. We have considered three systems representative of the current manycore-based hardware trends. The first system is composed of dual-socket 18-core Intel(R) Xeon(R) Haswell CPU E5-2699 v3 @ 2.3 GHz with 256 GB of main memory. The second system hosts the latest Intel commodity chip with dual-socket 14-core Intel(R) Xeon(R) Broadwell CPU E5-2680 v4 @ 2.4 GHz with 128 GB of main memory. The third system has the latest Intel(R) Xeon Phi(TM) Knights Landing manycore 7210 chips with 64 cores @ 1.30 GHz with 128 GB of main memory, operating in quadrant/cache modes. For simplicity, each system is named after its chip codename. Our TLR implementations have been compiled with Intel C compiler v16 and linked against sequential Intel MKL v11.3.1. We have run ten times each test configuration and report the average time as the consistent metric.

9.2 Memory Footprint Assessment

Theoretical Memory Footprint for Fixed Rank. For native dense Cholesky factorization, the memory footprint of the input matrix is simply $\frac{N^2}{2}$. For TLR Cholesky factorization, assuming fixed rank, the memory footprint can be calculated as follows. The numbers of diagonal and off-diagonal tiles are $ndt = \frac{N}{nb}$ and $nodt = \frac{(ndt*ndt)-ndt}{2}$, respectively. Therefore, assuming double precision and given a rank k, the required memory footprint for TLR is $8 * (ndt * \frac{nb*(nb+1)}{2} + 2 * nodt * nb * k) \approx 4 * ndt * nb^2 + 16 * nodt * nb * k$.

Actual Memory Footprint for Fixed Accuracy. Figure 11(a) shows the memory footprint for dense and TLR Cholesky factorization up to $200K \times 200K$ covariance matrix size. The fixed accuracy of 10^{-9} is used, as required by the application. As seen in the figure, the TLR-based compression scheme exhibits more than an order of magnitude memory footprint saving with respect to naive dense Cholesky factorization.

Actual Operation Count for Fixed Accuracy. Figure 11(b) shows the operation count performed by dense and TLR Cholesky factorization up to $200K \times 200K$ covariance matrix size. Similarly, the fixed accuracy of 10^{-9} is used. As seen in the figure, the TLR Cholesky requires significantly less number of operations with respect to naive dense Cholesky factorization.

In both Figs. 11(a) and (b), the data points for matrix size of $73984 = 16^2 * 17^2$ are below the general trend for TLR-based scheme. This finding can be attributed to the better compression effect of the global Morton ordering for matrix sizes that are multiple of power of 2, as explained at the end of Sect. 4.

9.3 Performance of TLR Compression

Although the compression phase is important, it is performed only once, while generating the covariance matrix on the fly. Figure 12 reports the performance and scalability of TLR compression on the Haswell system for various tile sizes. We benchmark both DGESVD and DGESDD as MKL SVD implementations. DGESDD is faster thanks to its efficient divide-and-conquer at the expense of

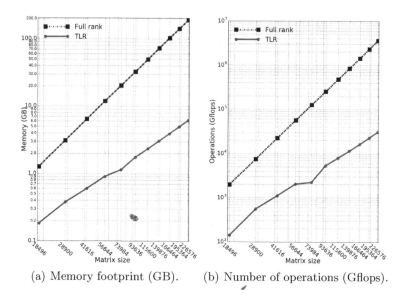

(a) Memory footprint (GB).   (b) Number of operations (Gflops).

Fig. 11. Memory footprint and number of flops (accuracy is set to $1e - 9$).

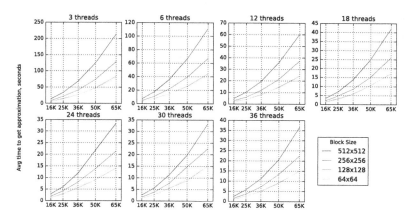

Fig. 12. Time to solution to approximate all tiles of a TLR matrix by DGESDD on various numbers of threads and block sizes.

requiring eight times more memory allocation than DGESVD. This explains the increase in time of approximation routine, when increasing the number of threads. TLR matrices with larger tiles tend to use more memory per tile and may saturate the memory bus bandwidth on the system due to the memory-bound character of the approximation phase. The scalability may be further improved through cross approximation techniques or randomized SVD kernel instead of ordinary dense SVD.

9.4   Performance of TLR Cholesky Factorization on Climate/Weather Modeling Applications

Figure 13 depicts the time to solution of the TLR Cholesky factorization (referred to as TLR-HiCMA_dpotrf) on various hardware architectures using an accuracy of 10^{-9}, as required by the application. In this figure, the time for compression has not been included, since this initial phase may only be done once before

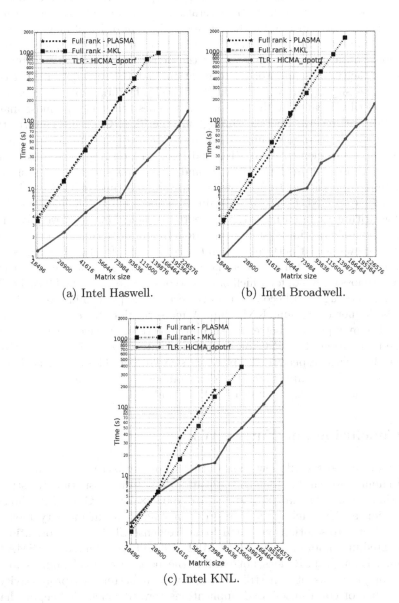

(a) Intel Haswell.   (b) Intel Broadwell.

(c) Intel KNL.

Fig. 13. Time to solution for TLR Cholesky factorization using an accuracy of 10^{-9}.

the matrix computation starts. Optimal tile sizes nb have been selected from empirical experiments for each Cholesky factorization variant, depending on the matrix size (e.g., for TLR Cholesky, $nb = 1156$ turns out to be the most effective). The naive interface of PLASMA_dpotrf call requires an out-of-place data translation, which doubles the memory footprint and prevents PLASMA from further scaling up. For all experiments in this section, we used almost the whole systems' resources as described in Sect. 9.1, except one or two cores, which are left to ensure that basic tasks of the operation system do not interfere with our experiments. As seen in Fig. 13, there is more than an order of magnitude time difference between TLR and dense Cholesky factorizations across all architectures. Some data points are missing for the dense approaches due to physical memory capacity. It is noteworthy to mention that the ranks after TLR compression have slightly grown after TLR Cholesky factorization, especially the off-diagonal tiles located at the bottom right. These tiles are the most manipulated tiles and receive updates throughout the TLR Cholesky factorization. Regarding the three architectures, the elapsed times of the full dense Cholesky factorization, as implemented in MKL and PLASMA on KNL, are considerably lower than those obtained for Haswell and Broadwell systems, thus showing the compute capability of KNL. However, the elapsed time of TLR Cholesky is slightly higher on KNL than those obtained on the other two architectures, due to the low arithmetic intensity of the sequential kernels. Moreover, we rely on the OpenMP dynamic runtime system to schedule the tasks on the different systems. While this shows decent performance on the commodity Intel CPU architectures with two sockets for which all cores share the same L3 cache, it does suffer from performance loss on KNL, for which only two cores share the same L2 cache. The overhead of moving data becomes a bottleneck, while performing work stealing across the higher core count KNL chip. A more regular static scheduling with data locality may perform better for such architecture. One can also notice that the time to solution of TLR Cholesky for the matrix size of $73984 = 17^2 16^2$ is relatively less with respect to the problem size growth. The reason is that the obtained rank after compression and total number of operations for this matrix size are less, as previously seen in Figs. 11(a) and (b).

10   Conclusion and Future Work

We have presented the tile low rank (TLR) Cholesky factorization in the context of climate/weather modeling application based on geospatial statistics on a Gaussian covariance matrix of size up to $200K \times 200K$. Our TLR Cholesky factorization achieves more than an order of magnitude in memory footprint saving and time to solution compared to native dense Cholesky factorization, as implemented in vendor optimized Intel MKL [19] and open-source PLASMA [27] libraries. Although TLR does not exhibit the best theoretical bounds for $\mathcal{H}$-matrix computations, it can still leverage, with a better user-productivity, a wide number of covariance-based applications toward much challenging hardware machines such as distributed-memory systems equipped with hardware accelerators so that larger-scale problem dimensions can be covered. This will lead to new scientific research opportunities, especially for simulation workloads relying on the mainstream R software project. Moving forward, we would like to investigate batch algorithms by redesigning the current TLR Cholesky factorization from a tile-centric to a kernel-centric representation. This will help in compensating the kernel launch overhead due to the low arithmetic intensity, while increasing the hardware occupancy.

Acknowledgment. We would like to thank R. Kriemann from Max Planck Institute for Mathematics in the Sciences and M. Genton, A. Litvinenko, Y. Sun, and G. Turkiyyah from KAUST for fruitful discussions. We would like also to thank A. Heinecke from Intel for helping us tuning the codes on KNL. This work has been partially funded by the Intel Parallel Computing Center Award.

References

1. The R Project for Statistical Computing (2016). r-project.org
2. Agullo, E., Demmel, J., Dongarra, J., Hadri, B., Kurzak, J., Langou, J., Ltaief, H., Luszczek, P., Tomov, S.: Numerical linear algebra on emerging architectures: the PLASMA and MAGMA projects. J. Phys: Conf. Ser. **180**, 012037 (2009)
3. Ambikasaran, S., Darve, E.: An $\mathcal{O}(N \log N)$ fast direct solver for partial hierarchically semiseparable matrices. J. Sci. Comput. **57**(3), 477–501 (2013)
4. Amestoy, P., Ashcraft, C., Boiteau, O., Buttari, A., L'Excellent, J.Y., Weisbecker, C.: Improving multifrontal methods by means of block low-rank representations. SIAM J. Sci. Comput. **37**(3), A1451–A1474 (2015)
5. Amestoy, P.R., Duff, I.S., L'Excellent, J.Y.: Multifrontal parallel distributed symmetric and unsymmetric solvers. Comput. Methods Appl. Mech. Eng. **184**(2), 501–520 (2000)
6. Aminfar, A., Darve, E.: A fast sparse solver for finite-element matrices. arXiv:1403.5337 [cs.NA], pp. 1–25 (2014)
7. Anderson, E., Bai, Z., Bischof, C.H., Blackford, L.S., Demmel, J.W., Dongarra, J.J., Croz, J.J.D., Greenbaum, A., Hammarling, S., McKenney, A., Sorensen, D.C.: LAPACK User's Guide, 3rd edn. SIAM, Philadelphia (1999)
8. Augonnet, C., Thibault, S., Namyst, R., Wacrenier, P.A.: StarPU: a unified platform for task scheduling on heterogeneous multicore architectures. Concurr. Comput.: Pract. Exp. **23**(2), 187–198 (2011)
9. Börm, S.: H2Lib 2.0. Max-Planck-Institut, Leipzig (1999–2012)
10. Börm, S.: Efficient numerical methods for non-local operators: $\mathcal{H}^2$-Matrix compression, algorithms and analysis. EMS Tracts in Mathematics, vol. 14. European Mathematical Society, Zürich (2010)
11. Duputel, Z., Rivera, L., Fukahata, Y., Kanamori, H.: Uncertainty estimations for seismic source inversions. Int. Geophys. J. **190**(2), 1243–1256 (2012)
12. Duran, A., Ferrer, R., Ayguadé, E., Badia, R.M., Labarta, J.: A proposal to extend the OpenMP tasking model with dependent tasks. Int. J. Parallel Prog. **37**(3), 292–305 (2009)
13. The FLAME project, April 2010. http://z.cs.utexas.edu/wiki/flame.wiki/FrontPage
14. Hackbusch, W.: A sparse matrix arithmetic based on $\mathcal{H}$-matrices. Part i: introduction to $\mathcal{H}$-matrices. Computing **62**(2), 89–108 (1999)

15. Hackbusch, W., Börm, S.: Data-sparse approximation by adaptive $\mathcal{H}^2$-matrices. Computing **69**(1), 1–35 (2002)
16. Hackbusch, W., Khoromskij, B., Sauter, S.: On $\mathcal{H}^2$-Matrices. In: Bungartz, H.J., Hoppe, R., Zenger, C. (eds.) Lectures on Applied Mathematics, pp. 9–29. Springer, Heidelberg (2000)
17. Hackbusch, W.: Hierarchical Matrices: Algorithms and Analysis, vol. 49. Springer, Heidelberg (2015)
18. Hackbusch, W., Börm, S., Grasedyck, L.: HLib 1.4. Max-Planck-Institut, Leipzig (1999–2012)
19. Intel: Math Kernel Library (2016). software.intel.com/en-us/intel-mkl
20. Kriemann, R.: $\mathcal{H}$-LU factorization on many-core systems. Comput. Vis. Sci. **16**(3), 105–117 (2013)
21. Ltaief, H., Gratadour, D., Charara, A., Gendron, E.: Adaptive optics simulation for the world's largest telescope on multicore architectures with multiple GPUs. In: Proceedings of the Platform for Advanced Scientific Computing Conference, PASC 2016. pp. 9:1–9:12. ACM, New York (2016)
22. Meuer, H., Strohmaier, E., Dongarra, J., Simon, H.: The Top500 List, November 2016. http://www.top500.org
23. Rouet, F.H., Li, X.S., Ghysels, P., Napov, A.: A distributed-memory package for dense hierarchically semi-separable matrix computations using randomization. ACM Trans. Math. Softw. **42**(4), 27:1–27:35 (2016)
24. Sun, Y., Stein, M.L.: Statistically and computationally efficient estimating equations for large spatial datasets. J. Comput. Graph. Stat. **25**(1), 187–208 (2016)
25. Tyrtyshnikov, E.E.: Mosaic-skeleton approximations. Calcolo **33**(1), 47–57 (1996)
26. YarKhan, A., Kurzak, J., Dongarra, J.: QUARK users' guide: QUeueing and runtime for kernels. Technical report ICL-UT-11-02, University of Tennessee Innovative Computing Laboratory (2011)
27. YarKhan, A., Kurzak, J., Luszczek, P., Dongarra, J.: Porting the PLASMA numerical library to the OpenMP standard. Int. J. Parallel Program. **45**(3), 612–633 (2017). doi:10.1007/s10766-016-0441-6

EDGE: Extreme Scale Fused Seismic Simulations with the Discontinuous Galerkin Method

Alexander Breuer[1]([✉]), Alexander Heinecke[2], and Yifeng Cui[1]

[1] University of California, San Diego, 9500 Gilman Drive, La Jolla, CA 92093, USA
anbreuer@ucsd.edu
[2] Intel Corporation, 2200 Mission College Blvd., Santa Clara, CA 95054, USA

Abstract. This article introduces EDGE, a solver package for fused seismic simulations. Fused seismic simulations are a novel technique addressing one of the grand challenges of computational seismology: large ensemble runs of geometrically similar forward simulations. Application fields include, but are not limited to: uncertainty quantification in the context of seismic hazard analysis or the accurate derivation of velocity models through tomographic inversion. For efficient and accurate handling of complex model geometries (topography, fault geometries, material heterogeneities), EDGE utilizes the Discontinuous Galerkin (DG) method for spatial and Arbitrary high order DERivatives (ADER) for time discretization, implemented for unstructured tetrahedral meshes. EDGE's ADER-DG scheme requires sparse and dense matrix-matrix multiplications at the kernel level. By choosing a sufficient memory layout and relying on runtime code generation and specialization, both, sparse and dense operations, can be efficiently vectorized on wide-SIMD machines. We present a convergence study of single and fused seismic simulations, code verification in an established benchmark, as well as a detailed performance assessment for different discretization orders. As target architecture we select the recently released Intel Xeon Phi processor, which powers the Theta and Cori-II supercomputers. For a single sixth order seismic forward simulation we achieved 10.4 PFLOPS of hardware performance and 5.0 PFLOPS for fused simulations in fourth order, both occupying 9,000 nodes of Cori-II. From a throughput perspective, fused seismic simulations can outperform a single forward simulation by $1.8\times$ to $4.6\times$, depending on the chosen order of the method.

1 Introduction

A popular approach for accurate numerical simulations of seismic wave propagation are Finite Difference Methods (FDM) [8,10,28,36]. FDM approximate the partial derivatives through stencils, which combine adjacent grid points. While low dispersion errors can be reached through high-order stencils, accurate modeling of sharp material contrasts remains an ongoing challenge for FDM due to the underlying Cartesian meshes [3,29,34]. Further, the seismic wave field is often highly heterogeneous, resulting in inefficiencies for FDM since adaptive refinement in space and time is a highly non-trivial task, often limited to moderate patch-based adaptivity [2,19,32].

© Springer International Publishing AG 2017
J.M. Kunkel et al. (Eds.): ISC High Performance 2017, LNCS 10266, pp. 41–60, 2017.
DOI: 10.1007/978-3-319-58667-0_3

Finite Element Methods (FEM) overcome many limitations intrinsic to FDM, if the mesh honors major material heterogeneities. Continuous Galerkin (CG-) FEM, often in combination with diagonal mass matrices, obtained through mass lumping or a special choice of quadrature and interpolation nodes, became a prominent option [16,21,26,35]. Here, the widely used Spectral Element Methods (SEM) rely almost exclusively on hexahedral meshes and have been applied with great success on a global scale to forward runs and, more recently, to inverse problems [7,21,31]. However, on a local scale, the complexity of the resolved geometric features is limited by the difficult hexahedral meshing, leaving tetrahedral meshes as the only practical option [31,33]. While the generalization of SEM to more flexible elements remains ongoing work, the CG scheme in [17] couples hexahedral and tetrahedral meshes, but is limited by low convergence rates. In contrast, Discontinuous Galerkin (DG-) FEM using tetrahedral meshes have reached a mature status in the last decade [9,11,30]. DG-FEM allow discontinuities in the numerical solution between elements and the corresponding discretized materials, which greatly simplifies the integration of sharp heterogeneities. Classical finite volume methods [5] are closely related to DG-FEM.

While the accurate numerical simulation of seismic wave propagation is already demanding, many of the grand challenges in computational seismology require large ensembles of geometrically similar forward simulations. In detail these ensembles cover few, but very complex model geometries with a broad range of variation influencing only the source descriptions. Important examples include uncertainty quantification in the context of seismic hazard analysis or the accurate derivation of velocity models through tomographic inversion. Interpretation of the similarities in the source descriptions as input parallelism offers large potential for reduced time-to-solution.

In this work we present EDGE, a new software package addressing some of the hardest challenges in computational seismology. EDGE's forward solver for seismic wave propagation relies on the flexibility of the ADER-DG scheme [9,20]. Our software supports different element types and hyperbolic partial differential equations. However, in this work, we will focus on unstructured meshes with 4-node tetrahedral elements and the elastic wave equations. EDGE enables ensemble-based, high-dimensional studies with an unprecedented complexity by *fusing* multiple forward simulations into one execution of the solver. Therefore this paper makes following novel contributions: (1) EDGE as an open source solver package (BSD-3), which was created from scratch to support fused simulations for maximum throughput, and (2) a runtime code generation approach for highest performing kernels when running fused simulations on wide-SIMD architectures.

2   Discretization

For an isotropic medium the 3-D elastic wave equations in velocity-stress formulation are given by a system of hyperbolic partial differential equations:

$$q_t + A_1 q_{x_1} + A_2 q_{x_2} + A_3 q_{x_3} = 0. \tag{1}$$

Time is given by $t \in \mathbb{R}^+$ and location in space by $\boldsymbol{x} = (x_1, x_2, x_3)^T \in \mathbb{R}^3$. $q(\boldsymbol{x}, t) = (\sigma_{11}, \sigma_{22}, \sigma_{33}, \sigma_{12}, \sigma_{23}, \sigma_{13}, u, v, w)^T \in \mathbb{R}^9$ is the vector of quantities. Here, σ_{11}, σ_{22}, and σ_{33} are the normal stress components in x_1-, x_2-, and x_3-direction. The shear stresses are given respectively by σ_{12}, σ_{13}, and σ_{23}. $A_1(\boldsymbol{x}), A_2(\boldsymbol{x}), A_3(\boldsymbol{x}) \in \mathbb{R}^{9 \times 9}$ are the three space-dependent Jacobians. The Jacobians characterize the wave propagation in our hyperbolic system and are derived from the material parameters, given by the mass density $\rho(\boldsymbol{x})$, and Lamé constants $\lambda(\boldsymbol{x})$ and $\mu(\boldsymbol{x})$. By applying the DG-machinery in space and the explicit ADER-scheme in time, we obtain the fully discrete form of Eq. 1 as a series of integration kernels. These kernels describe time-, volume-, and surface-integration and might be formulated as series of small matrix-matrix products.

Our fully discrete formulation divides the computational domain Ω into K pair-wise disjunct tetrahedral elements T_k: $\Omega = \bigcup_{k=1}^{K} T_k$. The numerical solution in every element k is given by a set of $9 \times \mathcal{B}(\mathcal{O})$ time-dependent Degrees Of Freedom (DOFs) $Q_k(t) \in \mathbb{R}^{9 \times \mathcal{B}}$. $\mathcal{O}$ is the order of our ADER-DG discretization with $\mathcal{O} = \mathcal{P}-1$, where $\mathcal{P}$ is the degree of our orthogonal, hierarchical, polynomial basis. We use the same order in time and space, which can be arbitrarily high. Further, we assume piecewise constant material parameters in every element T_k, leading to per-element, constant Jacobians.

Time Kernel: Our first kernel uses the Cauchy-Kovalewski procedure to integrate the element-local DOFs Q_k for a full time step $t^n \to t^{n+1} = t^n + \Delta t$ in time:

$$\mathcal{I}_k^n = \mathcal{I}(Q_k^n) = \sum_{d=0}^{\mathcal{O}-1} \frac{\Delta t^{d+1}}{(d+1)!} \cdot \frac{\partial^d}{\partial t^d} Q_k, \tag{2}$$

where the time derivatives, with the DOFs Q_k^n at time step t^n as initial conditions, $\partial^0 / \partial t^0 Q_k = Q_k^n = Q_k(t^n)$, are obtained recursively through:

$$\frac{\partial^{d+1}}{\partial t^{d+1}} Q_k = -\sum_{c=0}^{3} A_{k,c}^* \left(\frac{\partial^d}{\partial t^d} Q_k \right) (K_{\xi_c})^T. \tag{3}$$

Here, matrices $A_{k,c}^* \in \mathbb{R}^{9 \times 9}$ are linear combinations of the element-local Jacobians, and matrices $K_{\xi_c} \in \mathbb{R}^{\mathcal{B} \times \mathcal{B}}$ the three stiffness matrices, formulated in terms of the unique reference tetrahedron T_{ref} and multiplied with the diagonal, inverse mass matrix in initialization.

Volume Kernel: The volume kernel computes the volume integration based on the element's time integrated DOFs:

$$V_k^n = \mathcal{V}(\mathcal{I}_k^n) = \sum_{c=1}^{3} A_{k,c}^* (\mathcal{I}_k^n) K_{\xi_c}. \tag{4}$$

Surface Kernel: Our last kernel computes the net-updates of the surface integration based on the element's time-integrated DOFs $\mathcal{I}_k^n$ and those of the four face-adjacent elements $\mathcal{I}_{k_i}^n$:

$$S_k^n = \mathcal{S}(\mathcal{I}_k^n, \mathcal{I}_{k_1}^n, \ldots, \mathcal{I}_{k_4}^n) = \sum_{i=1}^{4} A_{k,i}^- (\mathcal{I}_k^n) F^{-,i} + \sum_{i=1}^{4} A_{k,i}^+ (\mathcal{I}_k^n) F^{+,i,j_k,h_k} \tag{5}$$

$A_{k,i}^{-} \in \mathbb{R}^{9 \times 9}$ and $A_{k,i}^{+} \in \mathbb{R}^{9 \times 9}$ are the flux solvers, computing the numerical fluxes. Matrices $F^{-,i} \in \mathbb{R}^{\mathcal{B} \times \mathcal{B}}$ and $F^{-,i,j_k,h_k} \in \mathbb{R}^{\mathcal{B} \times \mathcal{B}}$ are the flux matrices. Index i is the local face of element k w.r.t. the reference element. Indices $j_k(i) \in \{1, 2, 3, 4\}$ and $h_k(i) \in \{1, 2, 3\}$ depend on the vertices both adjacent elements k and k_i share with respect to their transformation to the reference element [9].
Time Step: Our ADER-DG scheme splits a time step $t^n \rightarrow t^{n+1}$ into two steps. First, we compute all element-local operations, not requiring any data from adjacent elements. This is the time kernel and the first update step consisting of the volume kernel $\mathcal{V}_k^n$, and the local part of the surface kernel $\mathcal{S}_k^n$:

$$\bar{Q}_k^{n+1} = Q_k^n + \mathcal{V}_k^n + \sum_{i=1}^{4} A_{k,i}^{-} (\mathcal{I}_k^n) F^{-,i} \tag{6}$$

Here, we use the recently computed time integrated DOFs $\mathcal{I}_k^n$ directly and store them for later use in our second step. The second step contains the remainder of the surface kernel, and thus updates the elements' DOFs with data of face-adjacent tetrahedrons:

$$Q_k^{n+1} = \bar{Q}_k^{n+1} + \sum_{i=1}^{4} A_{k,i}^{+} (\mathcal{I}_k^n) F^{+,i,j_k,h_k}. \tag{7}$$

3   Fused Simulations

A non-fused setup defines fixed input i, and runs the forward solver s to obtain observations $o = s(i)$. Now, if we are interested in results for n different inputs, e.g., different seismic sources, we would specify a set of inputs $I_n = (i_1, i_2, \ldots, i_n)$ and run the non-fused forward solver s on all these inputs to obtain the set of observations $O_n = (o_1, o_2, \ldots, o_n) = (s(i_1), s(i_2), \ldots, s(i_n))$. Typically, the n executions of the solver are completely decoupled, which means that potential parallelism and shared data between two instances $s(i_k)$ and $s(i_l)$ is not utilized.

Fused simulations in EDGE exploit this potential by integrating the concept of multiple but similar input parameters into the forward solver. Thus, we introduce a new forward solver S_m which is capable of handling a set of $m \leq n$ inputs $I_m = (i_1, i_2, \ldots, i_m)$ in a single execution: $O_m = (o_1, o_2, \ldots, o_m) = S_m(I_m)$. We achieve this by a fundamental paradigm in EDGE's data layout, which sets the m forward runs as the fastest dimension in all respective data structures. For example the two most important data structures in our ADER-DG solver for seismic simulations (see Sect. 2) are the DOFs Q_k^n and the time integrated DOFs $\mathcal{I}_k^n$. Here, we use the K elements as slowest dimension, followed by the 9 quantities, the $\mathcal{B}$ modes and finally the m simulations as fastest dimension. Each element is therefore represented by a 3D-tensor.

Note, that one might interpret the different input parameters as multiple right-hand sides of the PDEs, which would lead to the term *parallelization over multiple right-hand sides* in literature [4, 27]. However, in this work we prefer the more general term *fused simulation* due the diverse advantages of the approach,

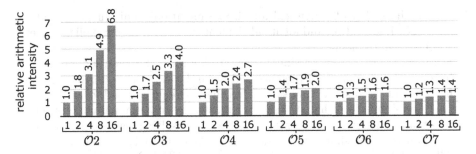

Fig. 1. Arithmetic intensity if the material parameters and mesh are shared in an elastic ADER-DG setup. Shown is the relative improvement over a non-fused simulation in dependency of the order ($\mathcal{O}2$-$\mathcal{O}7$) and the number of fused runs (1, 2, 4, 8, 16).

and settings where interpretation as a right-hand side is more complex, e.g., in multi-physics setups. We identify four key advantages of EDGE's fused approach over non-fused simulations:

1. By fusing multiples of the vector-width, we are able to perform full vector operations, even when using sparse matrix-operations, whereas non-fused settings require dense matrix operations (which have up-to a 50% zero padding overhead) for best performance [14].
2. Data structures are automatically aligned by fusing multiples of the cache line size. Zero-padding [14] for fast aligned loads and stores is not needed.
3. Read-only data structures might be shared among all runs. As illustrated in Fig. 1 for our seismic setup of Sect. 2, this results in substantially increased arithmetic intensities. For example, a non-fused fourth order accurate simulation theoretically requires 8,640 bytes per element. 67% of this requirement is read-only data. By fusing eight runs, we only need 28,800 bytes, which reduces this ratio to 20% and therefore increases the arithmetic intensity by 2.4×. Analogue, for a sixth order configuration, the memory footprint per element only increases from 13,824 to 70,272 bytes, which corresponds to a 1.6× higher arithmetic intensity.
4. Fused simulations are less sensitive to memory latencies and conditional jumps, due to less frequent context switches. Here, the increased, fused workload per memory operation or conditional jump effectively reduces the performance penalty of start-up latencies or branch mispredictions. Analogue, they are less sensitive to network latencies due to larger MPI-messages having identical exchange-frequencies. See [1] for details on memory latencies of Knights Landing and [25] for the relation of message sizes and bandwidth.

However, there are also requirements and limitations. I_m, the set of m inputs has to be "similar enough" for exploitation in fused forward simulations. If a parameter space beyond the following fusing-limitations is studied, we simply distribute the $n \geq m$ inputs to respective fused and non-fused runs. Considering our seismic use case (see Sect. 2), we formulate the following requirements for EDGE on a set of input parameters to be fused into a single forward run:

1. The mesh needs to be identical for all m simulations. This ensures identical adjacency information and identical element sizes, used in our explicit solver's stability requirements.
2. Start- and end-time of all simulations are identical. Further, all simulations have the same order of convergence and share the same characteristics of wave field output (frequency) and seismic receivers (frequency and location).
3. All fused simulations share the same element-local material parameters. Thus, we obtain identical update patterns, since the resulting wave speeds, in combination with the shared mesh, determine the element-local time step.
4. All simulations are allowed to have arbitrary initial DOFs. The location of seismic sources is shared among all m simulations, but moment-rate time histories are private and thus arbitrary. A similar approach would apply if EDGE is extended with internal dynamic rupture boundary conditions [14] in future work.

Nevertheless, all of these limitation and requirements are fulfilled by ensemble simulations and therefore fused simulation are the perfect tool to increase hardware efficiency and simulation throughput.

4   EDGE in a Nutshell

4.1   Runtime Code Generation of DG-FEM Kernels

Section 2 shows that that the speed of EDGE's integrators heavily depends on the performance of small dense or sparse matrix-matrix operators. In the case of fused simulations, a sparse matrix needs to be multiplied with a 3D-tensor, which represents the DOFs Q_k^n, time derivatives $\partial^d/\partial t^d Q_k^n$, or time integrated DOFs $\mathcal{I}_k^n$ for a given mesh element. Previous work showed, that code generation is the ideal tool to speed up single forward runs and yields extremely high hardware efficiencies (greater than 50%) in a portable manner [14]. All previously discussed tricks (c.f., [6]) for an efficient implementation of the ADER-DG scheme for a single simulation have been enabled in EDGE and needed kernels are runtime code generated in EDGE's setup phase leveraging LIBXSMM [15]. As these techniques are covered in the literature, we are not recapping them here.

Instead, we focus on runtime code generation for the required 3D-tensor manipulations of fused simulations. Specifically, this requires two operations to be optimized:

- $K1$: sparse-matrix × 3D-tensor = 3D-tensor, this operation is needed for multiplication with Jacobians and flux-solvers. In BLAS-notation, the sparse matrix A is a 9×9 matrix, whereas B and C are dense 3D-tensors. Matrix A is applied to all planes enumerated by the inner-most dimension f of this tensor, which corresponds to the number of fused forward runs.
- $K2$: 3D-tensor × sparse-matrix = 3D-tensor, this operation is needed for multiplication with stiffness or flux matrices. The dimensions of the sparse matrix B depend on the order and which stage of the integration kernels is performed. Again, this matrix has to be applied to all forward simulations, which are stored in the inner-most dimension f of the 3D-tensor.

Algorithm 1. Code generator sketch of kernel *K1*

1: **for all** $m = 1$ to #quantities **do**
2:    $a_{\#\text{Entries}} \leftarrow \text{row}_A[m+1] - \text{row}_A[m]$
3:    **for** $k = 1$ to $a_{\#\text{Entries}}$ **do**
4:      $a \leftarrow A[\text{row}_A[m] + k]$
5:      **for all** $n = 1$ to #modes **do**
6:        $C[m][n][1:f] \leftarrow \text{fma}(\text{bcst}(a), B[\text{col}_A[\text{row}_A[m] + k]][n][1:f], C[m][n][1:f])$
7:      **end for**
8:    **end for**
9: **end for**

In this work, we focus on a length of f that matches the SIMD-length of the underlying architecture. As we target Intel's Xeon Phi processor, code-named Knights Landing, we leverage AVX-512, offering a double precision vector length of 8 entries. Thus, the number of fused simulations in this work is $f = 8$. We are using slightly different specifiers as in Sect. 2 to allow for a BLAS-related naming.

Under these assumptions, the code generator of *K1* can be realized straight-forward and is sketched in Algorithm 1. We store the entries of all sparse matrices in Compressed Sparse Row Format (CSR). However, the row pointer (row_A in Algorithm 1) and column indices (col_A in Algorithm 1) are only used for the runtime code generation at EDGE's initialization. Thus, the loops hardwire the sparsity pattern of matrix A by fully unrolling *K1*'s implementation and therefore eliminating any access to row or column index structures. As A is sparse, we have unstructured accesses to full vectors over the fused quantities in input tensor B, c.f., line 6. Since the scalar entry of A can be reused across all fused forward simulations, we broadcast it and we can maintain a contiguous access pattern to the result tensor C. During the surface computation, matrix A, the flux solver, is a dense matrix. In this case we disable unrolling over the number of quantities to reduce code size. Additionally, for code used in the neighboring update (7), our code generator supports insertion of last-level cache software prefetching instructions. These help to accelerate EDGE by roughly 10% as the negative impact of accessing face-adjacent elements in the unstructured mesh can be mitigated.

Generating an efficient implementation of *K2* is more challenging and we cover the details by a step-by-step explanation of Algorithm 2. From a high-level point of view, we follow the same approach as in Algorithm 1. However, since now the right hand side operator, matrix B, is sparse we end up with unstructured accesses to the result tensor C, which depend on B's sparsity pattern. From a performance perspective we cannot afford frequent read and write access to C, as we already consume all L1 cache bandwidth for reading the input tensor A and matrix B. We therefore create an in-register scratchpad for a C accumulator set, indexed by the quantities, c.f., line 2 for loading and line 10 for storing this scratchpad. It contains all modes for all forward simulations for a given quantity.

Algorithm 2. Code generator sketch of kernel $K2$

1: **for all** $m = 1$ to #quantities **do**
2:      **for all** $n = 1$ to #modes **do** $c_n[1 : f] \leftarrow C[m][n][1 : f]$ **end for**
3:      **for all** $k = 1$ to #modes **do**
4:          $b_{\#\mathrm{Entries}} \leftarrow \mathrm{row}_B[k + 1] - \mathrm{row}_B[k]$
5:          **for** $n = 1$ to $b_{\#\mathrm{Entries}}$ **do**
6:              $j \leftarrow \mathrm{col}_B[\mathrm{row}_B[k] + n]$
7:              $c_j[1 : f] \leftarrow \mathrm{fma}(A[m][k][1 : f], \mathrm{bcst}(B[\mathrm{row}_B[k] + n]), c_j[1 : f])$
8:          **end for**
9:      **end for**
10:     **for all** $n = 1$ to #modes **do** $C[m][n][1 : f] \leftarrow c_n[1 : f]$ **end for**
11: **end for**

This now allows us to implement unstructured access to C, as we only need to pick the corresponding register in the dot product calculation, c.f., lines 6 and 7.

In summary, both kernels $K1$ and $K2$ are able to achieve 25–40% of hardware efficiency on a single core of the Intel Xeon Phi processor using AVX512. However, they have a higher L2-cache pressure than dense kernels and therefore are limited by the shared L2 cache interface of two cores in Xeon Phi's computing tile for two reasons: (a) latencies due to unstructured tensor entry accesses (b) L2 cache bandwidth is shared. Therefore at full chip level we can expect a kernel compute efficiency of roughly 20%.

On an AVX512-capable processor, we can generate kernels for up to 31 modes efficiently without additionally blocking as the architecture offers 32 vector registers. In this work we limit ourself to a maximum of fourth order runs which have $\mathcal{B}(4) = 20$ modes. Having Fig. 1 in mind, this limitation is only minor as the expected runtime benefit decreases for higher orders. Nevertheless, an additional blocking is planned as future work. Such a feature will also allow to use older vector instruction sets such as AVX2 which offer a small register file with only 16 entries.

4.2   Parallelization and Data Layout

Our parallelization strategy strictly separates between shared and distributed memory parallelization. For the latter one we use the Message Passing Interface (MPI) and assign one rank to every of the P available nodes, sharing a memory space. Therefore, we require exactly P partitions of our unstructured mesh for utilization of P nodes. This reduces the pressure on the partitioner, e.g., the Metis-library [18], and reduces relative communication costs defined as the volume-to-surface ratio of the partitions.

In addition to using fused simulations as fastest dimension of the data layout, EDGE also follows the distributed memory parallelization for the sorting of entity-data in memory. Focusing on a single partition $p \in P$, we store inner-entities first, send-entities second and recv-entities last. Here, we follow the naming scheme of corresponding MPI-functions: Values of inner-entities are not communicated, values of send-entities are send to other ranks and values of recv-entities received from other ranks. In terms of our ADER-DG solver for seismic wave propagation in Sect. 2, our MPI-partitions only exchange time integrated DOFs $\mathcal{I}_k^n$, required in the second update step (7). Here, our inner-elements are owned by partition p and are, within a time step, independent of element-data owned by other partitions. Send-elements are owned by p, but their associated $\mathcal{I}_k^n$ are required for application of Eq. (7) to send-elements of other partitions. Similar recv-elements are owned by an adjacent partition and the respective $\mathcal{I}_k^n$ are required for updating the DOFs of p's send-elements in Eq. (7). We further sort the send- and recv-elements by their corresponding neighboring rank. If one of these elements is connected to more than one MPI-rank through its faces, we logically duplicate the element in our data layout. Within the inner-elements and the per-rank groups of the send- and receive-elements, we sort the elements by an unique but arbitrary identifier. Therefore, we are able to directly use our data layout for sending and receiving MPI-messages without the need for artificial communication buffers.

Our shared memory parallelization uses the OpenMP library. Compared to other work [14], we only use minimal functionality of OpenMP in the time marching loop. After synchronization, e.g., after initialization or wave field output, we open a single parallel-region until we reach the next synchronization point. Out of a total of T threads, we use the first $1 \leq W < T$ threads as workers and the $W + 1$'th thread as management and communication thread. The workers perform the numerical operations described in Sect. 2. Here, the distribution of work, e.g., *"compute Eq. (6) for all send-elements"* to workers is performed statically at initialization. This approach is similar, to traditional, static OpenMP annotation of for-loops, but allows for fine-grained load balancing and removes unnecessary, implicit barriers. For example, a thread might directly continue with Eq. (6) for inner-elements, after finishing its part of the send-elements. The $W + 1$'th thread initiates communication through MPI_Isend and MPI_Irecv, progresses communication through MPI_test, and ensures correctness by resolving dependencies and signaling the workers where to head next.

Considering different layers of memory, such as High Bandwidth Memory (HBM) and traditional DDR4 RAM in case of the Intel Xeon Phi x200 processor, we follow the general strategy of [13]. Here, we distribute data to the different layers, if our simulation size exceeds the size of near-memory and if the memory layers are available at application level, e.g., in flat-quadrant mode. In our seismic setup (see Sect. 2), we place the time-integrated DOFs $\mathcal{I}_k^n$, having high access frequencies and unstructured accesses, in near-memory. Further, EDGE provides high-bandwidth scratch memory for temporary storage of intermediate results, to avoid performance penalties of large stack-based memory chunks.

5   Experiments and Results

For the purpose of this work, we solely relied on double precision arithmetic for every of EDGE's floating point operations and used following machines:

- **Theta** is a Cray XC40 that comprises 3,200 Intel Xeon Phi 7230 64-core processors at 1.3 GHz (with Intel Turbo Boost enabled), 16 GB of in-package HBM and 192 GB of DDR4 RAM. Here, we used the performance-related modules intel/17.0.1.132, craype/2.5.8, PrgEnv-intel/6.0.3, cray-mpich/7.5.0, cray-memkind, craype-mic-knl, and the performance-related compile-flags -O2, -xMIC-AVX512, and -qopenmp for our scaling studies.
- **Cori-II** is a Cray XC40 that combines 9,304 Intel Xeon Phi 7250 68-core processors at 1.4 GHz (with Intel Turbo Boost enabled), 16 GB of in-package HBM and 96 GB of DDR4 RAM. Except for craype/2.5.7 and cray-mpich/7.4.4, we used the same performance-related modules and flags, as on Theta, on Cori-II.

5.1 Benchmarks

Convergence Analysis. Our first benchmark explores EDGE's high order convergence. Similar to [9], we use a cubic domain of size $[0, 100]^3$ and generate 24 setups by dividing the domain regularly into cubes with descending edge lengths: $\frac{100}{2} = 50, \frac{100}{4} = 25, \ldots, \frac{100}{50} = 2$. Within every setup, each of the cubes is then subdivided into five tetrahedral elements. Material parameters are $\rho = 1$, $\lambda = 2$, $\mu = 1$, while the initial DOFs discretize plane waves traveling in diagonal direction with a P-wave velocity of 2 and a S-wave velocity of 1. Additionally we use periodic boundary conditions, such that the solution of the setup can be derived analytically after a given time [9]. We simulate for a total time of $\sqrt{3} \cdot 100$. Therefore, the resulting exact solution is identical to our initial setup. Figure 2 shows two convergence plots derived from our setups. The plot on the left shows convergence when executing EDGE in non-fused mode. The plot on the right presents convergence when running EDGE with $m = 8$ fused simulations. Here, we shifted the initial setup of the respective simulations

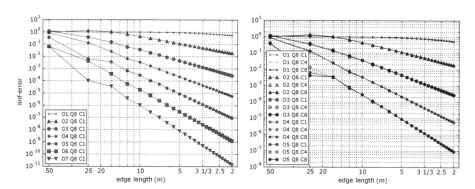

Fig. 2. Convergence of EDGE in the L^∞-norm. Shown are orders $\mathcal{O}1-\mathcal{O}7$ for the eighth quantity v (Q8) in non-fused runs on the left. The right plot shows orders $\mathcal{O}1 - \mathcal{O}5$ for v (Q8) when utilizing EDGE's fusion capabilities with shifted initial conditions. For clarity, from the total of eight fused simulations, only errors of the first (C1), fourth (C4) and last simulation (C8) are shown. (Color figure online)

by $(0, 0, 0)^T, (5, 5, 5)^T, \ldots, (35, 35, 35)^T$ to obtain true input-parallelism. We see that EDGE obtains the convergence rates reported in literature when ADER-DG is applied to seismic wave propagation [9]. The different fused simulations show almost identical convergence behavior.

Layer Over Halfspace Benchmark 1 (LOH.1). Our second configuration is the LOH.1 benchmark, which is part of *The Spice Code Validation* [22]. We used a domain covering $[-26 \, km, 32 \, km] \times [-26 \, km \times 32 \, km] \times [0 \, km, 33 \, km]$. All boundary-conditions are outflow, except for $z = 0$, where free-surface boundary conditions are set. The one seismic source of the benchmark is a point dislocation at $(0, 0, 693 \, m)$ with $M_{xy} = M_{yz} = M_0 = 10^{18} \, Nm$ being the only non-zero entries in the moment tensor. The moment time history is given by $M_0(1 - (1 + \frac{t}{T})exp(-\frac{t}{T}))$ with $T = 0.1 \, s$. The LOH.1 benchmark compares a total of nine receivers at the surface. The material parameters are $\rho = 2600 \, \frac{kg}{m^3}$, $\lambda = 20.8 \, GPa$, and $\mu = 10.4 \, GPa$ up to a depth of 1 km. In the remainder of the domain the parameters are given by $\rho = 2700 \, \frac{kg}{m^3}$, $\lambda = 32.4 \, GPa$, and $\mu = 32.4 \, GPa$.

We used the software gmsh [12] to generate a problem-adapted tetrahedral mesh. The material interface was integrated into the surface mesh, which resulted in interface-aligned faces of our tetrahedral elements. We specified a characteristic length of 100 m in $[-5 \, km, 13.67 \, km] \times [-5 \, km \times 15.392 \, km] \times [0 \, km, 1 \, km]$, 257 m in $[-5 \, km, 13.67 \, km] \times [-5 \, km \times 15.392 \, km] \times [1 \, km, 7 \, km]$, and 771 m everywhere else. To ensure smooth mesh coarsening in the 1 km thick layer, we additionally defined an attractor and used the overall minimum characteristic length for meshing. Further, we used gmsh's built-in optimizer and Netgen-interface to improve mesh quality. The final mesh consisted of 11,060,982 tetrahedral elements. We used fourth order in space and time and 256 nodes of Cori-II to simulate the 9 s of the benchmark. To ensure correctness of EDGE's full capabilities, we fused eight simulations. However, we simply used identical input for all fused simulations and therefore obtained eight identical solutions.

Figure 3 examplary compares EDGE's obtained particle velocity in x-direction u to the reference solution. We see that the solutions match very well, which is confirmed by Table 1, showing the single-valued envelope misfit

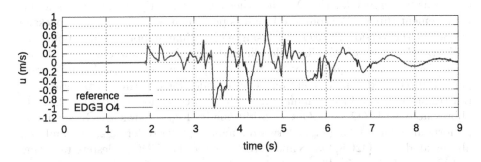

Fig. 3. Synthetic seismogram of EDGE for quantity u at the nith seismic receiver located at $(8647 \, m, 5764 \, m, 0)$ in red. The reference solution is shown in black. (Color figure online)

Table 1. Single-valued envelope misfit EM and single-valued phase misfit PM in percent for the nine receivers in the LOH.1 benchmark. The misfits are given for non-zero seismograms of the reference solution in a frequency range between 0.13 Hz and 5 Hz.

	location (m)			u (%)		v (%)		w (%)		max (%)	
	x	y	z	EM	PM	EM	PM	EM	PM	EM	PM
1	0	693	0	0.75	0.29					0.75	0.29
2	0	5543	0	1.20	0.16					1.20	0.16
3	0	10392	0	1.17	0.17					1.17	0.17
4	490	490	0	0.80	0.31	0.74	0.34	1.05	0.23	1.05	0.34
5	3919	3919	0	1.06	0.15	1.10	0.15	0.97	0.19	1.10	0.19
6	7348	7348	0	1.12	0.17	1.13	0.17	0.96	0.19	1.13	0.19
7	577	384	0	0.84	0.32	0.73	0.33	1.09	0.23	1.09	0.33
8	4612	3075	0	0.94	0.15	1.37	0.17	0.98	0.19	1.37	0.19
9	8647	5764	0	1.01	0.18	1.33	0.18	0.96	0.19	1.33	0.19

EM and single-valued phase misfit PM [23,24] for all nine seismic receivers and three particle velocities u, v, and w. Here, the misfits stay well below the threshold of 5%, referring to the highest accuracy level of the benchmark.

5.2   Single Node Performance

In this section we discuss EDGE's single node performance when running the LOH.1 benchmark (see Sect. 5.1), discretized with a total of 350,264 tetrahedral elements. Additionally, as in all following performance studies, we greatly limited the number of time steps to avoid unnecessary computations. All runs in this section were carried out on a single node of Cori-II in flat-quadrant mode and with all memory allocated in HBM through numactl's membind-feature. We used a setting identical to our per-node layout in distributed memory runs by utilizing only 66 cores for computations in EDGE. The first of the two remaining cores was left empty for the OS, the other core hosted the communication and management thread. We compare EDGE's performance to the software package SeisSol in the version *201511* [13] using global time stepping and support for AVX512. Here, we left the first tile idle and pinned the communication thread to the last core, as required by SeisSol for highest performance. Figure 4 compares the required time-to-solution of both codes for 500 time steps. First, we ran traditional, non-fused simulations with both codes for orders $\mathcal{O} = 2,\ldots,6$, abbreviated with O2C1,...,O6C1. Additionally, Fig. 4 shows EDGE's relative performance when fusing eight forward simulations for orders $\mathcal{O}2$, $\mathcal{O}3$, and $\mathcal{O}4$, abbreviated with O2C8, O3C8 and O4C8. We see that EDGE, despite targeting at fused simulations, is able to maintain a high fraction of SeisSol's performance when running single, non-fused forward simulations. In the case of O2C1, EDGE even outperforms SeisSol since SeisSol's zero-padding introduces a significant

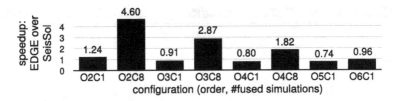

Fig. 4. Speedup of EDGE over SeisSol. For convergence rates $\mathcal{O}2 - \mathcal{O}6$ results for a single non-fused forward simulations (O2C1-O6C1) are presented. Additionally, respective per-simulation speedups for orders $\mathcal{O}2 - \mathcal{O}4$ are presented when using EDGE's full capabilities by fusing eight simulations (O2C8-O4C8).

overhead overturning improvements of alignment to cache lines. However, for orders higher than $\mathcal{O}2$ these optimizations pay off, leading to a higher performance of SeisSol. For the sixth order configuration O6C1, EDGE reaches 96% of SeisSol's performance. The reason for this relatively higher performance, compared to O4C1 and O5C1, is given by the $\mathcal{B}(6) = 56$ basis function of this setting. $\mathcal{B}(6)$ is a multiple of 8 and naturally leads to 64-byte aligned DOFs Q_k^n and time integrated DOFs $\mathcal{I}_k^n$ in EDGE since the base pointers of all our heap data structures are aligned 4,096 byte boundaries.

Comparing EDGE's performance on a simulation-by-simulation basis to SeisSol, when running eight fused simulations, we observe a factor 1.8-4.6 improvement in time-to-solution. This result confirms our theoretical discussion in Sect. 3, where we identified higher arithmetic intensities and increased regularity of fused simulations as key advantages. As shown in Fig. 1, the potential speedup offered by the higher arithmetic intensities is largest in the memory-bound, low order regime. Moving to the compute-bound high order simulations, the increased regularity becomes more important, leading to a substantial, but relatively smaller, 1.8× speedup over SeisSol for O4C8.

5.3   Weak Scaling

The setup of our weak scaling study follows the convergence analysis in Sect. 5.1. However, to further avoid unnecessary computations, we replaced the initial value computation of the DOFs, requiring an L2-projection, with zero values and disabled the error-norm computation. Instead, we added a total of 8 seismic sources, where only one of the sources was active in a single forward simulation. Further, in comparison to other work [14], we left the more demanding periodic boundary conditions intact, which is supported by EDGE for regular meshes and enables convergence studies in distributed memory setups. We used a total of 276,480 tetrahedral elements per node and studied the performance of fourth and sixth order convergence. In the case of the sixth order runs we present results for a single, non-fused simulation (O6C1). For the fourth order runs we present performance for a single forward simulation (O4C1) and eight fused simulations (O4C8). Considering the memory consumption of the heavy data structures touched in the time marching loop – $Q_k^n, \mathcal{I}_k^n, A_{k,c}^*, A_{k,i}^\pm$ in Eqs. (3), (4), and (5) – our weak scaling setup only has

54   A. Breuer et al.

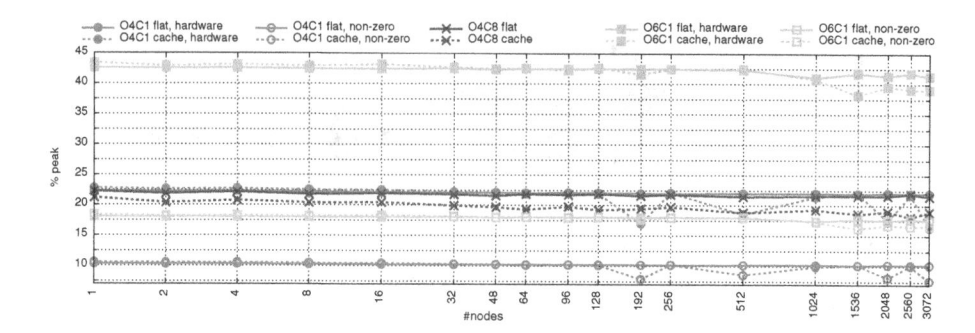

Fig. 5. Weak scaling study on Theta. Shown are hardware and non-zero hardware peak efficiencies of all configurations in cache and flat mode. O denotes the order and C the number of fused simulations. (Color figure online)

a moderate size, underlining the relevance of this scaling study. O4C1's matrices consume 2.2 GiB per node, O4C8's matrices 7.4 GiB and O6C1's matrices 3.6 GiB per node

Figure 5 shows the hardware and non-zero peak efficiencies of our weak scaling on 1 to 3,072 nodes of Theta. Here, the hardware peak efficiency counts every of the double-precision floating point operation performed in hardware, while the non-zero peak efficiency only considers those of non-zero entries in our kernel's matrices (see Sect. 2). We see that EDGE obtains more than 38% of hardware peak efficiency in cache mode and more than 41% in flat mode for all O6C1 runs on Theta. The highest sustained hardware performance on Theta was obtained in flat mode and is 3.4 PFLOPS, which corresponds to a non-zero performance of 1.4 PFLOPS and a parallel efficiency of 97%. Moving to the fourth order configurations O4C1 and O4C8, EDGE is able to maintain the single node speedup (see Fig. 4) offered by its fusion capabilities at scale. In fact O4C8 outperforms O4C1 in per-simulation time-to-solution by 2.1× when running in flat mode at scale. Due to O4C8's sparse matrix-operators, this corresponds to a hardware and nonzero peak efficiency of 21.5% on 3,072 nodes, which is equivalent to a sustained performance of 1.8 PFLOPS and a parallel efficiency over 96%.

Figure 6 shows our weak scaling study on 1 to 9,000 nodes of Cori-II. The obtained peak efficiencies are almost identical to Theta and, once again, show EDGE's high hardware and non-zero peak efficiencies. On Cori-II, we sustained 10.4 PFLOPS in hardware when running O6C1 in flat mode on 9,000 nodes. To the best of our knowledge, this is the highest obtained peak performance for seismic simulations with ADER-DG, outperforming 24,576 cards of Tianhe-2, reaching 8.6 PFLOPS [14]. Further, O4C8 in flat mode has a 2.0× higher single simulation throughput than O4C1 on 9,000 nodes with a sustained hardware and non-zero peak efficiency of 18.1%, corresponding to 5.0 PFLOPS.

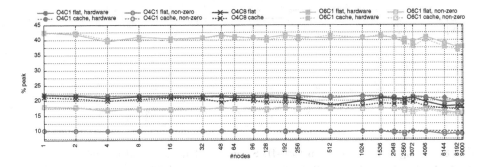

Fig. 6. Weak scaling study on Cori-II. Shown are hardware and non-zero hardware peak efficiencies of all configurations in cache and flat mode. O denotes the order and C the number of fused simulations. (Color figure online)

5.4   Strong Scaling

Our final performance study consists of two strong scaling setups of the LOH.1 benchmark (see Sect. 5.1). Here, we used a total of 172,386,915 tetrahedral elements on 32 to 3,072 nodes of Theta and a total of 340,727,199 tetrahedrons on 128 to 8,192 nodes of Cori-II. EDGE required a total of 1.7 TiB of memory for O4C1, 4.7 TiB for O4C8, and 2.6 TiB for O6C1 on Theta. Analogue, the setup consumed a total of 3.5 TiB for O4C1, 9.4 TiB for O4C8, and 5.2 TiB on Cori-II.

Figure 7 shows the hardware and non-zero peak efficiencies of the cache and flat mode runs on Theta. We observe that the efficiencies are close to the weak scaling depicted in Fig. 5. Here, we have to remember that the weak scaling study relied on a perfectly balanced, artificial setup, while our strong scaling's mesh is fully unstructured and partitioned by Metis. When analyzing the performance of the O4C8-runs in detail, we see a plateau between 192 and 2048 nodes with performance dropping below and afterwards. The reason for the lowered performance below 192 nodes is the total memory requirements of the computational data structures exceeding Xeon Phi's 16 GB of HBM, required

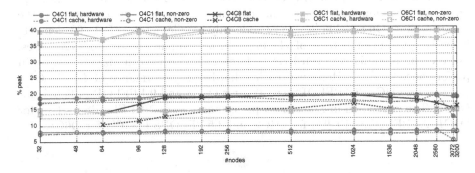

Fig. 7. Strong scaling study on Theta. Shown are hardware and non-zero peak efficiencies of all configurations in cache and flat mode. O denotes the order and C the number of fused simulations. (Color figure online)

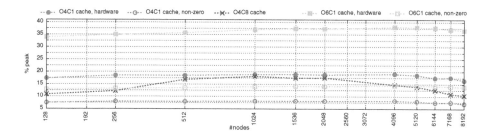

Fig. 8. Strong scaling study on Cori-II. Shown are hardware and non-zero hardware peak efficiencies of all configurations in cache mode. O denotes the order and C the number of fused simulations. (Color figure online)

for optimal performance of Eq. (7). For high node counts, we see a degradation due to the extreme layout of the strong scaling, reaching a 50× increase of O4C8 and 100× of O4C1 and O6C1 at 3,200 nodes. Comparing the stable flat mode performance of O4C1 to that of O4C8, we see that the parallel efficiency of O4C8 drops sooner. Recalling Sect. 3, this is property of the fused simulations, since the communication volume simply grows one-to-one with the number of fused simulations. However, the simulation throughput of O4C8 is greatly increased, which leaves less time spent in computations for hiding communication. The highest hardware performances were obtained in flat mode on 3,200 nodes: 1.6 PFLOPS (19.1) for O4C1, 1.4 PFLOPS (16.3%) for O4C8, and 3.4 PFLOPS (39.6%) for O6C1. With respect to non-zero peak performances, this corresponds to 0.7 PFLOPS (8.2%) for O4C1, 1.4 PFLOPS (16.3%) for O4C8 due to sparse matrix-matrix operators, and 1.3 PFLOPS (15.1%) for O6C1.

Figure 8 takes our strong scaling one step further, with a cache mode node-range of 128 to 8,192 on Cori-II. As already observed in the weak scaling in Fig. 6, the relative performance of all runs is slightly lower on Cori-II than on Theta, due to the higher per-socket performance. Again we observe an plateau for O4C8 due to HBM, but dropping performance for all runs at higher node counts. These drops are most severe for the O4C8 runs since our high single-node speedup (see Fig. 4) significantly decreases the time per simulation and time step, but keep the communication volume constant, exposing communication in the strong scaling. On 8,192 nodes every node only handles a total of 41,593 elements in average, facing an increase of 64× in potential computer power from 128 nodes. Since cache mode is very sensitive to large compute we can observe a drop in performance at scale. Here, we reach a hardware performance of 4.1 PFLOPS (16.4%) for O4C1, 2.6 PFLOPS (10.4%) for O4C8 and 9.1 PFLOPS (36.6%) for O6C1. The corresponding non-zero performances are 1.8 PFLOPS (7.1%) for O4C1, 2.6 PFLOPS (10.4%) for O4C8 and 3.5 PFLOPS (13.9%) for O6C1.

6 Conclusions

This article has introduced EDGE[1], a novel solver for fused seismic simulations which aims at increasing the throughput of extreme scale seismic ensemble simulations. For highest accuracy, EDGE utilizes the Discontinuous Galerkin (DG) method for spatial and the Arbitrary high order DERivatives (ADER) scheme for time discretization, implemented for unstructured tetrahedral meshes. The occurring kernel routines, small sparse and dense matrix-matrix multiplications, are accelerated by a sophisticated runtime code generation approach. This technique allows for hardware efficiencies of more than 40% for single runs (10–20% non-zero efficiency) and more than 20% of non-zero efficiency when conducting fused simulations. Depending on the chosen order, fused simulations can offer an increased throughput of $1.8\times$ to $4.6\times$. With respect to achieved raw performance EDGE weak-scaled to 9,000 nodes of the Cori-II supercomputer, while running at 10.4 PFLOPS at order six. For a fused fourth order run EDGE achieved 5.0 PFLOPS of non-zero/non-padded performance using small sparse matrix kernels. In addition to these excellent weak-scaling results, EDGE also exhibits nearly the same performance in case of strong scaling. This is achieved by a carefully designed parallel implementation, which minimizes threading overhead and maximizes MPI message progression. When strong scaling by $100\times$ on Theta and $64\times$ on Cori-II, EDGE sustained a performance of 3.4 PFLOPS and 9.1 PFLOPS, respectively.

Acknowledgements. Only the great support of experts at NERSC and ALCF made our extreme-scale results possible. In particular, we thank J. Deslippe, S. Dosanjh, R. Gerber, and K. Kumaran. This work was supported by the Southern California Earthquake Center (SCEC) through contribution #16247. This research used resources of the National Energy Research Scientific Computing Center, a DOE Office of Science User Facility supported by the Office of Science of the U.S. Department of Energy under Contract No. DE-AC02-05CH11231. This research used resources of the Argonne Leadership Computing Facility, which is a DOE Office of Science User Facility supported under Contract DE-AC02-06CH11357. This work used the Extreme Science and Engineering Discovery Environment (XSEDE), which is supported by National Science Foundation grant number ACI-1053575.

Optimization Notice: Software and workloads used in performance tests may have been optimized for performance only on Intel microprocessors. Performance tests, such as SYSmark and MobileMark, are measured using specific computer systems, components, software, operations and functions. Any change to any of those factors may cause the results to vary. You should consult other information and performance tests to assist you in fully evaluating your contemplated purchases, including the performance of that product when combined with other products. For more information go to http://www.intel.com/performance. Intel, Xeon, and Intel Xeon Phi are trademarks of Intel Corporation in the U.S. and/or other countries.

---

[1] EDGE is available under the 3-clause BSD license at http://dial3343.org.

References

1. Reinders, J., Jeffers, J., Sodani, A. (eds.) Intel Xeon Phi Processor High Performance Programming Knights Landing Edition (2016). Ch. 4 and Ch. 6
2. Aoi, S., Fujiwara, H.: 3D finite-difference method using discontinuous grids. Bull. Seismol. Soc. Am. **89**(4), 918–930 (1999)
3. Appelö, D., Petersson, N.A.: A stable finite difference method for the elastic wave equation on complex geometries with free surfaces. Commun. Comput. Phys. **5**(1), 84–107 (2009)
4. Bastian, P., et al.: Hardware-based efficiency advances in the EXA-DUNE project. In: Bungartz, H.-J., Neumann, P., Nagel, W.E. (eds.) Software for Exascale Computing - SPPEXA 2013-2015. LNCSE, vol. 113, pp. 3–23. Springer, Cham (2016). doi:10.1007/978-3-319-40528-5_1
5. Benjemaa, M., Glinsky-Olivier, N., Cruz-Atienza, V.M., Virieux, J.: 3D dynamic rupture simulations by a finite volume method. Geophys. J. Int. **178**, 541–560 (2009)
6. Breuer, A., Heinecke, A., Rettenberger, S., Bader, M., Gabriel, A.-A., Pelties, C.: Sustained petascale performance of seismic simulations with SeisSol on SuperMUC. In: Kunkel, J.M., Ludwig, T., Meuer, H.W. (eds.) ISC 2014. LNCS, vol. 8488, pp. 1–18. Springer, Cham (2014). doi:10.1007/978-3-319-07518-1_1
7. Chaljub, E., Komatitsch, D., Vilotte, J.-P., Capdeville, Y., Valette, B., Festa, G.: Spectral-element analysis in seismology. Adv. Geophys. **48**, 365–419 (2007). Advances in Wave Propagation in Heterogenous Earth, http://www.sciencedirect.com/science/article/pii/S0065268706480079
8. Chaljub, E., Maufroy, E., Moczo, P., Kristek, J., Hollender, F., Bard, P.-Y., Priolo, E., Klin, P., de Martin, F., Zhang, Z., Zhang, W., Chen, X.: 3-D numerical simulations of earthquake ground motion in sedimentary basins: testing accuracy through stringent models. Geophys. J. Int. **201**(1), 90–111 (2015)
9. Dumbser, M., Käser, M.: An arbitrary high-order discontinuous galerkin method for elastic waves on unstructured meshes - II. The three-dimensional isotropic case. Geophys. J. Int. **167**(1), 319–336 (2006)
10. Duru, K., Dunham, E.M.: Dynamic earthquake rupture simulations on nonplanar faults embedded in 3D geometrically complex, heterogeneous elastic solids. J. Comput. Phys. **305**, 185–207 (2016)
11. Etienne, V., Chaljub, E., Virieux, J.: An hp-adaptive discontinuous Galerkin finite-element method for 3-D elastic wave modelling. Geophys. J. Int. **183**(2), 941–962 (2010)
12. Geuzaine, C., Remacle, J.-F.: Gmsh: A 3-D finite element mesh generator with built-in pre-and post-processing facilities. Int. J. Numer. Methods Eng. **79**(11), 1309–1331 (2009)
13. Heinecke, A., Breuer, A., Bader, M., Dubey, P.: High order seismic simulations on the intel Xeon Phi processor (Knights Landing). In: Kunkel, J.M., Balaji, P., Dongarra, J. (eds.) ISC High Performance 2016. LNCS, vol. 9697, pp. 343–362. Springer, Cham (2016). doi:10.1007/978-3-319-41321-1_18
14. Heinecke, A., Breuer, A., Rettenberger, S., Bader, M., Gabriel, A.-A., Pelties, C., Bode, A., Barth, W., Liao, X.-K., Vaidyanathan, K., et al.: Petascale high order dynamic rupture earthquake simulations on heterogeneous supercomputers. In: Proceedings of the International Conference for High Performance Computing, Networking, Storage and Analysis (2014)

15. Heinecke, A., Henry, G., Hutchinson, M., Pabst, H.: LIBXSMM: accelerating small matrix multiplications by runtime code generation. In: Proceedings of the International Conference for High Performance Computing, Networking, Storage and Analysis (2016)
16. Ichimura, T., Fujita, K., Quinay, P., Maddegedara, L., Hori, M., Tanaka, S., Shizawa, Y., Kobayashi, H., Minami, K.: Implicit nonlinear wave simulation with 1.08T DOF and 0.270T unstructured finite elements to enhance comprehensive earthquake simulation (2015)
17. Ichimura, T., Hori, M., Bielak, J.: A hybrid multiresolution meshing technique for finite element three-dimensional earthquake ground motion modelling in basins including topography. Geophys. J. Int. **177**(3), 1221–1232 (2009)
18. George, K., Vipin, K.: MeTis: Unstructured Graph Partitioning and Sparse Matrix Ordering System, version 4.0 (2009)
19. Kang, T.-S., Baag, C.-E.: An efficient finite-difference method for simulating 3D seismic response of localized basin structures. Bull. Seismol. Soc. Am. **94**(5), 1690–1705 (2004)
20. Käser, M., Dumbser, M., Puente, J., Igel, H.: An arbitrary high-order discontinuous galerkin method for elastic waves on unstructured meshes - III. viscoelastic attenuation. Geophys. J. Int. **168**(1), 224–242 (2007)
21. Komatitsch, D., Tromp, J.: Spectral-element simulations of global seismic wave propagation-II. Three-dimensional models, oceans, rotation and self-gravitation. Geophys. J. Int. **150**(1), 303–318 (2002)
22. Moczo, P., Ampuero, J.P., Kristek, J., Day, S.M., Kristekova, M., Pazak, P., Galis, M., Igel, H.: Comparison of numerical methods for seismic wave propagation and source dynamics - the SPICE code validation. In: Third International Symposium on the Effects of Surface Geology on Seismic Motion. Actes des journées scientifiques du LCPC. Laboratoire central des ponts et chaussées, Paris, France, pp. 1–10 (2006). ISBN 9782720824654
23. Kristeková, M., Kristek, J., Moczo, P.: Time-frequency misfit and goodness-of-fit criteria for quantitative comparison of time signals. Geophys. J. Int. **178**(2), 813–825 (2009)
24. Kristeková, M., Kristek, J., Moczo, P., Day, S.M.: Misfit criteria for quantitative comparison of seismograms. Bull. Seismol. Soc. Am. **96**(5), 1836–1850 (2006)
25. Liu, J., Chandrasekaran, B., Wu, J., Jiang, W., Kini, S., Yu, W., Buntinas, D., Wyckoff, P., Panda, D.K.: Performance comparison of MPI implementations over InfiniBand, Myrinet and Quadrics. In: Proceedings of the 2003 ACM/IEEE Conference on Supercomputing (2003)
26. Ma, S., Liu, P.: Modeling of the perfectly matched layer absorbing boundaries and intrinsic attenuation in explicit finite-element methods. Bull. Seismol. Soc. Am. **96**(5), 1779–1794 (2006)
27. Malas, T., Kurth, T., Deslippe, J.: Optimization of the sparse matrix-vector products of an IDR Krylov iterative solver in EMGeo for the Intel KNL manycore processor. In: Taufer, M., Mohr, B., Kunkel, J.M. (eds.) ISC High Performance 2016. LNCS, vol. 9945, pp. 378–389. Springer, Cham (2016). doi:10.1007/978-3-319-46079-6_27
28. Moczo, P., Kristek, J., Vavryčuk, V.: 3D heterogeneous staggered-grid finite-difference modeling of seismic motion with volume harmonic and arithmetic averaging of elastic moduli and densities. Bull. Seismol. Soc. Am. **92**(8), 3042–3066 (2002)

29. Moczo, P., Robertsson, J.O.A., Eisner, L.: The finite-difference time-domain method for modeling of seismic wave propagation. Adv. Geophys. **48**, 421–516 (2007). Advances in Wave Propagation in Heterogenous Earth, http://www.sciencedirect.com/science/article/pii/S0065268706480080

30. Modave, A., St-Cyr, A., Warburton, T.: GPU performance analysis of a nodal discontinuous Galerkin method for acoustic and elastic models. Comput. Geosci. **91**, 64–76 (2016)

31. Peter, D., Komatitsch, D., Luo, Y., Martin, R., Goff, N., Casarotti, E., Loher, P., Magnoni, F., Liu, Q., Blitz, C., Nissen-Meyer, T., Basini, P., Tromp, J.: Forward and adjoint simulations of seismic wave propagation on fully unstructured hexahedral meshes. Geophys. J. Int. **186**(2), 721–739 (2011)

32. Pitarka, A.: 3D elastic finite-difference modeling of seismic motion using staggered grids with nonuniform spacing. Bull. Seismol. Soc. Am. **89**(1), 54–68 (1999)

33. Shepherd, J.F., Johnson, C.R.: Hexahedral mesh generation constraints. Eng. Comput. **24**(3), 195–213 (2008)

34. Symes, W.W., Vdovina, T.: Interface error analysis for numerical wave propagation. Comput. Geosci. **13**(3), 363–371 (2009)

35. Taborda, R., Bielak, J.: Large-Scale earthquake simulation: computational seismology and complex engineering systems. Comput. Sci. Eng. **13**(4), 14–27 (2011)

36. Cruz-Atienza, V.M., Virieux, J., Aochi, H.: 3D finite-difference dynamic-rupture modeling along nonplanar faults. Geophysics **72**(5), 123–137 (2007)

LAMMPS' PPPM Long-Range Solver for the Second Generation Xeon Phi

William McDoniel[1]([✉]) [iD], Markus Höhnerbach[1], Rodrigo Canales[1],
Ahmed E. Ismail[2], and Paolo Bientinesi[1]

[1] RWTH Aachen University, 52062 Aachen, Germany
mcdoniel@aices.rwth-aachen.de
[2] West Virginia University, Morgantown 26506, USA

Abstract. Molecular Dynamics is an important tool for computational biologists, chemists, and materials scientists, consuming a sizable amount of supercomputing resources. Many of the investigated systems contain charged particles, which can only be simulated accurately using a long-range solver, such as PPPM. We extend the popular LAMMPS molecular dynamics code with an implementation of PPPM particularly suitable for the second generation Intel Xeon Phi. Our main target is the optimization of computational kernels by means of vectorization, and we observe speedups in these kernels of up to 12×. These improvements carry over to LAMMPS users, with overall speedups ranging between 2–3×, without requiring users to retune input parameters. Furthermore, our optimizations make it easier for users to determine optimal input parameters for attaining top performance.

1 Introduction

Molecular dynamics simulations are used to compute the evolution of systems of atoms in fields as diverse as biology, chemistry, and materials science. Such simulations target millions or billions of particles, are frequently run in parallel, and consume a sizable portion of supercomputers' cycles. Since in principle each atom interacts with all the other atoms in the system, efficient methods to compute the pairwise forces are vital. The most widespread method for electrostatic interactions is the "Particle-Particle Particle-Mesh" (PPPM) method [1], which makes it possible to efficiently compute even the interactions between distant particles.

Due to its popularity, we target the open-source LAMMPS code [2], which offers the PPPM method. LAMMPS is a C++ code designed for large parallel simulations using MPI, and is written to be modular and extensible. LAMMPS can be compiled with a variety of packages that provide different implementations of key methods for the calculation of short-range and long-range interactions. For example, the USER-OMP package includes versions of methods such as PPPM which are specifically designed for shared-memory parallelism. In this paper, we extend the LAMMPS molecular dynamics simulator with a version of PPPM that is especially suitable for architectures with wide vector registers,

© Springer International Publishing AG 2017
J.M. Kunkel et al. (Eds.): ISC High Performance 2017, LNCS 10266, pp. 61–78, 2017.
DOI: 10.1007/978-3-319-58667-0_4

such as the Xeon Phi. In the past, long-ranged solvers have been optimized for GPUs, with issues similar to those encountered with Xeon Phi accelerators [3,4].

On these systems, one of the main routes towards high-performance is the exploitation of the wide (512-bit) vector registers. To this end, we create vectorized kernels for all the computational components that are not directly supported by highly optimized math libraries (e.g. FFTs). These routines account for between 20% and 80% of the time spent in PPPM. As such, their optimization leads to notable speedups in the overall performance of the simulation.

One challenge is that the innermost loops of said computational routines are very short, with trip-counts between 3 and 7. This is a common problem for vectorizing molecular dynamics even outside of PPPM. For example, it was encountered by Höhnerbach et al. in their multi-platform vectorization of the extremely short loops of the Tersoff potential [5]. It turns out that work can be saved elsewhere by increasing these trip counts, simultaneously enabling efficient vectorization. Similarly, work can be shifted away from poorly-scaling FFTs and into newly-optimized functions, and, within the optimized functions, memory bandwidth can be traded against additional computation.

In this paper, in addition to discussing vectorization techniques, we also provide insights into the parametrization of PPPM for performance. In particular, we consider three tunable parameters: the real-space cutoff, the interpolation order, and the differentiation mode. Many users will stick to the default choices where such exist, since these promise accurate and reasonably performant calculations. Others will have taken time to tune these parameters for their particular problems, but even expert users often make suboptimal choices that can up to double time-to-solution for a given desired accuracy, depending on the problem [6]. We achieve 2–3× speedups for a wide range of input parameters, and our optimizations also make the careful tuning of several parameters unnecessary by making particular options superior to the others for almost all cases.

The code presented in this paper is contributed to the USER-INTEL package of LAMMPS [7]. It has been shown that this package can not just yield impressive speedups on Intel architecture, but also improve the energy efficiency of the calculation [8].

2   Molecular Dynamics and PPPM

2.1   An Algorithmic Overview

The interaction between atoms in a molecular dynamics simulation is governed by a so-called potential function. For example, the Lennard-Jones (LJ) and the Coulombic ($Coul$) potentials are given by:

$$V_{LJ}^{ij} = 4\epsilon_{ij} \left[\left(\frac{\sigma_{ij}}{r_{ij}} \right)^{12} - \left(\frac{\sigma_{ij}}{r_{ij}} \right)^{6} \right], \quad \text{and} \quad V_{Coul}^{ij} = \frac{C \, q_i \, q_j}{\varepsilon \, r_{ij}}. \tag{1}$$

For a given pair of atoms (i, j), the potential depends on the distance between them, r_{ij}, as well as their charges q_i and q_j (in the Coulombic case), or the parameters ϵ_{ij} and σ_{ij} (in the Lennard-Jones case), which describe the minimum of the potential function and its root. In order to obtain the forces on atoms, MD simulations can compute these potential functions for all pairs of atoms, but $\mathcal{O}(n^2)$ pairs have to be evaluated, and this quickly becomes infeasible.

A simple solution is to introduce a cutoff. One only considers interactions among atoms within a given cutoff radius r_C of each other. Consequently, the number of pairs to be evaluated decreases to $\mathcal{O}(nr_C^3)$. Since all the potential functions (e.g., Eq. 1) fall off with distance, the cutoff provides a reasonable strategy to approximate the total potential on atoms.

There are, however, numerous situations in which long-range interactions between atoms cannot be neglected, and instead have to be approximated numerically. A plain cutoff strategy does not work well for Coulomb interactions, which are relevant when a system contains charged particles or polar molecules, because the potential falls off only as r^{-1}. In contrast, the cutoff is perfectly fine for the Lennard-Jones potential, as long as the system is uniform.

In non-uniform problems, such as those featuring an interface, even Lennard-Jones interactions may need to be calculated using a long-ranged solver and can not be approximated [9]. In these cases, it is necessary to approximate these long-range interactions without explicitly computing pair-wise potential functions; for this task, Particle-Particle Particle-Mesh is often the method of choice. PPPM approximates long-range interactions in a periodic system by obtaining the potential of the entire system of atoms as a function of space, discretized to a grid [1]. While originally developed for electrostatics, the method was later adapted to the r^{-6} term of the Lennard-Jones potential [10].

In this work, we focus on PPPM for electrostatics, i.e., the Coulomb potential. PPPM uses an idea due to Ewald, and splits the potential into two components [11]. The first component, the "short-ranged" part of PPPM, contains the discontinuity due to the r^{-1} term, and a smooth screening term that limits the support to a small spherical region around a given atom; this component can be calculated directly between each atom and its neighbors in a certain cutoff radius r_C. The second component is the "long-ranged" part of PPPM; due to its smooth nature, this can be solved accurately on a grid.

The efficient solution of the long-ranged component is the key ingredient of the PPPM method. Since we are operating with smooth quantities, the electrostatic potential is related to the charge distribution ρ via Poisson's equation

$$\nabla^2 \Phi = -\frac{\rho}{\epsilon_0}. \tag{2}$$

From the electrical potential Φ, one can compute the forces on all the atoms due to it. The forces on an atom j with charge q_j can be obtained from the gradient of the potential evaluated at the particle's position:

$$\boldsymbol{F}_j = -q_j \nabla \Phi. \tag{3}$$

PPPM approximates these forces on each particle by proceeding in three steps:

1. First, particle charges are mapped to a grid using a stencil, obtaining a discretized form of the charge distribution ρ.
2. Second, Poisson's equation (Eq. 2) is solved in order to obtain the potential Φ. This is done by first taking the 3D Fourier transform of the charge distribution, as Poisson's equation is easier to solve in reciprocal space, and then performing one or more inverse FFTs to obtain a result in real space.
3. Third, this result is mapped back to the atoms with the same stencil used when mapping charges.

The forces are obtained from the gradient of the potential, and this gradient can be taken in reciprocal or real space, determined by the user-specified differentiation mode. For IK differentiation, the gradient is calculated in reciprocal space, immediately after solving Poisson's equation, and three inverse FFTs bring it back into real space, where its components are mapped to the atoms. For AD differentiation, one inverse FFT yields the scalar potential in real space, and this is mapped to the atoms using different sets of coefficients for each component of the gradient to be obtained.

Our optimizations focus especially on the mapping steps (steps 1 and 3). Step 2 is not as interesting for manual optimization since it is dominated by FFT calculations, for which highly optimized libraries exist. The mapping steps, on the contrary, are deeply nested loops performing calculations on data that is likely already in cache. We will show that optimizations, especially proper vectorization, will speed up these steps by at least a factor of four.

2.2 Related Work

Besides LAMMPS, many other popular molecular dynamics codes contain long-ranged solvers. Examples include, but are not limited to, Gromacs [12], DL_POLY [13], AMBER [14], Desmond [15], and NAMD [16]. These codes tend not to implement PPPM itself, in favor of related schemes such as PME [17], SPME [18], and k-GSE [19]. The main differences with respect to PPPM lie in the function used to interpolate atom charges onto the grid and back, and in the corresponding Green's function used to solve for the smooth part of the potential. There also exist schemes for long-ranged force evaluation that are not based on Fourier transforms, such as lattice Gaussian multigrid [20], Multilevel Summation [21], and r-GSE [19].

2.3 Parametrization of PPPM

Since LAMMPS is used for a wide variety of problems, users have many choices about input parameters for the target physical system. Several of these parameters influence the accuracy and/or speed of the simulation, including the cutoff distance (r_C), the prescribed error in forces relative to a reference (ϵ), the stencil size (S), and the differentiation mode, IK or AD. r_C expresses the distance within which pair-wise interactions are computed directly, and outside of which the interactions are approximated using the PPPM grid; the short-ranged calculations scale with r_C^3. The work done when computing FFTs is controlled by ϵ; LAMMPS automatically determines the coarseness of the FFT grid to satisfy this accuracy constraint, depending on the values chosen for the other parameters. A 7^3 stencil ($S = 7$) causes writing to, and reading from, about 2.7 times as many grid cells compared to the default 5^3 stencil. A higher-order stencil produces more accurate results, and LAMMPS takes this into account when deciding the resolution of the PPPM grid. Therefore, a higher-order stencil shifts work out of the FFT functions, and into the mapping functions. Users can also choose between the IK and AD differentiation modes described above, and LAMMPS again takes their different accuracies into account when setting up the FFT grid, with the IK mode yielding a slightly coarser grid.

Users will typically want to use a set of inputs that nearly minimize runtime, subject to an accuracy constraint. Unfortunately, short of trial-and-error for a specific problem it can be difficult to find a good set of parameters. In a recent work [6], Fabregat et al. developed a method for automatically searching the space of input parameters to find a good set, guided by cost and accuracy models; their case studies suggest that even expert users systematically underestimate the expense of PPPM: they invariably predicted lower-than-optimal cutoffs, which minimize the work done in computing pair interactions while forcing a finer FFT grid. The impact of stencil size was not considered, leaving the choice at LAMMPS' default. In the next sections we demonstrate that an appropriate choice of stencil size is needed to achieve good vectorization.

2.4 Profiling

In order to investigate the effects of the input parameters on runtime, we execute our baseline on a single core of a KNL machine with a single thread. The system is an Intel Xeon Phi 7210 chip (64 cores and 16 GB of HBM RAM) in quadrant and flat memory mode, connected to other nodes via OmniPath. Our software is based on the May 11, 2016 version of LAMMPS with the RIGID, USER-OMP and USER-INTEL packages enabled. It was compiled using the Intel C++ Compiler version 16.01 (build 20151021), and uses Intel MPI 5.0 (build 20150128). The reference runs use the code provided by the USER-OMP package, and our runs are based on code from USER-INTEL package running in mixed precision mode. Our benchmark is an SPC/E water simulation [22], a benchmark provided with LAMMPS. We modified it to have a cubic domain.

Since all the atoms in the system carry partial charges, the simulation uses PPPM to calculate forces. Unless otherwise specified, the default settings that we use are relative error $\epsilon = 10^{-4}$, and short-range cutoff $r_C = 5$ Å. The basecase contains 36,000 atoms, and will later be scaled up for more extensive benchmarks.

Figure 1 shows timings as the cutoff, relative error, and differentiation mode vary. The vertical sections denote the time spent in FFTs ("PPPM FFT"), and in PPPM aside from FFTs ("PPPM non-FFT"), the time spent in the pair-wise short-ranged interactions ("Pair"), and everything else ("Other").

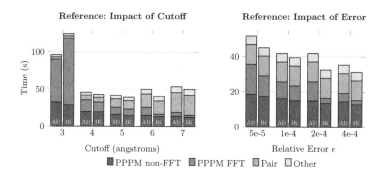

Fig. 1. Profile of SPC/E water test case running single-threaded on one core of a KNL. Left bar: IK differentiation, right bar: AD differentiation.

For cutoff, there actually is a minimum of the runtime, i.e., reducing the cutoff will not reduce runtime beyond a certain point where the long-ranged part gets less efficient: The $r_C = 3$ Å case spends a disproportionate amount of time in PPPM. The cutoff mostly impacts the "Pair" time—since it scales as $\mathcal{O}(r_C^3)$—and the "PPPM FFT" time—since it forces the grid to grow or shrink.

For ϵ, there of course is no minimum—lower accuracy results in faster simulations—mostly due to less time spent in FFT calculations (i.e. smaller grids). Outliers in FFT performance can be attributed to pathological cases (in terms of size) of the FFT library.

In both panels of Fig. 1, the "Other" and the "PPPM non-FFT" sections are largely unaffected by changes in cutoff or relative error. In both, AD differentiation performs best (except for one outlier). For cutoff-optimal cases, the majority of the runtime is spent on long-ranged calculation, suggesting that optimization in that area might be quite fruitful.

3 Optimizations

The optimizations for the different stages of the algorithm are discussed here. In particular, we cover the functions that map atoms to grid points and grid values to atoms, the Poisson solver, and the routines responsible for the short-ranged contribution.

3.1 Mapping Functions

All three mapping functions—*Map-Charge* and both the IK and the AD versions of *Distribute-Force*—share the same structure: a loop over all atoms, the calculation of stencil coefficients, and then a loop over stencil points. *Map-Charge* multiplies the particle charge by the stencil coefficient and adds that value to a point on the grid. *Distribute-Force* proceeds in a slightly different way depending on the differentiation mode. The IK mode multiplies the grid values for each spatial dimension at each grid point by the corresponding stencil coefficient, then adds them to three totals, one for each dimension; after the loop over stencil points, these components are multiplied by the atom's charge and a scaling factor to obtain force components. The AD mode multiplies the scalar potential at a grid point by three different stencil coefficients to obtain a vector, which is added on the atom; after the loop over stencil points, substantially more calculation than is required for IK differentiation transforms these totals into the components of the force vector.

The stencil coefficients are the product of three polynomials of order equal to the stencil size, one for each dimension. The iteration over stencil points consists of a triple loop (one for each dimension of the stencil). This represents the bulk (80%+) of the work, and accounts for almost all the memory accesses in the mapping functions. *Map-Charge* accesses only a single value at each grid point, but does very little computation. The IK mode of *Distribute-Force* uses three different values at each grid point. The AD mode uses only one value at each grid point, but performs more floating point operations. The arithmetic intensity of all these routines is relatively low, and memory access patterns will determine the best approach to vectorization.

Since the number of grid points is typically comparable to or smaller than the number of atoms, and NS^3 stencil points are touched when looping over N atoms, there is a great deal of data reuse. With so few calculations being performed on data which is almost always found in cache, managing vectorization overhead will prove to be vital. In general, we find that it is important to minimize the amount of data shuffling or masking required to prepare for vector operations; whenever possible, a full vector should be pulled from memory, operated on, and returned.

With an understanding of the structure of the mapping functions, we now walk through our process of optimizing each one, pointing out what worked and what did not. A summary of progressive speedups for each function is shown in Fig. 2.

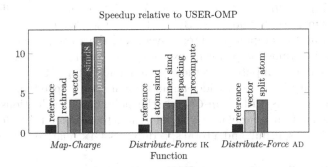

Fig. 2. Speedups for different implementations of each of the three mapping functions relative to the USER-OMP baseline version. Charge mapping timings were obtained from simulations using IK differentiation.

Function *Map-Charge*

Rethread: To avoid race conditions when writing to the grid, the USER-OMP package has threads own disjoint chunks of the grid, and uses conditional statements in the innermost loop over stencil points. By giving threads disjoint sets of atoms and maintaining private copies of the grid—which are then summed together—we achieve a $\sim2\times$ speedup.

Vector: We vectorize the innermost loop over stencil points, which features unit stride memory accesses as it iterates through grid points. We target a new default stencil size of 7, instead of 5, to make better use of 256-bit vector registers. This implementation achieves another factor of ~2 speedup ("vector" implementation), which is significant but not close to the theoretical $7\times$ we might hope for.

Simd8: Masking associated with the 7-iteration loop is a significant overheard. By explicitly setting the loop length to 8 and padding the stencil coefficient arrays with zeros, we avoid masking and obtain a total of $\sim6\times$ speedup over the re-threaded scalar version.

Precompute: Rather than evaluating polynomials to obtain the stencil coefficients for each atom every time step, we precompute 5000 values for each polynomial and refer to the nearest entry in this lookup table instead. This brings total speedup to over $12\times$ of the baseline.

Function *Distribute-Force* (IK Differentiation)

Atom Simd: Since *Distribute-Force* performs reads from the grid rather than writes, the atom loop can be vectorized easily, yielding a $\sim2\times$ speedup. The gather operations required to read grid point values cause this to be a poor choice.

Inner Simd: Reproducing the inner loop vectorization from *Map-Charge*, setting the loop length to 8, produces a $\sim3.7\times$ speedup over the scalar implementation.

Repacking: *Distribute-Force* for IK differentiation uses three different grids with their own force components. By modifying the Poisson solver to instead output the x and y components interweaved, and the z component interweaved with 0 s, the innermost loop can be extended to 16 iterations and the x and y components can be computed together by taking advantage of the 512-bit vector register on Xeon Phi. This provides an additional $\sim1.1\times$ speedup.

Precompute: As with *Map-Charge*, the polynomial evaluations to obtain stencil coefficients can be replaced with references to a lookup table, for a similar $\sim1.1\times$ additional speedup and a total speedup of $\sim4.4\times$ relative to the reference.

Function *Distribute-Force* (AD Differentiation)

Vector: Transferring over all of the optimizations from the IK mode of *Distribute-Force*, except the inapplicable repacking of the Poisson solver output, yields speedup below $3\times$ relative to the reference. This is because the extra work after the loop over stencil points has become relatively expensive.

Split Atom: We split the loop over atoms in two. The first atom loop ends after the triple loop over stencil points, having summed weighted potentials into three arrays of length equal to the number of atoms. The second atom loop operates on these arrays to obtain force components, and can be vectorized as it contains no inner loops and has unit stride access to the weighted potential arrays. This brings the overall speedup to just above 4×.

3.2 Poisson Solver

The Poisson solver is a poorly-scaling, communication-intense function which performs 3D FFTs, solves Poisson's equation in reciprocal space, and then performs a number of inverse 3D FFTs depending on the differentiation mode (3 for IK and 1 for AD). These 3D FFTs are performed in parallel as a series of 1D FFTs with communication steps in between. The FFT functions are from high-performance libraries (in our case MKL) and we do not attempt to optimize them. Our optimization of the solver comes from three ideas.

Shift Work: Switching to a stencil size of 7 creates more work in the mapping functions, but causes LAMMPS to choose a coarser grid resolution, requiring fewer calculations to perform the FFTs.

2D FFTs: The series of 1D FFTs is inefficient [23]. We replace it with a 2D FFT followed by a 1D FFT, and in the first communication step we ensure that planes of data are located on each MPI rank. This saves one communication step and is roughly (∼10%) faster. Even for poorly load-balanced cases, where the number of necessary 2D FFTs is only slightly greater than the number of MPI ranks, it does not perform worse.

Adjust Grid Sizes: The FFT calls of Intel's MKL library do not perform well for particular unfortunate values, which can catch users by surprise (compare time spent in FFTs across the cases in Fig. 1). A simple fix that catches many problem cases is to check whether the number FFT grid points in any dimension is a multiple of 16, and increase it by 1 if necessary. Users will now only rarely find that their simulations run substantially slower after making a tiny change to their input file, and, as an added bonus, these simulations will gain slightly improved accuracy.

3.3 Short-Ranged Interactions

To avoid shifting the bottleneck to the short-range calculation, it is desirable that it be vectorized. Mike Brown of Intel contributed code vectorizing the pair potential used in simulations containing electrostatic interactions (optionally with cut off Lennard-Jones interactions), where his strategy was to vectorize the loop over each atom's neighbors. This achieves a ∼3× speedup (for example, compare the time spent in "Pair" between the reference and optimized versions in Fig. 3). We provide similar code compatible with the Buckingham potential, optimized for PPPM and USER-INTEL, and also versions of pair potentials compatible with PPPM for dispersion.

4   Results

We now present comparisons between the reference and optimized versions of LAMMPS using full simulations, profiling the code as in Fig. 1, to show how the various parts of the code contribute to total runtime. We also investigate the opaque way in which the user-facing knobs impact accuracy, and provide evidence that our optimizations do not sacrifice accuracy. The experiments were conducted on a single core, a full node, and multiple nodes. While the speedup is both problem dependent and parameter dependent, the optimized version is faster in every case simulated.

Because of our decision to target a new default stencil size of 7, it would not be fair to make like-to-like comparisons between the reference and our optimized versions. Further, LAMMPS' input files do not even require an explicit choice of stencil size, so many users will just allow it to take on its default value. Figure 3 compares the two versions as stencil order varies for our baseline test cases, using IK differentiation to demonstrate that the new value is faster for the optimized version. We simulate the standard 5 Å case on a single core and a 64× scaled-up 7 Å case on a full KNL node, which are nearly-optimal cutoff radii for each case. The trend in total runtime is expected: on both a single core and the full node the reference version is fastest with a stencil size of 5 while the new version is fastest with a value of 7. For all future cases presented, the reference code uses $S = 5$ while ours uses $S = 7$.

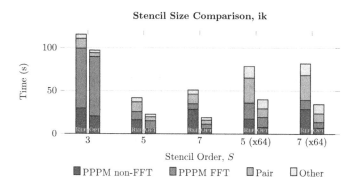

Fig. 3. Profiles of SPC/E water as stencil size varies for both single-core and scaled-up full-node cases. Left bar: reference, right bar: optimized.

4.1   Accuracy

Since the optimizations proposed involve both parameter-tuning and numerical approximations, we now verify that our code is as accurate as the reference. To this end, we compare to an Ewald summation run with a relative error of 10^{-5}, and a cutoff of 10 Å.

Table 1. RMS errors for force after one timestep compared to Ewald summation

Version	Mode	r_c	S	Precompute	RMS error	Version	Mode	r_c	S	RMS error
ref	IK	7 Å	7	-	0.0186	ref	AD	7 Å	7	0.0189
opt	IK	7 Å	7	-	0.0186	ref	IK	3 Å	7	0.5853
opt	IK	7 Å	7	500 points	0.0313	ref	IK	5 Å	7	0.0124
opt	IK	7 Å	7	5000 points	0.0188	ref	IK	7 Å	3	0.0197
opt	AD	7 Å	7	5000 points	0.0188	ref	IK	7 Å	5	0.0194

As seen in Table 1, without stencil coefficient precomputation, the optimized and reference versions obtain almost identical forces for both differentiation modes. 5000 precomputed stencil polynomial evaluations are sufficient to retain overall accuracy with our approximation. In addition, the optimized version conserves momentum (the sum of forces on all atoms remains nearly zero) and the macroscopic temperature difference between reference and optimized simulations after 100 time steps is always small ($\sim$0.1%), and nearly zero without stencil precomputation.

Many users may not expect that their choice of cutoff can have a large effect on accuracy, and LAMMPS' internal accuracy model does not do as good of a job with stencil size as it does with differentiation mode. After 100 time steps, the temperature is almost 10 degrees higher for a 3 Å cutoff than for cutoffs greater than or equal to 4 Å. In addition to speedup, our optimized version becomes slightly more accurate by moving to a stencil size of 7.

4.2   Single-Core Simulations

We first compare simulations using our optimized version to the reference cases we presented earlier in Fig. 1. Figure 4 shows both versions as cutoff varies for IK and AD differentiation, respectively. As with the reference version, there is a runtime-optimal cutoff for the optimized version at 5 Å where a balance is struck between the pair interactions and the FFTs. Total speedup at this optimal cutoff is 2.21× for IK and 2.75× for AD differentiation. With our optimizations, AD differentiation goes from being only marginally faster at the runtime-optimal cutoff to being 32% faster, making it a compelling choice even for serial simulations where the FFTs do not take up much time.

The calculation of long-range interactions, inclusive of the mapping functions, the FFTs, and various minor functions (PPPM FFT plus PPPM non-FFT), is sped up by a factor of 3.44× for AD differentiation. The calculation of the long-range interactions *excluding* the FFTs has actually sped up by a higher factor of 3.61× despite the larger stencil requiring looping over 2.74 times as many grid points. The calculation of pair interactions is sped up by about 2.5×. AD differentiation is now faster than IK differentiation for every cutoff, due to the smooth decrease in time spent performing FFTs as cutoff increases.

The relative penalty for choosing a poor cutoff has not changed much except for cases where an unfortunate number of FFT grid points was doubling the cost

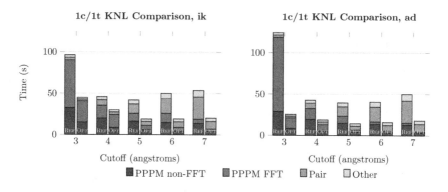

Fig. 4. Profiles of SPC/E water test case running single-threaded on one core of a KNL as cutoff varies. Left bar: reference, right bar: optimized.

of FFTs. In general, an overestimate of the runtime-optimal cutoff is much less penalizing than an underestimate because the cost of the FFTs increases rapidly as cutoff decreases. Because the optimized long-range calculations are sped up by about as much as the optimized short-range calculations, users will find that pre-existing input files and intuitions about runtime-optimal cutoffs still yield good results.

Figure 5 compares the optimized implementation to the reference as relative error varies. Speedups are between 2.1× and 2.77× for all cases, without an apparent pattern other than that AD differentiation has gained more from the optimizations than IK differentiation. There is not a clear optimal relative error, since users will want to adjust this parameter depending on how important accuracy is in the long-range calculation for their specific problems.

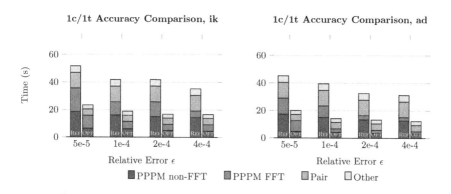

Fig. 5. Profiles of SPC/E water test case running single-threaded on one core of a KNL as PPPM relative error varies. Left bar: reference, right bar: optimized.

4.3   OpenMP and MPI Parallelism

With the additional complication of parallelism, we do not attempt to determine optimal choices of input parameters for our test case, though users will go through this complex process for their individual problems, often settling on a suboptimal set of parameters [6]. Here we just show that ouroptimized version is much faster than the reference for a range of cutoffs on a full KNL node, for varying numbers of cores on up to two full nodes, and for varying numbers of OpenMP threads per rank.

LAMMPS is intended to be scalable to very large numbers of cores, but this scalability is highly dependent on the details of the simulation. As the number of MPI ranks increases, the runtime-optimal input parameters change. Using just one set of input parameters might result in poor scalability (if the chosen set is optimal for small numbers of ranks) or good scalability (if the chosen set is optimal for a large number of ranks). As the number of ranks grows, FFTs and other functions requiring communication become relatively more expensive. This increases the runtime-optimal cutoff and can also make using a stencil size of 7 more efficient even for reference LAMMPS. Parallelism provides yet more knobs for users to consider. These include the number of MPI ranks per node and a number of OpenMP threads per rank. The optimal choice is again problem-dependent, but generally LAMMPS should be run with around 1 core per rank and 1–2 threads per core.

Figure 6 contains results for running a proportionally scaled-up benchmark on an entire KNL node with all 64 of its cores. Now we present results for cutoffs from 4 to 9 Å instead of 3 to 7 Å, since at 3 Å the FFTs for both versions take much longer. For reference LAMMPS the runtime-optimal cutoff is now at 7 Å. The optimized version is fastest at 6 Å, although 7 Å is only slightly slower. This set of simulations features the same number of atoms per core as Fig. 4, but its efficiency is reduced by parallelism overhead. For the single-core optimal cutoff of 5 Å, this scaled-up simulation takes 2.5 times as long per atom with our optimized code. It still takes about twice as long even at the new optimal cutoff of 6 Å. The reference version fares a little better, taking "only" twice as long at 5 Å and 1.4 times as long at its new optimal cutoff of 7 Å. If instead we compare the times required at the new runtime-optimal cutoffs to that required for the single-core optimal cutoff, the full node simulations take 1.8 and 2.1 times longer for the reference and optimized codes, respectively. Scalability aside, however, the same general patterns are apparent here as were seen earlier. Total speedup is about 2.4× for optimal cutoffs, lower than for the single-core case due to the relative increase in the expense of communication-intensive functions.

As it appears on the LAMMPS website, the SPC/E water benchmark we use here defaults to a cutoff of 9.8 Å. This is of course far higher than the runtime-optimal cutoff on a single core—the simulation takes more than twice as long as at 5 Å for reference LAMMPS and about twice as long for our optimized version. However, this exhibits much better scalability since runtime-optimal cutoffs are higher for higher core counts. This is because less time is spent performing poorly-scaling FFTs while more time is spent computing short-range

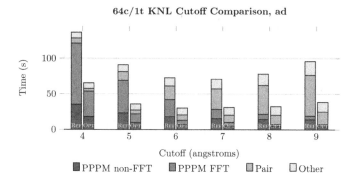

Fig. 6. Profiles of SPC/E water test case scaled up by 64× running single-threaded on a full KNL node as cutoff varies, for AD differentiation. Left bar: reference, right bar: optimized.

pair interactions. Figure 7a shows core-seconds taken to simulate a fixed-size problem as the number of cores used increases. There is one MPI rank per core and 1 thread per rank. For the 10 Å case this scales well up to 32 cores, but for the full KNL node parallel efficiencies are 82% for reference LAMMPS and 63% for optimized LAMMPS. Running on 128 cores across two full nodes is very inefficient; the optimized version actually runs faster on one node, in part due to using an unfortunate number of FFT grid points, although it remains faster than the reference. Both versions see a comparable increase in core-seconds as communication costs rise, and this has a larger relative impact on the optimized version because it was faster to begin with. These observations are consistent with benchmarks published on the LAMMPS website, which exhibit large losses in parallel efficiency after about 16 processors for a variety of systems when running fixed-size benchmarks.

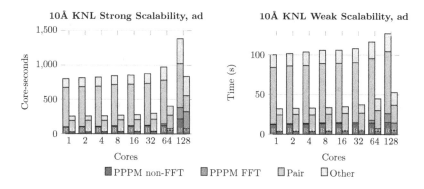

Fig. 7. Strong and weak scalability comparisons up to 2 full KNL nodes. Left bar: reference, right bar: optimized.

More commonly, users will simulate large problems on large numbers of cores. Figure 7b shows core-seconds per atom as problem size and core count both vary, such that there are 36k atoms per core in each simulation. Parallel efficiencies on a full KNL node are now 85% and 71% for the reference and optimized versions, respectively, and 79% and 60% for two full nodes. Again we see the optimized version scaling less well because the rise in communication costs with core count is roughly the same for both versions, but it remains 2–3× faster over the entire range.

Users can also make use of OpenMP parallelism, by either assigning multiple cores to each MPI rank or using multiple threads per physical core, or both. Figure 8 shows profiles for the same 64×-scale water test case being simulated on a full KNL node, where the number of MPI ranks and OpenMP threads per rank is varied. We use a cutoff of 6 Å, as this was close to the runtime-optimal cutoff for this case on the full node when using 64 MPI ranks and 1 thread per rank. Best results are obtained when using one MPI rank per core, which is expected when not running on many nodes—the behavior on two full nodes is similar. Slight performance gain is obtained by using two OpenMP threads per core, which helps a little when computing the short-range interactions. The optimized version behaves similarly to the reference, and is at least twice as fast except when using too few MPI ranks.

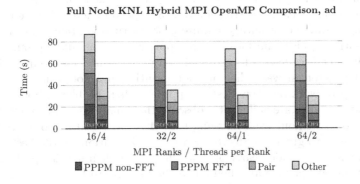

Fig. 8. Profiles of 64×-scale SPC/E water test case running on a full KNL node, for AD differentiation, varying the number of MPI ranks and OpenMP threads per rank. The reference user-omp implementation is on the left and our optimized implementation is on the right. The reference cases were run with a stencil size of 5 and the optimized cases with a stencil size of 7. Left bar: reference, right bar: optimized.

5   Conclusion

Efficient vectorization proved to be key to attaining significant speedups over reference LAMMPS. For the PPPM functions, we tested several approaches and found memory access patterns to be particularly important. However, because the contiguous memory accesses were to be found in loops over stencil points, the stencil size limited vectorization efficiency. At the same time, as other parts of the code were optimized, the FFTs became relatively more expensive. And from the beginning we were concerned with users having difficulty choosing an optimal stencil size.

All of these problems turn out to have the same solution. Targeting a higher default stencil size allowed whole rows of a larger stencil to be computed at once, enabling efficient vectorization. Work shifted away from the FFTs and into newly-optimized functions when LAMMPS automatically adjusted the FFT grid to preserve accuracy. And users who do not test a variety of stencil sizes are no longer missing out on potential performance, because $S = 7$ is optimal for every case and can be made the default. The relatively more expensive FFTs also made another previously-hard choice much easier, as now AD differentiation is significantly faster than IK differentiation due to its requiring only half as many FFTs. Although not discussed here, most of our optimizations are applicable to 256-bit vector registers and yield significant speedup on Xeon architectures, and similar speedup is also observed for different types of physical problems, such as an interfacial system where half of the domain is a vacuum.

LAMMPS is an extremely flexible program that allows and requires users to make numerous choices when simulating their different physical problems, and our optimized code is a significant improvement over reference LAMMPS, regardless of a user's particular needs, for simulations which make use of the PPPM method for electrostatics. We achieve 2–3× speedup across a wide range of cutoff radii, for different accuracy requirements of the long-range solver, for both differentiation modes, and for different approaches to parallelization.

Many of these choices have a large impact on performance and even on simulation accuracy, often in ways that are not intuitive and not transparent to users as they try to work out how best to approach their problems. Some, like the choice of stencil size, are sufficiently obscure that many users likely use the default value, some without even knowing that they even had a choice. Other users will have gone to great lengths to set up their simulations in the best possible way, and will have made nearly-optimal choices for their specific problems. Our optimizations are particularly helpful to the first group because several of the user-facing knobs now have clearly best settings for a range of problem sizes, and these settings can be clearly communicated without much qualification as to which cases they work for, or they can even be made the default selections. Users with long experience and carefully-crafted input files will benefit from significant speedup for their existing set of inputs and can also expect that the optimal inputs for the new version are close to what they were already using.

Acknowledgments. The authors gratefully acknowledge financial support from the Deutsche Forschungsgemeinschaft (German Research Association) through grant GSC 111, and from Intel Corporation via the Intel Parallel Computing Center initiative.

References

1. Hockney, R.W., Eastwood, J.W.: Computer Simulation Using Particles. Hilger, Bristol (1988)
2. Plimpton, S.: Fast parallel algorithms for short-range molecular dynamics. J. Comput. Phys. **117**(1), 1–19 (1995)
3. Brown, W.M., Kohlmeyer, A., Plimpton, S.J., Tharrington, A.N.: Implementing molecular dynamics on hybrid high performance computers - particle - particle particle-mesh. Comput. Phys. Commun. **183**(3), 449–459 (2012)
4. Harvey, M.J., De Fabritiis, G.: An implementation of the smooth particle mesh Ewald method on GPU hardware. J. Chem. Theor. Comput. **5**(9), 2371–2377 (2009). doi:10.1021/ct900275y
5. Höhnerbach, M., Ismail, A.E., Bientinesi, P.: The vectorization of the tersoff multibody potential: an exercise in performance portability. In: Proceedings of the International Conference for High Performance Computing, Networking, Storage and Analysis, SC 2016, pp. 7:1–7:13. IEEE Press, Piscataway (2016)
6. Fabregat-Traver, D., Ismail, A.E., Bientinesi, P.: Accelerating scientific codes by performance and accuracy modeling, In: CoRR (2016). http://arxiv.org/abs/1608.04694
7. Brown, W.M., Carrillo, J.-M.Y., Gavhane, N., Thakkar, F.M., Plimpton, S.J.: Optimizing legacy molecular dynamics software with directive-based offload. Comput. Phys. Commun. **195**, 95–101 (2015)
8. Brown, W.M., Semin, A., Hebenstreit, M., Khvostov, S., Raman, K., Plimpton, S.J.: Increasing molecular dynamics simulation rates with an 8-fold increase in electrical power efficiency. In: Proceedings of the 2016 ACM/IEEE Conference on Supercomputing, SC 2016, IEEE, New York (2016)
9. in 't Veld, P.J., Ismail, A.E., Grest, G.S.: Application of Ewald summations to long-range dispersion forces. J. Chem. Phys. **127**(14), 144711 (2007)
10. Isele-Holder, R.E., Mitchell, W., Ismail, A.E.: Development and application of a particle-particle particle-mesh Ewald method for dispersion interactions. J. Chem. Phys. **137**(17), 174107 (2012)
11. Ewald, P.P.: Die Berechnung optischer und elektrostatischer Gitterpotentiale. Ann. Phys. **369**(3), 253–287 (1921)
12. Berendsen, H., van der Spoel, D., van Drunen, R.: GROMACS: a message-passing parallel molecular dynamics implementation. Comput. Phys. Commun. **91**(1), 43–56 (1995)
13. Todorov, I.T., Smith, W., Trachenko, K., Dove, M.T.: DL_POLY_3: new dimensions in molecular dynamics simulations via massive parallelism. J. Mater. Chem. **16**, 1911–1918 (2006)
14. Salomon-Ferrer, R., Case, D.A., Walker, R.C.: An overview of the Amber biomolecular simulation package. Wiley Interdisc. Rev.: Comput. Mol. Sci. **3**(2), 198–210 (2013)
15. Bowers, K.J., Chow, E., Xu, H., Dror, R.O., Eastwood, M.P., Gregersen, B.A., Klepeis, J.L., Kolossvary, I., Moraes, M.A., Sacerdoti, F.D., Salmon, J.K., Shan, Y., Shaw, D.E.: Scalable algorithms for molecular dynamics simulations on commodity clusters. In: Proceedings of the 2006 ACM/IEEE Conference on Supercomputing, SC 2006, ACM, New York (2006)
16. Phillips, J.C., Braun, R., Wang, W., Gumbart, J., Tajkhorshid, E., Villa, E., Chipot, C., Skeel, R.D., Kalé, L., Schulten, K.: Scalable molecular dynamics with NAMD. J. Comput. Chem. **26**(16), 1781–1802 (2005)

17. Darden, T., York, D., Pedersen, L.: Particle mesh Ewald: an n log(n) method for Ewald sums in large systems. J. Chem. Phys. **98**(12), 10089–10092 (1993)
18. Essmann, U., Perera, L., Berkowitz, M.L., Darden, T., Lee, H., Pedersen, L.G.: A smooth particle mesh Ewald method. J. Chem. Phys. **103**(19), 8577–8593 (1995)
19. Shan, Y., Klepeis, J.L., Eastwood, M.P., Dror, R.O., Shaw, D.E.: Gaussian split Ewald: a fast Ewald mesh method for molecular simulation. J. Chem. Phys. **122**(5), 054101 (2005)
20. Sagui, C., Darden, T.: Multigrid methods for classical molecular dynamics simulations of biomolecules. J. Chem. Phys. **114**(15), 6578–6591 (2001)
21. Hardy, D.J., Wu, Z., Phillips, J.C., Stone, J.E., Skeel, R.D., Schulten, K.: Multilevel summation method for electrostatic force evaluation. J. Chem. Theor. Comput. **11**(2), 766–779 (2015). doi:10.1021/ct5009075
22. Berendsen, H.J.C., Grigera, J.R., Straatsma, T.P.: The missing term in effective pair potentials. J. Phys. Chem. **91**(24), 6269–6271 (1987)
23. Wende, F., Marsman, M., Steinke, T.: On enhancing 3D-FFT performance in VASP. In: CUG Proceedings (2016)

Communication Reducing Algorithms for Distributed Hierarchical N-Body Problems with Boundary Distributions

Mustafa Abduljabbar[1]([✉]) [iD], George S. Markomanolis[2], Huda Ibeid[1],
Rio Yokota[3], and David Keyes[1]

[1] Extreme Computing Research Center (ECRC),
King Abdullah University of Science and Technology (KAUST),
Thuwal, Saudi Arabia
mustafa.abduljabbar@kaust.edu.sa
[2] KAUST Supercomputing Laboratory (KSL),
King Abdullah University of Science and Technology (KAUST),
Thuwal, Saudi Arabia
[3] Global Scientific Information and Computing Center (GSIC),
Tokyo Institute of Technology (TITECH), Tokyo, Japan

Abstract. Reduction of communication and efficient partitioning are key issues for achieving scalability in hierarchical N-Body algorithms like Fast Multipole Method (FMM). In the present work, we propose three independent strategies to improve partitioning and reduce communication. First, we show that the conventional wisdom of using space-filling curve partitioning may not work well for boundary integral problems, which constitute a significant portion of FMM's application user base. We propose an alternative method that modifies orthogonal recursive bisection to relieve the cell-partition misalignment that has kept it from scaling previously. Secondly, we optimize the granularity of communication to find the optimal balance between a bulk-synchronous collective communication of the local essential tree and an RDMA per task per cell. Finally, we take the dynamic sparse data exchange proposed by Hoefler et al. [1] and extend it to a *hierarchical* sparse data exchange, which is demonstrated at scale to be faster than the MPI library's MPI_Alltoallv that is commonly used.

Keywords: N-body methods · Fast multipole method · Load balancing · Communication reduction

1 Introduction

The N-body problem is a kernel in many scientific simulations in which the behavior of the system is defined from mutual interactions between discrete entities (e.g., molecules, charges, astrophysical bodies). The N-body algorithm sums up contributions due to all particles in the system, which results in quadratic complexity. The Barnes-Hut treecode, which subdivides the 2D/3D domain into

© Springer International Publishing AG 2017
J.M. Kunkel et al. (Eds.): ISC High Performance 2017, LNCS 10266, pp. 79–96, 2017.
DOI: 10.1007/978-3-319-58667-0_5

quad/octrees, brings the complexity down to $\mathcal{O}(N \log N)$ by hierarchically clustering the sources into multipole expansions. FMM clusters the targets into local expansions to bring the complexity further down to $\mathcal{O}(N)$. For mathematical foundations of the multipole expansions, see [2–4]. Among the applications of FMM are [5,6] where protein-protein encounter within a biomolecular dynamics solver is accelerated by using FMM to solve the boundary integral equation, which is used to discretize the linearized Possion-Boltzmann equation. In [7] all-atom molecular dynamics is performed to simulate the conditions of living cells by calculating energy at target proteins in a solvent and a molecular crowder using FMM. It is also used to speedup the matrix-vector multiplication, which arises from electromagnetic scattering problems [8]. Other applications include gravity simulations [9,10].

Due to their increased importance in large-scale simulations, there is now a considerable literature on implementing parallel hierarchical N-body solvers, e.g., FMM. Also, since they are among Berkeley's seven dwarfs, the numerical methods that are believed to be the most impactful in science and engineering according to [11], it is important to address issues arising at exascale especially the increasing cost of data movement (through memory hierarchy or network) as opposed to floating point operations. Even though many of the current FMM implementations are scalable to the full machine they run on, a communication reducing approach that works on at least an order of magnitude more nodes tends to be rarely the emphasis of these implementations. This tendency is justified in accordance to the trend in enhancing a node with multi/many-core capabilities. However, even within a many-core node, more sophisticated methods should be used to place and exchange data to get the maximum performance reported by the vendor. This is already implied in equipping the second generation of Intel® Xeon Phi™ processors code-named Knights Landing (KNL) with memory 'clustering modes'. Therefore, ideas presented in this paper complement the literature although they mainly target distributed memory.

An example work that achieves full machine scalability using GPUs is that of Bédorf et al. [9], where a parallel algorithm for sparse tree construction and traversal that works completely on the GPU is introduced. At the construction phase, they map the 3D coordinates to Hilbert's linear (n-bit) addresses, then particles are sorted to achieve locality in memory. To avoid the typical sequential insertions to build Hilbert trees [12], one particle is assigned per GPU thread. A level-wise mask is applied successively on each particle to discover its predecessors such that cells with less than N_{leaf} are considered leaves. Grouping of particles is done using parallel compact algorithm. To exploit the massively parallel GPU threads, a breadth-first traversal is used to carry out the computation. They report a processing rate of 2.8 million particles per second. This work was extended to an MPI parallel version where 24.77 PFlop/s (mixed precision) on the full Titan system [13] was achieved.

Speck et al. [14] report scalability on up to 262,144 cores by introducing temporal parallelism (parallel-in-time algorithm) on top of MPI/Pthreads spatial decomposition to overcome the strong scaling limits when the number of particles per node becomes too small. The scalability is shown for up to 4M particles; then when they take advantage of shared and distributed memory parallelism, and exploit the overlap of data-exchange and computation, they calculate 2 billion particles on 262,144 cores of JUGENE, according to [15]. Lashuk et al. [16] propose an FMM implementation that scales on up to 196,608 cores by providing a novel domain-specific bulk synchronous all-reduce algorithm for remote tree communication. They report communication complexity of $O(\sqrt{P} * (\frac{N}{P})^{2/3})$, which comes from their hypercube alltoall communication scheme. Hoefler et al. [1] discuss the time and memory complexity of the common protocols used for the dynamic sparse data exchange problem and develop the non-blocking exchange protocol ($\mathcal{NBX}$) with constant memory overhead. Their novel algorithm improves the runtime of sparse data-exchange up to 8,192 processors of Bluegene/P by a factor of 5.6. They prove and model a generic time complexity of $O(\log P)$ using the LogGP model.

Zandifar et al. [17] provide a parallel FMM implementation as a benchmark for their high-level skeletons (abstract parallel patterns) framework which executes on top of the STAPL runtime system that dynamically schedules task on highly heterogeneous architectures. They reuse several parallel patterns like the bucket-sort and alltoall to perform geometric bisection and to aggregate the local essential tree (LET) respectively. They achieve comparable performance to the corresponding base MPI implementation by taking advantage of the underlying data-driven execution and asynchronous task scheduling guaranteed by the runtime system. Many features of Charm++ like task migration and Structured Control Flow are augmented in [18] to overlap computation with the communication of the local essential tree (LET).

Contributions of the present work can be summarized as follows:

- A novel demonstration that shows a weakness in Hilbert's space-filling interval partitioning for boundary element distributions.
- A communication scheme with adjustable granularity, which enables the overlap of local essential tree communication with computation that otherwise cannot be overlapped.
- Introduction of the adaptive hierarchical sparse data exchange ($\mathcal{HSDX}$), a neighborhood collective communication algorithm for exchanging the global tree in a few steps by direct near-field communication only.

In Sect. 2, we describe our adopted partitioning techniques and justify our choice in detail. Section 4 describes different communication strategies that we adopt in order to avoid bulk synchronous LET communication. We also describe the adopted load-balancing strategies and the communication complexity analysis of our approach. Finally, we demonstrate our scalability and evaluation results.

2 Partitioning Schemes for the Fast Multipole Method (FMM)

There are two traditional objectives associated with good partitioning of the N-body problem: evenly splitting data among partitions to achieve work balance, and providing efficient access to non-local data. There is no optimal approach that can simultaneously handle these two objectives, because of strict considerations on locality of data for high arithmetic intensity, granularity, and the size of communication, which can vary based on space-time proximity of partitions.

2.1 Preliminaries

Partitioning schemes for fast N-body methods can be categorized into orthogonal recursive bisections (ORB) [19] or hashed octrees (HOT) [20].

Orthogonal Recursive Bisection (ORB). The ORB [19] forms a balanced binary tree by finding a geometric bisector that splits the number of particles equally at every bisection of the tree. The direction of the geometric bisector alternates orthogonally $(x, y, z, x, \ldots)$ to form a cascade of rectangular subdomains that contain equal number of particles similar to Fig. 1(c). For nonuniform distributions the aspect ratio of the subdomain could become large, which leads to suboptimal interaction list size and communication load. This problem can be alleviated by choosing the direction of the geometric bisector to always split in the longest dimension. The original method is limited to cases where the number of processes is a power of two, but the method can be extended to non-powers-of-two by using multi sections instead of bisections [21].

Hashed Oct-Tree (HOT). In HOT, initially proposed by [20], the domain is partitioned by splitting Morton/Hilbert ordered space filling curves into equal segments as shown in Fig. 1(a) and (b). Morton/Hilbert ordering maps the geometrical location of each particle to a single key. The value of the key depends on the depth of the tree at which the space filling curve is drawn. Three bits of the key are used to indicate which octant the particle belongs to at every level of the octree. Therefore, a 32-bit unsigned integer can represent a tree with 10 levels, and a 64-bit unsigned integer can represent a tree with 21 levels. Directly mapping this key to the memory address is inefficient for non-uniform distributions since most of the keys will not be used. Therefore, a hashing function is used to map the Morton/Hilbert key to the memory address of particles/cells.

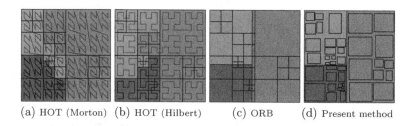

(a) HOT (Morton)   (b) HOT (Hilbert)   (c) ORB   (d) Present method

Fig. 1. Schematic of different partitioning schemes. (a) Shows the hashed octree with Morton keys. (b) Shows the hashed octree with Hilbert keys. (c) Shows the orthogonal recursive bisection with an underlying global tree. (d) Is the present method using an orthogonal recursive bisection with independent local trees and tight bounding boxes.

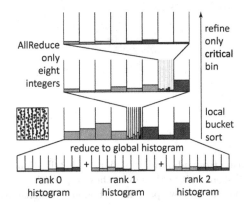

Fig. 2. Histogram-based partitioning scheme.

2.2 Adopted Partitioning Strategies

Parallel Sampling-Based Techniques for Finding Splitters/Bisectors.
Parallel sampling-based techniques have proven to be useful for both finding the
bisectors in ORB [21] and finding the splitting keys in HOT [22]. Both ORB and
HOT are constructing parallel tree structures, but in different ways. There is an
analogy between parallel tree construction and parallel sorting. The idea behind
ORB is analogous to merge sort, where a divide and conquer approach is taken.
HOT is analogous to radix sort, where each bit of the key is examined at each
step. Therefore, sampling-based techniques that are known to be effective for
parallel sorting are also effective for parallel tree partitioning. The partitioning
can be separated into two steps. The first step is to find the bisectors/key-
splitters by using a sampling-based parallel sorting algorithm. An example of
such sampling-based partitioning is shown in Fig. 2. Sorting is only performed
among the buckets (not within them) and this is done only locally. The only
global information that is communicated is the histogram counts, which is only
a few integers and can be done efficiently with an MPI_allreduce operation. The
bins can be iteratively refined to narrow the search for the splitter of the HOT
key or ORB bisector. This will determine the destination process for each particle. The second step is to perform an all-to-all communication of the particles.
Since the ORB bisector is one floating point number and the HOT key is one
integer, it is much less data than sending around particle data at each step of
the parallel sort.

Weakness in Space-Filling Partitioning for Boundary Distributions. It
is well-known that the main advantage of Hilbert curve as opposed to Morton is
its locality preserving properties in 2D. It is not clear, however, to what extent
we can generalize this property in higher dimensions [23]. As a counterexample
to the locality property, we observe that it is not entirely preserved in case of
3D boundary element distributions, which increases the distributed interaction
list size. The reason for that comes from the intuitive notion of space-filling

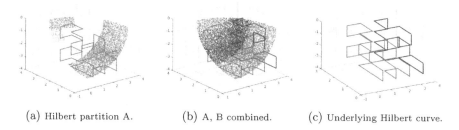

(a) Hilbert partition A.   (b) A, B combined.   (c) Underlying Hilbert curve.

Fig. 3. A Hilbert partition from a boundary spherical distribution viewed from different perspectives. A space discontinuity exists even though partitions are in correct Hilbert order due to the existence of hollow space in orthogonal dimensions.

curves, that is, when the space is not filled, e.g., in boundary spherical distribution, interpolation of spatial points to Hilbert curve does not necessarily map to keys that are continuous in space. This is attributable to the fact that keys are not interpolated in their natural order, since points are spread out on surface patches. Figure 3 shows particles laid out in their respective Hilbert order. Due to the geometry of the space-filling curve, movement across dimensions happens orthogonally, hence, if hollow space is encountered in the orthogonal direction, it will introduce discontinuity in the partition as in Fig. 3(a). Clearly, this does not apply to uniform dense distributions, which comprise many classical applications of FMM, making HOT partitioning an optimal choice in such cases.

Hybrid Partitioning. In our implementation, we choose a modified version of ORB over HOT for a few other reasons. One of the main reasons is that we were able to improve a major defect of ORB – partition-cell alignment issue. Since geometrically closer points interact more densely with each other, it is crucial to keep the particles in the same cell on the same process in order to minimize communication. However, if a global Morton/Hilbert key is used to construct the local trees, the ORB may place a bisector in the middle of a cell as shown in Fig. 1(c). This results in an increase in the interaction list size. We avoid this problem by using local Morton/Hilbert keys that use the bounds of the local partition. This may at first seem to increase the interaction list near the partition boundaries since two misaligned tree structures are formed. However, when one considers the fact that the present method squeezes the bounding box of each cell to tightly fit the particles as shown in Fig. 1(d), it can be seen that the cells are not aligned at all in the first place. Furthermore, our flexible definition of the multipole acceptance criteria optimizes the interaction list length for a given accuracy regardless of the misalignment.

3   Communication of the Local Essential Tree

Once particles are partitioned, those in the local domain are used to construct a local tree. We use a completely local construction of the octree using the local bounding box, instead of using a global Morton/Hilbert key that is derived from the global bounding box. This allows us to reuse all parts of the serial code and only add a few routines for the partitioning, grafting of trees, and communication. Therefore, any modification in the serial code is immediately reflected in the parallel code.

After the local tree structure is constructed, a post-order traversal is performed on the tree structure and Particle-to-Multipole (P2M) and Multipole-to-Multipole (M2M) kernels are executed bottom up. The P2M kernel is executed only at the leaf cells. It loops over all particles in the leaf cell to form the multipole expansion at the center of the leaf cell. The M2M kernel is executed only for the non-leaf cells. It loops over all child cells and translates the multipole expansions from its children's centers to its center.

Once the multipole expansions for all local cells have been determined, the multipole expansions are sent to the necessary processes in a sender-initiated fashion [24]. This reduces the latency by communicating only once, rather than sending a request to remote processes and then receiving the data. Such sender-initiated communication schemes were common in cosmological N-body codes since they tend to use only monopoles, and in this case the integer to store the requests is as large as the data itself if they were to use a request-based scheme. This data is used to construct the local essential tree (LET), that is, the union of all trees representing the entire domain as seen by the local process [25]. It gets coarser depending on the distance of the remote cell. In the present method, it is formed by simply grafting the root nodes of the remote trees. In conventional parallel FMM codes, a global octree is formed and partitioned using either HOT or ORB. Therefore, the tree structure was severed in many places, which caused the merging of the LET to become quite complicated. Typically, code for merging the LET would take a large portion of a parallel FMM code, and this made it difficult to implement new features such as periodic boundary conditions, mutual interaction, more efficient translation stencils, and dual tree traversals. ExaFMM[1] is able to incorporate all these extended features and still maintain a fast pace of development because of this simplification in how the global tree structure is geometrically separated from the local tree structure.

While the remote information for the LET is being transferred, the local tree can be traversed. Conventional fast N-body methods overlap the entire LET communication with the entire local tree traversal. The LET communication becomes a bulk-synchronous MPI_alltoallv type communication, where processes corresponding to geometrically far partitions send logarithmically less information, thus resulting in $O(\log P)$ communication complexity where P is the number of processes. Nonetheless, in traditional fast N-body codes this part is performed in a bulk-synchronous manner.

---

[1] ExaFMM is an open-source code base to utilize fast multipole algorithms, in parallel, and with GPU capability. Algorithms pertaining to partitioning and communication reduction are all available on the public repository https://github.com/exafmm/exafmm.

4   Communication Reduction for the Adaptive Tree

In the following sections, we present different novel techniques that can be used to do the hierarchically sparse data exchange ($\mathcal{HSDX}$) of the adaptive FMM tree, which are generally applicable to a variety of algorithms constituting Definition 1. The optimization of global tree communication is essential to achieve strong scaling especially at a large scale. Such class of communication becomes very challenging due to the fact that ExaFMM has a highly optimized serial code that utilizes many-core parallelism, making communication dominates even when overlapped with computation. The natural solution to this problem is to strong scale communication, but to our knowledge, it is not straightforward to achieve this for practical reasons such as network congestion, growing interaction lists, and the different implementations of some MPI collectives that do not scale by definition e.g., MPI_Alltoallv. Therefore, it is important to look at these caveats while implementing a domain-specific communication scheme of the global FMM tree.

Definition 1. *Let $\mathcal{T}$ be a global adaptive tree with $\mathcal{L}$ levels numbered from $l_0 - l_k$ (coarse to fine) and partitioned to $\mathcal{P}$ processes. s is the "essential" subtree size such that $0 < s < \mathcal{S}$. $P_i, P_j \subset l_k$, if the finest level P_i, P_j share is k. We have a hierarchically sparse data exchange $\mathcal{HSDX}$ if for $P_i, P_j \subset l_1$ and $P_i, P_v \subset l_2$, $s_1 < s_2$ and $s_1! = 0$*

4.1   Overlapping Computation Depending on Communication Granularity

Asynchronous communication is a limiting factor to performance at exascale especially when done collectively. This appears to be the case for hierarchical algorithms such as FMM and Multigrid method (MG). Hence, communication needs to be balanced and efficiently overlapped with local work. In FMM, it is known that a substantial amount of time is spent in doing local Multipole-to-Local (M2L) and Particle-to-Particle (P2P) computations, but the question is how often we need to communicate to reduce blocking for data given the problem size, distribution and scale. To answer this question, we have parametrized our FMM to accept different granularities of communication represented by the size of the LET's subset. The subsets may contain non-leaf cells requiring $O(p)$ steps for $p = $ order of multipole expansion (higher p increases arithmetic intensity for low-level kernels) or leaf cells requiring $O(N/P)^2$ steps for $P = $ number of processes. The typical case would be to call a blocking MPI_Recv on the expected tag because there is no useful work to do in the current context; however, since MPI does not provide guarantees on the order of messages when used in mixed mode, our code consumes the available subtree and marks it as "traversed". This mechanism will maximize concurrency and minimize the message queuing time. The calling task will keep traversing until requested cell is received or traversed by another task.

Conventional parallel N-body methods use a bulk-synchronous MPI_alltoallv to communicate the whole LET at once, and overlap this communication with the local tree traversal to hide latency. One could over-decompose the

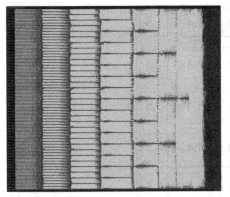

(a) Hypercube communication of 256 MPI processes. Interactions get coarser as we move right and finish in LogP steps.

(b) A zoomed-in version of the flat communication of 256 MPI processes, potentially causing contention when scaling on a supercomputer's network.

Fig. 4. Implemented communication patterns in FMM as visualized by Extrae. (Color figure online)

LET down to a per cell request, and then aggregate the communication to the optimal granularity. The bulk-synchronous communication model can be thought of as an extreme case of aggregation, while something like an RDMA per task per cell would be at the other end of the granularity spectrum. There is a caveat: We still require further tuning to reduce global communication by indirectly relaying multipoles through neighbor processes, as we will show in Sect. 4.2 using Algorithm 1.

4.2   Hierarchical Sparse Data Exchange Protocol ($\mathcal{HSDX}$)

Lashuk et al. [26] define a set of parameters that denote the interaction lists, i.e., U-, V-, W- and X-lists of the FMM tree. The same analogy can be used for describing the relationship between adjacent processes such that exchanging the entire LET can happen in a few steps. The mentioned lists constitute the adjacent nodes/processes through which global cells that contribute to the local tree are relayed. For the majority of the spatial N-Body partitioning methods, we can use the subdomain's bounding box to depict partitions that share a face, an edge or a vertex in $O(1)$ steps using Lemma 1. This enables us to create a breadth-first data exchange graph that starts from the local tree and covers all the cells from the essential tree. Each node in the graph contains the corresponding partition id and the adjacent partition id, which is needed since communication strictly happens between adjacent nodes. Figure 5 shows the exchanges needed to receive the entire LET by target process (3,3), with overlapping direct clusters enclosed in dashed squares. The corresponding data exchange graph of node (3,3) contains a node with id (1,5) and an adjacent id of (2,4), meaning that cell data of (1,5) can be acquired through (2,4) in the second stage of exchanges. To inherently achieve algorithmic balance, we hardwire edges in such a way that

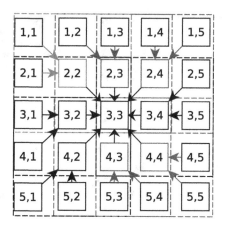

Fig. 5. The underlying data exchange graph of central process (3,3) within a uniform 2D grid of processes.

messages are evenly distributed over direct neighbors. If we start with direct neighbor (2,4), a naive approach would exhaust all its direct neighbors, namely {(1,3), (1,4), (1,5), (2,5), (3,5)}, thus overloads its buffers and causes imbalance. The next neighbor (3,4) will only have (4,5) data to relay. Therefore, we design our communication graph such that for internal processes in a uniform domain, the average number of messages received from direct neighbors in each step is $\left\lceil \frac{5^D - 3^D}{3^D - 1} \right\rceil$. Using notations from Table 2, we can generalize this formula to non-uniform domains if we turn it into

$$NB = \left\lceil \frac{\tau(P, 1) - \zeta(\Omega(P))}{\zeta(\Omega(P)) - 1} \right\rceil \tag{1}$$

We finally reach a stage where each process has access to the near and far-field interactions, thus accomplishing global communication using multiple calls to `MPI_Neighbor_alltoallv`. Algorithm 1 and Table 2 summarize our method.

Time Complexity of the adaptive $\mathcal{HSDX}$. A good lower bound complexity for $\mathcal{HSDX}$ is $\mathcal{NBX}$ i.e. $\Omega(\log P)$ from [1], when non-neighbor data exchange is extremely sparse or non-existent. The hierarchical sparsity in Definition 1 increases as we move away from target processes. The data exchange graph can be mapped to a tree since there is exactly one path from P_i to P_j, with an order bounded by Eq. 1. An upper bound is analogous to a fully dense communication, such that $O(\log P)$ exchanges happen $O(\log P)$ times, which is equivalent to $O(\log^2 P)$. Table 1 shows FMM communication complexity for uniform domains.

Lemma 1. *A partition P' is added to the adjacency list of P iff for any dimension D $maxBound(P'_x) - maxBound(P_x) > \epsilon$ and $minBound(P_x) - minBound(P'_x) > \epsilon$*

Table 1. Communication complexity of FMM.

Reference	Communication complexity
Teng [27]	$\mathcal{O}\left(P(N/P)^{2/3}(\log N + \mu)^{1/3}\right)$
Lashuk *et al.* [26]	$\mathcal{O}\left(\sqrt{P}(N/P)^{2/3}\right)$
Lashuk *et al.* [16]	$\mathcal{O}\left(\log P + (N/P)\right)$
Yokota *et al.* [28]	$\mathcal{O}\left(\log P + (N/P)^{2/3}\right)$

Table 2. $\mathcal{HSDX}$ Algorithm communication symbols.

Symbol	Indication
P and P'	Local and global partitions
$\Omega(P)$	Subdomain boundary
$\zeta(\Omega(P))$	Direct neighbors of P
$\mathcal{T}$	Level-by-level communication adjacency graph

Algorithm 1. $\mathcal{HSDX}$ - Hierarchical Sparse Data Exchange

---

    input : A list l_{in} of cells and destinations
    output: A list l_{out} of cells and sources

1 **foreach** P' *in* $\Omega(P,\beta)$ **do**
2   add(P',$\zeta(\Omega(P))$)
3 **end**
4 $\mathcal{T} \leftarrow$ `BuildCommTree`$(\zeta(\Omega(P)))$;
5 create distributed MPI graph topology;
6 **foreach** l *in* $\mathcal{T}.Levels$ **do**
7   **foreach** P' *in* $\zeta(\Omega(P))$ **do**
8   reduce tree based on the bounding box and forward to P';
9   **end**
10   exchange meta data;
11   call `MPI_Neighbor_alltoallv`;
12 **end**

4.3 Pairwise Exchange for Reducing Contention

It is observed at large scale that direct communication between sources and targets results in network contention which can be amortized by relaying multipoles through neighbor processes while utilizing the well-known pattern of N-Body interactions. Therefore, to mimic $O(\log P)$ complexity for boundary distributions, we implement a modified version of the well-known hypercube (butterfly) global communication scheme which starts out by the fine neighbor interactions depicted by $(P \oplus 2^i)$ and gets coarser as we move towards the ($\log P$) step. This is clearly visualized in Fig. 4 using Extrae, a tool that uses different interposition mechanisms to inject probes into the target application so as to gather information regarding the application performance. During this work, the tool is used to better understand the performance of the application pertaining to the used communication techniques. In Fig. 4, the horizontal axis represents the visualized timeline and the vertical axis represents the MPI processes. The yellow colors declare communication links, whereas the blue colors represent computation and red color symbolizes MPI_Wait calls. One of the main advantages of carrying out communication in ($\log P$) steps, as in is Fig. 4(a), is that subtrees received at intermediate stages can be asynchronously traversed, which otherwise cannot be done if communication is done with blocking collectives.

5   Performance Analysis

5.1   Experimental Setup

Our experiments are on Shaheen XC40, the rank 15 supercomputer according to the November 2016 Top500 list, located at King Abdullah University of Science and Technology. It has 196,608 physical cores and HPL performance of 5.537 PFlop/s. Each node is equipped with dual socket Intel Xeon E5-2698v3 16C 2.3 GHz and Cray Aries interconnect with dragonfly topology.

Throughout the following experiments, the underlying FMM code is compiled with the Laplace kernel, Cartesian coordinates, $P = 4$ (order of expansion) and spherical boundary distribution unless otherwise stated. Problems have been partitioned using the hybrid partitioning from Sect. 2.2. To demonstrate the effectiveness of the presented methodologies, we start by showing how optimal grain size for a specific problem is chosen, then assessing the scalability with the tuned granularity of communication. Then, results from using $\mathcal{HSDX}$ vs. existing communication reducing approaches are presented. Good scalability shows that an inordinate cost is not paid for intra-node communication, as opposed to the conventional bulk-synchronous approach, for which performance depends on the underlying network topology, the implementation of collectives like alltoall or allgather, the available memory size and bandwidth, and the frequency at which synchronization is triggered.

5.2   Communication Time for Different Granularities

In order to show the direct effect of asynchronous traversal on performance, we gradually vary the grain-size and measure the communication time, which is the most dominant factor at a large scale. Optimal granularity is a tuning parameter that varies with problem size, distribution and other factors as depicted by the average communication time in Fig. 6, where subtree size is gradually increased. The unit of communication is a subtree, which has 2, 4, 8, etc., cells as shown in the X-axis. The is a subset of the local essential FMM tree as we explain in Sect. 3. Communication time is measured by accumulating times of individual asynchronous sends and receives per process and taking their arithmetic mean.

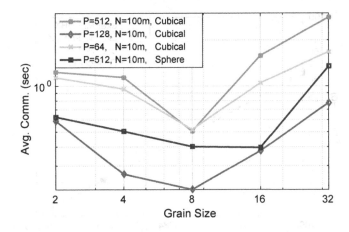

Fig. 6. Average communication time for different sizes and distributions as grain-size is varied.

The theoretical maximum subtree size is the entire LET. We stop at a certain threshold (32 in this case) because when it is increased further, a huge jump in time occurs. This is attributable to the change in communication protocol as per the Cray® MPICH specification from Eager Message to Rendezvous Message Protocol. When the message size exceeds a specific threshold (8 KB in this case), MPICH2 GNI NetMod alters the pathways towards a more relaxed algorithm for point-to-point inter-node messaging. A similar approach is developed in other MPI implementations like Open MPI and Intel® MPI. Hence, the remote tree traversal enables us to tune the performance by reducing the communication time enough to increase the impact of latency hiding.

5.3 Scalability of Spherical Boundary Distribution with $\mathcal{HSDX}$

In Fig. 7, we test the strong scalability at optimal grain size using $\mathcal{HSDX}$ for a large problem of 10^{10} particles. It follows that we have an efficient asynchronous communication when remote calls are non-blocking, have tunable granularity and when control is handed over to useful work rather than waiting immediately. To show this, we have integrated and compared several communication protocols within ExaFMM in Fig. 7. We note that $\mathcal{HSDX}$ is the closest to ideal scaling and has the advantage of fastest time-to-solution since it limits the inter-rack communication penalty on the dragonfly network by solely exchanging data through neighbors. By just looking at Fig. 7, it is hard to see that $\mathcal{HSDX}$ is at potential advantage for the exascale era. So we find it useful to present Table 3, which shows a more detailed analysis of the strong scalability. We notice a 6-fold increase in performance gain (from 3.87% to 23.44%) over the corresponding MPI_Alltoallv implementation as more cores are added. The parallel efficiency decreases, however, as the problem gets smaller while communication overhead prevails. Conventional $O(P)$ communication schemes stop

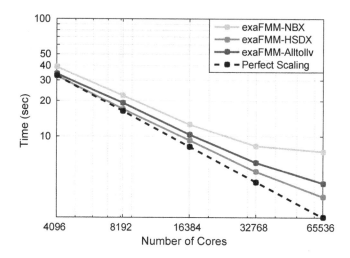

Fig. 7. Strong scaling across different communication protocols with 10^{10} particles.

Table 3. $\mathcal{HSDX}$ strong scalability analysis with FMM.

P	4,096	8,192	16,384	32,768	65,536
HSDX	32.72	17.02	9.27	5.008	3.05
Rel. Speedup	1	1.92	3.53	6.53	10.70
Efficiency	-	0.96	0.88	0.81	0.66
Enhancement	3.87%	11.41%	10.55%	16.27%	23.44%

scaling after 2048 nodes (65,536 cores) of Shaheen XC40. According to our largest setup that has an input of $N = 10^{10}$, we have an update rate of approximately 10^9 particles/second.

PVFMM is a large-scale FMM library that uses a kernel independent implementation, thus widens its target range of applications that require calculation of potential for elliptic kernels [29]. In this experiment, we attempt to compare the strong-scaling performance of PVFMM to our ExaFMM branch. It is worth noting that citing independent work is not meant to deem one superior to the other, but on the contrary, it is to give rise to our promising performance boosting strategies that tackle problematic communication and partitioning issues that are likely to arise in the near exascale era. In their most recent reports on PVFMM, Malhotra et al. [29] report perfect scalability up to 256 cores when running the Laplace kernel to compute potentials for 10^8 distributed on the surface of an ellipsoid. From that point onwards, communication cost starts to grow. They achieve 95% speedup corresponding too about 37% parallel efficiency. We switch to neighborhood collective communication presented in Sect. 4.2 for this comparison, since it vastly reduces network contention by propagating cells through direct neighbors only. Figure 8(a) shows consistent weak-scalability of communication

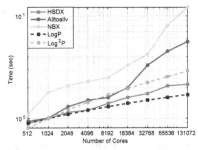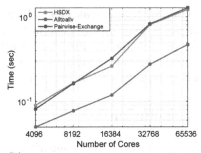

(a) Big example comparison of different communication protocols when weak-scaling 15m particles.

(b) Small example comparison of different communication protocols when weak-scaling 200k particles

Fig. 8. Communication scaling for big and small examples.

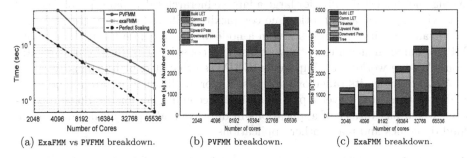

(a) ExaFMM vs PVFMM breakdown.   (b) PVFMM breakdown.   (c) ExaFMM breakdown.

Fig. 9. Strong scaling 2^{31} unknowns for sphere distribution and $P = 4$ and comparing ExaFMM while using $\mathcal{HSDX}$ communication and PVFMM.

over the conventional MPI_Alltoallv implementation. The presented approach shows a faster time-to-solution in ExaFMM vs. PVFMM when computing 2 billion unknowns as in Fig. 9. We cannot claim that scaling will persist indefinitely beyond the depicted number of cores, but when we have an exascale application that requires orders of magnitude larger problems that can fit in the machine's memory, we have a strong evidence of strong scalability.

5.4   Evaluation of Neighborhood Collective Communication Using $\mathcal{HSDX}$

Figure 8(a) compares $\mathcal{HSDX}$ using neighborhood collectives to $\mathcal{NBX}$ and MPI_Alltoallv. For the class of problems that constitute a hierarchically sparse data exchange defined in 1, $\mathcal{HSDX}$ is asymptotically bounded by the $c_1 \log P$ and $c_2 \log^2 P$. This behavior is shown for the boundary distribution solving Laplace Cartesian FMM kernels with $P = 4$ (order of expansion). However, the figure does not suggest that $\mathcal{HSDX}$ can generally replace its rivals; we still believe that $\mathcal{NBX}$ would outperform our algorithm in the general sparse data exchange, because it has the advantage of both $O(\log P)$ upper bound in addition to the use of a non-blocking barrier and synchronized sends [1].

Figure 8(b) weak scales a small example in order to reduce the effect of non-neighbor communication. The fact that $\mathcal{HSDX}$ and Pairwise exchange exhibit similar performance is anticipated since they almost have identical $logP$ behavior in such cases. They seem to lose herein against `MPI_Alltoallv` because of the initialization overhead included in communication time.

6 Conclusion

In this work, we propose algorithms that improve data locality, remote data access, and load-balance of the N-body problem. These algorithms contribute to producing an FMM solver that exploits communication redundancy and computation overlap. We show that Hilbert space-filling curves may not be the most optimal choice to partition boundary domain distributions. $\mathcal{HSDX}$ shows good strong and weak scalability for large adaptive hierarchically sparse problems, and falls within proven asymptotic time complexities. Shared memory parallelism is important to utilize resources within a node and to alleviate the problems with MPI resource management; thus we need to consider it in future implementations. We are working on improving $\mathcal{HSDX}$ so that it exploits the advantages of $\mathcal{NBX}$ to widen its range of use cases. As for application, we are intending to make the presented solver a part of an FMM preconditioner for the Poisson equation, which has variety of applications in diffusive and equilibrium processes in fluid dynamics and many other applications.

Acknowledgment. This work was supported by JSPS KAKENHI Grant-in-Aid for Young Scientists A Grant Number 16H05859. This work is partially supported by "Joint Usage/Research Center for Interdisciplinary Large-scale Information Infrastructures" and "High Performance Computing Infrastructure" in Japan. The authors are grateful to the KAUST Supercomputing Laboratory for the use of the Shaheen XC40 system.

References

1. Hoefler, T., Siebert, C., Lumsdaine, A.: Scalable communication protocols for dynamic sparse data exchange. In: Proceedings of the 15th ACM SIGPLAN Symposium on Principles and Practice of Parallel Programming, ser. PPoPP 2010, pp. 159–168. ACM, New York (2010)
2. Appel, A.W.: An efficient program for many-body simulation. SIAM J. Sci. Stat. Comput. **6**(1), 85–103 (1985)
3. Greengard, L., Rokhlin, V.: A fast algorithm for particle simulations. J. Comput. Phys. **73**(2), 325–348 (1987)
4. Beatson, R., Greengard, L.: A short course on fast multipole methods. Wavelets Multilevel Methods Elliptic PDEs **1**, 1–37 (1997)
5. Lu, B., Cheng, X., Huang, J., McCammon, J.A.: Order N algorithm for computation of electrostatic interactions in biomolecular systems. Proc. Natl. Acad. Sci. **103**(51), 19314–19319 (2006)
6. Yokota, R., Bardhan, J.P., Knepley, M.G., Barba, L.A., Hamada, T.: Biomolecular electrostatics using a fast multipole BEM on up to 512 GPUs and a billion unknowns. Comput. Phys. Commun. **182**(6), 1272–1283 (2011)

7. Ohno, Y., Yokota, R., Koyama, H., Morimoto, G., Hasegawa, A., Masumoto, G., Okimoto, N., Hirano, Y., Ibeid, H., Narumi, T., et al.: Petascale molecular dynamics simulation using the fast multipole method on K computer. Comput. Phys. Commun. **185**(10), 2575–2585 (2014)
8. Rui, P., Chen, R.: An efficient sparse approximate inverse preconditioning for FMM implementation. Microw. Opt. Technol. Lett. **49**(7), 1746–1750 (2007)
9. Bédorf, J., Gaburov, E., Zwart, S.P.: A sparse octree gravitational N-body code that runs entirely on the GPU processor. J. Comput. Phys. **231**(7), 2825–2839 (2012)
10. Price, D., Monaghan, J.: An energy-conserving formalism for adaptive gravitational force softening in smoothed particle hydrodynamics and N-body codes. Mon. Not. R. Astron. Soc. **374**(4), 1347–1358 (2007)
11. Asanovic, K., Bodik, R., Catanzaro, B.C., Gebis, J.J., Husbands, P., Keutzer, K., Patterson, D.A., Plishker, W.L., Shalf, J., Williams, S.W., et al.: The landscape of parallel computing research: a view from Berkeley. Technical report UCB/EECS-2006-183, EECS Department, University of California, Berkeley (2006)
12. Warren, M.S., Salmon, J.K.: A fast tree code for many-body problems. Los Alamos Sci. **22**(10), 88–97 (1994)
13. Bédorf, J., Gaburov, E., Fujii, M.S., Nitadori, K., Ishiyama, T., Portegies Zwart, S.: 24.77 Pflops on a gravitational tree-code to simulate the Milky Way Galaxy with 18600 GPUs. In: Proceedings of the 2014 ACM/IEEE International Conference for High Performance Computing, Networking, Storage and Analysis, pp. 1–12 (2014)
14. Speck, R., Ruprecht, D., Krause, R., Emmett, M., Minion, M., Winkel, M., Gibbon, P.: A massively space-time parallel N-body solver. In: Proceedings of the International Conference on High Performance Computing, Networking, Storage and Analysis, p. 92. IEEE Computer Society Press (2012)
15. Winkel, M., Speck, R., Hubner, H., Arnold, L., Krause, R., Gibbon, P.: A massively parallel, multi-disciplinary barnes-hut tree code for extreme-scale N-body simulations. Comput. Phys. Commun. **183**(4), 880–889 (2012)
16. Lashuk, I., Chandramowlishwaran, A., Langston, H., Nguyen, T.-A., Sampath, R., Shringarpure, A., Vuduc, R., Ying, L., Zorin, D., Biros, G.: A massively parallel adaptive fast multipole method on heterogeneous architectures. Commun. ACM **55**(5), 101–109 (2012)
17. Zandifar, M., Abdul Jabbar, M., Majidi, A., Keyes, D., Amato, N.M., Rauchwerger, L.: Composing algorithmic skeletons to express high-performance scientific applications. In: Proceedings of the 29th ACM on International Conference on Supercomputing, ser. ICS 2015, pp. 415–424. ACM, New York (2015)
18. AbdulJabbar, M., Yokota, R., Keyes, D.: Asynchronous execution of the fast multipole method using charm++. arXiv preprint arXiv:1405.7487 (2014)
19. Salmon, J.K.: Parallel hierarchical N-body methods. Ph.D. dissertation, California Institute of Technology (1991)
20. Warren, M.S., Salmon, J.K.: A parallel hashed oct-tree N-body algorithm. In: Proceedings of the 1993 ACM/IEEE Conference on Supercomputing, pp. 12–21. ACM (1993)
21. Makino, J.: A fast parallel treecode with GRAPE. Publ. Astron. Soc. Jpn. **56**, 521–531 (2004)
22. Solomonik, E., Kalé, L.V.: Highly scalable parallel sorting. In: Proceedings of the 2010 IEEE International Symposium on Parallel and Distributed Processing (IPDPS), pp. 1–12 (2010)
23. Haverkort, H.: An inventory of three-dimensional Hilbert space-filling curves. arXiv preprint arXiv:1109.2323 (2011)

24. Dubinski, J.: A parallel tree code. New Astron. **1**, 133–147 (1996)
25. Warren, M.S., Salmon, J.K.: Astrophysical N-body simulations using hierarchical tree data structures. In: Proceedings of the 1992 ACM/IEEE Conference on Supercomputing, ser. Supercomputing 1992, pp. 570–576. IEEE Computer Society Press, Los Alamitos (1992)
26. Lashuk, I., Chandramowlishwaran, A., Langston, H., Nguyen, T.-A., Sampath, R., Shringarpure, A., Vuduc, R., Ying, L., Zorin, D., Biros, G.: A massively parallel adaptive fast multipole method on heterogeneous architectures. In: Proceedings of the Conference on High Performance Computing Networking, Storage and Analysis (2009)
27. Teng, S.-H.: Provably good partitioning and load balancing algorithms for parallel adaptive N-body simulation. SIAM J. Sci. Comput. **19**(2), 635–656 (1998)
28. Yokota, R., Turkiyyah, G., Keyes, D.: Communication complexity of the fast multipole method and its algebraic variants. Supercomput. Front. Innov.: Int. J. **1**(1), 63–84 (2014)
29. Malhotra, D., Biros, G.: PVFMM: a parallel kernel independent fmm for particle and volume potentials. Commun. Comput. Phys. **18**(3), 808–830 (2015)

EvoGraph: On-the-Fly Efficient Mining of Evolving Graphs on GPU

Dipanjan Sengupta[1] and Shuaiwen Leon Song[2(✉)]

[1] Georgia Tech, Atlanta, USA
dsengupta6@gatech.edu
[2] Pacific Northwest National Lab, Richland, USA
Shuaiwen.Song@pnnl.gov

Abstract. With the prevalence of the *World Wide Web* and social networks, there has been a growing interest in high performance analytics for constantly-evolving dynamic graphs. Modern GPUs provide massive amount of parallelism for efficient graph processing, but the challenges remain due to their lack of support for the near real-time streaming nature of dynamic graphs. Specifically, due to the current high volume and velocity of graph data combined with the complexity of user queries, traditional processing methods by first storing the updates and then repeatedly running static graph analytics on a sequence of versions or snapshots are deemed undesirable and computational infeasible on GPU. We present EvoGraph, a highly efficient and scalable GPU-based dynamic graph analytics framework that incrementally processes graphs on-the-fly using fixed-sized batches of updates. The runtime realizes this vision with a user friendly programming model, along with a vertex property-based optimization to choose between static and incremental execution; and efficient utilization of all hardware resources using GPU streams, including its computational and data movement engines. Extensive experimental evaluations for a wide variety of graph inputs and algorithms demonstrate that EvoGraph achieves up to *429* million updates/sec and over *232x* speedup compared to the competing frameworks such as *STINGER*.

1 Introduction

High performance machines are increasingly using GPUs to leverage their scalability and low dollar to FLOPS ratios [1–4]. As a result, GPUs have become the main compute engines for today's HPC supercomputers such as Titan in Oak Ridge [5]. Another recent trend is the gain in popularity of GPU processing in many domains such as social networks, e-commerce, advertising, and genomics. This has motivated the growing interest in large-scale real-world graph processing for both scientific and commercial applications, as well as the recent efforts in accelerator-based graph processing frameworks such as MapGraph [6], CuSha [7], GraphReduce [8,9], and so on. An important aspect of real-world graphs, like Facebook friend lists or Twitter follower graphs, is that they are dynamic and evolving. Given the billions of Facebook [10] users sharing more than 100 billion

© Springer International Publishing AG 2017
J.M. Kunkel et al. (Eds.): ISC High Performance 2017, LNCS 10266, pp. 97–119, 2017.
DOI: 10.1007/978-3-319-58667-0_6

photos and posts per month, let alone the volume on Twitter [11], there is a huge need to quickly analyze this high velocity stream of graph data.

However, state-of-the-art graph analytics for dynamic graphs [12–14] follow a store-and-static-compute model that involves batching these updates into discrete time intervals, applying all of the updates to the total graph, and then rerunning the static analysis. There is considerable redundancy and inefficiency in this approach to analyzing this *evolving* graph sequence. Static graph analytics on a single version of the evolving graph, even when leveraging massive amount of parallelism offered by thousands of cores in a GPU, can be very slow due to the large scale of many real-world graphs (e.g., one Facebook graph purportedly has a trillion edges [10]) and/or because of the complexity of the graph queries that are traditionally both compute and memory intensive. Second, data movement of the entire input graph repeatedly between the host and the GPU over the slow *PCIe* link can result in substantial overhead, which in turn can overshadow the benefits from the massive parallelism offered by a GPU. Finally, there are real world graph analytics problems that inherently require soft or hard real-time guarantees, e.g., real-time anomaly detection, disease spreading, etc., and hence cannot use the traditional static recomputation model. Beyond just hardware performance, we also note that the skills to write high-performance GPU code are substantially different from the coding skills that many analysts have learned. As one can therefore see, the many demands of high velocity graph data, both commercial and scientific, have outstripped the traditional, batched static graph analytics models when using GPUs.

To address this, we propose a two-pronged approach to deal with both the performance and programmability challenges. We introduce an accelerator-based incremental graph processing framework named EvoGraph. EvoGraph employs a new variant of the popular *Gather-Apply-Scatter* (GAS) programming model [15–17], which we call *Incremental-GAS* (or I-GAS), to incrementally process a batched stream of updates (i.e., edge/vertex insertions and deletions) on-the-fly. The key insight is that I-GAS algorithms are designed to work over a dynamically determined sub-graph of the previous version of the evolving graph. For many popular graph algorithms and real-world graphs, the corresponding I-GAS logic affects only a fractional portion of the graph; this reduction in problem size can result in tremendous performance benefits compared to the traditional static recomputation on the entire graph. The modest additions of the I-GAS model to the already-published GAS model interface enable an easy transition of analysts from coding in a static sequential to a dynamic streaming environment.

From a simplistic view, it would seem that incremental methods would always be preferable. However, there are scenarios when a streamed update may affect a very large portion of the graph, and incremental processing may become worse than static recomputation due to the overheads from incremental execution. One such counterexample is in the incremental version of Breadth First Search (BFS), where updates that affect vertices close to the source/root node will affect nearly the entire BFS tree. Thus the incremental run can at best perform as good as the static re-run. In order to handle such scenarios, we employ a *per batch*, property-based mechanism named *'property-guard'*, which dynamically selects between incremental and static graph processing. Utilizing user-defined and built-in properties (e.g., *vertex degree* and *parent ID*) along with programmable control policies, EvoGraph analyzes each update batch and dynamically decides whether to process the graph incrementally using I-GAS or to fall back to static recomputation. To the best of our knowledge, EvoGraph is the first GPU-based graph analytics framework that enables efficient online processing of evolving graphs.

Contributions. We make the following contributions:

- *EvoGraph*, an accelerator-based high-performance incremental graph processing framework built on top of GraphReduce [8], processes evolving graphs by avoiding the naive static graph recomputation approach. It seamlessly maps users' sequential codes for incremental graph algorithms onto GPU for acceleration.
- Improved GPU core utilization via dynamic merging of GPU contexts (or *context packing*) from different graph applications, and additional hardware parallelism extracted using deep copy operations on separate CUDA streams[1] to leverage multiple GPU hardware queues.
- An extensive evaluation of three general classes of graph algorithms (i.e., *Stateful, Partially Stateless* and *Fully Stateless*) on real-world and synthetic graph datasets demonstrates that *EvoGraph* can significantly outperform the existing static recomputation approaches. Compared to competitive frameworks like *STINGER*, *EvoGraph* achieves a speedup of up to *232x* and overall throughput of *429* million updates/sec.
- Graph-property-based performance optimization called *property-guard* to dynamically decide between static and dynamic graph execution based on user-defined and built-in graph properties, resulting in a speedup of up to *18.4x* over a common streaming approach.

2   Background and Motivation

2.1   Computation Abstraction

As introduced in the previous work [8, 15–17], the *Gather-Apply-Scatter* (GAS) computation model has been widely adopted in research and industry to simply and effectively express a broad range of graph algorithms (e.g., heat simulation, nuclear trafficking and sparse linear algebra). Under GAS, the input data can be described as a directed graph, $G = (V, E)$, where V denotes the vertex set and E denotes the directed edge set. A GAS-based computation iterates over three sequential phases, the eponymous *Gather, Apply* and *Scatter*. The iteration process continues until the vertex state no longer changes. In the Gather phase, in-coming messages are processed and combined (reduced) into one message.

---

[1] In this paper, we use the NVIDIA CUDA terminology to describe the GPU architecture. However, our work is independent of the terminology itself.

In the Apply phase, vertices use the combined message to update their states. Finally, in the Scatter phase, vertices can send a message to their neighbors along their edges. Depending on whether the Scatter and Gather phases iterate over and update edges or vertices, there are three ways to implement GAS-based algorithms: *vertex centric* [18], *edge centric* [19] and hybrid [8].

2.2   Motivation and Challenges

Compared to its counterpart CPU, GPU often provides superior acceleration for general graph algorithms because of their unparalleled massive amount of parallelism. Figure 1 demonstrates that for processing three real-world in-memory graphs under BFS, recent frameworks for processing *static graphs* on GPU [6–8] significantly outperform one of the state-of-the-art CPU-based graph analytics (i.e., X-Stream [19]). This motivates us to leverage GPU's high computation power for processing *dynamic graphs*.

Figure 2 shows an example of an evolving Linkedin social network graph, in which a subgraph (circled by red dashed line) is going through *update batches* (e.g., insert:(1,4) and delete:(1,3)) at different time points. Different colors of dots on the social network represent work fields. Processing such common constantly-evolving social network graphs on GPU is very challenging because (i) highly efficient computation model and convenient programming constructs do not exist

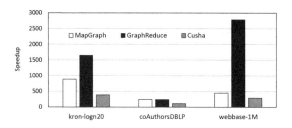

Fig. 1. State-of-the-art GPU frameworks (i.e., MapGraph, GraphReduce and Cusha) for processing static graphs under BFS significantly outperform a CPU-based framework X-Stream (baseline). X-Stream runs on a 16-core Xeon E5-2670 CPU with 32 GB memory. GPU frameworks run on a NVIDIA Tesla K40c GPU with 15 SMX and 12 GB GDDR5 RAM.

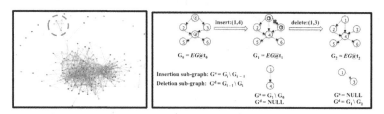

Fig. 2. A subgraph of a Linkedin social network has been updated over time but the majority of the network remains unchanged. (Color figure online)

for programmers to effectively express their algorithms on GPU, (ii) how to efficiently utilize the parallelism provided by GPU to deal with the computation and data storage overlap in dynamic graphs is complicated, and (iii) how to extract the most throughput from GPU without burdening the users with hardware details is unclear. To address these challenges, we designed a runtime graph analytics framework named *EvoGraph* to enable online processing of complex evolving graphs on modern GPUs. Under EvoGraph, users only need to write sequential codes and the sophisticated runtime will seamlessly map the incremental graphs to GPU for acceleration.

3   Design Choices

In general, there are two major strategies for processing evolving graphs: (1) Offline evolving graph processing where multiple versions of the graph are stored and analyzed for the change in certain graph properties over time. (2) Online evolving graph processing that involves real-time continuous query processing over streaming updates on an evolving graph. EvoGraph is a framework designed for (2).

From the design perspective, we will discuss the four key aspects of evolving graphs that dictate the design decisions for EvoGraph in this section.

3.1   Computation Overlap and Programming Model

As shown in Fig. 2, across multiple versions or snapshots of an evolving graph, the vertex states or values for many vertices remain the same over time, and thus their recomputation is essentially redundant. We define an *inconsistent vertex* as a vertex for which one or more properties are affected when an update batch is applied. For instance, when calculating out-degree of vertices, an insertion or deletion of edge (v_i, v_j) only makes vertex v_i inconsistent. However, under BFS (Breadth-First Search) algorithm, insertion of edge (v_i, v_j) makes v_j and all the vertices that are descendants of v_j *inconsistent*. One may consider the entire vertex set V to be inconsistent by default. But for many real-world evolving graphs (e.g., social network), changes affect only a very small subset of the graph. Therefore, computing the vertex states only for those inconsistent vertices while maintaining the vertex states for the rest will significantly reduce the computation time. To enable this, we propose *Incremental GAS Programming Model* (or **I-GAS**) based on the classic GAS abstraction (Sect. 2.1) for incremental graph processing. To reduce overheads, I-GAS builds a group of inconsistent vertex sets and sub-graphs that are affected by an update batch and then reduce the incremental graph problem to a sub-problem under GAS. We provide detailed discussion for I-GAS in Sect. 4.3.

3.2   Working Set Overlap and Data Structure Choice

Another key observation is that there can be a significant overlap in the edge and vertex sets between the consecutive versions of an evolving graph. For instance, if a graph evolved from G to G' during a certain time epoch T and let $\delta_1 = G' - G$ (insertions), $\delta_2 = G - G'$ (deletions), then $G \cap G' = G - \delta_2 = G' - \delta_1$ is the overlap between the working sets of the two consecutive versions.

There are multiple options for choosing data structures to store an evolving graph. Assume the graph has n vertices and m edges at certain time point. *Adjacency matrices* allow fast update (i.e., $O(1)$ time cost) with both insertions and deletions but require $O(n^2)$ space. *Adjacency lists* are space efficient ($O(m+n)$) and allow fast update, but graph traversals are very inefficient due to the non-contiguous memory nodes in the adjacency edge list. *Compressed Sparse Row* (CSR) [20] formats provide both space efficiency and fast traversal through storing offsets rather than all the valid fields in an adjacency matrix. But its insertions and deletions are very expensive because each update requires shifting of the graph data throughout the compressed array to match the compressed format. To allow efficient updates and processing for both the incremental and static graph algorithms, EvoGraph applies a hybrid data structure: edge-lists to store incremental updates and compressed format to store the previous static version of the graph. As mentioned previously, the edge-list will allow faster updates without adversely affecting the performance of the incremental computation. Meanwhile, the compressed matrix format allows faster traversal over the static version of the graph. EvoGraph merges both whenever required (Sect. 4.3).

3.3 Static vs. Dynamic Runtime

Runtime of online graph analytics varies widely depending on the algorithm and the update mechanism. On one hand, there are cases in which incremental algorithms affect only a small local portion of the entire graph (e.g., making a small subset of the graph inconsistent). As demonstrated in [21–23], per-vertex properties that depend on a fixed radius affect only a local portion of the graph and hence the runtime is proportional to the update batch size (e.g. triangle counting algorithm). On the other hand, there are classes of incremental algorithms whose properties depend on the graph path which may cause a large portion of the graph to be inconsistent, resulting in a complete recomputation of the graph. Under such scenario, incremental processing will not achieve any performance benefit over static recomputation, and may even suffer from a performance degradation due to the overheads associated with the incremental execution. To effectively handle both scenarios, EvoGraph applies a heuristic to select the execution path: incremental processing or static recomputation. The decision is made dynamically based on a set of built-in or user-defined graph property checks (e.g., vertex degree information) and the fraction of inconsistent vertices in the update batch that meets the criteria. More specifically, if the update is predicted to affect a small portion of the graph then the incremental execution path is taken. Otherwise, the update is merged with the static graph, which will then be recomputed. Take BFS as an example. If 90% of the inconsistent vertices in an update batch are of high degree, a large portion of the graph is likely to be impacted, so the static execution path will be taken. The metadata for making decisions on the execution path will be discussed later.

3.4   Context Packing and Multi-level GPU Sharing

During the graph processing, some incremental computation may only affect a small portion of the graph, resulting in GPU cores being significantly underutilized. This gives us opportunities for GPU resource sharing among static and incremental graph computation. Taking NVIDIA GPUs for example, since the CUDA runtime does not allow more than one host process to share the same GPU context (or *protection domain*), the GPU workloads of two different applications cannot run concurrently on a single GPU. When processing incremental graphs, this could result in high context switching overhead and potential core idling. To avoid this, EvoGraph enables '*Context Packing*' which packs different application contexts into a single protection domain. Specifically, all the graph workloads (static and incremental) collocated on a GPU are dynamically mapped to separate host threads of the same per GPU host process, with their respective GPU operations invoked via separate CUDA streams shown in Fig. 3. Using a single GPU context to host all applications enables (i) the cross-application sharing of GPU resources, i.e., graph operations from different applications can run concurrently on a single GPU, thereby achieving the benefits of space and time sharing- a true multi-tenancy, (ii) minimal context switching overhead reduced further by pinning the per GPU host threads to certain CPU cores, (iii) high scalability achieved with GPU requests being channelized through separate CUDA Streams, thereby reducing the overheads of request synchronization and pipelined execution to the minimum, and (iv) high fault tolerance as the faults due to one corrupt graph application can be localized to certain threads and will not affect other graph applications. One specific advantage of leveraging CUDA streams is that all three GPU engines, (a) memory copy from host to device (*H2D*), (b) from device to host (*D2H*), and (c) *computation*, can be concurrently executed by different applications.

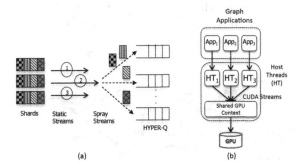

Fig. 3. Context packing and multi-level GPU sharing: (a) Deep copy mechanism between host and device. (b) Context packing mechanism for true multi-tenancy.

4   EvoGraph: The Runtime Framework

EvoGraph can efficiently process evolving graphs that incrementally change over time due to edge or vertex insertions and/or deletions by leveraging hundreds of cores available on GPU. The continuous stream of updates is divided into fixed size batches prior to being processed by EvoGraph in the order of their arrival. EvoGraph simplifies evolving graph analytics programming by supporting a *multi-phase, asynchronous, property guarded* execution model. Figure 4 shows the general software architecture of EvoGraph which consists of five major components: *Static-/Meta-computation Engine, Stream Engine, Inconsistency Graph Builder, I-GAS Engine and Graph Merger.* All of them support GAS-based APIs.

4.1   User Interface

Table 1 shows the six user-defined functions for representing the different computation phases in EvoGraph. By customizing these functions, programmers can simply write sequential graph algorithms on the host CPU side. The runtime of EvoGraph will then generate parallelized code to incrementally process evolving graph updates and execute them on the targeted GPU. The user-defined functions including *meta_computation(), build_inconsistency_list(), property_guard(), frontier_activate(), update_inconsistency_list()* and *merge_state()* correspond to the five computation phases of EvoGraph which are summarized as follows:

1. **Processing Static Graph and Metadata:** computing the static version of the graph and any optional metadata that will be used later for incremental processing.
2. **Extracting Graph Inconsistency:** creating a list of inconsistent vertices, and optionally, an inconsistent subgraph.
3. **Determining the Execution Path:** using the user-defined and built-in property list to examine the current update batch to proactively decide between incremental processing vs. static recomputation.

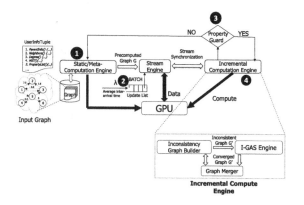

Fig. 4. The software architecture diagram of EvoGraph.

Table 1. Implementing graph algorithms in EvoGraph

Examples	EvoGraph computation phases and APIs						
	Categories	Phase I meta_computation()	Phase II build_inconsistency_list()	Phase III property_guard()	Phase IV frontier_activate()	update_inconsistency_list()	Phase V merge_state()
Breadth First Search (BFS)	Stateful	Parent ID & Vertex degree	Inconsistency list contains vertices with incorrect depth values with MIN_PRIORITY. (2) $G' = G$	Check BFS depth property	Activate inconsistent vertices with minimum depth value	Remove frontier vertices and add inconsistent successors to inconsistency list	(1) Apply all insertions and deletions to G
Connected Components (CC)	Partially stateless	Vertex degree	For each edge insertion add an edge in G' if the endpoints belong to different components. (2) G' is also known as component graph	Check disjoint component property	Activate all the vertices in G'	Clear inconsistency list	(1) Apply only deletions to G. (2) Relabel components in G using G'
Triangle Counting (TC)	Fully stateless	Vertex degree	(1) Inconsistency list contains endpoints of every edge inserted and / or deleted and their respective neighbors. (2) G' consists of inconsistent vertices and edge incident on them in G	Check vertex degree property	Activate all the vertices in G'	Clear inconsistency list	(1) Applying insertions and deletions to G not required. (2) Update triangle counts and degree information in G using G'

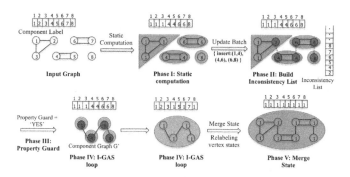

Fig. 5. Computation phases of CC in EvoGraph with inconsistent vertices marked red. (Color figure online)

4. **Incremental GAS (I-GAS)** [24,25]: applying incremental version of the GAS programming model to move the computational frontier one step per iteration.
5. **Merging:** Merging the incremental and static graph states.

As examples, Fig. 5 illustrates the five computation phases in Connected Component (CC) algorithm. CC requires a separate inconsistent subgraph G' in Phase IV. Before discussing each of these phases in detail, we first look into the **Stream Engine** shown in Fig. 4, which conducts multi-level GPU related optimizations.

4.2   Stream Engine: Data Movement and Context Packing

The *Stream Engine (SE)* is mainly responsible for (i) efficient asynchronous data transfer between host and GPU, (ii) context merging of static and incremental computation, and (iii) context packing of multiple graph workloads on the same GPU to enable multi-level GPU sharing.

For (i), SE leverages CUDA Streams, double buffering, and hardware support like *Hyper-Qs* provided by the architecture to effectively overlap data streaming and computation. SE spawns separate CUDA Streams to launch multiple kernels simultaneously and transfer batches of incremental updates to the graph asynchronously, overlapping memory copies within and across computation phases. Furthermore, as shown in Fig. 3(a), EvoGraph uses separate CUDA Streams to enable deep copy operations [26] in order to take advantage of the large number of hardware queues offered by modern GPU architectures. This is motivated by the fact that an update batch in EvoGraph is not a single contiguous byte-array, but consists of many sub-arrays that contain edge, vertex, and vertex/edge property update information. EvoGraph exploits this by not moving the entire update batch in one copy performed by a single CUDA stream, but instead making SE to dynamically spawn multiple CUDA Streams to move these sub-arrays to GPU. The outcome is the concurrent usage of the GPU's many hardware queues, which consequently improves the overall throughput.

As shown in Fig. 3(b), SE achieves (ii) and (iii) by packing multiple applications' GPU contexts into a single protection domain on-the-fly to maximize GPU resource utilization and avoid core idling. When a GPU request from a graph application (static or incremental computation) arrives, SE creates a separate CUDA stream object for it by calling *cudaStreamCreate()*, the handler to which is stored in a thread local storage. Using this handler, subsequent requests from this application is dispatched over this designated stream. Upon application exit, SE tears down the stream by calling *cudaStreamDestroy()* on the stream handler. To ensure all the applications packed into a single GPU context associated with a particular GPU are not blocked when one of them explicitly synchronizes its host thread with the device, EvoGraph dynamically maps all device synchronization calls to their respective stream synchronization counterparts (e.g., cudaDeviceSynchronize() is converted to cudaStreamSynchronize()). Next we discuss each computation phase in detail.

4.3   Computation Phases in EvoGraph

Phase I: Static Graph and Metadata Preprocessing. Shown as ❶ in Fig. 4 and *meta_computation()* in Table 1, this phase has two main purposes. First, it computes the static version of the input graph based on the traditional GAS model. In theory, any GAS-based static graph processing frameworks can be applied here for the static computation. In this work, we chose the highly optimized GPU-based static-graph processing framework *GraphReduce* [8] as our static computation engine. Due to its hybrid GAS-based programming model and ability to handle out-of-memory big graph inputs, GraphReduce fits well into our overall design methodology. Second, this phase computes the graph property metadata, such as parent id, vertex degree and minimum spanning tree (MST). These property metadata plays an important role in processing incremental graph algorithm in the upcoming phases. Table 1 lists what metadata is required to be computed in Phase I using *meta_computation()* for different incremental graph algorithms.

Phase II: Marking Out Graph Inconsistency. As illustrated in Fig. 5, this is the phase where incremental graph processing begins. This phase identifies the inconsistent part of the graph after applying the update batch (❷ in Fig. 4) using the *build_inconsistency_list()* function shown in Table 1. This user-defined function takes the update batch information (e.g., edge/vertex insertions and/or deletions) and the priority attribute of each vertex to build a list of inconsistent vertices. EvoGraph also provides an option for users to construct an inconsistent sub-graph G' which can be used later. Table 1 lists the action items from Phase II for three different graph algorithms.

Phase III: Determining the Execution Path Through Property Checking. (❸) This is the phase that decides which execution path, incremental processing or static recomputation, should be taken based on the area effect caused by the incremental graph algorithms. Specifically, if an incremental algorithm causes the majority portion of the graph to become inconsistent, incremental processing may not be a better option than static recomputation due to its extra execution overheads. Such overheads may occur in multiple phases, including (1) marking inconsistent vertices and/or building an optional inconsistent subgraph, (2) resolving such inconsistencies in the I-GAS computation loop, and (3) merging the incremental states with the static graph. The static computation does not have these overheads of finding inconsistencies or merging different vertex states.

For every update batch, EvoGraph uses a selected set of graph properties (e.g., *vertex degree, neighbor info, distance, depth,* etc.) that will affect the runtime performance of the algorithm to make the selection for execution path. Table 1 shows such essential graph properties for different graph algorithms, and the corresponding API call *property_guard()*. Using BFS as an example, for each batch update, EvoGraph will check the vertex depth threshold below which incremental processing will degrade the performance, and the inconsistency fraction which is the percentage of inconsistent vertices that are under the vertex depth. For instance, EvoGraph with batch X will stop benefiting from incremental processing if more than 80% (inconsistency fraction) of the inconsistent vertices have vertex depth less than 3. We want to emphasize that these selected graph properties are input and algorithm dependent and can be tuned for optimal performance by users.

Listing 1.1. I-GAS computation loop per update batch

```
While(!inconsistency_list.empty())
  //activate vertices in the inconsistency_list
  frontier = frontier_activate(G,inconsistency_list)
  IGAS(G')
  update_inconsistency_list(G',inconsistency_list,frontier)
```

Phase IV: Incremental GAS. (④) As mentioned previously, we propose Incremental GAS (or I-GAS) to compute the vertex states only for those inconsistent vertices that are affected by the batch updates, while maintaining the vertex states for the rest to reduce computation overhead. I-GAS will only incrementally operate on the new computational frontiers[2], avoiding the processing of the overlap between two consecutive versions of the graph. More specifically, I-GAS has four key differences from the classic GAS, including (1) identifying the vertex state inconsistencies, (2) determining incremental computation order by the priority attributed to each inconsistent vertice (Phase II), (3) providing an option for user-defined heuristics to choose between static and incremental execution, and (4) merging the incremental vertex states with the original graph. Figure 5 shows the example of I-GAS loops for CC. A typical I-GAS computation loop per update batch is demonstrated in Listing 1.1. Basically, EvoGraph maintains a inconsistency list and the three functions will iterate until the list becomes empty. Note that in each iteration function *frontier_activate()* will activate new

---

[2] *Computational frontier* describes the number of inconsistent/active vertices in a given iteration.

computational frontiers using the vertex priority to feed *IGAS()*, which then calls incremental versions of *Gather, Apply and Scatter*. Finally, the new frontier information will update the inconsistency list.

Phase V: State-Merging. (④) During this phase, EvoGraph merges the updated vertex property with the previous version of the graph. Based on individual algorithms' *merge pattern*, it decides if edge insertions or deletions are required to be applied to the recent version of the static graph G before processing the next update batch. Table 1 shows three general classes of merge patterns represented by three graph algorithms: *Stateful* (Breadth-First Search), *Partially Stateless* (Connected Components) and *Fully Stateless* (Triangle Counting). We summarize the characteristics of these patterns as follows:

- **Stateful:** This type of incremental algorithms typically operate on the graph properties that have global effects, and must apply all the updates (both insertions and deletions) of the current batch to G at the end of the I-GAS loop. For example, vertex depth calculation in BFS requires consideration of any added/deleted edges.
- **Partially Stateless:** In each incremental iteration, this type of algorithms has dependency on either deletions or insertions from the previous update batch, but not both. In other words, either deletions or insertions are required to be merged with G at the end of the I-GAS loop. Hence the rest of the updates that lack dependency can be processed anytime during the execution without influencing the final result, and their merger with G is **deferred** by EvoGraph. Connected Components belongs to this category.
- **Fully Stateless:** This category of incremental algorithms update the graph properties that only have local effects. In other words, neither insertions nor deletions within each incremental iteration have any dependency on the previous update batch. Therefore, both insertions and deletions are deferred by EvoGraph. Triangle Counting shown in Table 1 belongs to this category. Other examples include *Clustering Coefficients* and *Vertex-degree Counting*.

Next, we will showcase the implementation of these incremental algorithms representing the three merge patterns.

5   Case Studies

Stateful. Detailed in Table 1, BFS is an example of a Stateful algorithm as it requires all the updates from one batch to be merged with the original graph before processing the next batch. Phase I involves static computation of BFS depths from the source vertex (handled by GraphReduce [8]) and metadata computation of properties such as degree and parent vertex id information for each vertex in the graph. In Phase II, vertices that have incorrect depth values [27] after applying the current update batch are marked as inconsistent and added to a container with min-priority that is ordered by depth value. Phase III checks for any listed property to decide if the framework should run the incremental version or re-run the static recomputation algorithm. In BFS, we use *vertex depth* as the property and check if the fraction of inconsistent vertices with depth values below a certain threshold have surpassed a certain limit. In Phase IV, EvoGraph fixes the inconsistency in the vertices of the graph in the order of their minimum depth values, as described in the algorithm by Ramalingam and Reps [27]. Thus, in each iteration of I-GAS loop, inconsistent vertices with the minimum depth value (can be multiple vertices) are activated and made consistent; and the inconsistency list is updated. Phase V is trivial as the vertex states are shared and hence do not require merging.

Partially Stateless. Shown in Table 1 and Fig. 5, Connected Components (CC) is a partially stateless algorithm because only deletions are required to be merged with G. For deletions we need to re-run the static algorithm and there are few proposed optimizations [22,23] to eliminate false delections so that a component will not be broken. Phase I calculates the static version of CC. In Phase II, EvoGraph builds the inconsistent graph G' with *vertex ids* as the component labels in the original graph, and for each edge insertion in G it adds an edge in G' if the endpoints of the edge belong to different components. G' is also known as *component graph* [23]. Phase III checks for the fraction of inconsistent vertices that belong to disjoint components. Phase IV runs static connected components algorithm on G'. Note that EvoGraph has successfully reduced the incremental problem in G to a static problem in G'. Finally, Phase V relabels the vertices in G from the computed component labels in G'.

Fully Stateless. As illustrated in Table 1, Triangle Counting (TC), which measures the total number of closed triangles in a graph (representing small-worldness of a graph), is a fully stateless algorithm because both insertions and deletions from an update batch are not required to be merged with the original graph before processing the next batch. Phase I computes the static version of the algorithm and the degree property for each vertex. In Phase II, EvoGraph marks the endpoints of every edge inserted or deleted and their respective neighboring vertices as inconsistent. Then it builds the inconsistent graph G' with edges incident on every inconsistent vertex. Phase III checks for the fraction of inconsistent vertices in G that have degree above certain threshold. Phase IV is similar to that in CC, activating all the vertices in G' and then running the static algorithm on G'. Note that EvoGraph has again successfully reduced a fully dynamic (having both insertions and deletions) problem in G to a static problem in G'. Finally, Phase V updates the triangle counts and the degree info in G using the corresponding computed values in G'. A Bloom Filter version of the incremental algorithm can also be implemented for fast membership queries [21].

6   Evaluation

6.1   Experimental Setup

Evaluation Platform. We evaluate EvoGraph on a heterogeneous HPC node equipped with 12-core Intel Xeon X5660 processors running at 2.8 GHz with

12 GB of DDR3 RAM, and one attached NVIDIA Tesla K40c GPU with 15 SMX multiprocessors and 12 GB GDDR5 RAM. The Kepler GPU is enabled with CUDA 7.0 runtime and the version 352.79 driver, while the host CPU is running Fedora version 20 with kernel v.3.11.10-301 × 86. To evaluate the effectiveness of EvoGraph framework, we use GraphReduce [8], GraphMat [28] and STINGER [21,23,29] for performance comparisons. GraphReduce is a state-of-the-art GPU-based static graph processing framework that process larger-than-GPU-memory graphs. GraphMat is a state-of-the-art CPU-based high performance graph processing framework that takes vertex programs and compiles them into sparse matrix operations (e.g. sparse matrix-vector multiplication). GraphReduce and GraphMat are both used as the GPU- and CPU-based static engine of EvoGraph and hence act as our comparison baseline. Note that other static graph processing engine (e.g., BlazeGraph [30]) can also serve as the static engine in EvoGraph as long as they are based on GAS programming model. Since different static engines maintain very similar optimization opportunities in evolving graphs, they can be selected based on their base performance. Furthermore, shared-memory based STINGER [13] proposes an efficient representation for implementing evolving graphs (i.e., abstract data structures) to enable fast real-time processing of queries. STINGER's graph data structures have been used to implement several applications on shared-memory CPU-based systems, including Clustering Coefficients and Connected Components. Unlike EvoGraph, STINGER is not a graph analytics framework. Updates are provided in batches to EvoGraph and STINGER where each batch size can range from 100,000 up to one million and consist of 99% edge insertions and 1% deletions. The endpoints of the edges used for batch updates are generated randomly.

Graph Dataset and Evaluated Algorithms. For evaluating the performance of EvoGraph, we use a mix of real-world and synthetic datasets. Their graph properties are shown in Table 2. The five real-world datasets are from University of Florida Sparse Matrix Collection [31]. The synthetic datasets are obtained from the Graph500 RMAT data generator [32] using scale 19, 20 and 21 with

Table 2. Graph datasets under evaluation

Graph dataset	Type	#Vertices	#Edges
hollywood-2009	real world	1,139,905	113,891,327
indochina-2004	real world	7,414,866	194,109,311
ljournal-2008	real world	5,363,260	79,023,142
kron_g500-logn21	real world	2,097,152	182,082,942
uk-2002	real world	18,520,486	298,113,762
G19D16	synthetic	524,288	8,388,608
G20D16	synthetic	1,048,576	15,700,394
G21D16	synthetic	2,097,152	31,771,509

average degree of 16 per vertex, labeled as G19D16, G20D16, and G21D16 respectively. The three widely used graph algorithms discussed in Sect. 5 are evaluated, representing the three merge patterns. Algorithms requiring undirected graphs as inputs are stored as pairs of directed edges.

6.2   Results Summary: EvoGraph vs. Static Recomputation

To process evolving graphs, the state-of-the-art GPU framework, which only process static graphs, have to follow a store-and-static-compute model, repeatedly running static graph computation on the "snapshots" of the evolving graph. Here we showcase the benefits of our EvoGraph (incremental graph analytics) over such recomputation schemes. For the overall speedup, Fig. 6 shows that EvoGraph achieves an average performance improvement of 12278x, 9.13x and 1.16x over GraphReduce across all the datasets for TC, CC and BFS respectively, with the update batch size as high as 1 million updates. Additionally, Fig. 7 demonstrates that EvoGraph is able to achieve up to 429 million updates/sec (indochina-2004 for TC). Several factors contribute to such high performance improvement: (i) the use of incremental computation in the I-GAS execution model to compute the vertex states for only the inconsistent set of vertices, as opposed to executing the algorithm on the entire input graph (Sect. 3.3); (ii) asynchronous mode and deep copy operations between host and device leveraging CUDA Streams and *Hyper-Qs* to keep both compute and memory-copy engines occupied simultaneously; (iii) concurrent static and incremental graph processing via time and space sharing on GPU (Sects. 3.4 and 4.2), resulting in substantial reduction in context-switching overhead and GPU core idling. An important observation to make here is that the performance benefit of Evograph is inversely proportional to the number of inconsistent vertices after applying

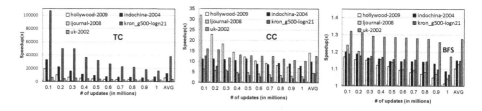

Fig. 6. EvoGraph's speedup over the static computation (GraphReduce) for TC, CC and BFS.

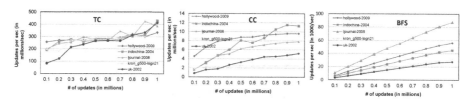

Fig. 7. Update rate that EvoGraph achieves for TC, CC and BFS.

the update batch, i.e., if the inconsistency graph G' is very small compared to the original graph after applying the updates, the performance benefit of Evo-Graph will be very large. But if the size of G' is too large the performance will be comparable to static recomputation or sometimes even worse (Sect. 6.4). This is why we see the large speedup in the case of fully-stateless applications like Triangle Counting where the inconsistency graph G' is small. Next, we draw key inferences as how the performance of the incremental execution in EvoGraph varies with algorithm type, update batch size and input graph size.

Effect of Graph Algorithm. Figure 6 shows that the maximum speedup achieved by EvoGraph over static recomputation occurs with TC (fully state-less), followed by CC (partially stateless) and then BFS (stateful). Also, the average system throughputs achieved across all graph algorithms for a batch size of 1 million updates are 372 million, 7.3 million and 50 K updates/sec for TC, CC and BFS, respectively. This drastic difference in performance across different merge patterns is because the fraction of the graph that becomes inconsistent after applying an update batch as the I-GAS loop unfolds increases in the order of fully-stateless, partially-stateless, and stateful. In other words, fully-stateless or partially-stateless algorithms only affect the graph locally, so the incremental runtime is bounded by the size of the update batch. On the contrary, since the stateful algorithms like BFS calculate a global property (e.g., vertex depth), the incremental computation affects a larger portion of the graph and hence achieves lower speedup. Furthermore, during the State-Merging phase of incremental BFS, the new update batch is applied or merged with the current static version which in turn is copied back to the GPU. This incurs some data transfer overhead, whereas for TC and CC the data transfers are of the order of the update batch size, keeping the memcpy time low.

Effect of Update Batch Size. Shown in Fig. 6, the speedup decreases as the update batch size increases due to the increasing problem size. We also observe that both the runtime and update rate (Fig. 7) increase with the batch size, which implies that speedup decreases slower with respect to the drastic update rate increase for larger batches.

Effect of Input Graph Size. Figure 7 shows that BFS's throughput increases with the batch size a lot faster for smaller graphs (e.g., ijournal-2008) than larger graphs (e.g., uk-2002). This happens because for the updates affecting a particular BFS level, the cost of incremental computation increases with the size of the inconsistent subgraph which in turn is proportional to the size of the input graph. However, the update rates of CC and TC show no correlation with the input size as the graph properties under consideration are local or semi-local.

6.3 Performance Implications of Graph Properties

We chose specific graph property for each of the three algorithms: vertex degree for TC, vertices with disjoint components for CC, and vertex depth from the source for BFS. These properties heavily impact the runtime of the static versions of these algorithms.

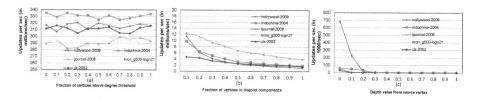

Fig. 8. Impact of properties on the update rate: (a) vertex degree: TC; (b) disjoint components: CC; and (c) vertex depth: BFS.

Triangle Counting (Vertex Degree): Figure 8(a) shows the change in the update rate for TC versus the fraction of updates (insertions and deletions) affecting vertices with degree greater than a certain threshold (e.g., *1900* for hollywood-2009). We vary the fraction of inconsistent vertices with degree higher than the threshold degree in a given update batch and then evaluate its effect on the incremental runtime and the update rate. From the figure we can observe that vertex degree does not have a significant impact on the update rate for TC. This is because TC is a stateless algorithm for both insertions and deletions, and hence the size of the sub-graph G' created in Phase II (Table 1) as well as the incremental runtime are independent of the vertex degree. Thus the update rate remains relatively constant even when more edges are inserted and/or deleted near high degree vertices.

Connected Components (Disjoint Components): Figure 8(b) shows that the update rate for CC decreases as the fraction of edges inserted (whose endpoints belong to different components in the original graph) is increased, with a maximum slowdown of *10.2x* across all the datasets. This slowdown of update rate is caused by: (i) the endpoints of an edge falling in the same component results in a self-edge in the component graph which is ignored by EvoGraph; (ii) since EvoGraph reduces the problem of incremental CC processing on G to static CC processing on G', the size increase of G' caused by the increasing number of vertices with disjoint components subsequently increase the processing time.

BFS (Vertex Depth): Figure 8(c) shows that increasing the fraction of vertices with depth below a given threshold (MAX_DEPTH/4 in our case) causes a sharp decline in the update rate. This slowdown comes from more insertions and deletions on the lower-depth vertices closer to the root vertex, which results in the I-GAS loop making a much larger portion of the graph inconsistent with each increment. The maximum slowdown (max to min ratio of the update rate) across all datasets is *213x* which leads to drastic system performance degradation and hence motivates our *property-guard* heuristic design.

6.4   Property-Guard Heuristic

In these sets of experiments we show how EvoGraph uses property information to adapt to situations where the incremental processing performs worse than the static recomputation. Figure 9 shows that the performance of incremental BFS

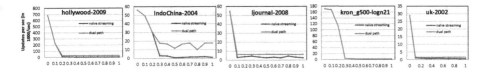

Fig. 9. Property-guard heuristic vs. naive streaming in incremental BFS using vertex depth property for five graph inputs. The x-axis represents the fraction of vertices below depth threshold of MAX_DEPTH/4.

for naive streaming without considering the property information of the current update batch falls relative to the static processing beyond a threshold (measured by the fraction of vertices with depth threshold below MAX_DEPTH/4). For hollywood, Indochina, ijournal, kronLogn21 and uk-2002, this threshold fraction is 0.2, 0.3, 0.1, 0.5 and 0.1 respectively. The reason for this degradation in incremental performance is that a larger number of updates to the lower-depth vertices results in a large portion of inconsistent graph and hence significant increase in processing time. In phase III, EvoGraph analyzes the current update batch for the depth threshold and if the batch has a fraction of vertices beyond a certain threshold, it processes the update batch with static recomputation. This ensures the worst-case performance has the same lower bound as static recomputation instead of proceeding to I-GAS incremental execution. We achieve a maximum speedup of *18.4x* using this heuristic over a naive streaming approach (Indochina-2004).

6.5   EvoGraph vs. STINGER

Figure 10 shows the comparison between the update rate for EvoGraph vs. STINGER [29] for TC and CC. For fairness, data transfer time between host and GPU has been included for EvoGraph computation while STINGER (a shared memory solution) is not subject to such overhead. Across all 3 synthetic datasets, STINGER shows a max update rate of 2.1 million updates/sec versus 488 million updates/sec from EvoGraph (S19D16), a *232.4x* increase in throughput. EvoGraph also shows better scalability as batch size increases because of

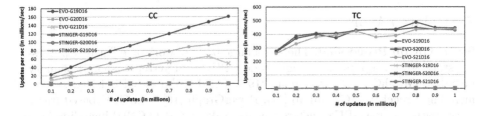

Fig. 10. EvoGraph vs STINGER throughput comparison for (a) Connected Components and (b) Triangle Counting.

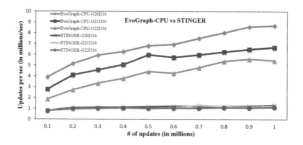

Fig. 11. CPU-EvoGraph vs STINGER throughput for Triangle Counting (TC).

(1) the massive parallelism provided by context packing and multi-level GPU sharing from EvoGraph is sufficient to overcome the overheads from the data movement over PCIe, (2) EvoGraph's hybrid data structure of edge-list for incremental updates and compressed matrix format for static versions of the graph. STINGER uses edge-list based data structures for both the static and incremental graph processing, which results in faster data structure update but slower traversal time. EvoGraph's hybrid data structure enables faster updates (via the edge-list) as well as faster static computation (via compressed matrix format).

In order to compare performance of CPU-based STINGER with pure I-GAS programming model based EvoGraph (without GPU), we implemented a CPU-version of EvoGraph with GraphMat as its static engine. As shown in Fig. 11, triangle counting (TC) using STINGER attains a maximum update rate of 1.32 million/sec as compared to 8.7 million updates/sec with EvoGraph using CPU-based GraphMat as the static engine for the G20D16 case, which results in 6.6× speedup in throughput. The reason for such high performance are two folds. First, the use of incremental computation in the I-GAS execution model to compute the vertex states for only the inconsistent vertices, as opposed to executing the graph algorithm for the entire input graph in the static case avoids a lot of redundant computation and results in large speedup. Second, unlike STINGER, which uses edge-list based data structures for both static and incremental graph processing, EvoGraph's hybrid data structure of edge-list for incremental updates enabling faster updates and compressed matrix format for static versions of the graph enabling fast static computation on the triangle counting subproblem.

7   Related Work

Static Graph Processing. There is a large body of work on efficiently processing static graph inputs on a single node CPU-based systems (shared memory) including GraphChi [18], X-Stream [19], etc.; distributed CPU-based systems including Pregel [15], GraphLab [17], PowerGraph [16]; and GPU-based frameworks (either single GPU or heterogeneous scale-up CPU+GPU) including Map-Graph [6], Cusha [7], GraphReduce [8] etc. EvoGraph is a scale-up heterogeneous solution for processing evolving graphs that can be integrated into the distributed CPU-based solutions, especially the ones using GAS programming models (e.g., Pregel and PowerGraph). Most of the GPU frameworks above can be used as the static graph processing core of EvoGraph (Sect. 4.3 Phase I). In this work, we applied the recent GraphReduce [8] as our static graph processing engine due to its unique features and high throughput achieved by mapping sub-graphs to the different memory abstractions of slow and fast memory [33].

Evolving Graph Processing. Broadly, there are two categories of evolving graphs processing (1) offline mining of evolving graphs that involves the generation, storing, and analysis of a sequence of versions or time-stamped snapshots of the evolving graphs (i.e., historic data) for the calculation of some global graph property; and (2) online processing of evolving graphs that enables real-time, continuous query processing over streaming updates. *EvoGraph is a framework designed to address (2).*

- *Offline Mining of Evolving Graphs:* Chronos [12], GraphScope [13], and TEG [14] are some examples of the most recent work in offline evolving graph processing. Chronos [12] supports incremental processing on temporal graphs using a graph representation that places graph vertex data from different versions together leading to good cache locality. GraphScope [13] proposes encoding for evolving graphs for community discovery and anomaly detection. Both Chronos and GraphScope are shared-memory CPU-based solution. TEG [14] provides a distributed CPU-based solution focusing on partitioning time evolving graphs across nodes and enables subgraph queries.
- *Online Processing Providing Real-time Continuous Query:* This type of approach implies certain memory constraints that may not allow keeping multiple versions of the evolving graph as historical data for future processing. STINGER [29] defines an efficient *data structure* to represent streaming graphs that enables fast, real-time insertions and/or deletions to the graph. Unlike STINGER which uses a single data structure for both static and dynamic graph analysis, EvoGraph applies a novel hybrid data structure that allows for incremental computation on edge lists and a compressed format for static graph computation. More importantly, STINGER is not a highly efficient runtime framework that maximizes the heterogeneous (CPU + GPU) performance in a single node and provides unified virtual functions for users to write sequential graph algorithms to process complex evolving graphs. Thus all the complex runtime and architecture-specific optimizations become the burden of the users. Built upon STINGER, DSTINGER [34] provides a distributed CPU-based graph representation (data structure) to store and process streaming updates, but it neither unleashes the massive computation power of CPU+GPU heterogeneous system nor provides a unified programming framework.

8   Conclusions and Future Work

This paper presents EvoGraph, an accelerator-based high-performance incremental graph analytics framework for processing time-evolving graphs. Technical advances offered by EvoGraph include: (1) an incremental variant of Gather-Apply-Scatter called I-GAS to compute graph properties only for the inconsistent subgraphs, (2) a user-tunable property-based optimization called property-guard for switching between I-GAS and static recomputation, (3) GPU context packing and deep memory copy operations for improved asynchronous computation and communication performance, and (4) an hybrid data structure for efficient incremental updates and static graph storage. Evaluation on a variety of graph inputs and algorithms demonstrates that EvoGraph achieves a system throughput of up to *429* million updates/sec and a *232x* speedup when compared to competitive frameworks like STINGER. Furthermore, the property-guard optimization on BFS (Stateful type) achieves a speed up of up to *18.4x* over a naive streaming approach. Future work will look at incorporating EvoGraph in distributed setups which will help the community study extreme-scale datasets and scenarios.

References

1. Luk, C.-K., Hong, S., Kim, H.: Qilin: exploiting parallelism on heterogeneous multiprocessors with adaptive mapping. In: Proceedings of MICRO 2009. ACM (2009)
2. Tarditi, D., Puri, S., Oglesby, J.: Accelerator: using data parallelism to program GPUs for general-purpose uses. SIGOPS Oper. Syst. Rev. **40**(5) (2006)
3. Sengupta, D., et al.: Scheduling multi-tenant cloud workloads on accelerator-based systems. In: Proceedings of the SC 2014. IEEE Press (2014)
4. Sengupta, D., Belapure, R., Schwan, K.: Multi-tenancy on GPGPU-based servers. In: Proceedings of the VTDC 2013. ACM (2013)
5. Top 500 List. http://www.top500.org/system/177975
6. Fu, Z., et al.: Mapgraph: a high level API for fast development of high performance graph analytics on GPUs. In: GRADES 2014. ACM (2014)
7. Khorasani, F., Vora, K., Gupta, R., Bhuyan, L.N.: Cusha: vertex-centric graph processing on GPUs. In: Proceedings of HPDC 2014. ACM (2014)
8. Sengupta, D., Song, S.L., et al.: Graphreduce: processing large-scale graphs on accelerator-based systems. In: Proceedings of the SC 2015. ACM (2015)
9. Sengupta, D., et al.: Graphreduce: large-scale graph analytics on accelerator-based HPC systems. In: IEEE IPDPSW (2015)
10. Ching, A., Edunov, S., Kabiljo, M., et al.: One trillion edges: graph processing at facebook-scale. Proc. VLDB Endow. **8**(12), 1804–1815 (2015)
11. Twitter Statistics. http://tinyurl.com/kcuhdcw
12. Han, W., Miao, Y., Li, K., et al.: Chronos: a graph engine for temporal graph analysis. EuroSys (2014)
13. Sun, J., Faloutsos, C., Papadimitriou, S., Yu, P.S.: Graphscope: parameter-free mining of large time-evolving graphs, KDD 2007. ACM (2007)
14. Fard, A., Abdolrashidi, A., Ramaswamy, L., Miller, J.: Towards efficient query processing on massive time-evolving graphs. In: CollaborateCom, October 2012
15. Malewicz, G., Austern, M.H., Bik, A.J., et al.: Pregel: a system for large-scale graph processing, SIGMOD 2010. ACM (2010)
16. Gonzalez, J.E., Low, Y., Gu, H., et al.: Powergraph: distributed graph-parallel computation on natural graphs. In: OSDI 2012. USENIX, Hollywood (2012)

17. Low, Y., Bickson, D., Gonzalez, J., et al.: Distributed graphlab: a framework for machine learning and data mining in the cloud. Proc. VLDB Endow. **5**, 716–727 (2012)
18. Kyrola, A., Blelloch, G., Guestrin, C.: Graphchi: large-scale graph computation on just a PC. In: OSDI 2012. USENIX Association, Berkeley (2012)
19. Roy, A., Mihailovic, I., Zwaenepoel, W.: X-stream: edge-centric graph processing using streaming partitions. In: SOSP 2013. ACM (2013)
20. Bell, N., Garland, M.: Efficient sparse matrix-vector multiplication on CUDA. NVIDIA Corporation, NVIDIA Technical report NVR-2008-004, December 2008
21. Ediger, D., Jiang, K., Riedy, J., Bader, D.: Massive streaming data analytics: a case study with clustering coefficients. In: IPDPSW 2010, pp. 1–8, April 2010
22. McColl, R., Green, O., Bader, D.: A new parallel algorithm for connected components in dynamic graphs. In: HiPC, December 2013
23. Ediger, D., Riedy, J., Bader, D., Meyerhenke, H.: Tracking structure of streaming social networks. In: IPDPSW 2011, May 2011
24. Sengupta, D., et al.: GraphIn: An Online High Performance Incremental Graph Processing Framework. Springer International Publishing, Cham (2016)
25. System design principles for heterogeneous resource management and scheduling in accelerator-based systems (2016). http://hdl.handle.net/1853/55607
26. CUDA 7.0. https://developer.nvidia.com/cuda-downloads/
27. Ramalingam, G., Reps, T.: An incremental algorithm for a generalization of the shortest-path problem. J. Algorithms, **21**(2) (1996)
28. Sundaram, N., Satish, N., Patwary, M.M.A., et al.: Graphmat: high performance graph analytics made productive. Proc. VLDB Endow. **8**(11), 1214–1225 (2015)
29. Ediger, D., McColl, R., Riedy, J., Bader, D.: Stinger: high performance data structure for streaming graphs. In: HPEC, September 2012
30. BlazeGraph. https://www.blazegraph.com/
31. University of Florida Sparse Matrix Collection. http://tinyurl.com/hh8g3n9
32. Murphy, R.C., Wheeler, K., Barrett, B., Ang, J.A.: Introducing the graph 500. In: Cray User's Group (CUG) (2010)
33. Sengupta, D., et al.: A framework for emulating non-volatile memory systems with different performance characteristics. In: Proceedings of the ICPE 2015. ACM (2015)
34. Feng, G., Meng, X., Ammar, K.: Distinger: a distributed graph data structure for massive dynamic graph processing. In: Big Data. IEEE (2015)

High-Performance Incremental SVM Learning on Intel® Xeon Phi™ Processors

Dipanjan Sengupta$^{(\boxtimes)}$, Yida Wang⬡, Narayanan Sundaram,
and Theodore L. Willke

Intel Corporation, 2200 Mission College Blvd., Santa Clara, CA 95054, USA
{dipanjan.sengupta,yida.wang,narayanan.sundaram,ted.willke}@intel.com

Abstract. Support vector machines (SVMs) are conventionally batch trained. Such implementations can be very inefficient for online streaming applications demanding real-time guarantees, as the inclusion of each new data point requires retraining of the model from scratch. This paper focuses on the high-performance implementation of an accurate incremental SVM algorithm on Intel® Xeon Phi™ processors that efficiently updates the trained SVM model with streaming data. We propose a novel *cycle break* heuristic to fix an inherent drawback of the algorithm that leads to a deadlock scenario which is not acceptable in real-world applications. We further employ intelligent caching of dynamically changing data as well as other programming optimization ideas to speed up the incremental SVM algorithm. Experiments on a number of real-world datasets show that our implementation achieves high performance on Intel® Xeon Phi™ processors ($1.1 - 2.1\times$ faster than Intel® Xeon® processors) and is up to $2.1\times$ faster than existing high-performance incremental algorithms while achieving comparable accuracy.

Keywords: High-performance · Incremental SVM · Intel Xeon Phi processor

1 Introduction

Support Vector Machine (SVM) [24] has established itself as one of the most popular and successful methods in example-based learning as an effective pattern classification tool where after training on a series of examples, the resulting model can generalize well on new input samples. Conventionally, SVMs are trained in batch mode, which can be formulated as a quadratic optimization problem. Several special-purpose optimization algorithms have been proposed for batch SVM learning, among which Sequential minimal optimization (SMO) [15] is one of the most commonly used. SVMs are widely applied to many application areas from scientific computing such as neuroscience and bioinformatics to Internet-based information retrieval like text classification, etc.

Intel, Xeon and Intel Xeon Phi are trademarks of Intel Corporation or its subsidiaries in the U.S. and/or other countries.

© Springer International Publishing AG 2017
J.M. Kunkel et al. (Eds.): ISC High Performance 2017, LNCS 10266, pp. 120–138, 2017.
DOI: 10.1007/978-3-319-58667-0_7

The batch training algorithms assume that the training set is fixed. If there is any sample addition/deletion/modification on the training set, the batch algorithms have to retrain the model on the entire data set from scratch to produce a new model, which is inefficient and expensive. However, in many cases datasets are under change. For example, when training on a data stream, the model should be updated incrementally after getting a new sample (incremental training). Also, an efficient way to do cross validation on a dataset is to train a model on all data and update it by removing different sets of left-out samples (decremental training).

Standardized packages for batch SVM training such as *LibSVM* [4] and SVM^{light} [11] have been around for years. There are also highly optimized implementations on top of them targeted towards many-core architectures like GPU [3] and the first generation of Intel Xeon Phi products [25]. However, incremental SVM algorithms are not widely popular in machine learning community because there are no efficient implementations of the proposed algorithms readily available for use.

An accurate incremental and decremental SVM learning algorithm has been previously proposed by Cauwenberghs and Poggio [16] and their approach was adapted to other variants of kernel machines [12,13]. When a single sample is added (or removed) this algorithm updates the exact optimal solution recursively without retraining it from scratch. The key idea is to retain the Karush-Kuhn-Tucker (KKT) conditions [24] on all previously trained samples, while adding (or removing) a new sample to the solution. In principle, this is better than other incremental algorithms such as [2,21] which tweak the model without globally optimal solution guarantee. A detailed comparison to related work is in Sect. 6.

Although theoretically possible, there are several challenges to implement a practical, especially high-performance version of incremental SVM algorithm that can be used by potential practitioners in real-world applications on modern many-core architectures. First, an incremental SVM algorithm is usually a multi-stage solution with varying compute and memory requirements. Therefore, a per stage detailed analysis of compute efficiency and memory access pattern is required to design well-tailored data structures and intelligent computation techniques to achieve maximal performance. Moreover, the algorithm involves multiple branching cases (Sect. 3.3) which makes it quite challenging to parallelize. Second, the incremental algorithm may have inherent limitations for convergence in particular scenarios where it fails to making progress as trapping into an infinite loop [12]. In real-world applications such behavior is not acceptable and requires to be handled intelligently. Third, as the algorithm dynamically updates the model, i.e. the support vector set, with each insertion (or deletion) of a sample, in order to get desired running performance, it needs an efficient data caching mechanism to deal with the dynamic change of the support vector set and other corresponding data structures.

In this paper, we propose and implement a high-performance incremental SVM algorithm that runs efficiently on Intel Xeon Phi processors based on Intel Many Integrated Core architecture (referred to hereinafter as *MIC processors*).

We are in the progress of open-sourcing the code. In brief, this paper makes following key contributions:

1. We propose *cycle-breaking*, a practical heuristic to avoid scenarios where the incremental algorithm stops making progress (happening on average once every 27 samples - Sect. 5.3).
2. We conduct several programming optimizations. Caching dynamically changing data results in up to 3.3× speedup for the overall application. Intelligently using efficient data structures and memory access patterns tailored for each stage of the incremental algorithm towards the MIC processors further gives an overall speedup of up to 1.5×.
3. Compared to existing incremental SVM algorithms such as warm-start SMO (described and discussed in Sects. 5.1 and 6), our algorithm is up to 2.1× faster. Our implementation is faster than warm-start SMO for over 90% of samples.
4. Our incremental SVM training algorithm optimized for the MIC processors is up to 1.3× faster than running on the Intel Xeon processors. For performing Leave-One-Out cross validation using the decremental variation of our incremental algorithm, running on the MIC processors is up to 2.1× faster than Intel Xeon processors.

The rest of the paper is organized as follows: Sect. 2 gives a brief overview of the MIC processors. Section 3 explains the incremental SVM training algorithm and our algorithmic contributions. Section 4 explains our optimization ideas for improving the performance on many-core architectures. Section 5 discusses the results and shows how we outperform other batch and incremental SVM algorithms without sacrificing accuracy. We compare our work to the related work in Sect. 6 and conclude in Sect. 7.

2   Intel® Xeon Phi™ Processors

The Intel® Xeon Phi™ processor is based on the Intel® Many Integrated Core (MIC) architecture. Unlike the graphic processing units (GPUs), this many-core processor provides a general-purpose programming environment similar to that of a regular Intel Xeon processor.

We describe the high-level architecture of Intel Xeon Phi processor 7250 (formerly codenamed Knights Landing or KNL) used in this paper. This processor has 68 cores, each of which runs at a processor base frequency of 1.40 GHz and supports up to 4 hardware threads. The cores are tiled in pairs, with each core having 32 KB L1 data cache, 32 KB L1 instruction cache and 1 MB unified L2 cache shared within the tile. The tiles are interconnected via 2D mesh. Cache coherence across cores/tiles is maintained via a global-distributed tag directory provided by caching/home agent (CHA). In this paper, the tiles are clustered in *quadrant mode* [20] for better performance and productivity trade-off.

Each core has two 512-bit vector processing units (VPUs), which allows 16 single precision or 8 double precision floating point numbers to be processed in a single CPU cycle. This makes vectorization challenging and critical to the performance. The theoretical peak floating point performance of the processor is 6.10 TFLOPS for single precision and 3.05 TFLOPS for double precision.

This processor has 16 GB multi-channel DRAM (MCDRAM) with bandwidth larger than 400 GB/s, and supports up to 384 GB DDR4 memory. In order to have the full control of the MCDRAM usage, in this paper we configured the memory subsystem in *flat mode* [20], working as a NUMA system in which MCDRAM serves the local memory to all cores.

3   Algorithm

In this section, we start from the SVM batch training to describe the incremental SVM algorithm we implemented in detail. We also highlight the changes we made to scale up the incremental algorithm to practical problem sizes on the MIC processors.

3.1   Support Vector Machine and KKT Conditions

Suppose we have a set of training data and their labels given by $\mathrm{T} = \{(x_i, y_i), i = 1 \ldots m\}$, where $x_i \in \mathrm{X} \subseteq \mathbb{R}^d$ is the input, $y_i \in \{-1, +1\}$ is the corresponding output label. We can write out the classification function as:

$$f(x) = w^T \Phi(x) + b \tag{1}$$

where $\Phi(x)$ is a fixed feature space transformation mapping the input x to a vector in feature space F. The model parameters can be obtained by solving the optimization problem:

$$\max_{\alpha} \ \mathbb{W}(\alpha) = \sum_{i=1}^{m} \alpha_i - \frac{1}{2} \sum_{i=1}^{m} \sum_{j=1}^{m} Q_{ij} \alpha_i \alpha_j$$
$$s.t. \sum \alpha_i y_i = 0 \tag{2}$$
$$0 \leq \alpha_i \leq C, \ i = 1, \ldots, m$$

where $C \in \mathbb{R}^+$ is the regularization parameter that controls the relative weighting between maximizing the margin and minimizing the error rate, and $Q_{ij} = y_i y_j K(x_i, x_j)$ is the kernel matrix where $K(x_i, x_j) = \Phi(x_i)^T \Phi(x_j)$ is a kernel function [19].

Given the solution to (2), the optimal classification function $f : \mathrm{X} \to \mathbb{R}$ in formula (1) can be written as $f(x) = \sum_{i=1}^{m} \alpha_i y_i K(x_i, x_j) + b$.

From the Karush-Kuhn-Tucker (KKT) conditions, the margin function $g(x_i) = y_i f(x_i) - 1$ and the corresponding α_i must satisfy the following relationship at the optimal solution:

$$g(x_i) \geq 0; \ \alpha_i = 0$$
$$g(x_i) = 0; \ 0 < \alpha_i < C \tag{3}$$
$$g(x_i) \leq 0; \ \alpha_i = C$$

This partitions the samples in training set T into three categories. Let us define the following partitioned index sets:

$$S := \{i : y_i f(x_i) = 1, 0 < \alpha_i < C\} \text{ (On-margin support vectors)}$$
$$E := \{i : y_i f(x_i) \leq 1, \alpha_i = C\} \text{ (Error support vectors)} \quad (4)$$
$$R := \{i : y_i f(x_i) \geq 1, \alpha_i = 0\} \text{ (Within-margin vectors)}$$

The incremental SVM algorithm essentially moves the samples across these three sets to reach an optimal solution.

3.2   Incremental SVM Algorithm

The incremental SVM algorithm updates the previously trained SVM model with the inclusion of a new sample point (x_c, y_c) to the training set T instead of batch training the entire training set plus the new sample point. Figure 1 shows the complete software workflow of incremental SVM including the optimizations proposed in this paper. The key idea of the algorithm is to change the coefficient α_c (initialized to 0) corresponding to the new sample x_c in discrete steps with largest possible increments under the constraint that the change is small enough to keep other elements in training set T satisfying the KKT optimality conditions, i.e. no old training samples move across S, E or R sets. The update ends when the new sample satisfies the KKT optimality conditions.

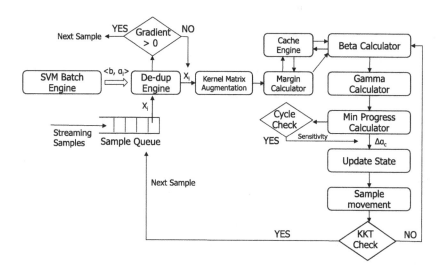

Fig. 1. Software workflow of incremental SVM.

Let us define the indices of the samples in the margin set S as $\{s_1, s_2, \ldots, s_{l_S}\}$. As derived in [16], we need to solve:

$$\mathbb{Q} \begin{bmatrix} \Delta b \\ \Delta \alpha_{s_1} \\ \vdots \\ \Delta \alpha_{s_{l_S}} \end{bmatrix} = -QSc \cdot \Delta \alpha_c \tag{5}$$

where $\mathbb{Q} = \begin{bmatrix} 0 & y_{s_1} & \cdots & y_{s_{l_S}} \\ y_{s_1} & Q_{s_1 s_1} & \cdots & Q_{s_1 s_{l_S}} \\ \vdots & \vdots & \ddots & \vdots \\ y_{s_{l_S}} & Q_{s_{l_S} s_1} & \cdots & Q_{s_{l_S} s_{l_S}} \end{bmatrix}$ and $QSc = \begin{bmatrix} y_c \\ Q_{s_1 c} \\ \vdots \\ Q_{s_{l_S}} \end{bmatrix}$ (6)

If we define $\beta = -R \cdot QSc$ with $R = \mathbb{Q}^{-1}$ then the bias and coefficients can be expressed in terms of $\Delta \alpha_c$ as:

$$\Delta b = \beta_0 \Delta \alpha_c \tag{7}$$
$$\Delta \alpha_j = \beta_j \Delta \alpha_c, \quad \forall j \in S \tag{8}$$

The margin for all the sample points change according to:

$$\Delta g(x_i) = \gamma_i \Delta \alpha_c \; \forall \in T \cup \{c\}$$
$$where, \; \gamma_i = Q_{ic} + \sum_{j \in S} Q_{ij} \beta_j + y_i \beta_0 \tag{9}$$
$$and \; \gamma_i = 0 \; \forall i \in S$$

As γ_i is non-zero if $i \notin S$ set, we define $N = \{E \cup R\} = \{n_1, n_2, \ldots, n_{l_N}\}$ and rewrite γ in matrix form:

$$\gamma = \begin{bmatrix} Q_{n_1 c} \\ Q_{n_2 c} \\ \vdots \\ Q_{n_{l_N} c} \end{bmatrix} + QNS \cdot \beta + \begin{bmatrix} y_{n_1} \\ y_{n_2} \\ \vdots \\ y_{n_{l_N}} \end{bmatrix} \beta_0$$

$$where, \; QNS = \begin{bmatrix} Q_{n_1 s_1} & \cdots & Q_{n_1 s_{l_N}} \\ \vdots & \ddots & \vdots \\ Q_{n_{l_N} s_1} & \cdots & Q_{n_{l_N} s_{l_N}} \end{bmatrix} \tag{10}$$

To summarize, given $\Delta \alpha_c$ we can update α_i for $i \in S$ and bias b using the Eqs. (7) and (8), and update $\Delta g(x_i)$ for $i \in \{E \cup R\}$ using Eq. (9).

3.3   Accounting: Largest Increment $\Delta \alpha_c$

Equations (5) and (9) hold only when there are no changes to the S set. Once the newly included sample affects the S set, the updated SVM state cannot be directly computed from these equations. Using KKT conditions (3) and Eq. (7), we can also observe that $\Delta\alpha_i$, $\forall i \in S$ and $\Delta\alpha_c$ affect the composition of S. Therefore, in the process of incrementing α_c towards the optimal solution, the SVM parameters are required to be updated in discrete steps with the largest possible $\Delta\alpha_c$ such that KKT optimality conditions are not violated for any of the existing samples. The following bookkeeping is required to ensure that KKT conditions are not violated in each of the discrete steps:

1. If $g(x_c)$ changes from $g(x_c) < 0$ to $g(x_c) = 0$, the new sample x_c is moved to set S and the algorithm terminates. The proposed $\Delta\alpha_c^S = \frac{-g_c}{\gamma_c}$.
2. If α_c changes from $\alpha_c < C$ to $\alpha = C$, the new sample x_c is moved to set E and the algorithm terminates. The proposed $\Delta\alpha_c^E = C - \alpha_c$.
3. $\forall i \in$ set S with $0 < \alpha_i < C$:
   - If $\beta_i < 0$ and α_i changes to $\alpha_i = 0$, sample x_i is moved from S to R set and the proposed $\Delta\alpha_c^{SR} = \min_{i \in S} \frac{-\alpha_i}{\beta_i}$.
   - If $\beta_i > 0$ and α_i changes to $\alpha_i = C$, sample x_i is moved from S to E set and the proposed $\Delta\alpha_c^{SE} = \min_{i \in S} \frac{C - \alpha_i}{\beta_i}$.
4. $\forall i \in$ set E, if $\gamma_i > 0$ and $g(x_i)$ changes from $g(x_i) < 0$ to $g(x_i) = 0$, sample x_i is moved from E to S set and the proposed $\Delta\alpha_c^{LE} = \min_{i \in E} \frac{-g_i}{\gamma_i}$.
5. $\forall i \in$ set R, if $\gamma_i < 0$ and $g(x_i)$ changes from $g(x_i) > 0$ to $g(x_i) = 0$, sample x_i is moved from R to S set and the proposed $\Delta\alpha_c^{LR} = \min_{i \in R} \frac{-g_i}{\gamma_i}$.

The above five cases are used to determine the allowed values of $\Delta\alpha_c$, among which the minimum value is chosen to ensure that the KKT conditions hold for all samples in the training set.

$$\Delta\alpha_c = min(\Delta\alpha_c^S, \Delta\alpha_c^E, \Delta\alpha_c^{SR}, \Delta\alpha_c^{SE}, \Delta\alpha_c^{LE}, \Delta\alpha_c^{LR}) \tag{11}$$

Finally, the algorithm terminates on either $\alpha_c = C$ or $g_c = 0$.

3.4   Incremental Update of R Matrix

R matrix must be updated whenever the S set changes but it is impractical to invert the matrix $\mathbb{Q}$ every time this happens. We apply the Sherman-Morrison-Woodbury formula for block matrix inversion [7] that recursively updates R matrix to avoid the explicit computation of matrix inverse [16]. To add a sample x_c to the S set, R is expanded as:

$$R = \begin{bmatrix} & & 0 \\ & R & \vdots \\ & & 0 \\ 0 \cdots 0 & 0 \end{bmatrix} + \frac{1}{\gamma_c} \begin{bmatrix} \beta_0 \\ \beta_{s_1} \\ \vdots \\ \beta_{s_{l_S}} \\ 1 \end{bmatrix} \begin{bmatrix} \beta_0 & \beta_{s_1} & \cdots & \beta_{s_{l_S}} & 1 \end{bmatrix} \tag{12}$$

To remove the kth support vector x_{s_k} from set S, R matrix can be contracted as follows:

$$R_{ij} = R_{ij} - \frac{1}{R_{kk}} R_{ik} R_{kj} \forall i, j \in S \cup \{0\}; i, j \neq k \tag{13}$$

3.5   Convergence and Breaking Immediate Cycling

One of the key characteristics of the incremental algorithm proposed in [16] is that it converges in a finite number of steps only if in each of these steps a non-zero update $\Delta\alpha_c$ is found. This brings us to 'zero-progress' scenarios where $\Delta\alpha_c = 0$ is encountered. We next discuss in detail two such scenarios, namely *empty support vector set* and *immediate cycling*.

Empty Support Vector Set: Equation (5) requires that the support vector set S to be non-empty. Otherwise the matrix $\mathbb{Q}$, which is to be inverted to get R, is an empty matrix. To handle this special case, we first try to find a sample point $x_i : i \in \{E \cup R\}$ with $g(x_i) = 0$. If this sample exists, we can move it to the S set which does not violate the KKT conditions and continue with the algorithm.

Otherwise, the expression for the margin update (formula (9)) reduces to:

$$\Delta g(x_i) = y_i \Delta b, \ \forall i \in \{E \cup R\} \cup \{c\} \tag{14}$$

Using this we can find the maximum change in Δb such that $g(x_i)$ for one of the samples becomes 0 and hence can be moved to the S set. With the S set being non-empty, we can continue with the algorithm.

Immediate Cycling and Cycle Breaking: There is another scenario in which $\Delta\alpha_c = 0$ and the algorithm fails to making progress. In this scenario, a sample migrating from one set to another is immediately removed from that set in the very next iteration without making any progress towards convergence. For example, suppose a sample x_i moves from R to S set in an iteration, $\alpha_i = 0$ because x_i was in the R set. In the next iteration, $\Delta\alpha_i = 0$ if $\beta_i < 0$, hence x_i becomes a potential candidate to be selected as the sample with the minimum $\Delta\alpha_c$. This results in a transition from S set back to R set and because the algorithm does not make any progress in the previous iteration it falls into this infinite loop of transitioning x_i back and forth between S and R sets. This is called *immediate cycling*. Laskov et al. [12] showed that it is theoretically impossible to encounter an immediate cycle if the symmetric augmented kernel matrix $\mathbb{Q}$ is positive semi-definite. But in the real world setup $\mathbb{Q}$ matrix might not always be positive semi-definite so that the immediate cycle is inevitable. One simple solution to this issue is to fall back to retrain the model from scratch which is usually not acceptable in streaming applications. Hence there is a need for solutions that can handle such scenarios incrementally without retraining from scratch.

One of the reasons for the $\mathbb{Q}$ matrix becoming non semi-positive is the existence of duplicate sample points in the training set. Hence, as shown in Fig. 1, in the *De-duplication* stage, the framework ensures that a newly arrived sample is ignored if its duplicate already exists in the training set.

Sample deduplication only fixes one kind of immediate cycling. We use a heuristic when other immediate cycling occurs. The heuristic involves two steps:

(1) *cycle detection* and (2) *cycle break*. The cycle detection step identifies the zero-progress scenario and the corresponding sample responsible for it. In particular, going from $(t-1)^{th}$ to t^{th} iteration, the cycle detection conditions are as follows:

$$\beta_i > 0 \ and \ \alpha_i = C; \ i^{t-1} \in E \wedge \ i^t \in S$$
$$\beta_i < 0 \ and \ \alpha_i = 0; \ i^{t-1} \in R \ \wedge \ i^t \in S \tag{15}$$

After the sample x_i, which is responsible for the cycle, has been detected, the heuristic artificially adds a small positive perturbation in the cycle break step, using a user defined *sensitivity* parameter, ensuring $\Delta \alpha_c > 0$. This is achieved by modifying the coefficient α_i of x_i using the following rule:

$$\alpha_i = C \cdot sensitivity; \ i^{t-1} \in R \wedge \ i^t \in S$$
$$\alpha_i = C \cdot (1 - sensitivity); \ i^{t-1} \in E \ \wedge \ i^t \in S \tag{16}$$
$$where \ sensitivity \in [0,1]$$

Note that *sensitivity* controls the progress rate of convergence. Choosing very small values for sensitivity might require a lot of iterations for a new sample x_c, that encountered a cycle, to reach the optimal solution. Choosing a large value (≈ 1) might deteriorate the accuracy of the SVM solution. In all our experiments we have chosen a sensitivity of 0.01.

3.6 Algorithm Summary and Runtime Analysis

We summarize the incremental SVM algorithms in Algorithm 1. As revealed in the pseudo-code as well as in the flow chart of Fig. 1, the incremental algorithm can be viewed as a multi-stage pipeline, involving arithmetic (matrix-vector and matrix-matrix multiplications) and memory operations, which is iterated until convergence. These iterations also involve sample migration between S, R and E sets before the algorithm converges to an optimal solution. We list the stages as follows, assuming that an existing SVM model is available.

- **Deduplication:** This is the preprocessing stage to check for duplication. Only unseen samples to the model is allowed to enter the pipeline since duplicated ones do not carry additional information to the model.
- **Kernel Matrix Augmentation:** A new row and a new column corresponding to the new sample x_c are computed using $Q_{ij} = y_i y_j K(x_i, x_j)$ to augment the kernel matrix Q.
- **Gradient/Margin Calculation:** The margin or gradient g_i for each of the sample x_i is calculated. This stage is computationally intensive involving a matrix-vector multiplication ($GEMV$) between the kernel matrix Q and the sample coefficient vector α.
- **γ Calculation:** This stage involves a matrix-vector multiplication of matrix QNS and vector β (Eq. 10). Note that QNS is a data structure that depends on the S set which dynamically changes between iterations. Because S set

Algorithm 1. Incremental SVM algorithm

1: Read sample x_c, compute gradient g_c, $\alpha_c \leftarrow 0$.
2: **if** $CheckDuplicate(x_c) =$ true or $g_c > 0$ **then**
3:     **return**
4: **end if**
5: **while** $g_c > 0$ and $\alpha_c < C$ **do**
6:     **if** Margin g not in $Cache$ **then**
7:         $g \leftarrow CalculateMargin()$
8:     **end if**
9:     $\beta \leftarrow CalculateBeta()$
10:     $\gamma \leftarrow CalculateGamma()$
11:     $\Delta\alpha_c \leftarrow FindMinProgress()$
12:     **if** $\Delta\alpha_c = 0$ **then**
13:         $\Delta\alpha_c \leftarrow BreakCycle(sensitivity)$
14:     **end if**
15:     /* **Update SVM solution state***/
16:     $\alpha_c \leftarrow \alpha_c + \Delta\alpha_c$
17:     $\alpha_s \leftarrow \beta\Delta\alpha_c, \forall s \in S$
18:     $g_n \leftarrow \gamma\Delta\alpha_c, \forall n \in \{R \cup E\}$
19:
20:     $MoveVector()$ {See Sect. 3.3}
21:     Incrementally update R matrix. {see Sect. 3.4}
22: **end while**

has substantial temporal and spacial locality between consecutive iterations, efficient storage and caching of QNS can avoid expensive recomputation and irregular memory accesses.

- **Minimum Progress and Cycle Check:** Using the accounting rules of Sect. 3.3, all possible $\Delta\alpha_c$ values are calculated from five different cases and the minimum is used as the maximum progress towards optimal solution without violating KKT conditions for other samples. If zero-progress scenarios is encountered i.e. $\Delta\alpha_c = 0$: empty support vector set is handled using Eq. (14) and immediate cycling using $CycleBreak$ heuristic (see Sect. 3.5).
- **Update SVM State:** Using (8), (7) and (9) we update the coefficient α_i, bias b and gradient g_i for every sample $x_i \in T$.
- **Sample Movement:** After updating the coefficient α_i, some samples might need to be migrated to different sample sets due to the change of memberships. Using the migration rules described in Sect. 3.3 and the case that was responsible for the minimum $\Delta\alpha_c$, a particular sample is migrated to an appropriate destination set. If in this process S set changes (grows or shrinks), then matrix R is updated using the incremental update trick described in Sect. 3.4.
- **KKT Condition Check:** Finally, the KKT optimality conditions for x_c are checked to terminate the iteration if $\alpha_c = C$ or $g_c = 0$.

3.7 Decremental Algorithm

The decremental algorithm is very similar to the incremental version with minor changes. When a sample x_c is removed from the training set T, the algorithm gradually decreases the value of the coefficient α_c to zero, while ensuring that all other samples satisfy the KKT conditions. In other words, it finds the maximum decrement in the value of α_c instead of maximum increment (as in case of incremental algorithm) following the rules described in Sect. 3.3. Based on the previously discussed incremental version, the decremental algorithm makes the following specific changes:

- If sample $x_c \in R$ set, then remove it from the training set without making any change to the SVM solution.
- There is no case 1 in Sect. 3.3 as the removed sample x_c will never be moved to S set.
- Case 2 is modified to: if α_c changes from $\alpha_c > 0$ to $\alpha_c = 0$, remove the sample x_c and the algorithm terminates.

4   Optimization

In this section, we describe how we optimize the incremental and decremental SVM algorithms described in Sect. 3. The codebase we used to implement the incremental SVM algorithms is originally from a well optimized high-performance GPU-based batch SVM implementation [3], which was also successfully adapted to run efficiently on the previous version of Intel Xeon Phi products [25].

4.1 Caching Dynamic Data Structures

Caching S Set Related Buffer: As mentioned previously, S, R and E sets dynamically change due to sample migrations as the algorithm progresses towards the optimal solution. Because most of the data structures are either dependent on the cardinality of T ($|T| = m$) or S set, we focus on dynamic data structures related to $|S|$. We make two key observations about S: (1) $|S| << m$ (from bounds on error expectation for SVMs [23]), and (2) between two consecutive iterations, S set either remains the same or, grows or shrinks by one sample.

The dynamically changing buffers dependent on S set are β, R, QSc, Q and QNS. Since $|S| << m$, the buffer with the most significant memory footprint among all is QNS. QNS is required in the gamma calculation stage and with a changing S set this buffer also dynamically changes every iteration. Recomputing the entire QNS matrix every time S set changes is very computationally intensive. On the other hand, copying all the corresponding elements from the cached kernel matrix Q to create QNS will cause a lot of cache misses because of the large memory footprint of both Q and QNS. Therefore, we employ an efficient caching mechanism for QNS and dynamically grow and shrink it as the algorithm progresses. To track the dynamics of the buffer between iterations we maintain two copies of S set indices: S^{t-1} and S^t, corresponding to index set for support vectors in iteration t-1 and t respectively. Hence, if there are no changes to the S set from the previous iteration, we use QNS from previous iteration. Otherwise, we compute the difference between S^{t-1} and S^t set: $\delta_1 = S^t - S^{t-1}$ (grow), $\delta_2 = S^{t-1} - S^t$ (shrink). If δ_1 is not empty, we grow QNS by copying only the corresponding elements from the row in Q matrix indexed by the newly migrated support vector. If δ_2 is not empty, we erase the corresponding row in QNS indexed by the sample removed from support vector set from previous iteration. It is worth noting that all buffers including Q matrix are stored in row-major fashion except for QNS which is stored in column major fashion. This is to make sure that both 'grow' and 'shrink' operations in QNS can be indexed using support vector indices.

Caching Gradient Vector: The gradient information of samples is used in the calculation of minimum progress $\Delta\alpha_c$ as described in the accounting rules of Sect. 3.3 and hence is required to be updated every single iteration. Note that gradient calculation is a computationally expensive operation involving a matrix-vector multiplication between huge kernel matrix Q of size $m \times m$ and sample coefficient vector α. Hence whenever possible gradient information is cached from previous iterations and is reused to avoid this expensive recomputations. Using formula (9) we update the gradient for each sample and reuse it in the next iteration. Note that because the gradients are cached as SVM state, they can be reused across samples as well i.e. we also avoid the gradient recomputation whenever a new sample is inserted.

4.2   Memory Access Pattern

In the incremental SVM training process, a lot of operations (e.g. *GEMV*) are memory-bound. Therefore, it makes sense to place data to MCDRAM which has larger memory bandwidth when running it on the MIC processors. However, since the capacity of MCDRAM is limited (typically 16 GB), we cannot fit the entire working set in. Instead, we explicitly allocated the frequently retrieved data (e.g. QNS matrix, R matrix) to be in MCDRAM using the memkind library. As described above, QNS is a matrix of $m \times |S|$, and R is a $|S| \times |S|$ square matrix. The fact that $|S| << m$ makes it possible to fit QNS and R in MCDRAM.

As an $m \times |S|$ matrix, QNS is maintained in column-major fashion to facilitate the memory access of an entire column corresponding to the kernel values of a specific support vector. And both QNS and R are aligned to 64 bytes so that the vectorization can easily take the entire cache line in for achieving the high performance.

4.3   Parallelization and Vectorization-Friendly Workflow

The workflow of incremental SVM contains multiple stages with various branches. For example, in the bookkeeping process of sample movement, there are five different conditions and within each condition the samples in the same set are handled differently according to their own situations. This characteristics largely prevents the thread-level parallelization and vectorization within a loop.

To facilitate thread-level parallelization, we carefully define stages of the workflow (Fig. 1), so that within each stage the thread-level parallelization can be conducted via OpenMP easily. The philosophy is to make the parallel granularity as large as possible to reduce the OpenMP thread launching overhead while making sure all available cores are utilized. For enabling the vectorization within a loop, we simplify the control flow logic by reducing the number of branches.

5   Evaluation

5.1   Experimental Setup

We tested our implementation of incremental SVM on both the MIC processors and Intel Xeon processors (referred to hereinafter as processors). The configuration of the MIC processors we used was described in Sect. 2. In the experiments we launched 67 threads, one per core, leaving the last core for OS usage. Regarding the processors, we used Intel Xeon E5-2699 v4 (codenamed Broadwell) with 22 cores running at 2.2 GHz. In the experiments we launched 22 threads, one per core.

Table 1 summarizes the datasets we used for evaluation. They are all real datasets in various domains. We z-scored the datasets to bring values of every dimension to the same scale. covtype is originally with multiple classes, we converted it into binary classification for our usage.

Table 1. Summary of datasets

Dataset	#samples	#dimensions
covtype [5]	50,000	54
cod-rna [22]	49,466	7
ijcnn [18]	49,990	22
susy [1]	60,000	18

In addition to our incremental algorithm, for comparison purpose we also ran another incremental SVM algorithm named warm-start SMO which is used in [26]. The warm-start SMO shares the same high-performance SVM training codebase as our incremental SVM code. Therefore, it is a decent baseline which is supposed to largely outperform the off-the-shelf SVM packages, let alone most of them do not have incremental training component built in. In the warm-start SMO, when a new sample is added, the training takes place from the state of the current model until it gets converged again. Both our incremental algorithm and the warm-start SMO are based on a batch trained model with $C = 1$ and Gaussian kernel with $\gamma = 1/\#dimensions$.

5.2 Overall Performance

We first thoroughly test out the performance of the incremental SVM algorithms by starting from very small models that contain only tens of samples, and incrementally training all the way to the entire dataset, except for 500 samples kept for accuracy testing. Table 2 shows the running time of both our incremental algorithm and the warm-start SMO on the MIC processors. From the table we can see that our incremental algorithm runs $1.1 - 2.1\times$ faster than warm-start SMO.

Table 2. Performance of incremental SVM and warm-start SMO on MIC processors

Dataset	Incremental (s)	Warm-start (s)
covtype	238.5	397.6
cod-rna	240.2	454.9
ijcnn	192.5	409.7
susy	3069.5	3344.4

We compared the models we obtained using our incremental algorithm, the warm-start SMO and batch training to verify the correctness of the methods in Table 3. We counted the number of support vectors (the samples in S set plus E set) as well as applied the models to the left-out 500 samples of each dataset. The results show that the models obtained from our incremental SVM is close to the batch training and warm-start SMO training, which verifies the correctness of our implementation.

Table 3. SVM model comparison

Dataset	Incremental		Warm-start		Batch	
	#SV	Accuracy	#SV	Accuracy	#SV	Accuracy
covtype	7593	77.8%	7552	77.0%	7704	77.2%
cod-rna	7807	94.2%	7764	95.6%	7805	95.8%
ijcnn	4849	96.8%	4772	98.0%	4843	98.0%
susy	27742	80.6%	27825	80.4%	27881	80.6%

In practice, the incremental training may take place on top of a model trained from a large number of samples in batch. For example, in a real-time data analysis application, one may want to tweak a well-trained model using the incoming data stream. For this scenario, we evaluated the running time of adding 100 samples to a model trained via tens of thousands of samples on both the MIC processors and the processors in Table 4. The results show that running on the MIC processors outperforms the processors by $1.1 - 1.3\times$, which is limited by the unavoidable sequential code spread in the workflow.

Table 4. Streaming in 100 samples on different processors

Dataset	MIC processors (s)	Processors (s)
covtype	4.61	5.59
cod-rna	0.84	1.04
ijcnn	0.65	0.73
susy	12.75	15.94

We also investigated the time it takes to incorporate each new sample using both our incremental algorithm and the warm-start SMO on the MIC processors. Similar to what we have done in Table 4, we streamed in 100 samples of each dataset and record the time it took to process them one by one. Figure 2 depicts the results sorted by processing times, from which we see that in most of the cases (90% of the samples) our incremental algorithm processes the samples faster. Especially, for the samples that do not affect the distinguishing hyperplane, the processing rate using our incremental algorithms is more than 10× faster than the warm-start SMO (e.g. 0.3 ms/sample vs. 4 ms/sample). Even for the samples that requires longer training (hundreds of milliseconds), the incremental training is still much faster than batch which typically takes seconds to tens of seconds.

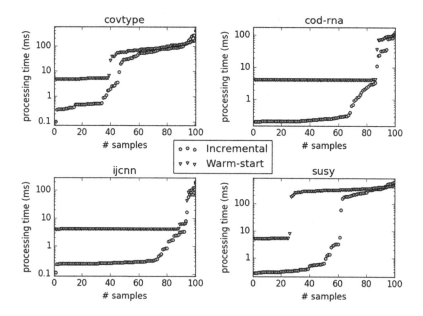

Fig. 2. The time duration of processing single samples in logarithmic scale.

5.3   Performance Gain of Optimization

This subsection shows the performance gain of our proposed optimizations to the incremental SVM algorithm. We summarized the optimization speedup in Table 5 by streaming in 1000 samples to each dataset. Overall, our optimization speed up the algorithm by $4.2-4.8\times$. Table 5 also listed the number of immediate cycles (Sect. 3.5) encountered during the incremental training. We observed a considerable amount of immediate cycles (in average 1 cycle per 27 samples across all datasets), which suggests that our cycle breaking heuristic is critical in achieving high-performance incremental SVM training.

Table 5. Speedup of optimization and the immediate cycles broken whiling training

Dataset	Caching dynamic data	Memory and vectorization optimization	#cycles
covtype	2.8×	1.5×	28
cod-rna	3.2×	1.5×	6
ijcnn	3.3×	1.4×	7
susy	3.0×	1.5×	108

5.4   Leave-One-Out Cross-Validation

Cross-validation (CV) [10] is a popular method to assess the generalization ability of a machine learning model by dividing the dataset into disjoint training and validation sets for training in rotation. Leave-one-out cross-validation (LOOCV) which maintains a one-sample validation set is useful especially when the dataset size is small. In batch processing of SVM, LOOCV can be expensive as retraining of the entire dataset but one sample is required for each sample. LOOCV can be implemented much more efficiently using the decremental variation of our incremental SVM algorithm as follows:

1. Learn the SVM parameter for the entire dataset T in batch;
2. For each sample $x_i \in T$, using the decremental algorithm described in Sect. 3.7, remove x_i to learn the model of $T - \{x_i\}$ to apply to x_i;
3. Summarize the overall classification accuracy on all samples.

We randomly chose 100 samples from each dataset shown in Table 1 to simulate small datasets and ran LOOCV using both batch training and decremental training. From Table 6, we can observe that the decremental algorithm achieves substantial performance benefit over the batch training on the MIC processors. Furthermore, our decremental algorithm on the MIC processors outperforms the processors by $1.1-2.1\times$.

Table 6. LOOCV speedup using decremental training

Dataset	Incremental on MIC processors vs. batch on MIC processors	Incremental on MIC processors vs. incremental on processors
covtype	121.3×	1.6×
cod-rna	11.7×	1.1×
ijcnn	108.0×	2.2×
susy	15.4×	2.1×

6   Related Work

Incremental training is a popular technique for many machine learning classifiers. For algorithms built by techniques like stochastic gradient descent etc., it is quite simple to train incrementally. For example, incremental learning of neural networks [17] already exist.

Support vector machine training, on the other hand, relies on the convexity of the data space. Therefore, the batch training algorithms are much more efficient than techniques like gradient descent. Techniques such as Sequential Minimal Optimization (SMO), decomposition based SVM^{light} [11] etc. are only slightly worse than linear time in practice [15]. Efficient implementations of SVM training exist in many software packages optimized for different hardware platforms including GPU [3] and the first generation of Intel Xeon Phi products [25].

A good incremental SVM training algorithm in practice must both perform precisely to produce similar results, if not identical, to the batch training, and run in high-performance. Incremental SVM training algorithms such as [2,21] do not solve the problem to full optimality. They are only approximate approaches by applying updates to the set of support vectors instead of the full dataset. Errors can accumulate if these algorithms run for a large number of samples. Incremental SVM training algorithms based on SMO (called warm-start SMO which trains from the previously converged states) [6,8,9,27] have been proposed earlier, but perform slowly especially for the non-support vector new samples.

Our work uses the incremental algorithm presented in [16] which can be used to update models when adding or removing samples. This algorithm was not practical to use due to two reasons - (1) there were no good methods to break out of cycles (Sect. 3.5) and (2) naive implementation of this algorithm would not be faster than warm-start SMO. [12] characterizes the cycling phenomenon but does not propose a feasible solution beyond doing batch retraining. Incremental SVM training is particularly challenging to implement on many-core architectures because of its highly irregular workflow (Sect. 3) and branch-heavy code. As a consequence, there is no existing implementation optimized for highly parallel platforms. We largely relieve these limitations to present a usable and efficient implementation of the algorithm optimized for the MIC processors in this paper. Given that other work [13,14] has extended [16] to support vector regression, our improvements should apply to those techniques as well.

7   Conclusions and Future Work

This paper discussed how to construct an efficient implementation of the incremental SVM training algorithm that runs well on many-core architectures such as Intel Xeon Phi processors. We started from a known algorithm [16] and fixed several issues (immediate cycle, data recompuation, irregular memory access pattern, lack of parallelization and vectorization) to improve the performance. We have shown that our implementation is up to 2.1× faster than warm-start SMO, another high-performance incremental SVM algorithm, on average. Our algorithm is better than warm-start SMO for 90% of samples. The code is planned to be released as open source and we hope it will benefit SVM training in real-time and other streaming-oriented applications in various domains.

Our further work focuses on scaling up the current incremental SVM implementation for very large datasets. The major limitation of current implementation is that the support vectors are required to be maintained in the memory for the entire learning process. Two largest data structures in play are Q and QNS, with memory complexities $O(|S|^2)$ and $O(m * |S|)$ respectively, where $|S|$ is the size of the support vector set, and m is the number of all training samples. From [24], we know that for an SVM solution to generalize well on test set, $|S| << m$ holds. Hence the size of Q matrix in all practical scenarios should not become the bottleneck. However QNS can be too large to fit in the main memory. Therefore, in order to scale the algorithm to a very large m ($m \rightarrow \infty$), we would need an intelligent way to handle the QNS matrix efficiently. For example, we may extend the algorithm implementation to more than one MIC processor.

References

1. Baldi, P., Sadowski, P., Whiteson, D.: Searching for exotic particles in high-energy physics with deep learning. Nat. commun. **5** (2014)
2. Bordes, A., Ertekin, S., Weston, J., Bottou, L.: Fast kernel classifiers with online and active learning. J. Mach. Learn. Res. **6**, 1579–1619 (2005)
3. Catanzaro, B., Sundaram, N., Keutzer, K.: Fast support vector machine training and classification on graphics processors. In: Proceedings of the 25th International Conference on Machine Learning, pp. 104–111 (2008)
4. Chang, C.-C., Lin, C.-J.: LIBSVM: a library for support vector machines. ACM Trans. Intell. Syst. Technol. **2**(3), 1–27 (2011)
5. Collobert, R., Bengio, S., Bengio, Y.: A parallel mixture of SVMs for very large scale problems. Neural Comput. **14**(5), 1105–1114 (2002)
6. Fliege, J., Heseler, A.: Constructing Approximations to the Efficient Set of Convex Quadratic Multiobjective Problems. Citeseer, Princeton (2002)
7. Golub, G.H., Van Loan, C.F.: Matrix Computations, 3rd edn. Johns Hopkins University Press, Baltimore (1996)
8. Gondzio, J.: Warm start of the primal-dual method applied in the cutting-plane scheme. Math. Program. **83**(1–3), 125–143 (1998)
9. Gondzio, J., Grothey, A.: Reoptimization with the primal-dual interior point method. SIAM J. Optim. **13**(3), 842–864 (2002)

10. Hastie, T.J., Tibshirani, R.J., Friedman, J.H.: The Elements of Statistical Learning: Data Mining, Inference, and Prediction. Springer Series in Statistics. Springer, New York (2009)

11. Joachims, T.: Svmlight: support vector machine. SVM-Light Support Vector Mach. **19**(4) (1999). University of Dortmund, http://svmlight.joachims.org/

12. Laskov, P., Gehl, C., Krüger, S., Müller, K.-R.: Incremental support vector learning: analysis, implementation and applications. J. Mach. Learn. Res. **7**(Sep), 1909–1936 (2006)

13. Ma, J., Theiler, J., Perkins, S.: Accurate on-line support vector regression. Neural Comput. **15**(11), 2683–2703 (2003)

14. Martìn Muñoz, M.: On-line support vector machines for function approximation. Technical report, Universitat Politecnica de Catalunya, Departament de Llengatges i Sistemes Informatics (2002)

15. Platt, J.: Sequential minimal optimization: a fast algorithm for training support vector machines. Technical report MSR-TR-98-14, Microsoft Research, April 1998

16. Poggio, T., Cauwenberghs, G.: Incremental and decremental support vector machine learning. Adv. Neural Inf. Process. Syst. **13**, 409 (2001)

17. Polikar, R., Byorick, J., Krause, S., Marino, A., Moreton, M.: Learn++: a classifier independent incremental learning algorithm for supervised neural networks. In: Proceedings of the 2002 International Joint Conference on Neural Networks, IJCNN 2002, vol. 2, pp. 1742–1747 (2002)

18. Prokhorov, D.: IJCNN 2001 neural network competition. Slide Present. IJCNN **1**, 97 (2001)

19. Smola, A.J., Schölkopf, B.: A tutorial on support vector regression. Stat. Comput. **14**(3), 199–222 (2004)

20. Sodani, A.: Knights landing (KNL): 2nd generation Intel® Xeon Phi^{TM} processor. In: 2015 IEEE Hot Chips 27 Symposium (HCS), pp. 1–24. IEEE (2015)

21. Syed, N.A., Huan, S., Kah, L., Sung, K.: Incremental learning with support vector machines (1999)

22. Uzilov, A.V., Keegan, J.M., Mathews, D.H.: Detection of non-coding RNAs on the basis of predicted secondary structure formation free energy change. BMC Bioinf. **7**(1), 1 (2006)

23. Vapnik, V., Chapelle, O.: Bounds on error expectation for support vector machines. Neural Comput. **12**(9), 2013–2036 (2000)

24. Vapnik, V.N.: The Nature of Statistical Learning Theory. Springer-Verlag New York Inc., New York (1995)

25. Wang, Y., Anderson, M.J., Cohen, J.D., Heinecke, A., Li, K., Satish, N., Sundaram, N., Turk-Browne, N.B., Willke, T.L.: Full correlation matrix analsis of fMRI data on Intel® Xeon Phi^{TM} coprocessors. In: Proceedings of the International Conference for High Performance Computing, Networking, Storage and Analysis, SC 2015, November 2015

26. Wang, Y., Keller, B., Capotă, M., Anderson, M.J., Sundaram, N., Cohen, J.D., Li, K., Turk-Browne, N.B., Willke, T.L.: Real-time full correlation matrix analysis of fmri data. In: 2016 IEEE International Conference on Big Data (Big Data). IEEE (2016)

27. Yildirim, E.A., Wright, S.J.: Warm-start strategies in interior-point methods for linear programming. SIAM J. Optim. **12**(3), 782–810 (2002)

Accelerating Seismic Simulations Using the Intel Xeon Phi Knights Landing Processor

Josh Tobin[1]([✉]), Alexander Breuer[1], Alexander Heinecke[2], Charles Yount[2], and Yifeng Cui[1]

[1] University of California, San Diego, 9500 Gilman Drive, La Jolla, CA 92093, USA
rjtobin@ucsd.edu
[2] Intel Corporation, 2200 Mission College Blvd., Santa Clara, CA 95054, USA

Abstract. In this work we present AWP-ODC-OS, an end-to-end optimization of AWP-ODC targeting homogeneous, manycore supercomputers. AWP-ODC is an established community software package simulating seismic wave propagation using a staggered finite difference scheme which is fourth order accurate in space and second order in time. Recent production simulations, e.g. using the software for the computation of seismic hazard maps, largely relied on GPU accelerated supercomputers. In contrast, our work gives a comprehensive overview of the required steps to achieve near-optimal performance on the Intel® Xeon Phi™ x200 processor (code-named Knights Landing), and compares our competitive performance results to the most recent GPU architectures.

At the level of a single vector operation, we apply the vector folding technique to AWP-ODC-OS, yielding a 1.6× performance increase over traditional vectorization. Further, we present a novel strategy utilizing both DDR4 RAM and High Bandwidth Memory, increasing the maximum problem size by 26% while still operating at maximum performance. The presented shared and distributed parallelization carefully schedules work to the cores and ensures overlapping communication and computation. We conclude with a detailed study of AWP-ODC-OS's full-application performance on the Intel Xeon Phi x200 processor, achieving up to 98.5% of the most recent P100 GPU generation's performance. Additionally, our weak scaling study on up to 9,000 nodes of the supercomputer Cori Phase II achieves a parallel efficiency of greater than 91%, equivalent to the performance of over twenty thousand NVIDIA Tesla K20X GPUs.

Keywords: Seismic · Wave propagation · Xeon Phi · Knights Landing · KNL · Earthquake · Large scale · Stencil vectorization · Finite difference method

1 Introduction

Finite difference schemes are the most popular choice for the simulation of seismic waves. These schemes are attractive for a variety of reasons: the implementation is simple and efficient due to stencil-approximations of the partial

© Springer International Publishing AG 2017
J.M. Kunkel et al. (Eds.): ISC High Performance 2017, LNCS 10266, pp. 139–157, 2017.
DOI: 10.1007/978-3-319-58667-0_8

differentials; there are very low dispersion errors if high-order stencils are used; and the literature contains a vast number of model extensions, allowing computational scientists to incorporate many advanced physical features. In the past many of those extensions have greatly increased the accuracy of earthquake simulations [1, 3, 8, 12, 14–16, 18, 23]. For example, state-of-the-art finite difference solvers are able to handle realistic dynamic rupture source descriptions and detailed physics-based anelasticity together with small-scale heterogeneities and near-surface nonlinearity.

AWP-ODC is a widely-used code that simulates the propagation of seismic waves through a viscoelastic medium, using a staggered grid finite difference scheme. It has been crucial in many high impact projects including the San Andreas fault scenarios in the TeraShake simulations [19], the "M8" simulation, revealing a wave-guide amplification for the Los Angeles area [6], a Pacific Northwest megathrust scenario [20], and a realistic earthquake ground motion simulation reaching a frequency content up to 10 Hz on OLCF's Titan [7]. The software is used by many academic institutions worldwide and is part of the computational platform of the Southern California Earthquake Center (SCEC), e.g. high-frequency ground motion forward simulations (High-F), inverse problems (F3DT) or seismic hazard analysis in the CyberShake studies [5].

In this project, we present AWP-ODC-OS[1], our end-to-end optimization of AWP-ODC targeting self-hosted manycore architectures, in particular the Intel Xeon Phi Knights Landing processor. AWP-ODC-OS is an open source code that unifies both the newly optimized Xeon Phi targeting code, and the previous GPU optimized code. AWP-ODC, or "Anelastic Wave Propagation - ODC" is named after the initials of three of its initial main developers. It began as a personal research code of Kim Olsen at the University of Utah [21] and has existed in several different incarnations over the following two decades. Recently, AWP-ODC was heavily optimized for heterogeneous, GPU-accelerated supercomputers [6, 7, 22]. Consequently, the processor based implementations fell behind in terms of optimization for modern hardware. This project aims to address this, and empower AWP-ODC and its users to take full advantage of current and future generations of manycore architectures.

In Sect. 2 we give an overview of the governing partial differential equations and the numerical scheme that AWP-ODC-OS employs to solve these equations. In Sect. 3 we exploit the technique of *vector folding* [24, 26] which promotes data locality, and ensures that the stencil code is vectorized. Since this technique relies on carefully constructed data structures and vector permutation instructions for optimal performance, we use the YASK[2] software package [26] to generate the stencil operators of our code. This general approach of using tool-generated kernels in AWP-ODC has been undertaken previously, using the PATUS code generation framework [4]; these PATUS kernels targeted AMD and Intel® Xeon™ CPUs using traditional vectorization, rather than the vector folding technique we consider here. In addition to vector folding, we present a novel scheme that

---

[1] https://github.com/HPGeoC/awp-odc-os.
[2] https://github.com/01org/yask.

utilizes both DDR and MCDRAM bandwidths to increase available problem size while retaining or improving pure-MCDRAM performance. We give a detailed description of these contributions, as well as our OpenMP and MPI parallelization schemes, in Sect. 3. In Sect. 4 we present weak and strong scaling studies. In the largest of these simulations, we utilized 9,000 nodes of NERSC's Cori Phase II supercomputer, attaining an aggregate performance that is equivalent to 20,400 NVIDIA Tesla K20X GPUs. Finally we present our conclusions in Sect. 5.

2   Numerics

2.1   Governing Equations

The AWP-ODC-OS code simulates the propagation of seismic waves, by solving a velocity-stress formulation of the three-dimensional elastodynamic equations. The governing hyperbolic partial differential equations are

$$\delta_t v = \frac{1}{\rho} \nabla \cdot \sigma$$
$$\delta_t \sigma = \lambda (\nabla \cdot v) I + \mu (\nabla v + \nabla v^T)$$

(where ρ represents density, λ, μ are the Lamé parameters of the medium, σ is the stress tensor and v is the vector of velocities v_x, v_y, v_z). Component-wise, these equations yield a system of nine equations in nine variables, one for each of the three components of the velocity v and six upper-triangular elements of the stress tensor σ. This system is solved using a staggered-grid finite difference scheme, with time derivatives approximated by second-order accurate central differences:

$$\delta_t v(t) \approx \frac{v(t + \Delta t/2) - v(t - \Delta t/2)}{\Delta t}$$
$$\delta_t \sigma(t + \Delta t/2) \approx \frac{\sigma(t + \Delta t) - \sigma(t)}{\Delta t}$$

Similarly, space derivatives are approximated by fourth-order accurate central differences:

$$\delta_x \Phi_{i,j,k} \approx \frac{c_1 (\Phi_{i+1/2,j,k} - \Phi_{i-1/2,j,k}) + c_2 (\Phi_{i+3/2,j,k} - \Phi_{i-3/2,j,k})}{h}$$

where Φ represents either a velocity or stress component, $c_1 = 9/8$, $c_2 = -1/24$, and h is the mesh spacing (partial derivatives in the y and z directions are approximated similarly).

Due to the staggered grid, to perform a single timestep update first the entire velocity grid is updated, and then the stress grid is updated using the newly updated velocity values. The velocity components and the diagonal stress components $\sigma_{xx}, \sigma_{yy}, \sigma_{zz}$ are updated using 13-point stencils, while the off-diagonal stress components use 9-point stencils.

2.2   Boundary Conditions

AWP-ODC-OS currently supports absorbing boundary conditions and free surface boundary conditions. For the absorbing boundaries, a sponge layer is applied to the velocity and stress components [2]. These absorbing boundary conditions are applied on all of the faces of the domain excluding the $z = z_{\max}$ face. On the $z = z_{\max}$ face, which represents the free surface of the Earth, the free surface boundary conditions denoted FS2 in [13] are applied.

2.3   Anelastic Attenuation and Source Terms

To accurately simulate the propogation of seismic waves, it is necessary to incorporate the effects of anelastic attenuation, which is quantified by a quality factor denoted by Q. The effects of anelasticity potentially depend on the entire history of the stress tensor, which imposes infeasible memory requirements on a simulation. To resolve this problem, accurate approximations have been developed which require only a constant number of "memory variables" per grid point [10]. AWP-ODC-OS uses the coarse-grained approach of [9], which requires a single memory variable for each component of the stress tensor.

Many previous seismic simulations that have incorporated anelastic attenuation use a value of Q that is a constant, independent of frequency. As noted in [23], this scheme becomes inappropriate at frequencies higher than 1 Hz. Instead, the authors of [23] propose a model where Q follows a power-law above a certain threshold and is constant below that threshold, and incorporate this into the coarse-grained approach. We adopt these same numerics in AWP-ODC-OS.

AWP-ODC-OS supports kinematic point source descriptions, which are input as moment-rate time histories applied to a number of grid points in the computation domain, using a custom binary format. These point sources can be arranged along a fault plane to represent a finite source.

3   Implementation

3.1   Overview

In this section we describe the implementation of AWP-ODC-OS, from the prospective of a single core, to a single node, to multiple nodes. We begin with a high-level overview of the control flow.

Upon initialization, the background velocity model, consisting of the density and Lamé parameters, and the source terms are read from disk, and the necessary data structures are allocated and initialized. In total there are 26 regular three-dimensional grids used: a velocity grid for each of the x, y and z components; six stress grids, representing the upper-triangular components of the stress tensor; a grid for the density ρ and Lamé parameters λ, μ; a grid for the Cerjan sponge layer; and finally 13 grids for the anelastic attenuation, composed of the six upper-triangular components of the memory matrix and seven grids for the coarse-grained attenuation.

A timestep in AWP-ODC-OS's time marching loop consists of a velocity stencil update of the whole domain, followed by a stress stencil update, source term updates and possibly output. Additionally, if the domain has a free surface boundary, there are velocity and stress free surface computations applied on that boundary, which occur after the velocity and stress stencil updates respectively. A schematic diagram of this control flow is given in Fig. 1.

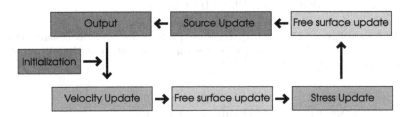

Fig. 1. Diagram of AWP-ODC-OS's control flow. Green boxes represent domain-wide stencil updates, free surface boundary updates are in grey and all other procedures are in blue. For multinode runs, MPI communication also occurs as part of the velocity and stress grid updates. (Color figure online)

3.2   Architecture Description

The Intel Xeon Phi x200 family of processors, codenamed Knights Landing (KNL), is the second generation in the Intel Xeon Phi product line, and the first generation to be available as a self-hosted processor.

A Knights Landing processor contains up to 36 active *tiles*. Each tile contains two cores and a 1 MB L2 cache shared between these cores. Each core contains two Vector Processing Units, which support 512-bit wide vector instructions, and a 64 KB L1 cache (broken into 32 KB for instructions and data). Each core supports up to four hyperthreads, giving a total of up to 288 logical cores. AWP-ODC-OS performs best with a single thread per core, and this is the setting we will use throughout this work.

In addition to 6 DDR controllers (supporting up to 384 GB), each KNL part is equipped with 16 GB on-package high-bandwidth MCDRAM. This memory can be used in one of several modes, chosen at boot time. In *Flat* mode, this memory is accessible as a separate NUMA node. The programmer can either explicitly allocate memory on this node, or rely on a utility such as *numactl* to intercept all allocations in an existing executable and place them in MCDRAM. In *Cache* mode, MCDRAM acts as a large direct-mapped last level cache. This provides many benefits of high-bandwidth memory without requiring code changes; however, it provides the programmer less control, since in this mode MCDRAM cannot be accessed directly. In addition, *hybrid* modes exist, in which some percentage of MCDRAM is exposed as a NUMA node and the remainder acts as a cache, as in Cache mode. In this work, when allocating memory in MCDRAM in Flat mode, we perform these allocations using libnuma. Additionally KNL provides various *clustering modes*; for all of our Flat mode results, we use the Quadrant clustering mode.

We will evaluate the performance of AWP-ODC-OS on a variety of Intel Xeon Phi installations, in addition to a number of other architectures, including Haswell-generation Intel Xeon processors and NVIDIA Tesla P100 GPUs. In Table 1 we summarize the different KNL machines which we have used for benchmarking, including two local nodes and two clusters: the TACC Stampede KNL Upgrade and NERSC Cori Phase II at LBNL.

Table 1. A summary of the KNL systems used for AWP-ODC-OS benchmarks. For each system, we list which Xeon Phi processor is present, and the output of the STREAM Triad benchmark [17].

Name	SKU	Triad	Description
KNL-LC	7210	470 GB/s	Local KNL
KNL-STMP	7250	480 GB/s	TACC Stampede KNL
KNL-CORI	7250	480 GB/s	NERSC Cori Phase II
KNL-FAST	7290	490 GB/s	Local KNL

3.3   Single Core

Since memory bandwidth is the principal performance bottleneck for AWP-ODC-OS, to optimize performance on a single core, we exploit spatial data locality in the stencil updates. To achieve this, we utilize the *vector folding* technique [24].

Vector folding is based on the observation that neighboring data values are often reused between consecutive stencil computations. When this reuse occurs along the same dimension that SIMD vectorization is applied, memory bandwidth can be reduced because many of the values in a previous vector can be reused. Vector folding extends this reuse from the traditional one dimension to multiple dimensions; typically 2D is used, but higher dimensionality is possible. When performing the SIMD stencil calculations, small multi-dimensional tiles of data are stored within each SIMD register. For example, in traditional 1D vectorization, a 512-bit SIMD register might contain 16 consecutive single precision floating-point values in the x dimension, but when using vector-folding, a SIMD register of the same size might contain a 4×4 tile of values in the x and y dimensions, or a $4 \times 2 \times 2$ tile in three dimensions [25]. Figure 2 illustrates three different ways of "folding" data in an 8-element SIMD format and how each of these folds would be applied to calculate 8 results in a simple 25-point stencil. The benefit of vector folding can be seen by observing that fewer unique elements need to be loaded in the 2D and 3D formats compared to the traditional 1D format, even though the number of results calculated in each case is the same.

To enable this SIMD-element reuse and to also reduce the number of memory loads, the memory layout must also be modified to match the vector folding

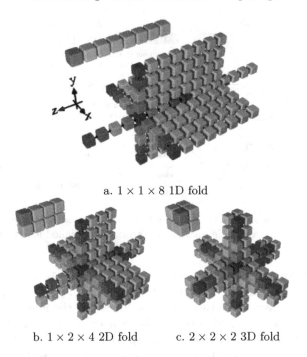

a. $1 \times 1 \times 8$ 1D fold

b. $1 \times 2 \times 4$ 2D fold   c. $2 \times 2 \times 2$ 3D fold

Fig. 2. Various folds of 8 elements [24]. The smaller diagram in the upper-left of each sub-figure illustrates a single SIMD layout, and the larger diagram shows the input values needed to calculate an example 25-point stencil for the entire vector.

scheme. For example, if 4×4 vector folding is used in the SIMD representation, each 16 consecutive elements in memory must also contain values from a 4×4 tile as specified by the logical multi-dimensional indices of the problem domain. This more efficient layout comes at the cost of added complexity when constructing folded SIMD tiles from their constituent elements when the access is unaligned, e.g. when one or more indices are not a multiple of the folded vector length in its corresponding dimension. Figure 3 compares the traditional 1D memory layout to the 4×4 example layout and illustrates the added complexity of assembling unaligned data. Creating the shuffle and permutation instructions required to properly assemble the unaligned data can be tedious and error-prone. We use the stencil compiler from the YASK software package [26] to automate this task.

To determine the most efficient vector fold scheme for AWP-ODC-OS, we explored the performance of a variety of vector-fold dimensions using a performance proxy that is part of the YASK software. Since AWP-ODC-OS uses single-precision floating point arithmetic, we considered vector folds consisting of 16 elements each to fill 512-bit SIMD registers.

Table 2 shows the performance for a range of vector-fold sizes $x \times y \times z$ on **KNL-LC**. Performance is measured by number of millions of lattice update points completed per second (MLUPS), where one lattice update includes both

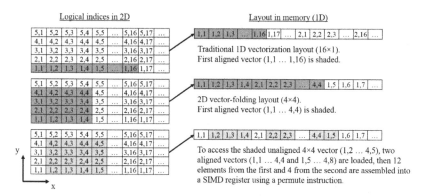

Fig. 3. Exploiting data locality of vector folding requires modifying the memory layout and generating code to assemble unaligned vectors from aligned loads [26].

a velocity and stress update. We observe that a $1 \times 1 \times 16$ vector fold has the lowest performance, while $4 \times 4 \times 1$ fold attains the highest performance, with a factor of 1.6 between these two extremes. Since z is the innermost dimension in our grids, $1 \times 1 \times 16$ fold corresponds to a traditionally-vectorized kernel with no vector folding (i.e. 1D vectorization). Thus, the vector-folding technique provides a 1.6× speedup compared to using a traditional SIMD representation and memory-layout. Additionally, we can see that overall the best performing fold sizes are those orthogonal to the innermost dimension z. This matches our expectations, since a vector fold of this type has a higher proportion of data dependencies in the innermost dimension, which will generally already be in cache. Since a fold of size $4 \times 4 \times 1$ achieves the best performance, this is the size that we have used for the remainder of the Xeon Phi results in this work.

Table 2. Comparison of performance of velocity and stencil kernels for different vector fold sizes. Given is the performance in MLUPS for each choice of vector fold size, and the relative performance of that fold size compared to the best observed performance. A domain size of $1024 \times 1024 \times 64$ was used, and all performances were measured using YASK, which provides a performance proxy for measuring performance of kernels under different folding sizes.

Fold size	$1 \times 1 \times 16$	$1 \times 16 \times 1$	$2 \times 8 \times 1$	$4 \times 1 \times 4$	$4 \times 4 \times 1$	$8 \times 2 \times 1$	$16 \times 1 \times 1$
MULPS	812	1140	1311	1280	1313	1273	1260
Relative perf	1.00	1.40	1.61	1.58	1.62	1.57	1.55

In addition to vector folding, we exploit the AVX-512ER instruction set extension. AWP-ODC-OS's stencils require 8 divisions per timestep. We can replace these divisions with the single precision reciprocal approximation instruction, RCP28, which is accurate to 2^{-23} and has a reciprocal throughput several times smaller than VDIVPS. This achieves almost IEEE 754 single precision, which has 24 mantissa bits. The resulting performance gain is 7%.

3.4   Task Scheduling on a Single Node

We have developed a dynamic scheduling scheme for AWP-ODC-OS, with a single dedicated management core which assigns *work packages* to the remaining cores (which we refer to as *computation cores*); where a work package is a stencil update in a subset of the domain, or MPI communication to one of the adjacent nodes. Although we are using the OpenMP library, within the main loop we manage the parallelism directly using thread IDs, rather than using OpenMP annotated `for` loops. This allows us greater control and more flexibility in our scheme. During the initialization phase of the code however, where performance is less critical, we do make use of standard OpenMP annotated loops.

Since each timestep in the main loop is composed of the same computations, the set of work packages required for each timestep is identical, and can be generated at initialization. There are two types of work packages:

1. A velocity or stress stencil update on a portion of the domain, of fixed size $w_x \times w_y \times w_z$. If the domain size on a node is $N_X \times N_Y \times N_Z$, then the total number of work packages of this type per timestep is $N_{\text{stencil}} = 2 \lceil \frac{N_X}{w_x} \rceil \lceil \frac{N_Y}{w_y} \rceil \lceil \frac{N_Z}{w_z} \rceil$. The factor of two is due to the fact that there is both a velocity and stress stencil update every timestep.
2. MPI communication that sends and receives velocity or stress halo regions to or from all MPI neighbors of that node. There are two such work packages per timestep, $N_{mpi} = 2$: one for the communication of velocity boundaries and one for stress boundaries. During such a work package, first `MPI_Isend` and `MPI_Irecv` are posted for each MPI neighbor, and then `MPI_Test` is repeatedly called until all requests are complete.

Additionally, each stencil update work package contains metadata to denote if free surface boundary conditions should be applied after the stencil update. The total number of work packages is then given by $N_{wp} = N_{\text{stencil}} + N_{mpi}$. For optimal load balancing, this number should be large compared to the number of computation cores. For example, for a problem size $512 \times 512 \times 512$, the optimal work package size for stencil updates is $16 \times 16 \times 128$, yielding $N_{wp} = 8194$ (determined by comparing a range of sizes on the system **KNL-LC**).

The management core assigns work to a computation core via two integers which are accessible only to that computation core and the management core. These integers represent the next work package index that a core should complete, and are initially negative to signal that no work package is ready. First each computation core continually checks the corresponding two integers until it reads a positive number, at which point it begins that work package. Upon completion, it sets that integer to be negative. The management core continually loops through these integers, and when it encounters a negative integer it checks if there is a work package with no outstanding dependencies, and if so it sets that integer to be that work package index. For simplicity, the work packages are arranged in an order so that work package i is assigned to a computation core only when all work packages $j < i$ have already been assigned (though not necessarily completed).

During each timestep, there are several dependencies among the work packages. For example a stress stencil update requires all nearby velocity stencil updates have completed, and an MPI work package cannot begin until all MPI boundary computations are complete. These dependencies can be expressed by sorting the work packages accordingly and insisting that no work package after some index i can be assigned until all work packages with index $j \leq d_i$ are complete. In order to reduce the time spent waiting for dependencies, the work packages are arranged so that the difference $i - d_i$ is large compared to the number of computation cores.

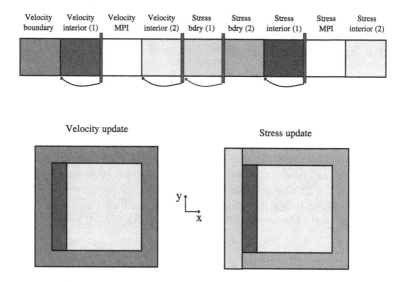

Fig. 4. Illustration of our shared memory parallelization scheme. On top, the ordering of work packages is listed; barriers are depicted by vertical lines, and their corresponding dependency indicated by arrows. On the bottom, a two dimensional representation of the domain is given, indicating the order in which the stencil updates are applied.

The ordering of the work packages and the corresponding dependencies are illustrated in Fig. 4. The first work packages to be assigned are the velocity updates for the parts of the domain which will need to be sent to that node's MPI neighbors. These MPI messages cannot be sent until the boundary computations are completed; this dependency barrier is depicted by the first vertical red bar in Fig. 4. To prevent computation cores idling until this dependency is met, some additional work packages are ordered before the MPI communication, with the aim that by the time the dependency barrier is reached, the boundary computations are complete and no core will idle. The next dependencies are for the stress MPI boundary computations, which cannot be completed until the neighboring rank has finished its boundary velocity updates and our `MPI_Irecv` of the velocity has completed. To mitigate the impact of these barriers, the stress boundary is broken into two parts, where the first part depends only on work packages up to the velocity MPI work package. The second part of the boundary is then started only when all of the velocity updates are finished. The final dependency barrier ensures that the stress MPI communication does not begin until the stress boundary updates have completed; this is arranged in the same way as the velocity MPI communication, described above.

3.5 Multiple Node Parallelism

In this subsection we describe the multiple node parallelism scheme we have developed for AWP-ODC-OS, as well as an alternative scheme that is more efficient in cases where MPI scheduling becomes a bottleneck. Multinode parallelism in AWP-ODC-OS utilizes an overlapping MPI scheme, and currently supports domain decomposition in the X and Y dimensions. To perform a single update of both velocity and stress, a node requires a layer of width two from the velocity and stress grids from all neighboring nodes, where two nodes are considered neighbors if they share a face.

Each node communicates with its MPI neighbors twice during each timestep, once for each kernel. These MPI communications are scheduled like all other work packages, in particular, there is no dedicated communication core. As illustrated in Fig. 4, the work packages are ordered so that first the boundaries are computed, with the MPI communication work package being placed soon after the boundary computations. The MPI communications cannot begin until all boundaries have been updated, which introduces a dependency in our work scheduling. In order to reduce the impact of this dependency, a small portion of the interior computation occurs between the end of the boundary computation and the MPI communication.

An alternative MPI scheduling scheme is provided to enhance performance in cases when the above scheme is not appropriate. For example, if the domain is small enough that there are more cores than work packages on the boundary then some cores will remain idle until the boundary computations are complete. The alternative scheme enables a dedicated communication core, and then removes the MPI work packages from the queue. This sacrifices a core, but in return removes two dependencies, and ensures that the MPI communication will begin immediately after the required stencil updates have completed.

3.6 Simultaneously Utilizing MCDRAM and DDR

In order to increase available memory bandwidth, when operating in Flat mode we utilize both MCDRAM and DDR simultaneously. By placing a small number of the grids storing the 26 variables in DDR and leaving the remaining grids in MCDRAM, we reduce the load on MCDRAM while ensuring that DDR bandwidth does not become a bottleneck. Additionally, since the AWP-ODC-OS kernels exhibit a substantial read/write imbalance (approximately 5:1), by placing heavily-read grids in DDR we can reduce this imbalance which yields an

increase in the theoretical peak MCDRAM bandwidth. As an additional benefit, this increases the total memory available, thereby allowing us to run larger
simulations on a single node.

Since we have 26 grids, there is a large number of possible partitions of
these grids between MCDRAM and DDR. We want to reduce the read/write
imbalance in MCDRAM accesses, so the 6 stress and 3 velocity grids which
are heavily written to are poor candidates to be placed in DDR. Furthermore,
more computation time is spent in the stress kernel than the velocity kernel,
and the sets of grids accessed by each kernel are not the same. This further
suggests which grids are good candidates to be placed in DDR. There are still
many combinations to check, and since the different grids are accessed quite
asymmetrically, it is difficult to predict which precise combination will perform
best. So we employed a search, using these initial observations as a guide to
reduce the search space, for example by always placing the velocity and stress
grids in MCDRAM.

The performance of all combinations of up to three grids in MCDRAM was
exhaustively checked, and for the remaining possibilities a random sample was
taken. The results are presented in Fig. 5. The best performing combination
involved placing four grids in DDR, attaining a performance increase of 5%.
Moreover, it is possible to place seven grids in DDR without decreasing overall
performance, thereby increasing the available memory by a factor of 7/26, or a
total of 21.89 GB. If we only place the 9 grids corresponding to velocity and stress
components in MCDRAM and place the remaining 17 grids in DDR, performance
degrades by a factor of two, while increasing available memory to 46.2 GB.

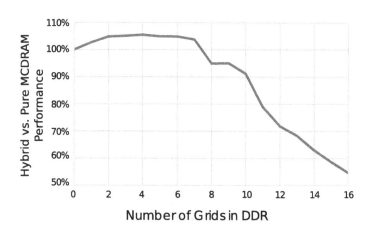

Fig. 5. Best performance improvement obtained by moving a fixed number of grids
from MCDRAM to DDR. For one to three grids, all possible combinations were tested,
for the remaining values a random sample was used instead. In each case, performance
was measured for 400 timesteps on a domain of size $128 \times 96 \times 192$.

4 Experiments and Results

4.1 Architecture Comparison

For the purposes of comparison, we ran AWP-ODC-OS on a variety of architectures. We tested two different code branches: Firstly, a GPU branch which we have tested on several NVIDIA cards: a Tesla K20X, an Tesla M40 and a Tesla P100 (250 W PCIE part); and secondly an x86 version, which was tested on **KNL-FAST** and **KNL-CORI** and a single-socket Intel Xeon E5-2630v3. These two branches contain independent implementations of the same numerics, with identical physical features, including viscoelasticity through frequency-dependent attenuation described in Sect. 2.

In Fig. 6, the performance of AWP-ODC-OS is shown for each of these architectures. In each case, a problem size was chosen that resulted in the best performance, and for the KNL systems and the GPUs, this size was fixed to occupy a large fraction of MCDRAM capacity and device memory capacity, respectively. In the case of Xeon Phi the problem dimensions were $512 \times 256 \times 1024$, for the K20X and M40 $160 \times 320 \times 512$ was used, for the P100 $320 \times 320 \times 1024$ was used and finally for the Xeon a problem size of $1024 \times 1024 \times 64$ was used. In addition to the performance of AWP-ODC-OS, memory bandwidth is benchmarked. For the Xeon and KNL systems, we measured this by the STREAM-Triad benchmark [17]. In the case of the Flat mode KNL systems, the bandwidth listed is the aggregate of the MCDRAM and DDR STREAM-Triad results, since we utilize both. For the GPUs, bandwidth is measured by the HPCG-SpMV benchmark [11], which is bound by read-bandwidth, in order to accurately capture the read/write imbalance of AWP-ODC-OS. As we can see these bandwidth test can

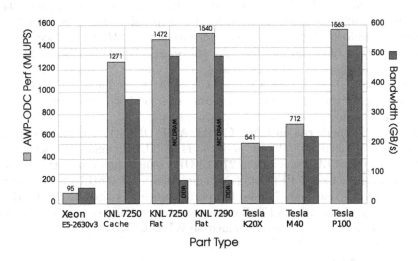

Fig. 6. AWP-ODC-OS performance on a variety of architectures, as well as memory bandwidth for each system (measured by the HPCG-SpMV benchmark for the GPUs and STREAM-Triad for the other architectures).

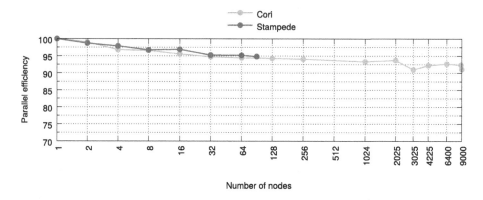

Fig. 7. Weak scaling performance on up to 9,000 nodes of NERSC Cori and 90 nodes of TACC Stampede KNL Upgrade, in Flat mode. On 9,000 nodes, a parallel efficiency of 91% is attained.

be regarded as proxy for AWP-ODC-OS maximum possible performance. It also demonstrates the high degree of tuning in AWP-ODC-OS as the entire solver is able to achieve close to peak bandwidth.

4.2   Weak Scaling

We completed two weak scaling studies of AWP-ODC-OS, both in Flat mode. Scaling plots are presented in Fig. 7. On **KNL-CORI**, this scaling ranges from 1 to 9,000 nodes, out of a total of 9,300 KNL nodes in the cluster, and a parallel efficiency of above 91% is achieved. On **KNL-STMP**, it ranges from 1 to 90 nodes, of the 96 available Flat mode nodes, with a parallel efficiency above 94%.

In both scaling studies, each node was responsible for a computational domain of size $512 \times 512 \times 512$, which corresponds to 13 GB per node to store the grids for each of the 26 variables. We utilize the scheme described in Sect. 3.6 where 7 variables are stored in DDR and 19 variables in MCDRAM, which corresponds to 9.5 GB in MCDRAM and 3.5 GB in DDR. There are 7,744 point sources active for the first 400 time steps, out of a total of 2,000 time steps. Two cores were set aside for use by the operating system.

For the 9,000 node run on **KNL-CORI**, AWP-ODC-OS attained an average performance of 1,230 MLUPS per node, or 11.07 TLUPS aggregate between all nodes. Since every LUP consists of 270 FLOPS (single precision), this yields a total perfomance of 2.989 PFLOPS (single precision). 1,230 MLUPS corresponds to a performance that is 2.27 times the performance of a single NVIDIA K20X card. It would require 20,430 K20X cards, running at 100% parallel efficiency to match the performance we have attained on **KNL-CORI**.

4.3   Strong Scaling

We completed strong scaling studies on both **KNL-CORI** and **KNL-STMP**, ranging from 4 nodes to 128 nodes on **KNL-CORI** and from 4 nodes to 80

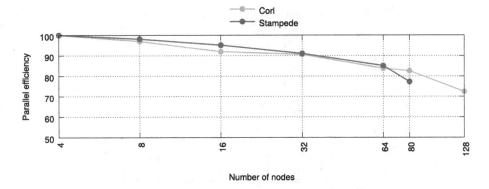

Fig. 8. Strong scaling performance on up to 128 nodes of Cori and 80 nodes of Stampede. Both studies begin with 4 nodes, representing a scaling factor of 32 on Cori and 20 on Stampede. In both cases, we achieve greater than 80% parallel efficiency when scaling to a factor of 16.

nodes on **KNL-STMP**. In both cases, the total problem size across all nodes was $2560 \times 1536 \times 192$, and all runs were completed in Flat mode, using the DDR/MCDRAM hybrid scheme, where we place 7 of the 26 variable grids in DDR. Additionally, since for strong scaling the ratio of communication to computation time increases as the number of nodes grows, we used the variant MPI scheme with a dedicated communication core.

The results of both studies are presented in Fig. 8. Parallel efficiency remained above 80% while scaling to a factor of 16. Beyond this, parallel efficiency began to decay reapidly, as it became increasingly difficult to hide the communication time behind computation time. Additionally, as the number of nodes increases the total number of work packages becomes smaller relative to the number of cores, and this increases time spent by cores waiting for previous, dependent work packages to be completed. For example, for the 128 node run on **KNL-CORI**, there are a total of only 120 stencil update work packages for each stencil, and 64 computation cores.

4.4 Memory Mode Comparison

As large KNL installations are deployed, there is great interest in the relative performance of the different memory modes it provides. Cache mode aims at providing the benefits of MCDRAM without requiring that the developer undertake code changes, while Flat mode requires some action on the part of the developer but provides much more control. From the comparatively low arithmetic intensity (and from Fig. 6), it is clear that AWP-ODC-OS is sensitive to the amount of memory bandwidth available, and hence there are large performance improvements to be gained on KNL if MCDRAM is fully exploited.

In Fig. 9, the performance of AWP-ODC-OS over a range of combinations of memory modes and problem sizes is presented, measured on **KNL-STMP**.

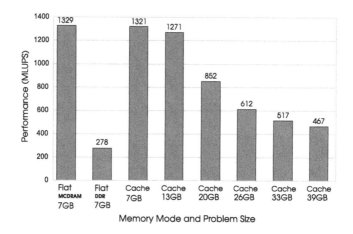

Fig. 9. Comparison of AWP-ODC-OS performance on a single KNL node, in different memory modes and with different problem sizes, measured on **KNL-STMP**.

For the 7 GB problem sizes, a domain of $512 \times 512 \times 256$ was used, and the larger problem sizes were attained by taking $512 \times 512 \times 256$ and multiplying the z dimension as necessary to achieve the desired size. Firstly, as a reference point the performance for Flat mode running completely from MCDRAM and running completely from DDR are given. The Cache mode performances all lie within these two extremes, with performance in Cache mode degrading as the problem size decreases. This is as we expect: if the problem size is much smaller than 16 GB we expect relatively few MCDRAM cache conflicts, and then Cache mode should provide similar performance to Flat mode running entirely from MCDRAM. On the other hand, as the problem size gets larger there are necessarily MCDRAM cache misses as we iterate over the domain, and we then increasingly depend on DDR bandwidth to supply data. Note that when running completely from MCDRAM we are not using the hybrid MCDRAM/DDR technique, and the measurements in this section were completed on a system without the tickless kernel setting. These two factors, combined with a different problem size, account for the difference in performance observed in this section and in the Architecture Comparison section.

Overall, for problem sizes smaller than MCDRAM, Cache mode provides similar performance to Flat mode. For example, for the 13 GB problem size we observe 95.6% of Flat mode performance. We conclude that Cache mode is a viable option for AWP-ODC-OS in terms of single node performance, though Flat mode is superior in terms of performance and control. For a 39 GB problem size we see a performance drop to 35% of Flat mode performance. As was noted in Sect. 3.6, by placing some grids in DDR in Flat mode, we can increase the available problem size to 46 GB with performance of 50% of the maximum observed performance. This is an improvement on using Cache mode in this case, which means that especially for problem sizes larger than 16 GB, Flat mode is advantageous.

5   Conclusion

We have presented AWP-ODC-OS, an end-to-end optimization of the seismic simulation code AWP-ODC, enabling this widely-used code to run close to optimally on the Intel Xeon Phi Knights Landing microarchitecture. In recent years AWP-ODC has primarily run on GPU accelerated supercomputers, and the developments we have made will allow this code to additionally exploit a new range of current and upcoming HPC installations.

We have optimized AWP-ODC for Xeon Phi from end-to-end: from the level of a single vector processing unit via the vector folding technique, which yields a factor of 1.6 improvement over traditional vectorization; to single- and multiple-nodes via a custom dynamic scheduling scheme, which promotes efficient load balancing and allows for overlapping computation and communication. The performance of the resulting code is competitive with the cutting-edge of GPU offerings, including the NVIDIA Tesla P100, compared to which AWP-ODC-OS on Xeon Phi achieves 98.5% performance. On a large scale weak scaling study on the supercomputer Cori Phase II, AWP-ODC-OS achieved a parallel efficiency of greater than 91%. The combined performance of this run is equivalent to 20,430 NVIDIA Tesla K20X GPUs, running at 100% parallel efficiency. This very promising result demonstrates that Knights Landing supercomputers are a prime candidate for future high-impact simulations using AWP-ODC-OS.

Acknowledgements. We acknowledge support from the National Energy Research Scientific Computing Center (NERSC) for access to the Cori supercomputer. We acknowledge the Texas Advanced Computing Center (TACC) at The University of Texas at Austin for providing HPC resources that have contributed to the research results reported within this paper. We thank Jack Deslippe, Sudip Dosanjh and Richard Gerber at NERSC and Lars Koesterke, Tommy Minyard and Dan Stanzione at TACC. The UCSD team was supported by NSF awards ACI-1450451, EAR-1349180, EAR-1135455 and Keck Foundation grant 005590-00001.

Optimization Notice: Software and workloads used in performance tests may have been optimized for performance only on Intel microprocessors. Performance tests, such as SYSmark and MobileMark, are measured using specific computer systems, components, software, operations and functions. Any change to any of those factors may cause the results to vary. You should consult other information and performance tests to assist you in fully evaluating your contemplated purchases, including the performance of that product when combined with other products. For more information go to http://www.intel.com/performance. Intel, Xeon, and Intel Xeon Phi are trademarks of Intel Corporation in the U.S. and/or other countries.

References

1. Aochi, H., Ulrich, T., Ducellier, A., Dupros, F., Michea, D.: Finite difference simulations of seismic wave propagation for understanding earthquake physics and predicting ground motions: advances and challenges. **454**(1), 012010 (2013)
2. Cerjan, C., Kosloff, D., Kosloff, R., Reshef, M.: A nonreflecting boundary condition for discrete acoustic and elastic wave equations. Geophysics **50**(4), 705–708 (1985)

3. Chaljub, E., Maufroy, E., Moczo, P., Kristek, J., Hollender, F., Bard, P.-Y., Priolo, E., Klin, P., de Martin, F., Zhang, Z., Zhang, W., Chen, X.: 3-D numerical simulations of earthquake ground motion in sedimentary basins: testing accuracy through stringent models 201(1), 90–111 (2015)
4. Christen, M., Schenk, O., Cui, Y.: Patus for convenient high-performance stencils: evaluation in earthquake simulations. In: 2012 International Conference for High Performance Computing, Networking, Storage and Analysis (SC), pp. 1–10. IEEE (2012)
5. Cui, Y., Poyraz, E., Zhou, J., Callaghan, S., Maechling, P., Jordan, T.H., Shih, L., Chen, P.: Accelerating cybershake calculations on the XE6/XK7 platform of blue waters. In: 2013 Extreme Scaling Workshop (XSW 2013), pp. 8–17. IEEE (2013)
6. Cui, Y., Olsen, K.B., Jordan, T.H., Lee, K., Zhou, J., Small, P., Roten, D., et al.: Scalable earthquake simulation on petascale supercomputers. In: Proceedings of the 2010 ACM/IEEE International Conference for High Performance Computing, Networking, Storage and Analysis, pp. 1–20. IEEE Computer Society (2010)
7. Cui, Y., Poyraz, E., Olsen, K.B., Zhou, J., Withers, K., Callaghan, S., Larkin, J., Guest, C., Choi, D., Chourasia, A., et al.: Physics-based seismic hazard analysis on petascale heterogeneous supercomputers. In: Proceedings of the International Conference on High Performance Computing, Networking, Storage and Analysis, p. 70. ACM (2013)
8. Dalguer, L.A., and Day, S.M.: Staggered grid split node method for spontaneous rupture simulation. J. Geophys. Res.: Solid (2007)
9. Day, S.M.: Efficient simulation of constant Q using coarse-grained memory variables. Bull. Seismol. Soc. Am. 88(4), 1051–1062 (1998)
10. Day, S.M., Bradley, C.R.: Memory-efficient simulation of anelastic wave propagation. Bull. Seismol. Soc. Am. 91(3), 520–531 (2001)
11. Dongarra, J.: Toward a new metric for ranking high performance computing systems. Sandia Report, SAND2013-4744, p. 312 (2013)
12. Duru, K., Dunham, E.M.: Dynamic earthquake rupture simulations on nonplanar faults embedded in 3D geometrically complex, heterogeneous elastic solids 305, 185–207 (2016)
13. Gottschämmer, E., Olsen, K.B.: Accuracy of the explicit planar free-surface boundary condition implemented in a fourth-order staggered-grid velocity-stress finite-difference scheme. Bull. Seismol. Soc. Am. 91(3), 617–623 (2001)
14. Kristek, J., Moczo, P.: Seismic-wave propagation in viscoelastic media with material discontinuities: a 3D fourth-order staggered-grid finite-difference modeling 93(5), 2273–2280 (2003)
15. Cruz-Atienza, V.M., Virieux, J., Aochi, H.: 3D finite-difference dynamic-rupture modeling along nonplanar faults 72(5), SM123–SM137 (2007)
16. Madariaga, R., Olsen, K., Archuleta, R.: Modeling dynamic rupture in a 3D earthquake fault model. Bull. Seismol. (1998)
17. McCalpin, J.D.: A survey of memory bandwidth and machine balance in current high performance computers. IEEE TCCA Newsl. 19–25 (1995)
18. Moczo, P., Robertsson, J., Eisner, L.: The finite-difference time-domain method for modeling of seismic wave propagation 48 (2007)
19. Olsen, K.B., Day, S.M., Minster, J.B., Cui, Y., Chourasia, A., Faerman, M., Moore, R., Maechling, P., Jordan, T.: Strong shaking in Los Angeles expected from southern San Andreas earthquake. Geophys. Res. Lett. 33(7) (2006)
20. Olsen, K.B., Stephenson, W.J., Geisselmeyer, A.: 3D crustal structure and long-period ground motions from a M9.0 megathrust earthquake in the pacific northwest region. J. Seismolog. 12(2), 145–159 (2008)

21. Olsen, K.B.: Simulation of three-dimensional wave propagation in the Salt Lake Basin. Ph.D. thesis, University of Utah (1994)
22. Roten, D., Cui, Y., Olsen, K.B., Day, S.M., Withers, K., Savran, W.H., Wang, P., Mu, D.: High-frequency nonlinear earthquake simulations on petascale heterogeneous supercomputers. In: Proceedings of the International Conference for High Performance Computing, Networking, Storage and Analysis, p. 82. IEEE Press (2016)
23. Withers, K.B., Olsen, K.B., Day, S.M.: Memory-efficient simulation of frequency-dependent Q. Bull. Seismol. Soc. Am. (2015)
24. Yount, C.: Vector folding: improving stencil performance via multi-dimensional simd-vector representation. In: High Performance Computing and Communications (HPCC), pp. 865–870, August 2015
25. Yount, C., Duran, A.: Effective use of large high-bandwidth memory caches in HPC stencil computation via temporal wave-front tiling. In: Proceedings of the 7th International Workshop in Performance Modeling, Benchmarking and Simulation of High Performance Computer Systems Held as Part of ACM/IEEE Supercomputing 2016 (SC 2016), PMBS 2016, November 2016
26. Yount, C., Tobin, J., Breuer, A., Duran, A.: Yask-yet another stencil kernel: a framework for HPC stencil code-generation and tuning. In: Proceedings of the 6th International Workshop on Domain-Specific Languages and High-Level Frameworks for High Performance Computing Held as Part of ACM/IEEE Supercomputing 2016 (SC 2016), WOLFHPC 2016, November 2016

A Framework for Out of Memory SVD Algorithms

Khairul Kabir[4], Azzam Haidar[1]([✉]), Stanimire Tomov[1], Aurelien Bouteiller[1],
and Jack Dongarra[1,2,3]

[1] University of Tennessee, Knoxville, USA
haidar@icl.utk.edu
[2] Oak Ridge National Laboratory, Oak Ridge, USA
[3] University of Manchester, Manchester, UK
[4] Nvidia, Santa Clara, USA
kkabir@nvidia.com

Abstract. Many important applications – from big data analytics to information retrieval, gene expression analysis, and numerical weather prediction – require the solution of large dense singular value decompositions (SVD). In many cases the problems are too large to fit into the computer's main memory, and thus require specialized *out-of-core* algorithms that use disk storage. In this paper, we analyze the SVD communications, as related to hierarchical memories, and design a class of algorithms that minimizes them. This class includes out-of-core SVDs but can also be applied between other consecutive levels of the memory hierarchy, e.g., GPU SVD using the CPU memory for large problems. We call these *out-of-memory* (OOM) algorithms. To design OOM SVDs, we first study the communications for both classical one-stage blocked SVD and two-stage tiled SVD. We present the theoretical analysis and strategies to design, as well as implement, these communication avoiding OOM SVD algorithms. We show performance results for multicore architecture that illustrate our theoretical findings and match our performance models.

1 Introduction

The singular value decomposition (SVD) of an $m \times n$ matrix A finds two orthogonal matrices U, V, and a diagonal matrix Σ with non-negative numbers, such that $A = U\Sigma V^T$. The diagonal elements of Σ are called the singular values, and the orthogonal matrices U and V contain the left and right singular vectors of A, respectively. The SVD is typically done by a three-phase process: (1) *Reduction phase*: orthogonal matrices Q and P are applied on both the left and the right side of A to reduce it to a bidiagonal form matrix, B; (2) *Solver phase*: a singular value solver computes the singular values Σ, and the left and right singular vectors $\widetilde{U}$ and $\widetilde{V}$, respectively, of the bidiagonal matrix B; (3) *Singular vectors update phase*: if required, the left and the right singular vectors

© Springer International Publishing AG 2017
J.M. Kunkel et al. (Eds.): ISC High Performance 2017, LNCS 10266, pp. 158–178, 2017.
DOI: 10.1007/978-3-319-58667-0_9

of A are computed as $U = Q^T \widetilde{U}$ and $V = P \, \widetilde{V}$. In this work, we are interested in the computation of the singular values only. When the matrix A is too large and does not fit in-memory, our goal is to design efficient algorithms to perform the computation while A is out-of-memory (e.g., A could be in the hard disk drive, flash memory, or fast buffer when a CPU computation is considered, or in the CPU memory for GPU or Xeon Phi computations). The memory bottleneck of the SVD computation is the first phase (e.g., illustrated by the difference in columns 7 and 8 in Tables 4 and 5 from the experimental results section). Once A is reduced, B consists of two vectors that fit (in general) in-memory, where the singular value solver will be able to compute the singular values of B in-memory. If the singular vectors are needed, the second phase also requires the use of OOM techniques. To reduce a general matrix to bidiagonal form we can use either the standard approach which is implemented in LAPACK (we call it one-stage algorithm since it reduces the matrix to bidiagonal in one step), or a two-stage algorithm which reduces the matrix to a bidiagonal form in two steps: first to a band, and then to the bidiagonal form.

Since A resides out-of-memory, the communications to bring parts of A in-memory and back will have a high impact on the overall run time of any OOM algorithm. Thus, to develop efficient OOM SVDs, first and foremost we must study the SVD computational processes and communication patterns, in order to successfully design next the algorithms that minimize communications, as well as overlap them with computation as much as possible.

2   Related Work

A number of dense linear algebra algorithms have been designed to solve problems that are too large to fit in the main memory of a computer at once, and are therefore stored on disks [4,6,18]. Called *out-of-core*, these algorithms mainly targeted one-sided factorizations (LU, QR, and Cholesky). Similar algorithms can be derived between other levels of the memory hierarchy, e.g., for problems that use GPUs but can not fit in the GPU's memory and therefore also use CPU memory, e.g., called non-GPU-resident in [19,20].

Similar algorithms are computationally not feasible for the standard eigensolvers or SVD problems in LAPACK, as we show in this paper, and therefore have not been developed before. Exceptions are special cases, e.g., SVD on tall-and skinny matrices, where a direct SVD computation is replaced by an out-of-core QR first, followed by an in-core SVD of the resulting small R [17].

The development of two-stage eigensolvers and SVD algorithms made it feasible to consider designing their out-of-core counterparts. A two-step reduction for the generalized symmetric eigenvalue problem was reported for the first time in the context of an out-of-core solver [8,9]. Later, the two-stage approach [2,14] was generalized to a multi-stage implementation [3] to reduce a matrix to tridiagonal, bidiagonal, and Hessenberg forms. The two-stage approach was applied to the TRD (Triangular Reduction) [12] and to SVD [13,15,16] in combination with tile algorithms and runtime scheduling based on data dependences between tasks that operate on the tiles. This resulted in very good performance but has never been used to compute the singular vectors.

We note that the principle of the two-stage approach is similar to [12], as in both cases the matrix is first reduced to condensed forms. However, the final form and the transformations used are different, e.g., [12] is for symmetric eigenvalue problems, so reduction is to block diagonal and symmetry is preserved, while the reduction for SVD is to band with shape as shown in Fig. 2. The second stages are also different in terms of transformations, their application, and final matrix shape (tridiagonal vs. bidiagonal). Figure 7 shows the effect of specific strategies for retaining data in memory vs. a generic approach, e.g., that would follow the computation as coded in [12].

More recently, a new parallel, high-performance implementation of the tile reduction phase on homogeneous multicore architectures was introduced [15]. It used a two-stage approach and a runtime scheduler that keeps track of data dependences. Algorithmically, the two-stage approach is the latest development in the field.

3 Contributions

The primary goal of this paper is to design communication avoiding OOM SVD algorithms and their efficient implementations that overlap communications with computations as much as possible. An efficient (and acceptable) OOM SVD design must perform the computation in a realistic time and hide the communication overhead to the fullest. Our main contributions towards achieving this goal are as follows:

- We developed and presented the analysis of the communication costs for the one-stage and two-stage SVD algorithms on hierarchical memories, e.g., CPU memory for main memory and disk for out-of-memory storage, or the GPU/Coprocessor memory for main memory and CPU DRAM memory for out-of-memory storage;
- We investigated different communication avoiding strategies and developed a design with optimal communication pattern;
- We created techniques, along with their theoretical analysis, to hide communication overheads for OOM SVD;
- We also designed a communication avoiding OOM SVD algorithm and developed an optimized implementation for multicore architecture. We showed performance results that illustrate its efficiency and high performance.

4 Background

The first phase of the SVD computation is called *bidiagonal reduction* or BRD, and as mentioned, is considered to be the most expensive part of the computation. In particular, when only singular values are to be computed, it takes more than 90% of the time on modern computer architectures. The BRD's computation cost in terms of floating point operations (flops) is $O(\frac{8}{3}n^3)$. The two main approaches for the BRD phase are:

- **One-stage approach:** the standard one-stage approach as implemented in LAPACK [1], applies Householder transformations in a blocked fashion to reduce the dense matrix to bidiagonal form in one step;
- **Two-stage approach:** the newly developed two-stage approach [12] reduces the general matrix to band form in a first stage, and then reduces the band matrix to bidiagonal form in a second stage.

4.1 The One-Stage Algorithm for SVD

The one-stage reduction of a matrix A to bidiagonal form, as is implemented in LAPACK, applies orthogonal transformation matrices on the left and right side of A. The transformations are applied from both left- and right-side of A, and therefore BRD is also called a "two-sided factorization." The blocked BRD [5] proceeds by "panel/trailing matrix update" and can be summarized as follows. The panel factorization zeroes the entries below the subdiagonal and above the diagonal. It goes over its "nb" columns and rows (red portion of Fig. 1) and annihilates them one after another in an alternating fashion (a column followed by a row, as shown in Fig. 1). The panel computation requires two matrix-vector multiplications: one with the trailing matrix to the right of the column that is being annihilated, and a second one with the trailing matrix below the row that is being annihilated. The panel computation generates the left and right reflectors U and V, and the left and right accumulation X and Y. Once the panel is done, the trailing matrix is updated by two matrix-matrix multiplications:

$$A_{s+nb:n,s+nb:n} \leftarrow A_{s+nb:n,s+nb:n} - U \times Y^\mathsf{T} - X \times V^\mathsf{T},$$

where s denotes the step and nb denotes the panel width. The process is repeated until the whole matrix is reduced to bidiagonal form.

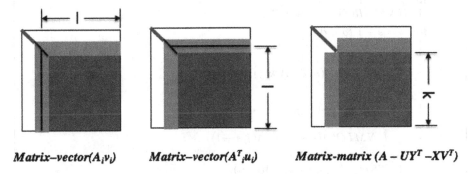

$Matrix{-}vector(A_i v_j)$ $Matrix{-}vector(A^T_i u_i)$ $Matrix{-}matrix\ (A - UY^T - XV^T)$

Fig. 1. LAPACK one-stage blocked algorithm: illustration of the main BLAS kernels used. (Color figure online)

4.2 The Two-Stage Algorithm for SVD

Because of the cost of the reduction step, renewed research has focused on improving this step, resulting in a novel technique based on a two-stage reduction [3,5,7,10,12]. The two-stage reduction is designed to overcome the limitations of the one-stage approach by exchanging memory-bound operations for compute intensive ones. It relies heavily on compute-intensive operations so that performance scales up with CPU core count. As the name implied, the two-stage approach splits the original one-stage approach into two phases - the first stage reduces the general matrix to band form and the second stage reduces the band matrix to bidiagonal form. The first stage is compute-intensive and heavily depends on Level 3 BLAS, whereas the second stage which represents a small percentage of the flops and is memory bound, but can be implemented with cache-friendly and memory-aware kernels to make it efficient.

First Stage: Compute-Intensive. The first stage reduces general matrix to band form using a sequence of blocked Householder transformations. Compared with the one-stage algorithm, this stage eliminates matrix-vector operations and replaces them with matrix-matrix multiply kernels. Conceptually the matrix of size $n \times n$ is split into $u \times u$ tiles of size nb each, where $u = n/nb$. The algorithm then proceeds as a collection of interdependent tasks that can be scheduled for execution by either static or dynamic scheduler. Algorithm 1 shows the tile algorithm for the reduction of general matrix to band form. Figure 2 shows the execution foot-print for the second step of the reduction to band (stage 1) algorithm. The process consists of a QR sweep followed by an LQ

---

for $s = 1$ *to* u **do**
   $GEQRT(A(s,s))$;
   for $j = s + 1$ *to* u **do**
      $\lfloor$ $UNMQR(A(s,s),\ A(s,j))$;
   for $k = s + 1$ *to* u **do**
      $TSQRT(A(s,s),\ A(k,s))$;
      for $j = s + 1$ *to* u **do**
         $\lfloor$ $TSMQR(A(s,j),\ A(k,j),\ A(k,s))$;

   if $(s < u)$ **then**
      $GELQT(A(s,s+1))$;
      for $j = s + 1$ *to* u **do**
         $\lfloor$ $UNMLQ(A(s,s+1),\ A(j,s+1))$;
      for $k = s + 2$ *to* u **do**
         $TSLQT(A(s,s+1),\ A(s,k))$;
         for $j = s + 1$ *to* u **do**
            $\lfloor$ $TSMLQ(A(j,s+1),\ A(j,k),\ A(s,k))$;

Algorithm 1. Two-stage algorithm to reduce a general matrix to band form.

sweep at each step. A QR factorization (GEQRT) is computed for the tile $A_{2,2}$ (the red tile). When this QR factorization is finished, all the tiles to right of $A_{2,2}$ (the light blue tiles of Fig. 2a) are updated by the UNMQR function (each tile is updated by multiplying it on the left by Q^T). At the same time, all the tiles $A_{\bullet,2}$ (the magenta tiles of Fig. 2a) can also be factorized using the TSQRT kernel (computing the QR factorization of a matrix built by coupling the R factor of the QR of $A_{2,2}$ and the $A_{\bullet,2}$ tiles) one after another as all of them modify the upper triangular portion of $A_{2,2}$. Once the factorization of any of the tiles $A_{i,2}$ (for example the dark magenta tile of Fig. 2a), is finished, all the tiles of the block row i (the dark yellow tiles of Fig. 2a) are updated by the TSMQR kernel. Moreover, when all the operation on tile $A_{2,3}$ are finished, LQ factorization (GELQT) can now proceed for this tile (the green tile of Fig. 2b). Just like the QR process, all the tiles in the third column $A_{3:u,3}$ (the light blue tiles of Fig. 2b) are now updated by the Householder vectors computed during the LQ factorization (UNMLQ). Note, however, that this last update has to wait until the prior QR operations have completed. Similarly, all the tiles $A_{2,4:u}$ (the blue tiles of Fig. 2b) can also be factorized (TSLQT), and once any of the tiles $A_{2,i}$ (for example, the dark blue tile of Fig. 2b) finish it factorization, it enables the update of the tiles in the block column i (the dark yellow tiles of Fig. 2b) using the TSMLQ kernel. The interleaving of QR and LQ factorization at each step, as explained above, repeats until the end of the algorithm. At the end, it generates a band matrix of band size nb. Such restructuring of the algorithm removes the fork-join bottleneck of LAPACK and increases the overall performance efficiency.

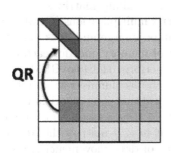

(a) QR factorization of tile $A_{2,2}$ (b) LQ factorization of tile $A_{2,3}$

Fig. 2. Kernel execution of the BRD algorithm during the first stage. (Color figure online)

Second Stage: Cache-Friendly Computational Kernels. The band form is further reduced to the final condensed form using the bulge chasing technique. This procedure annihilates the extra off-diagonal elements by chasing the created fill-in elements down to the bottom right side of the matrix using successive orthogonal transformations. Since the band "nb" is supposed to be small, we consider that the data of this phase fit into the main memory and thus an in-memory algorithm can be applied. This stage involves memory-bound operations that require irregular memory accesses throughout the band matrix. In other words, a straightforward implementation will start accumulating substantial latency overheads each time different portions of the matrix are loaded into cache memory, and the loads can not be compensated for by the low execution rate of the actual computations on that data. To overcome these critical limitations, we employ a bulge chasing technique – originally designed for symmetric eigenvalue problems (tridiagonal reductions) [12] – to extensively use cache friendly kernels combined with fine-grained, memory-aware tasks in an out-of-order scheduling technique, which considerably enhances data locality. This reduction has been designed for newest architectures, and results have shown its efficiency. It has been well optimized so that it takes between 5% to 10% of the global time of the reduction from dense to tridiagonal on modern multicore architectures. We refer the reader to [10, 12] for a detailed description of the technique.

5   An Analytical Study of the Communication Cost of Data Movement

In this section we develop and present the communication minimization pattern for the OOM reduction to bidiagonal form. We provide the analysis for the two techniques – one-stage v.s. two-stage – that we use to design OOM SVDs minimizing the communication cost.

As described in Sect. 4.1, the one-stage bidiagonal reduction needs two matrix-vector multiplications (GEMV) with the trailing matrix at every column and row annihilation, and two matrix-matrix multiplications (GEMM) after every panel computation. Thus, when the matrix is large and does not fit into the main memory, it must be loaded from out-of-memory once for each column and once for each row annihilation (e.g., to perform the two GEMV operations) as well as loaded and stored once after each nb columns/rows annihilation (e.g., after each panel) for the two GEMM operations. The algorithm requires $2(m \times nb + n \times nb)$ in-memory workspace to hold the panel (U and V) and the arrays X and Y of Eq. (4.1). Therefore, for an $m \times n$ matrix, the amount of words to be read and written (i.e., the amount of data movement) is given by the following formula:

Read A for dgemv #1 + Read A for dgemv #2 + Read/Write A for dgemm

$$= \sum_{s=0}^{n-1}(m-s)(n-s) + \sum_{s=0}^{n-1}(m-s)(n-s-1) + 2\sum_{s=1}^{n/nb}(m-s \times nb)(n-s \times nb).$$

Thus, for an $n \times n$ matrix, the amount of word movements is about $\approx \frac{2}{3}n^3 + \frac{1}{nb} \times \frac{2}{3}n^3$.

On the other hand, for the two-stage approach, there is no notion of panel and trailing matrix update. We also note that, since the whole band matrix of size $\min(m, n) \times nb$ is considered to fit into the main memory, the second stage runs efficiently in-memory, and the main attention must be brought to the first stage (i.e., reduction from dense to band), which needs to be performed in on OOM fashion. Overall, if we follow the description in Sect. 4.2, we find that a tile that needs to be updated must be "loaded from/stored to" out-of-memory (e.g., disk) once every step. As a result, for an $m \times n$ matrix and band of width nb, the amount of data movement is given by:

Read/Write A for QR + Read/Write A for LQ

$$
= 2 \times \sum_{s=0}^{n/nb-1} (m - s \times nb)(n - s \times nb) + 2 \times \sum_{s=0}^{n/nb-1} (m - s \times nb)[n - (s+1) \times nb]
$$

$$
\approx \frac{2}{nb}(mn^2 - \frac{n^3}{3}).
$$

Thus, for an $n \times n$ matrix, the amount of word movements is about $\frac{4n^3}{3nb}$.

From this formulation, one can easily observe that the classical one-stage algorithm for the reduction to bidiagonal requires $O(n^3)$ more word transfers between the in-memory and the out-of-memory storage than the two-stage approach. This is a huge amount of extra communication that dramatically affects the performance. To highlight the importance of the communications, we start by giving an example. Consider a matrix of size $n = 100,000$. The classical one-stage algorithm needs $\frac{2}{3}n^3 + \frac{1}{nb} \times \frac{2}{3}n^3$ word movements. In double precision arithmetic, for a recent Hard Drive, Solid State Drives (SSD), or out-of-GPU memory where the communication bandwidths are about 150 MB/s, 500 MB/s, and 8 GB/s, respectively, the standard one-stage technique requires 411, 123, and 7.72 days, respectively, to perform the reduction. The two-stage technique needs approximatively $\frac{1}{nb} \times \frac{4}{3}n^3$ word movements, and thus, in double precision, it necessitates 5.14, 1.54, and 0.09 days, respectively (with nb equal 160). Figure 3

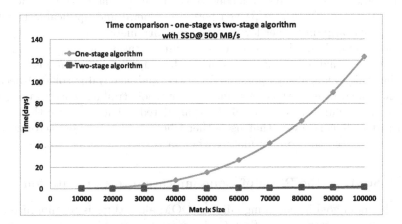

Fig. 3. OOM SVD time comparison between the one-stage and two-stage algorithms.

compares the times required to reduce a general matrix to bidiagonal form, using either the one-stage or the two-stage algorithm for different matrix sizes when the matrix resides in SSD. In conclusion, these results illustrate that it is unacceptable to build an OOM algorithm based on the one-stage approach. For that, it has long been thought that an OOM SVD implementation is practically impossible.

To further emphasize the choice of the two-stage approach, consider one more example where the matrix fits in-memory, and therefore word movements are between the main memory and the cache levels. For a recent hardware, like the Intel Haswell E5-2650 v3 multicore system, achieving a bandwidth of about 60 GB/s, the one-stage takes about 24.71 h to finish the reduction to bidiagonal form in double precision arithmetic, while the two-stage algorithm takes about 0.31 h (with nb equal 160).

6   A Theoretical Study of the Design of an OOM SVD Solver

In this section, we present the theoretical analysis of the OOM algorithm and provide a detailed study of the communication pattern required by the OOM algorithm. Also, we investigate different strategies to design one that is provably optimal in term of data movement and performance. Using the conclusion from the previous section, the design path for an efficient OOM SVD must follow the two-stage approach. The reduction from dense to band form is thus the main component that needs to be studied and implemented as an OOM algorithm. The algorithm starts with A stored out-of-memory, loads in-memory parts of A by block, performs computation on the in-memory data, and sends back results in order to allow other blocks to be loaded as the algorithm proceeds to completion. For simplicity, we use the specifics for out-of-core algorithms, where the matrix is on disk and the CPU DRAM is considered to be the main memory. However, the formulation and theorem proved here are general and applicable to OOM SVDs designs targeting other levels of the memory hierarchy.

Besides algorithmic designs to reduce communication, we create techniques to overlap the remaining communications with computation (when possible). We show that this is not always possible for SVD (and eigenvalue solvers) because of the two-sided process that must modify the whole trailing matrix in order to proceed from column to column of the (panel) reduction. We note that this is in contrast to linear solvers that use either Cholesky, LU, or QR factorizations, which do not need the trailing matrix when factorizing a panel [4,6,18,19].

6.1   A Study of the Ratio of Communication to Computation

While the main goal in designing efficient OOM algorithms is to minimize communication, as determined in Sect. 5, the second major objective is to overlap the remaining communications with computation (when possible). Ideally, communication is totally overlapped, in which case the OOM algorithm runs as fast

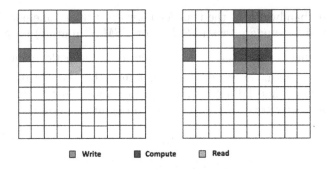

☐ Write   ■ Compute   ☐ Read

Fig. 4. Reduction of general matrix to band form – update (multi-threaded single task vs. sequential multi-task). (Color figure online)

as its in-core counterpart. We study and formulate a theorem that theoretically answers the question to what degree this overlap is possible for an OOM SVD. The basic principle that we apply to hide the communication overhead is: if a computation is using and operating on data of block k, we write back the data of block $k − 1$ and read the data of block $k + 1$. For full overlap, the communication must be in less or equal time to the computation task on the data of block k. The main and the most time consuming type of tasks in the two-stage algorithm are the update tasks (e.g., TSMQR and TSMLQ) [11]. Therefore, we focus our analysis and description on this type, as the substitution to other type can be derived easily. Figure 4 shows two scenarios for the update tasks: (1) All the threads are participating on the computation of a single task that we call *multi-threaded single task*. To hide communication we must write back the tile computed previously (pink color) and bring the next tile (cyan color) in memory in less time than the computation of the current tile (red color); and (2) Each thread works on a separate tile – called *sequential multi-task*. If there are p threads, we must write back the previously computed "p" tiles and load the next "p" tiles for the next computation while computation is happening on the current p tiles.

Theorem 1. *The OOM two-stage SVD reduction algorithm fully overlaps data communication with computation if the tile size b is at least $\dfrac{3.2\alpha}{\beta}$ for double precision (DP) arithmetic, where β is the communication bandwidth (in Bytes/s) and α is the computational performance capability of the system (in flops/s).*

Proof. First, we consider the case when all threads are working on a single task, as shown in Fig. 4 (left). A tile of size b consists of b^2 elements, which is $8b^2$ bytes in DP arithmetic. We use the DP arithmetic representation for all the subsequent formulations. Assuming that the read and write bandwidths are similar, the time t_{read} to read (or the time t_{write} to write) a tile of size b in seconds (s) is given by:

$$t_{read} = t_{write} = \frac{8b^2}{\beta},$$

where β is the bandwidth of the transfer between disk and memory. The computation cost of the update task (*TSMQR* or *TSMLQ* routine) for a tile of size b is $5b^3$ flops, yielding $t_{compute} = \dfrac{5b^3}{\alpha}$, where α is the performance capability in flops/s for the in-memory operation that must be performed (e.g., update operation; we note that TSMQR/TSMLQ reach about 80–85% of the machine peak). The necessary condition to hide the communication overhead is:

$$t_{compute} \geq t_{read} + t_{write}$$

$$=> \frac{5b^3}{\alpha} \geq \frac{16b^2}{\beta}$$

$$=> b \geq \frac{3.2\alpha}{\beta}.$$

Now consider the case where tasks are running in parallel (see Fig. 4 (right)) and each thread is working on a separate tile. If p tasks run in parallel, p tiles are brought in-memory and sent back to disk after the computation. Thus,

$$t_{read} = t_{write} = \frac{p \times 8b^2}{\beta} \quad \text{and} \quad t_{compute} = \frac{5b^3}{\frac{\alpha}{p}} = \frac{p \times 5b^3}{\alpha}.$$

Thus, to overlap communication with the computation, we must have $b \geq \dfrac{3.2\alpha}{\beta}$.

□

Table 1 shows the minimum tile sizes "b", required to completely overlap the communication with the computation for various systems. The higher the performance capability is, the larger the required tile size is in order to overcome the

Table 1. Minimum tile sizes needed in order to overlap communication time by computation for OOM SVD solver on various systems.

System	Communication bandwidth β (GB/s)	Update kernel performance (Gflop/s)	Minimum tile size to hide communication
Sandy Bridge E5-2670 WDC1002FAEX	0.05	250	16000
Haswell i7-5930K Samsung SSD EVO	0.5	200	1280
Haswell E5 2650V3 Seagate Constellation	0.15	300	6400
K40 PCI	8	960	384
P100 PCI	8	3760	1504
KNC PCI	8	768	308
KNL PCI	8	1600	640

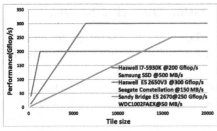
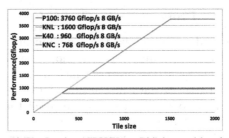

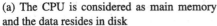

(a) The CPU is considered as main memory and the data resides in disk

(b) The Device (GPU/Xeon-Phi) is considered as main memory and the data resides in system DRAM memory

Fig. 5. Roofline performance model for the OOM SVD solver.

communication time. For example, a Sandy Bridge machine, having a computational performance of $\alpha = 250$ Gflop/s, connected to an HDD with bandwidth of $50\,\mathrm{MB/s}$, requires the tile to be of size $16,000$. Such big tile size is however not computationally feasible for the following reason:

- The tile size defines the width of the reduced band matrix. Band matrix of this size $(n \times b)$, may not fit in-memory for the second stage;
- Even if the band matrix fits in-memory, the second stage of the algorithm (reduction from band to bidiagonal form) will be extremely inefficient and will adversely affect the overall run-time.

The performance of the two-stage OOM SVD can be estimated by a roofline model for the update tasks. For double precision data, the update task computes $5b^3$ flops for a tile of size b, and communicates $16b^2$ bytes of data. In short update task computes $5b^3$ flop for $16b^2$ byte data. The arithmetic intensity, i.e. flop to byte ratio for update task is $\frac{5b}{16}$. If the system has bandwidth β, performance of two-stage OOM SVD is computed multiplying arithmetic intensity by system bandwidth, i.e. $\frac{5b \times \beta}{16}$. Figure 5 shows the roofline performance model of the OOM SVD solver for different tile sizes and for different types of systems. Figure 5 shows that the peak performance is not achievable with small tile size. At the same time, big tile sizes, that are required to reach peak performance, are also not feasible. Therefore, it can be concluded that the performance of the OOM two-stage algorithm is bounded by disk bandwidth.

7 Algorithmic Design

Sections 5 and 6 addressed the two main design considerations for OOM SVD. These are: (1) algorithms to minimize the communications between the in- and out-memory layers, and (2) overlapping the remaining communications with computation, respectively. In this section, since any system will have some available main physical memory, we analyze and develop strategies to further reduce the communication overhead for the two-stage OOM SVD algorithm by taking advantage of such memory holding data and reusing it as much as possible.

7.1 Proposition 1 - Global Communication Reducing Strategy

In order to minimize the communication overhead, our first strategy follows the idea to hold and keep in memory the tiles that are the most accessed during the whole reduction process which we call global access pattern. As we are reading and writing data in tile granularity, our first algorithmic design comprised of finding out the tiles that are used the most in order keep them in the main memory. If one tile of the matrix is held in memory, then, at each step of Algorithm 1, we can save one read and one write for the QR sweep, and similar for the LQ sweep till the step reach the tile index. For example if we hold the tile in the lower right corner, the amount of reads and writes that can be reduced by holding it in memory is $2(u-1)R + 2(u-1)W$. The most used tiles are in the lower right corner of the matrix as those tiles are used for both the QR and LQ sweeps in each step of the algorithm. Figure 6a shows the total number of reads (R) and writes (W) required during the process for each tile of a square matrix of $u \times u$ tiles. As a results, according to the proposed strategy, the available physical memory will be used to hold tiles from the lower right corner of the matrix based on their global access number of R/W. Our strategy is implemented as a decision maker engine which decide which tile is to keep in memory, when to release it back (write it back) as well as when to read it. Based on the decision a task with the corresponding dependencies is submitted to the runtime system and this task return the pointer to the data (that has been held, copied) that the next computational kernel will need. Similarly, when a computational task is done, the decision maker decide whether to keep it in memory or to initiate a task that send it back to the disk.

(a) Total number of R/W

1 R / 1 W	2 R / 2 W	u R / 2 W	....	u R / 2 W	u R / 2 W	u R / 2 W
(u−1) R / 1 W	3 R / 3 W	4 R / 4 W	....	(u+1) R / 4 W	(u+1) R / 4 W	(u+1) R / 4 W
(u−1) R / 1 W	u R / 3 W	5 R / 5 W	....	(u+2) R / 5 W	(u+2) R / 5 W	(u+2) R / 5 W
⋮	⋮	⋮	⋱	⋮	⋮	⋮
(u−1) R / 1 W	u R / 3 W	(u+1) R / 5 W	....	(2u−5) R / (2u−5) W	(2u−4) R / (2u−4) W	(2u−3) R / (2u−4) W
(u−1) R / 1 W	u R / 3 W	(u+1) R / 5 W	....	(2u−4) R / (2u−5) W	(2u−3) R / (2u−3) W	(2u−2) R / (2u−2) W
(u−1) R / 1 W	u R / 3 W	(u+1) R / 5 W	....	(2u−4) R / (2u−5) W	(2u−3) R / (2u−3) W	(2u−1) R / (2u−1) W

(b) number of R/W for 1 step

1 R / 1 W	2 R / 2 W	u R / 2 W	....	u R / 2 W	u R / 2 W	u R / 2 W
(u−1) R / 1 W	2 R / 2 W	2 R / 2 W	....	2 R / 2 W	2 R / 2 W	2 R / 2 W
(u−1) R / 1 W	2 R / 2 W	2 R / 2 W	....	2 R / 2 W	2 R / 2 W	2 R / 2 W
⋮	⋮	⋮	⋱	⋮	⋮	⋮
(u−1) R / 1 W	2 R / 2 W	2 R / 2 W	....	2 R / 2 W	2 R / 2 W	2 R / 2 W
(u−1) R / 1 W	2 R / 2 W	2 R / 2 W	....	2 R / 2 W	2 R / 2 W	2 R / 2 W
(u−1) R / 1 W	2 R / 2 W	2 R / 2 W	....	2 R / 2 W	2 R / 2 W	2 R / 2 W

Fig. 6. Snapshot of the amount of reads and writes required overall (left) and by step (right). (Color figure online)

7.2   Proposition 2 - Optimal Communication Reducing Strategy

We analyzed in detail the characteristic of the reduction algorithm. As mentioned above, it is composed of a QR followed by an LQ sweep or vice versa. The QR and the LQ sweeps consist of applying the Householder reflectors generated during the panel factorization at each step "i" to the trailing matrix. The QR and the LQ panels of a step "i" consists of the tiles in position A(:,i) and A(i,:) respectively, for example, the tiles highlighted in purple and green in Fig. 6b corresponds to the panels of step 1). The trailing matrix is the portion on the right/bottom side of the panel for the QR and LQ update respectively). Diving into the detail of the algorithm, we can find that the Householder reflectors generated at step "i" are needed as input data by all the update tasks corresponding to step "i". Thus, these tiles are read as many times as they are needed. Moreover, we can also observe that these tiles are never accessed in the upcomings steps $> i$. For example, the tiles highlighted in purple and green in Fig. 6b are read $(u - 1)$ and u times for the QR and LQ sweep, respectively. This is done only in step 1 and they are never referenced after that. As consequence of our analysis, holding one tile from the purple block during the QR sweep, then, when the QR is done, using the same space to hold one tile form the green area $(LQ$ sweep), saves about $2(u-2)$ reads in step $1, 2(u-3)$ reads in step 2, and so on. As a result, if we have physical memory to hold one tile, we can reduce $(u^2 - 3u + 2)$ reads using our proposition 2 compared to $2(u-1)R+2(u-1)W$ using proposition 1. Compared to the first strategy, we can expect a very large gain using this strategy.

Thus, if we consider that the minimum workspace of the OOM algorithm is composed of one panel (e.g., u tiles), we can find that the gain is about $\sum_{s=1}^{u-1}(u - s - 1)(u - s) + \sum_{s=1}^{u-1}(u - s - 1)(u - s - 1) = \frac{2}{3}u^3 - \frac{5}{2}u^2 + \frac{17}{6}u - 1$ reads. Since in practice the available space can be larger than a panel, then after holding the panel, we can start holding from the right bottom corner, since then these tiles become the most used step-wise or global-wise. Figure 7 compares the amount of the read that can be reduced by our two strategies. It is easy to notice that the optimal solution is the second strategy.

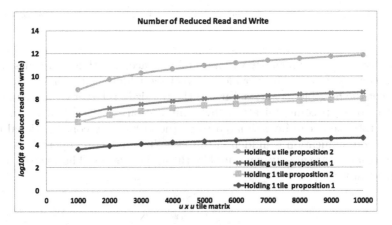

Fig. 7. Amount of reduced tile reads/writes by using the two new strategies that we propose.

8   Runtime Estimation Model for the OOM Two-Stage SVD Solver

In this section we define the model to estimate the run-time for reduction to band form of the OOM two-stage SVD solver. We first start by assuming that there is enough memory to store only u tiles for the panel and 4 tiles for temporary data. Since, as described in the above section, the algorithm is bound by the amount of tiles to be read/written, we compute the total number of tiles to be read/written. For a matrix of $u \times v$ tiles, we compute that the total number of tiles to be read or written is:

$$1 \times \sum_{s=0}^{v-1}(u-s) + 2 \times \sum_{s=0}^{v-1}(u-s)(v-s-1) = uv^2 - \frac{1}{3}v^3 + \frac{1}{2}v^2 - \frac{1}{6}v. \quad (1)$$

For a square matrix with $u \times u$ tiles, the amount of communication is $\frac{2}{3}u^3 + \frac{1}{2}u^2 - \frac{1}{6}u$ tiles to be read and $\frac{2}{3}u^3 + \frac{u^2}{2} - \frac{u}{6}$ tiles to be written (Fig. 8).

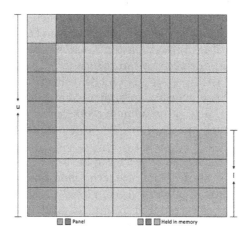

Fig. 8. Extra memory available used to hold tiles to reduce communications (Color figure online)

Usually the system memory will have more space, and thus more tiles can be kept in memory. In order to provide a correct model for the runtime estimation, we present the possible scenarios. First, if the tile size b is larger than the minimal needed to overlap communications by computation, as described in Sect. 6.1, then the total time can be estimated to be the in-memory computational time, since the communication is hidden in this case. The reduction operations $- \frac{8}{3}n^3$, where $n = u \times b$ – are mostly computed by the update kernel. Thus, the estimated time is equal to:

$$T_{est} = \frac{8n^3}{3\alpha},$$

where α is the performance of the update kernel.

The other scenario, which is commonly faced in practice for the DRAM/disk case, is when b is smaller than the minimal tile size required to entirely hide the communication. In this case, the estimated run-time is given by:

$$T_{est} = T_{read} + T_{write} + T_{compute},$$

where T_{read} and T_{write} are the times required for all the read and write, respectively, and $T_{computation}$ is the computation time. $T_{computation}$ is not straightforward to estimate. For the yellow area, it is equal to the computational time of the kernel since this data is in memory, while for the white tiles, it is equal to the communication time (since the tile size b is smaller than the minimal, the communication time is larger than the computation time). So, $T_{computation}$ will be included in T_{read} and T_{write}, and therefore, $T_{computation} = l^2 \frac{5b^3}{\alpha}$.

We define T_{opti} to be the time that has been optimized by avoiding the read and the write of the yellow area. From steps 1 to $u - l$, each tile in the yellow area is read twice and written twice (see Sect. 7.2 and Fig. 6b), meaning that at every step for each tile of the yellow area, we optimize 2 reads and 2 writes in terms of communication. Consequently, we optimize $(v - l) \times (2R + 2W)$. For the steps from $l + 1$ to u all the tiles are in memory and thus all the read and the write required for this area are avoided, which is $\frac{2}{3}l^3 + \frac{1}{2}l^2 - \frac{1}{6}l$ reads and $\frac{2}{3}l^3 + \frac{1}{2}l^2 - \frac{1}{6}l$ writes. Therefore:

$$T_{opti} = (2(v - l) + \frac{2}{3}l^3 + \frac{1}{2}l^2 - \frac{1}{6}l)(R + W).$$

Thus, the T_{read} or T_{write} is equal to the total amount of read needed without holding or optimizing, minus the T_{opti} for the read:

$$T_{write} = T_{read} = \frac{2}{3}u^3 + \frac{1}{2}u^2 - \frac{1}{6}u^2 - 2(v - l) - \frac{2}{3}l^3 - \frac{1}{2}l^2 + \frac{1}{6}l$$

Consequently, the model for estimating the time of the OOM SVD is defined by:

$$Test = \frac{4}{3}u^3 + u^2 - \frac{1}{3}u^2 - 4(v - l) - \frac{4}{3}l^3 - l^2 + \frac{1}{3}l + l^2 \frac{5b^3}{\alpha}. \tag{2}$$

9   Experimental Results

To evaluate the performance of the OOM two-stage algorithm, we have done a set of experiments. This section presents the results and analysis of the experimental data collected. We run our experiment on both Haswell i7-5930K and Haswell E5 2650 V3 machines. We use a few different systems to run our experiments. The details of the machines we used are given in Table 2. We first studied the effect of the bandwidth size on the performance. A low bandwidth predestines low performance for the OOM solver since communication will be dominant. The maximum performance in this case will be bound somewhere in the lower portion of the roofline model, since the block size must be small. Consequently,

Table 2. Machine configurations.

	SSD System: Haswell i7-5930K	Spindle System: Haswell Xeon E5 2650V3
Clock	3.5 GHz	2.3 GHz
Core	6	10
Memory	32 GB	32 GB
L2 Cache	15 MB	25 MB
Peak performance	336 Gflop/s	368 Gflops
Disk	Samsung SSD EVO 465 GB	Seagate ES.3 1000 GB

the generation of many small Read/Write tasks further increases disk traffic, and affects bandwidth of the disk negatively. Even though Samsung SSD and Seagate Constellation HDD have high theoretical R/W bandwidth, we are unable to achieve it because of complex access order and small tile sizes. Big tile sizes help to have less tasks and overcome some of these short comings, but at the same time increase run-time for the second stage (reduction of band matrix to bidiagonal form) of the two-stage algorithm. Table 3 shows the effect of tile size for the OOM SVD solver for $100k \times 60k$ matrix when we run it on the Spindle System. Basically, the second stage of the SVD solver is memory bound, and its performance depends on the memory bandwidth. Table 3 shows the execution time for both stages for two tile size. Big tile size, e.g., 512, improves the performance of the first stage compared to tiles of size 128, but it requires longer time for the second stage. However, since the second stage runs in-memory, its time remain negligible compared to the first stage.

Table 3. Effect of tile size on the runtime of the two-stage OOM SVD algorithm on the Spindle System, with a matrix of size $100k \times 60k$.

Tile size	Obtained disk bandwidth (GB/s)	Update kernel performance (Gflop/s)	First stage of two-stage SVD algorithm		Second stage of two-stage SVD algorithm time (hour)
			Estimated time (hour)	Obtained time (hour)	
128	80	300	13.42	13.90	0.06
512	110	300	3.94	3.68	0.53

Tables 4 and 5 present details of our experiments. We report the obtained bandwidth (e.g., the average of the measured bandwidth) as well as the performance of the main kernel (e.g., the update kernel) since our roofline performance model depends on it. We also report the estimated time to compute the first stage using Eq. 2 and the actual time obtained during our runs. Moreover, we report the time to performs the second stage, and thus the total time for the OOM reduction to bidiagonal using the two-stage algorithm. To give the reader a clear view about the benefit and the efficiency of our proposed OOM algorithm, we show the estimated runtime for an OOM reduction to bidiagonal using the standard one-stage algorithm. Our OOM SVD solver uses the maximum amount of memory that the system allows us to use (32 GB on these systems). From Tables 4 and 5 we can observe that the estimated execution time for the first stage is close to the observed run-time. This also highlights the importance of the performance analysis discussed above, and shows that our performance model is good enough. For example, in the Spindle System (e.g., Haswell E5 2650V3 machine), for $100k \times 100k$ matrix, the actual run time for the first stage is 19.04 h, whereas the estimated run-time using Eq. 2 is 19.70 h.

Table 4. Obtained and estimated runtime of the two-/one- stage algorithms on the SSD System.

Matrix	Size	Tile size	Benchmarking Bandwidth & Perf		two-stage BRD reduction				one-stage BRD reduction	
			Obtained bandwidth (MB/s)	Obtained Update kernel performance (Gflop/s)	Estimated OOM first stage time(h)	Obtained OOM first stage time(h)	Obtained second stage time(h)	Obtained OOM two-stage time(h)	Estimated OOM one-stage time(day)	Obtained OOM one-stage time
100k x 20k	16GB	128	180	160	0.32	0.33	0.05	0.38	1.50h	1.48h
100k x 40k	32GB	128	180	160	1.21	1.20	0.20	1.40	5.25h	5.2h
100k x 60k	48GB	512	145	160	4.50	4.36	0.48	4.84	184	N/A
100k x 80k	64GB	512	145	160	10.19	9.90	0.84	10.74	300	N/A
100k x 100k	80GB	512	145	160	17.73	17.21	1.30	18.51	426	N/A

Table 5. Obtained and estimated runtime of the two-/one- stage algorithms on the Spindle System.

Matrix	Size	Tile size	Benchmarking Bandwidth & Perf		two-stage BRD reduction				one-stage BRD reduction	
			Obtained bandwidth (MB/s)	Obtained Update kernel performance (Gflop/s)	Estimated OOM first stage time(h)	Obtained OOM first stage time(h)	Obtained second stage time(h)	Obtained OOM two-stage time(h)	Estimated OOM one-stage time(day)	Obtained OOM one-stage time
100k x 20k	16GB	128	130	300	0.174	0.171	0.005	0.176	1.4h	1.3h
100k x 40k	32GB	128	130	300	0.64	0.58	0.02	0.60	5.1h	5.0h
100k x 60k	48GB	512	110	300	3.94	3.68	0.53	4.22	242	N/A
100k x 80k	64GB	512	110	300	10.52	10.28	0.96	11.24	395	N/A
100k x 100k	80GB	512	110	300	19.70	19.04	1.54	20.57	562	N/A

Tables 4 and 5 show the overall runtime for the two-stage OOM SVD solver for both systems. We compare it to the obtained/estimated time for an OOM SVD solver by using the standard one-stage algorithm since both methods reduce a general matrix to bidiagonal form. To make the estimation as accurate as possible, we did not use the manufacturer data for the bandwidth and performance, instead, we used α and β obtained from benchmarking the bandwidth and the update kernel performance. As seen in the tables, and as expected based on our theoretical study presented in Sect. 5, the OOM two-stage algorithm is much faster than the one-stage algorithm, and can be used in practice, versus the non-practical use of the one-stage algorithm. For example, for $100k \times 100k$ matrix the two-stage OOM SVD algorithm is taking only 20.57 h, whereas the one-stage algorithm takes 562 days. Also, we notice that our optimized two-stage OOM SVD can solve big problems that are not possible to solve using the traditional SVD algorithm in limited time. This is because the two-stage OOM SVD reduces disk traffic significantly, using all the strategies and techniques explained above. In addition to what has been described and showed above in term of importance and efficiency of our proposed OOM SVD solver, we note that the $100k \times 20k$ and $100k \times 40k$ test case fits into the main memory, and thus, all algorithms run in-memory. We can see here that even for in-memory, our two-stage approach remains about 3–5 times faster than the standard one-stage approach. Last, we also note that simply using swap space in a memory constrained environment is not a viable option. We performed SWAP experiment, we force the algorithm to execute in a memory constrained environment by locking away 90% of physical memory from the application. The memory management is thus delegated to the operating system and inactive pages are sent to a disk-backed swap space. The observed disk bandwidth sampled during the execution of the algorithm is lower than 5 MB/s. The execution time of the two-stage reduction algorithm using disk SWAP was about 580 times more expensive for a small test case of size $10k \times 10k$, while the one using the one-stage algorithm cannot complete after a full two days of execution. For that, we consider that using the swap disk is not a acceptable option at all.

10   Conclusion

We developed and presented the analysis of the communication costs for the one-stage and two-stage SVD algorithms on hierarchical memories. Different communication avoiding strategies were investigated and a design with optimal communication pattern was developed. Moreover, techniques to hide communication overheads for the OOM SVD were created. Optimized implementations of the algorithms developed now enable us to solve efficiently SVD problems where the matrix is too large and does not fit into the system memory, and for which traditional SVD algorithms can not be used. We provided a clear picture about the possible optimizations and improvements. Future work includes efforts to further improve the performance of the OOM SVD by developing OOM QR factorization for tall matrices. The idea here is to precede the SVD by an OOM QR decomposition, and then perform an in-memory SVD on the small upper triangular matrix R. In case R does not fit in-memory, our OOM SVD can be applied to it to still benefit from R's smaller size.

Acknowledgments. This research was supported by the Exascale Computing Project (17-SC-20-SC), a collaborative effort of the U.S. Department of Energy Office of Science and the National Nuclear Security Administration.

References

1. Anderson, E., Bai, Z., Bischof, C., Blackford, L.S., Demmel, J.W., Dongarra, J.J., Du Croz, J., Greenbaum, A., Hammarling, S., McKenney, A., Sorensen, D.: LAPACK Users' Guide. SIAM, Philadelphia, (1992). http://www.netlib.org/lapack/lug/
2. Bischof, C., Lang, B., Sun, X.: Parallel tridiagonalization through two-step band reduction. In: Proceedings of the Scalable High-Performance Computing Conference, pp. 23–27. IEEE Computer Society Press (1994)
3. Bischof, C.H., Lang, B., Sun, X.: Algorithm 807: the SBR toolbox–software for successive band reduction. ACM TOMS 26(4), 602–616 (2000)
4. D'Azevedo, E.F., Dongarra, J.: The design and implementation of the parallel out-of-core ScaLAPACK LU, QR, and Cholesky factorization routines. Concurr. - Pract. Exp. 12(15), 1481–1493 (2000)
5. Dongarra, J.J., Sorensen, D.C., Hammarling, S.J.: Block reduction of matrices to condensed forms for eigenvalue computations. J. Comput. Appl. Math. 27(1–2), 215–227 (1989)
6. Dongarra, J.J., Hammarling, S., Walker, D.W.: Key concepts for parallel out-of-core LU factorization. Comput. Math. Appl. 35(7), 13–31 (1998)
7. Gansterer, W.N., Kvasnicka, D.F., Ueberhuber, C.W.: Multi-sweep algorithms for the symmetric eigenproblem. In: Hernández, V., Palma, J.M.L.M., Dongarra, J.J. (eds.) VECPAR 1998. LNCS, vol. 1573, pp. 20–28. Springer, Heidelberg (1999). doi:10.1007/10703040_3
8. Grimes, R., Krakauer, H., Lewis, J., Simon, H., Wei, S.-H.: The solution of large dense generalized eigenvalue problems on the cray X-MP/24 with SSD. J. Comput. Phys. 69, 471–481 (1987)
9. Grimes, R.G., Simon, H.D.: Solution of large, dense symmetric generalized eigenvalue problems using secondary storage. ACM Trans. Math. Softw. 14, 241–256 (1988)
10. Haidar, A., Tomov, S., Dongarra, J., Solca, R., Schulthess, T.: A novel hybrid CPU-GPU generalized eigensolver for electronic structure calculations based on fine grained memory aware tasks. Int. J. High Perform. Comput. Appl. (2012, accepted)
11. Haidar, A., Kurzak, J., Luszczek, P.: An improved parallel singular value algorithm and its implementation for multicore hardware. In: SC 2012: The International Conference for High Performance Computing, Networking, Storage and Analysis (2013)
12. Haidar, A., Ltaief, H., Dongarra, J.: Parallel reduction to condensed forms for symmetric eigenvalue problems using aggregated fine-grained and memory-aware kernels. In: Proceedings of SC 2011, pp. 8:1–8:11. ACM, New York (2011)
13. Haidar, A., Ltaief, H., Luszczek, P., Dongarra, J.: A comprehensive study of task coalescing for selecting parallelism granularity in a two-stage bidiagonal reduction. In: Proceedings of the IEEE International Parallel and Distributed Processing Symposium, Shanghai, China, 21–25 May 2012. ISBN 978-1-4673-0975-2
14. Lang, B.: A parallel algorithm for reducing symmetric banded matrices to tridiagonal form. SIAM J. Sci. Comput. 14, 1320–1338 (1993)
15. Ltaief, H., Luszczek, P., Dongarra, J.: High performance bidiagonal reduction using tile algorithms on homogeneous multicore architectures. ACM TOMS, 39(3) (2013, in publication)

16. Ltaief, H., Luszczek, P., Dongarra, J.: Enhancing parallelism of tile bidiagonal transformation on multicore architectures using tree reduction. In: Wyrzykowski, R., Dongarra, J., Karczewski, K., Waśniewski, J. (eds.) PPAM 2011. LNCS, vol. 7203, pp. 661–670. Springer, Heidelberg (2012). doi:10.1007/978-3-642-31464-3_67
17. Rabani, E., Toledo, S.: Out-of-core SVD and QR decompositions. In: PPSC (2001)
18. Toledo, S., Gustavson, F.G.: The design and implementation of SOLAR, a portable library for scalable out-of-core linear algebra computations. In: Proceedings of the Fourth Workshop on I/O in Parallel and Distributed Systems: Part of the Federated Computing Research Conference, IOPADS 1996, pp. 28–40. ACM, New York (1996)
19. Yamazaki, I., Tomov, S., Dongarra, J.: One-sided dense matrix factorizations on a multicore with multiple GPU accelerators*. Procedia Comput. Sci. **9**, 37–46 (2012)
20. Yamazaki, I., Tomov, S., Dongarra, J.: Non-GPU-resident dense symmetric indefinite factorization. Concurr. Comput.: Pract. Exp. (2016)

Proxy Applications

Neuromapp: A Mini-application Framework to Improve Neural Simulators

Timothée Ewart$^{(\boxtimes)}$ (iD), Judit Planas (iD), Francesco Cremonesi (iD), Kai Langen,
Felix Schürmann, and Fabien Delalondre

Blue Brain Project, École Polytechnique Fédérale de Lausanne, Genève, Switzerland
`timothee.ewart@epfl.ch`

Abstract. The increasing complexity and heterogeneity of extreme scale systems makes the optimization of large scale scientific applications particularly challenging. Efficiently leveraging these complex systems requires a great deal of technical expertise and a considerable amount of man-hours. The computational neuroscience community relies on an handful of those frameworks to model the electrical activity of brain tissue at different scales. As the members of the Blue Brain Project actively contribute to a large part of those frameworks, it becomes mandatory to implement a strategy to reduce the overall development cost. Therefore, we present *Neuromapp*, a computational neuroscience mini-application framework. Neuromapp consists of a number of *mini-apps* (small standalone applications) that represent a single functionality in one of the large scientific frameworks. The collection of several mini-apps forms a skeleton which is able to reproduce the original workflow of the scientific application. Thus, it becomes easy to investigate both single component and workflow optimizations, new software and hardware systems or future system design. New solutions can then be integrated into the large scientific applications if proved to be successful, reducing the overall development and optimization effort.

1 Introduction

In 2005, the Blue Brain Project (BBP) [2] was launched with the objective of systematic integration of the heterogeneous neuroscience data into unifying models of simulation-based research in neuroscience. For that purpose, a unique software infrastructure has been co-designed with neuroscientists resulting in a first-of-a-kind opportunity to perform *in silico* experiments on virtual tissues that are impossible using current experimental technique [12]. The HPC team of the BBP actively supports the scientists and the neuroscience community through contributions to three major neural simulators: Nest [14], NEURON [8] and STEPS [6]. These three simulators are complementary and simulate the brain and its components at different scales: $m$metric (point neuron scale), μmetric (cellular scale) and $n$metric (sub-cellular scale) respectively. All these simulators have years of development, even three decades for the NEURON simulator, and its half million lines of code (including DSL, scripting language and source to source compiler).

© Springer International Publishing AG 2017
J.M. Kunkel et al. (Eds.): ISC High Performance 2017, LNCS 10266, pp. 181–198, 2017.
DOI: 10.1007/978-3-319-58667-0_10

***In Silico* Experiments:** In a standard electrophysiological *in silico* exper-
iment, the neuroscientists define a portion of *in silico* tissue by specifying the
morphology of each neuron (the shape and geometry of all its cellular processes),
a set of connectivity rules (e.g. which neurons are connected by synapses) and a
stimulation protocol (incoming spike trains delivered to the dendrites of target
neurons) [5,11]. At the BBP, *in silico* circuits are populated with virtual neurons
in a data-derived, biologically realistic way through a multi-step procedure.

Once the portion of *in silico* tissue is defined, the neural simulation is executed. Neuroscientists typically change the stimulation protocol between experiments, in order to capture different aspects of the propagation of the electrical signals across the neural network. We consider here three kinds of stimulation patterns applied to the same neural circuit: *original-stim* is a strong
injection of current in a ring-shaped portion of the tissue, *weaker-stim* has
the same ring-pattern, but a weaker current, and finally, *Neocortical-stim* is
a stimulation pattern taken from [12] that is intended to mimic thalamocortical
innervations.

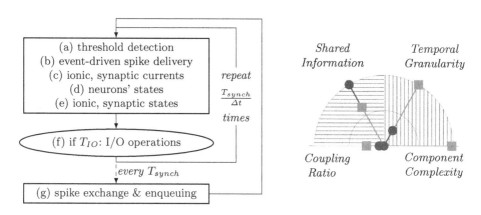

Fig. 1. Left: *In silico* experiments common algorithm. Right: performance metrics for
Diesmann *et al.* [3] (blue) and Markram *et al.* [12] (red). Vertical shading denotes
metrics that can be related to single node performance requirements in the roofline
model, whereas horizontal shading denotes metrics associated to network communication. *Component complexity* represents the number of variables to represent a single
neuron; *temporal granularity* is the inverse of the time step; *shared information* is the
number of variables communicated between neurons; *coupling ratio* is the number of
computation steps before a communication step is required. (Color figure online)

Even though *in silico* experiments can be quite different, and can even use
different software, it is possible to extract a common algorithm. The required
steps that any *in silico* experiment needs to go through are presented in Fig. 1.
The approach can be summarized as a hybrid clock-/event-driven algorithm.
In the event-driven part, spike events are issued for every neuron that satisfies
certain threshold conditions *(a)*, and spike events from other presynaptic neurons

are integrated *(b)*. For this phase, computation is performed only in case of an event. In the clock-driven part, first the contributions of ion channels and synapses to the membrane equations are computed *(c)*, then, the membrane equations are integrated numerically to update the states of neurons *(d)*, and, if needed, the states of channels and synapses[1] are also updated *(e)*. In this phase, computations are performed regularly at every time step. If the simulation time reaches a multiple of a user-defined parameter T_{IO}, expensive I/O operations are performed to output simulation results *(f)*. Finally, every few time steps (determined by the peculiar biological properties of the neural network being simulated) a synchronization step is performed to ensure all neurons receive the events they need to perform the next few states' updates *(g)*.

Computational Challenges in Neural Simulations: Simulating faithful models of the human brain requires a great amount of biological detail, thus making the effort intractable despite the constant improvement in overall performance of software and hardware technologies. Hardware improvement projections seem to indicate that a model of the scale of the human brain might become in reach within the exascale or post-exascale era. It is however anticipated that simulation software may experience delays to support the execution of extreme scale faithful models. The main reasons for this are of two folds: the complexity of large legacy software validated on numerous experiments over the years makes it hard to provide implementations able to fully exploit the rapidly changing hardware. The second main reason lies in the great diversity of biological models, each requiring a specific set of tailored solutions. This observation is illustrated in Fig. 1 where we consider two publications: a fully detailed model comprising 31,000 rat neurons [12] (i.e. a factor of 2.6 billion times smaller than the human brain) and a simplified model comprising 1.73 billion neurons [3] (i.e. 1% of the human brain scale). Figure 1 shows that different neuroscience models, whilst all representing the same biological entity, can have different performance profiles: detailed models appear to be bounded by on-node memory bandwidth whereas non-detailed models suffer more from interconnect communication specifications.

As exascale will likely require the development of unconventional solutions, a new strategy needs to be developed that allows rapid prototyping. Building on previous work presented in [4] initially focused on the NEURON software and the POWER8 platform, we introduce in this paper the *Neuromapp* framework. *Neuromapp* consists of a collection of mini-applications (generally less than a thousand lines of code) where each mini-app represents only a single critical algorithm extracted from one of the major computational neuroscientific frameworks. Each extracted mini-app provides a template from which further implementations and experiments can unfold. From these experiments, it becomes easier to verify the suitability of alternative implementations at low development cost before integrating it to the large scientific application. Furthermore,

---

[1] In the vocabulary of NEURON simulator, the synonym *mechanisms* is used for channels/synapses key word.

by assembling mini-apps together, one can reconstruct the skeleton of the original scientific application to experiment workflow optimization opportunities.

The novelty of *Neuromapp*, whose initial concept is based on efforts undertaken primarily in the US National Laboratories [7,16] lies in the fact that, on the one hand, it is only targeting application software used by the computational neuroscience community and, on the other hand, it makes an effort by design to attempt to break down large scientific applications using a very low level of algorithmic granularity. For the sake of this paper, we will only focus on a subset of mini-apps that were extracted to model the complete workflow of the NEURON software. Our hope is however that all major computational neuroscience frameworks will participate in this effort to identify common solutions and community-based performance requirements for future systems.

In summary, the key contributions of this paper are the following: (i) the development of Neuromapp, (ii) the validation of the mini-applications against parent code behaviors and (iii) the conclusions drawn from the performance analysis of the particular mini-applications.

The structure of the paper is as follows: the main concepts of the *Neuromapp* and their implementation are described in Sect. 2. Building on the framework, the following Sects. 3–6 describe four different case studies that model the aforementioned neuroscience applications. Each case study includes a detailed description of a mini-app, its performance analysis as well as a derived discussion. Finally, Sect. 7 concludes the paper.

2   Neuron Mini-application Framework

Neuromapp consists of a collection of mini-apps (generally less than a thousand lines of code) that represent the relevant functionalities of neural simulators. Individual mini-apps have multiple objectives and advantages as follows:

– **Simple:** Small portions of code extracted from the original frameworks and carefully interfaced are easy to understand, thus allowing several developers with complementary skills to rapidly become productive. The minimal set of dependencies provides opportunities for the community to share, participate and contribute to their development and improvement.
– **Fast:** The execution time of the mini-app is considerably faster than the full simulation execution time, thus, enabling faster experiments and developments. This allows faster prototyping of software/hardware solutions.
– **Realistic:** In order to ensure that the mini-apps can have a concrete impact on neuroscience software development, each mini-app is required to reproduce the same behavior as the original code with a great level of accuracy. In addition, it gives system designers the opportunity to extract performance requirements which form the basis of the co-design process.

A collection of mini-apps can be assembled to form the skeleton of the original scientific application offering the following opportunities:

- **Workflow optimization:** The optimization of scientific applications tends to focus on a small subset of major bottlenecks. By offering the possibility to quickly analyze the entire workflow, it becomes easier to identify kernel execution overlapping opportunities.
- **Software design:** mini-apps offer the possibility to suggest modifications of their programming interface and later on the original scientific application. In addition the definition of an application skeleton may require the implementation of common building blocks. These two factors favor software modularity and thus re-usability.
- **Community driven:** By extracting the key algorithms of multiple scientific applications within the same community, it becomes easier to identify commonalities and discrepancies. This favors the development of joint solutions and reusable software across the community.

Implementation: As the targeted hardware platforms come in a large variety that includes non-commodity hardware *e.g.* from Linux clusters to proprietary solutions like the IBM BlueGene/Q (BG/Q), the success of a mini-application framework lies in both its flexibility and simplicity of execution.

To this aim, Neuromapp implementation consists of a collection of libraries (to support shared memory applications) and applications (to support distributed memory applications), referred as *mini-apps* and organized around a main *driver*. The driver provides an interactive command line interface to the mini-app collection from which individual mini-apps can be accessed both for documentation (helper function implemented on top of Boost::program_options) and execution.

The distinction between shared and distributed applications in Neuromapp comes from the specificity of MPI program execution (or similar alternatives) when using schedulers such as SLURM. Schedulers require the total number of desired processors to be specified whereas the Neuromapp driver is expected to be serially executed, creating a discrepancy. To solve this issue, MPI provides the `mpi_comm_spawn` functionality which however may not always be well supported on unconventional hardware. To alleviate this issue and ensure the portability of the framework, the following options are supported in Neuromapp: The user can either start an MPI application using a system command (e.g. mpirun/srun) or directly start the mini-app MPI applications using their preferred scheduling environment. It is worthwhile to notice that such caveat does not exist in the case of shared memory applications as the threading environment is independent of the driver.

In either cases, the libraries or applications of the mini-apps must respect the simplest signature possible: `my_miniapp(int argc, char* argv[])`. This signature enables collaboration between the mini-apps to form a scientific application skeleton as long as the user sets the appropriate command line arguments for each mini-app. A summary of all the mini-apps included in Neuromapp with their inter-dependencies is shown in Table 1.

As previous performance studies [4] prove to be difficult on new hardware and sometimes required very specific solutions, Neuromapp does not provide

Table 1. Description of all mini-apps with the main hardware elements they evaluate

Mini-app	Objective
1-hello	Simple mini-app with a Hello World example
2-kernel	Reproduce the main computations of NEURON kernels (CPU)
3-solver	Linear algebra (Hines) solver of NEURON (CPU)
4-queue	Reproduce NEURON queueing (CPU)
5-cstep	Reproduce NEURON simple workflow (CPU)
6-event	Reproduce NEURON spike exchange (CPU, network)
7-synapse	Reproduce Nest synapse computation (CPU, network)
8-key/value	Generate I/O load to evaluate key/value libraries for neuroscience (I/O)
9-replib	Mimic ReportingLib (used by NEURON to store results) (I/O)

any specific performance analysis tools beyond the recording of time stamps for which utility functions are provided. It is therefore the responsibility of the developer to use external tools such as the PAPI or SCOREP libraries, to analyze performance and build performance models [15].

3   Case Study 1: Kernels

Motivation: The profiling of the NEURON simulator shows that approximately 85–90% of the computational time is spent in resolving the non-linear PDEs/ODEs representing biological mechanisms such as synapses and ion channels (step *(c)*, *(d)* and *(e)* in Fig. 1). Therefore, the goals of this mini-app is to measure the actual performance of the kernel implementation that includes gather/scatter operations, evaluate the capacity of the compiler to improve performance using vectorization and build performance models to identify which part of the hardware is limiting performance.

Description of Mini-app: The mini-app Kernel reproduces the three representative kernels of the NEURON simulator among hundreds: two ionic channels (*Na* and *Ih*) and one synapse. These are among the most common and computationally costly kernels in the fully detailed model from [12]. In NEURON, an application DSL describes biological mechanisms (such as synapses and ion channels) in "mod" files. The mod2c source-to-source utility converts the DSL language written in the "mod" files to generate a corresponding C implementation. All generated files are then compiled and linked against the rest of the NEURON framework. In the mini-app, for simplification, the C generated kernel is directly used and augmented by `#pragma` hints to facilitate vectorization (Fig. 2).

Performance Evaluation: In this section the benchmarking of one million mechanism instances are performed on the POWER8 processor. The investigated system comes in two sockets where each socket includes a POWER8 processor

```
1 #pragma ibm independent_loop
2 for (int i = 0; i < size; ++i) {
3   _v = pVEC_V[pni[i]];
4   _lvv = _v ;
5   _lmggate =
        1.0/(1.0+exp(0.062*-(_lvv))
        *(p_8[i]/3.57)));
6   _lg_AMPA =
        gmax_ProbAMPANMDA_EMS
7       *(p_21[i]-p_20[i]);
8   _lg_NMDA=gmax_ProbAMPANMDA_EMS
9       *(p_23[i]-p_22[i])*lmggate;
10  _lg = _lg_AMPA + _lg_NMDA ;
11  _lvve = (_lvv-p_7[i]) ;
```

```
12  _li_AMPA = _lg_AMPA*_lvve ;
13  _li_NMDA = _lg_NMDA*_lvve ;
14  _li = _li_AMPA+_li_NMDA ;
15  _rhs = _li;
16  _g = _lg_AMPA+_lg_NMDA;
17  _g *= 1.e2/ppvar0[i];
18  _rhs *= 1.e2/ppvar0[i];
19  pshadow_rhs[i] = _rhs;
20  pshadow_d[i] = _g;}
21 for (int i = 0; i < size; ++i) {
22  pVEC_RHS[pni[i]] -=
        pshadow_rhs[i];
23  pVEC_D[pni[i]] +=
        pshadow_d[i]; }
```

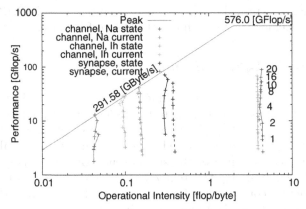

Fig. 2. Top: Example of the state functor extracted from the synapse mechanism (memory bound limited). Bottom: Roofline model of the different kernels when executing benchmark on 1 to 20 cores, with a single thread per core for both vectorized (plain line) and non-vectorized (dash-line) implementations. Peak bandwidth has been measured using the STREAM benchmark with 20 threads while the peak FLOP performance corresponds to the theoretical measure. Numbers correspond to the number of threads used for a dedicated experiment.

embarking 10 cores. Each core can manage up to 8 threads simultaneously (SMT technology). The compiler used as part of this experiment is the IBM-XLC 13.01 for its excellent auto-vectorization and prefetching capacity. Measurements of the bandwidth and FLOP performances are carried out using hardware counters provided by the PAPI library. A detailed description of the tested hardware and measurement method can be found in [4].

In this benchmark a single thread per core is used and the number of cores is increased until the maximum (20). The application performance is tested with and without vectorization. A roofline model is plotted using the best results obtained from a triad STREAM benchmark and the theoretical FLOP performance. From this plot, it can be observed that the performance of the kernels increases linearly. Most of the kernels reach peak memory bandwidth at 20 threads (memory-bound kernels). We can also observe from these results that if the vectorization is efficient it is not required for the memory bound kernels to reach hardware performance limits. The compute-bound kernels were on the other hand only able to reach 88 GFlop/s *i.e.* 15% FLOP peak performance with the *state* kernel of the *Na* mechanism. We believe that such a low performance is due to the dependency chain between instructions. However further investigations are needed to confirm this hypothesis.

Discussion: From the analysis of this mini-app, we can conclude that memory bandwidth is the key limiting factor of the NEURON simulator. We observe that vectorization can help with the compute bound kernels but is not a mandatory as most of the NEURON kernels prove to be memory bound. Therefore future system design aiming at providing optimal performance for the NEURON application must favor memory bandwidth over FLOP performance.

4   Case Study 2: Spike Exchange

The peculiarity of neural cells to exchange information via electrical and chemical connections, called synapses, is believed to be at the heart of the brain's ability to perform cognitive tasks. The spike exchange routine which supports this data exchange must ensure that any generated spike is communicated to all relevant targets before the delivery time of the spike event. Although there are many different strategies for enforcing this requirement, we focus here on the method at the basis of popular computational neuroscience software such as NEST and NEURON, which consists of: **(i)** Associating a synaptic delay to each connection between neurons corresponding to the time taken by the signal to travel through the axon; **(ii)** Performing a blocking communication step at fixed times during the simulation (depending on the minimum synaptic delay).

Motivation: Depending on the choice of neuron abstraction, the relative computational cost of the spike exchange routines in the simulation of biological networks can vary significantly (see Fig. 1). However it is still important to study its performance in details, in particular when trying to extrapolate performance at extreme scale. For example, even though historically only small improvements in performance were obtained after significant explorations on the possible implementations of the spike exchange algorithm [9], a recent study has shown that in a weak scaling scenario at extreme scales the relative importance of MPI routines begins to grow, thus causing a drop in weak scaling efficiency [13].

Description of Mini-app: This mini-app reproduces the spike exchange and enqueueing functionality of biological neural network simulators. In particular, it reproduces a hybrid shared/distributed memory implementation based on Address Event Representation (AER) [14] and blocking collective communications optimized using the concept of minimum synaptic delay [9]. The main data structures involved in the spike exchange algorithm are the following:

- **spike** contains spike time (`double`) and GID of the spiking neuron (`int`);
- **inter_thread_events** a buffer of spikes shared by all the threads on a rank;

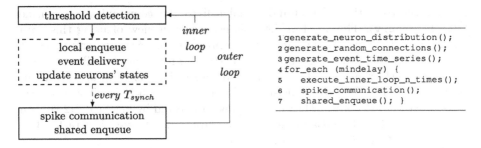

Fig. 3. Left: workflow of the core algorithm. Dashed boxes represent shared-memory, parallel tasks, whereas the non-dashed tasks are only performed by the master thread. Right: The corresponding listing of the core algorithm.

- **queue** a spikes' priority queue, local to each thread and sorted by time;
- **spikeout** a spikes buffer generated by neurons belonging to a given rank;
- **gid2out** a table of all the GIDs of neurons that are sources to at least one connection on a given rank.

Figure 3 shows the core algorithm, divided into six phases:

- **threshold detection** a condition is checked for every neuron to determine whether it generates a spike event at that time step; every spike event thus populates the spikeout buffer;
- **local enqueue** the inter_thread_events buffer is emptied and spikes are pushed to the local queue;
- **event delivery** a function is called for every spike on the queue whose delivery time is smaller than the current time step;
- **update** the states of all neurons are updated; all the sub-tasks that make up this task are lumped together, as they are irrelevant for understanding the spike exchange functionality;
- **communication** only performed whenever the simulated time exceeds a multiple of the minimum synaptic delay; it consists of two steps: first, a blocking call to MPI_Allgather is issued, during which every rank communicates to others how many spikes it intends to communicate; second a blocking call to MPI_Allgatherv is used to distribute the spike information;
- **shared enqueue** every rank consults the table gid2out to find out which spikes have a source GID relevant for itself, and populates the buffer of inter_thread_events.

The pseudo-code of the spike exchange mini-app is listed in Fig. 3. The fundamental assumption behind this mini-app is that, in contrast with an actual simulation, *the time series of events is generated a priori*.

Comparison with Original Code: The intended use case for this mini-app is to replicate the performance of the original application but with a simpler infrastructure. In this context, by performance we mean the measured wallclock time for the execution of each-individual call to the communication routine (MPI_Allgatherv). This level of detail is necessary in view of using this data to make analytical performance models and predictions. Care is taken to respect as much as possible the original data structures (with some flexibility) and to replicate exactly the original algorithm. We ran validation tests on two architectures: a small x86 cluster consisting of 8 Intel Xeon E5-2670 v2 @ 2.60 GHz nodes, each with 16 cores, 64 GB memory and connected by MVAPICH2 version 2.2b on a 100 Gb/s InfiniBand network; the larger architecture is 1 rack (1024 nodes) of BlueGene/Q (described in Sect. 6).

For validation purposes, we have implemented a version of the mini-app capable of replaying the exact same communication pattern of an actual simulation use case. We found that the required information consists of: distribution of neurons across ranks, times at which communication occurs, times and GIDs of each spike event. Inserting MPI_Barrier calls just before starting the timers and performing the Allgatherv collective operation appears to be sufficient to ensure a good degree of similarity on the small x86 cluster, but less so for the large-scale tests on BlueGene/Q. Figure 4 shows the 95% confidence intervals for the difference between measurements of the mini-app and the original code.

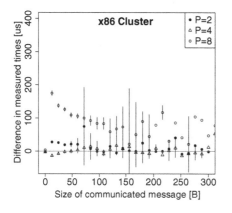 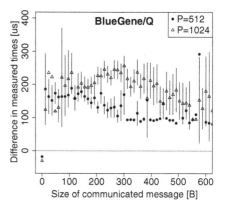

Fig. 4. Confidence intervals (level 0.95) for the mean difference between time measurements of the Allgatherv from the original code and the mini-app. Whenever the vertical lines cross the red line of value 0, there is no statistically significant difference between the code and the mini-app. (Color figure online)

On the x86 cluster, at least for $P = 2$ and $P = 4$, the value 0 lies within the confidence interval for several values of the total message size, thus allowing us to reject the hypothesis that the measurements were different. For $P = 8$, the mini-app predictions are quite good for message sizes in the range 100–200 B, but for smaller messages the mini-app consistently over-estimates the performance by roughly 100 us. On BG/Q as well the mini-app consistently over-estimates the performance by roughly 200 us; As a measure of comparison, sending a message of 100 B within an iteration of the CoreNeuron application costs roughly 40,80 and 140 us for $P = 2, 4$ and 8 on the x86 cluster; on the BlueGene/Q it costs 500 and 650 us for $P = 512$ and 1024, thus meaning that the 200 us error in prediction corresponds to roughly 30% of the original performance at larger scales.

Discussion: We demonstrated a mini-app capable of replicating exactly the communication workload of the spike exchange routines in the software CoreNeuron. Moreover, we demonstrated that the mini-app can reproduce the actual performance of the original code on small clusters of x86 hardware, but appears to consistently predict faster communication times on large architectures.

Once the validation step is completed and the mini-app produces performance predictions within an acceptable range, it is no longer necessary to provide all the detailed input information required by the validation. Instead, it becomes interesting to explore different configurations, or even different hardware architectures, by using a simpler version of the mini-app (e.g. one for which the distribution of neurons and events is determined randomly).

5   Case Study 3: Queueing

Motivation: During the execution of the spike exchange algorithm, the NEURON simulator may be considered as a discrete/event simulation. The simulator schedules events (spikes) that are enqueued and dequeued, *i.e.* removed and returned with the highest priority (smallest time). Support of this functionality is through the use of the *priority_queue* data structure for which NEURON implements a customization: a "splay tree".

The splay tree [10] is used in variable time step simulations. A splay tree is set up as a binary search tree: all items lower than the root are in the left subtree whereas those larger than the root are in the right subtree. Using comparators, the *dequeue* operation removes either the leftmost or the rightmost item. For enqueueing, the splay tree offers amortized $O(\log n)$ performance; and a sequence of M operations on an n-node splay tree takes $O(M \log n)$ time.

Description of Mini-app: This mini-app implements the queueing algorithm presented in Fig. 3. The benchmark evaluates the performance of the implementations and relies on a random generator with a uniform distribution. The goal of this mini-app is to evaluate the legacy container, comparing its performance against standard libraries (**boost** and **std**). Pseudo-code and results are reported in Fig. 5, the three test cases are referred as: *weaker-stim, Neocortical-stim* and *original-stim*. It is worthwhile to point out that through the development of this mini-app an alternative API to the legacy code based on the **std** one (push(T), pop() and top()) has been proposed.

Comparison with Original Code: This benchmark mimics the original code performance only in a single-thread version, for which an inter-thread buffer does not exist (it is merged with the single queue).

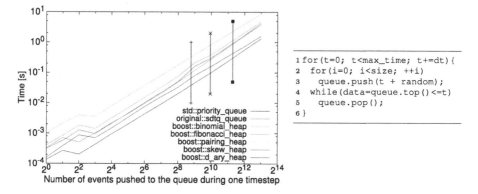

Fig. 5. Left: Benchmark suggested by Michael Hines, the x-axis is the number of elements pushed in the queue at each time step (line 3 of code on the left). $+-+$ indicates the *weaker-stim*, $\times - \times$ the *Neocortical-stim* and $\blacksquare - \blacksquare$ the *original-stim* case. Right: pseudo-code of the queueing algorithm for single thread version.

Performance Evaluation: Execution of the benchmark is carried out on an x86 cluster that includes Intel Xeon E2670@2.6 GHz nodes. Applications have been compiled using GCC 5.1 and Boost library version 1.54.

The obtained results show that `std::priority_queue` is the fastest, followed by `boost::d_ary_heap`, both using a contiguous buffer implementation. Those results show that the contiguous memory pattern increases performance as it allows better memory accesses, prefetching, *etc.* The legacy queue (splay tree) is approximately 10 times slower than the `std::priority_queue`, like all other implementations based on trees. However, we do not take into account the input random distribution; in fact, splay trees are efficient when using bias distribution.

Discussion: From this mini-app, we can conclude that `std::priority_queue` provides the best performance in the case of fixed/variable time step simulation respectively. Although the decrease in the overall time to solution of the full scientific application is negligible in the cases investigated by the neuroscientists so far (queuing being responsible for less than 2% of the total wall time), future use cases requiring faster than real time execution may benefit from this work. In addition, it is worthwhile to point out that this work allows suggesting a better interface of the queuing component which is currently under investigation for integration. Finally, as this version of the mini-app was only supporting the single thread use case, future experiments will focus on exploring the multi-threaded implementation which requires the use of an additional buffer and mutual exclusion mechanisms. One of the objectives will be to test alternative concurrent containers to avoid the use of dual containers.

6   Case Study 4: I/O Simulation Data

Although optimizing the execution of neuroscience frameworks is important, the process of creating simulation results plays a key role as well. In typical *in silico* experiments, first, the neural simulation produces and stores the results in persistent storage (usually hard disk) and, in a second step, neuroscientists use visualization or analysis tools to interpret the results. The amount of data produced varies from a few megabytes to hundreds of gigabytes or terabytes, directly impacting both simulation and analysis execution time. In some experiments, even output data is read, processed and rewritten by external applications on-the-fly, imposing a strong requirement in I/O performance. But, in any case, the step of storing simulation results is mandatory for their immediate or later analysis. For this reason, we created a mini-app to study the process of writing neural simulation results.

Motivation: NEURON offers the capability of connecting external libraries as plug-ins. At BBP, since the past ten years, neuroscientists have been using this feature to connect the simulation results to an I/O library that writes the data into a binary file. The I/O library is implemented on top of MPI and uses an in-house-defined structured format. It leverages from MPI I/O to write the simulation results in a single, large file stored in a parallel file system. Figure 6 shows how the results are structured in the file. Results are stored in a matrix format: for each simulation time step, a single row is written at once through the use of collective MPI I/O calls. Each cell of the row contains information about one neuron (GID) and there are as many cells as neurons in the simulated circuit. The contents of each cell depend on the simulation configuration set by the user: it can contain a single value per neuron or a set of values per neuron (usually, one value for each neuron compartment). Therefore, cells of the same color are written in the same collective call.

Since the real I/O bottleneck appears only when large results are produced, we mainly focus on these use cases: the process of storing a large report of neural activity. In this case study, the stimulation pattern explained and analyzed in the previous sections is not relevant, as the amount of data produced by the simulation depends only on the number of neurons and the amount of simulation time steps. However, the same configurations have been used to keep consistency across this paper. Understanding and addressing the writing problem with the real, in production application would be costly and complicated, as each simulation runs for, at least, a few hours. Moreover, understanding the code is not straightforward, so evaluating different approaches and layouts would be extremely complicated and time consuming. Therefore, trying to improve the I/O phase in this environment is not feasible.

Description of Mini-app: This mini-app reproduces the writing patterns of NEURON for output report generation. Since there are no simulation computations in the code, the mini-app just creates random data to represent the output of a real NEURON simulation and then writes the output data into a file. Even if the output data is generated randomly, different biological characteristics have been taken into account to make the output data as similar as possible to a real simulation output. For example, a *full-compartment voltage report* contains the voltage of all neuron compartments for each time step, represented as single-precision floating-point numbers. One biological characteristic of these values is that they are always in the range between -75.0 and $+75.0$. Therefore, we developed the mini-app very carefully to take all these characteristics into account.

Listing 1 shows the pseudo-code of the mini-app. First, the output data is generated randomly with the same values as a real output report could hold (line 1). Then, like NEURON does, output data is collected for several *simulation steps* (lines 3–5) and finally, written at once in a binary file (line 7). Although output data can be written at the end of each simulation step, NEURON aggregates the data of several simulation steps to get higher bandwidth. Therefore, there is one *reporting step* every few *simulation steps*. Since the mini-app does not do any simulation computation, a *sleep()* system call is performed in its place[2] (line 4), following an overwrite of the output data to avoid caching benefits (line 5). In addition, we added a timer (lines 6,8) in the mini-app to measure the performance of collective I/O. The mini-app can be configured with several parameters to test the I/O behavior in different situations. For example, the number of processes, the number of reporting steps, the number of simulation steps per one reporting step, etc. In addition, the specific amount of data written by each process can also be set, as well as the way all data blocks are combined in the file. With this last feature, we are able to run NEURON with a real use case once and generate a file with real data distributions per process. Then, the mini-app can read this file and use exactly the same data distributions.

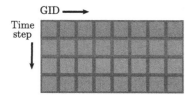

Fig. 6. Simulation results layout.

```
1 generate_random_output_data();
2 for"r"reporting_steps {
3   for"s" simulation_steps {
4     sleep_to_simulate_computing_phase();
5     overwrite_output_data(); }
6   start_io_timer();
7   MPI_collective_write(output_data);
8   stop_io_timer(); }
```

Listing 1. Mini-app pseudo-code.

The specific objectives of this mini-app are the following: (i) provide an easy-to-use tool that mimics the I/O pattern of a real neural simulator, (ii) understand the I/O behavior of the real framework and (iii) serve as the base to investigate new approaches to improve the I/O performance.

Comparison with Original Code: Before proceeding with any investigation, we must ensure that mini-app behavior matches the behavior of the original code, so any improvements obtained in the former will apply as well in the latter.

---

[2] One could argue that the sleeping phase is not needed, or it is even disturbing the I/O results, as it allows time for the I/O library to flush internal buffers in between two I/O calls. However, if we remove the sleep call, the mini-app would no longer mimic the behavior of the real framework and, therefore, any extrapolation to the real framework would be incorrect.

We added in NEURON a few lines of code to output how the real output data is distributed across process, i.e., which block of the output file is written by which process. With this information we can reproduce the exact I/O patterns of NEURON in the mini-app, and, in fact, we have checked that they match with exhaustive profiling and benchmarking. Since the data distribution is constant for each reporting time step, we just need to run the real neural simulator for one reporting time step. This execution takes in the order of a few minutes, so we can quickly get a real data distribution. Since NEURON distributes neurons across processors according to their computational weight, this leads to a scenario where different processes will write different amounts of output data. With the mini-app, it is very easy to change data distribution through command line arguments to explore which distributions give optimal performance.

Performance Evaluation: In this section, we use our mini-app to demonstrate its flexibility and adaptability to different types of systems. There is a large set of options to explore, but due to space limitations we focus on one use case and evaluate it across different systems. We run the mini-app for a certain number of reporting steps with different number of processes. Each process writes a data block of a given size at each step. The number of reporting steps was always large enough to generate a file with a final size of 10–100 GB, depending on the system, and running for at least 100 reporting steps. We determined that, on average, in a real simulation, each process writes in the order of 650 KB at each reporting step. Therefore, we chose this value as our starting point. Additionally, we include two extra points with lower and larger block sizes to evaluate their impact in bandwidth performance. The evaluation was performed on the following three systems:

- **BG/Q system**: the tests were always run on the same mid-plane of a 4-rack BlueGene/Q system (8 mid-planes in total). Each mid-plane has 512 nodes, each node has 16 IBM PowerPC A2 1.6 GHz and 16 GB SDRAM-DDR3. Nodes are connected through a 5D Torus-40 GBps network. Benchmark data was stored on GPFS. We used MPICH2 version 1.5 and IBM XL 12.01 to compile and run the mini-app.
- **x86 system**: We used 4 nodes of an x86 cluster. Each node has 8 Intel Xeon E5-1620 v3 3.50 GHz and 64 GB of DRAM. Nodes are connected through a 100 Gb/s InfiniBand network. Benchmark data was stored on a Lustre file system. We used GCC 5.3 and MVAPICH2 version 2.2b.
- **NVM system**: We used the same x86 system described above plus a set of 4 extra nodes with non-volatile memory (NVM). The nodes were provided by DDN, using their IME technology [1]. Each node has 2 Intel Xeon E5-2650 v2 2.6 GHz (16 cores/node) with hyper-threading enabled, 64 GB of DRAM and 12 Intel SSDs of 256 GB each. The total SSD capacity is 3 TB/node. IME offers a burst buffer technology from the client point of view over POSIX, MPI or IME interfaces. The SSDs of the servers are used as a caching system to the final file system. In our case, we used the MPI interface. All nodes are connected through the same InfiniBand network described before. We used GCC 5.3 and a customized implementation of MPI provided by DDN (based on MVAPICH2 version 2.1).

In order to perform the evaluation, we measured the bandwidth of the collective call `MPI_File_write_all()`. Only in the case of the NVM system tests, we disabled MPI's collective buffers, as suggested by IME developers.

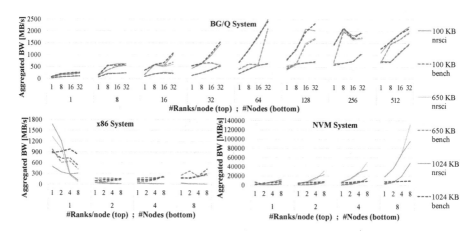

Fig. 7. I/O performance of the mini-app on different systems: BG/Q with GPFS (top), x86 system with Lustre (bottom left) and NVM system with IME (bottom right). (Color figure online)

Figure 7 shows the aggregated bandwidth reported by the mini-app on the different evaluated platforms. We evaluate three different cases where each rank writes a block of 100 KB (purple), 650 KB (orange) or 1024 KB (blue) at each I/O operation. The tag *nrsci* (solid lines) corresponds to the mini-app explained in this section, whereas the tag *bench* (dashed lines) corresponds to the mini-app without the simulation phase, so it behaves as a purely I/O benchmark.

We cannot explain all the results in the detail, but we would like to highlight the necessity of having a good representation of the application's I/O pattern. As we can see, the results substantially vary from the different block sizes used. In addition, in some cases, especially on the NVM system, the performance reported by an I/O benchmark does not match to the I/O impact that the application would experiment. The reason why the mini-app reports higher bandwidth is because the I/O library (IME) uses the simulation phase of the mini-app to flush internal buffers, thus resulting in a transparent overlapping of computation (on the mini-app side) and I/O flushing (on the I/O library side). In this case, increasing block size to match a large scale simulation output converges to a more realistic bandwidth, close to the *bench* values, but still slightly higher.

Discussion: We developed a mini-app that mimics how output reports are generated from a widely used neuroscience framework. With this, we demonstrate that (i) the I/O patterns of complex neuroscience frameworks can be extracted and simplified as a mini-app to be deeply analyzed and (ii) the ability of our mini-app to easily adapt to a wide range of hardware and software technologies and predict the expected performance of the real neural simulator. We test the mini-app on three different environments: a supercomputer, an x86 cluster and an NVM cluster, and proved its flexibility to adapt to any type of system. The power of this mini-app is that we can now present a simple, portable code to hardware vendors and software developers and work closely with them towards improving the performance of our real neuroscience framework.

7   Conclusions

Neural simulators are large frameworks used by neuroscientists on a daily basis to simulate the electrical activity of brain tissue. However, with the current software and hardware technologies, these frameworks are far from being able to simulate a human brain in real time at scale. Thus adapting these frameworks to the new, more powerful software and hardware technologies becomes a challenging necessity, especially when dealing with non-modular legacy community software.

To facilitate the long term development of the neuroscience community as well as future system design, we introduced in this paper the Neuromapp framework. Neuromapp consists of a set of small mini-apps that mimic individual parts of neural simulators which may be combined to form the original scientific application. Our approach offers numerous benefits to the computational neuroscience community, like **simplicity**, **flexibility** and, of course, they are a **faithful reproduction** of the original frameworks.

In this paper, we demonstrate that Neuromapp can be used to try new software or hardware solutions, analyze their performance and then extrapolate the results to decide whether they benefit the original framework. With our approach, we can considerably reduce the software development cycle by providing the infrastructure to quickly test new hardware and software design solutions.

We encourage the computational neuroscience community to actively contribute to it so that it becomes the place where key algorithms used in the community can be implemented. As future work, we plan to keep extending the framework with more mini-apps that cover a wider range of neural simulators and their functionalities, more specifically, the "in-memory compression" topic due to the huge amount of dynamic memory that brain simulators need. In addition, we expect additional positive outcomes such as code refactoring and redesign, but also the identification of common algorithms across scientific applications which could be better placed into a common library. Neuromapp source code can be found at: https://github.com/BlueBrain/neuromapp.

Acknowledgments. We would like to thank the HPC team of BBP, Till Schumann and Michael Hines for their discussions and contributions; DDN developers for the help and feedback provided and CSCS for the hardware resources and support provided. This work has been funded by the EPFL Blue Brain Project (funded by the Swiss ETH board) and the Supercomputing and Modeling for the Human Brain (SMHB) project supported by the German Helmholtz Association.

References

1. DDN IME. http://www.ddn.com/products/infinite-memory-engine-ime14k
2. EPFL: Blue Brain Project. http://bluebrain.epfl.ch
3. Diesmann, M.: Brain-scale neuronal network simulations on K. In: Proceedings of the 4th Biosupercomputing Symposium: Next-Generation Integrated Simulation of Living Matter (ISLiM) Program of MEXT (2012)
4. Ewart, T., et al.: Performance evaluation of the IBM power8 architecture to support computational neuroscientific application using morphologically detailed neurons. In: PMBS 2015, pp. 1:1–1:11. ACM, New York (2015)
5. Harris, K.D., Shepherd, G.M.G.: The neocortical circuit: themes and variations. Nat. Neurosci. **18**(2), 170–181 (2014)
6. Hepburn, I., et al.: Steps: efficient simulation of stochastic reaction-diffusion models in realistic morphologies. BMC Syst. Biol. **6**(1), 1–19 (2012)
7. Heroux, M.A., et al.: Improving performance via mini-applications. Technical report, Sandia National Laboratories (2009)
8. Hines, M.: NEURON, a program for simulation of nerve equations. In: Eeckman, F.H. (ed.) Neural Systems: Analysis and Modeling, pp. 127–136. Springer, Heidelberg (1993). doi:10.1007/978-1-4615-3560-7_11
9. Hines, M., et al.: Comparison of neuronal spike exchange methods on a Blue Gene/P supercomputer. Front. Comput. Neurosci. **5**(49) (2011)
10. Jones, D.W.: An empirical comparison of priority-queue and event-set implementations. Commun. ACM **29**(4), 300–311 (1986)
11. Markram, H., et al.: Interneurons of the neocortical inhibitory system. Nat. Rev. Neurosci. **5**(10), 793–807 (2004)
12. Markram, H., et al.: Reconstruction and simulation of neocortical microcircuitry. Cell **163**(2), 456–492 (2015)
13. Ovcharenko, A., et al.: Simulating morphologically detailed neuronal network at etreme scale. In: International Conference on Parallel Computing (ParCo) (2015)
14. Plesser, H.E., Eppler, J.M., Morrison, A., Diesmann, M., Gewaltig, M.-O.: Efficient parallel simulation of large-scale neuronal networks on clusters of multiprocessor computers. In: Kermarrec, A.-M., Bougé, L., Priol, T. (eds.) Euro-Par 2007. LNCS, vol. 4641, pp. 672–681. Springer, Heidelberg (2007). doi:10.1007/978-3-540-74466-5_71
15. Williams, S., Waterman, A., Patterson, D.: Roofline: an insightful visual performance model for multicore architectures. Commun. ACM **52**(4), 65–76 (2009)
16. Zerr, R.J., Baker, R.S.: SNAP: SN (discrete ordinates) application proxy: description. Technical report LA-UR-13-21070, Los Alamos National Laboratories (2013)

gearshifft – The FFT Benchmark Suite for Heterogeneous Platforms

Peter Steinbach[1(✉)] and Matthias Werner[2]

[1] Max Planck Institute of Molecular Cell Biology and Genetics,
01307 Dresden, Germany
`steinbac@mpi-cbg.de`
[2] Center for Information Services and High Performance Computing,
TU Dresden, 01062 Dresden, Germany
`Matthias.Werner1@tu-dresden.de`

Abstract. Fast Fourier Transforms (FFTs) are exploited in a wide variety of fields ranging from computer science to natural sciences and engineering. With the rising data production bandwidths of modern FFT applications, judging best which algorithmic tool to apply, can be vital to any scientific endeavor. As tailored FFT implementations exist for an ever increasing variety of high performance computer hardware, choosing the best performing FFT implementation has strong implications for future hardware purchase decisions, for resources FFTs consume and for possibly decisive financial and time savings ahead of the competition. This paper therefor presents `gearshifft`, which is an open-source and vendor agnostic benchmark suite to process a wide variety of problem sizes and types with state-of-the-art FFT implementations (`fftw`, `clFFT` and `cuFFT`). `gearshifft` provides a reproducible, unbiased and fair comparison on a wide variety of hardware to explore which FFT variant is best for a given problem size.

Keywords: Signal processing · FFT · fftw · cufft · clfft · GPU · GPGPU · Benchmark · HPC

1 Introduction

Fast Fourier transforms (FFTs, [31]) are at the heart of many signal processing and phase space exploration algorithms. Examples for their substantial usage include image reconstruction in life sciences [27,28], amino acid sequence alignment in bioinformatics [22], phase space reduction for weather simulations [23], option price analysis and prediction in financial mathematics [19] and machine learning [5] to just name a few.

An FFT is a fast implementation of the discrete Fourier transform which is a standard text-book mathematical procedure. The forward transform is a mapping from an array x of n complex numbers in the time domain to an array X of n complex numbers in the frequency domain (referred to as Fourier domain):

$$X[k] = \sum_{j=0}^{n-1} x[j] e^{\frac{-2\pi i j k}{n}} \tag{1}$$

© Springer International Publishing AG 2017
J.M. Kunkel et al. (Eds.): ISC High Performance 2017, LNCS 10266, pp. 199–216, 2017.
DOI: 10.1007/978-3-319-58667-0_11

with k being an integer index within $0 \le k < n$ and the imaginary unit $i^2 = -1$. This operation was found to be computable in $\mathcal{O}(n \log n)$ complexity by Cooley-Turkey [8], who rediscovered findings of Gauss [16]. The basis of the Cooley-Turkey approach is the observation that the DFT of size n can be rewritten by smaller DFTs of size n_1 and n_2 by the factorization of $n = n_1 n_2$. Given the indices $j = j_1 n_2 + j_2$ and $k = k_1 + k_2 n_1$, Eq. (1) can be re-expressed as:

$$X[k_1 + k_2 n_1] = \sum_{j_2=0}^{n_2-1} \left(\left(\sum_{j_1=0}^{n_1-1} x[j_1 n_2 + j_2] e^{\frac{-2\pi i j_1 k_1}{n_1}} \right) e^{\frac{-2\pi i j_2 k_1}{n}} \right) e^{\frac{-2\pi i j_2 k_2}{n_2}} \quad (2)$$

Equation (2) describes a decomposition that can be performed recursively [15]. Here, n_1 is denoted *radix* as it refers to n_1 transforms of size n_2. These smaller transforms are combined by a *butterfly* graph with n_2 DFTs of size n_1 on the outputs of the corresponding sub-transforms. Radix-2 DFTs (n being a power of two) are mostly implemented with the Cooley-Tukey algorithm [8]. Stockham's formulations of the FFT can be applied [29] to avoid incoherent memory accesses. Arbitrary and mixed radices can be tackled with the prime-factorization or Chirp Z-transform implemented by the Bluestein's algorithm [6].

The top ten list of the fastest worldwide computer installations (Top500 [24]) shows that the used hardware is by far not homogeneous in terms of vendor and composition. This trend can be even more observed in practice, where library architects and domain specialists are confronted with an essential question: Which FFT implementation works best on what hardware?

With increasing experimental data production [18] and simulation output bandwidths [23], input data to FFT libraries in the order of gigabytes becomes the standard. With the advent of graphics processing units (GPUs) for scientific computing around the beginning of the 21st century and the subsequent availability of general purpose programming paradigms to program these [11], vendor-specific and open-source libraries to perform FFTs on accelerators emerged (cuFFT [25] by Nvidia, open-source clFFT [3]) to offer performance which supersedes traditional high-performance implementations running on standard Central Processing Units (CPUs) such as the open-source fftw library [15] or the Intel specific MKL [20].

To our surprise, comprehensive and peer-reviewed benchmarks of FFT implementations across different hardware platforms have not been published extensively. Either only specific hardware is chosen for the benchmark [2,12,26] or only specific FFT implementation variants are tested [9,10]. In addition, many performance benchmarks are tied to domain-specific implementations [14] that either lack comprehensiveness or the ability to map the results obtained to other implementation requirements.

Thus, a new open-source benchmark package called gearshifft [17] has been developed. It is able to benchmark available state-of-the-art FFT libraries in a reproducible, automated, comprehensive and vendor-independent fashion on CPUs and GPUs. gearshifft helps library authors and domain-specific developers to choose the best FFT library available. The discussion above motivates the following design goals of gearshifft:

- open-source and free code
- standardized output format for downstream statistical analysis
- state-of-the-art build system
- open and extensible architecture with generic interface
- community-ready and vendor independent project infrastructure through version control and public accessibility

Given the multitude of mathematical formulations and the heterogeneity of hardware, `gearshifft` approaches the challenge of benchmarking a variety of FFT libraries from a user perspective. This means, that the following parameters should be easy to study:

- FFT dimension and radix-type (e.g. $32 \times 32 \times 32$ as radix-2 3D FFT)
- transform kinds, i.e. real-to-complex or complex-to-complex transforms
- precision, i.e. 32-bit or 64-bit IEEE floating point number representation
- memory mode
  - *in-place*: the input data structure is used for storing the output data (low memory footprint and low bandwidth are to be expected)
  - *out-of-place*: where the transformed input is written to a different memory location than where the input resides (high memory footprint and high bandwidth are to be expected)
- transform direction, i.e. forward (from discrete space to frequency space) or backward (from frequency space to discrete space)

The remainder of this article is organized as follows: the C++ implementation of `gearshifft` is discussed in Sect. 2 after an introduction to modern FFT APIs. The largest part of the paper is dedicated to the presentation of first results in Sect. 3, after which our conclusions are presented in Sect. 4.

2   Implementation

2.1   Using a Modern FFT Library

Before discussing the design of `gearshifft`, a brief introduction into the use and application programming interfaces (APIs) of modern FFT libraries is required to illustrate the design choices made. Many FFT libraries today, and particularly those used in this study, base their API on `fftw` 3.0.

Here, in order to execute an FFT on a given pointer to data in memory, a data structure for plans has to be created first using a planner. For this, the FFT problem is defined in terms of rank (1D, 2D or 3D), shape of the input signal (the dimensional extent), type of the input signal (single or double precision of real or complex inputs), type of the transformation (real-to-complex, complex-to-complex, real-to-half-complex) and memory mode of the transformation (in-place versus out-of-place). These parameters describing the FFT problem are then used as input to the planner.

The planner is a piece of code inside `fftw` that tries to find the best suited radix factorization based on the shape of the input signal. By default, it then

performs several FFTs derived from the mathematical descriptions discussed in
Sect. 1 on the input data to sample the runtime of different FFT implementations
available inside `fftw`. This ensemble of runtimes is then used to find the optimal
FFT implementation to use. After the plan has been created, it is used to execute
the FFT itself.

Listing 1. Minimal usage example of the `fftw` single precision real-to-complex planner
API. Memory management is omitted.

```
1 int shape[] = {32,32,32};
2 fftw_plan r2c_plan = fftw_plan_dft_r2c(
3   /* rank, here 3D       */   3,
4   /* shape of the input */   shape,
5   /* input data array   */   (float *) input_buffer,
6   /* output data array  */   (fftwf_complex *) output,
7   /* plan-rigor flag    */   FFTW_ESTIMATE );
8 fftwf_execute(r2c_plan);
```

Listing 1 illustrates the `fftw` API for a single precision real-to-complex out-
of-place transform. `fftw` offers the freedom to choose the degree of optimization
for finding the most optimal FFT implementation for the signal at hand by
means of the planner flag, also referred to as plan rigors. Listing 1 uses the
`FFTW_ESTIMATE` flag as an example, which is described in the `fftw` manual [13]:

"`FFTW_ESTIMATE` specifies that, instead of actual measurements of different
algorithms, a simple heuristic is used to pick a (probably sub-optimal) plan
quickly. With this flag, the input/output arrays are not overwritten during
planning."

`fftw` offers five levels for this planning flag, where two further descriptions are
given here:

"`FFTW_MEASURE` tells `fftw` to find an optimized plan by actually computing several FFTs and measuring their execution time. Depending on your
machine, this can take some time (often a few seconds).
`FFTW_WISDOM_ONLY` is a special planning mode in which the plan is only
created if wisdom is available for the given problem, and otherwise a NULL
plan is returned."

In `fftw` terminology, *wisdom* is a data structure representing a more or less
optimized plan for a given transform. The `fftw_wisdom` binary, that comes with
the `fftw` bundle, generates hardware adapted wisdom files, which can be loaded
by the wisdom API into any `fftw` application. `cuFFT` and `clFFT` follow this API
mostly, only discarding the plan rigors and *wisdom* infrastructure, cp. Listing 2.

Listing 2. Minimal usage example of the `cuFFT` single precision real-to-complex planner API. Memory management is omitted.

```
1 int N = 32;
2 cufftHandle plan;
3 cufftPlan3d(&plan, N, N, N, CUFFT_R2C);
4 cufftExecR2C(plan, input_buffer, output);
```

Table 1. Methods an FFT client in `gearshifft` has to implement

constructor	get_alloc_size	execute_forward
destructor	get_transfer_size	execute_inverse
allocate	get_plan_size	upload
destroy	init_forward	download
	init_inverse	

2.2 The Architecture of `gearshifft`

`gearshifft` is developed as an open-source framework using C++ (following the 2014 ISO standard [21]) and the Boost Unit Test Framework (UTF, [7]). One goal is to have a unified benchmark infrastructure and an extensible set of FFT library clients. The benchmark framework is independent of the used FFT library and provides the measuring environment, data handling and processing of results. `gearshifft` involves template meta-programming for a compile-time constant interface between the clients and the benchmark framework. Such a generic approach is necessary to obtain comparable results between FFT libraries and reproducible data for later statistical analysis while keeping code redundancy and overhead at a minimum.

In `gearshifft` a benchmark is meant to collect performance indicators of the operations in Table 1 defining the interface for the FFT clients. Different parameters such as precision, FFT extents, transform variant, device type or FFT library relate to different benchmarks. `gearshifft` controls many of them by command line arguments. The FFT libraries are related to different `gearshifft` binaries (`gearshifft_cufft`, ...). For the full documentation of `gearshifft` the reader is referred to [17].

There are common interfaces for the context management and for the FFT workflow. The user has to implement the context and the FFT client class. The `create` and `destroy` context methods of the client encapsulate time-consuming device and library initialization, which are measured separately and run only once. The library only must be initialized within the FFT client when the library stores plan information (cp. `fftw` wisdoms). The client's context class derives from `ContextDefault` which enables to access and extend the program options.

Listing 3. Required template arguments for FFT client implementation

```
1 template<
2   typename TFFT,        // e.g. gearshifft::FFT_Inplace_Real, ...
3   typename TPrecision,  // e.g. double, float, ...
4   size_t   NDim         // 1,..,3
5   /* .. further template types if needed .. */ >
6 struct MyFFTClient;
```

The FFT client implementation in Listing 3 is instantiated once per benchmark run and follows the *resource allocation is initialization* (RAII) idiom [30].

`gearshifft` invokes the FFT client methods listed in Table 1 to perform the benchmarks and to populate the benchmark data. The FFT client can assign user-defined template types to create different FFT client classes to mimic various use cases.

Depending on the FFT library, after a forward transform the same plan handle might be recreated for backward transform. This saves memory as there is only one plan allocated at any point in time. For example, a `cuFFT` plan allocation can be several times bigger than the actual signal data for the FFT. `fftw` can overwrite input and output buffers during the planning phase, when e.g. `FFTW_MEASURE` is used. Afterwards, the buffers can be filled with data. In turn, this plan handle cannot be recreated later on, as the result buffer of the previous plan would be overwritten at plan recreation. `gearshifft`'s compile-time interface supports this use case, where both plans are allocated before the round-trip FFT starts. The **gearshifft** interface also allows library-specific time measurements, which is only implemented for the `cuFFT` library at the moment, where CUDA events measure the runtime on GPU. For `fftw` and `clFFT`, the CPU timer exposed by the C++14 `chrono` header is used.

Listing 4. Define FFT client types for corresponding FFTs

```
1 namespace MyFFT {
2   using Inplace_Real = gearshifft::FFT<
3     gearshifft::FFT_Inplace_Real, MyFFTClient, TimerCPU >;
```

Listing 4 shows a type definition for the user implemented class `MyFFTClient` and specifies an in-place-real FFT (cp. Listing 3). This type is added to a list for the benchmark runner, as demonstrated in `benchmark.cpp` (Listing 5). The `gearshifft::List` is a compile-time constant list, which holds the different template instantiations of an FFT client. `FFT_Is_Normalized` denotes a compile time flag if the backward transformed data needs to be normalized in order to achieve identity with the input.

Listing 5. Using FFT client types to run the benchmarks

```
1  using namespace gearshifft;
2  using Context           = MyFFT::Context;
3  using FFTs              = List<MyFFT::Inplace_Real>;
4  using Precisions        = List<float, double>;
5  using FFT_Is_Normalized = std::false_type;
6  int main( int argc, char* argv[] ) {
7    try {
8      Benchmark<Context> benchmark;
9      benchmark.configure(argc, argv);
10     benchmark.run<FFT_Is_Normalized, FFTs, Precisions>();
11   } catch(const std::runtime_error& e) { \\ ...
```

The back-end of **gearshifft** uses the Boost Unit Test Framework to generate the benchmark instances within a tree data structure, which is referred to as the benchmark tree. The measurement layout and benchmark framework are

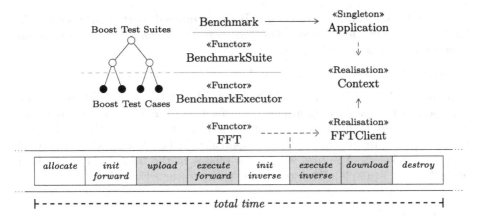

Fig. 1. The benchmark framework of `gearshifft` using Boost UTF and a realized FFT interface; Here, only FFT interfaces are shown, that are measured (gray operations are measured by device timers if provided); Context also has an implicit interface, which is omitted here.

illustrated in Fig. 1. One single run comprises time measurement of each operation (`allocate`, ...). The total time measures all from `allocate` to `destroy`. The size of the allocated buffers and the memory information of the FFT library (if available) is recorded as well. The functor `FFT` calls the FFT client operations wrapped with time measurements. The input data buffer, filled with a see-saw function in $[0, 1)$ in `BenchmarkData`, is held by the `BenchmarkExecutor`. A copy is given to the `FFT` functor in each run and is used for the output. For each benchmark configuration a number of warmups and benchmark repetitions is performed. After the last benchmark run the round-trip transformed data is validated against the original input data. The error ε is computed by the sample standard deviation of input and round-trip output. When that error is greater than 10^{-5}, the benchmark is marked as failed and `gearshifft` continues with the next configuration in the benchmark tree.

`gearshifft` adapts the API of the different FFT libraries to a common interface. The `FFT` functor defines the interface of the common FFT workflow. This pattern refers to Wrapper Facades and Static Adapter design pattern which provides static polymorphism at compile-time [4]. Currently, `gearshifft` implements three different FFT libraries, `cuFFT` (CUDA runtime, [25]) for Nvidia GPUs, `clFFT` (OpenCL runtime, [3]) for CPU and GPUs and `fftw` for CPU (C/C++ runtime, [15]). By this selection, an accelerator-only, a mixed CPU-GPU and a CPU-optimized library is covered. The `cmake` build system is used to setup build paths to construct one executable for each supported FFT library found by `cmake` as well as for collecting the include paths during the build process and library locations for linking later on. There are options for disabling FFT libraries or pointing to non-standard installation paths and to configure compile-time constants such as the error-bound as well as the number of warmups and repetitions.

For the command-line arguments, Boost is utilized, particularly for benchmark list creation and selection. There are several `gearshifft` program options to control benchmark settings, for example:

```
1 gearshifft_clfft −e 128x128 1024 −r */float/*/Inplace_Real −d cpu
```

Here, the `clFFT` benchmarks would first run a 128×128-point FFT and then a 1024-point FFT, performing in-place transforms with real input data in single-precision. The default setting instructs `gearshifft` to use all CPU cores and to store the results into result.csv. The `gearshifft` benchmark selection syntax supports wildcards. The first wildcard * relates to the title of the FFT client (`ClFFT` in this example). The second one refers to the FFT extents.

3   Results

3.1   Experimental Environment

This section will discuss the results obtained with `gearshifft v0.2.0` on various hardware in order to showcase the capabilities of `gearshifft`. Based on the applications in [27,28], 3D real-to-complex FFTs with contiguous single-precision input data are chosen for the experiments. If not stated, this is the transform type assumed for all illustrations hereafter. Expeditions into other use cases will be made where appropriate. The curious reader may rest assured that a more comprehensive study is possible with `gearshifft`, however the mere multiplicity of all possible combinations and use cases of FFT render it neither feasible nor practical to discuss all of them here.

This study concentrates on three modern and current FFT implementations available free of charge: `fftw` (3.3.6pl1, on x86 CPUs), `cuFFT` (8.0.44, on Nvidia GPUs) and `clFFT` (2.12.2, on x86 CPUs or Nvidia GPUs). This is considered as the natural starting point of developers beyond possible domain specific implementations. It should be noted, that this will infer not only a study in terms of hardware performance, but also how well the APIs designed by the authors of `fftw`, `clFFT` and `cuFFT` can be used in practice.

The results presented in the following sections were collected on three hardware installations: All systems presented in Table 2 will be used for the bench-

Table 2. Benchmark hardware

	Taurus		Hypnos	Islay
	HPC cluster [33]		HPC cluster [1]	Workstation
CPU family	Haswell Xeon	Sandybridge Xeon	Haswell Xeon	Haswell Xeon
CPU model	2× E5-2680 v3	2× E5-2450	2× E5-2603 v3	2× E5-2640 v3
RAM	64 GiB	48 GiB	64 GiB	64 GiB
GPU (PCIe3.0)	4x K80	2x K20x	1x P100	1x GTX 1080
GPU memory	4x 12 GiB	6 GiB	16 GiB	8 GiB
GPU driver	367.48	367.48	367.48	367.57
OS	RHEL 6.8	RHEL 6.8	Ubuntu 14.04.3	CentOS 7.2

marks in this section. Access was performed via an `ssh` session without running a graphical user interface on the target system. All measurements used the GNU compiler collection (GCC) version 5.3.0 as the underlying compiler. All used GPU implementations on Nvidia hardware interfaced with the proprietary driver and used the infrastructure provided by CUDA 8.0.44 if not stated otherwise. After a warmup step a benchmark is executed ten times. From this, the arithmetic mean and sample standard deviations are used for most of the figures.

3.2 Overhead of gearshifft

`gearshifft` is designed to be a lightweight framework with a thin wrapper for the FFT clients, where the interface between back-end and front-end is resolved at compile-time. Performance indicators of each benchmark are collected and buffered to be processed after the last benchmark finished. For validation purposes, a cuFFT standalone code [17] was created that provides a timer harness like `gearshifft` (referred to as *standalone*). In addition, the time to solution of a straightforward implementation of a round-trip FFT was measured as well (referred to as *standalone-tts*). Both invoke a warm-up step and ten repetitions of the entire round-trip FFT process. Figure 2 shows the impact of the `gearshifft` internal time measurement with cuFFT for two input signal sizes. Figure 2a illustrates that the time measurement distribution of `gearshifft` overlaps with *standalone* code using multiple timers. A comparison of *gearshifft* and *standalone-tts* visually shows a shift in the average obtained timing result (most likely due to timer object latencies), the scale of this shift resides in the regime below 2% which we consider negligible. We make this strong claim also because one of the goals of `gearshifft` is measuring individual runs of the benchmark for downstream statistical analysis, thus using one timer object would prohibit this core feature of the benchmark. Figure 2b shows the impact of larger input

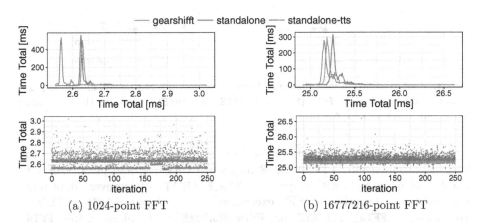

(a) 1024-point FFT   (b) 16777216-point FFT

Fig. 2. Time-to-solution measured in *gearshifft* (`cuFFT`), in a *standalone* `cuFFT` application using multiple timer objects and in a standalone application using one timer object (*standalone-tts*) for a single-precision in-place real-to-complex round-trip FFTs on the K80 [33].

signals on the time measurement result. Here, the difference between *gearshifft*, *standalone* and *standalone-tts* decreases even more and converges to a permille level (the longer duration of the benchmark mitigates timer object latencies).

3.3 Time to Solution

The discussion begins with the classical use case for developers that might be accustomed to small size transforms. As such, an out-of-place transform with `powerof2` 3D signal shapes will be assumed. The memory volume required for this operation amounts to the real input array plus an equally shaped complex output array of the same precision. Figure 3 reports a comparison of runtime results of `powerof2` single-precision 3D real-to-complex forward transforms from `fftw` and `cuFFT`. It is evident that given the largest device memory available of 16 GiB, the GPU data does not yield any points higher than 8 GiB. The more recent GPU models supersede `fftw` which used all 2×12 CPU Intel Haswell cores. Any judgment on the superiority of `cuFFT` over `fftw` can be considered premature at this point, as `fftw` was used with the `FFTW_ESTIMATE` planner flag.

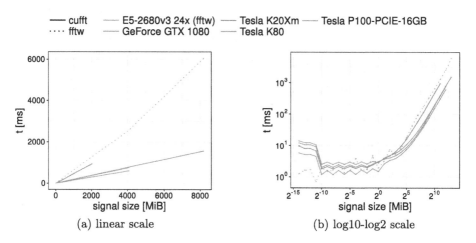

Fig. 3. Time-to-solution for `powerof2` 3D single-precision real-to-complex out-of-place forward transforms using `fftw` (`FFTW_ESTIMATE`) and `cuFFT`. (b) shows the same data as (a) but in a log10–log2 scale.

Figure 4 compares the time-to-solution to the actual time spent for the FFT operation itself. `FFTW_MEASURE` imposes a total runtime penalty of 1 to 2 orders of magnitude with respect to `FFTW_ESTIMATE`. It however offers superior performance considering FFT execution time compared to `FFTW_ESTIMATE`. To compare `FFTW_ESTIMATE` or `FFTW_MEASURE` with plans using `FFTW_WISDOM_ONLY`, wisdom files are generated with the `fftw_wisdom` binary. `fftw_wisdom` precomputed plans for a canonical set of sizes (powers of two and ten up to 2^{20}) in `FFTW_PATIENT` mode, which in all took about one day on Taurus

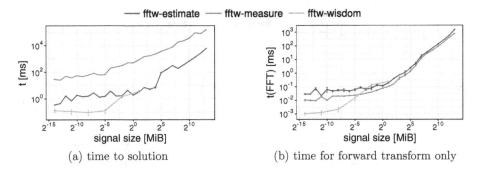

(a) time to solution

(b) time for forward transform only

Fig. 4. fftw on Intel E5-2680v3 CPU with FFTW_ESTIMATE, FFTW_MEASURE and FFTW_WISDOM_ONLY computing powerof2 3D single-precision real-to-complex in-place forward transforms. (a) reports the time to solution, whereas (b) shows the time spent for the execution of the forward transform only. Both figures use a log10–log2 scale.

[33] using (see [13] for command-line flag details): fftwf–wisdom −v −c −n − T 24 −o wisdomf.

As during plan creation, the *wisdom* has to be loaded from disk only, the planning times for calling the planner with FFTW_WISDOM_ONLY are drastically reduced. Figure 4b shows that the user is rewarded by pure FFT runtimes of less than an order of magnitude for small signal sizes. Unexpectedly, the FFT runtimes become larger than those of FFTW_ESTIMATE for input signal sizes of more than 32 KiB, which apparently contradicts the FFTW_PATIENT setting which should find better plans than FFTW_MEASURE. It must be emphasized that the planning times for FFTW_MEASURE become prohibitively long and reach minutes for data sets in the gigabyte range. This is a well-known feature of fftw as the authors note in [15]:

> "In performance critical applications, many transforms of the same size are typically required, and therefore a large one-time cost is usually acceptable."

gearshifft allows one to dissect this problem further and isolate the planning time only. Figure 5 illustrates the problem to its full extent. FFTW_MEASURE consumes up to 3–4 orders of magnitude more planning time than other planrigors and plans from GPU based libraries. The 3D planning is compared with its counterpart in 1D (see Fig. 5b). It is important to note that fftw planning in 1D appears to be very time consuming as the FFTW_MEASURE curve is very steep compared to Fig. 5a. At input sizes of 128 MiB in 1D, the planning phase exceeds the duration of 100s. The multi-threaded environment could be a problem for fftw (compiled against OpenMP): when using 24 threads in fftw the time to solution with FFTW_MEASURE was up to 6× slower than using 1 thread. Even worse, FFTW_PATIENT was up to 50× slower than in a single-thread environment. Unfortunately, the number of threads used for wisdoms, which usually run in FFTW_PATIENT mode, must be equal to the ones used by the client later on.

In practice, this imposes a challenge on the client to the fftw API. Not only is the time to solution affected by this behavior which is a crucial quantity

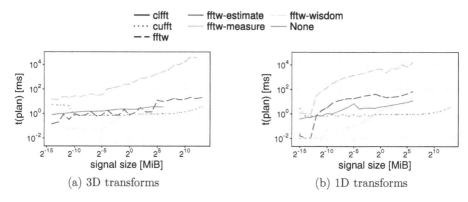

Fig. 5. Time-to-plan for `powerof2` single-precision in-place real-to-complex forward transforms using `fftw` (Intel E5-2680v3 CPU), `cuFFT` (K80 GPU) and `clFFT` (K80 GPU). (a) reports the complete time to plan for 3D FFTs and (b) for 1D FFTs. "None" refers to the planning with `cuFFT` or `clFFT` as they do not support the plan rigor concept. Both figures use a log10–log2 scale.

in FFT-heavy applications. Moreover, in an HPC environment the runtime of applications needs to be known before executing them in order to allow efficient and rapid job placement on compute resources. From another perspective, this asserts a development pressure on the developer interfacing with `fftw` as she has to create infrastructure in order to perform the planning of `fftw` only once and reuse the resulting plan as much as possible. Furthermore, based on these observations of Figs. 4 and 5 weighing plan time versus execution time, it becomes more and more unclear for a user of `fftw` which plan rigor to use in general.

3.4   Comparing CPU versus GPU Runtimes

The last section finished by discussing a design artifact, that the `fftw` authors introduced in their API and which other FFT libraries adopted. Another important and common question is whether GPU accelerated FFT implementations are really faster than their CPU equivalents. Although this question cannot be answered comprehensively in our study, there are several aspects to be explored. First of all, modern GPUs are connected via the PCIe bus to the host system in order to transfer data, receive instructions and to be supplied with power. This imposes a severe bottleneck to data transfer and is sometimes neglected during library design. Therefore, the time for data transfer needs to be accounted for or removed from the measurement. `gearshifft`s results data model offers access to each individual step of a transformation, see Fig. 1. Hereby it is possible to isolate the runtime for the FFT transform.

Figure 6 shows the runtime spent for computing the forward FFT for real single precision input data. This illustration is a direct measure for the quality of the implementation and the hardware underneath. For the 3D case in Fig. 6a `fftw` seems to provide compelling performance if the input data is not larger than

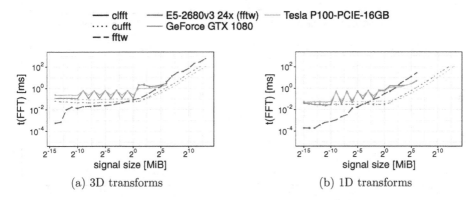

Fig. 6. Time for computing `powerof2` out-of-place single-precision real-to-complex forward transforms for 3D and for 1D shapes. Both figures use a log10-versus-log2 scale. Curves on the Intel E5-2680v3 based node were obtained with `fftw`, the data on Nvidia GPUs was obtained with `cuFFT` and `clFFT`.

1 MiB on a double socket Haswell Intel Xeon E5 CPU. Above this limit, the GPU implementations offer a clear advantage by up to one order of magnitude. The current Pascal generation GPUs used with `cuFFT` provide the best performance, which does not come by surprise as both cards are equipped with GDDR5X or HBM2 memory which are clearly beneficial for an operation that yields rather low computational complexity such as the FFT. In the 1D case of Fig. 6b, the same observations must be made with even more certainty. The cross-over of `fftw` and the GPU libraries occurs at an earlier point of 64 KiB.

Another observation in Fig. 6a is that the general structure of the runtime curves of GPU FFT implementations follows an inverse roofline curve [32]. That is for input signals smaller than the roofline turning point at 1 MiB the FFT implementation appears to be of constant cost, i. e. to be compute bound. Above the aforementioned threshold, the implementation appears to be memory bound and hence exposes a linear growth with growing input signals which corresponds to the $\mathcal{O}(n \log n)$ complexity observed in Sect. 1 and validates the algorithmic complexity in [32] as well.

Finally, it is not to our surprise that the `clFFT` results reported in Fig. 6 cannot be considered optimal. As we executed `clFFT` on Nvidia hardware interfacing with the OpenCL runtime coming with CUDA and interfaced to the Nvidia proprietary driver, OpenCL performance can not be considered a first-class citizen in this environment. Only in Fig. 6b, the `clFFT` runtimes are below those of `fftw`. These experiments should be repeated on AMD hardware where the OpenCL performance is expected to be better.

3.5 Non-`powerof2` Transforms

It is often communicated, that input signals should be padded to `powerof2` shapes in order to achieve the highest possible performance. With `gearshifft`

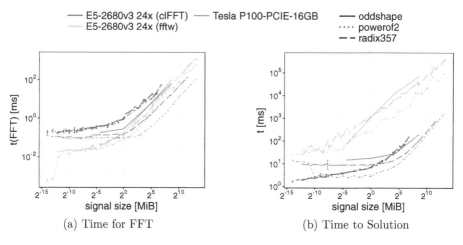

(a) Time for FFT   (b) Time to Solution

Fig. 7. fftw and clFFT on Intel E5-2680v3 CPU with 24 threads versus cuFFT on P100 GPU computing single-precision real-to-complex out-of-place forward transforms of 3D shapes. Both figures use a log10-versus-log2 scale.

the availability and quality of the common mathematical approaches across many FFT libraries can now be examined in detail. For the sake of brevity, only the results for fftw (Intel E5-2680v3 CPU) and cuFFT (P100) are presented here.

Figure 7 confirms that powerof2 transforms are generally faster than radix357 and oddshape transforms. Excluding the long planning time fftw offers the fastest FFT runtime until the turning point at 1 MiB, see Fig. 7a. However, looking at time to solution in Fig. 7b clFFT on the CPU outperforms fftw by 1 to 2 orders of magnitude due to the long planning times of fftw. At very small input signal sizes, cuFFT lacks behind clFFT on the CPU until 1 KiB for powerof2 shapes, where cuFFT offers superior or comparable runtimes thereafter. clFFT only offers support for powerof2 and radix357 shape types but has almost the same performance for either. cuFFT shows an FFT runtime difference of up to one order of magnitude on the P100 for large input signals (Fig. 7a) of powerof2 and oddshape type, where the time to solution converges due to planning and transfer penalties (Fig. 7a).

For a large range of input signal sizes between 2^{-10} MiB 2^7 MiB a padding to powerof2 might be justified when using cuFFT if enough memory is available on the device. For fftw non-powerof2 signals can be padded at signal sizes above 2^{-3} MiB $= 128$ KiB. clFFT on CPU is only a good choice, when short planning times are more important than transform runtime. clFFT provides similar performance on the P100 as on CPU, but it is not shown here.

3.6 Data Types

It is a common practice that complex-to-complex transforms are considered more performant than real-to-complex transforms. Therefore, in order to transform a real input array, a complex array is allocated and the real part of each datum is filled with the signal. The imaginary part of each datum is left at 0.

Figure 8 restricts itself to larger signal sizes in order to aid the visualization. Note that in Fig. 8a, a data point at the same number of elements of the input signal does have different size in memory. fftw exposes a factor of 2 and more of runtime difference for signals larger than 2^{15} elements comparing real and complex input data types in Fig. 8a. Below this threshold, the performance can be considered identical except for very small input signals although real FFTs always remain faster than complex ones. The situation is different for cuFFT, where the overall difference is smaller in general. In the compute bound region of cuFFT (below 2^{19} elements), complex transforms perform equally well than real transforms given the observed uncertainties. In the memory bound region (above 2^{19} elements), real transforms can be a factor of 2 ahead of complex ones which is clearly related to twice the memory accesses.

If single-precision can be used instead of double-precision, then the possible performance gain can be estimated by Fig. 8b. On the high grade server GPU, the Nvidia Tesla P100, the performance difference remains around 2× in the memory bound region due to double the memory bandwidth required. The results for fftw vary more around 1.5 to 2.5 fold regressions between single and double precision inputs across a wider input signal range.

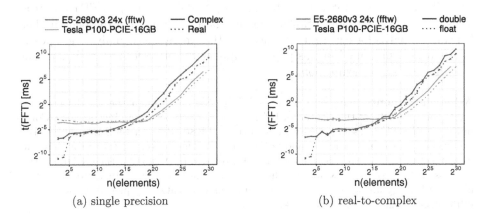

(a) single precision   (b) real-to-complex

Fig. 8. Time for computing a forward FFT using 3D powerof2 input signals using fftw and cuFFT on respective hardware versus the number of elements in the input signal. (a) computes a real-to-complex transform and compares it to a complex-to-complex transform for single precision input data, whereas (b) shows a real-to-complex transform for either single or double precision. Both figures use a log2-versus-log2 scale.

4   Summary

With this paper gearshifft is presented to the HPC community and other performance enthusiasts as an open-source, vendor-independent and free FFT benchmark suite for heterogeneous platforms. gearshifft is a C++14 modular benchmark code that allows to perform forward and backward FFT transforms on various types of input data (both in shape, memory organization, precision and data type). `gearshifft`'s design offers an extensible architecture to accommodate FFT packages with very low overhead. `gearshifft`'s design choices address both FFT practitioners, FFT library developers, HPC admins or integrators and decision makers supporting a wide range of use cases.

To showcase the capabilities of `gearshifft`, a first study of three common FFT libraries, `fftw`, `clFFT` and `cuFFT` is presented. The performances of CPU based implementations Haswell Xeon CPUs to state-of-the-art Pascal generation Nvidia GPUs are compared. The results indicate that for input signal sizes of less than 1 MiB, the CPU implementation is superior whereas for larger input data size the GPU offers better turn-around. The difference between runtimes of `powerof2`, `radix357` and power-of-19 shaped input data was demonstrated to be negligible for `fftw` and non-negligible for `cuFFT` transforms used in this study. The results further indicate runtime differences when using complex versus real arrays and when comparing double versus single precision data types.

As we warmly welcome contributions of benchmarks from various pieces of hardware, we hope to extend the `gearshifft` repository with many more data sets from platforms used in the HPC arena of today and tomorrow. It is planned to run `gearshifft` on non-x86 hardware to establish a basis for hardware performance comparisons. Connected to this, we plan to explore more state-of-the-art FFT libraries such as Intel IPPS, Intel MKL, AMD's rocFFT, cusFFT etc. It is a future task to consolidate the benchmark data structure and to open another benchmark paths for e.g. FFT callbacks, so that many more analyses are possible than were presented in this paper both in terms of performance exploration as well as energy consumption.

Acknowledgments. The work was funded by Nvidia through the GPU Center of Excellence (GCOE) at the Center for Information Services and High Performance Computing (ZIH), TU Dresden, where the K20Xm and K80 GPU cluster Taurus was used. We would like to thank the Helmholtz-Zentrum Dresden-Rossendorf for providing the infrastructure to host the Nvidia Tesla P100 (provided by Nvidia for the GCOE) in the Hypnos HPC cluster. We would also like to thank the Max Planck Institute of Molecular Cell Biology and Genetics for supporting this publication by providing computing infrastructure and service staff working time.

References

1. Helmholtz-Zentrum Dresden-Rossendorf Abteilung IT-Infrastruktur. Hypnos. http://www.hzdr.de/db/Cms?pOid=12231&pNid=852
2. Akin, B., Franchetti, F., Hoe, J.C.: FFTs with near-optimal memory access through block data layouts: algorithm, architecture and design automation. J. Sig. Proc. Syst. **85**, 67–82 (2015)
3. AMD. clFFT. A software library containing FFT functions written in OpenCL (2016). https://github.com/clMathLibraries/clFFT

4. Bachmann, P.: Static and metaprogramming patterns and static frameworks: a catalog. An application. In: Proceedings of the 2006 Conference on Pattern Languages of Programs, PLoP 2006, pp. 17:1–17:33. ACM, Portland (2006). ISBN: 978-1-60558-372-3. doi:10.1145/1415472.1415492

5. Bahrampour, S., Ramakrishnan, N., Schott, L., Shah, M.: Comparative study of caffe, neon, theano, and torch for deep learning. In: CoRR abs/1511.06435 (2015). http://arxiv.org/abs/1511.06435

6. Bluestein, L.: A linear filtering approach to the computation of discrete Fourier transform. IEEE Trans. Audio Electroacoust. **18**(4), 451–455 (1970). doi:10.1109/TAU.1970.1162132. ISSN: 0018-9278

7. C++ Boost. Libraries (2016). http://www.boost.org/

8. Cooley, J.W., Tukey, J.W.: An algorithm for the machine calculation of complex Fourier series. Math. Comput. **19**(90), 297–301 (1965)

9. Danalis, A., Marin, G., McCurdy, C., Meredith, J.S., Roth, P.C., Spafford, K., Tipparaju, V., Vetter, J.S.: The scalable heterogeneous computing (SHOC) benchmark suite. In: Proceedings of the 3rd Workshop on General-Purpose Computation on Graphics Processing Units, pp. 63–74. ACM (2010)

10. Dongarra, J., Luszczek, P.: HPC Challenge: Design, History, and Implementation Highlights. In: Contemporary High Performance Computing: From Petascale Toward Exascale (2013)

11. Du, P., Weber, R., Luszczek, P., Tomov, S., Peterson, G., Dongarra, J.: From CUDA to OpenCL: towards a performance-portable solution for multi-platform GPU programming. Parallel Comput. **38**(8), 391–407 (2012)

12. Eleftheriou, M., Fitch, B., Rayshubskiy, A., Ward, T.J.C., Germain, R.: Performance measurements of the 3D FFT on the Blue Gene/L supercomputer. In: Cunha, J.C., Medeiros, P.D. (eds.) Euro-Par 2005. LNCS, vol. 3648, pp. 795–803. Springer, Heidelberg (2005). doi:10.1007/11549468_87

13. FFTW User Manual, 29 November 2016. http://www.fftw.org/fftw3_doc/index.html#Top

14. Fialka, O., Cadik, M.: FFT and convolution performance in image filtering on GPU. In: Tenth International Conference on Information Visualisation (IV 2006), pp. 609–614. IEEE (2006)

15. Frigo, M., Johnson, S.G.: The design and implementation of FFTW3. Proc. IEEE **93**(2), 216–231 (2005). Special issue on "Program Generation, Optimization, and Platform Adaptation"

16. Gauss, C.F.: Theoria interpolationis methodo nova tractata, vol. 3, pp. 265–327. Königliche Gesellschaft der Wissenschaften, Göttingen (1866)

17. gearshifft: Benchmark Suite for Heterogeneous FFT Implementations (2016). https://github.com/mpicbg-scicomp/gearshifft

18. Huisken, J., Swoger, J., Del Bene, F., Wittbrodt, J., Stelzer, E.H.: Optical sectioning deep inside live embryos by selective plane illumination microscopy. Science **305**(5686), 1007–1009 (2004)

19. Hurd, T.R., Zhou, Z.: A Fourier transform method for spread option pricing. SIAM J. Fin. Math. **1**(1), 142–157 (2010)

20. MKL Intel. Intel math kernel library (2007)

21. Information technology — Programming languages — C++. Norm (2014)

22. Katoh, K., Misawa, K., Kuma, K.I., Miyata, T.: MAFFT: a novel method for rapid multiple sequence alignment based on fast Fourier transform. Nucleic Acids Res. **30**(14), 3059–3066 (2002)

23. Maronga, B., Gryschka, M., Heinze, R., Hoffmann, F., Kanani-Sühring, F., Keck, M., Ketelsen, K., Letzel, M.O., Sühring, M., Raasch, S.: The Parallelized Large-Eddy Simulation Model (PALM) version 4.0 for atmospheric and oceanic flows: model formulation, recent developments, and future perspectives. Geosci. Model Dev. Discuss. **8**(2), 1539–1637 (2015)

24. Meuer, H., Strohmaier, E., Dongarra, J., Simon, H.D.: Top. 500 supercomputing sites. Technical report top. 500.org (2011). https://www.top.500.org/lists/2016/11/

25. NVIDIA. CUFFT library. Version (2010). https://developer.nvidia.com/cufft

26. Park, Y.S., Park, K.R., Kim, J.M., Jeong, H.Y.: Fast Fourier transform benchmark on X86 Xeon system for multimedia data processing. Multimedia Tools Appl., 1–16 (2015)

27. Preibisch, S., Amat, F., Stamataki, E., Sarov, M., Singer, R.H., Myers, E., Tomancak, P.: Efficient Bayesian-based multiview deconvolution. Nat. Methods **11**(6), 645–648 (2014)

28. Schmid, B., Huisken, J.: Real-time multi-view deconvolution. Bioinformatics **31**(20), 3398–3400 (2015)

29. Stockham Jr., T.G.: High-speed convolution and correlation. In: Proceedings of the April 26–28, 1966, Spring Joint Computer Conference, pp. 229–233. ACM (1966)

30. Stroustrup, B.: The Design and Evolution of C++. Pearson Education India, Hoboken (1994)

31. Van Loan, C.: Computational Frameworks for the Fast Fourier Transform, vol. 10. SIAM, New Delhi (1992)

32. Williams, S., Waterman, A., Patterson, D.: Roofline: an insightful visual performance model for multicore architectures. Commun. ACM **52**(4), 65–76 (2009)

33. Zentrum für Informationsdienste und Hochleistungsrechnen, TU Dresden. Taurus. https://doc.zih.tu-dresden.de/hpc-wiki/bin/view/Compendium/SystemTaurus

An Overview of MPI Characteristics of Exascale Proxy Applications

Benjamin Klenk$^{(\boxtimes)}$ and Holger Fröning

Institute of Computer Engineering, Ruprecht Karls University Heidelberg,
Mannheim, Germany
{benjamin.klenk,holger.froening}@ziti.uni-heidelberg.de

Abstract. The scale of applications and computing systems is tremendously increasing and needs to increase even more to realize exascale systems. As the number of nodes keeps growing, communication has become key to high performance.

The Message Passing Interface (MPI) has evolved to the de facto standard for inter-node data transfers. Consequently, MPI is well suited to serve as proxy for an analysis of communication characteristics of exascale proxy applications.

This work presents characteristics like time spent in certain operations, point-to-point versus collective communication, and message sizes and rates, gathered from a comprehensive trace analysis. We provide an understanding of how applications use MPI to exploit node-level parallelism, always with respect to scalability, and also locate parts which require more optimization. We emphasize on the analysis of the message matching and report queue lengths and associated matching rates.

It is shown that most data is transferred via point-to-point operations, but the most time is spent in collectives. Message matching rates significantly depend on the length of message queues, which tend to increase with the number of processes. As messages are also become smaller, the matching is important to high message rates in large-scale applications.

1 Introduction

While there are many challenges on the road toward exascale computing, communication is key to both performance and energy efficiency. It is projected that an exascale computing system comprises 50 times more nodes than systems deployed in 2010 [1]. Additionally, the number of available processing elements increases even more as nodes become more parallel themselves, including massively parallel and heterogeneous processors.

Data movement within such highly parallel environments cannot rely on a single paradigm, but needs to be hierarchical and specialized. A single global address space is just as unpromising as solely relying on message passing. Computing has become heterogeneous and thus the processor's different execution models require different communication models [2].

Nonetheless, message passing has become the de facto standard for data movement between nodes as it abstracts communication to a well understood

© Springer International Publishing AG 2017
J.M. Kunkel et al. (Eds.): ISC High Performance 2017, LNCS 10266, pp. 217–236, 2017.
DOI: 10.1007/978-3-319-58667-0_12

concept of messages being sent and received by a source and destination process. Besides high productivity, message passing allows messages to be sent asynchronously to overlap communication with computation, and provides collective operations, such as *barrier* and *broadcast*. In particular, the Message Passing Interface (MPI) is in wide use, especially in large scale applications. In spite of increasing heterogeneity, message passing is expected to remain the dominating communication model for data exchanges across operating system (OS) boundaries, even in future hierarchical communication systems.

With exascale computing ahead of us, application developers as well as system architects need to understand how data is exchanged. Applications have to be optimized to minimize communication overhead and systems have to provide an environment for the application to achieve best possible performance. Both cases require communication to be well understood in order to tweak applications and systems for performance.

Consequently, a set of MPI applications has been compiled by the U.S. Department of Energy (DOE), representing applications that are expected to run on exascale systems. Traces are provided that reflect the communication behavior on current systems with varying scale.

In this work, we analyze these trace files to provide an understanding of various aspects of message passing for such large-scale applications. Besides general statistics, such as overall communication time, message size, and data transfer volume, we provide a comprehensive analysis with regard to the message matching. The matching process significantly adds latency if long queues have to be searched in order to find a matching message. The matching is important, as it has been shown that solely speeding up the matching process can reduce an application's run time by a factor of 3.5× [3]. We report queue lengths as well as search depths and message rates of various exascale-like applications.

The results of this work can be used by application developers to understand consequences of various MPI aspects. Furthermore, systems architects learn about applications' demands, hence systems can be tailored to further accelerate common patterns. We also want to motivate programmers to consider similar analyses for their applications. In summary, we provide the following contributions:

- Comprehensive analysis of exascale proxy applications with respect to communication characteristics, such as message size and rate, number of communication partners, and time spent in particular MPI routines
- Analysis of queue lengths and search depths to further understand performance and implications of the matching process
- Based on our data, we discuss our observations and show limitations and challenges that arise at large scale.

The remainder of this work is structured as follows: Sect. 2 provides the background on MPI and our methodology. Section 3 shows related work, followed by an overview of the applications we are analyzing in Sect. 4. Next, Sect. 5

reports general MPI statistics, while Sect. 6 particularly assesses the message matching process. We discuss our observations in Sect. 7 before we conclude in Sect. 8.

2   Background

In this section we want to introduce MPI as prominent and widely used message passing system. A brief overview of our methodology completes this section.

2.1   The Message Passing Interface

MPI has become the de facto standard for data transfers in High Performance Computing (HPC) systems, due to its productivity and abstract interface. Each data transfer is declared as a message that is sent and received by two processes. Messages are delivered according to their origin and destination, but also require to be annotated with a tag and communicator. The tag allows for selection of messages between the same process pair and the communicator is a subset of all available processes, but can also comprise all processes of an application.

A process receives messages by calling a *recv* routine. The receive request needs to be matched with the right message, based on origin, tag, and communicator. This is widely known as *tag matching* and can significantly contribute to latency [4].

An important aspect of the matching performance is the length of the Unexpected Messages Queue (UMQ) and Posted Receive Queue (PRQ). Any incoming message for which a receive request has not been posted yet is added to the UMQ. Similarly, any receive request is added to the PRQ for which no message has been received yet. With longer queues, the search time and thus latency is increased, particularly limiting the rate at which small messages are exchanged.

Apart from direct messages between two distinct processes, MPI allows multiple processes to participate in collective communication routines. Collectives are executed by all processes of the communicator that is passed to the MPI routine and allow for synchronization, such as the barrier. Others enable collective data processing, such as determining the maximum of data that is distributed across multiple processes, namely (all-)reduce operation. Collectives for plain data distribution are implemented by broadcast, gather, and scatter operations.

Other MPI extensions, such as one-sided semantics, are beyond of this work's scope as we did not encounter them in the traces we analyzed.

2.2   Methodology

The foundation of our work are the exascale proxy application traces, made available by the U.S. Department of Energy (DOE) [5]. The traces cover a wide range of applications with different communication patterns and characteristics. Traces of the *Design Forward* program comprise only a single iteration, whereas the other programs do not provide any information on this manner.

For our analyses, we developed a script-based framework in Python and R to parse and analyze trace files and verified results with a different approach using bash commands. Traces are available in the *dumpi* format[1], whose library intercepts and logs every MPI call with its entrance and exit timestamp. In addition to the calls themselves, routine-specific meta data is logged. While an *MPI_Send* contains the destination rank and message size, an *MPI_Allreduce* also comprises the operation that is executed on the data. Traces are available for each rank separately.

While some data can be gathered by simply parsing the files, more complex characteristics require additional processing. For example, the determination of MPI queue length and search depth requires the queues to be rebuilt and searched for every occurring *MPI_Send*, *MPI_Recv*, and *MPI_Wait(all)*.

Although plenty of insights can be gained by a trace-based analysis, there are limitations. For example, not all traces provide information on custom data types, thus the exact size of messages cannot be reported for all applications. Instead, we can only report the number of elements in given messages. Similarly, if a new mapping of ranks is generated by *MPI_Cart_create*, for example, the queues cannot be rebuilt easily. Furthermore, it remains unclear whether and how much communication is overlapped with computation as *dumpi* tracks MPI calls only.

Unfortunately not all applications provide information on the systems the traces were generated on. Applications from the *Design Forward* program also offer Integrated Performance Monitoring (IPM) data[2], which contains MPI time, message size distribution, and load balancing information. Nonetheless, we want to report these metrics for all applications and chose to report numbers from our own analyses. Note that these numbers can differ since metrics are collected by different methods.

3   Related Work

There are two fields that are related to this work: general MPI statistics and the analyses of matching and queues, respectively. A brief overview of existing work is presented in the following.

Early work on analyzing communication characteristics focused on the NAS Parallel Benchmark (NPB) suite [6,7]. Their finding was that collectives are rather static, meaning that parameters can be determined at compile time and associated messages sizes are rather small. Furthermore, 5 out of 8 applications heavily use point-to-point communication with a share of more than 80%. Message sizes never exceed 64kB on 64 nodes in any NPB applications.

Vetter and Mueller [8] and Kamil et al. [9] looked at a small set of various applications and analyzed MPI metrics similar to our choice. They also found that in their set of applications the number of peer processes any rank communicates with and the message size of collective operations are rather small.

---

[1] http://sst.sandia.gov/about_dumpi.html.
[2] http://ipm-hpc.sourceforge.net/.

A similar analysis was done by Raponi et al. [10], in which MPI time and number of calls were studied. The set of applications differs from ours, except for *AMG*. However, they looked at small scale with only one application exceeding 512 ranks, while *AMG* was run with 128 ranks. The analysis showed similar results regarding the data transfer volume, which is strongly dominated by point-to-point communication. Traces were also analyzed by Lammel et al. [11], who proposes a trace analysis tool. Various MPI metrics are reported as well.

Other work also exists in the area of queue and matching analyses. UMQ and PRQ lengths were analyzed by Brightwell and Underwood [12], but only for the NPB applications again. They found that a significant amount of unexpected messages results in queue lengths of up to 200 entries with up to 140 processes. Furthermore, PRQ is always smaller than UMQ and average search lengths never exceed 30 entries. Note that they stated that it is necessary to analyze real applications, rather than benchmarks. Based on this, Underwood et al. [13] developed a list-acceleration unit in hardware. Benefits were shown as long as the queues fit in on-NIC memory. Keller and Graham [14] analyzed large-scale applications, showing that the UMQ length scales linearly with the process count for a thermodynamics application on the Jaguar and JaguarPF systems. However, ranks other than 0 differ significantly with not exceeding a queue length of 200. Reported UMQ lengths for other applications are much smaller, ranging between 10 and 30 entries.

New matching algorithms have been proposed by Zounmevo and Afsahi [15], aiming at reduced memory footprint and enhanced scalability. One algorithm uses multiple queues, statically assigned to ranks. Sequence numbers are used to comply with wildcards. Significant relative performance improvements were achieved for two applications (nbody and radix sort), but absolute numbers are missing. Flajslik et al. [3] also proposed a new matching algorithm, based on hash tables. Using this algorithm, the Fire Dynamics Simulator was run $3.5\times$ faster by only replacing the matching algorithm and no further optimization of the application. The authors in [4] proposed a dynamic matching algorithm and reported matching times for several benchmarks. However, no queue lengths or search depths were analyzed.

In previous work [16], we analyzed the GPU's capability to perform message matching and proposed an appropriate algorithm. We found that the message passing protocol would need to be relaxed with regard to wildcards and ordering to suit the GPU's execution model. The conclusions can also be applied to the CPU's protocol to allow for more optimizations and faster matching, especially as the number of cores per CPU keeps increasing.

4   Application Overview

This section provides an overview of the applications we are analyzing in this work. Table 1 summarizes the applications' communication pattern and general statistics for each application. Note that numbers of our scalability analysis can differ from this table since we did not include small scale configurations.

Table 1. Exascale proxy applications and various MPI characteristics (Non.Bl. S/R = share of non-blocking send/recv operations; Unxp.Msgs. = share of unexpected messages).

Application	Pattern	Ranks	MPI (comm) time	Unxp.Msgs.	Non-Bl. S/R	Peers
MOCFE (CESAR)*	Nearest neighbor (Near.N.)	64	74 (8)%	n/a	100/100%	2
		256	86 (6)%	n/a	100/100%	3
		1,024	92 (9)%	n/a	100/100%	4
NEKBONE (CESAR)	Nearest neighbor	64	11 (7)%	40%	99.9/99.9%	18
		256	34 (11)%	35%	99.9/99.9%	8
		1,024	78 (23)%	45%	99.9/99.9%	29
CNS (EXACT)	Nearest neighbor	64	3 (2)%	28%	0/92.5%	26
		256	24 (20)%	40%	0/98.5%	44
CNS Large (EXACT)	Nearest neighbor	64	3 (3)%	30%	0/60.8%	26
		256	11 (11)%	27%	0/85.7%	20
		1,024	43 (39)%	34%	0/98.4%	72
MultiGrid (EXACT)	Nearest neighbor	64	6 (3)%	27%	0/100%	14
		256	16 (12)%	47%	0/100%	37
MultiGrid Large (EXACT)	Nearest neighbor	64	3 (1)%	40%	0/100%	14
		256	5 (3)%	31%	0/100%	17
		1,024	22 (18)%	33%	0/100%	20
LULESH (EXMATEX)	Nearest neighbor	64	1 (1)%	21%	100/100%	14
		512	8 (8)%	29%	100/100%	19
CMC 2D (EXMATEX)	Nearest neighbor	64	76 (76)%	n/a	n/a	n/a
		256	78 (78)%	n/a	n/a	n/a
		1,024	84 (84)%	n/a	n/a	n/a
AMG (DF)	Nearest neighbor	216	3 (3)%	44%	100/100%	57
		1,728	1 (1)%	46%	100/100%	79
		13,824	0 (0)%	48%	100/100%	92
AMR Boxlib (DF)	Irregular	64	9 (5)%	27%	0/99.9%	18

(*continued*)

Table 1. (*continued*)

Application	Pattern	Ranks	MPI (comm) time	Unxp.Msgs.	Non-Bl. S/R	Peers
		1,728	12 (10)%	37%	0/99.9%	35
BigFFT (DF)	Many-to-many	100	99 (3)%	n/a	n/a	n/a
		1,024	99 (3)%	n/a	n/a	n/a
		10,000	99 (0)%	n/a	n/a	n/a
BigFFT Medium (DF)	Many-to-man	100	72 (29)%	n/a	n/a	n/a
		1,024	81 (19)%	n/a	n/a	n/a
		10,000	99 (1)%	n/a	n/a	n/a
Crystal Router (DF)	Staged all-to-all	10	23 (23)%	46%	0/100%	3
		100	63 (63)%	31%	0/100%	6
Fill Boundary (DF)	Nearest neighbor	125	40 (27)%	34%	0/100%	16
		1,000	52 (44)%	30%	0/100%	20
		10,648	72 (70)%	32%	0/100%	23
MultiGrid (DF)	Nearest neighbor	125	40 (17)%	41%	0/100%	14
		1,000	66 (58)%	39%	0/100%	10
		10,648	70 (69)%	38%	0/100%	8
MiniDFT (DF)*	Many-to-many	125	15 (15)%	n/a	32/3.4%	19
		424	11 (11)%	n/a	31.3/2.2%	30
MiniFE (Mantevo)*	Staged all-to-all	144	7 (6)%	n/a	0/100%	12
		1,152	7 (6)%	n/a	0/100%	15
PARTISN (DF)*	Near.N	168	51 (50)%	n/a	0/0%	1
Average	n/a	*n/a*	41 (21)%	36%	n/a	23

*The queue analysis of this application was not possible since rank numbers are renamed, resulting from MPI's cart create.

The second column of the table shows the communication pattern of the applications. Although we analyze a wide range of applications, it seems that nearest neighbor communication is by far the most prominent one, whereas no application relies on pure all-to-all communication. Only *Crystal Router* and *MiniFE*, both from the *Design Forward* program, implement a staged form of all-to-all. *Crystal Router* and *AMG* use send/receive operations only and refrain from using any collective data transfer operation. *BigFFT (Design Forward)* and *EXMATEX's CMC 2D*, on the other hand, completely rely on collective communication.

We determine the number of peer ranks a rank is communicating with by counting how many different ranks are addressed with all send and receive operations together. On average across all applications, only a mean of 23 ranks participate in point-to-point communication with any given rank. It suggests that point-to-point communication is rather local, which allows for optimizations regarding process mapping and topology.

We also want to constitute that except for two applications, namely *MiniDFT* and *MiniFE*, we did not see any wildcard for the source specifier in any *MPI_Recv* operation. Wildcards introduce additional complexity in the message matching process, which seems quite unnecessary for the vast majority of applications. Additionally, we could not find tag wildcards in any trace file either, questioning whether MPI needs to support wildcards at the cost of complex matching algorithms. However, it is possible that trace files omit MPI's initialization phases, in which wildcards may be used more often. It would still be desirably if MPI allows the user to refrain from using wildcards during compute phases to allow for optimized message matching algorithms [3,15].

Although messages within different communicators can be matched in parallel by replicating the associated data structures, applications do not seem to use multiple communicators. We observe that only *MiniDFT* groups ranks in 7 different communicators for point-to-point messages and *Nekbone* in 2, respectively, while all other applications rely on a single communicator. Given that communicators can be matched independently, we advocate to use multiple communicators to reduce matching overhead, allowing for higher message rates to be achieved.

The fifth column of the table shows the share of all messages that are unexpected. On average across all applications, 36% of all messages do not find a matching receive upon arrival and need to be placed in the UMQ. This is distributed as follows: applications and configurations with less than 100 ranks send 30% unexpected messages (15 samples), less than 500 ranks 34% (28 samples), and more than 1,000 ranks 39% (8 samples). Although the number of unexpected messages seems to increase with the scale of the application, the increment is not significant. Nonetheless, we observe a significant increase of unexpected messages with the number of ranks in the *AMG (Design Forward)* application, from 12% with 8 processes to 46% with 216 processes. However, increasing the scale to 1,728 processes has no further impact. Another example is *Crystal Router*, for which we observe that the number of unexpected messages increases with scale, from 31% at 10 processes to 46% at 100 processes. However, more samples would be needed to allow for more profound statements.

A mechanism to avoid unexpected messages is to post non-blocking *MPI_Irecv* operations in advance to provide MPI with the appropriate userspace buffer for the expected message. We count occurrences of blocking and non-blocking send and receive operations for each application and found that no general statement for all applications can be made and refer to the results shown in the table. Nonetheless, it seems to be a common pattern to send messages in a blocking way and receive them by non-blocking receive operations.

We also want to state that *Design Forward's MiniDFT* is the only application that uses *MPI_Rsend* and *MPI_Sendrecv_replace* in addition to the standard blocking and non-blocking send routines. We have not observed any synchronous or buffered send operations in any other application.

Another important metric of any large-scale application is how much time is actually spent for data transfers versus computation. The accumulated time of all MPI calls is divided by the total application time, which is determined here by the first and last MPI operation that appears in the traces. Although this approach does not represent the exact application time as it does not account for non-MPI operations, it still allows for a good estimate. Second, the communication time is the accumulated time for all data transferring or synchronizing MPI calls, such send/recv, collectives, and *MPI_Wait(all)*. Comparing both times provides insights on how much MPI overhead an application contains. For example, overhead is increased by creating new datatypes, communicators, or groups. Both MPI and communication time are determined for rank 0.

The time spent in MPI routines averages about 36% of the application time across all applications and configurations (67 samples). If we consider only applications with less than 100 ranks, the MPI time averages 20% (24 samples), whereas applications with less than 500 ranks spent 27% (48 samples) of their time in MPI functions. The larger the scale the more time is spent in MPI, as applications with more than 500 ranks show an average MPI time of 57% (19 samples) and more than 1,000 ranks result in 60% (16 samples). This is not surprising as most traces are generated with the same input and problem size and the impact of communication usually increases with strong scaling. The actual communication time, however, is lower with an average of 20% across all applications and only 12% for applications with less than 100 ranks. Again, increasing the scale also increases the communication time as applications with more than 500 ranks show an average of 29%.

On average, 73% of the MPI time is spent for communication routines like send/recv or collectives. However, there are a few applications with significantly higher MPI than communication time. *Mocfe* and *BigFFT* both contain the most overhead with spending only 10–20% of their MPI time for communication and synchronization. For example, *Mocfe* (1,024) spends 75% of its application time a single MPI_Cart_create call. Thus, actual communication times may be higher during the application after initialization is complete.

Traces for different problem sizes are also available for some applications, namely *BigFFT (Design Forward)*, and *EXACT*'s *CNS* and *MultiGrid*. In all cases the MPI time is lower for larger problem sizes due to an increased amount of computation.

5   General MPI Statistics

This section presents our findings regarding general MPI characteristics, such as data volume, message size, and usage of various MPI operations and features.

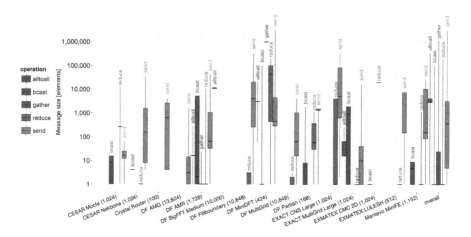

Fig. 1. Message sizes for various MPI operations and applications.

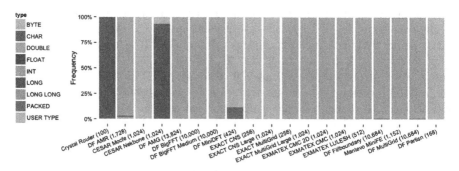

Fig. 2. Datatype distribution for each application.

Message Size: The message size for common MPI operations and various applications is depicted in Fig. 1. The graph shows the message size as a boxplot (1st, 2nd, and 3rd quartile, minimum, maximum) and considers all messages from all ranks of a given application and configuration. At last, an overall message size distribution is shown across all applications and configurations, however, applications are not equally represented as some applications exchange much more messages. Generally it can be said that point-to-point messages contain more elements than collective messages. In fact, collectives are often called with a single data element.

Taking the scale of applications into account, point-to-point messages tend to become smaller with an increasing number of ranks. This is observed in half of the applications (6 out of 12), whereas *Crystal Router*, *DF MiniDFT*, and *DF MultiGrid* show an increase in message size at larger scale. Contrary, messages remain roughly constant in *Mocfe*, *Fillboundary*, and *LULESH*.

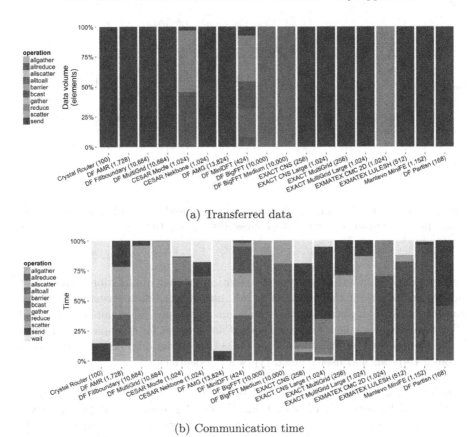

(a) Transferred data

(b) Communication time

Fig. 3. Transferred data and communication time, broken into various MPI operations

Broadcasts are mostly unaffected by scale as only *MiniDFT* shows an increase in message size while other applications' messages remain constant in size. The message size of *alltoall* operations always decreases with an increasing number of ranks. This is observed in *BigFFT*, *EXACT MultiGrid*, and *AMR*.

The most prominently used collective operation is *(all-)reduce*. Here, the message size is constant over scale in two-thirds of the applications (6 out of 9). However, *MiniDFT* and *AMR* show an increase in message size. *Nekbone*, however, first uses larger messages when the scale is increased from 64 to 256 processes, but messages become smaller again for 1,024 processes.

Summarizing it can be said that messages tend to become smaller or remain constant in size at larger scale. Nonetheless, a few applications show an increased message size, for example *MiniDFT*'s messages become larger for both point-to-point and collective messages.

Note that we cannot report the exact size of messages in terms of bytes since some traces lack information on the composition of user-defined types.

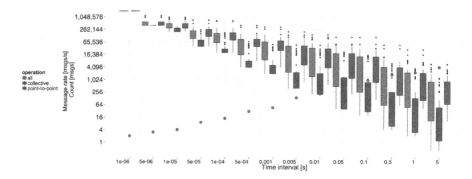

Fig. 4. Message rates for various time intervals, measured across all applications. The orange points indicate the number of messages (mean) that fall into a given time interval.

However, Fig. 2 shows the datatype distribution for each application. While most applications represent their data as *double*, user defined data structures are also prominent. Most applications use the same datatypes for point-to-point and collectives, however, there are exceptions. *Fillboundary*, for example, mainly uses *double* for point-to-point and *long* for collective operations. *Nekbone* uses *char* for point-to-point and user-defined types for collectives.

Transferred Data Volume: Figure 3(a) breaks down the total volume of transferred data into various MPI operations. As can be seen, most data is sent via point-to-point communication, except for a few workloads that primarily rely on collective operations for data movement. For example, *CESAR's Mocfe* and *EXMATEX's CMC* heavily rely on reduce and allreduce, respectively. *Design Forward's MiniDFT* almost entirely exchanges the data via all-to-all. Nonetheless, it is surprising how many applications rely on send/receive communication for data movement.

An interesting aspect is the data volume transferred during an application's run time. However, this is relative since we can only determine how many elements are sent, rather than the exact number of bytes. The most communication-intensive applications are *Crystal Router* (100 ranks) with 5.7 G elements per application time, and *BigFFT* (1,024 ranks) and *Fillboundary* (10,648 ranks) with 3.3 G elements/s each. Substituting application time with communication time yields different results. Here, *BigFFT* (10,000 ranks) is by far the most communication-intensive application with 112 G elements/s, followed by *AMG* (13,824) and *LULESH* (512) with 37G and 24 G elements/s, respectively. The lowest rate is achieved by *CMC* with 1.2K (64 ranks) to 24K (1,024) elements per communication time. *DF MultiGrid* shows also low rates with an average of about 100K elements/s across 125, 1000, and 10648 ranks.

The transfer rate can also be determined with regard to the number of ranks. Here, *MiniFe* (18 ranks) shows the highest rate with 900M elements per communication time and rank, followed by *LULESH* (16) and *Crystal Router* (10) with each yielding about 400M elements/s per rank. Again, *CMC* also shows the lowest rate in this analysis.

The vast majority of applications responds to an increase in scale with a decrease in transferred elements per communication time. As we have shown earlier, messages tend to become smaller at larger scale and thus communication and synchronization overhead predominates at some point as well. Contrary, the total data volume tends to increase with scale in most applications.

Communication Time: Besides transferred data volume, the time spent in certain MPI operations is used to break down the MPI time. Results are shown in Fig. 3(b). Although each application behaves differently, collective operations tend to contribute most to the application's MPI time. This is due their implicit synchronization and dependency on all ranks of the collective's communicator, whereas point-to-point communication just depends on two ranks, thus imbalances are less impactful regarding the operation's latency. However, only small amounts of data are moved by collective operations.

Looking at the graph suggests that point-to-point operations take less time than collectives, however, due to non-blocking send and receive operations the time spent in *MPI_Wait(all)* routines needs to be factored in as well. For example, *Design Forward's Crystal Router and AMG* spent most of their communication time on waiting for non-blocking operations to be completed, as it only uses non-blocking receive operations (see Table 1). Barriers, on the other hand, are especially time consuming in large-scale applications, such as *Fillboundary* and *MultiGrid*, both comprising 10,648 ranks.

Optimization of MPI communication needs to focus on collective operations and load balancing at large scale. While the data volume is lower than for point-to-point communication, the time spent in collectives is substantially higher.

Message Rate: The message rate of an application can be determined by counting all messages that are sent during an application and divide the result by the application's run time. However, this does not reflect the application's requirements regarding the network's performance. A better approach is to define a time interval and count all messages that fall into it. If a bulk of messages is sent before a long period of computation, the message rate during the actual communication phase can demand high message rates from the network while the network could idle during computation.

Figure 4 shows the message rate observed across all applications for a given time interval and the number of messages that were counted during the time slot (orange points). As expected, high message rates are measured for short intervals, but the actual number of messages is fairly low. For example, 2 messages are exchanged within $1\,\mu s$, resulting in a message rate of 2M messages/s. The sample size is also low with 4 applications out of 48. We believe $100\,\mu s$ to be more representative as at least the median of the message count amounts to about 10 messages. The associated message rate is above 100k messages/s for half of the applications with the maximum being 500k messages/s. It can also be seen that the time between subsequent collective operations is larger than between

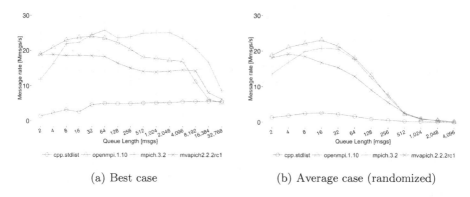

(a) Best case   (b) Average case (randomized)

Fig. 5. Matching rate of different MPI implementations for best and average cases.

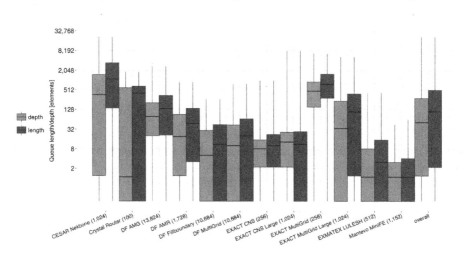

Fig. 6. Length and depth of the UMQ.

point-to-point operations, also an effect that is caused by collective's implicit synchronization.

6   MPI Message Matching

Two-sided communication requires messages to be matched with the target's receive requests. The matching is complex as MPI guarantees in-order delivery of messages and allows for source and tag wildcards. Also, messages can arrive unexpectedly.

Matching Performance: Messages and receive requests that cannot be matched need to be stored in queues, although all major MPI implementations implement lists. The length of these queues, or lists respectively, contributes to the memory

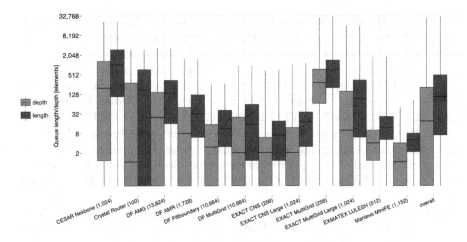

Fig. 7. Length and depth of the PRQ.

footprint and increases latency if matching elements are found toward the queues' tail. Figure 5 shows the matching performance for two synthetic scenarios: best case, in which each receive request matches the head of the UMQ and average case with a randomized match position within the queue. The experiment has two MPI processes running on the same node, whereas one process sends a certain number of messages to the other process, followed by a barrier. The second process receives all messages after the barrier. The match position is determined by the tag used in the send and receive functions. The tag is ascending linearly for the best case and randomized for the average case. Our test system is a single node with an Intel Xeon CPU E5-2630 (Ivy Bridge) processor at 2.60 GHz with 1600 MHz DDR3 memory. We evaluate *OpenMPI 1.10*, *MPICH 3.2*, *MVAPICH 2.2.2rc1*, and a list implementation based on C++'s Standard Template Library (STL). Results are reported as average of thousands of iterations.

Results indicate that *OpenMPI* is optimized for small queues, while *MPICH* becomes superior for queues longer than 64 elements. The STL implementation is outperformed by far, demonstrating how MPI's lists are optimized for the matching purpose. Note that STL's queue container performs even worse due to its costly remove operation of elements at arbitrary positions.

Regarding the average case, matching rates drop significantly for queues longer than 32 elements, reaching half of the peak matching rate at queue lengths of about 128 elements. This can be observed for all MPI implementations. Note that we also determined the worst case matching rate with receive requests always matching the tail of the UMQ, however, the course of performance is similar to the average case with slightly lower absolute matching rates.

Queue Lengths and Search Depth: As shown, the length of the queues has a significant impact on the matching time, thus also on latency and message rate. On the other side, if receive requests always match messages at the queue's head, the actual length is unconcerned, though memory footprint is still affected. Consequently, the search depth is another important aspect. Together with the length, the search depth is shown in Figs. 6 (UMQ) and 7 (PRQ).

Generally, both UMQ and PRQ show similar lengths and search depths, although the UMQ tends to be slightly larger in most applications. The longest queues are observed in Nekbone and MultiGrid with the median length being about 1,024. Overall, the length is smaller than 128 elements in half and smaller than 512 in 75% of the measured moments. Note that we determine the queue length and search depth in any event of send/recv or wait operation and especially toward the end of the application the queues become often zero in length. Thus, queues may be larger during the application's most active communication periods.

Furthermore, it is also interesting to compare search depth and length. If both are similar, matches tend to be found rather at the end of the queue. However, if the search depth is smaller than the length matches are often found near the head of the queue. Regarding the UMQ, search depth is never significantly lower than the measured length. Significantly lower would mean that the depth's median is below the length's 1st quartile. This is different from the PRQ, where at least 6 applications show significant lower depth than length.

While lengths of UMQ and PRQ are similar, the PRQ's search depth tends to be lower. If a receive is posted, the UMQ needs to be searched for a matching message and according to our results, the message tends to be found somewhere near the end of the queue. However, if a message arrives the matching receive tends to be found near the head of the PRQ. That suggests that the order of which receive requests are posted likely matches the order of which messages arrive, or receive requests match with multiple messages.

The median of all applications' search depth ranges below 100 elements, both for UMQ and PRQ. Combining this with the average case matching performance in Fig. 5, the effective matching rate in most cases amounts to less than 18M matches/s. This is about 30% lower than the peak rate of 25M matches/s. Again, communication intensive periods might show even longer queues and thus the matching rate drops even further.

Strong Scaling Effects: The overall mean search depth of the mean across all of the application's ranks with less than 100 processes amounts to 29 elements, while the median is 6. *CESAR's Nekbone's* search depth is 140 for 64 ranks, significantly adding to the mean. Considering all applications with less than 500 ranks, the mean search depth increases to 68, while the median increases to 14. On the other hand, the mean search depths for applications with more than 500 ranks amounts to 143 with a median of 38. The UMQ shows the same trends with higher absolute values. With applications sending more messages at larger scale, it is not surprising that queue lengths increase accordingly.

7 Discussion

This section summarizes the results and discusses our findings. While some insights are already widely assumed to be true in the community, this work aims to quantify these believes.

MPI Time: We observed that a significant amount of time is spent in MPI routines, averaging about 36% across all studied applications. Directing research towards optimizing communication, especially MPI, is therefore important. Especially at large scale, MPI can easily contribute to more than half of the total application time. On the other hand, strong scaling applications show an increased amount of messages and data volume, but also a decreased amount of data per message. Consequently, large scale applications tend to send a significant amount of small messages. This emphasizes the need for low latency communication, thus rendering the matching of messages and receive requests even more important.

Breaking down the MPI time into various operations, we have shown that collective operations consume a significant amount of time compared to plain send/receive communication. This is mainly due to the implicit synchronization and the large number of processes that are involved. Contrary, the amount of data that is transferred collectively is rather small since the bulk of data is transferred via send/receive operations. We advise to use MPI's non-blocking collective operations to hide synchronization time through overlap with computation. Non-blocking collectives were introduced in MPI 3 [17].

Similar recommendations apply to send/receive communications as we suggest using non-blocking operations whenever possible. Note that instead of *MPI_Wait*, a non-blocking scheme using *MPI_Test* can be implemented to avoid busy waiting on requests. On average across all applications, almost 40% of messages are unexpected and all applications heavily use non-blocking receive operations. Nonetheless, *Design Forward's Crystal Router* and *AMG* spend still more than 80% of their MPI time in *MPI_Wait(all)*, possibly allowing for further optimization.

The last important factor that contributes to MPI time is the barrier. We observed that almost every application uses only a single communicator, even at large scale. Hence, a large number of processes participate in barriers, penalizing imbalances. Barriers need to be used carefully and programmers need to consider using more communicators and groups to avoid synchronization at large scale, as also advocated in [18]. However, we understand that this might not be applicable for all applications. Another solution could be the non-blocking barrier, introduced with MPI 3. Instead of busy waiting on the arrival of all processes, useful work could be done in the meantime.

It would be interesting to analyze the MPI time of certain operations even further to obtain a detailed understanding of limiting aspects. For example, the actual time spent for message matching can be assessed for point-to-point operations. However, traces in the present form do not allow for such an analysis and a more detailed profiling framework is required.

Message Matching: The most dominant process within the whole matching of messages and receive requests is to search through unexpected messages and posted receives, respectively. We presented queue lengths and search depths to assess the matching performance. As we have seen, an optimistic 70% of the peak matching performance is achieved in most cases.

With an increased amount of messages and them becoming smaller at large scale, the importance of the matching increases as well. While the choice of algorithms is limited by MPI's in-order delivery, source and tag wildcards, and support for unexpected messages, not all of these features are required [16]. Although we understand that out-of-order delivery could require to restructure applications, we do not see a strong need for wildcards. Regarding the applications, none of them uses the tag wildcard and only two apply wildcards to the source. Alternative matching algorithms [3,4,15] steer in the right direction, but are still limited by wildcards. We suggest to support a mechanism that allows users to disable wildcards and select a more performant messaging mode. As for out-of-order delivery, tags can be used to re-establish ordering on user level. This allows to replace queue structures with hash tables, for example, enabling better performance.

Message Rate and Throughput: Surprisingly, we observed that message rates are rather low in all applications we have studied. Within $100\,\mu s$, which we found to be a reasonable time interval, a median message rate of 100k messages/s is achieved with a maximum of 500k messages/s. Together with most applications' mean message size of about 1K elements/s for point-to-point and collective operations, an effective message rate of 100M elements/s is achieved. This translates to a throughput of about $400\,MB/s$ for single precision and 800MB/s for double precision data, respectively. Since messages are most likely not aggregated, this is in the order of PCIe 2.0's bandwidth [19]. While it can also suggests that the message rate is limited by PCIe's bandwidth, our trace-based methodology is not sufficient to answer this question. Nonetheless, extremely fast interconnects are still limited by PCIe at end-point level. Tighter coupling of networking hardware and processors certainly steer into the right direction and will help to increase the network injection bandwidth.

8 Conclusion

We have presented and discussed several MPI characteristics of exascale proxy applications like time spent in certain operations, message size and rate, and queue lengths. Taking all applications with various scale into account, an application spends 36% of its time in MPI routines. Strong scaling applications with more than 1,000 ranks average an MPI time of even 60%. Most of this time is spent in collective operations, while the majority of data is transferred by point-to-point operations. We showed that messages become smaller at larger scale, emphasizing the importance of message matching.

We showed that search depth and queue length for both UMQ and PRQ are similar in most cases, suggesting that matching messages are rather found toward the end of the queues. Across all applications again, the median queue length amounts to about 100 elements. This translates to a matching rate of 70% of peak performance. Again, scaling applications to a large number of processes renders queues longer and reduces matching rates even further.

Another important aspect we have shown is the effective message rate. We observed that message rates are rather low, so that within a time interval of 100 μs only a median of 10 messages was counted, resulting in a message rate of 100k messages/s. Message sizes, on the other hand, show a median of about 512 elements/s for point-to-point and around 10 for collective operations.

While we gained valuable insights from the trace-based analysis, there are limitations and not all questions can be answered. The MPI time, for example, needs to be analyzed in more detail to understand what exactly is causing overhead. We assume that load imbalances lead to significant overhead for collective operations, but this needs to be verified using more detailed profiling frameworks, which is not trivial at large scale.

We also encourage operators of large computing facilities to provide more traces of their applications as access to these systems is often restricted. This allows for more applications to be analyzed and understood.

Acknowledgments. We would like to thank Hans Eberle and Larry Dennison from NVIDIA Corp. for insightful discussions that shaped the idea of this work. We also appreciate the U.S. DOE's effort of making the traces available to the public and thank all contributors for generating and providing the trace data.

References

1. The opportunities and challenges of exascale computing, summary report of the advanced scientific computing advisory committee (ASCAC) subcommittee at the US DOE Office of Science. Technical report (2010)
2. Klenk, B., Oden, L., Fröning, H.: Analyzing communication models for distributed thread-collaborative processors in terms of energy and time. In: IEEE International Symposium on Performance Analysis of Systems and Software (ISPASS), Philadelphia, PA (2015)
3. Flajslik, M., Dinan, J., Underwood, K.D.: Mitigating MPI message matching misery. In: International Conference on High Performance Computing (ISC), Frankfurt, Germany (2016)
4. Bayatpour, M., Subramoni, H., Chakraborty, S., Panda, D.K.: Adaptive and dynamic design for MPI tag matching. In: 2016 IEEE International Conference on Cluster Computing (CLUSTER) (2016)
5. U.S. DOE: Characterization of the DOE Mini-apps. https://portal.nersc.gov/project/CAL/doe-miniapps.htm. Accessed 25 Oct 2016
6. Faraj, A., Yuan, X.: Communication characteristics in the NAS parallel benchmarks. In: IASTED International Conference on Parallel and Distributed Computing Systems (PDCS), Cambridge, MA (2002)
7. Riesen, R.: Communication patterns. In: Workshop on Communication Architecture for Clusters (CAC), Rhodes Island, Greece (2006)

8. Vetter, J.S., Mueller, F.: Communication characteristics of large-scale scientific applications for contemporary cluster architectures. J. Parallel Distrib. Comput. **63**(9) (2003)

9. Kamil, S., Oliker, L., Pinar, A., Shalf, J.: Communication requirements and interconnect optimization for high-end scientific applications. IEEE Trans. Parallel Distrib. Syst. **21**(2) (2010)

10. Raponi, P.G., Petrini, F., Walkup, R., Checconi, F.: Characterization of the communication patterns of scientific applications on Blue Gene/P. In: IEEE International Symposium on Parallel and Distributed Processing Workshops (IPDPSW) and Ph.D. Forum, DC, USA, Washington (2011)

11. Lammel, S., Zahn, F., Fröning, H.: SONAR: automated communication characterization for HPC applications. In: Taufer, M., Mohr, B., Kunkel, J.M. (eds.) ISC High Performance 2016. LNCS, vol. 9945, pp. 98–114. Springer, Cham (2016). doi:10.1007/978-3-319-46079-6_8

12. Brightwell, R., Underwood, K.D.: An analysis of NIC resource usage for offloading MPI. In: IEEE International Parallel and Distributed Processing Symposium (IPDPS), Santa Fe, NM (2004)

13. Underwood, K.D., Hemmert, K.S., Rodrigues, A., Murphy, R., Brightwell, R.: A hardware acceleration unit for MPI queue processing. In: IEEE International Parallel and Distributed Processing Symposium (IPDPS), Denver, CO (2005)

14. Keller, R., Graham, R.L.: Characteristics of the unexpected message queue of MPI applications. In: Keller, R., Gabriel, E., Resch, M., Dongarra, J. (eds.) EuroMPI 2010. LNCS, vol. 6305, pp. 179–188. Springer, Heidelberg (2010). doi:10.1007/978-3-642-15646-5_19

15. Zounmevo, J.A., Afsahi, A.: An efficient MPI message queue mechanism for large-scale jobs. In: IEEE Conference on Parallel and Distributed Systems (ICPADS), Singapore (2012)

16. Klenk, B., Fröning, H., Eberle, H., Dennison, L.: Relaxations for high-performance message passing on massively parallel SIMT processors. In: IEEE International Parallel and Distributed Processing Symposium (IPDPS), Orlando, FL (2017)

17. Hoefler, T., Kambadur, P., Graham, R.L., Shipman, G., Lumsdaine, A.: A case for standard non-blocking collective operations. In: Cappello, F., Herault, T., Dongarra, J. (eds.) EuroPVM/MPI 2007. LNCS, vol. 4757, pp. 125–134. Springer, Heidelberg (2007). doi:10.1007/978-3-540-75416-9_22

18. Balaji, P., Chan, A., Thakur, R., Gropp, W., Lusk, E.: Toward message passing for a million processes: characterizing MPI on a massive scale Blue Gene/P. Comput. Sci. Res. Dev. (CSRD) **24**(1), 11–19 (2009)

19. Koop, M.J., Huang, W., Gopalakrishnan, K., Panda, D.K.: Performance analysis and evaluation of PCIe 2.0 and quad-data rate InfiniBand. In: IEEE Symposium on High Performance Interconnects (2008)

Fast Matrix-Free Discontinuous Galerkin Kernels on Modern Computer Architectures

Martin Kronbichler[1]([⊠]) [iD], Katharina Kormann[2,3], Igor Pasichnyk[4],
and Momme Allalen[5]

[1] Institute for Computational Mechanics, Technical University of Munich,
Boltzmannstr. 15, 85747 Garching, Germany
kronbichler@lnm.mw.tum.de
[2] Max–Planck–Institute for Plasma Physics,
Boltzmannstr. 2, 85748 Garching, Germany
[3] Zentrum Mathematik, Technical University of Munich,
Boltzmannstr. 3, 85747 Garching, Germany
[4] IBM Deutschland, Boltzmannstr. 1, 85748 Garching, Germany
[5] Leibniz-Rechenzentrum der Bayerischen Akademie der Wissenschaften,
Boltzmannstr. 1, 85748 Garching, Germany

Abstract. This study compares the performance of high-order discontinuous Galerkin finite elements on modern hardware. The main computational kernel is the matrix-free evaluation of differential operators by sum factorization, exemplified on the symmetric interior penalty discretization of the Laplacian as a metric for a complex application code in fluid dynamics. State-of-the-art implementations of these kernels stress both arithmetics and memory transfer. The implementations of SIMD vectorization and shared-memory parallelization are detailed. Computational results are presented for dual-socket Intel Haswell CPUs at 28 cores, a 64-core Intel Knights Landing, and a 16-core IBM Power8 processor. Up to polynomial degree six, Knights Landing is approximately twice as fast as Haswell. Power8 performs similarly to Haswell, trading a higher frequency for narrower SIMD units. The performance comparison shows that simple ways to express parallelism through `for` loops perform better on medium and high core counts than a more elaborate task-based parallelization with dynamic scheduling according to dependency graphs, despite less memory transfer in the latter algorithm.

1 Introduction

The increasing accuracy requirements when simulating partial differential equations in engineering applications can often not be satisfied by simply scaling up existing codes. A limitation in the solver design of many codes is their heavy use of sparse linear algebra routines, with matrices coming from some low-order discretization on unstructured meshes. Sparse matrix algebra is heavily memory bandwidth bound and has only seen moderate performance gains from the advances in computer architecture during the last decade. On systems with a limited amount of high-bandwidth memory, such as the 16 GB of MCDRAM on

© Springer International Publishing AG 2017
J.M. Kunkel et al. (Eds.): ISC High Performance 2017, LNCS 10266, pp. 237–255, 2017.
DOI: 10.1007/978-3-319-58667-0_13

the Intel Knights Landing architecture, the sheer memory consumption of sparse matrices can further limit the applicability of legacy implementations.

In iterative linear solvers which are dominated by matrix-vector products, an alternative to matrix-based schemes is an evaluation on the fly without actually constructing the matrix. Stencil-based realizations such as finite differences often impose too strong restrictions on the computational mesh. On the other hand, the integrals underlying a matrix-vector product in a finite element discretization are amenable to fast matrix-free implementation by sum factorization [6] for meshes consisting of quadrilaterals or hexahedra. A generic sum factorization finite element kernel was introduced to the deal.II finite element library [1] in [11]. For polynomial degrees two and higher, it has been shown to be several times faster than matrix-based schemes.

For discretization of complex transport phenomena, higher-order discontinuous Galerkin (DG) methods are very attractive: As opposed to continuous finite elements, they do not strongly impose the continuity of the solution over element interfaces but rather link the elements by integrals involving numerical fluxes as a combination of the solution on both sides. This flexibility allows for taking directionality into account, such as upwinding [2], and makes the method robust also in complex flow scenarios. Furthermore, the independent definition of the solution on each element in DG avoids the indirect addressing inherent to the access of degrees of freedom in continuous spectral element methods [6] in favor of "packed" data access. Its combination of highly desirable characteristics makes DG an essential building block in next-generation solvers and motivates the development of efficient and tuned implementations. The present work has its background in a high-order discontinuous Galerkin solver for simulating incompressible turbulent flow described by the Navier–Stokes equations, where one of the central algorithmic components is a solver for the pressure Poisson equation which is implemented via the multigrid infrastructure described in [12].

For this purpose, we have extended the sum-factorization finite element framework presented in [11] to discontinuous elements with face integrals. In this work, we consider single node code optimizations. Two central aspects of high-performance DG implementations on modern compute architecture are addressed, namely efficient SIMD vectorization and shared-memory parallelization. These two components form the basis for hybrid codes that additionally use MPI to span over several nodes. Our shared memory parallelization is realized with the Intel Threading Building Blocks (TBB) library (tightly integrated into `deal.II`) with support for both parallel `for` loops as well as task-based parallelism that schedules according to dependencies [13].

A major contribution of the present study is the identification of code patterns that provide best performance in shared memory, given several options. Most previous HPC implementations of DG use patterns similar to what we identify as the loop variant in the following, which also we find to perform best when parallelized. However, the pure performance metrics in terms of memory transfer are better for the alternative task implementation adapted from [9] as seen in Sect. 5.1, thus motivating our comparative analysis.

The second major contribution is the documentation of the absolute performance of our kernels on contemporary hardware, namely an Intel Xeon Phi system based on the Knights Landing architecture, a dual-socked Intel Haswell system, and an IBM Power8 system. Table 1 lists the key characteristics of these systems. While the Haswell and Power8 systems are conventional (latency-optimized) CPUs with a moderate number of cores, the KNL system is throughput-oriented with more parallelism but slower two-wide cores derived from the Intel Atom processor [5]. The Knights Landing architecture also comes with a new memory technology, a high bandwidth on-package memory called Multi-Channel DRAM (MCDRAM) in addition to the traditional DDR4 memory. MCDRAM provides up to 5× the bandwidth of DDR4 but is of lower capacity (16 GB), accessible through the "cache", "flat" and "hybrid" modes, respectively. The optimal usage of MCDRAM is an open issue, and addressed in our work by memory-lean kernels that can fit into this fast memory.

Table 1. Specification of hardware systems used for evaluation. Memory bandwidth on KNL according to the STREAM benchmark.

	Xeon Phi KNL	Haswell	Power8
Cores	64	14	16
Threads	4 Threads/core	2 Threads/core	8 Threads/core
Frequency	1.3 GHz/core	2.6 GHz/core	3.8 GHz/core
L1 cache	32 kB/core	32 kB/core	64 kB/core
L2 cache	1 MB/(2 cores)	256 kB/core	512 kB/core
Memory	16 GB MCDRAM @ 430 GB/s	L3 Cache: 2*17.5 MB	L3 Cache: 8 MB
	384 GB DDR4 @ 90 GB/s	2.3 GB/core	8 GB/core
SIMD	512 bit	256 bit	128 bit

The remainder of this text is structured as follows. Section 2 presents the fluid dynamics application underlying the tuning. Section 3 gives an overview of the implementation used for benchmarking. In Sect. 4, tuning steps of the code are described. Section 5 compares the performance on three systems using relevant test cases.

2   Application Background and Discretization

Incompressible fluid flow is governed by the Navier–Stokes equations,

$$\frac{\partial u}{\partial t} + \nabla \cdot \left(u \otimes u + pI - \frac{1}{\text{Re}}(\nabla u + \nabla u^{\text{T}}) \right) = f,$$

$$\nabla \cdot u = 0, \tag{1}$$

where $\boldsymbol{u}$ denotes the (non-dimensional) fluid velocity, p is the pressure, and $\boldsymbol{f}$ represents body forces. For large Reynolds numbers Re, the flow becomes turbulent and develops instationary and small-scale features that needs high resolution and efficient solvers. The physically relevant scale range in space and time behaves as Re^3. For moderate to large Reynolds numbers $\text{Re} = 10^4 \ldots 10^8$ whose resolution requirements exceed even the power of large supercomputers, modeling approaches such as large or detached eddy simulation complement direct numerical simulation.

For time discretization of Eq. (1), splitting schemes are most common at larger Reynolds numbers, such as the dual-splitting approach by Karniadakis et al. [7], where each time step involves an explicit convection step, a pressure Poisson equation, a projection to make the velocity field divergence-free, and an implicit viscous step. In Fig. 1, the result of a direct numerical simulation of the turbulent flow around a periodic hill is shown, i.e., a highly resolved computation that covers all length scales relevant to the flow physics. The simulation results have been obtained for a polynomial degree $k = 4$ on a mesh of $128 \times 64 \times 64$ elements, producing 260 million spatial degrees of freedom that are followed over several million time steps.

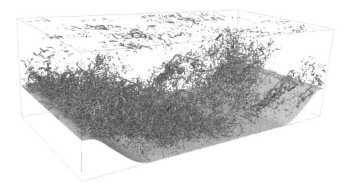

Fig. 1. Turbulent flow along a periodic hill, visualized through the Q-criterion, on a computation on a $128 \times 64 \times 64$ boundary-fitted mesh with fourth-degree elements involving 260 million degrees of freedom.

Table 2 details the distribution of run time in the four phases of a time step in this application, the fraction of time spent in integration kernels similar to the matrix-vector product analyzed in the sequel of this work, and the active access of memory of each step. The active memory can be compared to the global resident memory of 332 GB as measured by accumulation over all 128 nodes involved in the computation. The most demanding part is to solve the pressure Poisson equation with 65 million equations. To ensure optimal complexity and thus efficient use of computational resources, we use an iterative conjugate gradient solver preconditioned by a geometric multigrid V-cycle [12]. The smoothing

Table 2. Run times of the sub-steps involved in one time step of the incompressible flow solver with 260 million degrees of freedom when running on 2048 Sandy Bridge cores. The projection step includes a stabilization according to [10], which invokes fast local conjugate gradient solvers independently for each element.

	Run time	# iterations	Share mat-vec	Memory accessed
Explicit convective step	0.012 s	—	100%	59 GB of 332 GB
Pressure Poisson equation	0.29 s	11	77%	41 GB of 332 GB
Projection step	0.045 s	20–50	100%	26 GB of 332 GB
Viscous step	0.066 s	3	73%	36 GB of 332 GB

on each level is done by the Chebyshev iteration which only needs access to the inverse of the entries on the matrix diagonal besides the matrix-vector product.

The numbers in Table 2 highlight that code optimizations need to concentrate on the matrix-vector product which accounts for approximately 80% of the total run time. Note that the implementation according to [11] uses a generic interface to integration and improvements made for one kernel typically translate to similar profits in the other variants of the integration loops and thus the whole complex application code. Besides the times for a time step listed in the table, the code also consists an initial setup phase and small data analysis parts take less than 1% of overall run time.

A discretized partial differential operator corresponds to a matrix-vector product in our model. We assume a triangulation of the computational domain into elements $K \in \mathcal{T}_h$. The set of interior faces is denoted by $\mathcal{F}_h^i$ with p^- and p^+ the pressure solution on the respective side of the face, and the set of boundary faces by $\mathcal{F}_h^b$. The bilinear forms $(a, b)_K = \int_K a \odot b \, d\boldsymbol{x}$ and $\langle a, b \rangle_F = \int_F a \odot b \, d\boldsymbol{x}$ denote the inner product of the two quantities and subsequent integration over the element K or the face F, respectively. Using this notation, the discretization of the pressure Poisson equation finds p_h such that the equation

$$
\sum_{K \in \mathcal{T}_h} (\nabla q_h, \nabla p_h)_K + \sum_{F \in \mathcal{F}_h^i} \left[\langle q_h^- - q_h^+, \sigma(p_h^- - p_h^+) \rangle_F \right.
$$
$$
\left. - \left\langle (q_h^- - q_h^+) \boldsymbol{n}^-, \frac{\nabla p_h^- + \nabla p_h^+}{2} \right\rangle_F - \left\langle \frac{\nabla q_h^- + \nabla q_h^+}{2}, \boldsymbol{n}^-(p_h^- - p_h^+) \right\rangle_F \right]
$$
$$
+ \sum_{F \in \mathcal{F}_h^b} \langle q_h, 2\sigma p_h \rangle_F - \langle q_h \boldsymbol{n}, \nabla p_h \rangle_F - \langle \nabla q_h, \boldsymbol{n} p_h \rangle_F = \sum_{K \in \mathcal{T}_h} \left(q_h, -\frac{\gamma_0}{\Delta t} \nabla \cdot \hat{\boldsymbol{u}} \right)_K
$$

$$(2)$$

holds for all test functions q_h. In this equation, $\frac{\gamma_0}{\Delta t} \nabla \cdot \hat{\boldsymbol{u}}$ is the forcing given by the divergence of some intermediate-step velocity $\hat{\boldsymbol{u}}$ that is usually used in a slightly modified form with integration by parts including central fluxes for the velocity for stability reasons according to [10]. The interior penalty parameter is denoted by σ and penalizes jumps of the solution over faces, see e.g. [2].

3   Implementation

The operator evaluation is realized by fast integration, using an extension of the framework presented in [11] to discontinuous Galerkin. For the linear operator $\mathcal{L}$ implementing the left hand side of Eq. (2), an input vector $\boldsymbol{P}$ is interpreted by its solution function p_h and tested by all basis functions q_h, giving rise to an output vector $\boldsymbol{Q}$,

$$Q = \mathcal{L}P. \tag{3}$$

The integrals are performed according to Eq. (2) on both cells K and faces F. For the cell integrals, the degrees of freedom related to the cell from the global vector are extracted, the local operator is evaluated by integration and tested by all local basis functions and, finally, the local integrals are written into the global result vector. In the integrals, the gradient operators ∇ with respect to the spatial variable $\boldsymbol{x}$ in Eq. (2) are replaced by gradients in the reference coordinate $\boldsymbol{\xi} \in (0,1)^3$ and multiplied by the Jacobian of the transformation in the usual finite element fashion [11]. The unit-cell operation is the same on all elements and implemented by sum factorization kernels for hexahedra [6,8]. The Jacobian transformation on Cartesian meshes is the same throughout an element (and possibly over many different elements), whereas a separate $d \times d$ matrix for each quadrature point is necessary for curved meshes. Our realization makes use of these optimizations if the mesh allows for that, significantly reducing memory transfer in the Cartesian mesh case.

The face integrals involve interpolated solutions from the two neighboring cells, tested by basis functions and integrated by a quadrature formula on the faces. In order to avoid double computations when evaluating the integrals to all faces of a cell, we use a separate loop indexing for the faces. Integrals on inner faces combine the information from both adjacent cells in a single step.

The evaluation complexity per degree of freedom with sum factorization is $\mathcal{O}(k + 1)$ in the polynomial degree k for cell integrals [11] and $\mathcal{O}(1)$ for face integrals. The proportionality constants are such that the number of arithmetic operations for on-the-fly integration is lower than with the final matrix "stencils" starting at polynomial degrees three to four for continuous elements [11] and at degree two to three of discontinuous ansatz spaces. Since a matrix-based scheme is usually heavily memory-bandwidth bound, matrix-free evaluation is the fastest available evaluation option already for quadratic shape functions. The specific characteristics of the method allow for an almost constant run time per degree of freedom for a wide range of polynomial degrees $2 \leq k \leq 8$ [11,12], making the polynomial degree essentially a parameter that can be adapted to the complexity of the geometry to be meshed: A more complex geometry will use more elements of somewhat lower polynomial degree. On more regular domains, the higher solution quality of high-order shape functions can be leveraged. Our kernels are integrated into the deal.II finite element library [1], which provides the infrastructure of the mesh, definition of degrees of freedom and parallelization for our application code. This allows for implementing weak forms such as the Laplacian (2) in compact form with only up to a few dozens of lines of code.

Despite their generality, the matrix-free kernels outperform the benchmark code from the HPGMG project[1] by 1.5 to 2.5 times on continuous elements [12], which is due to the careful selection of stored data structures vs. on-the-fly computation. The arithmetic intensities of the resulting algorithms are between 1 and 6 FLOP/byte, depending on the geometry, i.e., close to the ridge of memory-bound and computation-bound algorithms [12]. This characteristic makes it necessary to consider both memory efficiency as well as optimizations addressing arithmetics and instruction scheduling.

Since several faces compute integral contributions to the same cell in this layout, the face computations cannot be simply split into subranges within a parallel for loop over the faces, and they cannot be arbitrarily mixed with cell integrals in order to avoid race conditions when accessing the global result vector Q in Eq. (3). In the following, we discuss two shared-memory parallelizations that avoid these race conditions in different ways. We focus on implementation with the Intel TBB library which is the main thread parallelism paradigm in deal.II. An alternative OpenMP-based implementation of our loops has shown very similar performance. We do not consider atomic operations or locks in this work because they have been found to be less efficient on preliminary tests. For the former, no vectorized versions are implemented in CPU hardware yet, reducing efficiency.

3.1   Parallel Evaluation Through Tasks

The task-based parallel scheme adapts the partition-partition scheme described in [9] for finite element operator application. In the discontinuous Galerkin setting, each task includes operations on a range of cells, a range of inner faces, and a range of boundary faces. The latter two ranges are associated with the cell range in order to leverage solution data already in caches from the cell integrals. A race condition can appear if one task operates on an inner face accessing cells K_1 and K_2 and another task simultaneously operates on another inner face involving either K_1 or K_2 or a cell integral on $K_{1/2}$. We note that at least one of the two cells—the one the face is associated with—will be part of the same task and not conflict. However, this does not necessarily hold true for the other cell.

The idea of the partitioning strategy is to compute the connectivity between tasks based on the access pattern of face integrals. The connectivity graph is then split in such a way that layer i is only connected to layers $i-1$ and $i+1$. With this layout, the cells in all even partitions can be parallelized without race conditions. Afterwards, all odd partitions can be run in parallel. Starting with a group of cells for the first partition, the size of the partitions can increase and the total number of partitions might be rather small. In order to create enough parallelism, we therefore create another layer of partitions inside each partition. Each partition on the second level is a multiple of a certain block size in order to make sure that vectorization is possible. The idea is related to graph coloring

---

[1] https://hpgmg.org.

but adapted such that only local synchronization points between the adjacent tasks are necessary, as opposed to global synchronization when running parallel loops on one color at a time, see [9].

The algorithm can be summarized as follows

- Preprocessing: Find the connectivity structure where each cell is associated with a list of cells that share a face with it.
- Assign each block to one partition:
  - Assign the first cells (up to a user-specified grain size) to partition zero.
  - Assign all cells that are connected with cells in partition zero, but not already assigned a partition to partition one. If the number of cells is not a multiple of the grain size, add neighbors of the cells in partition one. This fill-up avoids empty lanes when vectorizing over several cells as described in Sect. 3.3 below.
  - Repeat this procedure until all cells are assigned to a partition.
- For each partition, create a second layer of partitions analogously.
- Create an integer cell indexing according to the double partitioning.

Note that the algorithm is analogous to one described in [9] with the only difference that the connectivity graph uses the dependency of the face integrals instead of the degrees of freedom shared at the element boundary in continuous finite elements.

3.2   Parallel Evaluation Through for loops

An alternative approach to avoid simultaneous writes into the same vector positions is to introduce temporary data structures that hold information for each face integral separately. A common approach in discontinuous Galerkin methods [2,3] is to interpolate the function u^h to all the faces. In the context of integration where the differential operator is implemented by quadrature and tensor products are involved, the most efficient approach is to perform an interpolation step in face-normal direction and store this data in a global auxiliary variable. This gives the following algorithm for the SIP discretization (2):

1. Loop over all cells $K \in \mathcal{T}_h$:
   - Read values from input vector.
   - Interpolate elemental input values to all $2d$ faces for both values and the reference-cell normal derivative. This gives $2(k+1)^{d-1}$ data values per face that are stored in a global auxiliary vector.
   - Perform cell integration by sum factorization and write result into destination vector.
2. Loop over all inner faces $F \in \mathcal{F}_h^i$:
   - Load the values and normal derivatives from the global auxiliary vector from the element storage on both elements K^- and K^+ and local face numbers f^- and f^+ involved in the face.
   - Sum factorization provides values and reference gradients in face quadrature points.

- On each quadrature point, implement all face terms involved in (2).
- Sum over quadrature points and multiplication by test function $v_h^{\pm}$ and unit cell gradient $\nabla v_h^{\pm}$ with sum factorization.
- Write the resulting contribution to value and normal derivative to be tested back into the global auxiliary vector, indexed by the element numbers K^- and K^+ and local face numbers f^- and f^+ involved in the face.
3. Loop over all boundary faces $F \in \mathcal{F}_h^b$: Similar steps to inner faces.
4. Loop over all cells $K \in \mathcal{T}_h$:
   - Read global auxiliary vector for values and normal derivatives on each face.
   - Finalize integration step by expanding the test functions into the elements.
   - Add resulting contribution into destination vector.

This algorithm has the advantage that all quantities accessed inside the loops are independent from one another. This includes the face loops where different faces access different sections in the auxiliary vector also when they refer to the same element. Thus, a simple parallel `for` loop can be used. The price to pay for this alternative is the global auxiliary vector which needs to be transferred from/to main memory five times, twice for the initial write operation (write, including read-for-ownership), twice during the face loops (read and write), and once for the final interpolation (read). This increased memory access possibly reduces performance in memory-constrained situations.

3.3 Vectorization

An essential ingredient to high performance of the matrix-free operator evaluation is to use SIMD instructions. Automatic vectorization or OpenMP-SIMD annotations apply vectorization to the innermost loops, which is not the optimal strategy for the complex data flow in local integration with sum factorization that runs through the local vectors in different orders when passing through one direction at a time. Also, the subsequent operations on quadrature points use yet another data access pattern. Thus, full vectorization would involve a series of cross-lane permutations on each element. In addition, some lanes might remain empty or non-vectorized peel and remainder loops arise in case the number of degrees of freedom per direction, $k + 1$, is not a multiple of the SIMD width, reducing the effective throughput. Finally, we note that vectorization in the sum factorization kernel alone is not enough, as the operation on quadrature points can account for 10 to 50% of the instructions on non-vectorized code [11], with higher values for more complex operators like the convective term in the incompressible Navier–Stokes equations.

Instead, our work follows the approach proposed in [11], evaluating the contributions from several cells or faces within a SIMD instruction. This is profitable since the operation on each element is the same, albeit with different data from the vector and different geometries and coefficients. This approach only involves a single cross-lane or gather operation when the global vector data is read and written in the task-based algorithm according to Sect. 3.1. The data in solution vectors is stored contiguously for each element and needs to be "transposed" in this step for putting the same nodal point on all elements involved in the SIMD array next to each other. This transposition transforms an array of structures into a structure-of-array data layout. For the loop-based approach from Sect. 3.2, there are two additional transpose operations involved, one when cells access the auxiliary vector in steps 1 and 4 and one when faces access the auxiliary vector in steps 2 and 3, the latter accessing different components as compared to the cell. Note that some transpositions could be avoided by storing the solution vector in an array-of-structure-of-array data layout. However, the access into at least half of the faces would be considerably more complicated, involving gather and scatter operations where each index points into different cache lines, an operation which typically serializes the data access on contemporary hardware implementations and is less efficient than the vectorized access proposed here.

On Haswell, SIMD instructions process four cells/faces (double precision) or eight cells/faces (single precision) at once. On Knights Landing, the numbers are eight for double precision and 16 for single precision, whereas the numbers are two and four on Power8. A disadvantage of the proposed vectorization scheme is that the size of the scratch data fields holding temporary results from sum factorization increases with increasing vector width. The size of the scratch data used for processing a cell integral scales as $6(k+1)^d$, which is multiplied by 32 or 64 bytes in case of Haswell and Knights Landing, respectively. Thus, the scratch data spills L1 caches of Haswell for $k = 5$ and for $k = 4$ on KNL, relying on fast next-level caches for higher degrees. However, the results below show that memory hierarchies are sufficiently capable on both systems, with the exception of KNL on high degrees $k \geq 9$ when the L2 cache capacity is exhausted.

4   Performance Tuning

The performance tuning is driven by identifying the most significant bottlenecks in our code and making appropriate changes that reduce or eliminate the effect of these bottlenecks. Node level tuning is performed using the Intel VTune Amplifier Tool [4]. We conduct our analysis and optimization on a dual-socket Intel Xeon E5-2697 v3 according to Table 1 using the double-precision matrix-vector product. To reduce the amount of collected information the hot spot analysis is performed using one thread. The vector load intrinsic operation _mm256_loadu_pd which is called several times from the function vectorized_load_and_transpose is the most time-consuming operation as can be seen from the top-down view of the function call stack for the case of the Cartesian grid configuration shown in Fig. 2, which appears inside the aforementioned transposition step. The loop in the function vectorized_load_and_transpose_base performs vector load operations based on offset values inside a loop. We could improve this code by moving the redundant calculation of the offset indices outside the loop by introducing double pointers that can be held in registers.

Furthemore the same function `vectorized_load_and_transpose` appears in the code vectorization analysis performed by Intel Advisor. The analysis shows an inefficient use of vector registers due to the complex structures of the array indices. Keeping this in mind, we modify the function `vectorized_load_and_transpose` correspondingly. To help the compiler performing vectorization of the loop we additionally inserted an OMP SIMD pragma.

Function / Call Stack	CPU Time ≪		CPI Rate
	Effective Time by Utilization ▼ ≫ ▌I... ▌Poc ▌OI ▌I... ▌Ove		
▼ _mm256_loadu_pd	6.4%		3.089
dealii::vectorized_load_and_transpose<double>	6.4%		3.089
▼ _mm256_storeu_pd	6.2%		3.017
▶ dealii::vectorized_transpose_and_store<double>	6.2%		3.017
▼ _mm256_loadu_pd	5.4%		2.980
▶ dealii::vectorized_load_and_transpose<double>	5.4%		2.980
▼ _mm256_loadu_pd	4.5%		2.903
dealii::vectorized_load_and_transpose<double>	4.5%		2.903

Fig. 2. Top-down view of the function call stack for the Cartesian grid case.

Going to the case of a curvilinear grid configuration, Fig. 3 identifies the same function `vectorized_load_and_transpose` among the hot spots. However, the most time consuming function in this case is the overloaded `+=` operation called from the function `get_gradient`. The source code has multiple layers of abstractions for performing SIMD data additions. However, this function representing the actual arithmetic work maps to optimal assembler code, including fused multiply-add instruction identified by the compiler.

Function / Call Stack	CPU Time ≪		CPI Rate
	Effective Time by Utilization ▼ ≫ ▌I... ▌Poc ▌OI ▌I... ▌Ove		
▼ dealii::VectorizedArray<double>::operator+=	11.8%		2.858
▶ ↖ dealii::FEEvaluationAccess<(int)3, (int)1, double, (bool)0>::get_gradient ← ▐	11.8%		2.858
▼ dealii::VectorizedArray<double>::operator+=	6.4%		1.837
▶ ↖ dealii::FEEvaluationBase<(int)3, (int)1, double, (bool)1>::get_normal_gradie	6.4%		1.837
▼ _mm256_loadu_pd	6.3%		3.934
▶ dealii::vectorized_load_and_transpose<double>	6.3%		3.934
▼ _mm256_storeu_pd	5.1%		3.908
▶ dealii::vectorized_transpose_and_store<double>	5.1%		3.908

Fig. 3. Top-down view of the function call stack for curvilinear grid case.

5 Performance Comparison

All code was compiled with the `gcc` compiler, version 6.2, at optimization level `-O3 -march=native`. The performance with `gcc` is within 2% of the performance with the Intel compiler (v. 16.0 and 17.0) when compiled at `-O3 -xhost` on Haswell. The similar performance is due to the explicit vectorization and it depends on the particular instruction scheduling and loop unrolling which of these two compilers performs slightly better. On KNL, the code generated by gcc provides around 1.5 times higher throughput because the Intel compiler for KNL is not able to merge vectorized multiplications and additions arising in the high-level C++ implementation in deal.II into fused multiply-add instructions for __m512d data types. For the Power8 system the code is compiled using the Advanced Toolchain for PowerLinux.9.0 with the IBM's Mathematical Acceleration Subsystem (MASS) libraries. It exploits the advanced capabilities for the POWER vector instruction set from the Vector Multimedia eXtension (VMX). Scalability tests on Power8 are performed by varying the number of hardware threads in each core via the SMT option.

All times are reported as the minimal run time of the matrix-vector product out of ten experiments. Since Intel TBB dynamically distributes the tasks to threads without direct pinning [13], we use the "affinity partitioner" in the for loop variant to ensure that repeated loops run on the same threads. This is beneficial for the non-uniform memory access on the Haswell system where a first-touch page assignment of the data stored on cells such as Jacobian transformations for the loop-based algorithm from Sect. 3.2 is used. No affinity can be used for the task-based scheme. For KNL, MCDRAM memory is configured in "flat" mode where it is mapped to physical address space and exposed as a NUMA node (allocatable memory) in all experiments except the detailed analysis in Sect. 5.4.

5.1   Comparison of Task and Loop Parallelization

Figure 4 compares the parallel scaling of a code with Q_4 elements and 32.8 million degrees of freedom for the two algorithmic variants presented in Sect. 3 on the Haswell, Knights Landing, and Power8 architectures.

On a single Haswell core, the task-based scheme is faster than the loop-based scheme that splits computations into several parts, using 0.72 s rather than 1.17 s. This is due to the lower memory transfer and better cache utilization. An analysis of the matrix-vector product with the likwid tool[2] on a single core reports 0.63 GB of read transfer and 0.32 GB of write transfer to main memory for the layout from Sect. 3.1 (one solution vector: 0.26 GB). Conversely, the for loop from Sect. 3.2 involves 2.76 GB of reads and 1.82 GB of writes (size of auxiliary vector: 0.63 GB).

Despite the advantage in terms of memory transfer, the parallel task implementation scales considerably worse than the for loops. Therefore, the latter reaches 0.068 s on 28 Haswell cores, faster than the task-based scheme at 0.092 s. Power8 is slower with a single thread than Haswell due to the narrower SIMD width, but reaches similar performance to Haswell at higher thread counts and in particular with SMT thanks to more parallelism inside the cores and presumably a better memory controller.

---

[2] https://github.com/RRZE-HPC/likwid, retrieved on September 18, 2016.

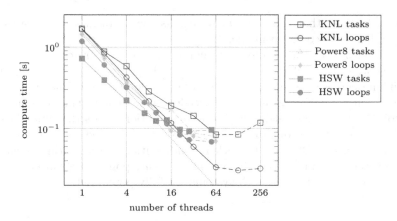

Fig. 4. Parallel scaling study of various task parallelization schemes on Haswell and Knights Landing using a problem with Q_4 elements on a 64^3 Cartesian mesh, using 32.7 million degrees of freedom. Dashed lines indicate the step to logical cores with simultaneous multithreading (SMT).

On a single core, the Knights Landing system is slowest with a wall time of around 1.7 s according to Fig. 4. Given that a KNL core is weak with only half the clock frequency of Haswell and restricted capabilities, a slowdown of only about 30% is remarkable particularly for the loop kernel and shows the effect of wider vectorization. The loop-based algorithm shows excellent strong scaling when increasing the core count to 64, reaching a parallel speedup of more than 50 (and 55 when going to 128 cores). For comparison, the parallel speedup is 17 on the Haswell system.

The task-based parallelization from Sect. 3.1 shows worse behavior on both Intel systems, in particular the KNL system with more cores. Since the code analysis shows that CPUs are mostly busy in that case, we suspect that the dynamic scheduling of tasks with complex dependencies results in less optimal usage of the memory hierarchy such as prefetchers and caches.

5.2   Analysis of Vectorization

In order to leverage the higher performance of single-precision arithmetics, our solvers use mixed precision: The outer residual computations and matrix-vector products according to Eq. (2) are done with double precision for algorithmic stability, whereas it is enough to use single precision for preconditioning the linear systems, which applies to the full multigrid V-cycle in the Poisson solver. Thus, the throughput of operator evaluation is recorded for both single precision and double precision. Figure 5 displays the number of degrees of freedom processed per second on the Haswell and Knights Landing architectures, respectively. For large problem sizes, evaluation in single precision is between 1.6 and 1.9 times as fast. The gap to the ideal factor 2 is mainly because the global loops are half as long when the number of element batches due to SIMD halves. This can be seen from the fact that the gap still widens as the problem size increases and more parallelism becomes available.

When turning to the absolute throughput numbers, our results show that the dual-socket Haswell system can evaluate the DG operator (2) for up to 480 million degrees of freedom per second in double precision, whereas Knights landing reaches 1.1 billion degrees of freedom per second. This speedup of a factor of 2.3 at a somewhat lower power consumption shows the capabilities of the KNL system for throughput-oriented tasks such as the massively parallel integration tasks in DG. On the other hand, initialization routines including many indirections and a mix of integer and floating point code run half as fast on KNL as on Haswell when both systems are fully populated.

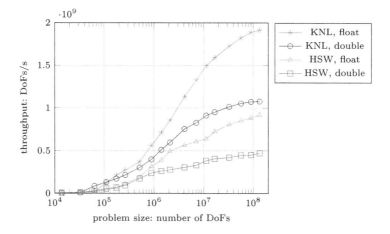

Fig. 5. Performance of matrix-vector product on discontinuous $\mathcal{Q}_3$ elements. Loop parallelization from Sect. 3.2.

Figure 6 evaluates the effectiveness of the explicit vectorization over elements as described in Sect. 3.3 by comparison with auto-vectorization explored by the compiler. In order to increase the possibilities for automatic vectorization, the pointers inside the sum-factorization kernels are annotated with the C/C++ _restrict keyword and OMP SIMD pragmas to exclude pointer aliasing. In all configurations, the explicit vectorization holds a clear performance advantage with up to a factor of 4.3. For Knights Landing with wider vector units, the gain with explicit vectorization is larger than on Haswell. Likewise, single precision shows larger gains than double precision. We note that the explicit vectorization path performs essentially all arithmetic operations in packed form. Measurements of the Haswell code with the likwid tool shows that more than 99% of floating point instructions in the relevant sections are on 256-bit packed data, whereas only up to 15% of arithmetic operations are vectorized by auto-vectorization according to the likwid analysis, both measured for $\mathcal{Q}_3$ elements. Despite a potential fourfold improvement for AVX vectorization on Haswell,

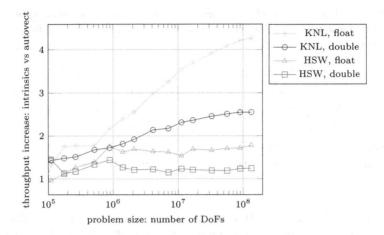

Fig. 6. Effectiveness of vectorization measured as the ratio in throughput of auto-vectorized code and the explicit vectorization over several elements with intrinsics according to Sect. 3.3 for Q_3 elements. Numbers larger than 1 point to an advantage of the explicit vectorization.

the actual speedup is between 20% and 80% because of memory bottlenecks in the wider code. This is explained by a substantially higher instruction throughput for the non-vectorized code at 2.38 instructions per clock cycle versus 1.47 instructions per cycle for the explicitly vectorized code.

The comparison of vectorization efficiency of Haswell and KNL also allows for projections about the run time on future systems: As soon as Intel Xeon CPUs move to AVX-512 instructions with the Skylake Server architecture, we expect them to surpass KNL in efficiency on computation bound kernels on Cartesian meshes with twice the theoretical throughput of Haswell. However, we expect KNL to remain faster due to the higher memory throughput of MCDRAM on the curved mesh which is memory bound.

5.3   Performance Metrics of Loop Kernel

Table 3 details the run time of the individual components in the loop parallelization according to Sect. 3.2 together with an analysis of memory transfer and arithmetic operations measured with the likwid tool. Steps $2 + 3$ as well as the part that computes the cell integral in step 1 involve more arithmetics as compared to the other operations. For the cell integration, Haswell reaches an arithmetic throughput of almost 400 GFLOP/s when counting FMA instructions as two operations.[3] About 55% of the arithmetic instructions are FMAs and the others separate additions and multiplications. This relatively low proportion of FMAs is due to our implementation that targets minimal execution

---

[3] As a complement to the numbers given by likwid that count FMAs as one FLOP, we recorded FMAs and additions and multiplication separately with the Intel software development emulator.

Table 3. Run time analysis of loop-parallel code in terms of memory transfer and GFLOP/s as measured with the likwid tool on 32.7 million degrees of freedom with Q_4 elements.

	Haswell 56 threads			KNL 128 threads		
	time [s]	GB/s	GFLOP/s	time [s]	GB/s	GFLOP/s
Step 1, all	0.026	80	230	0.013	160	460
Step 1, cell part	0.012	67	386	0.0092	87	510
Steps 2 + 3	0.024	55	210	0.012	110	420
Step 4	0.020	60	72	0.0063	190	220

time rather than maximal FLOP rates by using the so-called even-odd decomposition [8]. With these numbers, the cell integration part from step 1 reaches more than 60% of arithmetic peak on Haswell. In the memory-dominated parts, the complicated access patterns and possible issues in the memory pipeline prevent the implementation to reach the full memory performance which is measured as 95 GB/s for the STREAM add kernel on the Haswell system and 430 GB/s on KNL. Due to different memory intensities in these four steps, the complete matrix-vector product is relatively far away from the performance limits of the architectures, reaching 67 GB/s and 182 GFLOP/s on Haswell and 150 GB/s and 406 GFLOP/s on KNL. KNL is generally a bit farther from theoretical performance limits, showing the impact of the weaker core with instruction-scheduling bottlenecks.

As a metric for the performance in different application scenarios, Fig. 7 shows the throughput of the matrix-vector product as a function of the polynomial degree. Results have been generated for problem sizes between 16 and 134 million degrees of freedom on the Cartesian mesh and 4.5 to 25 million degrees of freedom on the curved mesh, both chosen such that the local kernels fit into the 16 GB MCDRAM memory of KNL that is operated in flat mode. As the polynomial degree increases, there are jumps in the number of elements which have a slight effect on the throughput, namely between $k = 3$ and $k = 4$ and between $k = 7$ and $k = 8$, respectively. The results show more than a two-fold advantage of KNL over Haswell on moderate polynomial degrees $k \leq 6$. Moreover, the advantage is more pronounced on the curved mesh case which has a lower arithmetic intensity (2 FLOP/byte versus 5 FLOP/byte). This result highlights the importance of fast MCDRAM memory as compared to the Haswell system, see also the results in Table 4 below.

5.4 Memory Mode of KNL

For the KNL system, the fast MCDRAM is an essentially ingredient to reach high performance, in particular due to the high dependence on memory throughput documented by the kernel analysis in Sect. 5.3. In Table 4 the performance of "flat" mode is compared to "cache" mode. For the "flat" mode, we use `numactl` to ensure

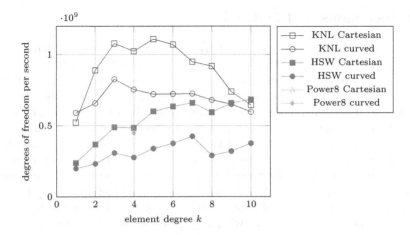

Fig. 7. Performance of double-precision matrix-vector product on discontinuous elements as a function of the polynomial degree.

that all memory allocations go to the MCDRAM or the DDR4 RAM, respectively. In flat mode, the code runs two to three times faster from MCDRAM than from DDR4 memory. When comparing the results of the flat mode with the cache mode, we see that the cache mode reaches similar or even slightly better performance than the flat mode for algorithms which repeatedly access the same memory. According to the numbers shown in Table 2, the fluid dynamics application is an ideal target for this mode: The application code does not need to specify at compile time where the memory should be allocated (like when using `hbwmalloc` through `memkind` [5] going to MCDRAM): In case the whole application fits into MCDRAM, full performance is reached in the steady state of many time steps. In case the overall program exceeds the MCDRAM cache, all steps except for the explicit convection step (with only one sweep through data) involve iterations with repeated access to at most one tenth of global resident memory.

Table 4. Comparison of memory modes on KNL, measured as degrees of freedom processed per second (DoFs/s).

	Cache mode		Flat mode	
	1st run	Avg 100 runs	MCDRAM	DDR4
Cartesian mesh Q_2	$0.46 \cdot 10^9$	$0.89 \cdot 10^9$	$0.89 \cdot 10^9$	$0.53 \cdot 10^9$
Curved mesh Q_2	$0.25 \cdot 10^9$	$0.68 \cdot 10^9$	$0.66 \cdot 10^9$	$0.20 \cdot 10^9$
Cartesian mesh Q_4	$0.44 \cdot 10^9$	$1.22 \cdot 10^9$	$1.08 \cdot 10^9$	$0.59 \cdot 10^9$
Curved mesh Q_4	$0.24 \cdot 10^9$	$0.82 \cdot 10^9$	$0.75 \cdot 10^9$	$0.24 \cdot 10^9$
Cartesian mesh Q_8	$0.41 \cdot 10^9$	$1.16 \cdot 10^9$	$0.92 \cdot 10^9$	$0.53 \cdot 10^9$
Curved mesh Q_8	$0.30 \cdot 10^9$	$0.75 \cdot 10^9$	$0.68 \cdot 10^9$	$0.22 \cdot 10^9$

254 M. Kronbichler et al.

6 Conclusions and Outlook

In this paper, we have discussed the portability of a matrix-free discontinuous Galerkin code to the new KNL and Power8 architectures. We have analyzed and optimized node-level performance by vectorization and thread parallelism with two different algorithms. The first algorithm is based on tasks scheduled according to nearest-neighbor dependencies, while the second is based on simple `for` loops. While the latter parallelization scheme is simpler and allows for more regular data access, it comes with the overhead of additional transfer from RAM memory for temporary face data buffers. Due to the memory overhead this option performs generally worse for low order elements where the amount of face data as compared to cell data is larger and the arithmetic intensity is lower. Nonetheless, it performs considerably better when parallelized on the many-core KNL, highlighting that `for` loops with regular scheduling is beneficial.

Our code implements an explicit vectorization of the integrals which improves runtime significantly as compared to automatic vectorization. This effect is more pronounced for wider vector units, rendering this feature essential for new Intel architectures with 512-bit vector units. Explicit vectorization makes the double-precision kernel run around 2.5 times faster and the single-precision kernel more than four times faster on KNL. When going from Haswell to KNL, we obtain a speedup of a factor 1.5 to 2.5 for our matrix-vector products. Despite different hardware architectures, the IBM Power8 and the Intel Haswell system showed very similar performance, with a slight advantage of the former on memory-heavy operations and a slight advantage of the latter on more arithmetic-heavy parts.

In the future, we plan to combine shared-memory performance obtained on single KNL nodes with MPI in a hybrid parallelization scheme to obtain results in computational engineering with unprecedented accuracy on emerging KNL clusters.

Acknowledgements. The authors acknowledge the support given by the Bayerische Kompetenznetzwerk für Technisch-Wissenschaftliches Hoch- und Höchstleistungsrechnen (KONWIHR) in the framework of the project *High performance finite difference stencils for modern parallel processors*. This work was supported by the German Research Foundation (DFG) under the project *High-order discontinuous Galerkin for the exa-scale* (ExaDG) within the priority program *Software for Exascale Computing* (SPPEXA). The authors gratefully acknowledge the Gauss Centre for Supercomputing e.V. (www.gauss-centre.eu) for funding this project by providing computing time on the GCS Supercomputer SuperMUC at Leibniz Supercomputing Centre (LRZ, www.lrz.de) through project id pr83te.

The authors acknowledge collaboration with Benjamin Krank, Niklas Fehn, and Matthias Brehm.

References

1. Bangerth, W., Davydov, D., Heister, T., Heltai, L., Kanschat, G., Kronbichler, M., Maier, M., Turcksin, B., Wells, D.: The `deal.II` library, version 8.4. J. Numer. Math. **24**(3), 135–141 (2016). doi:10.1515/jnma-2016-1045. www.dealii.org

2. Hesthaven, J.S., Warburton, T.: Nodal Discontinuous Galerkin Methods: Algorithms, Analysis, and Applications. Texts in Applied Mathematics, vol. 54. Springer, New York (2008). doi:10.1007/978-0-387-72067-8
3. Hindenlang, F., Gassner, G., Altmann, C., Beck, A., Staudenmaier, M., Munz, C.D.: Explicit discontinuous Galerkin methods for unsteady problems. Comput. Fluids **61**, 86–93 (2012). doi:10.1016/j.compfluid.2012.03.006
4. Intel Corporation: Intel VTune Amplifier XE 2017. https://software.intel.com/en-us/intel-vtune-amplifier-xe
5. Jeffers, J., Reinders, J., Sodani, A.: Intel Xeon Phi Processor High Performance Programming, Knights Landing Edition. Morgan Kaufmann, Cambridge (2016)
6. Karniadakis, G.E., Sherwin, S.J.: Spectral/hp Element Methods for Computational Fluid Dynamics, 2nd edn. Oxford University Press, Oxford (2005). doi:10.1093/acprof:oso/9780198528692.001.0001
7. Karniadakis, G.E., Israeli, M., Orszag, S.A.: High-order splitting methods for the incompressible Navier-Stokes equations. J. Comput. Phys. **97**(2), 414–443 (1991). doi:10.1016/0021-9991(91)90007-8
8. Kopriva, D.: Implementing Spectral Methods for Partial Differential Equations. Springer, Dordrecht (2009). doi:10.1007/978-90-481-2261-5
9. Kormann, K., Kronbichler, M.: Parallel finite element operator application: graph partitioning and coloring. In: Proceedings of the 7th IEEE International Conference on eScience, pp. 332–339 (2011). doi:10.1109/eScience.2011.53
10. Krank, B., Fehn, N., Wall, W.A., Kronbichler, M.: A high-order semi-explicit discontinuous Galerkin solver for 3D incompressible flow with application to DNS and LES of turbulent channel flow. arXiv preprint arXiv:1607.01323 (2016)
11. Kronbichler, M., Kormann, K.: A generic interface for parallel cell-based finite element operator application. Comput. Fluids **63**, 135–147 (2012). doi:10.1016/j.compfluid.2012.04.012
12. Kronbichler, M., Wall, W.A.: A performance comparison of continuous and discontinuous Galerkin methods with fast multigrid solvers. arXiv preprint arXiv:1611.03029 (2016)
13. Reinders, J.: Intel Threading Building Blocks. O'Reilly, Sebastopol (2007)

A New Parallel Research Kernel to Expand Research on Dynamic Load-Balancing Capabilities

Rob F. Van der Wijngaart[1]([⊠]), Evangelos Georganas[1], Timothy G. Mattson[1], and Andrew Wissink[2]

[1] Parallel Computing Lab, Intel Corp, Santa Clara, CA, USA
`rob.f.van.der.wijngaart@intel.com`
[2] US Army Aviation Development Directorate - AFDD (AMRDEC), Moffett Field, Sunnyvale, CA, USA

Abstract. The Parallel Research Kernels (PRK) are a tool to study parallel architectures and runtime systems from an application perspective. They provide paper and pencil specifications and reference implementations of elementary operations covering a broad range of parallel application patterns. Most of the current PRK are trivially statically load-balanced. In a prior study we described a novel PRK that requires dynamic load balancing, and demonstrated its effectiveness to assess automatic dynamic load balancing capabilities of runtimes. While useful, it did not fully represent the problem of greatest interest to researchers of extreme scale computing systems, namely the occurrence of localized, discrete, transient disturbances (system noise). For that purpose we introduce a new PRK, inspired by Adaptive Mesh Refinement (AMR) applications, which provides a proxy for the most detrimental property of noise, namely abrupt and discrete change of local system load. We give a detailed specification of the new PRK, highlighting the challenges and corresponding design choices that make it compact, arbitrarily scalable and self-verifying. We also present an implementation of the AMR PRK in MPI, with application-specific load balancing, as well as one in Adaptive MPI that leverages the MPI version, but adds runtime orchestrated dynamic load balancing, along with a set of performance results. These show that for applications that can be load balanced statically, but experience occasional local changes in computational load, automatic dynamic load balancing typically does not offer an advantage.

1 Introduction

The Parallel Research Kernels (PRK) [13,29] are a suite of kernels to study the efficiency of distributed and parallel computer systems, including all software and hardware components that make up the system. They cover a wide range of common parallel application patterns, especially from the area of High Performance Computing (HPC). The original kernels were all comprised of regular operations whose work and data could easily be distributed evenly statically among the computational resources. This approach was chosen to avoid measuring load imbalance, which carries no useful information for the system designer or analyst. However, load imbalance is a major factor in the execution of applications, and its importance is growing as the sizes of computer systems keep growing and as applications become more dynamic algorithmically.

We define load balancing as the process of ensuring that computational resources reach synchronization points at the same time, and hence are never idle. While a perfectly balanced load, i.e. full resource utilization, need not lead to optimal performance, a bad load balance is often the hallmark of poor performance, and application and runtime designers go to great lengths to avoid it.

In our prior work [13] we introduced a new kernel, the Particle-in-Cell (PIC) PRK, specifically designed to measure objectively, precisely, and in a controlled fashion the efficiency and effectiveness of techniques and technologies to balance load dynamically. While a useful tool, it did not fully capture the most troublesome source of load imbalance on large scale systems, namely localized and transient discrete system disturbances, which we term "noise."

In this paper we describe another kernel that better fills this gap. It is based on adaptive mesh refinement (AMR) workloads, which compute a certain quantity across an entire spatial domain, and create local refinements where extra resolution is needed. As in the case of PIC, the source of load imbalance in the AMR PRK is deterministic, which means it can be exercised at any system and problem scale, an important practical consideration. Unlike PIC's, AMR's load imbalances do not grow continually, but occur at discrete points in time, and have a duration and severity that can be specified precisely.

We provide a serial and multiple parallel implementations in open source (github.com/ParRes/Kernels/Kernels/tree/master/{SERIAL, MPI1, AMPI}/ AMR), and discuss our experiences with them to demonstrate utility of AMR as a tool. However, the true contribution of the AMR PRK is not the quality of its implementations, but its specification.

The remainder of this paper is organized as follows. Section 2 describes the context of this work and its specific contribution. Section 3 contains the paper-and-pencil specification of the kernel. The multiple reference implementations are described in Sect. 4, and experimental results with these implementations are discussed in Sect. 5. Conclusions and plans for future work are in the last section.

2   Related Work

Many studies have been published about dynamic load balancing techniques. We are especially interested in general solutions, applicable in various contexts, that require little effort by the application programmer. Usually, such solutions come in the form of frameworks covering a certain application domain (e.g. Zoltan [10], PREMA [1], JOVE [26], ARMaDA [8], Uintah [21], Scotio [11]), or even as parts of general-purpose runtimes (e.g. Charm++ [19], Chapel [7], Grappa [22], HPX [27], X10 [25], Legion [2]).

However, not much work has been done on methodologies for assessing and comparing the merits of such solutions. A notable exception is the UTS benchmark [23]. It represents workloads whose source of load imbalances is strictly the emergence of local new work during program execution. There is no global field data on which UTS operates, so the load balancing consists mostly of (re-) distribution of work, not data. In addition, new work occurs in (pseudo-)random locations on the system, which means that the past can not be used as a predictor for new work. That is a particularly harsh test for load balancing technologies, though these are greatly helped by the fact that only meta-data data of negligible size needs to be transferred along with work.

In contrast, HPC usually involves sizeable arrays, and changing data dependencies are important sources of load imbalance, and affect the efficiency with which load balancers can operate. But most HPC applications are of an iterative nature, and depending on the speed with which data dependencies change or the frequency with which new work shows up, the past can be used as a predictor for the future, which can be exploited by load balancers.

We list two more tools to assess dynamic load balancing technologies, namely workloads in the SPLASH-2 [33] and PARSEC [6] suite of programs. While useful for determining the effect of dynamic load balancing, they do not come with paper and pencil specifications, and for each workload they provide only one implementation for distributed memory systems–the focus of our interest–so that it is not possibe to compare different approaches.

The main reason for the dearth of test cases of sources of load imbalance is that such workloads tend to be complicated, and hence not easily ported to new environments and runtimes. They also tend to be quite domain specific, limiting their utility to the scientific community at large. The Particle-In-Cell (PIC) Parallel Research Kernel [13] was developed especially with the goals of simplicity, compactness, and portability in mind, as well as with the ability to adjust the type and severity of load skewing events.

It proved an insightful tool to study dynamic load balancing capabilities, especially in the context of runtime-orchestrated load balancing (i.e. without explicit programmer intervention). We used PIC to compare such capabilities when sources of load imbalances are present continually. While a research version of PIC also allowed the discrete injection and removal of work (i.e. particles), it did not have very precise control over actual load imbalance, because the injection/removal would be superimposed on an already fluctuating load signature. The new AMR PRK allows such precise control that it is possible to determine the actual load (im)balance analytically, see Sect. 5.1. In addition, it only features discrete changes in the load signature, so complements the continuous evolution of the load signature of PIC.

3   The Adaptive Mesh Refinement PRK

3.1   Algorithmic Structure of Adaptive Mesh Refinement Codes

Adaptive Mesh Refinement [5] is a technique used by computational science applications to focus computational work in numerical simulations that span a range of disparate length and time scales. It dynamically increases local grid resolution to resolve important fine scale features in the solution, achieving a more efficient computation than one in which a globally-uniform fine grid is applied. The approach has been used in numerous scientific computing applications, including Monte-Carlo simulations [12], geophysics [15], flame physics [4], airborne dispersion [30], helicopter wake resolution [32], and many others.

A number of successful Cartesian AMR meshing infrastructures are in use to support the complex mesh generation, adaptation, parallelization, and to various degrees, solvers and interfaces to solver packages. These include Chombo [9] and BoxLib [3] from Lawrence Berkeley National Laboratory, GrACE [24] from Rutgers University, PARAMESH [20] from NASA Goddard, and SAM-RAI [14,16,31] from Lawrence Livermore National Laboratory. These infrastructures have played a key role in advancing adaptive meshing capabilities to new applications in computational physics. By isolating much of the meshing and parallel computing complexity in the infrastructure, they provide the scientist with a way to introduce adaptive meshing into their application in much less time than would be required to develop this capability in their own standalone codes.

In Cartesian AMR techniques new grid points are introduced as entire blocks of points or Refinement Grids (RGs) with the same topology as the original mesh or Background Grid (BG), but with a finer spacing. Some of the advantages of this approach are that memory access is very regular, locality is good, and logic is simple (no time spent exploring local mesh topology). AMR methods generally consist of the following phases.

1. Create and initialize a background grid (BG).
2. Advance solution on BG.
3. Monitor local BG solution error and create RGs where needed.
4. Initialize RG solution, interpolating data from BG.
5. Advance solutions on BG and RG(s).
6. Depending on the problem, inject computed solution on RG back onto BG.
7. Monitor solution and remove RG when error has diminished sufficiently.

Steps 2–7 are carried out in an iterative fashion.

The parallelization of general AMR codes poses numerous challenges, see the references cited above. We focus specifically on the load imbalances triggered by the RGs, and minimize work not strictly related to reducing the impact of those imbalances. Note that we deliberately do *not* create a full-fledged, numerically accurate AMR application. It would be too involved (hard to implement/port), too domain specific to be useful for scientists in different subject areas, and not exactly verifiable, and thus would not satify our PRK requirements [13,29]. Consequently, we simplify steps 3 and 7, and completely skip step 6.

3.2   Specification of the Adaptive Mesh Refinement PRK

We define a BG of a certain size, and start/stop work on smaller RGs with a specified frequency. An RG does not necessarily have fewer points than the BG, as it can have a much finer mesh spacing. We apply the same stencil operation, S, implementing the discrete divergence, to all *interior* grid points (see specification of the Stencil PRK [28]).

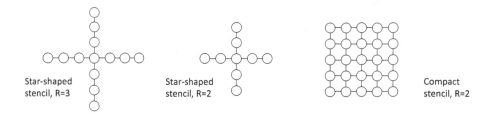

Star-shaped
stencil, R=3

Star-shaped
stencil, R=2

Compact
stencil, R=2

Fig. 1. Examples of stencils with different shapes and radii.

At any time at most one RG is active. RGs are aligned with the BG and are totally contained within it, and each point of the BG that falls within an RG coincides with a grid point of that RG. These two criteria ensure that inter-polation from BG to RG is simple and inexpensive, so that for most practical purposes we can ignore its cost.

Problem parameters:

- T: total number of iterations on BG.
- R: radius of difference stencil; see Fig. 1 for examples of stencils.
- n: linear dimension of square BG (n^2 points). The mesh spacing is one.
- r: refinement level (mesh spacing of RG is 2^{-r}).
- k: linear dimension of square RG in terms of BG points, so $((k-1)*2^r+1)^2$ refinement points.
- P: duration in terms of iterations on the BG of one full cycle of activation of one RG until that of the next RG (*period*).
- D: duration in terms of iterations on the BG of activity on each RG; $D \leq P$.
- d: number of iterations on a RG per iteration on the BG.

Initialization. The BG input field IN_{bg} is initialized with function $U(x,y)$, which is linear in the coordinates: $U(x,y) = c_x x + c_y y$, with $c_x, c_y \geq 0$. The bottom left corner of the BG coincides with the origin of the coordinate system. A set of four distinct RGs is created at the start of the program. Their input fields are initialized to all zeroes: $IN_i \equiv 0, i \in \{0,1,2,3\}$. Note that the subscript i is always used to indicate a refinement with index i, and that it can assume integral values beween 0 and 3. The output fields on BG and RGs are all initialized to all zeroes: $OUT_{bg} \equiv OUT_i \equiv 0$.

Computations. The result of each application of the stencil operation on the BG (an *iteration* or *time step*) is accumulated in OUT_{bg}, i.e. $OUT_{bg} = OUT_{bg} + S(R)IN_{bg}$, ($R$=stencil radius) after which the input field IN_{bg} is uniformly incremented by one. When an RG is actived, its input values are interpolated from the BG input values at that time, using bi-linear interpolation[1]. Subsequently, for each of the D iterations on the BG, d stencil iterations are carried out on the activated RG i, the results of which are accumulated in its corresponding output field, i.e. $OUT_i = OUT_i + S(R)IN_i$. After each iteration on RG i, its input field IN_i is uniformly incremented by one.

Refinements. We define a set of four RGs, located at the bottom left, top right, top left, and bottom right corners of the BG, respectively, that are activated and deactivated cyclically in that order. The bottom left corners of the RGs coincide with the following points of the BG, respectively: $\{(0,0), (n-k, n-k), (0, n-k), (n-k, 0)\}$. The iteration on the BG at which refinement i is activated for the ath time is: $P * (i + 4a), a = 0, 1, 2, \cdots$. This cyclic pattern does not qualify as real noise, due to its fixed frequency and amplitude. However, its block wave nature does provide the salient aspect of system noise, namely the abrupt, discrete, and localized variation of system load. It is possible, in principle, for a runtime to detect the fixed frequency and take preemptive action, but we are not aware of any runtimes that do this. In Fig. 2 we show an example configuration with grid and refinement parameters $n = 10$, $r = 2$, and $k = 3$, duration $D = 4$, and period $P = 8$. The BG has 100 points, and each RG has 81 points.

Verification. After all iterations have finished we compute the L^1 norm of the computed divergence over the interior points of the BG and all RGs, normalized by the respective numbers of grid points. These values are compared to the analytical values. Absolute values of the differences must satisfy a fixed error tolerance.

To determine the analytical values of the OUT array on a grid we need to know how many times τ it has been visited. For RG i we find: $\tau_i = d * \{ \lfloor T/(P * 4) \rfloor * D + \min(\max[0, T \bmod (P * 4) - i * P], D) \}$. The relative complexity of this formula is due to the fact that RGs emerge intermittently, and may not complete an entire cycle of $P * 4$ iterations before the total number of iterations, T, on the BG is reached and the code terminates. If T were divisible by $P*4$, we would find $\tau_i = d*T*D/(P*4)$. For the BG, τ_{bg} simply equals T. Only the linear terms of the input fields contribute to the divergence, and these do not change. Each iteration on a grid adds $c_x + c_y$ to the divergence at each point, where c_x and c_y are the constant coefficients of the linear BG initialization function. Consequently, the verification value of the divergence on any grid equals $\tau * (c_x + c_y)$. This function is linear in the total number of time steps, and while this may ultimately result in arithmetic overflow, it is considered stable in a numerical sense, since growth is less than exponential.

Performance Metric. Performance of this kernel is reported in terms of nominal floating point operations related to the application of the stencil, to the

---

[1] Bi-linear interpolation is a standard technique in which two 1D linear interpolations are combined to compute interpolations in 2D. See, e.g. [18], Appendix D. Taking advantage of the regular structure of BG and RGs, we can implement it with just three floating point operations per RG point.

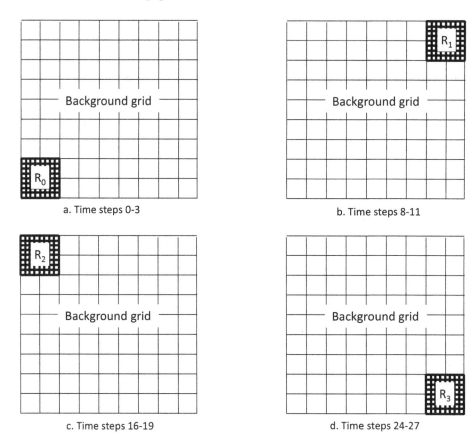

Fig. 2. Example BG with successive refinements R_0–R_3; $n = 10$, $r = 2$, and $k = 3$, duration $D = 4$, and period $P = 8$.

update of the input fields, and to the interpolation, divided by the time it took to carry out all computations. If the spacing of the RGs equals that of the BG, no floating point operations are assigned to the interpolations, since these can be implemented efficiently and conveniently as copy operations. In all other cases we assign a fixed number of floating point operations to each RG point to carry out the interpolation, corresponding to the number of operations necessary to determine the interpolant at each point.

Rationale. As for all PRK, we ensure that all required work is done, and that any work that is skipped or incorrectly carried out results in verification failure. Hence, each operation on the BG and the RGs needs to have an effect on the final result that can be verified. We therefore accumulate each computed result into the output fields in each iteration, rather than overwriting the output fields.

In a real stencil application there is usually no distinction between input and output field; a single solution field that is updated during each iteration. To evaluate the stencil of the solution field near grid partition boundaries requires communications to exchange ghost point values before each iteration. To make such communication necessary in this kernel as well, we change the BG and RG input field values after each iteration. The additon of a constant throughout has no influence on the computed divergence, which simplifies the verification test.

To keep the amount of state that needs to be preserved during the execution of the kernel constant, we opt for a fixed set of refinements that are statically determined, but that are activated and deactivated periodically. This allows us to accumulate results on refinements into a small, fixed set of arrays.

Note that the special initialization, particular positioning of RGs, and the accumulation and unit increment operations solely serve to catch errors and facilitate verification. The stencil operations on BG and RGs and the potential for load imbalance–the true focus of this kernel–are agnostic of these features.

4   Parallel AMR PRK Reference Implementations

The AMR PRK differs fundamentally from the Particle-In-Cell PRK when it comes to parallel implementation. There are essentially only two different states of the execution, one with active refinement, and one without. While the RGs occupy different parts of the BG, depending on which one is active, they are all of the same size and involve the same amount of work, so can all be treated similarly. Either of the two distinct states can be load balanced easily by the programmer, but alternation in time between the two requires important trade-offs. We describe the three most plausible methods for making those tradeoffs, assuming MPI as the basic parallelization method.

– FINE-GRAIN: The configuration *without* an RG is evenly distributed among all ranks. When an RG is activated, its work is distributed evenly among some or all of the existing ranks, without regard for communications between BG and RG needed to initialize RG. Each rank is responsible for one Cartesian subset (a *tile*) of BG data and one tile of each actived RG. This always produces a balanced load, but can cause very fine granularity.
– NO-TALK: The configuration *without* an RG is evenly distributed among all ranks. When an RG is activated, its work is distributed among the ranks, such that no communication is required to initialize it. Each rank is responsible for one BG tile and potentially one RG tile with which its BG tile coincides when that RG is active. This leads to a balanced load when no RG is active, but becomes unbalanced upon RG activation. The smaller the extent of an RG relative to the BG, the worse the load imbalance.
– HIGH-WATER: The configuration *with* an RG is evenly distributed among all ranks. Each rank is responsible either for one tile of the BG, or for one of the active RG. This means the load is only balanced when an RG is active. Granularity is typically coarser than FINE-GRAIN.

Each of these approaches can be optimal under certain conditions. When communications are very fast, the fully load-balanced FINE-GRAIN would be

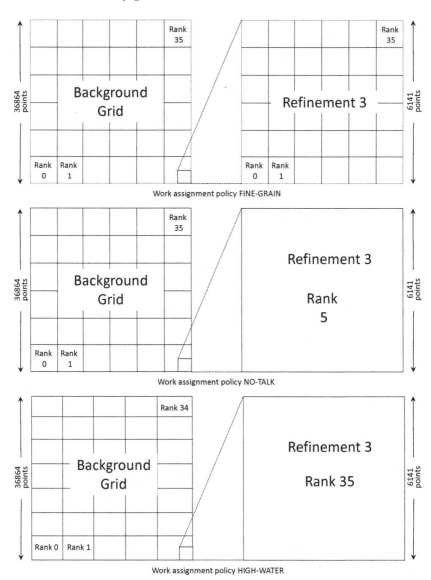

Fig. 3. Example of different work assignment policies for a mesh configuration of BG size $n = 36864$, RG size $k = 1536$, and refinement level $r = 2$.

optimal. When communication costs are significant, NO-TALK offers the benefit of no communication between grid levels, but can become very unbalanced during refinements, especially with small RGs with a higher level of refinement. In Fig. 3 we give an give an example of how a particular choice of BG and RGs–which we also use for shared memory experiments in Sect. 5–fares under the above three work distribution approaches.

Note that load balance of NO-TALK and HIGH-WATER could be improved by over-decomposing BG and RGs and assigning multiple tiles of these grids to each rank. The programmer would have to determine the proper tile-to-rank assignment, including how that assignment would change when refinements appear or disappear. We deliberately do not provide this option, as it leads to substantially more complicated programming, and is covered–in principle–by dynamic runtimes of the type discussed in Sect. 4.1. In addition, we want to mimic the scenario in which one does not know in advance which rank becomes overloaded with extra work, since that is the result of noise at large system scales.

4.1 Dynamic Load Balancing with Adaptive MPI

Adaptive MPI (AMPI) is an implementation of MPI, built on top of the Charm++ runtime [17], that supports dynamic load balancing and multithreading for MPI applications. According to the AMPI execution model, multiple user-level threads, named virtual processors, each representing an MPI rank, are assigned per operating system process, and typically one OS process is mapped to a single processor core, or–in the case of shared memory nodes with non-trivial extent–to a single node. The main strategy for implementing an application with AMPI is to over-decompose the problem to more ranks than the number of available physical cores and delegate the load balancing task to the runtime. The AMPI runtime utilizes the Charm++ scheduler to coordinate the execution and, more importantly, the migration of ranks to different system resources.

Porting an existing MPI application to AMPI is conceptually trivial; Any MPI application is a valid AMPI code as long as it does not include static or global variables. Every MPI process is mapped to a different virtual process and therefore the over-decomposition results in merely creating more MPI processes than resources. Additionally, AMPI provides the function `AMPI_Migrate()`, which activates the Charm++ load balancer. The duration of load monitoring and the frequency of triggering the load balancer, along with the degree of the over-decomposition, are tunable parameters. Finally, the heap allocated data can be migrated either automatically by employing the `isomalloc` memory allocation infrastructure that comes with the AMPI runtime, or the user can provide appropriate packing/unpacking (PUP) routines. We opt for PUP on distributed-memory memory systems, as it yields higher performance. On shared memory systems isomalloc is faster, because it does not require actual heap data movement, but simple pointer exchange. Consequently, we select this option for our experiments on a single shared-memory node.

5 Experimental Results

In this section we present experiments that provide examples of how to use the new AMR PRK to assess the performance of runtime assisted load balancing.

We compare the performance of the parallel implementations described in Sect. 4 (we used the Intel® C compiler icc version 15.0.1, Intel® MPI Library for Linux version 5.0, and Adaptive MPI with Charm++ version 6.7.1) in both shared and distributed memory settings. A few quick checks after installation of icc compiler version 17.0.0 on our shared memory system showed no impact on the performance of the AMR PRK.

First, we need to construct our experiments carefully to make sure they represent scenarios of interest. We focus on the NO-TALK policy, and an RG that is sufficiently small that even for the finest partitioning it fits within one tile of the BG assigned to each rank. This choice implies that whenever an RG appears, no additional communication and synchronization is incurred by the rank that needs to work on it. It proxies a scenario in which a single core at a time is slowed down because of synthetic noise. To be specific, we choose the number of points in the RG such that it requires the same amount of computational work as one tile of the BG, see Sect. 5.1. Consequently, whenever an RG appears, the rank that is responsible for it under the NO-TALK policy suddenly has its computational load doubled. For the canonical MPI implementation without overdecomposition or rank migration this is nominally equivalent to an abrupt halving of the frequency of the core whose rank receives the RG.

5.1 Shared Memory Experiments

Our shared-memory experiments are conducted on a workstation equipped with two 18-core Intel® Xeon® E5-2699 processors at 2.30 GHz, with total memory of 64 GB. We choose a total problem size that can be accommodated by the machine, without much space to spare. We keep the size fixed, and use all available cores. The BG/RG configuration corresponds to that of Fig. 3. The full list of fixed numerical and configuration parameters is as follows.

- $T = 400$: total number of iterations
- $R = 2$: radius of difference stencil
- $n = 36864$: linear dimension of BG ($36,864^2$ points)
- $r = 2$: refinement level
- $k = 1536$: linear dimension of RG in terms of BG points (6141^2 refinement points)
- $d = 1$: number of iterations on a RG per iteration on the BG
- $NP = 36$: number of physical cores used (full system)

For the following parameters we choose ranges to determine sensitivity to their variation.

- $D \in \{10, 20, 40, 80\}$: duration in terms of iterations on the BG of activity on each RG
- $P = 2 * D$: duration in terms of iterations on the BG of one full cycle of activation of one RG until that of the next RG (*period*)
- $Z \in \{1, 2, 4, 8\}$: overdecomposition factor, i.e. number of MPI ranks per core
- $LB \in \{\text{RefineLB}, \text{GreedyLB}\}$: Charm++ load balancing strategy

- $\Delta \in \{0,1,2,3,4\}$: delay in BG iterations between the change in grid configuration (activation or deactivation of an RG) and the invocation of `AMPI_Migrate()`

Because the ratio of P and D is fixed, increasing D corresponds to a decrease in the synthetic noise frequency, with a fixed fraction of time spent in the RG-activated and deactivated epochs.

The quartet $(r,d,n,k) = (2,1,36864,1536)$ ensures that with full system occupation and minimal assignment of one MPI rank to each core, the amount of computational work for the core working on an RG is nominally double that of a core that only works on the BG (number of discretization points in the BG tile and the RG are equal). With exactly two ranks per core the overloaded core has 1.5 times as much work as all others. In general, with exactly Z ranks per core the overloaded core has $2-1/Z, Z>1$ as much work as the other cores. We define load imbalance Φ as $1-T_{avg}/T_{max}$, where T_{max} equals the time the slowest core takes to reach successive synchronization points, and T_{avg} the time it takes all cores on average. It is a solid measure of total idle time (resources wasted) due to load imbalance. If epochs of RG activation and deactivation are equally long, load imbalance without rank migration would be, assuming a one-to-one correspondence between computational work and wall clock time:

$$\Phi_{static}(Z) = 1/3 \tag{1}$$

If ranks are allowed to migrate, the core responsible for an RG would move all (or all but one) of the ranks responsible for BG tiles to other cores during times of refinement, but no more than one BG tile extra per core. This would lead to the following load imbalance.

$$\Phi_{adapt}(Z) = \frac{1}{2Z+1} \tag{2}$$

These functions are depicted in Fig. 4. Without migration the load imbalance is constant at 0.33, the same as for the plain MPI version. With migration the load imbalance can be made arbitrarily small, but at the cost of very fine granularity.

We executed each of the experiments four times, and picked the best of the four results to represent that case. Even though the tests were run on an unloaded system, there was a fair amount of noise on the data. However, the results showed clearly that there was no correlation between parameter settings and performance, except with respect to the load balancer. Obviously, the best migration strategy would be the one described above (and captured by Eq. (2)), namely distributing just a few ranks from the overloaded core evenly among neighboring cores, and leaving everybody else alone. The RefineLB load balancing strategy indeed focuses on local migration only, whereas GreedyLB always moves work from the most overloaded core to the least overloaded, in a recursive fashion. Any Charm++ load balancing strategy requires load information from the runtime, as it has no knowledge of the actual workload. To obtain

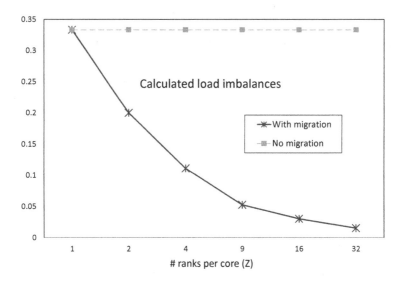

Fig. 4. Analytical load imbalance $(1 - T_{avg}/T_{max})$ for both shared and distributed-memory scenarios, with and without rank migration

that, the runtime monitors core idle times caused by synchronizations. To give the runtime sufficient opportunity to collect such data after each change in the grid configuration, we insert a (variable) delay, Δ, between such change and the execution of the rank migration scheme.

The performance figures for RefineLB and GreedyLB load balancers for the entire range of parameters tested were 42.2 GFlops and 35.3 GFlops, respectively, with corresponding standard deviations of 1.2% and 5.3%. These numbers correlate strongly with the average numbers of ranks migrated in each load balancing step, which were $(0, 4.6, 10.2, 17.9)$ and $(34.8, 69.5, 140.0, 280.4)$ for RefineLB and GreedyLB, respectively, for total numbers of ranks of $(36, 72, 144, 288)$. Obviously, the GreedyLB algorithm is too aggressive in moving ranks (almost 100% of all ranks migrate, even if there is only one rank per core, in which case–to first order–migration cannot improve load balance), and will no longer be considered. We also note that the number of ranks moved in each migration by the RefineLB algorithm differed substantially from one load change to the next within the same program execution, often by as much as 50%, even though there are only two distinct, repeated load states during the execution. In principle, all ranks save one (during refinement) have the exact same load, but noise and effects such as being close to a grid boundary can introduce small variations. Evidently, this leads to somewhat erratic scheduling decisions by the load balancer. At the longest duration of the refinements of $D = 80$ (lowest synthetic noise frequency), one such activation period equaled 26 s.

Keeping the work on BG and RGs the same, but changing the RGs' extent by increasing their size by a factor of four in both directions, while at the same time dropping the refinement level r to 0 (RG and BG are equally fine) produces a configuration in which some communication within RGs is required. This did not affect the performance numbers under Adaptive MPI, which points to the fact that communication costs within RGs can be ignored.

We repeated the original experiment using the plain MPI implementation and the same NO-TALK work-to-rank assignment. In this case each core receives one rank, which never migrates. Performance was identical to that of Adaptive MPI with the Refine load balancer, i.e. 42.2 GFlops for the range of refinement frequencies used. The absence of variation between different refinement frequencies is to be expected, since no new communications are introduced by the refinements, and the only thing that counts is the ratio of times the grid system spends in a refined and non-refined state. This ratio is constant across refinement frequencies in our experiments.

We also did experiments without any refinements, using the standard MPI Stencil PRK (see [28]), with as input sizes the full BG size ($36,864^2$ points) for 36 ranks, and the full RG size (6141^2 points) for 1 rank. The RG computation (5.3 GFlops) could be finished much faster than the BG computation (43.8 GFlops), among others because of the need for the ranks in the BG run to communicate. Average times per iteration were 0.14 and 0.58 for the RG and BG computations, respectively. The formulas for load balancing, Eqs. (1) and (2) do not take this effect into account. In general, when the ratio of the times it takes to finish computations on RG and BG, respectively, equals α, the scenario without migration has a load imbalance of $\Phi_{static}(\infty) = \alpha/(2+\alpha)$, which in this case equals 10.8%. The observed reduction in performance of the AMR PRK without migration, relative to the plain Stencil PRK with the $36,864^2$ grid, is actually less than 10.8%, namely appoximately 4%, and is not affected by the level of overdecomposition. In case migration is allowed, the load imbalance can again be made arbitrarily small, but with a high communication cost.

Finally, we also repeated the Adaptive MPI experiment with the same ratio of work between BG and RGs, but with a smaller overall problem size. Specifically, we reduced the linear BG and RG dimensions by a factor of four (so work on each reduced by a factor of 16), and kept all other parameters in our experiment the same. This resulted in an increase in frequency of synthetic noise by a factor of 16. Again, there was no observable correlation between number of ranks per core and performance, but there was one for the duration of the refinement. For durations of 10, 20, and 40 iterations we recorded performance of 32.4, 42.6, and 42.8 GFlops, respectively. While the migration for durations 20 and 40 again did not offer any improvement (nor deficit) over regular MPI runs without migration, the higher frequency corresponding to duration 10 evidently incurred significant overhead. For this small problem size the total activation of one refinement at this highest frequency lasted approximately 0.52 s.

5.2 Distributed Memory Experiments

Distributed-memory experiments are conducted on Edison, a Cray XC30 system located at NERSC. Edison has a peak performance of 2.57 petaflops/sec, with 5,576 compute nodes, each equipped with 64 GB RAM and two 12-core Intel®

Xeon® E5-2695 processors at 2.40 GHz for a total of 133,824 compute cores. The nodes are interconnected with the Cray Aries network using a Dragonfly topology.

In this case we kept the size and level of refinement of the RGs the same, but adjusted the size of the BG as follows. A full node contains 24 cores, so we multiply the size of the baseline BG by approximately 24/36 to maintain the same ratio of work on the RG and on one tile of the BG assigned to a single rank (without overdecomposition) as in the shared memory case. Consequently, the baseline BG size is $n = 30,000$ for a single node. With more nodes we employ weak scaling, so that the amount of BG work assigned to each rank remains constant. Since the size of the RG is also constant, a nominally fixed (source of) load imbalance holds. We also fix the overdecomposition factor at $Z = 4$, and the migration delay at $\Delta = 2$, since these did not show noticeable influence on performance in the shared memory case. We did vary the duration of the RG existence as before ($D \in \{10, 20, 40\}$), and varied the number of nodes from 1 to 64.

The performance results are shown in Fig. 5, along with the corresponding results for plain MPI (no overdecomposition or rank migration). All performance data are normalized by dividing aggregate performance by that of the AMPI code

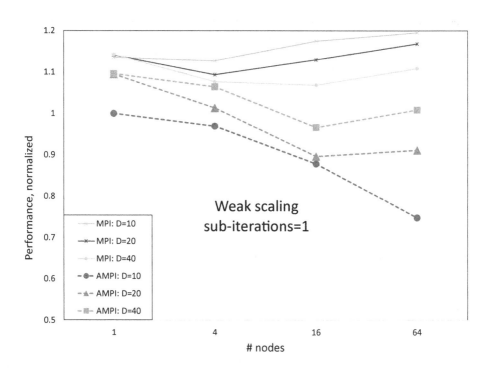

Fig. 5. Normalized performance (MFlops/node divided by AMPI performance on one node with $D = 10$, one RG sub-iteration per BG time step) of AMR weak scaling experiment on Edison, with one RG sub-iteration per time step

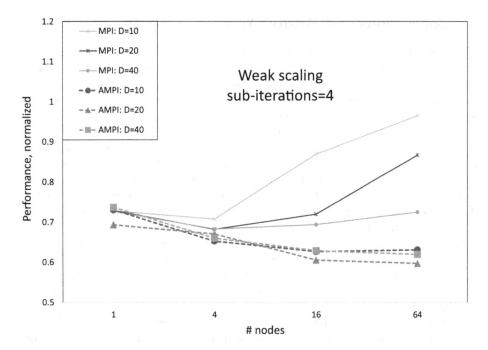

Fig. 6. Normalized performance (MFlops/node divided by AMPI performance on one node with $D = 10$, one RG sub-iteration per BG time step) of AMR weak scaling experiment on Edison, with four RG sub-iterations per time step

with one node, one RG sub-iteration, and a duration of $D = 10$, as well as by the number of nodes used. Evidently, in this case dynamic load balancing was even less favorable than in the shared memory case, especially for the shorter durations (higher frequency synthetic noise).

In the final experiment, illustrated in Fig. 6, we set the number of sub-iterations on RGs to $d = 4$. This means that the intensity of the source of load imbalance increased by a factor of four, compared to the previous experiment. In this case we would expect a more beneficial effect of dynamic load balancing compared to the plain MPI implementation, because of the greater imbalance caused by the refinements. That worsened load imbalance is evident from the reduced performance of the plain MPI code (compare Fig. 5, which uses the same scale). However, as Fig. 6 demonstrates, the dynamic load balancing again does not deliver any benefit for any of the noise frequencies. We note that the *expected* performance of the plain MPI implementation is independent of the refinement duration, but our results show that shorter duration corresponds with higher performance. This was repeatable. We do not yet have an explanation for this phenomenon.

6   Conclusions and Future Work

The first observation we can make is that the newly developed AMR Parallel Research Kernel has sufficient flexibility to construct relevant, fully-parameterized scenarios in large-scale computing with respect to the salient disruptive effect of localized system noise. That includes the capability to construct carefully tuned sources of load imbalance.

The second is that in our investigations of runtimes that are capable of executing automatic dynamic load balancing policies based on overdecomposition of the computational domain, which focused on the employment of Adaptive MPI in this paper, we could not find any parameter settings that led to better performance than a simple, dual-phase, static domain decomposition in standard MPI. This is true, even though the latter can not remove the load imbalances caused by the recurring introduction of adaptive refinements prescribed by the AMR kernel. Our tests covered shared as well as distributed memory experiments. Even for relatively low frequency synthetic noise caused by the refinements (up to 26 s), the adaptive runtime experiments did not improve performance over standard MPI. The performance deficit was largest for the highest frequency of synthetic noise.

We conjecture that part of the reason for the failure of our experiments is the fundamental nature of the load imbalances incurred by the AMR kernel. There are only two different load states, which are entered and exited abruptly, so that each load transition creates a "shock," as unpredictable noise would. Consequently, the runtime cannot properly use the past to predict the future, and always operates in a reactive mode.

In the future we plan to use the AMR PRK to investigate other runtimes that offer automatic dynamic load balancing capabilities. We will also construct some experiments that reflect an aspect of synthetic system noise that the experiments in this paper did not cover. Specifically, when we defined the refinement scenarios in Sect. 5, we ensured that even in case of overdecomposition only a single rank at a time was affected by the appearance of a refinement. But if actual system noise would slow down an entire core for a certain period of time, *all* ranks owned by that core would be affected. Simulating that effect requires a revision of our experiments.

Acknowledgement. This research used resources of the National Energy Research Scientific Computing Center, a DOE Office of Science User Facility supported by the Office of Science of the U.S. Department of Energy under Contract No. DE-AC02-05CH11231.
    *Other names and brands may be claimed as property of others.
    Intel and Xeon are trademarks of Intel Corporation in the U.S. and/or other countries. Software and workloads used in performance tests may have been optimized for performance only on Intel microprocessors. Performance tests, such as SYSmark and MobileMark, are measured using specific computer systems, components, software, operations and functions. Any change to any of those factors may cause the results to vary. You should consult other information and performance tests to assist you in fully evaluating your contemplated purchases, including the performance of that product when combined with other products. For more information go to http://www.intel.com/performance.

References

1. Barker, K., Chernikov, A., Chrisochoides, N., Pingali, K.: A load balancing framework for adaptive and asynchronous applications. IEEE Trans. Parallel Distrib. Syst. **15**(2), 183–192 (2004)
2. Bauer, M., Treichler, S., Slaughter, E., Aiken, A.: Legion: expressing locality and independence with logical regions. In: Proceedings of the International Conference on High Performance Computing, Networking, Storage and Analysis, p. 66. IEEE Computer Society Press (2012)
3. Bell, J., Rendleman, C.: CCSE application suite
4. Bell, J.B., Day, M.S., Grcar, J.F., Lijewski, M.J., Driscoll, J.F., Filatyev, S.A.: Numerical simulation of a laboratory-scale turbulent slot flame. Proc. Combust. Inst. **31**(1), 1299–1307 (2007)
5. Berger, M.J., Oliger, J.: Adaptive mesh refinement for hyperbolic partial differential equations. J. Comput. Phys. **53**(3), 484–512 (1984)
6. Bienia, C., Li, K.: Parsec 2.0: a new benchmark suite for chip-multiprocessors. In: Proceedings of the 5th Annual Workshop on Modeling, Benchmarking and Simulation (2009)
7. Chamberlain, B.L., Choi, S.-E., Deitz, S.J., Navarro, A.: User-defined parallel zippered iterators in chapel. In: Proceedings of Fifth Conference on Partitioned Global Address Space Programming Models, pp. 1–11 (2011)
8. Chandra, S., Parashar, M.: ARMaDA: an adaptive application-sensitive partitioning framework for SAMR applications. In: IASTED PDCS, pp. 441–446 (2002)
9. Colella, P., Graves, D., Ligocki, T., Martin, D., Modiano, D., Serafini, D., Van Straalen, B.: Chombo software package for AMR applications-design document (2003)
10. Devine, K.D., Boman, E.G., Heaphy, R.T., Hendrickson, B.A., Teresco, J.D., Faik, J., Flaherty, J.E., Gervasio, L.G.: New challenges in dynamic load balancing. Appl. Numer. Math. **52**(2), 133–152 (2005)
11. Dinan, J., Krishnamoorthy, S., Larkins, D.B., Nieplocha, J., Sadayappan, P.: Scioto: a framework for global-view task parallelism. In: 37th International Conference on Parallel Processing, ICPP 2008, pp. 586–593. IEEE (2008)
12. Garcia, A.L., Bell, J.B., Crutchfield, W.Y., Alder, B.J.: Adaptive mesh and algorithm refinement using direct simulation Monte Carlo. J. Comput. Phys. **154**(1), 134–155 (1999)
13. Georganas, E., Van der Wijngaart, R.F., Mattson, T.G.: Design and implementation of a Parallel Research Kernel for assessing dynamic load-balancing capabilities. In: 2016 IEEE International Parallel and Distributed Processing Symposium, pp. 73–82. IEEE (2016)
14. Hornung, R.D., Kohn, S.R.: Managing application complexity in the SAMRAI object-oriented framework. Concurr. Comput.: Pract. Exp. **14**(5), 347–368 (2002)
15. Hornung, R.D., Trangenstein, J.A.: Adaptive mesh refinement and multilevel iteration for flow in porous media. J. Comput. Phys. **136**(2), 522–545 (1997)
16. Hornung, R.D., Wissink, A.M., Kohn, S.R.: Managing complex data and geometry in parallel structured AMR applications. Eng. Comput. **22**(3–4), 181–195 (2006)
17. Kale, L.V., Krishnan, S.: CHARM++: a portable concurrent object oriented system based on C++, vol. 28. ACM (1993)
18. Kirkland, E.J.: Linear image approximations. In: Kirkland, E.J. (ed.) Advanced Computing in Electron Microscopy, pp. 19–39. Springer, Heidelberg (1998)

19. Koenig, G., Kale, L.V., et al.: Optimizing distributed application performance using dynamic grid topology-aware load balancing. In: IEEE International Parallel and Distributed Processing Symposium, IPDPS 2007, pp. 1–10. IEEE (2007)
20. MacNeice, P., Olson, K.M., Mobarry, C., de Fainchtein, R., Packer, C.: PARA-MESH: a parallel adaptive mesh refinement community toolkit. Comput. Phys. Commun. **126**(3), 330–354 (2000)
21. Meng, Q., Berzins, M., Schmidt, J.: Using hybrid parallelism to improve memory use in the Uintah framework. In: Proceedings of the 2011 TeraGrid Conference: Extreme Digital Discovery, p. 24. ACM (2011)
22. Nelson, J., Holt, B., Myers, B., Briggs, P., Ceze, L., Kahan, S., Oskin, M.: Latency-tolerant software distributed shared memory. In: 2015 USENIX Annual Technical Conference (USENIX ATC 15), Santa Clara, CA. USENIX Association, July 2015
23. Olivier, S., Huan, J., Liu, J., Prins, J., Dinan, J., Sadayappan, P., Tseng, C.-W.: UTS: an unbalanced tree search benchmark. In: Almási, G., Caşcaval, C., Wu, P. (eds.) LCPC 2006. LNCS, vol. 4382, pp. 235–250. Springer, Heidelberg (2007). doi:10.1007/978-3-540-72521-3_18
24. Parashar, M., Browne, J.C.: Systems engineering for high performance computing software: the HDDA/DAGH infrastructure for implementation of parallel structured adaptive mesh. In: Baden, S.B., Chrisochoides, N.P., Gannon, D.B., Norman, M.L. (eds.) Structured Adaptive Mesh Refinement (SAMR). IMA, vol. 117, pp. 1–18. Springer, New York (2000). doi:10.1007/978-1-4612-1252-2_1
25. Paudel, J., Amaral, J.N.: Hybrid parallel task placement in irregular applications. J. Parallel Distrib. Comput. **76**, 94–105 (2015)
26. Sohn, A., Biswas, R., Simon, H.D.: A dynamic load balancing framework for unstructured adaptive computations on distributed-memory multiprocessors. In: Proceedings of the Eighth Annual ACM Symposium on Parallel Algorithms and Architectures, pp. 189–192. ACM (1996)
27. Tabbal, A., Anderson, M., Brodowicz, M., Kaiser, H., Sterling, T.: Preliminary design examination of the parallex system from a software and hardware perspective. ACM SIGMETRICS Perform. Eval. Rev. **38**(4), 81–87 (2011)
28. Van der Wijngaart, R.F., et al.: Comparing runtime systems with exascale ambitions using the parallel research kernels. In: Kunkel, J.M., Balaji, P., Dongarra, J. (eds.) ISC High Performance 2016. LNCS, vol. 9697, pp. 321–339. Springer, Cham (2016). doi:10.1007/978-3-319-41321-1_17
29. Van der Wijngaart, R.F., Mattson, T.G.: The parallel research kernels: a tool for architecture and programming system investigation. In: Proceedings of the IEEE High Performance Extreme Computing Conference, HPEC 2014. IEEE Computer Society (2014)
30. Wissink, A., Kosovic, B., Berger, M., Chand, K., Chow, F.K.: Adaptive Cartesian methods for modeling airborne dispersion. Adv. Comput. Infrast. Parallel Distrib. Adapt. Appl. 79 (2010)
31. Wissink, A.M., Hornung, R.D., Kohn, S.R., Smith, S.S., Elliott, N.: Large scale parallel structured AMR calculations using the SAMRAI framework. In: ACM/IEEE 2001 Conference on Supercomputing, p. 22. IEEE (2001)
32. Wissink, A.M., Potsdam, M., Sankaran, V., Sitaraman, J., Mavriplis, D.: A dual-mesh unstructured adaptive cartesian computational fluid dynamics approach for hover prediction. J. Am. Helicopter Soc. **61**(1), 1–19 (2016)
33. Woo, S.C., Ohara, M., Torrie, E., Singh, J.P., Gupta, A.: The splash-2 programs: characterization and methodological considerations. In: ACM SIGARCH Computer Architecture News, vol. 23, pp. 24–36. ACM (1995)

Architecture and System Optimization

Extreme Event Analysis in Next Generation Simulation Architectures

Stephen Hamilton[1][(✉)] , Randal Burns[1], Charles Meneveau[2] ,
Perry Johnson[2] , Peter Lindstrom[3] , John Patchett[4],
and Alexander S. Szalay[5]

[1] Department of Computer Science, Johns Hopkins University, Baltimore,
MD 21218, USA
{stephenh,randal}@cs.jhu.edu
[2] Department of Mechanical Engineering, Johns Hopkins University, Baltimore,
MD 21218, USA
{meneveau,pjohns86}@jhu.edu
[3] Lawrence Livermore National Laboratory, Livermore, CA 94550, USA
pl@llnl.gov
[4] Los Alamos National Laboratory, Los Alamos, NM 87545, USA
patchett@lanl.gov
[5] Department of Physics and Astronomy, Johns Hopkins University, Baltimore, USA
szalay@jhu.edu

Abstract. Numerical simulations present challenges because they generate petabyte-scale data that must be extracted and reduced during the simulation. We demonstrate a seamless integration of feature extraction for a simulation of turbulent fluid dynamics. The simulation produces on the order of 6 TB per timestep. In order to analyze and store this data, we extract velocity data from a dilated volume of the strong vortical regions and also store a lossy compressed representation of the data. Both reduce data by one or more orders of magnitude. We extract data from user checkpoints in transit while they reside on temporary burst buffer SSD stores. In this way, analysis and compression algorithms are designed to meet specific time constraints so they do not interfere with simulation computations. Our results demonstrate that we can perform feature extraction on a world-class direct numerical simulation of turbulence while it is running and gather meaningful scientific data for archival and post analysis.

1   Introduction

Supercomputing trends toward exascale motivate our research, specifically the increasing performance gap between processing and I/O. At exascale, simulations will output fewer than one byte for every 10^5 bytes of system state; they will produce 200–300 PB/s in memory [1] and only 1 TB/s [2] will be saved to persistent storage. Next generation architectures must define meaningful ways to output

---

The rights of this work are transferred to the extent transferable according to title 17 U.S.C. 105.

© Springer International Publishing AG 2017
J.M. Kunkel et al. (Eds.): ISC High Performance 2017, LNCS 10266, pp. 277–293, 2017.
DOI: 10.1007/978-3-319-58667-0_15

data that preserve scientific discovery on reduced data representations. The Trinity supercomputer at Los Alamos has deployed a burst buffer architecture [3] to fill the performance gap between cluster memory and disk filesystems. Burst buffers place the SSD storage on the fast network to catch I/O bursts that would overwhelm the filesystem. Data on burst buffers are short lived; they must be discarded or stored to file system in (tens of) minutes. Our experiments run on a research cluster with nodes designed to mimic the performance of Trinity's burst buffers and reduce data by orders of magnitude while preserving usable data for visualization and extreme event analysis [4]. Our experiences using the Johns Hopkins Turbulence Databases [5] (JHTDB) inform the choice of data products that we extract from burst buffers. Specifically, we create compressed lower precision representations of the full field velocity data and extract high-resolution velocity data from regions of relatively high vorticity. JHTDB contains multiple datasets from direct numerical simulations that range from tens to 150 TB. In particular, the isotropic turbulence dataset contains 5028 timesteps of velocity with three components of floating point values and one component of floating point pressure values on a 1024^3 spatially dense regular grid. This dataset provides scientists all over the world an opportunity to discover many aspects of turbulence without the need to run their own large simulation. A number of discoveries from the JHTDB have come from the combination of visualization and analysis of high vorticity regions. These include a vorticity hierarchy that is not evident on smaller scale simulations [6] and that magnetic flux freezing in high-conductivity plasmas fails in the presence of MHD turbulence, explaining why solar flares can erupt in minutes or hours rather than the millions of years predicted by flux freezing [7].

Going forward, the lack of I/O bandwidth to long term storage will slow down the simulation. Transferring output every few timesteps from a larger simulation (8192^3) would slow down the simulation by an order of magnitude; JHTDB's isotropic database stores every tenth timestep because the integration time-step for stably solving the system is smaller than that needed for analyses. Each timestep serves as a checkpoint which is utilized if a restart is required due to simulation failure. The I/O needed to checkpoint simulations to file systems has become the performance limiting workload in scalable HPC [8] and exposure to failure governs checkpoint frequency; they are taken much less frequently than needed for time-resolved analysis of the simulated processes of turbulence.

We develop methods that capture and extract relevant scientific data of a direct numerical simulation as it runs. We propose a model in which checkpoints are written to burst buffers at the frequency needed for analysis and then we extract a subset of the data and reduced representations that can be utilized for scientific analysis in real-time as well as post simulation. The extraction requires little processing power and it does not disrupt the running simulation. On Trinity [9], the burst buffers are located on additional nodes that are separate from compute nodes. Burst buffers in recent architectures collocate compute and SSDs [10] and extraction codes can be run within the burst buffer nodes.

In the first part of the process, we extract a subset of velocity data in 3D space only at points where the vorticity magnitude exceeds a defined threshold.[1] Next we dilate the volumes within this 3D space by a kernel size based on the requirements for post analysis and extract the velocity field in the dilated regions. The dilation allows us to capture data just outside the high vorticity regions needed for iso-surface extraction and Lagrangian interpolation in post-processing. Many filters and derivative equations also rely on this additional data gained from the dilation for interpolation kernels around the region, which makes the extracted data useful for scientific analysis.

This method deliberately leaves out regions of low vorticity. Understanding that we cannot save the entire dataset, we extract a separate dataset that contains full field lower precision data by using lossy compression. We leverage the zfp algorithm [12], which is specifically designed to compress floating point scientific data in 1D, 2D, or 3D space. zfp's lossy compression is *error-bounded*; it guarantees that the values differ from the original by less than a specified amount. zfp achieves an order of magnitude or more compression and the loss of accuracy is indistinguishable when visualizing the data. These characteristics lend themselves well to capturing exascale simulation data for visualization.

Combining these extraction techniques allows one to visualize the simulation while it runs and create an archival database that is exact in regions of high-vorticity and error-bounded elsewhere. The data products are an order of magnitude or more smaller than simulation output and suitable for scientific post analysis. Although our focus is on vorticity and velocity data from direct numerical simulation of the single-phase incompressible Navier Stokes equations, the velocity extraction technique generalizes to richer fluid mechanical simulations that may include magnetic field, magnetic potential and density, to other governing equations, such as Large Eddy Simulations, and to numerical simulations from other domains that run on regular and irregular grids, such as climate, material fracture, and combustion.

Our evaluation utilized 32 burst buffer nodes that contained either 4, 10, or 16 cores. For extracting velocity in high vorticity regions, we reduce an 8192^3 grid by one order of magnitude in under 10 min (the 4 core node was not able to meet this time constraint). For lossy compression of velocity for the entire grid, we reduced by one order of magnitude and it took approximately 10 min for a single timestep. These results inform us that having 32 burst buffer nodes with a minimum of 10 cores each would allow us to execute either extraction task in under ten minutes for a world-class turbulence Direct Numerical Simulation (DNS).

2   Related Work

Supercomputing continues to evolve with speed increases and hardware architecture changes that coincide with application development to leverage these new architectures. Bent et al. [13] explore burst buffer configurations and demonstrate

---

[1] Thresholds are easy to choose because turbulence has threshold values with physical meaning derived from the inverse Kolmogorov scale that describes the near absence of, medium, and high vorticity [11].

that placing SSDs between compute nodes and the storage array allow jitter-free co-processing of their visualization tasks and reduce total time to completion by up to thirty percent. We utilize a similar architecture in our work. Ma et al. [14] discuss in-situ data extraction and visualization. They modify the simulation code to provide data useful for visualization in-situ, whereas our work performs feature extraction in-transit via burst buffers without having to modify existing simulation codes. Ahrens et al. [15] describe and test methods of utilizing multi-core CPU and GPU based processors in the Roadrunner supercomputer to perform visualization of an exascale simulation in-situ. Chen et al. [16] utilize the HemeLB lattice-Boltzmann code for large-scale fluid flow. They discuss pre- and post-processing along with computational steering to modify simulation parameters in situ. This work differs from ours in the way the data is saved and utilized for post-processing. They create a multi-resolution data structure by storing their simulation output in a hierarchical order. This method allows for visualization without reading the entire dataset. In our work, we utilize the SSD burst buffers to read the entire timestep and perform thresholding and extraction of high-magnitude events on a per-timestep basis. Wang et al. [17] developed a file system (BurstFS) that aggregates I/O bandwidth from burst buffers and maintains a distributed key-value store of metadata for the files. This system allows an application to perform small non-contiguous read operations on the burst buffer. Because our feature extraction reads of all the data, this file system would not benefit our work.

We build upon the concept of burst buffers [18] to integrate non-volatile memory into the supercomputing storage hierarchy. We focus specifically on using the SSD to capture write bursts, particularly those from checkpoint workloads. Other concept papers have discussed using burst buffers more generally in the HPC memory hierarchy [19].

3   Problem Overview

Extreme scale simulations produce petabyte-scale data that must be read for feature extraction and/or down-sampling in real time without hindering the computation of the underlying simulation. This presents a host of challenges due to the competition for memory resources, bandwidth, I/O, and storage. The burst buffer architecture adds to the storage hierarchy to enable a temporary storage area in between permanent storage and resident RAM for fast reading and writing. Once a timestep is written, a feature extraction application must read, process, and store the extracted data prior to the simulation overwriting the burst buffer space with a subsequent timestep. Typically, burst buffer capacity is chosen to be more than two times cluster memory so that the burst buffer will hold two to three consecutive timesteps. In addition, the data reduction and the simulation must maintain synchrony throughout the simulation. The feature extraction must process data prior to the simulation writing the next timestep.

The primary problem with world-class numerical simulation data is the sheer size of the output. Our target fluid simulation has a desired output (not every solved timestep) with dimension 8192^3 over 4000 timesteps and produces

4 attributes: 1 component for pressure and 3 for a velocity vector with 4 byte floating point (single precision) values resulting in total data of

$$8192^3 * 4 * 4 * 4000 = 3.518 \times 10^{16}$$

bytes, or approximately 31.25 PB of data. Although our simulation generates a pressure field, the remainder of this paper focuses only on storing the velocity data. Each timestep contains about 6 TB of velocity data that must be read, processed, and written on the order of tens of minutes. This process must complete in time in order to maintain synchronization with the simulation to ensure data extraction successfully finishes. Any delay would cause the simulation to stall.

The data extraction itself presents a complex problem, because it takes computational power to perform the extraction and it must complete in a timely fashion. If we were to do in-situ analysis, extraction resources compete directly with the processing required to perform the simulation. Our method leverages burst buffers in order to perform this extraction in-transit without interfering with the simulation.

4   Methods of Extraction

We present our two methods of extraction: velocity data in regions of high vorticity and lossy compression of the full field. Extraction produces two datasets, each an order of magnitude or more smaller than simulation output. Prior to presenting methods, we motivate our use of Q-criterion for identifying vortices.

4.1   Calculating Highly-Vortical Regions

In turbulent flows, identification of coherent structures, specifically vortices, aids in scientific understanding of these flows. Inside and around these high vortical regions, energy dissipation and squared vorticity (enstrophy) are orders of magnitude higher than the mean values, which we refer to as extreme events [20]. There are various methods for identifying vortices. Vortices are defined by the velocity field that reflects the rotational qualities and there is not a single approved method to describe vortices. Dubief and Delcayre [21] examine four methods of vortex identification: pressure, vorticity magnitude, λ_2, and Q-criterion. Because pressure fails to capture fine details in isotropic turbulence [21] and λ_2 appears to be affected by small noise present in all data, we examine visualizations based on vorticity magnitude and Q-criterion. Each of these two methods provide good visualizations of vortical flow structure when utilized to generate iso-surfaces. However, one particular issue with vorticity magnitude is that the vorticity criterion does not distinguish between swirling motions and shearing motions. Thus, vorticity magnitude can also present layered structures that are vorticity sheets and not vortices [22]. Q-criterion is also not perfect as it fails to reliably identify Bödewadt vorticies. However note that such vorticies occur normal to a wall, and our isotropic turbulence dataset is periodic and does not contain any walls [23].

We chose to compare the performance of the vorticity magnitude and Q-criterion for generating vortical flow iso-surfaces on an isotropic turbulence dataset.

In order to compare Q-criterion versus vorticity performance we defined a threshold that is equivalent for each calculation. The thresholds and resulting data can be constrained based on either scientific concerns (the loss of accuracy when evaluating averages of gradient norms over the entire flow volume) or system resources that set a target data size. This adjustment allows us to produce data that fits within available storage in the computing center, while still gathering useful scientific data to study these high vorticity regions. In order to determine the threshold, we begin by using a multiple of the root-mean-square value of the vorticity fluctuations. This value is known a-priori, based on knowledge of the dissipation rate ϵ and fluid viscosity ν according to $\langle \boldsymbol{\omega} \cdot \boldsymbol{\omega} \rangle^{1/2} = \sqrt{\epsilon/\nu}$ [24] where ω is the vorticity vector (curl of the velocity). For the data from the JHTDB, this value is $\sqrt{.0928/.000185} = 22.4$, which is also the inverse Kolomogorov time scale τ_η. Since we are interested in high vorticity regions, we scale this low reference threshold to achieve a clear visual representation of high vorticity regions.

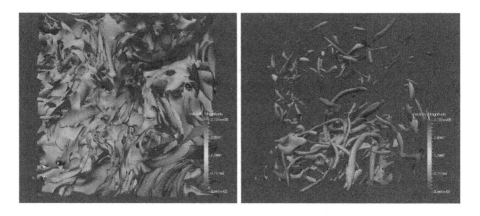

Fig. 1. Vorticity magnitude contour at threshold 22.4 (left) and 55.98 (right)

We tested various multiples of $1/\tau_\eta$ and found that a multiple of 2.5 presented clear vorticity structures without obvious erroneous surfaces. The threshold chosen in this case is $2.5 * 22.4 = 55.98$. The visualization of vorticity magnitude at this threshold was a much clearer representation of vortices than using a threshold of 22.4 as seen in Fig. 1.

Upon finding a reasonable threshold, we calculated the equivalent threshold for Q-criterion. In the absence of straining motions, the relationship between the threshold of vorticity and Q-criterion can be taken to be as follows: $Q = \frac{1}{4}\omega^2$. Therefore the threshold value for Q that we chose is $Q = .25(55.98)^2 = 783$.

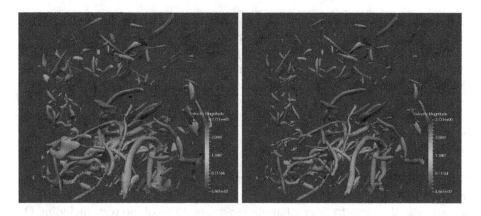

Fig. 2. Vorticity magnitude (left) and Q-criterion (right)

Figure 2 shows the visualization of vorticity magnitude contour versus the Q-criterion contour. Though they look very similar, the bottom left corner of the left image (vorticity magnitude) displays a structure that is not present in the Q-criterion visualization. This is due to shearing, because the vorticity magnitude does not differentiate between shearing and curl. In the definition of Q, strain is subtracted from vorticity which results in a lower Q value and filters out shearing.

We performed additional tests at various thresholds and cube dimensions (subsets of the full 8192^3 grid) to determine whether the computation of Q-criterion or vorticity magnitude has an impact on overall feature extraction time. Table 1 compares total computation times, which includes reading from and writing to the burst buffer. Our results show that Q-criterion computes slightly faster than vorticity regardless of cube size. As a result of these considerations and tests, we choose to use Q-criterion for all analyses in the remainder of this paper. We also note that Q-criterion is generally accepted in the turbulence community for vortex identification.

Table 1. Vorticity vs. Q thresholding in seconds total time per cube on a single core

Cube size	Vorticity threshold	Q threshold
64	.257	.222
128	1.597	1.375
192	5.070	4.500
256	11.120	9.522

4.2 Thresholded Vorticity Volumes

In order to capture the velocity data, we create a three-dimensional stencil that encompasses the regions of high-vorticity. This stencil masks out low Q regions and generates a sparse representation of velocity data within the regions. This sparse representation is a vtkUnstructuredGrid that consists of floating point coordinates in real space and the corresponding velocity vector at each point, thus each point contains six corresponding floating point values. This is not an ideal method of storage, however it works well enough in this application. Since the representation of vorticies in isotropic turbulence appear as worms, the goal is to capture velocities within all points within these worms, while discarding the velocity data outside of these structures. This data is the losslessly compressed to preserve the original values.

We begin by creating a stencil that "cuts out" high-vorticity regions from the full data. This includes points above the Q-criterion threshold. These regions are then dilated to include nearby points that are below the threshold. Dilating by four cells allows us to later compute most quantities of interest, including Q-criterion, vorticity magnitude, marching cubes for iso-surface extraction, velocity derivatives, and 4th-order Lagrangian interpolation. In order to create the stencil we create a bitmask dataset of the same dimensions of the original dataset and set all values above the threshold to one and those below to zero. Next we dilate this stencil with kernel size of four, meaning that each point that is already set to one sets all points within four voxels to one. Then we mask the velocity field with this zero/one data set, which extracts velocity values from the high vorticity regions and zeros out all other regions. The resultant data set contains a subset of velocity where each velocity vector retained contains a point coordinate to define its spatial location. The data can be utilized to reconstruct Q-criterion and iso-surfaces at or above the specified threshold. Figure 3 illustrates a visualization of dilated velocity volume utilizing the Q threshold of 783. Figure 4 demonstrates the ability to extract contours at higher thresholds from the thresholded velocity volume shown in Fig. 3.

4.3 Lossy Compression

While thresholding works well for scientists studying events specifically within extreme vortical regions, it may be necessary to save information outside those regions for post analysis. For example, vortex precursors may occur in initially weak vortical regions, which then act as seeds for subsequent vortex intensification. In addition, a researcher may need information about conditions where velocity may be relatively high, which may not be contained in our thresholded data due to the fact that vorticity is a measurement of curl or rotation. We present a method for storing *all* of the data in a lossy compressed form for post analysis and visualization. This does not provide exact raw simulation data, however, it provides data that is within a defined error tolerance. The error introduced on these data will be shown to be insignificant for the purposes of visualization, making the data desirable for post visualization analysis.

In order to store the data in a lossy form, we utilize a recent compression algorithm, zfp [12], designed specifically for the compression of multi-dimensional, floating-point scientific data. It contains various options for compression, one of which is to specify an absolute error tolerance. Utilizing this method at an error

Fig. 3. Visualization of a 256 cube of dilated velocity in regions above Q threshold of 783

Fig. 4. Iso-surface extraction from dilated velocity threshold at Q thresholds 1700 (left) and 2500 (right)

tolerance of 10^{-1} on the velocity data (the root-mean-square value of the velocity fluctuations is 0.686 while its mean is zero), we achieve an effective reduction of one order of magnitude from the raw velocity data. We note that this reduced dataset is intended for post analysis and visualization, and cannot be used as checkpoint data to restart the simulation.

While zfp operates on one scalar component, it contains a striding option that allows us to compress all three velocity vector components and store them as separate compressed blocks of data. We extended the Visualization Toolkit (VTK) [25] compression options to provide dimensions and component sizes to the compressor in order for zfp to have the information required to compress the data. Utilizing the striding option, each of the three velocity vector components (x, y, z) are compressed separately and stored as concatenated binary data. The data sizes for each axis are stored within the VTK XML file format as metadata in order for VTK to correctly decompress the data. During decompression, each component is decompressed into a separate array and interleaved back to their original representation creating a VTK float array of velocity vector values. If pressure or another scalar field were added, this could be compressed as well, and we would expect similar results.

5   Experimental Results

Experiments utilize the Visualization Toolkit version 7.1.0 by Kitware [25]. While we focus our experiments on finding high-Q vortical regions, VTK provides the flexibility of performing many other scientific computations on the simulation data. VTK provides a rich toolset for analysis and visualization. In addition to VTK, we utilize the zfp compression algorithm [12]. We compiled this natively into VTK in order to provide 3 dimensional lossy compression on VTK structured grid data.

We conducted all experiments on nodes in the Los Alamos National Lab development cluster called Darwin. We began by utilizing a partition built to emulate the performance of burst buffer nodes on Trinity which is used to test development software, such as the hierarchical input/output library [9]. Each node is equipped with a 6-core, 12-thread Intel Xeon E5-2630 2.30 GHz processor, 128 GB of RAM, and an Intel P3700 400 GB SSD that is rated for 2.8 GB/s of sequential throughput and up to 460 K random read IOPs.

5.1   Dilated Threshold

We perform a threshold and dilation velocity cutout operation on a cluster with SSD burst buffers that contains a single timestep of raw simulation data. We vary the cube size into which we decompose the problem in order to find the cube size that maximizes throughput. Smaller cubes reduce I/O throughput and reduce skew and memory pressure. Larger cubes increase I/O throughput, but reduce the efficacy of caching, particularly on smaller processor caches up the memory hierarchy. We find that a cube size of 256^3 maximizes throughput for this computation (Table 2). Above 192^3, performance is stable and degrades slightly above 256^3, which we attribute to increased cache misses.

Table 2. Comparison of I/O and computation times in seconds when processing a single cube

Size	Read	Q Comp	Thresh	Write	Total	Throughput
64	.029	.117	.0154	.0266	.222	13.51 MB/s
128	.043	.877	.064	.136	1.34	17.91 MB/s
192	.080	2.83	.206	.542	4.46	19.32 MB/s
256	.136	6.15	.399	1.08	9.522	20.17 MB/s
384	.373	20.68	2.23	5.67	34.337	18.87 MB/s
512	.788	48.76	5.31	13.17	78.86	19.47 MB/s

Averaged over all cubes, the extracted thresholded velocity data is reduced by a factor of 29 times. The raw size of 256^3 of velocity data is 192 MB and the dilated extraction averages 6.7 MB. As mentioned previously, if we increase the threshold, the extracted data size will decrease.

Based on the throughput in Table 2, we measured the resources required to perform a dilated velocity extraction of an 8192^3 grid on the order of ten minutes. Our results show that this can be done utilizing 32 nodes with 10 cores each (320 cores) and 6 TB of SSD storage to achieve a full extraction of the data within the time constraint.

Next, we performed read tests on the 32 heterogeneous nodes to compare the local hard drive throughput with the SSD. Of these nodes, 15 did not contain a spinning hard drive therefore there are no hard disk throughput results for those nodes. This test demonstrates the performance gains of the burst buffer by comparing it to the node's local hard disk. The burst buffer was between 5 to 20 times faster depending on the node as shown in Fig. 5.

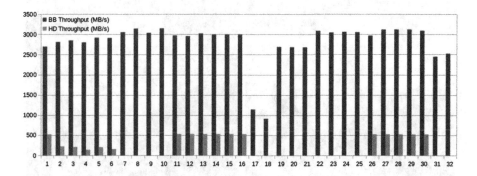

Fig. 5. Burst buffer throughput compared to hard disk throughput

5.2 Lossy Compression with zfp

The compression algorithm zfp provides an order of magnitude reduction by compressing scientific floating point data where the values spatially near each other have low variance. Although it provides many features like in-memory compression, we specifically use it for compressing data for storage with a predefined lossy tolerance of 10^{-1}. At this tolerance we achieve an order of magnitude of compression with visually lossless reconstruction, which is far superior to the default ZLib library utilized in VTK. We also note that while the error threshold is set at 10^{-1} our reconstructed data maximum error was .017. Table 3 shows the resulting size of compressing different sized cubes of isotropic turbulence data, along with the amount of time required to compress the cube. Visually the results of the lossy compression are indistinguishable from the original data as show in Fig. 6.

Table 3. zfp compression by cube and time

Cube size	Raw size	zfp size	Total time (s)	Reduction	Throughput
128	25 MB	2.3 MB	.334	×10.9	74.85 MB/s
192	81 MB	8.1 MB	1.05	×10	77.14 MB/s
256	192 MB	18 MB	2.09	×10.7	91.87 MB/s

zfp provides the ability to store the *entire* dataset in a lossy compressed mode. Each cube is saved as a VTK Image Data file which uses a few lines of XML for metadata about the object (for example, dimensions and array names), and a VTK float array that is compressed using zfp and saved as binary appended data to the XML file. Figure 6 shows a surface representation of a 256 cube of velocity data. The left figure is the raw velocity magnitude, while the right figure was

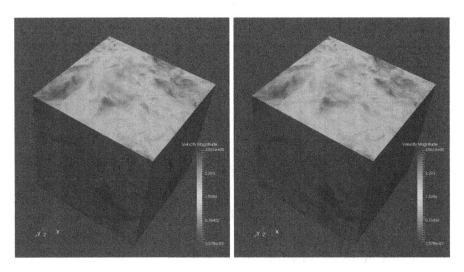

Fig. 6. Isosurface of a 256 cube of isotropic turbulence velocity data. Left: Raw velocity. Right: zfp compressed at 10^{-1} tolerance.

compressed by zfp and then decompressed for visual representation. The two cubes are indistinguishable in this figure and also when viewing at all zoom levels. Visual equivalence holds when deriving fields of interest from compressed velocity data, including Q-criterion and vorticity magnitude.

5.3 Compressing Dilated Threshold with zfp

We also evaluate using zfp as a compressor for threshold reduced data as compared with VTK's default ZLib and we conclude that ZLib is preferable; it is lossless and provides comparable compression. The data output from a threshold is sparse and best represented by an irregular grid.

While zfp does not work on an unstructured grid, version 0.5 added the capability of reducing storage of a block of 4^3 values to one bit if all values within a block are below the error tolerance, since then the block can be approximated as all zeros. To test zfp on sparse data, we performed another experiment to determine if zfp can be used instead of ZLib for our dilated threshold extraction. In this test, we compress a 256^3 block of dilated thresholded data. The data is stored on a structured grid with zero values where the threshold was not met. Utilizing ZLib compression, the result is 6.7 MB, and using zfp it was reduced to 5.8 MB. This compression was performed using a loss threshold of 1×10^{-1}. Using a decreased threshold of 1×10^{-2} resulted in a file size of 8.1 MB. Since the lossy compression did not create a significant reduction in data size, we recommend using a lossless compressor for dilated velocity extraction.

5.4 Multiprocessing Simulation Outputs

We move from microbenchmarks on individual cubes, to the parallel extraction of an entire simulation timestep across many nodes in order to demonstrate that extraction can meet the time constraints of data lifetimes in burst buffers. Our target is to scale these results to the Trinity supercomputer. However, we have to use the development cluster as a proxy. We start by examining the amount of parallelism appropriate for a single burst buffer node. Our treatment examines the amount of parallelism per node to maximize throughput. We initially utilized a node for testing that contained 6 cores and an SSD burst buffer. The results of executing velocity extraction in parallel are shown in Table 4.

The first test labled "Single" in the table displays the times for a single threaded extraction running on a single core. This test was performed in order to benchmark throughput on a single core. Next we performed the extraction in parallel across six cores. While the overall throughput is the combined speed of all six cores (approximately 93 MB/s), the individual throughput per core is less than when the extraction is performed on a single thread. Since I/O is shared on the burst buffer and memory, each core must compete for disk and memory I/O. The data shows that the resultant per core slowdown is about 25% for disk I/O and 20% for Q-Criterion computation. These results informs us that adding more cores to an extraction node will not linearly improve extraction throughput due to memory I/O contention.

Table 4. 256 Cube: Single vs. Multiprocessing I/O by core and averaged (in seconds). Multi throughput is the sum of throughput for all cores.

Core	Read	Q Comp	Write	Total	Speed
Single	.136	6.55	1.08	9.522	20.17 MB/s
Core 0	.179	8.28	1.81	12.34	15.56 MB/s
Core 1	.179	8.29	1.82	12.37	15.52 MB/s
Core 2	.181	8.37	1.77	12.38	15.51 MB/s
Core 3	.180	8.35	1.79	12.40	15.48 MB/s
Core 4	.183	8.37	1.79	12.41	15.47 MB/s
Core 5	.179	8.15	1.79	12.42	15.46 MB/s
Multi	.180	8.30	1.80	12.39	93 MB/s (total)

In the next step of testing, we utilized 32 burst buffer nodes to perform the computation in parallel on the number of cubes required to build an entire 8192^3 timestep. We performed dilated velocity extraction and zfp compression on 32,768 blocks of 256^3 raw velocity data (1024 blocks per node). Figure 7 shows the results of the total extraction time by node and extraction type. Since the Darwin cluster is heterogeneous, the number of cores per node are specified. As evidenced by nodes 27 through 32, four cores were not enough to complete either extraction in under ten minutes. However, nodes 1 through 26 were able to complete each extraction in less than ten minutes.

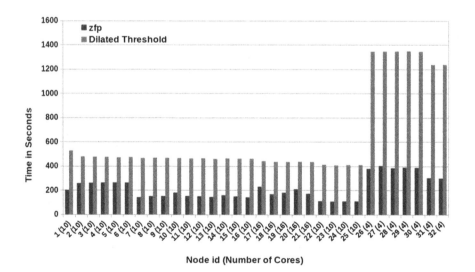

Fig. 7. Times per node for extraction and compression

For in-transit analysis and visualization, the extracted data could be read in place by a viewer such as Paraview to monitor the simulation during the run, and burst buffers provide fast reads in this process. For extracted data that needs to be saved for long term storage, a secondary process copies the results to a shared storage. The extracted data is significantly reduced in size, which also reduces the I/O burden when writing to shared storage. Due to the reduction, the write would not interfere with the simulation.

6 Recommendations for Exascale Simulations

Prior to performing an exascale simulation with the intent to store significant data, it is important to determine what data must be extracted to perform the post scientific analysis. Thus far, we have proposed a method to gather velocity data that contain high vorticity in a scientific dataset, while still capturing a broad view of the overall simulation utilizing a modern lossy data compression algorithm. These two methods combined present a state-of-the-art way to extract useful data from a world class computational fluid dynamics simulation. The lossy compression method with zfp can be used on virtually any scientific dataset that is on a dense structured grid. The compression works optimally on 3D data, but also can work on 2D and 1D floating point datasets. Our extraction techniques present a way forward on how to handle petabyte or even exabyte scale information. The essential part of these exascale simulations is to have a method to extract relevant data utilizing the architecture of modern supercomputers. Having a plan and understanding the data necessary to make scientific discoveries in the future is the key to gathering useful data from an exascale simulation.

7 Conclusion

We have demonstrated the ability to extract scientific data from a world class simulation using burst buffer SSD technology. We demonstrated a two-pronged approach that captures velocity in highly vortical regions along with a lossy compressed representation of the entire velocity dataset for concise storage and future scientific analysis. We demonstrated that we can reduce data by at least an order of magnitude for full field lossy compressed form, and nearly $30\times$ reduction for dilated velocity in high vorticity regions by utilizing the burst-buffer to read raw data and writing extracted and/or compressed data to shared storage. The extracted data can be utilized for various scientific applications from visualization to tracking highly vortical regions. The lossy compression can be utilized on any dense grid dataset, therefore this method is not limited to turbulence data.

8 Future Work

Since we have outlined and demonstrated the ability to create a meaningful dataset of an exascale simulation, we intend to gather data from an exascale simulation and ingest it into the Johns Hopkins Turbulence Databases a publicly accessible database, providing world-wide access to this compressed and high-Q velocity region dataset. The two-pronged approach will provide scientists the ability to query and perform analysis across the entire exascale simulation result. In addition, we will explore more efficient representations of sparse data. The vtkUnstructuredGrid primitive we utilized stores real space coordinates that result in each velocity vector containing three additional floating point coordinates. A custom representation method that more efficiently represents the points would allow us to even further reduce the space required for this data. In this work we defined a threshold for the simulation, however this may not be optimal in detecting all vortex structures. Our methodology could be expanded to utilize an adaptive threshold for feature extraction as explained in [26]. As scientific needs emerge and new practices for detecting high-vorticity regions are introduced, they could be implemented using our approach to feature extraction.

Acknowledgments. The authors would like to thank Los Alamos National Laboratory for providing compute resources. Specifically we would like to thank Ryan Braithwaite who configured the Darwin cluster and setup our reservation times to run our experiments. This work is supported in part by the National Science Foundation under Grants CMMI-0941530, OCI-108849, ACI-1261715, No. OCI-1244820, and AST-0939767, Johns Hopkins University's Institute for Data Intensive Engineering & Science, Lawrence Livermore National Laboratory under Contract DE-AC52-07NA27344, and was partially supported by the Exascale Computing Project (17-SC-20-SC), a collaborative effort of the U.S. Department of Energy Office of Science and the National Nuclear Security Administration, and under the auspices of the U.S. Department of Energy.

References

1. Sodani, A.: Race to exascale: opportunities and challenges. In: IEEE/ACM International Symposium on Microarchitecture, Micro-44 (2011)
2. Hick, J.: I/O requirements for exascale. In: Open Fabrics Alliance (2011)
3. Hemsoth, N.: Burst buffers flash exascale potential. HPC Wire, 1 May 2014 (2014)
4. Bent, J., Grider, G., Kettering, B., Manzanares, A., McClelland, M., Torres, A., Torrez, A.: Storage challenges at Los Alamos National Labs. In: 2012 IEEE 28th Symposium on Mass Storage Systems and Technologies (MSST), pp. 1–5, April 2012
5. Li, Y., Perlman, E., Wan, M., Yang, Y., Meneveau, C., Burns, R., Chen, S., Szalay, A., Eyink, G.: A public turbulence database cluster and applications to study lagrangian evolution of velocity increments in turbulence. J. Turbul. **9**(31), 1–29 (2008)
6. Bürger, K., Treib, M., Westermann, R., Werner, S., Lalescu, C.C., Szalay, A., Meneveau, C., Eyink, G.L.: Vortices within vortices: hierarchical nature of vortex tubes in turbulence. Computing Research Repository. arXiv:1210.3325 (2012)
7. Eyink, G., Vishniac, E., Lalescu, C., Aluie, H., Kanov, K., Bürger, K., Burns, R., Meneveau, C., Szalay, A.: Flux-freezing breakdown in high-conductivity magneto-hydrodynamic turbulence. Nature **497**(7450), 466–469 (2013)
8. Bent, J., Gibson, G., Grider, G., McClelland, B., Nowoczynski, P., Nunez, J., Polte, M., Wingate, M.: PLFS: a checkpoint filesystem for parallel applications. In: Proceedings of the Conference on High Performance Computing Networking, Storage and Analysis, SC 2009, pp. 21:1–21:12. ACM, New York (2009)

9. ACES Team: Trinity platform introduction and usage model. Los Alamos National Laboratories, number LA-UR-15-26834 (2015)

10. Ang, D.H., Brim, M., Parker, S., Watson, G., Bland, W.: Providing a robust tools landscape for coral machines. In: Workshop on Extreme Scale Programming Tools (2015)

11. Kanov, K., Lalescu, C., Burns, R.: Efficient evaluation of threshold queries of derived fields in a numerical simulation database. In: Extending Database Technology, pp. 301–312 (2015)

12. Lindstrom, P.: Fixed-rate compressed floating-point arrays. IEEE Trans. Vis. Comput. Graph. **20**(12), 2674–2683 (2014)

13. Bent, J., Faibish, S., Ahrens, J., Grider, G., Patchett, J., Tzelnic, P., Woodring, J.: Jitter-free co-processing on a prototype exascale storage stack. In: 2012 IEEE 28th Symposium on Mass Storage Systems and Technologies (MSST), pp. 1–5. IEEE, LA-UR-pending (2012)

14. Ma, K.-L., Wang, C., Hongfeng, Y., Tikhonova, A.: In-situ processing and visualization for ultrascale simulations. J. Phys: Conf. Ser. **78**(1), 012043 (2007)

15. Ahrens, J., Lo, L.-T., Nouanesengsy, B., Patchett, J., McPherson, A.: Petascale visualization: approaches and initial results. In: Workshop on Ultrascale Visualization UltraVis 2008, pp. 24–28, Nov 2008

16. Chen, F., Flatken, M., Basermann, A., Gerndt, A., Hetheringthon, J., Krüger, T., Matura, G., Nash, R.W.: Enabling in situ pre- and post-processing for exascale hemodynamic simulations - a co-design study with the sparse geometry Lattice-Boltzmann code HemeLB. In: 2012 SC Companion: High Performance Computing, Networking, Storage and Analysis (SCC), pp. 662–668, Nov 2012

17. Wang, T., Mohror, K., Moody, A., Sato, K., Yu, W.: An ephemeral burst-buffer file system for scientific applications. In: Proceedings of the International Conference for High Performance Computing, Networking, Storage and Analysis, SC 2016, pp. 69:1–69:12 (2016)

18. Liu, N., Cope, J., Carns, P., Carothers, C., Ross, R., Grider, G., Crume, A., Maltzahn, C.: On the role of burst buffers in leadership-class storage systems. In: 2012 IEEE 28th Symposium on Mass Storage Systems and Technologies (MSST), pp. 1–11, April 2012

19. Li, D., Vetter, J.S., Marin, G., McCurdy, C., Cira, C., Liu, Z., Yu, W.: Identifying opportunities for byte-addressable non-volatile memory in extreme-scale scientific applications. In: Proceedings of the 2012 IEEE 26th International Parallel and Distributed Processing Symposium, IPDPS 2012, pp. 945–956. IEEE Computer Society, Washington (2012)

20. Sreenivasan, K., Yeung, P.K., Zhai, X.M.: Extreme events in computational turbulence. Proc. Natl. Acad. Sci. U.S.A. **112**(41), 12633–12638 (2015)

21. Dubief, Y., Delcayre, F.: On coherent-vortex identification in turbulence. J. Turbul. **1**(11), 11 (2000)

22. Kida, S., Miura, H.: Identification and analysis of vortical structures. Eur. J. Mech. - B/Fluids **17**(4), 471–488 (1998)

23. Jeong, J., Hussain, F.: On the identification of a vortex. J. Fluid Mech. **285**, 69–94 (1995)

24. Tennekes, H., Lumley, J.L.: A first course in turbulence. M.I.T. Press, Cambridge (1972)

25. Schroeder, W., Martin, K., Lorensen, B.: Visualization Toolkit: An Object-Oriented Approach to 3D Graphics, 4th edn. Kitware, New York (2006)

26. Bremer, P.-T., Gruber, A., Bennett, J.C., Gyulassy, A., Kolla, H., Chen, J.H., Grout, R.W.: Identifying turbulent structures through topological segmentation. Commun. Appl. Math. Comput. Sci. **11**(1), 37–53 (2016)

An Analysis of Core- and Chip-Level Architectural Features in Four Generations of Intel Server Processors

Johannes Hofmann[1]([✉]), Georg Hager[2], Gerhard Wellein[2], and Dietmar Fey[1]

[1] Computer Architecture, University of Erlangen-Nuremberg,
91058 Erlangen, Germany
{johannes.hofmann,dietmar.fey}@fau.de
[2] Erlangen Regional Computing Center (RRZE), 91058 Erlangen, Germany
{georg.hager,gerhard.wellein}@fau.de

Abstract. This paper presents a survey of architectural features among four generations of Intel server processors (Sandy Bridge, Ivy Bridge, Haswell, and Broadwell) with a focus on performance with floating point workloads. Starting at the core level and going down the memory hierarchy we cover instruction throughput for floating-point instructions, L1 cache, address generation capabilities, core clock speed and its limitations, L2 and L3 cache bandwidth and latency, the impact of Cluster on Die (CoD) and cache snoop modes, and the Uncore clock speed. Using microbenchmarks we study the influence of these factors on code performance. We show that the energy efficiency of the LINPACK and HPCG benchmarks can be improved significantly by tuning the Uncore clock speed without sacrificing performance, and that the Graph500 benchmark performance may benefit from a suitable choice of cache snoop mode settings.

Keywords: Intel architecture · Performance modeling · LINPACK · HPCG · Graph500

1 Introduction

Intel Xeon server CPUs dominate in the commodity HPC market. Although their microarchitecture is ubiquitous and can also be found in mobile and desktop devices, many developers of numerical software hardly care about architectural details and rely on the compiler to produce "decent" code with "good" performance. If we actually want to know what "good performance" means we have to build analytic models that describe the interaction between software and hardware. Despite the necessary simplifications, such models can give useful hints towards the relevant bottlenecks of code execution and thus point to viable optimization approaches. The Roofline model [6,22] and the Execution-Cache-Memory (ECM) model [5,18] are typical examples. Analytic modeling requires simplified machine and execution models, with details about properties of execution units, caches, memory, etc. Much of this data is provided by manufacturers,

© Springer International Publishing AG 2017
J.M. Kunkel et al. (Eds.): ISC High Performance 2017, LNCS 10266, pp. 294–314, 2017.
DOI: 10.1007/978-3-319-58667-0_16

but many relevant features can only be understood via microbenchmarks, either because they are not documented or because the hardware cannot leverage its full potential in practice. One simple example is the maximum memory bandwidth of a chip, which can be calculated from the number, frequency, and width of the DRAM channels but which, in practice, may be significantly lower than this absolute limit. Hence, microbenchmarks such as STREAM [13] or likwid-bench [20] are used to measure the limits achievable in practice.

There has been some convergence in processor microarchitecures for high performance computing, but the latest CPU models show interesting differences in their performance-relevant features. Building good analytic performance models and, in general, making sense of performance data, requires intimate knowledge of such details. The main goal of this paper is to provide a coverage and critical discussion of those details on the latest four Intel architecture generations for server CPUs: Sandy Bridge (SNB), Ivy Bridge (IVB), Haswell (HSW), and Broadwell (BDW). The actual CPU models used for the analysis are described in Sect. 3.1 below.

1.1 Performance on Modern Multicore CPUs

Out of the many possible approaches to performance analysis and optimization (coined *performance engineering* [PE]) we favor concepts based on analytic performance models. For recent server multicore designs the ECM performance model allows for a very accurate description of single-core performance and scalability. In contrast to the Roofline model it drops the assumption of a single bottleneck for the steady-state execution of a loop. A brief introduction to the ECM model is given in Sect. 2 below. For a complete coverage we refer to [8,18]. The model has been shown to work well for the analysis of implementations of several important computational kernels [2,9,18,19,23].

In order to construct analytic models accurately, data about the capabilities of the microarchitecture and how it interacts with the code at hand is needed. For floating-point centric code in scientific computing, maximum throughput and latency numbers for arithmetic and LOAD/STORE instructions are most useful in all their vectorized and non-vectorized, single (SP) and double precision (DP) variants. On Intel multicore CPUs up to Haswell, this encompasses scalar, streaming SIMD extensions (SSE), advanced vector extensions (AVX), and AVX2 instructions. Modeling the memory hierarchy in the ECM model requires the maximum data bandwidth between adjacent cache levels (assuming that the hierarchy is inclusive) and the maximum (saturated) memory bandwidth. As for the caches it is usually sufficient to assume the maximum documented theoretical bandwidth (presupposing that all prefetchers work perfectly to hide latencies), although latency penalties might apply [9]. The main memory bandwidth and latency may depend on the cluster-on-die (CoD) mode and cache snoop mode settings. Finally, the latest Intel CPUs work with at least two clock speed domains: one for the core (or even individual cores) and one for the Uncore, which includes the L3 cache and memory controllers. Both are subject to automatic changes; in case of AVX code on Haswell and later CPUs

the guaranteed baseline clock speed is lower than the standard speed rating of
the chip. The performance and energy consumption of code depends crucially
on the interplay between these clock speed domains. Finally, especially when
it comes to power dissipation and capping, considerable variations among the
specimen of the same CPU model can be observed.

All these intricate architectural details influence benchmark and application
performance, and it is insufficient to look up the raw specs in a data sheet in
order to understand this influence.

1.2 Related Work

There is a large number of papers dealing with details in the architecture of CPUs
and their impact on performance and energy consumption. In [1] the authors
assessed the capabilities of the then-new Nehalem server processor for workloads in scientific computing and compared its capabilities with its predecessors
and competing designs. In [17], tools and techniques for measuring and tuning
power and energy consumption of HPC systems were discussed. The QuickPath
Interconnect (QPI) snoop modes on the Haswell EP processor were investigated
in [15]. Energy efficiency features, including the AVX and Uncore clock speeds,
on the same architecture were studied in [4,7]. Our work differs from all those by
systematically investigating relevant architectural features, from the core level
down to memory, via microbenchmarks in view of analytic performance modeling as well as important benchmark workloads such as LINPACK, Graph500,
and HPCG.

1.3 Contribution

Apart from confirming or highlighting some documented or previously published
findings, this paper makes the following new contributions:

- We present benchmark results showing the improvement in the performance
  of the vector gather instruction from HSW to BDW. On BDW it is now
  advantageous to actually use the gather instruction instead of "emulating" it.
- We fathom the capabilities of the L2 cache on all four microarchitectures and
  establish practical limits for L2 bandwidth that can be used in analytic ECM
  modeling. These limits are far below the advertised 64 B/cy on HSW and
  BDW.
- We study the bandwidth scalability of the L3 cache depending on the Cluster on Die (CoD) mode and show that, although the parallel efficiency for
  streaming code is never below 85%, CoD has a measurable advantage over
  non-CoD.
- We present latency data for all caches and main memory under various
  cache snoop modes and CoD/non-CoD. We find that although CoD is best
  for streaming and non-uniform memory access (NUMA) aware workloads in
  terms of latency and bandwidth, highly irregular, NUMA-unfriendly code

such as the Graph500 benchmark benefits dramatically from non-CoD mode with Home Snoop and Opportunistic Snoop Broadcast by as much as 50% on BDW.

- We show how the Uncore clock speed on HSW and BDW has considerable impact on the power consumption of bandwidth- and cache-bound code, opening new options for energy efficient and power-capped execution.

2   A Brief Introduction to the ECM Performance Model

In order to get a prediction of the single-core performance of a loop, the data transfer volumes through all levels of the cache hierarchy must be known. For instance, for a certain number of iterations a loop may transfer five cache lines (CLs) between L2 and L1, three between L3 and L2, and another three between memory and L3 (assuming an inclusive cache hierarchy here; the model is not restricted to inclusive caches, though). Each of those transfers takes a certain amount of cycles, which can be obtained by dividing the data volume by the theoretical bandwidth in bytes per cycle for each data path. In the example above, if the data paths between adjacent caches have a bandwidth of 32 bytes/cy and the CL size is 64 bytes, we get $T_{\mathrm{L1L2}} = 10\,\mathrm{cy}$ and $T_{\mathrm{L2L3}} = 6\,\mathrm{cy}$. For main memory transfers we use the saturated full-chip memory bandwidth (as obtained, e.g., from a suitable streaming benchmark) so that for a memory bandwidth of $50\,\mathrm{GByte/s}$ we get $T_{\mathrm{L3Mem}} = 3 \times 64\,\mathrm{bytes}/50\,\mathrm{GByte/s} \times f$, where f is the clock speed of the CPU in cycles per second.

Instruction execution on data in L1 takes a number of cycles, which can be predicted by manual analysis or by tools such as the Intel Architecture Code Analyzer (IACA)[1]. Here we distinguish between *non-overlapping time* (T_{nOL}), which encompasses data transfers between the L1 and the registers, and *overlapping time* (T_{OL}) for all the rest such as arithmetic, branching, etc.

Putting all these contributions together to get a prediction for execution time requires a *machine model*. The machine model for current Intel Xeon CPUs is to add all the data transfer contributions (including T_{nOL}) down to the level of the memory hierarchy where the working set resides to get a data transfer time prediction T_{data} and compare this to T_{OL}. The predicted time is then $\max(T_{\mathrm{OL}}, T_{\mathrm{data}})$. Other architectures call for different machine models; e.g., on the IBM Power8 most of the data transfer contributions overlap with each other, while on the Intel Xeon Phi "Knights Corner" we have to augment the transfer times with additional latency penalties [9].

A prediction for multiple cores is obtained by assuming perfect scalability until a bandwidth bottleneck (typically the main memory bandwidth) is saturated. In absence of other scalability limiters such as load imbalance, this makes it possible to determine the number of cores at which the performance will saturate.

The crucial difference between the ECM model and the Roofline model is that Roofline requires maximum bandwidth measurements for all possibly relevant

---

[1] http://software.intel.com/en-us/articles/intel-architecture-code-analyzer/.

data paths on the chip. A prediction is then obtained by taking the execution time determined by the data path that takes the longest time to deliver the data or the in-core execution, assuming perfect overlap of all contributions. The ECM model ideally only requires one measured value, which is the saturated memory bandwidth. All other measurable bandwidths are predicted.

3   Test Bed

3.1   Hardware Description

All measurements were performed on standard two-socket Intel Xeon servers. A summary of key specifications of the four generations of processors is shown in Table 1. According to Intel's "tick-tock" model, a "tick" represents a shrink of the manufacturing process technology; however, it should be noted that "ticks" are often accompanied by minor microarchitectural improvements while a "tock" usually involves larger changes.

SNB (a "tock") first introduced AVX, doubling the single instruction, multiple data (SIMD) width from SSE's 128 bit to 256 bit. One major shortcoming of SNB is directly related to AVX: Although the SIMD register width has doubled and a second LOAD unit was added, data path widths between the L1 cache and individual LOAD/STORE units were left at 16 B/cy. This leads to AVX stores requiring two cycles to retire on SNB, and AVX LOADs block both units. IVB, a "tick", saw an increase in core count as well as a higher memory clock; in addition, IVB brought speedups for several instructions, e.g., floating-point (FP) divide and square root; see Table 2 for details.

HSW, a "tock", introduced AVX2, extending the existing 256 bit SIMD vectorization from floating-point to integer data types. Instructions introduced by

Table 1. Key test machine specifications. All reported numbers taken from data sheets.

Microarchitecture	Sandy bridge-EP	Ivy bridge-EP	Haswell-EP	Broadwell-EP
Shorthand	SNB	IVB	HSW	BDW
Chip model	Xeon E5-2680	Xeon E5-2690 v2	Xeon E5-2695 v3	E5-2697 v4
Release date	Q1/2012	Q3/2013	Q3/2014	Q1/2016
Base freq.	2.7 GHz	3.0 GHz	2.3 GHz	2.3 GHz
Max all core turbo freq.	—	—	2.8 GHz	2.8 GHz
AVX base freq.	—	—	1.9 GHz	2.0 GHz
AVX all core turbo freq.	—	—	2.6 GHz	2.7 GHz
Cores/threads	8/16	10/20	14/28	18/36
Latest SIMD extensions	AVX	AVX	AVX2, FMA3	AVX2, FMA3
Memory configuration	4 ch. DDR3-1600	4 ch. DDR3-1866	4 ch. DDR4-2133	4 ch. DDR4-2400
Theor. mem. bandwidth	51.2 GB/s	59.7 GB/s	68.2 GB/s	76.8 GB/s
L1 cache capacity	8 × 32 kB	10 × 32 kB	14 × 32 kB	18 × 32 kB
L2 cache capacity	8 × 256 kB	10 × 256 kB	14 × 256 kB	18 × 256 kB
L3 cache capacity	20 MB (8 × 2.5 MB)	25 MB (10 × 2.5 MB)	35 MB (14 × 2.5 MB)	45 MB (18 × 2.5 MB)
L1→Reg bandwidth	2 × 16 B/cy	2 × 16 B/cy	2 × 32 B/cy	2 × 32 B/cy
Reg→L1 bandwidth	1 × 16 B/cy	1 × 16 B/cy	1 × 32 B/cy	1 × 32 B/cy
L1↔L2 bandwidth	32 B/cy	32 B/cy	64 B/cy	64 B/cy
L2↔L3 bandwidth	32 B/cy	32 B/cy	32 B/cy	32 B/cy

the fused multiply-add (FMA) extension are handled by two new, AVX-capable execution units. Data path widths between the L1 cache and registers as well as the L1 and L2 caches were doubled. A vector gather instruction provides a simple means to fill SIMD registers with non-contiguous data, making it easier for the compiler to vectorize code with indirect accesses. To maintain scalability of the core interconnect, HSW chips with more than eight cores move from a single-ring core interconnect to a dual-ring design. At the same time, HSW introduced the new CoD mode, in which a chip is optionally partitioned into two equally sized NUMA domains in order to reduce latencies and increase scalability. Starting with HSW, the system's QPI snoop mode can also be configured. HSW no longer guarantees to run at the base frequency with AVX code. The guaranteed frequency when running AVX code on all cores is referred to as "AVX base frequency," which can be significantly lower than the nominal frequency [12,14]. Also there is a separation of frequency domains between cores and Uncore. The Uncore clock is now independent and can either be set automatically (when Uncore frequency scaling (UFS) is enabled) or manually via model specific registers (MSRs).

As a "tick," BDW, the most recent Xeon-EP processor, offers minor architectural improvements. Floating-point and gather instruction latencies and throughput have partially improved. The dual-ring design was made symmetric and an additional QPI snoop mode is available.

3.2 Software and Benchmarks

The benchmarks LINPACK, HPCG, and Graph500 were chosen because they are de facto industry standards and are particularly suited to evaluate a chip's peak Flop/s, memory bandwidth, and latency properties. High-level language benchmarks (Graph500, HPCG) were compiled using Intel ICC 16.0.3. For Graph500 we used the reference implementation in version 2.1.4, and for LINPACK we ran the Intel-provided binary contained in MKL 2017.1.013, the most recent version available at the time of writing.

The LIKWID[2] tool suite in its current stable version 4.1.2 was employed in many of our experiments. All low-level benchmarks consisted of hand-written assembly. When available (e.g., for streaming kernels such as STREAM triad and others) we used the assembly implementations in the `likwid-bench` microbenchmarking tool. Latency measurements in the memory hierarchy were done with all prefetchers turned off (via `likwid-features`) and a pointer chasing code that ensures consecutive cache line accesses. Energy consumption measurements were taken with the `likwid-perfctr` tool via the RAPL (Running Average Power Limit) interface, and the clock speed of the CPUs was controlled with `likwid-setFrequencies`.

---

[2] http://tiny.cc/LIKWID.

4   In-Core Features

4.1   Core Frequency

Starting with HSW, Intel chips have provided different base and turbo frequencies for AVX and SSE or scalar instruction mixes. This is due to the higher power requirement of using all SIMD lanes in case of AVX. To reflect this behavior, Intel introduced a new frequency nomenclature for these chips.

The "base frequency," also known as the "non-AVX base frequency" or "nominal frequency" is the minimum frequency that is guaranteed when running scalar or SSE code on all cores. This is also the frequency the chip is advertised with, e.g., 2.30 GHz for the Xeon E5-2695v3 in Table 1. The maximum frequency that can be achieved when running scalar or SSE code on all cores is called "max all core turbo frequency." The "AVX base frequency" is the minimum frequency that is guaranteed when running AVX code on all cores and is typically significantly lower than the (non-AVX) base frequency. Analogously, the maximum frequency that can be attained when running AVX code on all cores is called "AVX max all core turbo frequency."

On HSW, at least core running AVX code resulted in a chip-wide frequency restriction to the AVX max all core turbo frequency. On BDW, cores running scalar or SSE code are allowed to float between the non-AVX base and max all core turbo frequencies even when other cores are running AVX code.

All relevant values for the HSW and BDW specimen used can be found in Table 1. According to official documentation the actually used frequency depends on the workload; more specifically, it depends on the percentage of AVX instructions in a certain instruction execution window. To get a better idea about what to expect for demanding workloads, LINPACK and FIRESTARTER [3] were selected to determine those frequencies. The maximum frequency difference between both benchmarks was 20 MHz, so Fig. 1 shows only results obtained with LINPACK. Figure 1a shows that HSW drops below the non-AVX base frequency of 2.3 GHz, but stays well above the AVX base frequency of 1.9 GHz

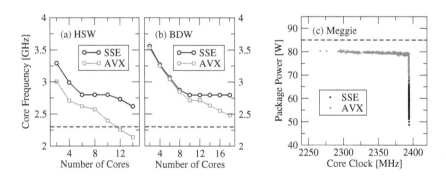

Fig. 1. Attained chip frequency during LINPACK runs on all cores on (a) BDW and (b) HSW. (c) Variation of clock speed and package power among all 1456 Xeon E5-2630v4 CPUs in RRZE's "Meggie" cluster running LINPACK.

while consuming 119.4 W out of a 120 W TDP. BDW, shown in Fig. 1b, can maintain a frequency well above the AVX *and* the non-AVX base frequency for workloads running at its TDP limit of 145 W (measured package power during stress tests was 144.8 W). When running SSE BDW consumes 141.8 W and manages to run at the max all core turbo frequency of 2.8 GHz. On HSW, running LINPACK with SSE instructions still keeps the chip at its TDP limit (119.7 W out of 120 W); the attained frequency of 2.6 GHz is slightly below the max all core turbo frequency of 2.7 GHz.

While it might be tempting to generalize from these results, we must emphasize that statistical variations even between specimen of the same CPU type are very common [21]. When examining all 1456 Xeon E5-2630v4 (10-core, 2.2 GHz base frequency) chips of RRZE's new "Meggie" cluster,[3] we found significant variations across the individual CPUs. The chip has a max all core turbo and AVX max all core turbo frequency of 2.4 GHz [14]. Figure 1c shows each chip's frequency and package power when running LINPACK with SSE or AVX on all cores. With SSE code, each chip manages to attain the max all core turbo frequency of 2.4 GHz. However, a variation in power consumption can be observed. When running AVX code, not all chips reach the defined peak frequency but stay well above the AVX base frequency of 1.8 GHz. Some chips do hit the frequency ceiling; for these, a strong variation can be observed in the power domain.

4.2 Instruction Throughput and Latency

Accurate predictions of instruction execution (i.e., how many clock cycles it takes to execute a loop body assuming a steady state situation with all data coming from the L1 cache) are notoriously difficult in all but the simplest cases, but they are needed as input for analytic models. As a "lowest-order" and most optimistic approximation one can assume full throughput, i.e., all instructions can be executed independently and are dynamically fed to the execution ports (and the pipelines connected to them) by the out-of-order engine. The pipeline that takes the largest number of cycles to execute all its instructions determines the runtime. The worst-case assumption would be an execution fully determined by the critical path through the code, heeding all dependencies. In practice, the actual runtime will be between these limits unless other bottlenecks apply that are not covered by the in-core execution, such as data transfers from beyond the L1 cache, instruction cache misses, etc. Even if a loop body contains strong dependencies the throughput assumption may still hold if there are no loop-carried dependencies.

Calculating the throughput and critical path predictions requires information about the maximum throughput and latency of all relevant instructions as well as general limits such as decoder/retirement throughput, L1I bandwidth, and the number and types of address generation units. The Intel Architecture Code Analyzer (IACA) can help with this, but the software and its models are proprietary with an unclear future development path and they do not always

---

[3] http://www.hpc.rrze.fau.de/systeme/meggie-cluster.shtml.

Table 2. Measured worst-case latency and inverse throughput for floating-point arithmetic instructions. For all of these numbers, lower is better.

μarch	Latency [cy]				Inverse throughput [cy/inst.]			
	BDW	HSW	IVB	SNB	BDW	HSW	IVB	SNB
vdivpd (AVX)	24	35	35	45	16	28	28	44
divpd (SSE)	14	20	20	22	8	14	14	22
divsd (scalar)	14	20	20	22	**4.5**	14	14	22
vdivps (AVX)	17	21	21	29	10	14	14	28
divps (SSE)	11	13	13	14	5	7	7	14
divss (scalar)	11	13	13	14	**2.5**	7	7	14
vsqrtpd (AVX)	35	35	35	44	28	28	28	43
sqrtpd (SSE)	20	20	20	23	14	14	14	22
sqrtsd (scalar)	20	20	20	23	**7**	14	14	22
vsqrtps (AVX)	21	21	21	23	14	14	14	22
sqrtps (SSE)	13	13	13	15	7	7	7	14
sqrtss (scalar)	13	13	13	15	**4**	7	7	14
vrcpps (AVX)	7	7	7	7	2	2	2	2
rcpps (SSE, scalar)	5	5	5	5	1	1	1	1
add	3,4[†]	3	3	3	1	1	1	1
mul	3	5	5	5	0.5	0.5	1	1
fma	5,6[‡]	5,6[§]	—	—	0.5	0.5	—	—

[†]SP/DP AVX addition: 3 cycles; SP/DP SSE and scalar addition: 4 cycles
[‡] SP/DP AVX FMA: 5 cycles; SP/DP SSE and scalar FMA: 6 cycles
[§]SP scalar FMA: 6 cycles; all other: 5 cycles

yield accurate predictions. Moreover, it can only analyze object code and does not work on the high-level language constructs. Thus one must often revert to manual analysis to get predictions for the best possible code, even if the compiler cannot produce it. In Table 2 we give worst-case[4] measured latency and inverse throughput numbers for arithmetic instructions in AVX, SSE, and scalar mode. In the following we point out some notable changes over the four processor generations.

The most profound change happened in the performance of the divide units. From SNB to BDW we observe a massive decrease in latency and an almost three-fold increase in throughput for AVX and SSE instructions, in single and double precision alike. Divides are still slow compared to multiply and add instructions, of course. The fact that the divide throughput *per operation* is the same for AVX and SSE is well known, but with BDW we see a significant rise in scalar

---

[4] The latencies of some instructions (e.g., FP division) depend on their operands. When working with "trivial" denominators, such as whole numbers, latency can be significantly lower than when operating on non-trivial floating-point numbers.

divide throughput, even beyond the documented limit of one instruction every five cycles. The scalar square root instruction shows a similar improvement, but is in line with the documentation.

The standard multiply, add, and fused multiply-add instructions have not changed dramatically over four generations, with two exceptions: Together with the introduction of FMA instructions with HSW, it became possible to execute two plain multiply (but not add) instructions per cycle. The latency of the add instruction in scalar and SSE mode on BDW has increased from three to four cycles; this result is not documented by Intel for BDW but announced for AVX code in the upcoming Skylake architecture. The fma instruction shows the same characteristic (latency increase from 5 to 6 cycles when using SSE or scalar mode).

One architectural feature that is not directly evident from single-instruction measurements is the number of address generation units (AGUs). Up to IVB there are two such units, each paired with a LOAD unit with which it shares a port. As a consequence, only two addresses per cycle can be generated. HSW introduced a third AGU on the new port 7, but it can only handle simple addresses for STORE instructions, which may lead to some restrictions. See Sect. 4.3 for details.

4.3   L1 Cache/AGU

The cores of all four microarchitectures feature two load units and one store unit. The data paths between each unit and the L1 cache are 16 B on SNB and IVB, and 32 B on HSW and BDW. The theoretical bandwidth is thus 48 B/cy on SNB and IVB and 96 B/cy on HSW and BDW; however, several restrictions apply.

An AVX vectorized STREAM triad benchmark uses two AVX loads, one AVX FMA, and one AVX store instruction to update four DP elements. On HSW and BDW, only two address generation units (AGUs) are capable of performing the necessary address computations, i.e., (base + scaled index + offset), typically used in streaming memory accesses; HSW's newly introduced third store AGU can only perform offset computations. This means that only two addresses per cycle can be calculated, limiting the L1 bandwidth to 64 B/cy. STREAM triad performance using only two AGUs is shown in Fig. 2a. One can make use of the new AGU by using one of the "fast LEA" units (which can perform only indexed and no offset addressing) to pre-compute an intermediate address, which is then used by the simple AGU to complete the address calculation. This way both AVX load units and the AVX store unit can be used simultaneously. When the store is paired with address generation on the new store AGU, both micro-ops are fused into a single micro-op. This means that the four micro-op per cycle front end retirement constraint should not be a problem: in each cycle two AVX load instructions, the micro-op fused AVX store instruction, and one AVX FMA instruction is retired. With sufficient unrolling, loop instruction overhead becomes negligible and the bandwidth should approach 96 B/cy. Figure 2 shows, however, that micro-op throughput still seems to be the bottleneck because bandwidth can be further increased by removing the FMA instructions from the loop body.

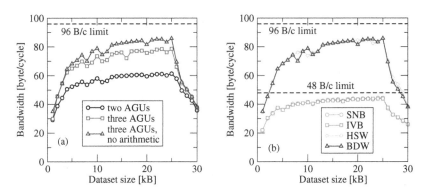

Fig. 2. (a) L1 bandwidth achieved with STREAM triad and various optimizations on BDW. (b) Comparison of achieved L1 bandwidths using STREAM triad on all microarchitectures.

Figure 2b compares the bandwidths achievable by different microarchitectures (using no arithmetic instructions on HSW and BDW for the reasons described above). On SNB and IVB a regular STREAM triad code can almost reach maximum theoretical L1 performance because it only requires half the number of address calculations per cycle, i.e., two AGUs are sufficient to generate three addresses every two cycles.

4.4 Gather

Vector gather is a microcode solution for loading noncontinuous data into vector registers. The instruction was first implemented in Intel multicore CPUs with AVX2 on HSW. The first implementation offered a poor latency (i.e., the time until all data was placed in the vector register) and using hand-written assembly to manually load distributed data into vector registers proved to be faster than using the gather instruction in some cases [10].

Table 3 shows the gather instruction latency for both HSW and BDW. The latency depends on where the data is coming from and, in case data is not in L1, over how many CLs it is distributed. We find that the instruction is 40% faster on BDW in L1. When data is coming from L2 on HSW and distributed

Table 3. Time in cycles per gather instruction on HSW and BDW depending on data distribution across CLs.

Microarchitecture	Haswell-EP				Broadwell-EP			
Location of data	L1	L2	L3	Mem	L1	L2	L3	Mem
Distributed across 1 CLs	12.3	12.3	12.4	15.5	7.3	7.3	7.7	13.3
Distributed across 2 CLs	12.5	12.5	13.2	23.0	7.5	7.6	11.0	24.5
Distributed across 4 CLs	12.5	12.7	20.6	42.7	7.5	9.9	20.0	47.5
Distributed across 8 CLs	12.3	18.4	38.5	89.3	7.3	18.1	38.2	94.4

across eight CLs, the latency is dominated by time required to transfer eight CLs from L2 to L1 cache. On BDW, this effect is already visible when data is coming from the L2 cache and distributed across four CLs. BDW's improvement of the instruction offers no returns when the latency is dominated by CL transfers, which is the case when loading more than four CLs from L2, two from L3, or one from memory.

5   L2 Cache

According to official documentation, the L2 cache bandwidth on HSW was increased from $32\,B/cy$ to $64\,B/cy$ compared to IVB. To validate this expectation, knowledge about overlapping transfers in the cache hierarchy is required. The ECM model for x86 assumes that no CLs are transferred between L2 and L1 in any cycle in which a LOAD instruction retires. Hence, the maximum of $64\,B/cy$ can never be attained by design but an improvement may still be expected. To derive the time spent transferring data, cycles in which load instructions are retired are subtracted from the overall runtime with an in-L2 working set. The resulting bandwidth should be compared with the documented theoretical maximum.

Table 4. Measured L1-L2 bandwidth on different microarchitectures for dot product and STREAM triad access patterns.

Pattern	Code	SNB	IVB	HSW	BDW
Dot product	dot+=A[i]+B[i]	28	27	43	43
STREAM triad	A[i]=B[i]+s*C[i]	29	29	32	32

Table 4 shows the measured bandwidths for a dot product (a load-only benchmark) and the STREAM triad. Both SNB and IVB operate near the specified bandwidth of $32\,B/cy$ for both access patterns. Although HSW and BDW offer bandwidth improvements, especially in case of the dot product, measured bandwidths are significantly below the advertised $64\,B/cy$.

The question arises of how this result may be incorporated into the ECM model. Preliminary experiments indicate that the ECM predictions for in-L3 data are quite accurate when assuming theoretical L2 throughput. We could thus interpret the low L2 performance as a consequence of a latency penalty, which can be overlapped when the data is further out in the hierarchy. Further experiments are needed to substantiate this conjecture.

6   Uncore

6.1   L3 Cache

Cluster-on-Die. Together with the dual-ring interconnect, HSW introduced the CoD mode, in which a single chip can be partitioned into two equally-sized

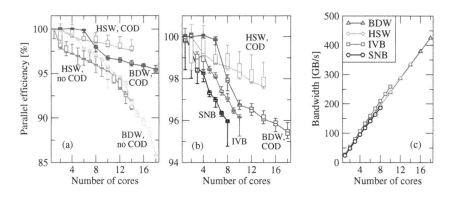

Fig. 3. (a) L3 scalability on HSW and BDW depending on whether CoD is used. (b) Comparison of microarchitectures regarding L3 scalability. (c) Absolute L3 bandwidth for STREAM triad as function of cores on different microarchitectures.

NUMA clusters. HSW features a so-called "eight plus x" design, in which the first physical ring features eight cores and the second ring contains the remaining cores (six for our HSW chip). This asymmetry leads to a scenario in which the seven cores in the first cluster domain are physically located on the first ring; the second cluster domain contains the remaining core from the first and six cores from the second physical ring. The asymmetry was removed on BDW: here both physical rings are of equal size so both cluster domains contain cores from dedicated rings. CoD is intended for NUMA-optimized code and impacts L3 scalability and latency and, implicitly, main memory bandwidth because it uses a dedicated snoop mode that makes use of a directory to avoid unnecessary snoop requests (see Sect. 6.2 for more details).

Figure 3a shows the influence of CoD on L3 bandwidth (using STREAM triad) for HSW and BDW. When data is distributed across both rings on HSW, the parallel efficiency of the L3 cache is 92%; it can be raised to 98% by using CoD. The higher core count of BDW results in a more pronounced effect; here, parallel efficiency is only 86% in non-CoD mode. Using CoD the efficiency goes above 95%. Figure 3b shows that HSW and BDW with CoD offer similar L3 scalability as SNB and IVB.

Given an n-core chip, the topological diameter (and with it the average distance from a core to data in an L3 segment) is smaller inside each of the $n/2$-core cluster domains in comparison to the non-CoD domain, consisting of n cores. Shorter ways between cores and data result in lower latencies when using CoD mode. On BDW, the L3 latency is 41 cycles when with CoD and 47 cycles without (see Table 5).

6.2   Memory

Snoop Modes. Starting with HSW, the QPI snoop mode can be selected at boot time. HSW supports three snoop modes: early snoop (ES), home snoop (HS), and directory (DIR) (often only indirectly selectable by enabling CoD in the BIOS) [11,15,16]. BDW introduced a fourth snoop mode called HS+opportunistic snoop broadcast (OSB) [16]. The remainder of this section discusses the differences among the modes and the immediate impact on memory latency and bandwidth.

On an L3 miss inside a NUMA domain, in addition to fetching the CL containing the requested data from main memory, cache coherency mandates other NUMA domains be checked for modified copies of the CL. Attached to each L3 segment is a cache agent (CA) responsible for sending and receiving snoop information. In addition to multiple CAs, each NUMA domain features a home agent (HA), which plays a major role in snooping.

In ES, snoop requests are sent directly from the CA of the L3 segment in which the L3 miss occurred to the respective[5] CAs in other NUMA domains. Queried remote CAs directly respond back to the requesting CA; in addition, they report to the HA in the requesting CA's domain, so it can resolve potential conflicts. ES involves a lot of requests and replies, but offers low latencies.

In HS, CAs forward snoop requests to their NUMA domain's HA. The HA proceeds to fetch the requested CL from memory but stalls snoop requests to remote NUMA domains until the CL is available. For each CL, so-called directory information is stored in its memory ECC bits. The bits indicate whether a copy of the CL exists in other NUMA domains. The directory bits only tell whether a CL is present or not in other NUMA domains; they do not tell which NUMA domain to query, so snoops have to broadcast to all NUMA domains. By waiting for directory data, unnecessary snoop requests are avoided at the cost of higher latency due to delayed snoops. By reducing snoop requests, overall bandwidth can be increased. As in ES, potentially queried remote CAs respond to the initiating CA and HA, which resolves potential conflicts.

In DIR, a two-step approach is used. Starting with HSW, each HA features a 14 kB directory cache (also called "HitMe" cache) holding additional directory information for CLs present in remote NUMA domains.[6] In addition to the directory information recorded in the ECC bits, the directory cache stores the particular NUMA domain in which the copy of a CL resides; this means that on a hit in the directory cache only a single snoop request has to be sent. This mechanism further reduces snoop traffic, potentially increasing bandwidth. When the directory cache is hit, latency is also improved in DIR compared to HS, because snoops are not delayed until directory information stored in ECC bits from main memory becomes available. In case of a directory cache miss, DIR mode proceeds similarly to HS. Note, however, that DIR mode is recommended only for NUMA-aware workloads. The directory cache can only hold data for a small number of

---

[5] CLs are mapped to L3 segments based on their addresses according to a hashing function. Thus, each CA knows which CA in other NUMA domains is responsible for a certain CL.

[6] Investigations using the HITME_* performance counter events indicate this cache is exclusively used in DIR mode.

Table 5. Measured access latencies of all memory hierarchy levels in base frequency core cycles

μarch	L1	L2	L3	MEM
SNB	4	12	40	230
IVB	4	12	40	208
HSW	4	12	37^b	168^f
BDW	4	12	47^a, 41^b	248^c, 280^d, 190^e, 178^f

^{a}COD disabled, ^{b}COD enabled, ^{c}ES
^{d}HS, ^{e}HS+OSB, ^{f}DIR

CLs. If the number of CLs shared between both cluster domains exceeds the directory cache capacity, DIR mode degrades to HS mode, resulting in high latencies.

BDW's new HS+OSB mode works similarly to HS. However, HAs will send opportunistic snoop requests while waiting for directory information stored in the ECC bits under "light" traffic conditions. Latency is reduced in case the directory information indicates snoop requests have to be sent, because they were already sent opportunistically. Redundant snoop requests are not supposed to impact performance under "light" traffic conditions.

The impact of snoop modes is largest on main memory latency. As expected, DIR produces the best results with 178 cy (see Table 5). Pointer chasing in main memory does not generate a lot of traffic on the ring interconnect, which is why HS+OSB will generate opportunistic snoops, achieving a latency of 190 cy. The difference in latency of 12 cy compared to DIR can be explained through shorter paths inside a single cluster domain in CoD mode. We measured an L3 latency of 41 cy for CoD and 47 cy for non-CoD mode. Since memory accesses pass through the interconnect twice (one to request the CL, once to deliver it) the memory latency of non-CoD mode is expected to be twice the L3 latency penalty of six cycles. In ES, the requesting CA has to wait for its HA to acknowledge that it received all snoop replies from the remote CAs, which causes a latency penalty. On BDW, the measured memory latency is 248 cy. As expected, HS offers the worst latency at 280 cy, because necessary snoop broadcasts are delayed until directory information becomes available from main memory.

Graph500 was chosen to evaluate the influence of snoop modes on the performance of latency-sensitive workloads. Figure 4a shows Graph500 performance for a single BDW chip. A direct correlation between latency and performance can be observed for HS, ES, and HS+OSB. DIR mode performs worst despite offering the best memory latency. This can be explained by the non-NUMA-awareness of the Graph500 benchmarks. Too much data is shared between both cluster domains; this means the directory cache can not hold information on all shared CLs. As a result, snoops are delayed until directory information from main memory becomes available. Figure 4b shows an overview of Graph500 performance

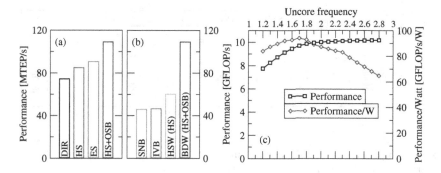

Fig. 4. (a) Graph500 performance in millions of traversed edges per second (MTEP/s) as function of snoop mode on BDW. (b) Graph500 performance of all chips. (c) HPCG performance and performance per Watt as function of Uncore frequency.

on all chips and the qualitative improvement offered by the new HS+OSB snoop mode introduced with BDW.

The effect of snoop mode on memory bandwidth for BDW is shown in Fig. 5. The data is roughly in line with the reasoning above. For NUMA-aware workloads, DIR should produce the least snoop traffic due to snoop information stored in the directory cache. This is reflected in a slightly better bandwidth compared to other snoop modes (with the exception of the non-temporal (NT) store access pattern, which seems to be a toxic case for DIR mode). DIR offers up to 10 GB/s more for load-only access patterns when compared to ES, which produces the most amount of snoop traffic. The effect is less pronounced but still observable when comparing DIR to HS and HS+OSB. Figure 6 shows the evolution of sustained memory bandwidth for all examined microarchitectures, using the best snoop mode on HSW and BDW. Increases in bandwidths over the generations is explained by new DDR standards as well as increased memory clock speeds (see Table 1).

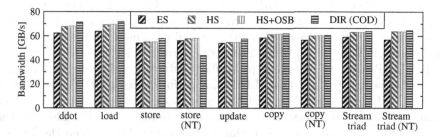

Fig. 5. Sustained main memory bandwidth on BDW for various access patterns. NT = nontemporal stores.

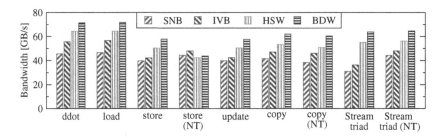

Fig. 6. Comparison of sustained main memory bandwidth across microarchitectures for various access patterns.

6.3   Uncore Clock, Bandwidth, and Energy Efficiency

Before HSW, the Uncore was clocked at the same frequency as the cores. Starting with HSW, the Uncore has its own clock frequency. The motivation for this lies in potential energy savings: When cores do not require much data via the Uncore (i.e., from/to L3 cache and main memory) the Uncore can be slowed down to save power. This mode of operation is called UFS. For our BDW chip, the Uncore frequency can vary automatically between 1.2–2.8 GHz, but one can also define custom minimum and maximum settings within this range via MSRs.

We examine the default UFS behavior for both extremes of the Roofline spectrum and use HPCG as a bandwidth-bound and LINPACK as a compute-bound benchmark. Our findings indicate that at both ends of the spectrum, UFS tends to select higher than necessary frequencies, pointlessly boosting power and in the case of LINPACK even hurting performance.

Figure 4c shows HPCG performance and energy efficiency versus Uncore frequency for a fixed core clock of 2.3 GHz on HSW. We find that the Uncore is the performance bottleneck only for Uncore frequencies below 2.0 GHz. Increasing it beyond this point does not improve performance, because main memory is now the bottleneck. Using performance counters the Uncore frequency was determined to be the maximum of 2.8 GHz when running HPCG in UFS mode. The energy efficiency of 64.7 GFLOP/s/W at 2.8 GHz is 26% lower than the 87.2 GFLOP/s/W observed at 2.0 GHz Uncore frequency, at almost the same performance. Energy efficiency can be increased even more by further lowering the Uncore clock; however, below 2.0 GHz performance is degraded.

For LINPACK, we observe a particularly interesting side effect of varying Uncore frequency. Figure 7 shows LINPACK performance on BDW as a function of core and Uncore clock. Note that in Turbo mode, the performance increases when going from the highest Uncore frequencies towards 1.8 GHz. This effect is caused by Uncore and cores competing for the chip's TDP. When the Uncore clock speed is reduced, a larger part of the chip's power budget can be consumed by the cores, which in turn boost their frequency. The core frequency in Turbo mode is 2479 MHz when the Uncore clock is set to 2.8 GHz (the Uncore actually only achieves a clock rate of 2475 MHz) vs 2595 MHz when the Uncore clock is set to 1.8 GHz. Below 1.8 GHz the CPU frequency increases further, e.g.,

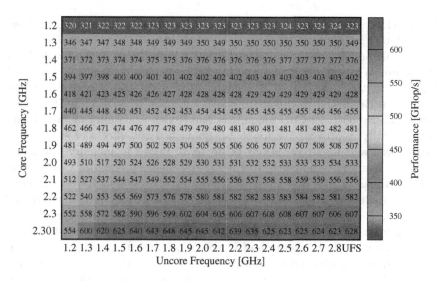

Fig. 7. LINPACK performance on BDW as a function of core and uncore frequency.

to 2617 MHz at an Uncore clock of 1.7 GHz and up to 2720 MHz at an Uncore clock of 1.2 GHz. LINPACK performance starts to degrade at this point despite an increasing core frequency due to the Uncore becoming a data bottleneck. In UFS mode, the Uncore is clocked at 2489 MHz and the cores run at 2491 MHz. Compared to the optimum, UFS degrades performance by 3%. Energy efficiency is reduced by 6% from 4.94 GFLOP/s/W at an Uncore clock of 1.8 GHz to 4.65 GFLOP/s/W in UFS. The most energy-efficient operating point for LIN-PACK is 5.74 GFLOP/s/W at a core clock of 1.6 GHz and an Uncore clock of 1.2 GHz.

7   Summary and Outlook

We have conducted an analysis of core- and chip-level performance features of four recent Intel server CPU architectures. On Broadwell the variability among chips of the same model in achieved AVX turbo frequencies and package power consumption that could already be observed on Haswell persists. Overall the documented instruction latency and throughput numbers fit our measurements, with slight deviations in scalar DP divide throughput; also, in contrast to documentation, scalar/SSE and AVX floating-point addition and multiply-add have different latencies on Broadwell. We could also demonstrate the consequences of limited instruction throughput and the special properties of Haswell's and Broadwell's address generation units for L1 cache bandwidth. The gather instruction, which was newly introduced with the AVX2 instruction set, is now faster than hand-crafted assembly on Broadwell. The L2 cache on Haswell and Broadwell does not keep its promise of doubled bandwidth to L1 but only delivers between

32 and 43 B/cy, as opposed to Sandy Bridge and Ivy Bridge, which get close to their architectural limit of 32 B/cy.

The scalable L3 cache was one of the major innovations in the Sandy Bridge architecture. While Sandy Bridge and Ivy Bridge achieved parallel L3 bandwidth efficiencies in the range of 96%, without Cluster on Die (CoD) the full-chip efficiency on Broadwell (at up to 18 cores) can drop to 85% while Haswell can maintain above 95%. In CoD mode, the bandwidth scalability of the L3 cache is substantially improved. We have also quantified the effects of snoop modes on Broadwell and found variations of up to 70 cycles in memory latency and 10 GB/s in memory bandwidth. In the L3 and memory domains CoD provides the highest bandwidth (except with streaming stores) and lowest latency as long as no cache line migration between the clusters is required. The Graph500 benchmark, where data migration occurs frequently, shows a 50% speedup when switching from non-CoD to Home Snoop with Opportunistic Snoop Broadcast.

Finally, our analysis of core and Uncore clock speed domains revealed that Uncore frequency scaling and manually set high Uncore frequencies can be detrimental to the performance of compute-intensive codes. For memory-bound codes analysis exhibited significant potential for saving energy in via a sensible setting of the Uncore frequency, without compromising time to solution.

Future work will include a thorough evaluation of the ECM performance model on all recent Intel architectures, putting to use the insights generated in this study. Additionally, existing analytic power and energy consumption models will be extended to account for the Uncore power more accurately. Significant changes in performance- and power-relevant features are expected for the upcoming Skylake architecture, such as (among others) an L3 victim cache and AVX-512 on selected models, and will pose challenges of their own.

References

1. Barker, K., Davis, K., Hoisie, A., Kerbyson, D.J., Lang, M., Pakin, S., Sancho, J.C.: A performance evaluation of the Nehalem quad-core processor for scientific computing. Parallel Proces. Lett. **18**(4), 453–469 (2008). http://dx.doi.org/10.1142/S012962640800351X
2. Gasc, T., Vuyst, F.D., Peybernes, M., Poncet, R., Motte, R.: Building a more efficient Lagrange-remap scheme thanks to performance modeling. In: Papadrakakis, M., et al. (ed.) Proceedings of the ECCOMAS Congress 2016, the VII European Congress on Computational Methods in Applied Sciences and Engineering, Crete Island, Greece, 5–10 June 2016. https://www.eccomas2016.org/proceedings/pdf/12210.pdf
3. Hackenberg, D., Oldenburg, R., Molka, D., Schöne, R.: Introducing FIRESTARTER: a processor stress test utility. In: 2013 International Green Computing Conference Proceedings. pp. 1–9, June 2013
4. Hackenberg, D., Schöne, R., Ilsche, T., Molka, D., Schuchart, J., Geyer, R.: An energy efficiency feature survey of the Intel Haswell processor. In: 2015 IEEE International Parallel and Distributed Processing Symposium Workshop, pp. 896–904, May 2015

5. Hager, G., Treibig, J., Habich, J., Wellein, G.: Exploring performance and power properties of modern multicore chips via simple machine models. Concurr. Computat.: Pract. Exper. (2013). doi:10.1002/cpe.3180

6. Hockney, R.W., Curington, I.J.: $f_{1/2}$: a parameter to characterize memory and communication bottlenecks. Parallel Comput. **10**(3), 277–286 (1989)

7. Hofmann, J., Fey, D.: An ECM-based energy-efficiency optimization approach for bandwidth-limited streaming kernels on recent Intel Xeon processors. In: Proceedings of the 4th International Workshop on Energy Efficient Supercomputing, E2SC 2016, pp. 31–38. IEEE Press, Piscataway (2016). https://doi.org/10.1109/E2SC. 2016.16

8. Hofmann, J., Fey, D., Eitzinger, J., Hager, G., Wellein, G.: Analysis of Intel's Haswell microarchitecture using the ECM model and microbenchmarks. In: Hannig, F., Cardoso, J.M.P., Pionteck, T., Fey, D., Schröder-Preikschat, W., Teich, J. (eds.) ARCS 2016. LNCS, vol. 9637, pp. 210–222. Springer, Cham (2016). doi:10. 1007/978-3-319-30695-7_16

9. Hofmann, J., Fey, D., Riedmann, M., Eitzinger, J., Hager, G., Wellein, G.: Performance analysis of the Kahan-enhanced scalar product on current multi-core and many-core processors. Concurr. Comput.: Pract. Exp. (2016). http://dx.doi.org/10.1002/cpe.3921

10. Hofmann, J., Treibig, J., Hager, G., Wellein, G.: Comparing the performance of different x86 SIMD instruction sets for a medical imaging application on modern multi- and manycore chips. In: Proceedings of the 2014 Workshop on Programming Models for SIMD/Vector Processing, WPMVP 2014, pp. 57–64. ACM, New York (2014). http://doi.acm.org/10.1145/2568058.2568068

11. Intel Corporation: Intel Xeon Processor E5-1600, E5-2400, and E5-2600 v3 Product Families - volume 2 of 2, Registers. http://www.intel.com/content/dam/www/public/us/en/documents/datasheets/xeon-e5-v3-datasheet-vol-2.pdf

12. Intel Corporation: Intel Xeon Processor E5 v3 Product Family. http://www.intel.com/content/dam/www/public/us/en/documents/specification-updates/xeon-e5-v3-spec-update.pdf

13. McCalpin, J.D.: Memory bandwidth and machine balance in current high performance computers. IEEE Comput. Soc. Tech. Comm. Comput. Archit. (TCCA) Newsl. **19**, 19–25 (1995)

14. Microway Inc.: Detailed specifications of the Intel Xeon E5-2600 v4 Broadwell-EP processors

15. Molka, D., Hackenberg, D., Schöne, R., Nagel, W.E.: Cache coherence protocol and memory performance of the Intel Haswell-EP architecture. In: Proceedings of the 44th International Conference on Parallel Processing (ICPP 2015). IEEE (2015)

16. Kottapalli, S., Geetha, V., Neefs, H.G., Choi, Y.: Patent US20130007376 A1: Opportunistic Snoop Broadcast (OSB) in directory enabled home snoopy systems. http://www.google.com/patents/US20130007376

17. Schöne, R., Treibig, J., Dolz, M.F., Guillen, C., Navarrete, C., Knobloch, M., Rountree, B.: Tools and methods for measuring and tuning the energy efficiency of HPC systems. Sci. Program. **22**(4), 273–283 (2014). http://dx.doi.org/10.3233/SPR-140393

18. Stengel, H., Treibig, J., Hager, G., Wellein, G.: Quantifying performance bottlenecks of stencil computations using the Execution-Cache-Memory model. In: Proceedings of the 29th ACM International Conference on Supercomputing, ICS 2015. ACM, New York (2015). http://doi.acm.org/10.1145/2751205.2751240

19. Treibig, J., Hager, G., Hofmann, H.G., Hornegger, J., Wellein, G.: Pushing the limits for medical image reconstruction on recent standard multicore processors. Int. J. High Perform. Comput. Appl. **27**(2), 162–177 (2013). http://dx.doi.org/10.1177/1094342012442424

20. Treibig, J., Hager, G., Wellein, G.: likwid-bench: an extensible microbenchmarking platform for x86 multicore compute nodes. In: Brunst, H., Müller, M., Nagel, W., Resch, M. (eds.) Tools for High Performance Computing, pp. 27–36. Springer, Heidelberg (2011)

21. Wilde, T., Auweter, A., Shoukourian, H., Bode, A.: Taking advantage of node power variation in homogenous HPC systems to save energy. In: Kunkel, J.M., Ludwig, T. (eds.) ISC High Performance 2015. LNCS, vol. 9137, pp. 376–393. Springer, Cham (2015). doi:10.1007/978-3-319-20119-1_27

22. Williams, S., Waterman, A., Patterson, D.: Roofline: an insightful visual performance model for multicore architectures. Commun. ACM **52**(4), 65–76 (2009). http://doi.acm.org/10.1145/1498765.1498785

23. Wittmann, M., Hager, G., Zeiser, T., Treibig, J., Wellein, G.: Chip-level and multi-node analysis of energy-optimized lattice Boltzmann CFD simulations. Concurr. Comput.: Pract. Exp. **28**(7), 2295–2315 (2016). http://dx.doi.org/10.1002/cpe.3489

Alleviating I/O Interference Through Workload-Aware Striping and Load-Balancing on Parallel File Systems

Yuichi Tsujita[1]([✉]), Tatsuhiko Yoshizaki[2], Keiji Yamamoto[1],
Fumichika Sueyasu[3], Ryoji Miyazaki[3], and Atsuya Uno[1]

[1] RIKEN AICS, Kobe, Hyogo, Japan
yuichi.tsujita@riken.jp
[2] Naniwa Calculate Center Co. Ltd., Osaka, Osaka, Japan
[3] FUJITSU Limited, Kawasaki, Kanagawa, Japan

Abstract. Nowadays parallel file systems have been widely used in many supercomputers. Lustre is one of the most used parallel file systems, and its enhanced file system named FEFS (Fujitsu Exabyte File System) has been used at K computer. The K computer has adopted two-layered file system consisting of a local file system and a shared global file system with data staging scheme in order to guarantee sufficient I/O throughput on the local file system during computation. However, huge data staging on the shared file system sometimes has led to big I/O interference in light-weight file accesses which have taken place at the same time. Alleviation of such I/O interference on shared file systems is an important issue in managing a big scale of parallel file systems in shared use. In this paper, we focus on I/O interference alleviation by using workload-aware striping and load-balancing. Appropriate striping configuration with effective load-balancing in service thread allocation for incoming I/O requests has improved performance of light-weight file accesses against huge data accesses without excessive sacrifice to data staging performance at the K computer. It is expected that the proposed optimization can be used as a system-wide I/O interference mitigation approach.

Keywords: Workload-awareness · Striping · Lustre · FEFS · Data staging · K computer

1   Introduction

High I/O throughput is the most important feature for parallel file systems. However, concurrent I/O accesses on the same file system sometimes cause I/O interference among I/O tasks [19]. Especially relatively light-weigh I/O tasks can be affected by heavy I/O tasks because such heavy tasks utilize almost all of I/O bandwidth [4]. Therefore, effective fair-share I/O load-balancing is one of the important issues.

© Springer International Publishing AG 2017
J.M. Kunkel et al. (Eds.): ISC High Performance 2017, LNCS 10266, pp. 315–333, 2017.
DOI: 10.1007/978-3-319-58667-0_17

Regarding parallel file systems, Lustre [8] has been widely used in many kinds of supercomputers. In using a huge scale of Lustre file system, striping configuration plays a big role to gain high I/O throughput. There have been many works focused on striping configuration optimization based on their experience or empirical performance studies [2,5,10,14,15]. Load-balancing among Object Storage Servers (OSSs) or Object Storage Targets (OSTs) is another optimization approach. Optimization for RPC request generations and I/O congestion elimination in network request scheduler (NRS) is addressing to have fair-share utilization in I/O bandwidth among multiple I/O tasks [7,11,12]. Topology-awareness and balanced data placement have solved I/O load imbalance and contention in accessing a Lustre file system [18]. Their work has focused on load-balancing by having cost model taking resource utilization frequency into account by using previous I/O requests generated from the same application in order to obtain balanced I/O workload. Congestion in scalable network system in a parallel file system is an another issue to be optimized. A research work in [3] has avoided such congestion by optimized I/O task placement with network topology-awareness. However, enough discussions have not been done about the way to reduce I/O interference caused by huge data accesses using workload-aware striping and load-balancing configuration without undue sacrifice to I/O performance.

The K computer [9] has been utilizing asynchronous data staging scheme [6] on two-layered parallel file system consisting of a local file system (LFS) and a global file system (GFS) using FEFS in order to guarantee enough I/O performance for programs running on compute nodes and effective job scheduling. Although the asynchronous data staging scheme has improved job scheduling efficiency and sufficient I/O performance on an LFS has been achieved during computation, I/O performance on a GFS in accesses from frontend servers was degraded by I/O interference caused by huge data accesses in data staging operations. We propose workload-aware striping configuration and load-balancing for data staging operation in order to mitigate I/O interference by huge data staging without reducing data staging performance. The optimization has two primary contributions; (1) stripe count configuration for balanced amount of I/O workload among OSTs and (2) available I/O resource management by limiting the number of service threads on FEFS [16,17] for effective load-balancing among multiple I/O tasks. Through our performance evaluation on the K computer, we have found that workload-aware striping configuration and load-balancing of FEFS have achieved balanced distribution of data among OSTs in data staging and effective load-balancing in service thread allocation for each I/O task. Consequently I/O interference by huge data staging has been mitigated without degrading data staging performance.

It should be remarked that our proposed scheme can also be implemented as system-wide I/O interference mitigation approach. However, for simplicity in demonstration on available huge system, we decide to start the proposed scheme at the K computer because it has a large scale of parallel file systems. Although the implementation and experimental context of our work are focused on the

K computer, the I/O workload-aware striping configuration and I/O load-balancing are not uncommon at other large scale supercomputers. Given the popularity of the Lustre file system, we think that our proposed scheme can find wider applicability in supercomputing community at large.

The rest of this paper is organized as follows. In Sect. 2, we give a detailed description of the K computer and discussions about related research works concerning our optimization proposal. Asynchronous data staging scheme using two-staged parallel file systems and observed I/O interference issues at the K computer motivate the design of the I/O workload-aware striping and load balancing scheme, which is elaborated in Sect. 3. Section 4 discusses our experimental strategy and evaluation results, followed by conclusion and future work in Sect. 5.

2   Background and Related Work

This section describes research background and related work. Since we evaluate our proposed scheme on the K computer, we describe a file system of the K computer briefly and the access response time degradation issue regarding huge data staging. Since the past and current research efforts on optimizations for Lustre motivate our proposed scheme, we review those works by comparing with our approach in the latter part of this section.

The K computer consists of 82,944 compute nodes, where each system rack consists of 96 compute nodes. Figure 1(a) depicts overview of the K computer system including its two-staged parallel file system using FEFS. Currently FEFS file systems at the K computer are based on Lustre version 1.8 technology. I/O nodes play a big role in accessing a GFS and an LFS.

Detailed configuration of I/O nodes associated with a GFS and an LFS is illustrated in Fig. 1(b). The K computer has 432 cabinets holding 192 compute nodes each, where one cabinet consists of two system racks. Every system rack is also equipped with I/O nodes, which are connected through Tofu interconnects [1]. Boot-I/O nodes (BIOs) are responsible for system software start-up. The LFS is accessible from compute nodes through local-I/O nodes (LIOs), and it is used for high performance file I/O during computation. Every system rack consists of three LIOs, and thus 6 LIOs per cabinet. The LFS has 2,592 OSSs and 5,184 OSTs, where each OSS running on LIO manages 2 OSTs. Network connections between OSSs and OSTs are established by FibreChannel. While a GFS is used to keep user's programs or data files, where a huge storage space is provided. More than 30 PB of the GFS is divided into multiple volumes, where each volume consists of 12 OSSs and 384 OSTs, except several volumes.

Every global-I/O node (GIO) in a system rack can access OSSs of each GFS volume via 4×QDR InfiniBand interconnects. Every OST is accessible by OSSs using FibreChannel. GIOs are responsible for asynchronous data staging, which is dedicated for efficient job scheduling at the K computer. Since every GIO is responsible for accessing up to 12 OSTs of the LFS, each GIO can manage up to 12 files at the same time in asynchronous data staging. Every GIO copies target

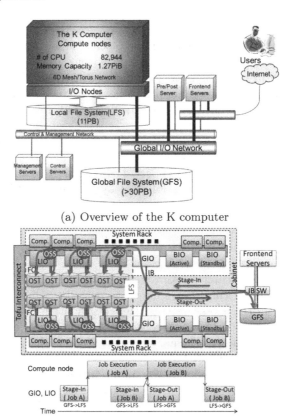

(a) Overview of the K computer

(b) I/O node configuration (upper) and typical asynchronous data staging scheme (lower)

Fig. 1. Overview of the K computer and I/O node configuration in a pair of system racks

files from the GFS through $4 \times$ QDR InfiniBand interconnects and writes them in target OSTs of the LFS in "stage-in" phase prior to computation phase, where "stage-in" phase is initiated in advance to catch up job start-up time with the help of staging and job scheduler systems at the K computer. After computation phase, "stage-out" phase moves specified data files from the LFS to the GFS in an asynchronous way during the next job runs on the used computation nodes. It is remarked that the number of GIOs is dependent on the 3D layout of used compute nodes. If we have A, B, and C in 3D layout for compute nodes in x, y, and z-directions, respectively, the number of available GIOs is $(A/2) \times (B/3) \times 2$ according to the K computer configuration.

Regarding storage spaces, a loop-back file system is employed in the LFS to provide individual local file system per MPI rank named "rank-directory" in addition to shared storage spaces. A single stripe count was configured for a rank-directory because we need to localize I/O accesses inside a rank-directory

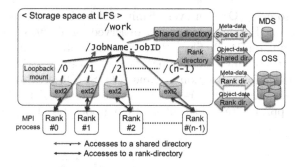

Fig. 2. Shared and rank-directories created on an LFS

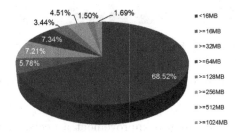

Fig. 3. Averaged file size of each completed job in stage-out phase during six months from October 2015

by creating it on a single OST. A rank-directory addresses to mitigate workload of FEFS's Meta Data Server (MDS) by meta data access distribution. Schematic view of the shared and rank-directories is depicted in Fig. 2. Shared directories are accessible from every MPI ranks, however accesses for many files lead to high MDS workload. While a rank-directory is accessible from only an associated MPI rank, thus leading to mitigation not only in MDS workload but also in I/O interference by other MPI ranks. In this context, rank-directories are recommended for applications generating files independently by each MPI rank.

The GFS is accessed by many I/O tasks not only in data staging but also in file accesses from frontend servers. When a huge scale of data accesses are done in "stage-out" phase, file accesses from frontend servers have been sometimes affected by such huge data staging. Figure 3 shows averaged file size distribution generated in stage-out phase among completed jobs during 6 months from October 2015. As seen in this figure, about 68% of generated files were below 16 MB. Although files more than or equal to 128 MB were about 11% for instance, applications that generated such big files utilized a large number of compute nodes, and took longer time in staging operations because of a large number of files and there sizes. Therefore, performance degradation by such huge data staging should be alleviated in case of accidental coincidence in shared accesses for the GFS.

Figure 4 shows a typical write performance degradation by huge data stage-out operation. Vertical axis represents write times for 1 MB using dd from a frontend server to every OST in every 5 min and horizontal axis denotes time-line in measurement. Big degradation was observed for about 3 h from 15:00 due to huge data staging for 24,000 files, which were amounted for about 58 TB, with a default single stripe count. Staging operation with a single stripe count for such huge data led to high load situation in some of OSSs (Object Storage Servers) or OSTs, and it resulted in a big increase in write time by dd. For suitable situation in file accesses, appropriate treatment in staging operation has been required.

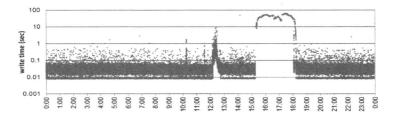

Fig. 4. Write performance degradation due to huge data stage-out operation

In the context of performance improvement aspects, many computer sites using Lustre have been working on tuning parameters including striping charac-teristics [2,5,10,14,15]. Tuning parameters was done based on empirical study or operation profiles in those works. On the other hand, our work has been trying to obtain a model to tune stripe count in order to achieve balanced I/O workloads among OSTs although relying on past operation profiles to some extent.

QoS management including load-balancing has been studied in many research works [7,11–13,18,20]. Qian et al. [11] proposed network request scheduler (NRS) by equipping optimized RPC requests that minimized seek operations and dead-line scheduling. They also proposed I/O congestion minimization using the sim-ilar technique in network congestion control. There have been extensive works about QoS policies concerning the NRS such as token bucket filter [7]. Those QoS implementations schedule RPC requests, while FEFS in our work provides different implementation managing RPC request dispatching to service threads based on source IP addresses of RPC request senders. The work in [13] guaran-teed network bandwidth for MPI communications by QoS of InfiniBand against heavy data staging. Another work in [20] realized QoS based on machine learn-ing to estimate I/O bandwidth for file I/O on PVFS2. Wang et al. [18] proposed balanced data placement among OSTs with topology-awareness for I/O perfor-mance improvements on a Lustre file system. Their approach addressed to have a cost model for I/O client placement regarding to multiple possible paths to reach the same OST via different I/O routers, OSSs, and so forth. The model took weighted average of how frequently different resources have been used by previ-ous I/O requests originating from the same application. However, performance impact of striping configuration has not been examined sufficiently. Congestion avoidance is another important issue to achieve high I/O performance. Since recent huge parallel file systems are built upon scalable interconnection technology, there is a chance to cause network congestion in accessing parallel file systems. Such congestion has been avoided by optimized I/O task placement with network topology-awareness [3].

Through examination of research works above, we have proposed two optimization approaches in our I/O framework. One is striping configuration and another is load-balancing to mitigate I/O interference caused by huge data accesses. Our proposal is different from the above works in terms of implementation approach and target situation. We focus on I/O interference alleviation coming from huge data accesses by a large number of files. Since such huge data accesses happen in a shared parallel file system at large scale of supercomputers, it is worth to study how to mitigate I/O interference in such case. In general, data staging scheme is implemented in an asynchronous way for effective scheduling as we explained in Fig. 1. Therefore preventing small I/O accesses from I/O interference is difficult because we need a kind of interrupt scheme to pose either of huge data accesses or small I/O accesses. Instead, we propose to incorporate I/O workload awareness in our optimization. Optimization in stripe count takes care of balanced I/O workloads among OSTs. Besides, fair-share approach has been adopted in our I/O load-balancing among heavy data accesses and small I/O accesses. Details of our proposal are described in the next section.

3   Alleviation of I/O Interference

In this paper, we focus on alleviation of I/O interference happened on GFS volumes by stage-out operations using rank-directories because rank-directories are utilized to generate files by every rank in huge scale of computation. Unlike shared file accesses among many processes such as collective MPI-IO, a large number of files are transferred between the LFS and the GFS at the same time in the data staging scheme. In order to alleviate degradation described in Sects. 1 and 2, we have adopted workload-aware stripe count configuration in data staging and load balancing service thread allocation between file accesses from frontend servers and data staging. The former one addresses to have same amount of data among OSTs for balanced I/O operations, while the latter one guarantee available service threads on OSSs for data staging and file accesses from frontend servers not to cause I/O interference by huge data accesses.

3.1   Stripe Count Optimization

In this subsection, we examine how to tune the number of stripe count by taking care of amount of data among OSTs. Here we consider data staging for n_{stg} files by N_{IO} client nodes using one volume of the GFS consisting of N_{OSS} OSSs and N_{OST} OSTs. In each OSS, l_{thr} service threads are invoked for incoming RPC requests from clients. When every client node manages up to k_{stg} files, the number of required iterations to complete data staging is calculated as

$$\lceil \frac{n_{stg}}{N_{IO} \cdot k_{stg}} \rceil.$$

Note that

$$k_{stg} = min(\frac{n_{stg}}{N_{IO}}, k_{stg}^{max}),$$ (1)

where k_{stg}^{max} is the maximum number of files that each GIO can manage in asynchronous data staging at the same time. For instance, $k_{stg}^{max} = 12$ at the K computer as we explained in Sect. 2. While RPC requests from $N_{IO} \cdot k_{stg}$ files are managed by $N_{OSS} \cdot l_{thr}$ service threads on OSSs for $\lceil (N_{IO} \cdot k_{stg})/(N_{OSS} \cdot l_{thr}) \rceil$ times if we assume that one RPC request per file is transferred to target service thread. Consequently the number of files that each service thread manages (α) is described as follows:

$$\alpha = \lceil \frac{n_{stg}}{N_{IO} \cdot k_{stg}} \rceil \cdot \lceil \frac{N_{IO} \cdot k_{stg}}{N_{OSS} \cdot l_{thr}} \rceil = \lceil \frac{n_{stg}}{N_{OSS} \cdot l_{thr}} \rceil.$$ (2)

On the other hand, the total number of striped files is $N_{IO} \cdot k_{stg} \cdot C_S$, where C_S is given stripe count, and the cumulative number of used OSTs is described as $\alpha \cdot N_{OST}$. According to the above numbers, the averaged number of striped files that each OST manages is described as

$$\lceil \frac{N_{IO} \cdot k_{stg} \cdot C_S}{\alpha \cdot N_{OST}} \rceil$$

if round-robin deployment of striped files among OSTs is applied. However, the number varies within a range of one striped file in realistic case even if we have balanced data layout among OSTs.

Concerning the amount of data on each OST, we discuss the amount of striped files of each OST. If we adopt the ideal number of files above, averaged size of striped files per OST (F_{OST}) is calculated as follows:

$$F_{OST} = \lceil \frac{N_{IO} \cdot k_{stg} \cdot C_S}{\alpha \cdot N_{OST}} \rceil \times \frac{F_{stg}}{C_S} = \lceil \frac{N_{IO} \cdot k_{stg} \cdot F_{stg}}{\alpha \cdot N_{OST}} \rceil,$$

where F_{stg} is an averaged size of files in data staging. It is noted that cumulative size of striped files per OST for each file is described as F_{stg}/C_S, and this size is a variance in the data size per OST. At least F_{stg}/C_S should be more than or equal to stripe size in our performance model. If we allow the variance in the data size per OST within a ratio of β of F_{OST},

$$\frac{F_{stg}}{C_S} = \beta \times F_{OST} = \lceil \beta \times \frac{N_{IO} \cdot k_{stg} \cdot F_{stg}}{\alpha \cdot N_{OST}} \rceil.$$

Consequently,

$$C_S = \lceil \frac{\alpha}{\beta} \times \frac{N_{OST}}{N_{IO} \cdot k_{stg}} \rceil.$$ (3)

An increase in stripe count leads to an increase in memory cache size on each client because client process prepares memory cache for every OST connections.

Besides, we can proceed a sort of multiple RPC data transfers, amounted by `max_rpcs_in_flight` × `max_pages_per_rpc` × (page size), to each OST in write operations before each OST receives RPC data. While Lustre's read-ahead scheme established for each OST improves read performance, where the maximum size of read-ahead data size is configured by `max_read_ahead_mb`. Therefore, we can expect to have enough memory cache to achieve higher I/O performance with utilizing a large number of OSTs in other words. However, further increase in stripe count leads to an increase not only in memory consumption on each client but also congestion in RPC request transfers between clients and OSSs. Therefore, stripe count should be tuned as small as possible to keep balanced amount of data among OSTs using the above calculation model.

3.2 Load Balancing Among I/O Tasks

As discussed in Sect. 2, shared accesses on a parallel file system without any load balancing awareness are sometimes degraded by I/O interference by a heavy file I/O task. Although there have been many research works about load-balancing in order to have fair-share utilization among a variety of I/O jobs, we propose alternative I/O workload balancing according to RPC request sources to suit for our data staging framework.

FEFS realizes I/O workload balancing function by limiting the number of available service threads for each I/O task [16]. Figure 5 depicts rough sketches of the load balancing by FEFS and our proposal to alleviate I/O interference by huge data staging from GIOs in light-weight accesses from frontend servers. Figure 5(a) shows I/O load-balancing by FEFS for multiple client groups such as clients A, B, C, and so forth. The function manages upper limit of available number of service threads (n_A, n_B, n_C, and so forth relative to the total number of threads denoted as N_{thr}) at server side of FEFS for each client group according to IP addresses of RPC clients. Therefore ratios of available I/O bandwidth relative to total I/O bandwidth for clients A, B, and C are described as $n_A/N_{thr}, n_B/N_{thr}$, and n_C/N_{thr}, respectively in rough estimation.

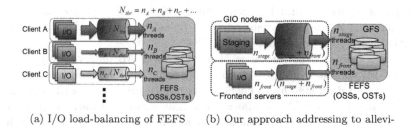

(a) I/O load-balancing of FEFS

(b) Our approach addressing to alleviate I/O interference by huge data staging at the K computer

Fig. 5. I/O load-balancing scheme by FEFS and its adoption in alleviation of I/O interference by huge data staging at the K computer

We have adopted the function to guarantee available I/O resources for data staging and I/O accesses from frontend servers as shown in Fig. 5(b). In case of the K computer, the GFS is accessed not only from GIOs in data staging but also from other nodes such as frontend servers. Therefore, effective I/O load balancing among different kinds of I/O tasks is essential to guarantee enough I/O throughput for each I/O task. Given the upper limit of number of threads for data staging and I/O accesses from frontend servers as n_{stage} and n_{front}, respectively, ratios of upper limit of guaranteed I/O bandwidth relative to total I/O bandwidth for data staging and I/O accesses from frontend servers are estimated as $n_{stage}/(n_{stage} + n_{front})$ and $n_{front}/(n_{stage} + n_{front})$, respectively. By using this function, we have addressed to alleviate interference by huge data staging to give enough I/O resources for file accesses from frontend servers in addition to the stripe count configuration.

4   Performance Evaluation

Performance evaluation has been carried out at the K computer to examine effectiveness of our proposal by using heavy data staging. We have used one volume of the GFS consisting 12 OSSs at the K computer, where each OSS managed 32 OSTs. Therefore one volume consisted of 384 OSTs in total. Each OSS deployed up to 256 service threads for incoming RPC requests. Note that the used GFS volume was isolated from shared use in order to eliminate noises from user applications, while data staging was scheduled by common job scheduler. Therefore start time of data staging was out of our control. In data staging, every GIO copied assigned target files from the GFS to a target rank-directory in stage-in phase, and vice-versa in stage-out phase. Every GIO was able to copy up to 12 files concurrently in data staging as explained in Sect. 2. Several stripe counts were arranged for file accesses on the GFS volume, while we had only a single stripe count for rank-directories on the LFS due to K computer configuration.

Dirty buffer sizes (max_dirty_mb) of a GIO for the GFS and the LFS were 1 MB and 4 MB, respectively. Regarding read-ahead operation, max_read_ahead_mb was 40 MB. Two parameters about RPC, max_rpcs_in_flight and max_pages_per_rpc, were 8 and 128, respectively. Note that page size of GIO was 8 KB, and thus it enabled advanced RPC transfers up to 8 MB (=8 × 128 × 8/1,024) before RPC management by OSSs.

We have evaluated performance of writing for 1 MB data on every OST of a target GFS volume from a frontend server using dd command in every 5 min during imitated data staging to check performance impacts in write operations from a frontend server. Meanwhile we also have evaluated data staging times. The data staging had both stage-in and stage-out between a target GFS volume and rank-directories built on the LFS with a default stripe size (1 MB). The data staging was imitated by moving data files in both stage-in and stage-out phases, where there was not any computation tasks. The imitated data staging job was executed twice for each parameter set, and we have picked up better performance value out of two.

Table 1. Parameters of data staging in performance evaluation

# compute nodes	Node layout	# GIO	File size	# files	Load-balancing
576	$12 \times 24 \times 2$	96	12 GB/file	576	No
288	$12 \times 24 \times 1$	96	24 GB/file	288	No
576	$12 \times 24 \times 2$	96	12 GB/file	576	Yes
41,472	$48 \times 54 \times 16$	864	512 MB/file	41,472	Yes

Table 1 shows parameters for data staging used in performance evaluation. The first two sets are aimed for evaluation to examine performance impact about the number of files that each GIO manages. Here we have the same total data size in data staging among the two sets. We address to examine our stripe count estimation model through results obtained from the two sets. The third case is same with the first case except the third case includes I/O load-balancing scheme of FEFS among data staging and I/O accesses by dd from a frontend server. Here we address to examine effectiveness of the load-balancing. The last one is for evaluation using the whole GIOs that the K computer has. Due to limited computing time to utilize whole GIOs, we minimize file size as 512 MB in order to get enough performance results for this paper. We discuss each performance results in the following subsections.

4.1 Workload-Aware Stripe Count Impact

At first, stripe count impact was examined using 576 compute nodes allocated in $12 \times 24 \times 2$ logical 3D layout, where 96 GIOs were responsible for data staging of 576 files against the one GFS volume consisting of 384 OSTs. Here 12 GB files were managed in data staging using rank-directories and every GIO managed 6 files ($k_{stg} = min(576/96, 12) = 6$) concurrently, and 576 files amounted for 6.75 TB in total were handled by the 96 GIOs.

Figure 6 shows write time distributions among 384 OSTs from a frontend server during data staging. Horizontal axis of these graphs represents time of measurement for 10 h, while vertical axis represents write time distribution among 384 OSTs. There is a horizontal bar on top of each graph and green and red colored rectangles on each bar indicate stage-in and stage-out, respectively. An attached blue-colored line starting from stage-in and ending-up by stage-out indicates the target staging job. An interval between stage-in and stage-out was waiting time to start stage-out phase because the imitated job did not consist of any computation tasks. The interval varied in time based on scheduling situation, and stage-out phase started once essential GIOs were available. In each graph, dark-blue colored region stands for OSTs with the shortest write times less than 0.01 s (OSTs in good response times). With an increase in write times for OSTs, color of each region changes from green, orange, and red. The worst case colored in black indicates write times more than or equal to 300 s.

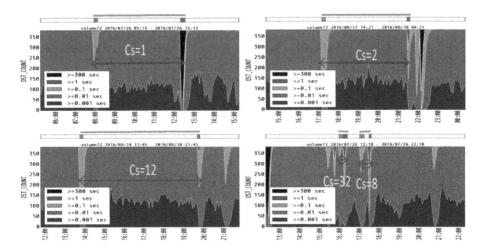

Fig. 6. Write time distributions over a period of 10 h against 384 OSTs during data staging for 576 files (12 GB/file) by 96 GIOs, where C_S represents stripe count (Color figure online)

Giving 1 in stripe count led to miserable situation as shown in the upper-left graph of Fig. 6. High I/O workload in each OST disturbed I/O accesses from frontend servers, and it resulted in such poor response times. In this case, every OST received a large number of RPC requests in a consecutive way from associated GIOs. Besides, this stripe count and RPC configuration against the GFS led to minimization of cache effect by client cache on each client and advanced RPCs in flight. Therefore each OST could not catch up with RPC requests from GIOs, thus leading to many retries of RPC requests. Consequently response time was degraded. Once we increased stripe count, degradation in dd's write response time was gradually mitigated because of I/O load-balancing improvements as shown in the lower left graph (stripe count = 12) of Fig. 6. However, stripe count at 32 increased response times as shown in the lower right graph of Fig. 6. A further increase in stripe count has a risk to incur congestion in RPC transfers, and thus leading to an increase in write response time by dd. It is remarked that degradation in write responses was big in stage-out phase compared with stage-in phase. It is considered that read-ahead scheme mitigated contention in I/O accesses happened in stage-in phase. While we had contention in stage-out phase because every client sent RPC requests once write function was called in stage-out phase.

The first five rows of Table 2 shows shorter data staging times out of two staging jobs by 96 GIOs in the above evaluation. Regarding times for stage-out, stripe count more than 2 is considered to be better. Although stage-out times were minimized with an increase in stripe count, dd's write times were increased as shown in Fig. 6. By taking the increase in write times into account, giving 12 in stripe count seems to be the best. On the other hand, times for stage-in were almost the same in terms of stripe count. This was due to single stripe

Table 2. Data staging times by 96 GIOs

File size	# files	Load-balancing	Stripe count for GFS	Stage-in (sec)	Stage-out (sec)
12 GB/file	576	No	1	776	838
			2	727	531
			8	751	426
			12	649	451
			32	711	416
24 GB/file	288	No	1	571	961
			2	571	621
			8	579	358
			12	612	379
			24	627	361
			32	609	427
12 GB/file	576	Yes	1	721	1,422
			2	761	739
			8	788	461
			12	794	444
			32	679	574

count configuration for each rank-directory, and we can say that staging times were dependent on stripe count configuration of destination. As we described, we focus on behavior and I/O interference alleviation in stage-out operations in this paper.

Figure 7 shows the amount of data among OSTs in four stripe count cases (1, 2, 12, and 32) out of evaluated 5 cases. In case of stripe count = 1, apparently unbalanced amount of data among OSTs is observed. By increasing the stripe count from 1 to 2, we see better balanced situation compared with the case of stripe count = 1. However, unbalanced situation is still observed. Some OSTs had smaller amount of data, while some other OSTs had larger amount of data. Differences between the minimum and maximum sizes were 12 GB (24 GB − 12 GB), which was the same with one file size. Compared with averaged amount of data per OST (18 GB), ratio in variance was about 66% ($\sim(12/18) \times 100$). As a result, unbalanced situation happened among OSTs in terms of cumulative amount of data. With an increase in stripe count, we obtained balanced situation as seen in the cases of 12 and 32 in stripe count. In those cases, difference between minimum and maximum sizes became small or negligible with an increase in stripe count. Giving 12 and 32 in stripe count led to the differences to be about 5% and 2% of the averaged data amount per OST, respectively. Giving 64 in stripe count led to about 1%, and it is turned out that such large number is excessive in terms of balanced I/O workloads. Giving 12 in stripe count was sufficient regarding both I/O interference mitigation observed in Fig. 6 and Table 2 and balanced data amount within 5% variances among OSTs shown in Fig. 7.

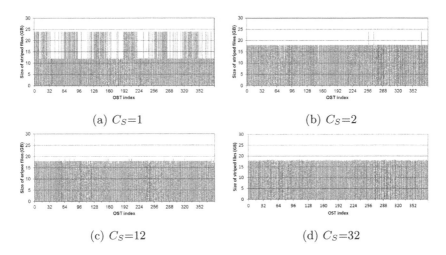

(a) $C_S=1$

(b) $C_S=2$

(c) $C_S=12$

(d) $C_S=32$

Fig. 7. Data amount distributions among 384 OSTs for striped 576 files in data staging by 96 GIOs about four stripe counts ($C_S = 1$, 2, 12, and 32)

In other words, we can estimate appropriate stripe count based on our model once we define upper limit in the variances. If we accept 10% ($\beta = 0.1$) of averaged amount of data per OST (18 GB) in variances, stripe count is estimated as 7 ($= \lceil (1/0.1) \times 384/(96 \times 6) \rceil$), where α in the stripe count calculation model is 1. If 10% is not acceptable for balanced I/O and upper limit is minimized within 5% ($\beta = 0.05$), stripe count is expected to be 14 ($= \lceil (1/0.05) \times 384/(96 \times 6) \rceil$), which is near from appropriate stripe count in the above evaluation.

The same evaluation was carried out by changing the number of files, where total amount of file sizes was the same with previous case. The evaluation was done by 288 compute nodes ($12 \times 24 \times 1$ in 3D layout) using 96 GIOs, where every GIO managed 3 files ($k_{stg} = min(288/96, 12) = 3$) and each file was 24 GB to have the same amount of total data size in the previous evaluation.

Our model estimated 27 in stripe count in this case if we accepted 5% in variances for data amount on OSTs. Figure 8 shows write time distributions during data staging. From this figure, giving 24 in stripe count is better than other cases. Roughly speaking, the estimated value is close to the preferable stripe count. Concerning stage-out times shown in the six rows ranging from sixth to eleventh ones of Table 2, stripe counts between 8 and 24 performed shorter times in stage-out, while we did not see significant differences in stage-in times as we saw in the previous evaluation.

4.2   FEFS Load Balancing

Service thread based load-balancing function of FEFS was additionally introduced in the above stripe count examination. Write time distributions under the data staging for 576 files (12 GB/file) by 96 GIOs were examined under the load

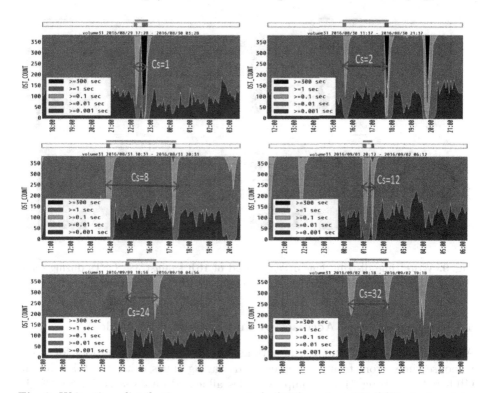

Fig. 8. Write time distributions over a period of 10 h against 384 OSTs during data staging of 288 files (24 GB/file) by 96 GIOs

balancing which guaranteed 20% of service threads for I/O accesses from frontend servers. Results are shown in Fig. 9. Here we show four stripe count cases (1, 2, 12, and 32). Compared with results in Fig. 6, I/O interference reduction is observed, especially big alleviation is seen when stripe count is 1. Thus the load-balancing is effective for I/O throughput guarantee even if we have heavy data staging.

Concerning data staging, lower five rows of Table 2 show staging times observed in the results in Fig. 9. Compared with results of the first five rows of Table 2, stage-out time increased when stripe count was 1. This is due to I/O load balancing of FEFS which limited the number of service threads in data staging. On the other hand, such heavy data staging with a single stripe count utilized almost all available service threads by beating other light-weight file accesses from a frontend server. With an increase in stripe count, stage-out time has been minimized and it has been in the same range with those times in the first five rows of Table 2. Consequently giving 12 in stripe count is the best case regarding with both I/O interference alleviation and staging performance. From these results, data amount aware striping configuration with the I/O load-balancing of FEFS is effective.

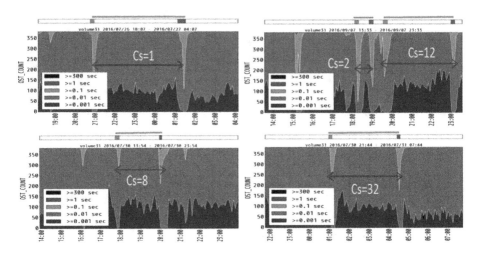

Fig. 9. Write time distributions over a period of 10 h against 384 OSTs during data staging for 576 files (12 GB/file) by 96 GIOs under FEFS load-balancing

4.3 Impact of Data Accesses by Full Scale of GIO Nodes

According to the performance evaluations, we did the same evaluations for write response times from frontend servers and staging times using the full scale of GIOs with utilizing 41,472 compute nodes allocated on $48 \times 54 \times 16$ 3D logical node layout. Figure 10 shows write time distributions among 384 OSTs in the range of 10 h in each graph. In this evaluation, every process managed 1 file amounted for 512 MB each, and those files were transferred between rank-directories on the LFS and the GFS. Because of limited times for such huge scale of execution at the K computer, we decreased file size so as to get performance results in reasonable time duration. As seen in this figure, giving 12 in stripe count minimized write response times among the evaluated five cases.

Table 3 shows staging times observed in the evaluations shown in Fig. 10. As seen in this table, giving 12 or 32 in stripe count minimized staging times. Considering both write response times and staging times, having 12 in stripe count was the best case among the evaluated stripe counts.

According to the estimation model in Eq. 3, appropriate stripe count is expected to be 11 $(=\lceil(14/0.05) \times (384/(864 \times 12))\rceil)$. This value is almost the same with the measured results, and thus the model is expected to perform prediction for stripe count in each staging scheme.

5   Conclusion and Future Work

We have proposed workload-aware striping and I/O load-balancing in order to alleviate I/O interference by huge data staging at the K computer. The proposed scheme consists of striping configuration in data staging for balanced amount of data on each OST and load-balancing by service thread allocation for incoming

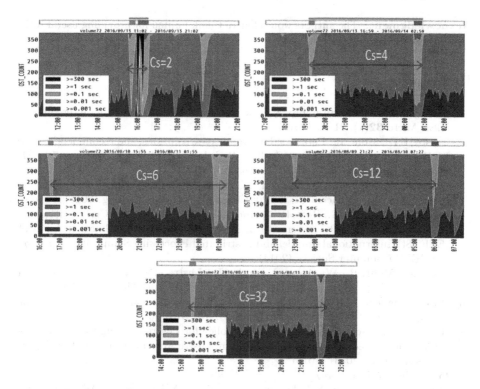

Fig. 10. Write time distributions over a period of 10 h against 384 OSTs during data staging for 41,472 files (512 MB/file) by 864 GIOs

Table 3. Data staging times by 864 GIOs

File size	# files	Load-balancing	Stripe count for GFS	Stage-in (sec)	Stage-out (sec)
512 MiB/file	41,472	Yes	2	1,039	1,898
			4	1,012	1,424
			6	910	1,433
			12	998	1,218
			32	1,130	1,168

RPC requests. Combination of the two optimizations has reduced I/O interference due to huge data staging impressively without excessive sacrifice to data staging performance in performance evaluation. As a future work, adoption of the optimizations in real machine operation is considered. Based on our model, we can tune stripe count once we give upper limit ratio in terms of data amount per OST. Load-balancing among many requests on an MDS is another challenge to mitigate heavy workload of MDS due to huge data accesses on shared storage spaces. Since FEFS development has been intended to contribute to Lustre development, we expect that our optimization scheme including the load-balancing function of FEFS will be adopted in future Lustre development.

Acknowledgment. The authors would like to thank Fujitsu for providing useful technical information about FEFS.

References

1. Ajima, Y., Inoue, T., Hiramoto, S., Takagi, Y., Shimizu, T.: The Tofu interconnect. IEEE Micro **32**(1), 21–31 (2012)
2. Crosby, L.D., Mohr, R.: Petascale I/O: challenges, solutions, and recommendations. In: Proceedings of the Extreme Scaling Workshop, BW-XSEDE 2012, pp. 7:1–7:7. University of Illinois at Urbana-Champaign (2012)
3. Dillow, D.A., Shipman, G.M., Oral, S., Zhang, Z.: I/O congestion avoidance via routing and object placement. In: 2011 Cray User Group Meeting (2011)
4. Dorier, M., Antoniu, G., Ross, R.B., Kimpe, D., Ibrahim, S.: CALCioM: mitigating I/O interference in HPC systems through cross-application coordination. In: 2014 IEEE 28th International Parallel and Distributed Processing Symposium, pp. 155–164. IEEE Computer Society (2014)
5. Ezell, M., Mohr, R., Wynkoop, J., Braby, R.: Lustre at petascale: experiences in troubleshooting and upgrading. In: 2012 Cray User Group Meeting (2012)
6. Hirai, K., Iguchi, Y., Uno, A., Kurokawa, M.: Operations management software for the K computer. Fujitsu Sci. Tech. J. **48**(3), 310–316 (2012)
7. Ihara, S.: A new quality of service (QoS) policy for Lustre utilizing the Lustre network request scheduler (NRS) framework. In: Lustre Administrator and Developers Workshop (LAD 2013) (2013)
8. Lustre. http://lustre.org/
9. Miyazaki, H., Kusano, Y., Shinjou, N., Shoji, F., Yokokawa, M., Watanabe, T.: Overview of the K computer system. Fujitsu Sci. Tech. J. **48**(3), 255–265 (2012)
10. Mohr, R., Brim, M., Oral, S., Dilger, A.: Evaluating progressive file layouts for Lustre (2016). http://lustre.ornl.gov/ecosystem-2016/
11. Qian, Y., Barton, E., Wang, T., Puntambekar, N., Dilger, A.: A novel network request scheduler for a large scale storage system. Comput. Sci. - Res. Dev. **23**(3), 143–148 (2009)
12. Qian, Y., Yi, R., Du, Y., Xiao, N., Jin, S.: Dynamic I/O congestion control in scalable Lustre file system. In: 2013 IEEE 29th Symposium on Mass Storage Systems and Technologies (MSST 2013), pp. 1–5. IEEE Computer Society (2013)
13. Rajachandrasekar, R., Jaswani, J., Subramoni, H., Panda, D.K.: Minimizing network contention in InfiniBand clusters with a QoS-aware data-staging framework. In: 2012 IEEE International Conference on Cluster Computing, pp. 329–336 (2012)
14. Reed, J., Archuleta, J., Brim, M.J., Lothian, J.: Evaluating dynamic file striping for Lustre. In: Proceedings of the International Workshop on the Lustre Ecosystem: Challenges and Opportunities (2015). http://arxiv.org/html/1506.05323
15. Saini, S., Rappleye, J., Chang, J., Barker, D., Mehrotra, P., Biswas, R.: I/O performance characterization of Lustre and NASA applications on Pleiades. In: 19th International Conference on High Performance Computing (HiPC), pp. 1–10 (2012)
16. Sakai, K., Sumimoto, S., Kurokawa, M.: High-performance and highly reliable file system for the K computer. Fujitsu Sci. Tech. J. **48**(3), 302–309 (2012)
17. Sumimoto, S.: An overview of Fujitsu's Lustre based file system. In: Lustre User Group 2011 (2011)

18. Wang, F., Oral, S., Gupta, S., Tiwari, D., Vazhkudai, S.S.: Improving large-scale storage system performance via topology-aware and balanced data placement. In: 2014 20th IEEE International Conference on Parallel and Distributed Systems (ICPADS), pp. 656–663. IEEE Computer Society (2014)
19. Yildiz, O., Dorier, M., Ibrahim, S., Ross, R., Antoniu, G.: On the root causes of cross-application I/O interference in HPC storage systems. In: 2016 IEEE 30th International Parallel and Distributed Processing Symposium, pp. 750–759. IEEE Computer Society (2016)
20. Zhang, X., Davis, K., Jiang, S.: QoS support for end users of I/O-intensive applications using shared storage systems. In: Proceedings of 2011 International Conference for High Performance Computing, Networking, Storage and Analysis, pp. 18:1–18:12. ACM (2011)

Designing Dynamic and Adaptive MPI Point-to-Point Communication Protocols for Efficient Overlap of Computation and Communication

Hari Subramoni$^{(\boxtimes)}$, Sourav Chakraborty, and Dhabaleswar K. Panda

Department of Computer Science and Engineering,
The Ohio State University, Columbus, OH, USA
{subramoni.1,chakraborty.52,panda.2}@osu.edu

Abstract. Broadly, there exist two protocols for point-to-point data transfer in the Message Passing Interface (MPI) programming model - Eager and Rendezvous. State-of-the-art MPI libraries decide the switch point between these protocols based on the trade-off between memory footprint of the MPI library and communication performance without considering the overlap potential of these communication protocols. This results in sub-par overlap of communication and computation at the application level. While application developers can manually tune this threshold to achieve better overlap, it involves significant effort. Further, the communication pattern may change based on the size of the job and the input requiring constant re-tuning making such a solution impractical. In this paper, we take up this challenge and propose designs for point-to-point data transfer in MPI which accounts for overlap in addition to performance and memory footprint. The proposed designs dynamically adapt to the communication characteristic of each communicating pair of processes at runtime. Our proposed full in-band design is able to transition from one eager-threshold to another without impacting the communication throughput of the application. The proposed enhancements to limit the memory footprint by dynamically freeing unused internal communication buffer is able to significantly cut down on memory footprint of the MPI library without affecting the communication performance.

Experimental evaluations show that the proposed dynamic and adaptive design is able to deliver performance on-par with what exhaustive manual tuning provides while limiting the memory consumed to the absolute minimum necessary to deliver the desired benefits. For instance, with the Amber molecular dynamics application at 1,024 processes, the proposed design is able to perform on-par with the best manually tuned versions while reducing the memory footprint of the MPI library by 25%. With the 3D-Stencil benchmark at 8,192 processes, the proposed design is able to deliver much better overlap of computation and communication as well as improved overall time compared to the default version.

This research is supported in part by National Science Foundation grants #CNS-1419123, #CNS-1513120, #ACI-1450440 and #CCF-1565414.

© Springer International Publishing AG 2017
J.M. Kunkel et al. (Eds.): ISC High Performance 2017, LNCS 10266, pp. 334–354, 2017.
DOI: 10.1007/978-3-319-58667-0_18

To the best of our knowledge, this is the first point-to-point communication protocol design that is capable of dynamically adapting to the communication requirements of end applications.

Keywords: MPI · Point-to-point communication · Overlap of communication and computation

1   Introduction

Message Passing Interface (MPI) [16] is a very popular parallel programming model for developing high-performance scientific applications. The MPI Standard [18] offers various point-to-point, collective, remote memory and synchronization operations. The point-to-point operation is a fundamental building block in MPI as one can orchestrate almost all higher level primitives that MPI provides using point-to-point operations. Point-to-point operations can be broadly classified as blocking and non-blocking depending on when the buffer that has been posted to the MPI library is available for reuse. While the semantics of blocking primitives (e.g.: MPI_Send, MPI_Recv) is geared towards delivering the best communication performance, non-blocking primitives (e.g.: MPI_Isend, MPI_Irecv) have the dual objective of delivering best performance while ensuring that applications can achieve overlap of computation and communication.

Over the last several years, point-to-point non-blocking communication has emerged as a popular method for application scientists to hide the communication overhead by overlapping communication and computation. While modern primitives like the Remote Memory Access (RMA) semantics proposed by the MPI-3 standard are specifically geared towards this, many popular application kernels and applications like conjugate gradient solvers [15], adaptive mesh refinement [12], multi-physics [26], molecular dynamics [7], and earthquake prediction codes [9] still take advantage of non-blocking point-to-point communication primitives to hide the communication overhead.

Although the concept of non-blocking point-to-point primitive seems simple and the benefits obvious, there are several caveats that need to be addressed before end applications can reap the benefits offered by this programming interface. One needs to carefully match the semantics expected by the programming interface to that offered by the underlying communication protocol in order to ensure optimal performance.

1.1   Motivation

There broadly exists two protocols for point-to-point data transfer in MPI — Eager and Rendezvous. Eager protocol sends data to the peer without waiting for an acknowledgment first and is thus used to transfer data of limited size to the receiver (typically small messages). The rendezvous protocol, on the other hand, uses control messages to ensure that the receiver has enough memory available to accommodate the incoming message. Thus it is typically used to transfer large messages. More details about these protocols are available in Sect. 2.1.

With modern multi-/many-core architectures and high-performance interconnects, there is always a "sweet-spot" where (1) the cost of exchanging the control information is not large enough to have an impact on the overall time of data transfer, and (2) the cost of memory copies to the internal buffer starts to be higher than the cost of exchanging control information. Most open source high-performance implementations of the MPI standard such as OpenMPI [8], MVAPICH2 [14], and MPICH [11] switch to the rendezvous protocol from eager protocol at this "sweet-spot" typically referred to as the "eager-threshold". In order to avoid the performance penalties seen with packetized data transfers, high-performance MPI libraries typically match the size of the internal communication buffers to be same as that of the eager-threshold. Thus, a secondary factor of consideration is the size of the internal communication buffers used to stage data in the eager protocol. Designers need to ensure that this is not so large that the memory footprint of the MPI library becomes too high.

As described above, while significant attention has been given to ensure that these protocols deliver best trade-off between performance and memory footprint, not much attention has been paid to the overlap aspect of these protocols. We employ a simple case-study with a 3D-stencil benchmark (described in Sect. 2.3) to clearly motivate the need to account for overlap of computation and communication. Note that this communication pattern is representative of several large applications mentioned in Sect. 1. Figure 1(a) compares the raw communication performance of the 3D-stencil benchmark run with the default eager-threshold value of 17 KB against a version where we manually forced the eager-threshold and the internal communication staging buffer to be 1 MB. These numbers were taken with 8,192 processes (512 nodes) on the Stampede supercomputing system at TACC [25]. As expected, a smaller eager threshold forces use of rendezvous protocol which provides better raw communication time for large messages. However, as seen in Fig. 1(b), this does not take into account the overlap potential of the different protocols. When there is computation that can be overlapped, use of the eager protocol is able to deliver better overall performance due to the higher overlap obtained. This is basically due to the fact that, with

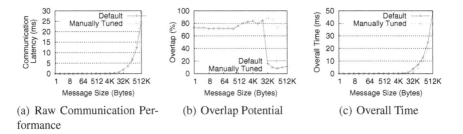

(a) Raw Communication Performance   (b) Overlap Potential   (c) Overall Time

Fig. 1. Performance and overlap offered by eager and rendezvous protocols for 3D-Stencil benchmark at 8,192 processes on Stampede

rendezvous transfer, the data transfer (which consumes the most time) does not start until an MPI_Wait or MPI_Waitall operation is called. However by switching to the eager protocol, the small loss of raw communication performance due to multiple memory copies are more than compensated by overlapping the most time-consuming data transfer part with computation, thereby reducing overall execution time Fig. 1(c).

While it is possible for application developers to manually tune this threshold to achieve better overlap, it involves significant effort and complexity. Modern high-performance MPI libraries have hundreds of tunable parameters each impacting a different aspect of communication. Thus, it is rather difficult for an application developer to effectively optimize a particular application using such manual tuning. Further, the communication pattern may change based on the size of the job and the input requiring constant re-tuning making such a solution impractical. To make matters worse, blindly increasing the eager-threshold can also have the negative consequence of increasing the overall memory footprint of the MPI library leaving less memory for the application to perform its science. Large internal communication buffers can also negatively affect the communication performance of small message operations due to poor cache locality on the sender and the receiver sides. Figure 2 shows the adverse effect of larger eager-threshold (and consequently larger communication buffers) on the message throughput. These issues lead us to the following broad challenge: **Can we design an adaptive and dynamic point-to-point communication mechanism for high-performance MPI libraries that can deliver the best communication performance, overlap of computation and communication, and memory footprint for all classes of applications?**

1.2   Contributions

In this paper, we take up this challenge and explore multiple point-to-point communication protocol designs to enable efficient overlap of computation and communication. We highlight the merits and deficiencies of each design and evaluate its performance with microbenchmarks and applications on modern HPC systems. Finally, we propose a dynamic and adaptive design for point-to-point communication that enables efficient overlap while ensuring basic communication performance and memory footprint is not adversely impacted. Our proposed full in-band design is able to transition from one

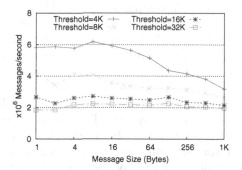

Fig. 2. Impact of changing Eager Threshold on performance of multi-pair message-rate benchmark with 32 processes on Stampede

eager-threshold to another without impacting the communication throughput of the application while taking care of all possible corner cases. The proposed enhancements to limit the memory footprint by dynamically freeing unused internal communication buffers is able to significantly cut down on memory footprint of the MPI library without affecting the communication performance. Our experimental results show that, our proposed dynamic and adaptive approach is able to deliver performance on par with what exhaustive manual tuning provides while cutting down on the overall memory footprint of the MPI library. For instance, with the Amber molecular dynamics application at 1,024 processes, the proposed design was able to perform on-par with the best manually tuned versions while reducing the memory footprint of the MPI library by 25%. With the 3D-Stencil benchmark at 8,192 processes, the proposed design is able to deliver much better overlap of computation and communication as well as improved overall time compared to the default version. To the best of our knowledge, this is the first point-to-point communication protocol design that is capable of dynamically adapting to the communication requirements of end applications. To summarize, the major contributions of this paper are:

- Study the interplay between communication pattern of applications and point-to-point communication protocols
- Propose, design, implement and study multiple dynamic and adaptive point-to-point communication protocols to deliver better overlap of computation and communication
- Explore alternate design approaches to overlap computation and communication and study its benefits and deficiencies
- Propose secondary designs to tackle the additional challenge of limiting memory footprint of the MPI library
- Demonstrate the benefits of the proposed scheme on performance with microbenchmarks and applications.

Figure 3 compares the default, manually tuned, and the new designs along the metrics of performance, productivity, memory scalability, and overlap achieved. In all axes, the higher value is better. As we can see, the proposed dynamic and adaptive design performs the best when all metrics are considered. For instance, the proposed design is able to deliver overlap of computation and communication and overall application performance comparable to the best manually tuned version while providing a high degree of productivity similar to the default versions. It is also able to significantly cut down on the

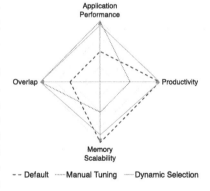

Fig. 3. Comparison of existing and proposed designs

memory requirement of the MPI library when compared to best manually tuned version.

2   Background

In this section, necessary background information for this paper is provided.

2.1   Protocols for High-Performance Point-to-Point Communication in MPI

Figures 4(a) and (b) depict how the eager and rendezvous protocol respectively are typically implemented. The eager protocol consists of four steps — (1) copying the data from application buffer to buffers internal to the MPI library, (2) initiating the data transfer to the remote process, (3) detecting the reception of data in buffers internal to the MPI library, and (4) copying the data back to the application buffer. With most high-performance networks like InfiniBand, the network itself takes care of the actual data transfer. Thus, initiating the data transfer at the sender and detecting the reception of the data at the receiver are low overhead tasks. So, apart from the time to transfer data over the network, the main costs involved in an eager transfer are the memory copies at the sender/receiver. Note that steps #1 and #2 happen inside the send function call itself. With a rendezvous protocol on the other hand (Fig. 4(b)), MPI designers take advantage of the RDMA feature that high-performance interconnects like InfiniBand offers and transfers data directly from the source application buffer to the target application buffer (with appropriate exchange of control information), thereby avoiding the extra large memory copies from the application buffer to internal communication buffers within the library.

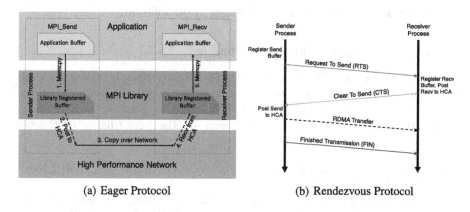

(a) Eager Protocol   (b) Rendezvous Protocol

Fig. 4. Point-to-point communication protocols in MPI

2.2   Amber

Amber [7] is a molecular dynamics package including numerous programs that work in conjunction to perform end-to-end molecular dynamics simulation (from the creation of input files to the analysis of results).

2.3   3D-Stencil Benchmark

The processes in the benchmark are mapped onto a 3D grid and each process talks to its neighbors in each dimension (6 neighbors). In every step, each process posts MPI_Irecv operations for all of the messages it expects and then posts all of the MPI_Isend calls. It waits for all of the transfers to complete with one MPI_Waitall call. At the end of each iteration, the benchmark executes a call to MPI_Allreduce to collect boundary information from all processes participating in the job. To calculate the overlap of communication and computation, we first measure the time to perform all the MPI_Irecvs and MPI_Isends immediately followed by a MPI_Waitall. The benchmark also computes the overall latency (the total time taken when computation is overlapped with communication), the communication and the computation time, and the overlap percentage. In addition, we are also time the initialization overhead and the wait time.

3   Common Challenges in Designing Dynamic and Adaptive Point-to-point Communication Protocols

Several applications tend to communicate with its peer processes using varying message sizes. Thus, one of the first design challenge is to enable the ability to have different eager-threshold values for different process pairs. To this end, we introduce two adaptive and dynamic designs — (1) partial in-band and (2) fully in-band that are capable of updating the eager-threshold for a pair of processes. However, there are some common design challenges that need to be addressed before such a change of eager-threshold can occur. We enumerate these challenges and our solutions to address these challenges in the following sub-sections.

3.1   Triggering Eager-Threshold Change

It is important for the MPI library to correctly identify when it needs to migrate to a higher eager-threshold in order to obtain better overlap of computation and communication. We find that two conditions need to hold for such a change of eager-threshold to have a positive impact on the performance of the end application:

1. The use of non-blocking send and/or recv operation (e.g.: MPI_Isend, MPI_Irecv) by the application
2. The time elapsed between posting non-blocking send/recv operation and polling for completion of the operation (through MPI_Wait, MPI_Waitall etc.) should be a reasonable proportion (50% or more) of the total estimated time for data transfer.

If either one of these conditions does not hold, then it is unlikely that the application will see any benefits because of the eager-threshold change. For instance, in an application using blocking send/recv operations there is no potential for overlap. On the other hand, if the time between posting the non-blocking operation and polling for completion is very fast (like in the case of a typical bandwidth benchmark), the potential for overlap is significantly reduced. Further, as shown in Sect. 1.1, incorrectly increasing the eager-threshold can negatively impact the performance of small messages due to the paging behavior at the receiver process. Finally, the initiating process must also ensure that there are enough resources available locally to allocate the resources necessary to perform an eager-threshold switch as described in Sect. 3.3.

3.2 Identifying the New Eager-Threshold

As the average size of messages being sent from process A to process B need not be the same as those being sent in the opposite direction, a "handshake" or "agreement" protocol is required to ensure that both processes settle on the same value for eager-threshold. This is very critical as different values for eager-threshold for a process pair can result in undefined communication behavior (like a hung data transfer). Further, it is possible that any one of the processes is unable to honor the eager-threshold change request (due to lack of resources or some internal errors). In this scenario, the process encountering the failure needs a mechanism to inform the peer process of its inability to proceed with the eager-threshold change.

We introduce two new packet types "NEW_CONN_HANDSHAKE_REQ" and "NEW_CONN_HANDSHAKE_REP" to address these issues. When a process decides to trigger an eager-threshold change (as identified in Sect. 3.1), it sends out a "NEW_CONN_HANDSHAKE_REQ" packet to its peer and marks the virtual communication channel that exists between the two processes to indicate that an eager-threshold change is in progress. This packet contains the new value of eager-threshold the initiating process wants the communication channel to be moved to. The new eager-threshold is calculated using the following equation:

$$Threshold_{new} = 2^{\left\lceil \log_2 \left(\frac{\sum sizeof(Rndv\ Msg + Pkt\ Header)}{Number\ of\ Rndv\ Msgs} \right) \right\rceil} + offset$$

The new threshold is chosen based on the average size of rendezvous messages being sent from the initiating process to the peer process. The goal here is to allow most of the large messages to go through the eager path while not increasing the eager-threshold to an unnecessarily large value. An "offset" of 1,024 bytes is added to ensure that messages falling right on the boundary of the new eager-threshold can also be accounted for with this change.

The remote process on receiving the "NEW_CONN_HANDSHAKE_REQ" packet, first checks if it can allocate the resources necessary to proceed with the eager-threshold change (as described in Sect. 3.3). If so, it proceeds to identify the local eager-threshold value using the formula described above. It then compares the local value with the value sent by the remote peer and uses the maximum of the two values as the new eager-threshold for the communication channel. This value is communicated to the peer process using a "NEW_CONN_HANDSHAKE_REP" message and the communication channel is marked as "in-active" indicating that an eager-threshold change is in progress. If, for some reason, the process is unable to allocate the necessary resources or is unable to proceed with the eager-threshold change for any other reason, it responds back with an eager-threshold value of "−1".

The initiating process on receiving the "NEW_CONN_HANDSHAKE_REP" packet extracts the value of eager-threshold indicated by peer. If the value is "−1", the peer has indicated that it cannot proceed with the eager-threshold change and the process marks the communication channel as being incapable of processing an eager-threshold change so that no future eager-threshold changes are initiated by this process for the communication channel with the peer. If the value is non-negative, the process initiates either the partially in-band or the fully in-band mechanism (described in Sects. 4.1 and 4.2 respectively) to establish a new connection with the larger eager-threshold.

3.3 Allocating Resources for Eager-Threshold Change

High-performance MPI libraries for InfiniBand typically use shared receive queues (SRQ) for improved scalability [22,24]. With this technology, a process can have just one queue to receive data from any peer process. However, the buffers that are posted to receive data on the shared receive queue must be large enough to hold the data any sender may possibly send to it in a gratuitous fashion. In other words, the buffers posted to the SRQ must be equal to the new eager-threshold size the process wants to use identified by the "handshake" protocol described in Sect. 3.2. We introduce a pool based design where each process creates a set of internal communication buffers whose size is equal to the new eager-threshold agreed upon by the pair of processes. If such a pool already exists (from a previous dynamic eager-threshold change with another process), the pool and the associated SRQ is reused. Otherwise, a new pool and the SRQ are created and added to the list of available pools. We limit the number of such pools that a process can create, to a value that can be set at runtime by the user through an environment variable (default value: 20).

4   Dynamic and Adaptive Design for Point-to-Point Communication Protocols

In this section we discuss the various alternative designs as well as their benefits and deficiencies. We use the open-source MVAPICH2 [14] library for the proposed designs and studies in this paper. However, the proposed designs are generic and can be incorporated into other MPI libraries.

4.1 Partial In-Band Design

We first explore a partial in-band design to re-establish the connections between the process pairs with an increased eager-threshold. The various messages

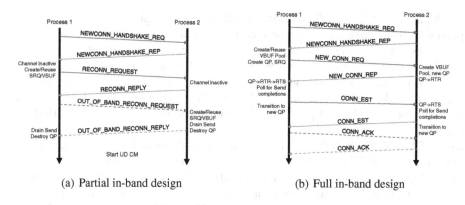

(a) Partial in-band design   (b) Full in-band design

Fig. 5. Connection establishment in partial and full in-band designs

exchanged in this design are depicted in Fig. 5(a). One of the major benefits of this approach is its ability to take advantage of the existing on-demand connection establishment design in MVAPICH2 [27,28]. Once the new eager-threshold has been successfully identified as described in Sect. 3.2, the design marks the communication channel as inactive to prevent the application from sending any further messages. The initiator process then allocates resources as described in Sect. 3.3 and sends a "RECONN_REQUEST" to the peer process. This will be the last message the initiator process transmits over the existing IB connection (also know as a queue pair - QP). The peer process on receiving the "RECONN_REQUEST" proceeds to mark the communication channel as inactive and replies back with a "RECONN_REPLY". This will be the last message that the peer process transmits over the existing QP. When the initiator process receives the "RECONN_REPLY", it initiates an "OUT_OF_BAND_RECONN_REQUEST" through the QP being used for the on-demand connection management design. On reception of the "OUT_OF_BAND_RECONN_REQUEST", the peer process allocates resources as described in Sect. 3.3, drains all the send completions from the existing QP and destroys it. After completing this successfully, it transmits a "OUT_OF_BAND_RECONN_REPLY" to the initiator. The initiator on receiving the request drains all the send completions from the existing QP, destroys it, and starts the on-demand connection establishment using the newly allocated resources. As we can see, one of the major cons of this approach is the duration of time for which the communication channel is marked as inactive. Such a long duration of inactivity has the potential to negatively impact the application throughput. Thus we discard this design from further consideration.

4.2 Full In-Band Design

In the full in-band design, we completely avoid using the on-demand connection management design in MVAPICH2 and instead use the regular communication channel to exchange messages. The various messages exchanged in this design are depicted in Fig. 5(b). The major benefit of this design when compared to the partial in-band design is that the communication channel is always active and thus does not affect the communication throughput of the application. Once the new eager-threshold has been successfully identified as described in Sect. 3.2, the initiator process allocates resources as described in Sect. 3.3, creates a QP for new eager-threshold and transmits a "NEW_CONN_REQ" message to the peer. The message contains the end-point information of the initiator process so that the peer can begin the process of IB connection management. The peer on receiving the "NEW_CONN_REQ" allocates resources as described in Sect. 3.3, extracts the initiator end-point information from the message, transitions the newly created IB QP to ready-to-receive (RTR) state, and responds to the initiator with a "NEW_CONN_REP" message containing the local end-point information.

The initiator process on receiving the "NEW_CONN_REP" extracts the peer processes end-point information and uses that to transition the new local QP to RTR and ready-to-send (RTS) states. At this point, the new QP is capable of gratuitously sending messages to the peer at the increased eager-threshold size. Once this is complete, the initiator will ensure that all the previous send operations on the existing QP has completed and will send out a "CONN_EST" message to the peer with the local end-point information. This will be the last message that is sent on the old QP. All future messages are sent over the newly created QP. The peer on receiving the "CONN_EST" message will transition its newly created QP to the RTS state and is thus capable of gratuitously sending messages to the peer at the increased eager-threshold size. After this, the process will ensure that all the previous send operations on the existing QP has completed and will send out a "CONN_EST" message to the peer with the local end-point information. This will be the last message that is sent on the old QP. All future messages are sent over the newly created QP.

The initiator on receiving the "CONN_EST" message responds back with a "CONN_EST_ACK" message over the new QP to indicate that there are no more messages in flight on the old QP. The peer on receiving this message will destroy the old QP and send a "CONN_EST_ACK" message over the new QP to indicate that the initiator can destroy the old QP as well thus completing the transition to the new eager-threshold size. As this design proceeds without having to throttle application communication, it has the potential to deliver the best performance. Thus we use the "Full In-band" design for all experimental evaluations in the paper.

4.3   Avoiding Message Loss During Threshold Migration

It should be noted that in our design, eager thresholds are not bidirectional, i.e. a message from Process A to Process B could go over the eager protocol while a message of the same size from Process B to Process A could go through the rendezvous path. Furthermore, each process can independently decide to change the eager-threshold for a peer process based on its past communication with said peer. To prevent loss of messages, both peers must be able to identify when to switch to the new QP as well as handle in-flight messages during the handshake. The handshake protocol used in the "Full In-band" design achieves this by ensuring that (a) the initiator process starts sending messages through the new QP only after the target process has acknowledged that it is ready to receive on the new QP, and (b) the target process destroys the old QP only after getting a confirmation from the initiator that it has processes send completions for all messages sent through the old QP.

4.4   Mitigating Memory Footprint Requirements

A major concern with manually and exhaustively tuning the eager-threshold and the proposed dynamic and adaptive design is the potential increase in memory footprint of the MPI library due to the increased size of internal communication buffers. To address this issue, we propose a design that dynamically identifies unused internal communication buffers and reclaims them. However, unless performed carefully, this operation can lead to a continuous cycle of allocation and freeing of internal communication buffers leading to poor performance.

Most high-performance MPI libraries dynamically allocate internal communication buffers as and when the library runs out of these buffers due to communication pressure from the application. Further, most applications have phases where the communication activity increases and decreases. Thus, if proposed design is too aggressive in freeing internal communication buffers, it could free a large number of buffers in the phase with low communication only to reallocate them when the communication pressure increases again. To avoid such a cycle, we add weights to the communication buffers and only free them if they have not been used for a specific period of time which is tunable. We have done extensive tuning of this value on multiple supercomputing systems and identified appropriate values for it to ensure that such cycles of allocation and freeing are avoided as much as possible. With such a design, we are able to significantly reduce the memory overhead caused by the dynamic and adaptive designs to less than 50% of what the manually tuned designs can offer.

4.5   Alternate Design Approaches

In this section, we explore possible alternate designs to avoid the requirement to exchange the control information in the rendezvous exchange which is the major cause for the lack of overlap. The ideal solution here would be to have a hardware component to which the rendezvous exchange can be offloaded. Unfortunately, such technology is still not available in the public domain. In this context, we create a new design that uses the "Receiver-Not-Ready" or RNR mechanism of InifniBand to avoid (1) the need to exchange control information and (2) the need for intermediate memory copies from the application buffer to internal MPI buffers and back. Figure 6 depicts how the communication proceeds in the RNR-based design.

In the RNR design, the sender and receiver create a special QP for each tag used for communication. Once the QP has been created, the sender directly registers the send buffer with the IB HCA and sends the data to the receiver's QP. At this point, the IB HCA takes over and continually checks with the target HCA as to whether it is ready to receive the data. The target HCA becomes ready to receive data when the receiver arrives and posts a corresponding receive operation to the special QP created earlier. Until this

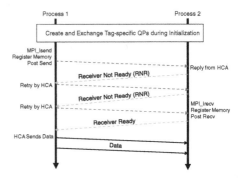

Fig. 6. Communication in RNR-based design

event occurs, the receiver HCA will respond back to the sender HCA's queries indicating that the receiver is not ready (RNR). Although there is a timeout after which the sender will stop trying to transmit the data to the receiver, we increase it so that the sender keeps retrying infinitely. Finally, when the receiver arrives, the target HCA indicates that the receiver is ready causing the sender to place the data in the buffer pointed to by the receive QP which happens to be the application level buffer in the RNR design. This design eliminates the need for the application to explicitly use control messages to stage the rendezvous transfer or to use intermediate memory copies to transfer the data using the eager protocol.

However, this design has several functionality and performance issues making it more constrained to use in real world applications. (1) Due to the lack of hardware-based tag matching, it cannot support wild cards such as MPI_ANY_SOURCE and MPI_ANY_TAG which is very common in MPI as well as application communication. Further, as described above each communicating process pair needs to use a separate QP for communication creating a scalability bottleneck. On the performance side, the RNR design is unable to send a continuous stream of data as a typical eager or rendezvous protocol does. This is mainly due to the fact that it cannot start a subsequent transfer until the previous transfer is complete. Thus, it is hard to keep the communication pipeline resulting in sub-par communication throughput. Due to these performance and functionality constraints, we discount this design from further performance evaluations.

5   Experimental Results

In this section, we describe the experimental setup, provide the results of our experiments, and give an in-depth analysis of these results. All numbers reported here are averages of a minimum of five runs. There was little to no variance between the different runs. As described in Sects. 4.1 and 4.5, we discard the Partial In-band design and RNR-based design from further performance evaluation due to their inherent design limitations. Thus, for the remainder of the performance evaluation section, "dynamic threshold" refers to the Full In-band design described in Sect. 4.2.

5.1   Experimental Setup

We used multiple high-performance computing systems to obtain the results for this paper:

Gordon @ SDSC [21]: Each node contains two 8-core 2.6 GHz Intel EM64T Xeon E5 (Sandy Bridge) processors and 64 GB of DDR3-1333 memory. The operating system used is CentOS release 6.4 (Final), with kernel version 2.6.32-431.29.2.el6. The network topology is a $4 \times 4 \times 4$ 3D torus with adjacent switches connected by three 4x QDR InfiniBand links (120 Gb/s). Compute nodes (16 per switch) and I/O nodes (1 per switch) are connected to the switches by 4x QDR (40 Gb/s).

Stampede @ TACC: Each node is equipped with an Intel SandyBridge series of processors using Xeon dual eight-core sockets, operating at 2.70 GHz with 32 GB RAM. Each host is equipped with MT4099 FDR ConnectX HCAs (54 Gbps data rate) with PCI-Ex Gen3 interfaces. The operating system used is CentOS release 6.7 (Final), with kernel version 2.6.32-431.17.1.el6, and OpenFabrics version 1.5.4.1. The network is a five-stage partial Fat-Tree with 5:4 oversubscription on the links.

5.2   Performance of 3D-Stencil Benchmark

In this section, we analyze the performance results of the 3D-stencil benchmark (described in Sect. 2.3) for different process counts on Stampede. In Fig. 7(a), we compare the raw communication performance of the default, manually tuned, and the proposed dynamic design at 8,192 processes. The default scheme provides the best pure communication time. However, when seen in conjunction with the overlapping computation, the default scheme performs worse than the manually tuned and proposed dynamic schemes as indicated by the overall time and overlap numbers in Figs. 7(c) and (b) respectively. We also observe that, while the default scheme is able to offer better communication initialization time by avoiding the large memory copies associated with eager protocol indicated in Sect. 2.1, it loses out significantly in the time spent in MPI_Wait. This is because, with the rendezvous protocol being used in the default scheme, almost all of the time consuming data transfer happens in the MPI_Wait operation with little or no overlap of computation and communication actually happening. Due to lack of space, we are unable to include the figures describing the initialization and wait times in the paper.

Finally in Fig. 8, we study the pure communication performance, overlap obtained, and overall communication time for the 128 KB message size of the 3D-stencil benchmark for various system sizes on Stampede. As we can see, while the proposed dynamic threshold design takes a slight hit in raw communication

348   H. Subramoni et al.

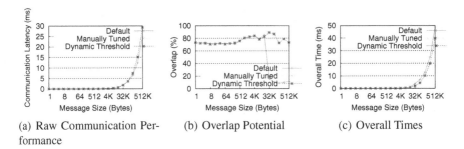

(a) Raw Communication Performance (b) Overlap Potential (c) Overall Times

Fig. 7. Performance and overlap offered by various point-to-point communication protocols for 3D-Stencil benchmark at 8,192 processes on Stampede

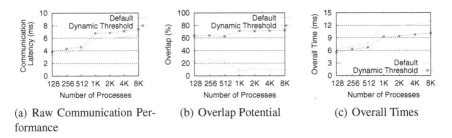

(a) Raw Communication Performance (b) Overlap Potential (c) Overall Times

Fig. 8. Comparison of performance and overlap offered by Default and Dynamic Threshold design for 128 KB messages in 3D-Stencil benchmark at different scales on Stampede

performance (depicted in Fig. 8(a)), is able to provide much better overlap (depicted in Fig. 8(b)) and overall time (depicted in Fig. 8(c)) when compared to the default design.

5.3 Performance of Amber

We perform an in-depth study and analysis of the performance of the Amber molecular dynamics code with the different point-to-point communication protocol designs in this section. Figure 9(a) shows the overall application execution time with the default design, various manual tuning options, and the proposed dynamic design. As we can see, for different system sizes, best performance is given by different manual tuning options. Such unpredictable behavior (as indicated in Sect. 1.1) makes this kind of manual tuning cumbersome, error prone, and impractical. The proposed dynamic design, on the other hand, is able to deliver performance on par with the best manual tuned design in a user transparent way making it a high-productivity and high-performance option for application developers.

Figure 9(b) illustrates the memory used for the internal communication buffers used by the MPI library to stage the data transfers. The data is plotted relative to the amount of memory taken by the default design for internal

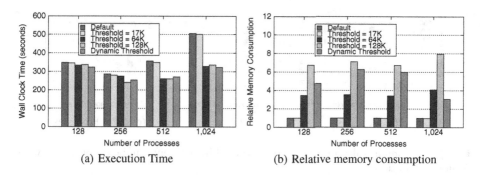

(a) Execution Time   (b) Relative memory consumption

Fig. 9. Performance of Amber on Gordon with different values of Eager-Threshold

communication buffers. As we can see, the default design gives best memory scalability. However, we also observe from Fig. 9(a) that, it is unable to deliver the best performance due to its inability to effectively overlap communication and computation. The proposed dynamic design, on the other hand, is able to keep the memory footprint to the absolute minimum required by the design described in Sect. 4.4.

Figure 10 depicts the number times various processes performed switches of eager thresholds during the execution of the program for different system sizes. Although, due to space limitations, we only show details of the larger system sizes, note that the trends for smaller system sizes are similar. As we can see, at 256 and 512 processes the processes perform a lot of eager-threshold changes. This is reflected as increased memory usage for the dynamic design for the corresponding system sizes in Fig. 9(b). However, at 1,024 processes, we observe that a large percentage of the processes perform no eager-threshold changes (indicated by the large value for zero in Fig. 10(c)). This trend translates to relatively lower memory consumption for the dynamic design (when compared to 256 and 512 processes) as seen in Fig. 9(b).

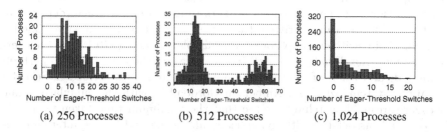

(a) 256 Processes   (b) 512 Processes   (c) 1,024 Processes

Fig. 10. Number of eager-threshold switches performed by different number of processes with Amber on Gordon

Figure 11 shows the maximum value of eager message size that various processes in the job end up with for different job sizes with Amber. We can

350   H. Subramoni et al.

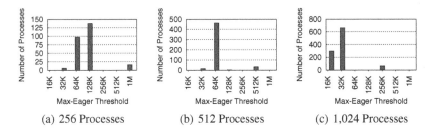

Fig. 11. Maximum value of eager-threshold used by different number of processes with Amber on Gordon

see a clear trend with the maximum value of the message continually decreasing as the size of the system increases. While the median max eager-threshold size with 256 processes is 128 KB, it reduces to 64 KB at 512 processes and further reduces to 32 KB at 1,024 processes. This indicates a distribution of computation load among the different processes - in other words, strong scaling. Another interesting trend to observe is the similarity in the number of processes whose max eager-threshold value is 17 KB (the default value) at 1,024 processes as depicted in Fig. 11(c) and the number of processes that perform no eager-threshold changes indicated by the large value for zero in Fig. 10(c). These values corroborate each other indicating that the processes that do not have to perform eager-threshold switch are actually those whose desired max eager-threshold value happens to be equal to the default value the MPI library is configured with.

Figure 12(a) depicts the average and maximum time taken for one eager threshold switch across all processes for various system sizes. As we can see, the maximum overhead of establishing a new connection is very low (of the order of 40 ms) indicating the efficiency of the proposed design. Figure 12(b) on the other hand measures the maximum and average cumulative time spent by each process for eager-threshold switching during the lifetime of the job. As we can see, while the maximum value fluctuates a little, it is still very low (<0.5 s). Note that this is for jobs that take 300 s to 350 s to execute on average (depicted in Fig. 9(a)). Thus, we can clearly see that even the maximum cumulative time for eager-threshold switching only forms a negligible percentage (0.1%) of the overall execution time. Finally in Fig. 12(c), we measure the time taken to perform dynamic de-allocation of internal communication buffers described in Sect. 4.4 for various system sizes with Amber on Gordon. As with the cumulative time for eager-threshold switching, we see that the maximum time taken to handle the overheads associated with dynamically allocating and freeing internal communication buffers are always less than one second. As we mentioned above, this only forms a negligible percentage (0.3%) of the overall execution time of the application.

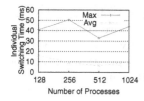
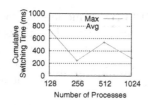
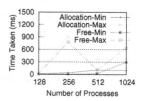

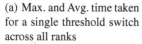

(a) Max. and Avg. time taken for a single threshold switch across all ranks

(b) Max. and Avg. cumulative time taken for threshold switching in each process

(c) Min. and Max. time taken for communication buffer allocation/free in each process across all ranks

Fig. 12. Time taken for switching eager-threshold and communication buffer allocation/free with different number of processes with Amber on Gordon

6   Related Work

The use of extra threads, commonly known as asynchronous progress threads, to progress communication in the background has been a popular method to progress communication in the background while the application is computing in the foreground. While this allows progression of messages without the application having to enter the MPI library to progress the communication, it takes away a valuable computation core away from the application process which can adversely affect the overall performance of the application.

Brightwell et al. [5] showed that eagerly sending large messages can improve latency for pre-posted receives. However, this scheme has to resend unexpected large messages in presence of application skew, which does not affect our design. In [3], Barrett et al. proposed the use of triggered operations in the portals [20] interface to perform large message rendezvous operations. This method is similar to the RNR-based design proposed in Sect. 4.5 and also suffers from the same drawbacks as the RNR-based design in that it is not able to handle wild cards in the MPI library (e.g.: MPI_ANY_SOURCE).

Researchers have also explored the use hardware-assisted tag matching techniques to offload rendezvous transfers to the hardware. While several high-performance network interconnect such as Intel Omni-Path, Myrinet [4], Quadrics [2], Bull BXI [10], and Mellanox [1] have proposed and are proposing solutions that expose such capabilities to high performance MPI libraries.

Automatic tuning for MPI libraries and applications has been explored by many researchers [6,17,19,23]. However, such tools generally cannot perform more targeted tuning, such as changing eager-threshold for a small number of peers. Although the introduction of MPI-T [13] might enable such fine-grained tuning, good designs are still required inside the MPI library to minimize the overhead involved.

The emerging remote memory access (RMA) model semantically relieves the remote process from having to actively participate in communication. Thus it has the potential to completely overlap computation and communication.

Although the use of the MPI3-RMA models is slowly catching up, the vast majority of scientific applications in use today still use the two-sided communication model. Further, collective operations, that are widely used across various scientific domains, still rely on two-sided point-to-point operations. Thus the proposed schemes are likely to remain very relevant in the future.

7   Conclusion and Future Work

In this paper, we proposed designs for point-to-point data transfer in MPI which accounts for overlap in addition to performance and memory footprint. The proposed designs dynamically adapt to the communication characteristic of each communicating pair of processes at runtime. Our proposed fully in-band design is able to transition from one eager-threshold to another without impacting the communication throughput of the application while taking care of all possible corner cases. The proposed enhancements to limit the memory footprint by dynamically freeing unused internal communication buffers is able to significantly cut down on memory footprint of the MPI library without affecting the communication performance. Our experimental evaluation showed that the proposed dynamic and adaptive design is able to deliver performance on-par with what exhaustive manual tuning provides while limiting the memory consumed to the absolute minimum necessary to deliver the desired benefits. For instance, with the Amber molecular dynamics application at 1,024 processes, the proposed design was able to perform on-par with the best manually tuned versions while reducing the memory footprint of the MPI library by 25%. With the 3D-Stencil benchmark at 8,192 processes, the proposed design is able to deliver much better overlap of computation and communication as well as improved overall time compared to the default version. To the best of our knowledge, this is the first point-to-point communication protocol design that is capable of dynamically adapting to the communication requirements of end applications.

As part of future work, we plan to study the benefits of the proposed design with multiple applications at scale.

References

1. Mellanox Technologies. http://www.mellanox.com
2. Quadrics Supercomputers World Ltd. http://www.quadrics.com/
3. Barrett, B.W., Brightwell, R., Hemmert, K.S., Wheeler, K.B., Underwood, K.D.: Using triggered operations to offload rendezvous messages. In: Cotronis, Y., Danalis, A., Nikolopoulos, D.S., Dongarra, J. (eds.) EuroMPI 2011. LNCS, vol. 6960, pp. 120–129. Springer, Heidelberg (2011). doi:10.1007/978-3-642-24449-0_15
4. Boden, N.J., Cohen, D., Felderman, R.E., Kulawik, A.E., Seitz, C.L., Seizovic, J.N., Su, W.: Myrinet: a gigabit-per-second local area network. IEEE Micro **15**, 29–36 (1995)
5. Brightwell, R., Underwood, K.: Evaluation of an eager protocol optimization for MPI. In: Dongarra, J., Laforenza, D., Orlando, S. (eds.) EuroPVM/MPI 2003. LNCS, vol. 2840, pp. 327–334. Springer, Heidelberg (2003). doi:10.1007/978-3-540-39924-7_46

6. Brunet, É., Trahay, F., Denis, A., Namyst, R.: A Sampling-based approach for communication libraries auto-tuning. In: 2011 IEEE International Conference on Cluster Computing (CLUSTER), pp. 299–307. IEEE (2011)
7. Case, D.A., Darden, T.A., Cheatham, T.E., Simmerling, C.L., Wang, J., Duke, R.E., Luo, R., Walker, R.C., Zhang, W., Merz, K.M., Roberts, B.P., Wang, B., Hayik, S., Roitberg, A., Seabra, G., Kolossváry, I., Wong, K.F., Paesani, F., Vanicek, J., Wu, X., Brozell, S.R., Steinbrecher, T., Gohlke, H., Cai, Q., Ye, X., Wang, J., Hsieh, M.-J., Cui, G., Roe, D.R., Mathews, D.H., Seetin, M.G., Sagui, C., Babin, V., Luchko, T., Gusarov, S., Kovalenko, A., Kollman, P.A.: Amber 2016, University of California, San Francisco (2016)
8. Open MPI: Open Source High Performance Computing. http://www.open-mpi.org
9. Cui, Y., Moore, R., Olsen, K., Chourasia, A., Maechling, P., Minster, B., Day, S., Hu, Y., Zhu, J., Majumdar, A., Jordan, T.: Toward petascale earthquake simulations. Acta Geotech. 4, 79–93 (2008). Springer
10. Derradji, S., Palfer-Sollier, T., Panziera, J.P., Poudes, A., Atos, F.W.: The BXI interconnect architecture. In: 2015 IEEE 23rd Annual Symposium on High-Performance Interconnects, pp. 18–25, August 2015
11. Gropp, W., Lusk, E., Doss, N., Skjellum, A.: A high-performance, portable implementation of the MPI, message passing interface standard. Technical report, Argonne National Laboratory and Mississippi State University
12. Heroux, M.A., Doerfler, D.W., Crozier, P.S., Willenbring, J.M., Edwards, H.C., Williams, A., Rajan, M., Keiter, E.R., Thornquist, H.K., Numrich, R.W.: Improving performance via mini-applications. Technical report SAND2009-5574, Sandia National Laboratories (2009)
13. Islam, T., Mohror, K., Schulz, M.: Exploring the capabilities of the new MPI_T interface. In: Proceedings of the 21st European MPI Users' Group Meeting, p. 91. ACM (2014)
14. Liu, J., Jiang, W., Wyckoff, P., Panda, D.K., Ashton, D., Buntinas, D., Gropp, W., Toonen, B.: Design and implementation of MPICH2 over InfiniBand with RDMA support. In: Proceedings of Int'l Parallel and Distributed Processing Symposium (IPDPS 2004), April 2004
15. Lu, Y., Yang, C., Du, Y.: HPCG on Tianhe2
16. Message Passing Interface Forum. MPI: A Message-Passing Interface Standard, March 1994
17. Miceli, R., et al.: AutoTune: a plugin-driven approach to the automatic tuning of parallel applications. In: Manninen, P., Öster, P. (eds.) PARA 2012. LNCS, vol. 7782, pp. 328–342. Springer, Heidelberg (2013). doi:10.1007/978-3-642-36803-5_24
18. MPI-3 Standard Document. http://www.mpi-forum.org/docs/mpi-3.0/mpi30-report.pdf
19. Pimenta, A., Cesar, E., Sikora, A.: Methodology for MPI applications autotuning. In: Proceedings of the 20th European MPI Users' Group Meeting, pp. 145–146. ACM (2013)
20. Portals Network Programming Interface. http://www.cs.sandia.gov/Portals/
21. San Diego Supercomputing Center. Gordon Supercomputer. http://www.sdsc.edu/services/hpc/hpc_systems.html#gordon
22. Shipman, G.M., Woodall, T.S., Graham, R.L., Maccabe, A.B., Bridges, P.G.: InfiniBand scalability in open MPI. In: Proceedings of the 20th International Conference on Parallel and Distributed Processing, IPDPS 2006, p. 100. IEEE Computer Society, Washington, DC (2006)

23. Sikora, A., César, E., Comprés, I., Gerndt, M.: Autotuning of MPI applications using PTF. In: Proceedings of the ACM Workshop on Software Engineering Methods for Parallel and High Performance Applications, pp. 31–38. ACM (2016)
24. Sur, S., Chai, L., Jin, H., Panda, D.K.: Shared receive queue based scalable MPI design for InfiniBand clusters. In: Proceedings of the 20th International Conference on Parallel and Distributed Processing, IPDPS 2006, p. 101. IEEE Computer Society, Washington, DC (2006)
25. Texas Advanced Computing Center. Stampede Supercomputer. http://www.tacc.utexas.edu/
26. The MIMD Lattice Computation (MILC) Collaboration. http://physics.indiana.edu/~sg/milc.html
27. Wu, J., Liu, J., Wyckoff, P., Panda, D.: Impact of on-demand connection management in MPI over via. In: Proceedings of the 2002 IEEE International Conference on Cluster Computing, pp. 152–159 (2002)
28. Yu, W., Gao, Q., Panda, D.K.: Adaptive connection management for scalable MPI over InfiniBand. In: Proceedings 20th IEEE International Parallel Distributed Processing Symposium, p. 10, April 2006

Diagnosing Performance Variations in HPC Applications Using Machine Learning

Ozan Tuncer[1]([✉]), Emre Ates[1], Yijia Zhang[1], Ata Turk[1], Jim Brandt[2],
Vitus J. Leung[2], Manuel Egele[1], and Ayse K. Coskun[1]

[1] Boston University, Boston, MA, USA
{otuncer,ates,zhangyj,ataturk,megele,acoskun}@bu.edu
[2] Sandia National Laboratories, Albuquerque, NM, USA
{brandt,vjleung}@sandia.gov

Abstract. With the growing complexity and scale of high performance computing (HPC) systems, application performance variation has become a significant challenge in efficient and resilient system management. Application performance variation can be caused by resource contention as well as software- and firmware-related problems, and can lead to premature job termination, reduced performance, and wasted compute platform resources. To effectively alleviate this problem, system administrators must detect and identify the anomalies that are responsible for performance variation and take preventive actions. However, diagnosing anomalies is often a difficult task given the vast amount of noisy and high-dimensional data being collected via a variety of system monitoring infrastructures.

In this paper, we present a novel framework that uses machine learning to automatically diagnose previously encountered performance anomalies in HPC systems. Our framework leverages resource usage and performance counter data collected during application runs. We first convert the collected time series data into statistical features that retain application characteristics to significantly reduce the computational overhead of our technique. We then use machine learning algorithms to learn anomaly characteristics from this historical data and to identify the types of anomalies observed while running applications. We evaluate our framework both on an HPC cluster and on a public cloud, and demonstrate that our approach outperforms current state-of-the-art techniques in detecting anomalies, reaching an *F-score* over 0.97.

1 Introduction

Application performance variations are among the significant challenges in today's high performance computing (HPC) systems as they adversely impact system efficiency. For example, the amount of variation in application running times can reach 100% on real-life systems [12,28,31]. In addition to leading to

---

The rights of this work are transferred to the extent transferable according to title 17 U.S.C. 105.

© Springer International Publishing AG 2017
J.M. Kunkel et al. (Eds.): ISC High Performance 2017, LNCS 10266, pp. 355–373, 2017.
DOI: 10.1007/978-3-319-58667-0_19

unpredictable application running times, performance variations can also cause premature job terminations and wasted compute cycles. Common examples of *anomalies* that can lead to performance variation include orphan processes left over from previous jobs consuming system resources [16], firmware bugs [1], memory leaks [6], CPU throttling for thermal control [15], and resource contention [12,18,28]. These anomalies manifest themselves in system logs, performance counters, or resource usage data.

To detect performance variations and determine the associated root causes, HPC operators typically monitor system health by continuously collecting system logs along with performance counters and resource usage data such as available network link bandwidth and CPU utilization. Hundreds of metrics collected from thousands of nodes at frequencies suitable for performance analysis translate to billions of data points per day [7]. As HPC systems grow in size and complexity, it is becoming increasingly impractical to analyze this data manually. Thus, it is essential to have tools that automatically identify problems through continuous and/or periodic analysis of data.

In this study, we describe a machine learning framework that can automatically detect compute nodes that have exhibited known performance anomalies and also diagnose the type of the anomaly. Our framework avoids data deluge by using easy-to-compute statistical features extracted from applications' resource utilization patterns. We evaluate the effectiveness of our framework in two environments: a Cray XC30m machine, and a public cloud hosted on a Beowulf-like cluster [33]. We demonstrate that our framework can detect and classify anomalies with an *F-score* above 0.97, while the *F-score* of the state-of-the-art techniques are between 0.89 and 0.97. Our specific contributions are:

- An easy-to-compute and fast statistical feature extraction approach that significantly reduces the amount of data required for performance analysis at runtime, while retaining relevant information for anomaly detection.
- A novel low-overhead method based on machine learning algorithms that can automatically detect and identify the anomalies that cause performance variations. We demonstrate that our approach outperforms the state-of-the-art techniques on identifying anomalies on two fundamentally different platforms: a CRAY XC30m HPC cluster and a public cloud.

The rest of the paper is organized as follows: Sect. 2 provides an overview of related work, Sect. 3 describes our machine-learning-based anomaly detection framework, Sect. 4 describes the state-of-the-art algorithms that we implement as baselines, Sect. 5 explains our experimental methodology, and Sect. 6 provides our experimental findings. Finally, we conclude in Sect. 7.

2   Related Work

Analysis of performance anomalies in large scale computing systems is a widely studied topic in the literature [25,32]. Some monitoring systems utilize raw data directly to define thresholds on monitored metrics to trigger alarms that warn system administrators about possible performance impasses [13]. Such approaches do not provide root cause analysis, and manually defining thresholds for root cause analysis requires expert knowledge and is hard to maintain.

A critical problem in automated anomaly diagnosis based on application performance and resource usage is the overwhelming volume of data monitored at runtime [25]. Time series analysis methods such as correlation and dynamic time warping [10] incur unacceptable computational overhead when used with high dimensional data. Various dimensionality reduction techniques such as principal component analysis (PCA) have been used to address this problem [20,23,27]. However, techniques focused on reducing the dataset can sometimes eliminate features that are useful for anomaly detection (see Sect. 6.1).

Another way of addressing the data volume problem is to generate fingerprints (i.e., signatures) by transforming monitored data. Bodik et al. [14] use quantiles of measured values (e.g., 95th percentile) at different time epochs to summarize the collected metric time series in a fingerprint. They further reduce this data using logistic regression to eliminate metrics that are irrelevant for anomaly detection. We use Bodik et al.'s technique as a baseline and demonstrate that our approach has superior anomaly detection accuracy (See Sect. 6).

Anomaly detection is typically orthogonal to dimensionality reduction techniques. Researchers have used statistical techniques and machine learning algorithms (i.e., either alone or after dimension reduction) for detecting and classifying specific subsystem anomalies such as high network congestion [11], poor file system performance [26], temperature-related issues [9], or out-of-memory errors [16]. These techniques can detect specific anomalies with high precision, but existing methods do not provide a generic framework to detect and classify anomalies occurring in compute nodes.

Most of the related work on automated anomaly detection use low-dimensional data collected via coarse-grained monitoring tools (e.g., 1 min or greater sampling period). Several researchers have demonstrated that a detailed view on how platform resources are being utilized using finer-grained monitoring (e.g., sampling every second) can provide better insight into application behavior and can be leveraged to more effectively discover anomalies. For this purpose, they use manually selected examples of power- and thermal-issues [15] as well as file system congestion and runaway memory demands [6]. These studies do not propose an automated method to discover these problems.

A large number of studies focus on anomaly detection via log file analysis (e.g., [19,21,24]). In this work, we use application resource usage and performance characteristics to detect anomalies instead of relying on system logs; hence, our work is orthogonal to log-file based anomaly detection approaches.

To the best of our knowledge, our work is the first to address the anomaly detection and classification problem using an automated framework in conjunction with fine-grained monitoring tools in HPC systems. By leveraging statistical features that are useful for time series clustering, our anomaly detection method is able to diagnose anomalies more accurately than other known approaches.

3   Anomaly Detection and Classification

Our goal is to detect anomalies that cause performance variations and to classify the anomaly into one of the previously encountered anomaly types. To this end, we propose an automated anomaly detection technique, which takes advantage of historical data collected from known healthy runs and anomalies, and builds generic machine learning models that can distinguish anomaly characteristics in the collected data. In this way, we are able to detect and classify anomalies when running applications with a variety of previously unobserved inputs. With a training set that represents the expected application characteristics, our technique is successful even when a known anomaly impacts an application we have not encountered during training.

Directly using raw time series data that is continuously collected from thousands of nodes for anomaly detection can incur unacceptable computational overhead. This can lead to significant time gaps between data collection and analysis, delayed remedies, and wasted compute resources. Instead of using raw time series data, we extract concise statistical features that retain the characteristics of the time series. This significantly reduces our data set, thus decreasing the computational overhead and storage requirements of our approach. We apply our anomaly diagnosis offline after application runs are complete. In future work, online or periodic anomaly detection can be performed by extending our framework. In the next subsections, we explain the details of our proposed approach on feature extraction and machine learning.

3.1   Feature Extraction

HPC monitoring infrastructures are rapidly evolving and new monitoring systems are able to periodically collect resource usage metrics (e.g., CPU utilization, available memory) and performance counters (e.g., received/transmitted network packets, CPU interrupt counts) during application runs [7]. This data provides a detailed view on applications' runtime characteristics.

While an application is running, we periodically collect resource usage and performance counter metrics from each node during the entire application run. Note that our technique is also applicable when metrics are collected for a sliding history window to investigate only recent data. The metrics we collect, as described in detail in Sect. 5.1, are not specific to any monitoring infrastructure and the proposed framework can be coupled with different HPC monitoring systems (e.g., [2,5,7]). From the time series of collected metrics, we extract the following easy-to-compute features to enable fast anomaly analysis:

- Simple order statistics that help differentiate between healthy and anomalous behavior: the minimum value, 5th, 25th, 50th, 75th, and 95th percentile values, the maximum value, and the standard deviation;
- Features that are known to be useful for time-series clustering [35]:
  - *Skewness* indicates lack of symmetry. In a time series X_t, skewness S is defined by $S = \frac{1}{n\sigma^3} \sum_{t=1}^{n} \left(X_t - \overline{X_t} \right)^3$, where $\overline{X_t}$ is the mean, σ is standard deviation, and n is the number of data points.

- *Kurtosis* refers to the heaviness of the tails of a distribution. The kurtosis coefficient is defined as $K = \frac{1}{n\sigma^4} \sum_{t=1}^{n} \left(X_t - \overline{X_t} \right)^4$.
- *Serial correlation* measures the noisiness in given data, and can be estimated by the Box-Pierce statistic [36].
- *Linearity* is a measure of how well a time series can be forecasted with traditional linear models [22].
- *Self-similarity* measures the long-range dependence, i.e., the correlation of X_t and X_{t+k} in time series X_t for large values of k.

The calculation of statistical features is a low-overhead procedure, and can be further optimized to work with data streams for on the fly feature generation. We provide an evaluation of the overhead of our implementation in Sect. 6.5.

3.2   Anomaly Diagnosis Using Machine Learning

Our machine-learning-based anomaly diagnosis approach is depicted in Fig. 1. As seen in the figure, during offline training, we run various types of applications (denoted as A, B, C in the figure) using different input sizes and input data (denoted with subscripts 1, 2, etc. in the figure). We gather resource usage and performance counter metrics from the nodes used by each application both when running without any anomaly and when we inject a synthetic anomaly to one of the nodes (see Sect. 5.2 for details on injected anomalies). When an application finishes executing, we compute statistical features using the metrics collected from individual nodes as described in Sect. 3.1. We label each node with the type of the introduced anomaly (or healthy). We use these labels and computed per-node features as input data to train various machine learning algorithms such as k-nearest neighbors and random forests. As machine learning algorithms do not use application type as input, they extract anomaly characteristics independent of applications.

At runtime, we again monitor application resource usage and performance counter metrics and extract their statistical features. We then use the machine learning models built during the training phase to detect anomalies and identify the types of anomalies in the nodes used by the application.

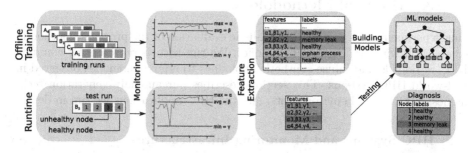

Fig. 1. Overall system architecture. Machine learning models built offline are used for classifying observations at runtime.

4 Baseline Methods

We implemented two state-of-the art methods as baselines of comparisons: the statistical approach proposed by Lan et al. [27] (referred as "ST-Lan"), and the fingerprinting approach of Bodik et al. [14] (referred as "FP-Bodik").

4.1 ST-Lan [27]

The core idea of ST-Lan is to detect anomalies based on distances between time series. ST-Lan applies Independent Component Analysis (ICA) to transform the monitored time series data into *independent components*, which represent the directions of maximal independence in data by using a linear combination of metrics. The first 3 independent components are used as a behavioral profile of a node. At runtime, the authors compare the behavioral profiles of the nodes that are used in new application runs to the profiles of known healthy nodes to identify whether the collected time series is an outlier using a distance-based outlier detection algorithm.

4.2 FP-Bodik [14]

This method first divides each metric's time series into equal-sized epochs. Each epoch is represented by three values: 25th, 50th, and 95th percentiles within that epoch. FP-Bodik further reduces data by selecting a subset of monitored metrics that are indicative of anomalies in the training set using logistic regression with L1 regularization. Next, a healthy range for the percentiles of each metric is identified using the values observed in healthy nodes while running applications. FP-Bodik then creates a *summary vector* for each percentile of each epoch based on whether observed metrics are within healthy ranges. The average of all summary vectors from a node constructs a *fingerprint* vector of the node. In order to find and classify anomalies, FP-Bodik compares L2 distances among these fingerprint vectors and chooses the nearest neighbor's category as the predicted anomaly type.

5 Experimental Methodology

Our experiments aim to provide a realistic evaluation of the proposed method in comparison with the baseline techniques. We run kernels representing common HPC workloads and infuse synthetic anomalies to mimic anomalies observed in real-world HPC systems. This section describes our anomaly generation techniques, experimental environments, and the HPC applications we run in detail.

5.1 HPC Systems and Monitoring Infrastructures

We use two fundamentally different environments to evaluate our anomaly detection technique: a supercomputer, specifically a Cray XC30m cluster named Volta, and the Massachusetts Open Cloud (MOC), a public cloud running on a Beowulf-like [33] cluster. We select these two environments as they represent modern deployment options for HPC systems.

Volta is a Cray XC30m cluster located at Sandia National Laboratories and accessed through Sandia External Collaboration Network[1]. It consists of 52 compute nodes, organized in 13 fully connected switches with 4 nodes per switch. The nodes run SUSE Linux with kernel version 3.0.101. Each node has 64 GB of memory and two sockets, each with an Intel Xeon E5-2695 v2 CPU with 12 2-way hyper-threaded cores, leading to a total of 48 threads per node.

Volta is monitored by the Lightweight Distributed Metric Service (LDMS) [7]. This service enables aggregation of a number of metrics from a large number of nodes. At every second, LDMS collects 721 different metrics as described below:

- Memory metrics (e.g., free, cached, active, inactive, dirty memory)
- CPU metrics (e.g., per core and overall idle time, I/O wait time, hard and soft interrupt counts, context switch count)
- Virtual memory statistics (e.g., free, active/inactive pages; read/write counts)
- Cray performance counters (e.g., power consumption, dirty, writeback counters; received/transmitted bytes/packets)
- Aries network interface controller counters (e.g., received/transmitted packets, flits, blocked packets)

Massachusetts Open Cloud (MOC) is an infrastructure as a service (IaaS) cloud running in the Massachusetts Green High Performance Computing Center, which is a 15 MW datacenter dedicated for research purposes [3].

In MOC, we use virtual machines (VMs) managed by OpenStack [30], where the compute nodes are VMs running on commodity-grade servers which communicate through the local area network. Although we take measurements from the VMs, we do not have control or visibility over other VMs running on the same host. Other VMs naturally add noise to our measurements, making anomaly detection more challenging.

We periodically collect resource usage data using the monitoring infrastructure built in MOC [34]. Every 5 s, this infrastructure collects 53 metrics, which are subset of node-level metrics read from the Linux `/proc/stat` and `/proc/meminfo` pseudo-files as well as `iostat` and `vmstat` tools. The specific set of collected metrics are selected by MOC developers and can be found in the public MOC code repository [4].

5.2 Synthetic Anomalies

We focus on node-level anomalies that create performance variations. These anomalies can result from system or application-level issues. Examples of such anomalies are as follows:

---

[1] http://www.sandia.gov/FSO/docs/ECN_Account_Process.pdf.

- *Out-of-memory:* When the system memory is exhausted in an HPC platform, the Linux out-of-memory killer terminates the executing application. This is typically caused by memory leaks [6].
- *Orphan processes:* When a job terminates incorrectly, it may result in orphan processes that continue using system resources such as memory and CPU [16,17].
- *Hidden hardware problems:* Automatic compensation mechanisms for hardware faults can lead to poor overall system performance. An example of such problems was experienced in Sandia National Laboratories' Redstorm system as slower performance in specific nodes, where several CPUs were running at 2.0 GHz instead of 2.2 GHz [32].

We run synthetic anomalies on a single node of a multi-node HPC application to mimic the anomalies seen in real-life systems by stressing individual components of the node (e.g., CPU or memory), emulating interference or malfunction in that component. As synthetic anomalies, we use the following programs with two different *anomaly intensities*:

1. *leak:* This program allocates a 16 MB char array, fills the array with characters, and sleeps for two seconds in an infinite loop. The allocated memory is never released, leading to a memory leak. If the available system memory is consumed before the running application finishes, the *leak* program restarts. In the low intensity mode, a 4 MB array is used.
2. *memeater:* This program allocates a 36 MB int array and fills the array with random integers. It then periodically increases the size of the array using realloc and fills in new elements. After 10 iterations, the application restarts. In the low intensity mode, an 18 MB array is used.
3. *ddot:* This program allocates two equally sized matrices of double type, using memalign, fills them with a number, and calculates the dot product of the two matrices repeatedly. We change the matrix size periodically to be 0.9, 5 and 10 times the sizes of the caches. It simulates CPU and cache interference by re-using the same array. The low intensity mode allocates arrays half the size of the original.
4. *dcopy:* This program again allocates two matrices of sizes equal to those of *ddot*, however it copies one matrix to the other one repeatedly. Compared to *ddot*, it has less CPU interference and writes back to the matrix.
5. *dial:* Repeatedly generates random floating point numbers, and performs arithmetic operations, thus stresses the ALU. In low intensity mode, the anomaly sleeps for 125 ms every 250 ms.

5.3 Applications

In order to test our system with a variety of applications, we use the NAS Parallel Benchmarks (NPB) [8]. We pick five NPB applications (bt, cg, ft, lu and sp), with which we can obtain feasible running times (10–15 min) for three different custom input sizes. Each application run uses 4 nodes on Volta and 4 VMs on

MOC. As some of our applications require the number of MPI ranks to be the square of an integer or to be a power of two, we adjust the number of ranks used in our experiments to meet these requirements and run applications with 64 and 16 ranks in Volta and MOC, respectively.

In our experiments, we run the selected 5 NPB applications for every combination of 3 different application input sizes and 20 and 10 randomized input data set in Volta and MOC, respectively. We repeat each of these runs 20 times: 10 without any anomaly, and 10 with one of the 4 application nodes having a synthetic anomaly for every combination of 5 anomaly types and 2 anomaly intensities. This results in 3000 application runs in Volta and 1500 in MOC, half of which use a single unhealthy node, i.e., a node with an anomaly.

We have observed that for the application runs with a single unhealthy node, the characteristics of the remaining (i.e., healthy) nodes are more similar to the nodes in a completely healthy application run than to an unhealthy node. This is because even when the runtime of an application changes due to inclusion of an unhealthy node, the characteristics that we evaluate do not change significantly on the remaining healthy nodes for the applications we use.

5.4   Implementation Details

We implement most of our preprocessing and classification steps in python. Before feature generation, we remove the first and last 30 s of the collected time series data to strip out the initialization and termination phases of the applications. Note that the choice of 30 s is based on these particular applications and the configuration parameters used.

During pre-processing, we take the derivative of the performance counters so that the resulting metrics represent the number of events that occurred over the sample interval (e.g., interrupts per second). This is automatically done in MOC, and can be easily integrated into LDMS in Volta.

Proposed Framework: For feature generation, we use the python `scipy-stats` package to calculate skewness and kurtosis. We use R to calculate Box-Pierce statistics, the `tseries` R package to calculate the Teräsvirta neural network test for linearity, and the `fracdiff` R package for self-similarity.

We evaluate the following machine learning algorithms: k-nearest neighbors, support vector classifiers with the radial basis function kernel, decision trees, random forests, and AdaBoost. We use python's `scikit-learn` packages [29] for the implementations of these algorithms.

ST-Lan: This algorithm uses the first $N = 3$ independent components determined by ICA as the behavioral profile of a node. The first 3 independent components do not capture the independent dimensions in our data because the metric set we monitor is significantly larger than that used by Lan et al. As the authors do not provide a methodology to select N, we have swept N values within $[3, 20]$ range and compared accuracy in terms of the percentage of correctly labeled nodes on both of our experimental platforms as shown in Fig. 2. $N = 7$ and

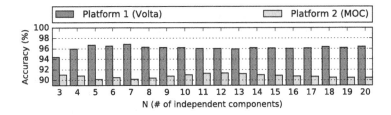

Fig. 2. Classification accuracy of ST-Lan w.r.t. number of independent components used in the algorithm for the two platforms used in this study.

$N = 12$ provide the highest accuracy on Volta and MOC, respectively. We settled on $N = 10$ as it provides a good middleground value that results in high accuracy on both platforms. In addition to selecting N, we extend ST-Lan to be able to do multi-class classification (i.e., to identify the type of an anomaly) as well by using a kNN classifier instead of the distance-based outlier detection algorithm used by the authors.

FP-Bodik: This algorithm uses divides the collected metric time series into epochs before generating fingerprints. In their work [14], Bodik et al. select the epoch length as 15 min with a sampling rate of a few minutes due to the restrictions in their monitoring infrastructure. In our implementation, we use the epoch length as 100 measurements, which corresponds to 100 s.

6   Results

We evaluate the detection algorithms using 5-fold stratified cross validation, which is a standard technique for evaluating machine learning algorithms, and is performed as follows: We randomly divide our data set into 5 equal-sized partitions with each partition having data from a balanced number of application runs for each anomaly. We use a single partition for testing while using the other 4 disjoint partitions for training; and repeat this procedure 5 times, where each partition is used once for testing. Furthermore, we repeat the 5-fold cross validation 10 times with different randomly-selected partitions.

We calculate the average *precision* and *recall* for each class across all test sets, where the classes are the 5 anomalies we use and "healthy", and precision and recall of class C_i are defined as follows:

$$precision_{C_i} = (\# \text{ of correct predictions})_{C_i}/(\# \text{ of predictions})_{C_i} \qquad (1)$$

$$recall_{C_i} = (\# \text{ of correct predictions})_{C_i}/(\# \text{ of elements})_{C_i} \qquad (2)$$

For each class, we report *F-score*, which is the harmonic mean of precision and recall. In addition, we calculate an overall F-score for each algorithm as follows: We first calculate the weighted average of precision and recall, where the precision and recall of each class is weighted by the number of instances of that class in our data set. The harmonic mean of these weighted average values is the overall F-score.

We use the following classifiers in our machine learning framework: k-nearest neighbors (kNN), support vector classifier (SVC), AdaBoost, decision tree (DT), and random forest (RF).

The rest of this section begins with comparing anomaly detection techniques when the disjoint training and test sets include data from the same applications, application input sizes, and anomaly intensities, but using different application input data. However, it is not a realistic scenario to know all the possible jobs that will run on an HPC system. Hence, in the following subsections, we evaluate the robustness of our approach and the baseline techniques to unknown application input sizes, unknown applications, and unknown anomaly intensities. Finally, we provide an experimental evaluation of the computational overhead of our anomaly detection approach.

6.1 Anomaly Detection and Classification

Figures 3 and 4 show the effectiveness of the anomaly detection approaches in terms of overall and per-anomaly F-scores in Volta and MOC environments, respectively. Note that half of our application runs use 4 healthy nodes and the other half use 3 healthy nodes and a single unhealthy node. Hence, the overall F-score of *majority voting*, which simply marks every node as "healthy", is 0.875 (represented by a dashed line in Figs. 3a and 4a).

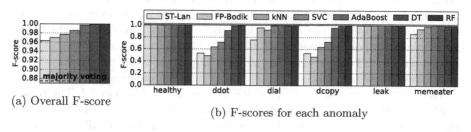

(a) Overall F-score

(b) F-scores for each anomaly

Fig. 3. F-scores for anomaly classification in Volta. ST-Lan and FP-Bodik are baseline algorithms. Majority voting in (a) marks everything as "healthy".

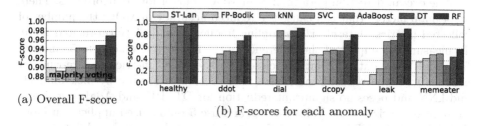

(a) Overall F-score

(b) F-scores for each anomaly

Fig. 4. F-scores for anomaly classification in MOC.

Table 1. The most important 10 features selected by RF in Volta

Source	Feature
/proc/stat	avg_user
/proc/stat	perc5_idle
/proc/stat	perc95_softirq
/proc/vmstat	std_dirty_backgnd_thrshld
/proc/stat	perc25_idle
/proc/vmstat	std_dirty_threshold
cray_aries_r	std_current_freemem
/proc/stat	perc50_idle
/proc/vmstat	perc95_pgfault
/proc/vmstat	min_numa_hit

Table 2. The most important 10 metrics selected by ST-Lan in Volta

Source	Metric
nic	WC_FLITS
/proc/meminfo	VmallocUsed
nic	WC_PKTS
/proc/meminfo	Committed_AS
/proc/vmstat	nr_page_table_pages
/proc/meminfo	PageTables
/proc/meminfo	VmallocChunk
nic	WC_BLOCKED
/proc/vmstat	nr_active_anon
/proc/meminfo	Active(anon)

In Volta, DT and RF result in close to ideal detection accuracy. As *ddot* and *dcopy* anomalies both stress caches, all algorithms tend to mislabel them as each other, resulting in lower F-scores.

The relatively poor performance on ST-Lan in Fig. 3 demonstrates the importance of feature selection. ST-Lan leverages ICA for dimensionality reduction and uses features that represent the maximal independence in data but are not necessarily relevant for anomaly detection. Table 1 presents the most useful 10 features selected by random forests based on the normalized total Gini reduction brought by each feature as reported by python `scikit-learn` package. For comparison, we present the metrics with the 10 highest absolute weight in the independent components used in ST-Lan in Table 2. Indeed, none of the top-level metrics used by ST-Lan is used in the most important features of RF.

In MOC, however, the important metrics in the independent components match with the important features of RF as shown in Tables 3 and 4. The reason is that we collect 53 metrics in MOC compared to 721 metrics in Volta; and hence, there is a higher overlap between the metrics in the first 10 independent components and those selected by decision trees. As the metric space increases, the independent components become less relevant for anomaly detection.

The overall detection performance in MOC is lower for all algorithms. There are 4 main factors that can cause the reduced accuracy in MOC: the number of collected metrics, dataset size, sampling frequency, and platform-related noise. To measure the impact of the difference in the metric set, we choose 53 metrics from the Volta dataset that are closest to the MOC metrics and re-run our analysis with the reduced metric set. This decreases F-score by 0.01 for SVC and kNN and poses no significant reduction for DT, RF, and AdaBoost. Next, we reduce the size of the Volta dataset and use 5 randomized application input data instead of 10. The combined F-score reduction due to reduced dataset size and metric set is around 0.02 except for DT, RF, and AdaBoost, where the F-score reduction is insignificant. We also measure the impact of data collection

Table 3. The most important 10 features selected by RF in MOC

Source	Feature
/proc/meminfo	std_free
/proc/meminfo	std_used
/proc/stat	avg_cpu_idle
vmstat	std_free_memory
/proc/meminfo	std_freeWOBuffersCaches
/proc/meminfo	std_used_percentage
vmstat	perc75_cpu_user
/proc/stat	max_cpu_idle
/proc/meminfo	std_usedWOBuffersCaches
/proc/stat	perc75_cpu_idle

Table 4. The most important 10 metrics selected by ST-Lan in MOC

Source	Metric
vmstat	cpu_user
/proc/stat	cpu_user
iostat	user
vmstat	cpu_idle
iostat	idle
vmstat	cpu_system
iostat	system
/proc/stat	cpu_system
/proc/meminfo	freeWOBuffersCaches
/proc/meminfo	usedWOBuffersCaches

period by increasing it to 5 s; however, the impact on classification accuracy is negligible. We believe that the reduction in accuracy in MOC mainly stems from the noise in the virtualized environment, caused by the interference due to VM consolidation and migration.

Considering both MOC and Volta results, our results indicate that RF is the best-performing algorithm with overall F-scores between 0.97 and 1.0 on both platforms, while the baselines have overall F-scores between 0.89 and 0.97.

6.2 Classification with Unknown Application Input Sizes

In a real-world scenario, we expect to encounter application input sizes other than those used during training. This can result in observing application resource usage and performance characteristics that are new to the anomaly detection algorithms. To evaluate the robustness of our approach against input sizes that have not been encountered before, we modify our training and test sets in our 5-fold cross validation, where we remove an unknown input size from all training sets and the other input sizes from all test sets. We repeat this procedure 3 times so that all input sizes are selected as the unknown size once. We also evaluate detection algorithms when two input sizes are simultaneously removed from the training sets, for all input size combinations.

Figure 5 presents the overall F-score achieved by anomaly detection algorithms for unknown input sizes. As we train the algorithms with a smaller variety of application input sizes, their effectiveness decrease as expected. In MOC, FP-Bodik's F-score decreases down to the majority voting level. However, the proposed machine learning approach consistently outperforms the baselines, with RF keeping its near-ideal accuracy in Volta.

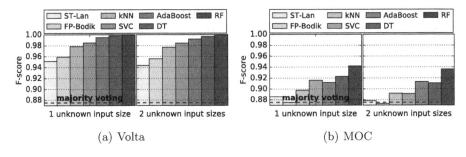

(a) Volta   (b) MOC

Fig. 5. Overall F-score when the training data excludes one or two input sizes and the testing is done using only the excluded input sizes

6.3   Classification with Unknown Applications

In order to evaluate how well our anomaly detection technique identifies anomaly characteristics independent of specific applications, we remove all runs of an application from the training sets, and then, remove all the other applications from the test sets. We repeat this procedure for all 5 applications we use.

Figure 6 shows the overall F-score of the detection algorithms for each unknown application. The most prominent result in the figure is that most algorithms have very poor classification accuracy in MOC when the unknown application is *ft*. Figure 7a illustrates how *ft* is different than other applications in terms of the most important two features used by DT to classify healthy runs. When not trained with *ft*, DT uses the threshold indicated by the dashed line to identify the majority of the healthy nodes, which results in most healthy *ft* nodes being marked as unhealthy. In Volta, however, the data has less noise due to the absence of VM interference and the number of metrics is significantly larger. Hence, DT is able to find more reliable features to classify healthy runs as depicted in Fig. 7b.

Figure 6 shows that the *F-score* of FP-Bodik also decreases significantly in both Volta and MOC when *ft* is the unknown application. This is because when

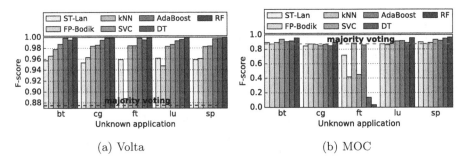

(a) Volta   (b) MOC

Fig. 6. Overall F-score when the training data excludes one application and the testing is done using only the excluded application

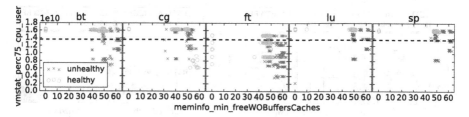

(a) MOC. When ft is excluded from the training set, DT classifies runs below the dashed line as unhealthy, which causes healthy ft nodes to be classified as unhealthy.

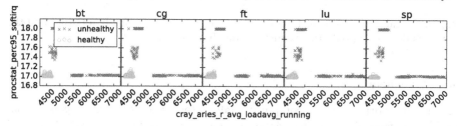

(b) Volta. The distinction between healthy and unhealthy clusters is clearly visible.

Fig. 7. The scatter plots of the datasets for the most important two features used by DT to classify healthy data.

not trained with *ft*, the generated fingerprint of the *memeater* anomaly by FP-Bodik is similar to the fingerprint of healthy *ft*, resulting in FP-Bodik marking healthy *ft* nodes as *memeater*.

These examples show that when the training set does not represent the expected application runtime characteristics, both our framework and the baseline algorithms may mislabel the nodes where unknown applications run. To avoid such problems, a diverse and representative set of applications should be used during training.

6.4   Classification with Unknown Anomaly Intensities

In this section, we evaluate the robustness of the anomaly detection algorithms when they encounter previously-unknown anomaly intensities. Thus, we train the algorithms with data collected when running with either high- or low-intensity anomalies test with the other intensity. Figure 8 shows the resulting F-scores in Volta and MOC environments. When the detection algorithms are trained with anomalies with high intensity, the thresholds placed by the algorithms are adjusted for highly anomalous behavior. Hence, when tested with low anomaly intensity, the algorithms misclassify some of the unhealthy nodes as healthy, leading to a slightly lower F-score. The baseline algorithms demonstrate a more robust behavior against unknown anomaly intensities compared to our approach except for RF, which outperforms the baselines on Volta and performs similarly on MOC when trained with low anomaly intensity.

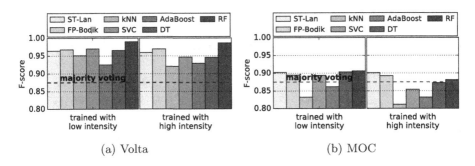

Fig. 8. Overall F-score when the training data excludes one anomaly intensity and the testing is done using only the excluded anomaly intensity

6.5 Overhead

In our framework, the most computationally intensive part is feature generation. Generating features for a 900-second time window in Volta, i.e., from a 48-thread server for 721 metrics with 1 s sampling period, takes 10.1 s on average using a single thread. This translates into 11 ms single-thread computational overhead per second to calculate features for the metrics collected from a 48-thread server. Assuming that these features are calculated on the server by monitoring agents, this corresponds to a total of $11/48 = 0.23$ ms computational overhead per second (0.02%) on Volta servers. Performing classification with trained machine learning algorithms takes approximately 10 ms and this overhead is negligible compared to application running times. With our implementations, the classification overheads of FP-Bodik and ST-Lan are 0.01% and below 0.01%, respectively. The training overhead of both the machine learning algorithms and the baseline algorithms is negligible as it can be done offline.

Regarding the storage savings, the data collected for a 4-node 15-minute run on Volta takes 6.2 MB as raw time series, and only 252 KB as features (4% of the raw data). This number can be further reduced for tree-based classifiers by storing only the features that are deemed to be important by the classifiers.

7 Conclusion and Future Work

Performance variation is an important factor that degrades efficiency and resiliency of HPC systems. Detection and diagnosis of the root causes of performance variation is a hard task due to the complexity and size of HPC systems. In this paper, we present an automated, low-overhead, and highly-accurate framework using machine learning for detection and identification of anomalies in HPC systems. We evaluate our proposed framework on two fundamentally different platforms and demonstrate that our framework is superior to other state-of-the-art approaches in detecting and diagnosing anomalies, and robust to previously unencountered applications and application characteristics.

In this work, we have focused on a subset of NPB applications, for which we have observed mostly flat profiles. As future work, we will explore runtime detection of anomalies considering applications that contain substantial variations in their resource usage. We are also planning to embed our solutions within the LDMS monitoring framework and evaluate our approach with a wider set of real-life applications.

Acknowledgments. This work has been partially funded by Sandia National Laboratories. Sandia National Laboratories is a multi-program laboratory managed and operated by Sandia Corporation, a wholly owned subsidiary of Lockheed Martin Corporation, for the U.S. Department of Energy's National Nuclear Security Administration under contract DE-AC04-94AL85000.

References

1. Cisco bug: Csctf52095 - manually flushing os cache during load impacts server. https://quickview.cloudapps.cisco.com/quickview/bug/CSCtf52095
2. Ganglia. ganglia.info
3. Massachusetts Open Cloud (MOC). http://info.massopencloud.org
4. MOC public code repository for kilo-puppet sensu modules. https://github.com/CCI-MOC/kilo-puppet/tree/liberty/sensu. Accessed 27 Oct 2016
5. Nagios. www.nagios.org
6. Agelastos, A., Allan, B., Brandt, J., Gentile, A., Lefantzi, S., Monk, S., Ogden, J., Rajan, M., Stevenson, J.: Toward rapid understanding of production HPC applications and systems. In: IEEE International Conference on Cluster Computing, pp. 464–473, September 2015
7. Agelastos, A., et al.: The lightweight distributed metric service: a scalable infrastructure for continuous monitoring of large scale computing systems and applications. In: Proceedings of the International Conference for High Performance Computing, Networking, Storage and Analysis (SC), pp. 154–165, November 2014
8. Bailey, D.H., et al.: The NAS parallel benchmarks - summary and preliminary results. In: Proceedings of the ACM/IEEE Conference on Supercomputing, pp. 158–165, August 1991
9. Baseman, E., Blanchard, S., Debardeleben, N., Bonnie, A., Morrow, A.: Interpretable anomaly detection for monitoring of high performance computing systems. In: Outlier Definition, Detection, and Description on Demand Workshop at ACM SIGKDD, San Francisco, August 2016
10. Berndt, D.J., Clifford, J.: Using dynamic time warping to find patterns in time series. In: Proceedings of the 3rd International Conference on Knowledge Discovery and Data Mining, vol. 10, pp. 359–370, August 1994
11. Bhatele, A., Titus, A.R., Thiagarajan, J.J., Jain, N., Gamblin, T., Bremer, P.T., Schulz, M., Kale, L.V.: Identifying the culprits behind network congestion. In: IEEE International Parallel and Distributed Processing Symposium (IPDPS), pp. 113–122, May 2015
12. Bhatele, A., Mohror, K., Langer, S.H., Isaacs, K.E.: There goes the neighborhood: performance degradation due to nearby jobs. In: SC, pp. 41:1–41:12, November 2013

13. Bodík, P., Fox, A., Jordan, M.I., Patterson, D., Banerjee, A., Jagannathan, R., Su, T., Tenginakai, S., Turner, B., Ingalls, J.: Advanced tools for operators at amazon.com. In: Proceedings of the First International Conference on Hot Topics in Autonomic Computing, June 2006

14. Bodik, P., Goldszmidt, M., Fox, A., Woodard, D.B., Andersen, H.: Fingerprinting the datacenter: automated classification of performance crises. In: Proceedings of the 5th European Conference on Computer Systems, pp. 111–124 (2010)

15. Brandt, J., et al.: Enabling advanced operational analysis through multi-subsystem data integration on trinity. In: Proceedings of the Cray User's Group (2015)

16. Brandt, J., Chen, F., De Sapio, V., Gentile, A., Mayo, J., Pebay, P., Roe, D., Thompson, D., Wong, M.: Quantifying effectiveness of failure prediction and response in HPC systems: methodology and example. In: Proceedings of the International Conference on Dependable Systems and Networks Workshops, pp. 2–7, June 2010

17. Brandt, J., Gentile, A., Mayo, J., Pébay, P., Roe, D., Thompson, D., Wong, M.: Methodologies for advance warning of compute cluster problems via statistical analysis: a case study. In: Proceedings of the 2009 Workshop on Resiliency in High Performance, pp. 7–14, June 2009

18. Dorier, M., Antoniu, G., Ross, R., Kimpe, D., Ibrahim, S.: Calciom: mitigating I/O interference in HPC systems through cross-application coordination. In: IPDPS, pp. 155–164, May 2014

19. Fronza, I., Sillitti, A., Succi, G., Terho, M., Vlasenko, J.: Failure prediction based on log files using random indexing and support vector machines. J. Syst. Softw. **86**(1), 2–11 (2013)

20. Fu, S.: Performance metric selection for autonomic anomaly detection on cloud computing systems. In: IEEE Global Telecommunications Conference, pp. 1–5, December 2011

21. Gainaru, A., Cappello, F., Snir, M., Kramer, W.: Fault prediction under the microscope: a closer look into HPC systems. In: SC, pp. 77:1–77:11, November 2012

22. Giannerini, S.: The quest for nonlinearity in time series. In: Handbook of Statistics: Time Series, vol. 30, pp. 43–63 (2012)

23. Guan, Q., Fu, S.: Adaptive anomaly identification by exploring metric subspace in cloud computing infrastructures. In: IEEE 32nd International Symposium on Reliable Distributed Systems, pp. 205–214, September 2013

24. Heien, E., LaPine, D., Kondo, D., Kramer, B., Gainaru, A., Cappello, F.: Modeling and tolerating heterogeneous failures in large parallel systems. In: SC, pp. 1–11, November 2011

25. Ibidunmoye, O., Hernández-Rodriguez, F., Elmroth, E.: Performance anomaly detection and bottleneck identification. ACM Comput. Surv. **48**(1), 4:1–4:35 (2015)

26. Kasick, M.P., Gandhi, R., Narasimhan, P.: Behavior-based problem localization for parallel file systems. In: Proceedings of the 6th Workshop on Hot Topics in System Dependability, October 2010

27. Lan, Z., Zheng, Z., Li, Y.: Toward automated anomaly identification in large-scale systems. IEEE Trans. Parallel Distrib. Syst. **21**(2), 174–187 (2010)

28. Leung, V.J., Phillips, C.A., Bender, M.A., Bunde, D.P.: Algorithmic support for commodity-based parallel computing systems. Technical report SAND2003-3702, Sandia National Laboratories (2003)

29. Pedregosa, F., et al.: Scikit-learn: machine learning in Python. J. Mach. Learn. Res. **12**, 2825–2830 (2011)

30. Sefraoui, O., Aissaoui, M., Eleuldj, M.: OpenStack: toward an open-source solution for cloud computing. Int. J. Comput. Appl. **55**(3), 38–42 (2012)

31. Skinner, D., Kramer, W.: Understanding the causes of performance variability in HPC workloads. In: IEEE International Symposium on Workload Characterization, pp. 137–149, October 2005
32. Snir, M., et al.: Addressing failures in exascale computing. Int. J. High Perform. Comput. Appl. **28**, 129–173 (2014)
33. Sterling, T., Becker, D.J., Savarese, D., Dorband, J.E., Ranawake, U.A., Packer, C.V.: Beowulf: a parallel workstation for scientific computation. In: Proceedings of the 24th International Conference on Parallel Processing, pp. 11–14 (1995)
34. Turk, A., Chen, H., Tuncer, O., Li, H., Li, Q., Krieger, O., Coskun, A.K.: Seeing into a public cloud: monitoring the Massachusetts open cloud. In: USENIX Workshop on Cool Topics on Sustainable Data Centers, March 2016
35. Wang, X., Smith, K., Hyndman, R.: Characteristic-based clustering for time series data. Data Min. Knowl. Disc. **13**(3), 335–364 (2006)
36. Wheelwright, S., Makridakis, S., Hyndman, R.J.: Forecasting: Methods and Applications. Wiley, Hoboken (1998)

Energy-Aware Computing

The Investigation of the ARMv7 and Intel Haswell Architectures Suitability for Performance and Energy-Aware Computing

Vojtech Nikl[✉], Michal Hradecky, Jakub Keleceni, and Jiri Jaros

IT4Innovations Centre of Excellence, Faculty of Information Technology,
Brno University of Technology, Bozetechova 2, 61200 Brno, Czech Republic
{inikl,jarosjir}@fit.vutbr.cz, hradec.m@gmail.com,
jakub.keleceni@gmail.com

Abstract. The reduction of the CPU frequency and voltage is a well-known approach to improve energy consumption of memory-bound applications. This is based on the conception that the performance of the main memory sees little or no degradation at reduced processor clock speeds while power consumption decreases significantly improving the overall energy efficiency. We study this effect on the Haswell generation of Intel Xeon processors as well as the ARMv7 generation of the 32-bit ARM big.LITTLE architecture. The goal is to analyse and compare computational performance, energy consumption and energy efficiency on a series of tasks, each focusing on different parts of the system and provide an analysis and generalisation to other similar architectures.

The benchmark suit consists of compute and memory intensive benchmarks as well as both single and multi-threaded scientific applications. The results show that frequency and voltage scaling can significantly improve algorithms' energy efficiency. Up to 2.5× on ARM and 1.5× on Intel compared to the maximum frequency. ARM is up to 2× more efficient than Intel.

Keywords: Haswell · ARMv7 · Odroid XU4 · k-Wave · LAMMPS · Energy efficiency

1 Introduction

Nowadays, the energy efficiency of modem processors is becoming more and more important next to the overall performance itself. Many programming tasks and problems do cannot use the hardware very efficiently due to being memory or communication-bound. Many clock cycles are wasted while waiting for data or a dependency conflict. Therefore, it is often not beneficial to use faster chips to achieve better runtimes. In this case, underclocking and undervolting, or employing slower low power processors or accelerators may be much more efficient. Mainly because of the possibility to get the same results using much less energy and often without any significant performance penalties.

© Springer International Publishing AG 2017
J.M. Kunkel et al. (Eds.): ISC High Performance 2017, LNCS 10266, pp. 377–393, 2017.
DOI: 10.1007/978-3-319-58667-0_20

An average Intel Xeon processor provides around 150–300 GFlop/s in double precision, with the Thermal Power Design (TDP) of 85–130 W. This gives roughly 2 GFlops/W of peak energy efficiency. These chips consist of about 6–18 cores being the most widely used CPUs in today's high performance clusters and supercomputers, according to the Top500[1] ladder.

Searching for even better efficiency, mobile ARM processors have attracted a lot of interest since their performance is comparable to the x86 CPUs. For example, an ARM based development board Nvidia Tegra X1[2] and its GPU can provide 512 GFlop/s while consuming only about 11 W of energy. This yields almost 50 GFlops/W in single precision.

The Green500[3] list provides a ranking of the most efficient supercomputers in the world. The most efficient machine reaches almost 10 GFlops/W using the nVidia DGX-1 system[4]. Current estimates indicate that processor efficiency will have to evolve to 50 GFlops/W for exascale machines to meet the realistic power budget of 20 MW.

Last but not least, an important reason to focus more on power efficiency is the resource allocation policy of supercomputing centers. Currently, resources are distributed among users based on core-hours. The energy efficiency of users' applications is defined simply by the runtime, faster is almost always more efficient. The processors are almost always running at the highest possible frequency, even when the application being executed may not fully utilise the processors' resources. This leads to a lot of wasted energy. However, due to rapidly increasing energy demands of modern clusters, the way the resources are allocated may change. Instead of using the core-hour metric, the users will be charged based on consumed kWhs. Hand to hand with this approach, users will be able to manually change hardware parameters such as frequency and voltage or shut down parts of the system. The SuperMUC[5] supercomputer already provides a frequency scaling options in the job scheduler for its users. The Taurus[6] supercomputer additionally allows users to change the processor frequency dynamically during job runtime. Taurus is able to measure the energy consumption of each of its Haswell nodes using a built-in FPGA probe. This is going to put much more emphasis on energy efficiency from both the software and hardware viewpoints. The hardware side will be much more dynamic and the ways to use provided resources as efficiently as possible will have to be exploited and optimised.

Much research effort in the area of the energy efficient computing makes use of the Dynamic Voltage and Frequency Scaling (DVFS) to improve energy efficiency [1,6,8,12]. The incentive is often that a system's main memory bandwidth is unaffected by reduced clock speeds, while the power consumption decreases significantly. The examples of memory-bound algorithms are sorting and searching

---

[1] https://www.top500.org/.

[2] http://www.nvidia.com/object/tegra-x1-processor.html.

[3] https://www.top500.org/green500/.

[4] http://www.nvidia.com/object/deep-learning-system.html.

[5] https://www.lrz.de/services/compute/supermuc/.

[6] https://doc.zih.tu-dresden.de/hpc-wiki/bin/view/Compendium/SystemTaurus.

algorithms, sparse vector-matrix algebra or multidimensional fast Fourier transforms, assuming the input data cannot fit into caches. These algorithms spend most of the time accessing the main memory and their compute intensity is often very low. Besides DVFS, another approach might be to switch off unneeded cores to save energy and let the others work at maximum frequency. However, this requires a direct hardware support.

This paper presents a study of DVFS and its impact on the energy efficiency. The investigated architectures are the latest Haswell generation of x86_64 Xeon systems from Intel and ARMv7 big.LITTLE architectures. A series of different benchmarks is tested, ranging from synthetic compute and memory ones to scientific applications.

2 Related Work

The Mont-Blanc project [10] based in Barcelona, Spain, has developed a high performance parallel system based on the ARMv7 architecture and its Cortex-A15 cores. The system was compared to a production supercomputer MareNostrum III composed of the Intel Xeon Sandy Bridge architecture. A single node of Mont-Blanc is $9\times$ slower while saving 40% energy. MPI applications are $3.5\times$ slower using the same number of processes, but consuming 9% less energy. A single node of Mont-Blanc consumes 5.3 W and 9.5 W while idle or load, respectively. Very similar architectures are compared in our paper, however, instead of focusing on MPI and GPUs, the emphasis is put on single-threaded and multi-threaded applications.

The READEX project [11] is improving energy efficiency of applications in the field of High Performance Computing by means of dynamic auto-tuning. This allows users to automatically exploit the dynamic behaviour of their applications by adjusting the hardware parameters to match the actual resource requirements. Their software consists of 3 main parts, the Periscope Tuning Framework (PTF) for design time analysis, the READEX Runtime Library (RRL) for tuning at runtime and the Score-P framework for the instrumentation and measurements of HPC applications. The outcome of the automatic READEX methodology is expected to be at least 50% of the manually achievable gains. Similarly to READEX, the goal is to analyse and find the optimal settings for a specific system running a given algorithm or its kernel. READEX exploits dynamism during the application's runtime on the Intel x86_64 architecture only. In this paper, a static frequency is set for each run.

Choi et al. [3] conducted a microbenchmarking study of the time, energy and power consumption on several existing platforms including modern GPUs, ARM (Arndale dual-core Cortex-A15) and Intel processors (Nehalem and mobile Ivy-Bridge) and an Intel Phi KNC accelerator. The dual-core ARM Cortex-A15 achieved 2.2 GFlops/W and 0.56 GB/W, Intel Nehalem achieved 0.62 GFlops/W and 0.14 GB/W using an architecture-specific hand-tuned benchmark. Our paper focuses only on the ARM and Intel x86 architectures, however, it provides a much wider set of benchmarks using actual scientific HPC applications.

Huang et al. [7] analyse the energy consumption of both the compute (HPL) and memory-bound (STREAM) problems on Haswell E5-2600 v3 architecture. The PAPI RAPL framework [14] is used to track the energy consumption of different parts of the system. The effect of different P-states, hyper-threading, socket power imbalance and core affinity on power consumption and performance were analysed. The results showed that different P-state settings provide up to 33% energy savings. Enabling the hyper-threading and core affinity improves energy efficiency by 19–48%. Minor power imbalances can be observed between the two sockets. Compiler optimisations improved the energy demands by 28.6%. Regarding to this paper, three different P-states are analysed in terms of performance and energy efficiency, threads and processes are always pinned to the cores, maximum compiler optimisations are used and a wider range of benchmarks is tested.

Hackenberg et al. [5] analyse a number of Haswell energy features, such as the enhanced RAPL implementation with better accuracy, integrated voltage and frequency regulators for each core, lower and unpredictable clock frequency for workloads with substantial amounts of AVX instructions and the P-state (voltage and frequency operation point) transition behaviour. The most important information for this paper is that RAPL measurements were verified using several microbenchmarks avoiding interference effects due to time synchronisation. The results show almost perfect correlation to the total system power consumption (AC) measured with high-accuracy power meter.

The contribution of our paper is the comparison of two architectures on a unique set of benchmarks. Two different methodologies are used for expressing the energy efficiency. A unique hardware setup of the Samsung Odroid-XU4[7] kit, based on a more powerful power supply, cooling and an accumulative power consumption sensor, is utilised.

3   Investigated Systems

The system configurations, all the benchmarks were run on, are summarised in Tables 1 and 2.

Table 1. Intel Haswell system hardware overview

Server	Supermicro 7048GR-TR	
Motherboard	Supermicro X10DRG-Q	
Processor	2× Intel Xeon E5-2620v3	TDP 2× 85 W, 2× 230.4 GFlop/s (SP, no Turbo), 2× 15 MB L3, 12× 256 KB L2, 12× 32 KB L1
RAM	2× 32 GB DDR4-2133	2× 59 GB/s, 2× 4 channels
Storage	SSD Crucial MX200 250 GB	

---

[7] http://www.hardkernel.com/main/products/prdt_info.php?g_code=G143452239825.

Table 2. Samsung ARMv7 system hardware overview

Device	Samsung Odroid-XU4	
Processor	Samsung Exynos5422 (4× Cortex-A15 + 4× Cortex-A7)	TDP ~15 W, 4 × 4 + 4 × 2.8 GFlop/s (SP) 2 × 2 MB L2, 8 × 32 KB L1
RAM	2 GB LPDDR3 933 MHz	14.9 GB/s, dual channel
Storage	eMMC5.0 HS400 Flash Storage	

The operating system was Ubuntu 16.04 on both systems.

On Intel, the energy measurements were taken using the **Intel Performance Counter Monitor**[8] and its **pcm-power** module, which can directly access the Running Average Power Limit Model Specific Registers (RAPL MSRs) of the CPU. It measures the energy consumption of three main components of each CPU - *package*, *powerplane* and *dram*. The package measures the whole socket including the memory controller. Powerplane only measures the cores themselves and dram measures the corresponding DRAM modules. The powerplane measurements are not supported by the Haswell architecture. The total power consumption in Watts was calculated as

$$package0 + dram0 + package1 + dram1 \tag{1}$$

The Samsung Odroid-XU4 kit does not support any hardware counters for measuring power consumption. The energy consumption was measured by the **KCX-017**[9] USB meter connected in-between the power supply and the power connector of the board to display actual electric voltage and current. The current is also accumulated into mAh used to manually calculate the overall energy consumption. Each benchmark ran long enough or was run multiple times in a loop to consume at least 20 mAh. The average deviation caused by reading the display manually is about 5 %.

The original Odroid power supply is not sufficient during high loads, the voltage dropped below 4.2 V and the kit got frozen. A programmable power supply **Diametral P230R51D**[10] was used instead.

The original cooler is also sufficient during high loads. It was replaced by **Primecooler PC-NBHP1**, originally used for motherboards' north bridges. The heat-conducting tape was replaced by the Arctic Ceramique paste. This dramatically improved the temperatures, however, due to the plastic heat spreader, 95 °C was often reached and the processor began throttling under High Performance Linpack at 2000 MHz on 4× Cortex-A15. This resulted in slightly poorer results in this particular test. All other tests performed within the range of safe temperatures and did not alter the performance. The complete hardware setup is shown in Fig. 1.

---

[8] https://software.intel.com/en-us/articles/intel-performance-counter-monitor.

[9] https://cdn.solarbotics.com/products/datasheets/kcx-017%20power%20bank%20testing.pdf.

[10] http://diametral.cz/ac-dc-zdroje/dc-regulovatelne-zdroje/laboratorni/laboratorni-zdroj-p230r51d-2x-030v/4a-1x-5v/3a.html.

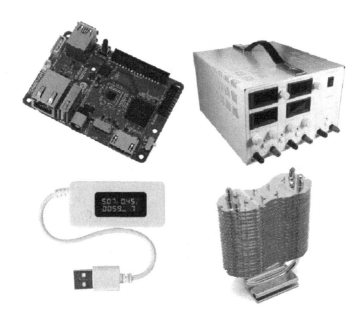

Fig. 1. A complete hardware setup for the Samsung Odroid-XU4 kit - the Diametral P230R51D power supply, the Primecooler PC-NBHP1 cooler and the KCX-017 power meter.

Our Haswell CPU supports frequencies ranging from 1.2 to 2.4 GHz, excluding the Intel Turbo boost. To be able to manually set a chosen frequency, the Intel P-state driver had to be replaced with the ACPI driver and the governor (power scheme for the CPU) was set from *balanced* to *userspace* using the system's **cpupower** utility. Similarly on Odroid, the **cpufreq-set** utility was used to change the frequency.

All the benchmarks were compiled using the **GNU Compiler Collection 5.3.0** compiler. The optimisation flags used for Haswell and ARM respectively were

$$-\texttt{O3} -\texttt{mavx2} -\texttt{mtune} = \texttt{native} -\texttt{march} = \texttt{native} \tag{2}$$

$$-\texttt{O3} -\texttt{mfpu} = \texttt{neon} - \texttt{vfpv4} -\texttt{mtune} = \texttt{cortex} - \texttt{a15} -\texttt{march} = \texttt{armv7} - \texttt{a} \tag{3}$$

On Haswell, three main frequencies for all the cores were chosen to be benchmarked, 1.2, 1.8 and 2.4 GHz. The Haswell architecture supports setting an individual frequency for each core, however, this feature is not utilised because all the benchmarks were run on all 2×6 cores. The single-threaded ones where the uniform frequency was set to keep the results comparable. Intel Turbo boost was turned off. Voltages for all frequencies were set automatically based on the default CPU stepping provided by Intel. On Odroid, 200, 800 and 1400 MHz were chosen for both A7 and A15, in addition to 2000 MHz for A15. The Exynos processor supports switching off all the cores except the first A7 core. However, using even a single core from either the A7 or A15 quadcore cluster keeps the whole cluster running. Therefore switching off the A15 cluster only proved beneficial. All benchmarks run on the A7 cluster were executed with the A15 cluster cores switched off to further isolate the A7 cores in terms of energy demands.

One parallel benchmark was parallelised using **OpenMPI 1.8.4**, the rest using OpenMP. Each MPI process was bound to its core using the **mpirun** binding arguments, non-MPI and serial processes were bound using the **taskset** system utility. If threading was used, each thread was bound to its core using the GOMP_CPU_AFFINITY variable. All data arrays were aligned using posix_memalign to 64 bytes, which is the cache line width on both architectures' memory.

The number of floating point operations of each test run was obtained using the **PAPI** [14] library and the PAPI_SP_OPS event for single precision and the PAPI_DP_OPS event for double precision floating point operations.

Two different metrics of understanding the energy demands are used in this paper called **the overall** and **the net**. The overall energy is the energy used by the whole system, in our case summing the RAPL readings from sockets and DRAMs on Haswell, or using the voltage and current readings from the USB meter on Odroid. The net energy is the overall energy minus the energy the system would require to run for the same amount of time in standby. This metric is marked ▼ in the following tables. For example, if the computation takes 10 s and the system's power consumption is 10 W under load and 2 W in idle, the overall energy demands are 100 Joules while the net energy demands are 80 Joules. This way, we can isolate the algorithm's energy requirements from the system's underlying overhead and also more accurately compare results across different architectures. Similar metrics are used in the READEX project [11].

4 Benchmarks

Three main groups of benchmarks were tested: synthetic ones focusing on CPU and memory, simple single-thread and parallel scientific applications.

The CPU's attainable performance was tested using the **High Performance Linpack 2.2** [4] compiled with the **ATLAS 3.10.3**[11] library. The compilation of ATLAS took over 24 h on a single Odroid kit. The memory and cache subsystem was benchmarked using **LMBench 3** [9], which can measure read/write bandwidth and latency on data of a chosen size.

The single-threaded benchmarks consisted of the **Linpack** benchmark, a recursive **quicksort**, an iterative **calculation of** π using a continued fraction, and a recursive **Fibonacci series** calculations. The quicksort focuses mainly on random data access and can be considered a memory-bound problem for large input data. The π calculation is a representative of common naive codes written by a non-HPC user. The Fibonacci series is similarly naive and focuses on the stack usage and its implementation.

The multi-threaded algorithms consisted of **LAMMPS** [2], a molecular dynamics simulator and its Fene bead/spring benchmark (polymer melt system with 32 000 atoms), the **k-Wave** toolbox [13], an ultrasound simulation

---

[11] http://math-atlas.sourceforge.net/.

toolkit based on a k-space pseudospectral method, and a 2D heat propagation algorithm using the 4th order Finite Difference Time Domain (FDTD) method in space and the 1st order in time.

5   Experimental Results

This section presents the results measured on both the Intel Haswell and ARMv7 architectures. Colours in tables represent the order of the particular result in a given group of results (red being the worst, yellow being the median and green being the best), tables with rows separated by a small vertical space have rows coloured separately.

5.1   Synthetic CPU and Memory Benchmarks

While Haswell being the most powerful CPU in the HPL benchmark, it is also the most energy efficient chip in both the overall and net parameters (see Fig. 2). Generally, an optimised compute-bound code which uses given resources efficiently should produce a low number of stalls and NOP operations. The static power is reduced by shorter runtimes and translating in a very good energy efficiency. Compute-bound problems are therefore not going to be very efficient on low power systems such as ARMs. Intel's more complex architecture is more preferred.

The LMBench memory benchmark shows the bandwidth of all level caches scales linearly with the frequency of the specific CPU (see Fig. 3 and the same data rearranged in Fig. 4b). This is expected, as the caches' frequency correspond to the core frequency of both architectures. In the main memory, Haswell looses only 4–5% bandwidth when downscaling the frequency by a factor of 2. The DRAM and memory controller frequency does not scale down with the CPU, which should be a considerable advantage mainly in memory-bound problems. On ARM, however, the DRAM bandwidth starts to decrease significantly once the CPU frequency drops below the DRAM frequency, which is 933 MHz. Above this point, the bandwidth is almost independent on the CPU frequency scaling showing only a slight drop probably due to an imperfect clock divider.

Comparing the maximum overall bandwidth of a dual-socket Haswell, A15 and A7 quadcores, Haswell is 7× faster in L1 cache, 15× faster in the last level cache and 20× faster in the main memory than A15. A15 is 4× faster in

	4x Cortex-A7			4x Cortex-A15				2x 6-core Xeon E5-2620v3		
	200MHz	800MHz	1400MHz	200MHz	800MHz	1400MHz	2000MHz	1200MHz	1800MHz	2400MHz
GFlop/s	0.293	1.15	1.98	1.21	4.77	7.68	9.34	201	251	300
GFlops/W	0.111	0.316	0.458	0.563	0.923	0.895	0.532	1.37	1.54	1.47
GFlops/W ▼	1.10	1.45	1.47	1.50	2.23	1.46	0.686	2.20	2.23	1.95

worst ▬▬▬▬▬▬ best (each row coloured separately)

Fig. 2. Performance, overall and net energy efficiency for High Performance Linpack. (Color figure online)

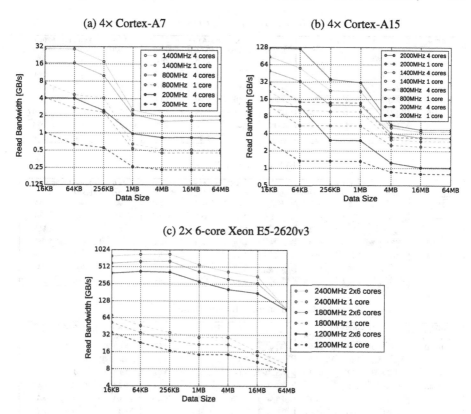

Fig. 3. Bandwidth comparison of memory and cache data read using LMBench.

L1 cache, $2\times$ faster in L2 cache and $2.5\times$ faster in the main memory than A7. These numbers roughly correspond to the differences in power consumption and theoretical performance of the CPU.

The single-core bandwidth shows that Haswell's performance drops almost $10\times$ across all cache levels and the main memory compared to employing all the 2×6 cores. At least 10 cores is necessary to fully saturate the data transfers. Lowering the frequency also negatively impacts the performance much more prominently. On ARM, the caches' bandwidth drops by a factor of unused cores, however, the main memory bandwidth reaches almost 70% compared to using all cores. Using 2 cores (not shown in the tables) saturates the main memory by almost 90% on both Cortexes. This fact could be exploited on appropriate ARM architectures in heavy memory-bound applications where most of the cores could be switched off to improve energy-efficiency without significant performance penalties.

The overall energy efficiency is presented in Fig. 4c. As long as data sits in caches, the lowest frequency of Haswell performs the best, followed by A15 on 1400 MHz and A7 on its maximum 1400 MHz. In the main memory, both Cortexes are the most efficient right around the frequency of their DRAM

(a) Bandwidth (single core)

GB/s	1x Cortex-A7			1x Cortex-A15				1x 1-core Xeon E5-2620v3		
Data Size	200MHz	800MHz	1400MHz	200MHz	800MHz	1400MHz	2000MHz	1200MHz	1800MHz	2400MHz
16 KB	1.01	4.12	7.32	2.87	11.9	21.8	29.8	35.3	52.9	70.6
64 KB	0.633	2.73	4.66	1.34	5.52	10.4	14.4	23.3	35.0	46.6
256 KB	0.553	2.29	4.10	1.33	5.48	9.63	13.8	17.0	25.5	35.2
1 MB	0.261	0.536	0.643	1.32	5.46	9.60	13.7	14.4	21.7	29.0
4 MB	0.230	0.450	0.518	0.853	2.51	3.15	3.45	14.5	21.7	29.0
16 MB	0.230	0.454	0.516	0.790	2.38	2.95	3.38	10.7	14.0	16.4
64 MB	0.229	0.455	0.516	0.794	2.33	2.96	3.38	7.3	8.4	9.9

(b) Bandwidth (all cores)

GB/s	4x Cortex-A7			4x Cortex-A15				2x 6-core Xeon E5-2620v3		
Data Size	200MHz	800MHz	1400MHz	200MHz	800MHz	1400MHz	2000MHz	1200MHz	1800MHz	2400MHz
16 KB	4.08	16.6	29.2	12.2	49.9	87.5	125.0	395	592	790
64 KB	4.05	16.5	29.1	11.8	32.9	55.9	121.7	424	635	847
256 KB	2.45	10.0	17.6	3.06	12.5	22.5	35.3	413	643	858
1 MB	0.974	2.12	2.53	3.04	12.4	21.8	31.2	281	420	557
4 MB	0.835	1.62	1.95	1.24	4.03	5.09	5.65	205	310	419
16 MB	0.838	1.66	1.97	1.02	3.39	4.28	4.68	176	264	348
64 MB	0.816	1.70	2.00	1.02	3.39	4.31	4.68	89.1	91.8	92.5

(c) Overall energy efficiency (all cores)

GB/W	4x Cortex-A7			4x Cortex-A15				2x 6-core Xeon E5-2620v3		
Data Size	200MHz	800MHz	1400MHz	200MHz	800MHz	1400MHz	2000MHz	1200MHz	1800MHz	2400MHz
16 KB	2.39	7.92	12.0	3.58	10.8	13.2	9.17	14.9	10.6	8.00
64 KB	2.33	8.30	11.5	3.52	7.12	8.12	9.31	15.5	11.0	8.37
256 KB	1.34	4.77	6.91	0.917	2.94	3.67	3.01	14.9	11.1	8.43
1 MB	0.490	0.913	0.975	0.954	2.73	3.30	2.61	9.14	6.56	4.96
4 MB	0.389	0.701	0.763	0.348	0.865	0.868	0.624	6.04	4.19	3.11
16 MB	0.396	0.777	0.698	0.284	0.694	0.653	0.512	4.10	2.60	2.24
64 MB	0.417	0.745	0.746	0.275	0.740	0.739	0.513	0.411	0.324	0.263

(d) Net energy efficiency (all cores)

GB/W ▼	4x Cortex-A7			4x Cortex-A15				2x 6-core Xeon E5-2620v3		
Data Size	200MHz	800MHz	1400MHz	200MHz	800MHz	1400MHz	2000MHz	1200MHz	1800MHz	2400MHz
16 KB	31.8	39.9	44.3	22.4	31.2	26.6	12.9	20.9	18.1	16.0
64 KB	39.0	42.7	39.2	23.3	20.8	15.7	13.3	21.7	18.8	16.7
256 KB	12.8	24.2	22.9	6.37	10.2	8.06	4.51	20.9	18.9	16.9
1 MB	2.77	3.33	3.09	9.48	8.21	6.65	3.89	12.8	11.2	9.91
4 MB	1.63	2.60	2.50	1.78	2.48	2.01	1.10	8.45	7.12	6.23
16 MB	1.73	3.66	1.89	1.39	1.83	1.33	0.895	5.74	4.42	4.48
64 MB	2.54	2.82	2.21	1.18	2.20	1.72	0.900	0.644	0.609	0.579

worst ▮▮▮▮▮▮▮▮▮▮▮ best (each row coloured separately)

Fig. 4. Memory and cache data read bandwidth and energy efficiency using LMBench. (Color figure online)

module (933 MHz). Dropping the frequency any lower results in a very poor efficiency mainly because of the increasingly prominent drop in bandwidth, and also because the static power becoming dominant as the computing time increases.

Figure 4d shows the net energy efficiency. This metric almost completely suppresses the effect of static power and computing time on the energy demands.

Lower frequencies become more favourable and even the lowest frequency is very often the most efficient one on all architectures. This metric suits both Cortexes better. The more efficient A7 as its overhead of the static power is more prominent due to the whole kit being measured for energy demands whereas only sockets' and DRAMs' hardware counters are taken into account on Haswell.

5.2   Single-Threaded Algorithms

All benchmarks run on a single core only (performance in Fig. 5) and therefore the overhead energy (mainly the static power) becomes much more significant (upper blue-coloured bars in Fig. 6). The overall energy (upper blue and bottom green bar pairs) is the lowest at the maximum frequency on all architectures except A15 being a bit more efficient calculating the Fibonacci and quicksort benchmarks on 1400 MHz. The cause is, similarly to the previous synthetic benchmarks but even more noticeable in this case, the static power of the system. Having only one core working and the other ones idling, the static power becomes the most dominant energy consumer and any decrease in frequency only prolongs the runtime and the system energy overhead problem.

The net energy, shown as green bars, can benefit from frequency scaling because it suppresses the effect of the static power, specifically on Intel, where each frequency drop results in a linear decrease in power demands. A15 is the most efficient around 800–1400 MHz and A7 at 800 MHz. A7 is overall the most efficient core.

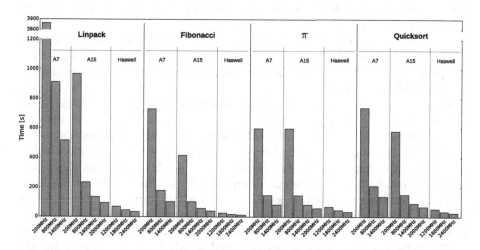

Fig. 5. Performance of single-threaded algorithms - Linpack using 4096 repetitions on 512×512 grid, recursive Fibonacci series calculating the 47th element, π calculation iteratively for 5×10^9 iterations and recursive quicksort sorting 150 000 000 elements. (Color figure online)

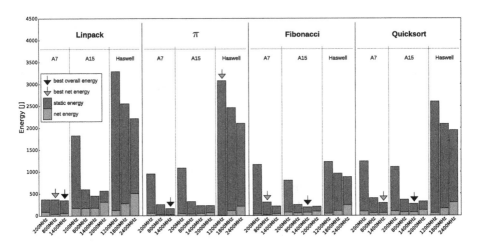

Fig. 6. Energy efficiency of single-threaded algorithms (bottom green part shows the net energy, blue and green together the overall, green arrow points to the lowest net energy of a given benchmark, black arrows points to the lowest overall energy) - Linpack using 4096 repetitions on 512×512 grid, recursive Fibonacci series calculating the 47th element, π calculation iteratively for 5×10^9 iterations and recursive quicksort sorting 150 000 000 elements. (Color figure online)

5.3 Multi-threaded Algorithms

The last group of benchmarks represents parallel algorithms corresponding to common HPC workloads.

The k-Wave toolbox [13] is based on the k-space pseudospectral method, which is characterised by high accuracy, fast convergence and a low number of grid points per wavelength. The 3D fast Fourier transforms are computed using the FFTW[12] 3.3.4 library.

Performance-wise, Haswell achieves more than 50 GFlop/s, which is about 15% of Linpack's performance. A15 is capable of almost 2.9 GFlop/s, almost a third of Linpack, and A7 achieves 0.85 Gflop/s, almost half of Linpack's performance. The CPUs are limited by the main memory bandwidth, and as the less powerful architecture is used, the performance is much closer to its theoretical limit. This can be observed even more prominently on the FDTD method.

Figure 7b shows all three CPUs behaving similarly in terms of the peak energy efficiency, achieving around 0.3 GFlops/W, A15 being the most efficient running at 800 MHz. Intel's efficiency drops considerably using the prime domain size of 257^3 (which is the worst case scenario and should be avoided), breaking the vectorisation and memory access patterns. Since the code is unable to be vectorised on ARM, because the FFTW library did not provide a support for Neon vectorisation at the time of writing this paper, A15's and A7's drops are not so significant.

---

[12] http://www.fftw.org/.

(a) Performance

GFlop/s	4x Cortex-A7			4x Cortex-A15				2x 6-core Xeon E5-2620v3		
Grid Size	200MHz	800MHz	1400MHz	200MHz	800MHz	1400MHz	2000MHz	1200MHz	1800MHz	2400MHz
128³ (112 MB)	0.140	0.527	0.847	0.352	1.33	2.10	2.66	29.3	36.8	43.8
256³ (896 MB)	0.146	0.483	0.755	0.382	1.46	2.08	2.88	33.2	44.3	51.8
257³ (907 MB)	0.063	0.250	0.446	0.144	0.571	0.955	1.29	2.91	4.87	6.15

(b) Overall energy efficiency

GFlops/W	4x Cortex-A7			4x Cortex-A15				2x 6-core Xeon E5-2620v3		
Grid Size	200MHz	800MHz	1400MHz	200MHz	800MHz	1400MHz	2000MHz	1200MHz	1800MHz	2400MHz
128³ (112 MB)	0.074	0.223	0.284	0.148	0.332	0.304	0.174	0.295	0.283	0.290
256³ (896 MB)	0.074	0.189	0.253	0.163	0.373	0.330	0.200	0.296	0.262	0.229
257³ (907 MB)	0.035	0.113	0.155	0.065	0.165	0.162	0.096	0.030	0.044	0.042

(c) Net energy efficiency

GFlops/W ▼	4x Cortex-A7			4x Cortex-A15				2x 6-core Xeon E5-2620v3		
Grid Size	200MHz	800MHz	1400MHz	200MHz	800MHz	1400MHz	2000MHz	1200MHz	1800MHz	2400MHz
128³ (112 MB)	0.575	0.732	0.681	0.536	0.605	0.429	0.211	0.561	0.445	0.421
256³ (896 MB)	0.451	0.526	0.608	0.617	0.698	0.485	0.247	0.509	0.363	0.290
257³ (907 MB)	0.371	0.432	0.390	0.296	0.348	0.246	0.121	0.059	0.077	0.061

worst ▬▬▬ best

Fig. 7. The k-Wave simulation toolbox (the k-space pseudospectral method). (Color figure online)

	4x Cortex-A7			4x Cortex-A15				2x 6-core Xeon E5-2620v3		
	200MHz	800MHz	1400MHz	200MHz	800MHz	1400MHz	2000MHz	1200MHz	1800MHz	2400MHz
GFlop/s	0.046	0.142	0.191	0.080	0.265	0.374	0.439	2.93	4.21	5.10
GFlops/W	0.023	0.057	0.062	0.037	0.073	0.067	0.039	0.042	0.044	0.042
GFlops/W ▼	0.132	0.177	0.140	0.130	0.136	0.103	0.051	0.125	0.094	0.070

worst ▬▬▬ best (each row coloured separately)

Fig. 8. Performance (double precision), overall and net energy efficiency comparison using the LAMMPS molecular dynamics simulator and its Fene benchmark. (Color figure online)

k-Wave's net energy efficiency (Fig. 7c) shows A7 as the most efficient at 800 MHz, followed by A15 also at 800 MHz and Haswell at 1200 MHz. Haswell is much closer to ARM compared to the FDTD method mainly because the raw performance is much higher using k-Wave.

LAMMPS is the only benchmark presented using MPI instead of a threading and double precision floating point arithmetic. The main difference is that ARMv7 does not support the double precision vectorisation, its 128-bit NEON registers support only a single precision. LAMMPS is a typical example of a problem with mutual interactions of a high number of independent and relatively simple elements. The performance of this algorithm class is often lower, however it should theoretically benefit even more from frequency scaling and the usage of low power architectures.

Performance-wise (see Fig. 8), Haswell achieves more than 5 GFlop/s, while A15 is about 11× slower and A7 is roughly 25× slower. Overall energy efficiency on A15 and A7 is about 1.5–2× better than on Haswell, which is the biggest difference of all the presented benchmarks. Net energy efficiency is the best on A7, followed by A15 and Haswell being the least efficient.

(a) Performance

GFlop/s	4x Cortex-A7			4x Cortex-A15				2x 6-core Xeon E5-2620v3		
Grid Size	200MHz	800MHz	1400MHz	200MHz	800MHz	1400MHz	2000MHz	1200MHz	1800MHz	2400MHz
128^2 (256KB)	0.238	0.990	1.75	0.475	1.95	3.42	4.81	10.2	12.9	16.0
256^2 (1MB)	0.219	0.846	1.34	0.479	1.98	3.44	4.91	11.5	16.8	22.3
512^2 (4MB)	0.171	0.637	1.04	0.320	1.24	1.89	2.20	10.5	16.1	20.0
1024^2 (16MB)	0.112	0.439	0.731	0.209	0.802	1.29	1.53	9.15	15.0	19.8

(b) Overall energy efficiency

GFlops/W	4x Cortex-A7			4x Cortex-A15				2x 6-core Xeon E5-2620v3		
Grid Size	200MHz	800MHz	1400MHz	200MHz	800MHz	1400MHz	2000MHz	1200MHz	1800MHz	2400MHz
128^2 (256KB)	0.135	0.485	0.651	0.223	0.561	0.551	0.338	0.156	0.164	0.173
256^2 (1MB)	0.120	0.396	0.470	0.222	0.581	0.547	0.319	0.174	0.210	0.234
512^2 (4MB)	0.097	0.301	0.366	0.140	0.343	0.319	0.178	0.162	0.201	0.208
1024^2 (16MB)	0.061	0.205	0.257	0.094	0.237	0.241	0.142	0.140	0.185	0.200

(c) Net energy efficiency

GFlops/W ▼	4x Cortex-A7			4x Cortex-A15				2x 6-core Xeon E5-2620v3		
Grid Size	200MHz	800MHz	1400MHz	200MHz	800MHz	1400MHz	2000MHz	1200MHz	1800MHz	2400MHz
128^2 (256KB)	1.07	2.20	1.76	1.07	1.19	0.819	0.413	0.527	0.454	0.375
256^2 (1MB)	0.787	1.55	1.15	1.03	1.26	0.807	0.383	0.576	0.563	0.490
512^2 (4MB)	0.766	1.20	0.902	0.538	0.698	0.485	0.226	0.559	0.539	0.434
1024^2 (16MB)	0.363	0.797	0.633	0.397	0.518	0.389	0.186	0.472	0.483	0.403

worst ▬▬▬▬▬▬▬ best

Fig. 9. The Finite Difference Time Domain method - 4th order in space, 1st order in time. (Color figure online)

The FDTD's performance overview is shown in Fig. 9a. FDTD is an example of a memory-bound problem because the number of operations per one byte of data is relatively low characterised by local data sharing only (no global information is needed), good scalability and a low number of cache misses.

In terms of performance, the dual-socket Haswell is almost 4–5× faster than A15, which is 2–3× more powerful than A7. While in the HPL benchmark, Haswell was more than 30× faster than A15, the difference in memory-bound applications shrinks quite dramatically. The 512^2 domain size does not fit into the L2 cache (two separate matrices are allocated for even and odd iterations and two matrices for heat conductivity properties of each point) of both Cortexes (2 MB) and the performance drop is quite radical. However, in the case of Haswell, exceeding the L3 cache size (15 MB) with the 1024^2 domain size does not hinder the performance. The 2048^2 and 4096^2 sizes were also tested (not shown in the table for the sake of brevity) and the performance stayed around the 20 GFlop/s mark, most likely because of the help of prefetcher.

Figure 9b displays the energy efficiency across all CPUs and domain sizes. A7 is the most efficient, capable of more than 0.6 GFlops/W running at 1400 MHz. A15's best frequency is between 800–1400 MHz, for Intel it is its highest - 2400 MHz.

The net energy efficiency, presented in Fig. 9c, shows A7 as the most efficient reaching 2.2 GFlops/W running at 800 MHz. A15 is about half as efficient as A7, running the most efficiently at 800 MHz. Intel is the least efficient giving best results at its lowest frequency - 1200 MHz.

6   Conclusion

In this paper, the effect of voltage and frequency scaling on performance and energy efficiency was studied comparing the Intel Xeon Haswell and ARMv7 big.LITTLE architectures. Two different techniques for measuring energy efficiency were presented, the overall and the net, isolating only the algorithm's energy demands.

The results showed that frequency scaling can bring significant energy savings mainly on the ARM architecture (1.5–2× on the optimal frequency compared to the maximum one). While Intel processors can also benefit from the frequency scaling, the profit is not so significant due to the higher energy demands for the rest of the system (the static power), mainly the DRAM modules and also lower flexibility regarding the frequency range.

The Samsung Odroid-XU4 board on the other hand provides a very flexible range of frequencies and a much lower energy overhead required to power the system around the processor. Overall, the lower range of frequencies does not prove to be efficient on any set of benchmarks. The "sweet spot" for both the Cortex-A7 and Cortex-A15 quadcores lies around the frequency of its DRAM, which is 933 MHz, providing better energy efficiency than the Haswell processors.

In High Performance Linpack, the peak performance of the dual-socket Haswell is 30× better than the Cortex-A15 quadcore. However, in parallel scientific applications, the difference shrank to about 5–15×, which results in a better performance to purchase price ratio in favour of ARM ($70 for the ARM kit vs. 2× $500 for only the Haswell processors).

Table 3 presents a 10-year lifetime comparison of all architectures running the LAMMPS simulator using the most energy-efficient setting. For ∼30× more energy consumed, Haswell provides ∼20× better performance.

Table 4 shows a complete comparison of all architectures and benchmarks relative to 4× Cortex-A15. For each benchmark, each architecture runs at the most overall energy-efficient frequency, and then, using the same frequency, the performance is compared. For example, in the HPL benchmark Haswell provides 1.67× more GFlops per Watt, while the performance is 52.6× better (251 GFlop/s at 1800 MHz vs. 4.77 GFlop/s at 800 MHz). The dual-socket Haswell is the most energy efficient in the synthetic benchmarks - HPL and LMBench, on average the efficiency is 0.66× worse than A15's for 14.1× better performance. Overall, Odroid is more energy-efficient in most of the presented benchmarks, but for the price of a significant performance drop.

Table 3. 10-year lifetime comparison running LAMMPS using the most overall energy-efficient setting (A7 1400 MHz, A15 800 MHz, Haswell 1800 MHz), considering €0.2 for 1 kWh.

Processor	Energy [MJ]	Electricity costs [€]	PFlops
4× Cortex-A7	0.975	194	60.2
4× Cortex-A15	1.16	232	83.6
2 × 6 Haswell	29 900	5 970	1 330

Table 4. Comparison of the overall energy efficiency and performance relative to $4\times$ Cortex-A15. For each benchmark and architecture, the most energy efficient frequency is chosen. The same frequency is then used to compare performance (higher number is better).

Algorithm	Overall energy efficiency			Performance		
	$4 \times$ A7	$4 \times$ A15	2×6 Haswell	$4 \times$ A7	$4 \times$ A15	2×6 Haswell
HPL	0.496	1	1.67	0.415	1	52.6
LMBench 16 KB (L1)	0.909	1	1.13	0.334	1	4.51
LMBench 1 MB (L2)	0.295	1	1.83	0.116	1	9.41
LMBench 64 MB (Main)	1.01	1	0.555	0.588	1	26.3
Linpack (single core)	1.29	1	0.204	0.259	1	3.04
Fibonacci (single core)	1.42	1	0.109	0.398	1	3.18
π (single core)	0.904	1	0.221	1.01	1	2.47
Quicksort (single core)	0.931	1	0.137	0.668	1	3.38
k-Wave 128^3	0.855	1	0.889	0.637	1	22.5
k-Wave 256^3	0.678	1	0.796	0.517	1	22.7
k-Wave 257^3	0.939	1	0.267	0.781	1	8.53
LAMMPS	0.849	1	0.603	0.721	1	15.9
FDTD 128^2	1.16	1	0.308	0.897	1	8.21
FDTD 256^2	0.809	1	0.403	0.677	1	11.3
FDTD 512^2	1.07	1	0.606	0.839	1	16.1
FDTD 1024^2	1.07	1	0.833	0.567	1	15.3
Average	0.918	1	0.660	0.589	1	14.1

The results presented in this paper can be used to save energy on similar systems. However, our study focuses only on single shared memory "nodes", leaving further measurements of power and energy on similar distributed systems for future work, which will focus on distributed ARMv8 clusters provided by the Mont-Blanc project.

Acknowledgement. This work was supported by The Ministry of Education, Youth and Sports of the Czech Republic from the National Programme of Sustainability (NPU II); project IT4Innovations excellence in science LQ1602. This work was also supported by the FIT-S-17-3994 Advanced parallel and embedded computer systems project.

References

1. Choi, K., Soma, R., Pedram, M.: Dynamic voltage and frequency scaling based on workload decomposition. In: Proceedings of the 2004 International Symposium on Low Power Electronics and Design, ISLPED 2004, pp. 174–179, August 2004
2. Cha, K.: Performance evaluation of LAMMPS on multi-core systems. In: High Performance Computing and Communications 2013 IEEE International Conference on Embedded and Ubiquitous Computing (HPCC_EUC), pp. 812–819, November 2013

3. Choi, J., Dukhan, M., Liu, X., Vuduc, R.: Algorithmic time, energy, and power on candidate HPC compute building blocks. In: Proceedings of the 2014 IEEE 28th International Parallel and Distributed Processing Symposium, IPDPS 2014, pp. 447–457. IEEE Computer Society, Washington, DC (2014). http://dx.doi.org/10.1109/IPDPS.2014.54
4. Davies, T., Karlsson, C., Liu, H., Ding, C., Chen, Z.: High performance Linpack benchmark: a fault tolerant implementation without checkpointing. In: Proceedings of the International Conference on Supercomputing, ICS 2011, pp. 162–171. ACM, New York (2011). http://doi.acm.org/10.1145/1995896.1995923
5. Hackenberg, D., Schöne, R., Ilsche, T., Molka, D., Schuchart, J., Geyer, R.: An energy efficiency feature survey of the Intel Haswell processor. In: 2015 IEEE International Parallel and Distributed Processing Symposium Workshop (IPDPSW), pp. 896–904, May 2015
6. Hsu, C., Feng, W.: A power-aware run-time system for high-performance computing. In: Proceedings of the ACM/IEEE SC 2005 Conference on Supercomputing, p. 1, November 2005
7. Huang, S., Lang, M., Pakin, S., Fu, S.: Measurement and characterization of Haswell power and energy consumption. In: Proceedings of the 3rd International Workshop on Energy Efficient Supercomputing, E2SC 2015, pp. 7:1–7:10. ACM, New York (2015). http://doi.acm.org/10.1145/2834800.2834807
8. Liang, W.Y., Chen, S.C., Chang, Y.L., Fang, J.P.: Memory-aware dynamic voltage and frequency prediction for portable devices. In: 2008 14th IEEE International Conference on Embedded and Real-Time Computing Systems and Applications, pp. 229–236, August 2008
9. McVoy, L., Staelin, C.: lmbench: portable tools for performance analysis. In: Proceedings of the 1996 Annual Conference on USENIX Annual Technical Conference, ATEC 1996, p. 23. USENIX Association, Berkeley (1996). http://dl.acm.org/citation.cfm?id=1268299.1268322
10. Rajovic, N., et al.: The mont-blanc prototype: an alternative approach for HPC systems. In: SC 16 (2016)
11. Schuchart, J., Gerndt, M., Kjeldsberg, P.G., Lysaght, M., Horák, D., Říha, L., Gocht, A., Sourouri, M., Kumaraswamy, M., Chowdhury, A., Jahre, M., Diethelm, K., Bouizi, O., Mian, U.S., Kružík, J., Sojka, R., Beseda, M., Kannan, V., Bendifallah, Z., Hackenberg, D., Nagel, W.E.: The readex formalism for automatic tuning for energy efficiency. Computing 1–19 (2017). http://dx.doi.org/10.1007/s00607-016-0532-7
12. Spiliopoulos, V., Kaxiras, S., Keramidas, G.: Green governors: a framework for continuously adaptive DVFS. In: 2011 International Green Computing Conference and Workshops (IGCC), pp. 1–8, July 2011
13. Treeby, B.E., Cox, B.T.: k-Wave: MATLAB toolbox for the simulation and reconstruction of photoacoustic wave-fields. J. Biomed. Opt. **15**(2), 021314 (2010)
14. Weaver, V.M., Johnson, M., Kasichayanula, K., Ralph, J., Luszczek, P., Terpstra, D., Moore, S.: Measuring energy and power with PAPI. In: 2012 41st International Conference on Parallel Processing Workshops, pp. 262–268, September 2012

Global Extensible Open Power Manager: A Vehicle for HPC Community Collaboration on Co-Designed Energy Management Solutions

Jonathan Eastep[✉], Steve Sylvester, Christopher Cantalupo, Brad Geltz,
Federico Ardanaz, Asma Al-Rawi, Kelly Livingston, Fuat Keceli,
Matthias Maiterth, and Siddhartha Jana

Power Pathfinding to Product (P3) Team, Data Center Group,
Intel Corporation, Hillsboro, OR, USA
jonathan.m.eastep@intel.com

Abstract. The power scaling challenge associated with Exascale systems is a well-known issue. In this work, we introduce the Global Extensible Open Power Manager (GEOPM): a tree-hierarchical, open source runtime framework we are contributing to the HPC community to foster increased collaboration and accelerated progress toward software-hardware co-designed energy management solutions that address Exascale power challenges and improve performance and energy efficiency in current systems. Through its plugin extensible architecture, GEOPM enables rapid prototyping of new energy management strategies. Different plugins can be tailored to the specific performance or energy efficiency priorities of each HPC center. To demonstrate the potential of the framework, this work develops an example plugin for GEOPM. This power rebalancing plugin targets power-capped systems and improves efficiency by minimizing job time-to-solution within a power budget. Our results demonstrate up to 30% improvements in the time-to-solution of CORAL system procurement benchmarks on a Xeon Phi cluster.

1 Introduction

Performance of future large-scale HPC systems will be constrained by power costs. Some HPC centers are already incentivized through government taxes to operate their systems at more energy-efficient points below peak performance and power [3]. Others may prefer peak performance today, but they face cost-pressure of a different kind to deploy more efficient systems in the future: system power draw is increasing by a substantial factor generation-over-generation, and without a breakthrough in system energy efficiency, industry trends forewarn that large-scale systems will exceed the limits of the existent power delivery infrastructure at typical centers by a 2–3× margin by 2022. This forces costly upgrades or limited system scale. Overcoming the 2–3× gap will require co-designed hardware and software system energy management solutions as well as increased collaboration between hardware vendors and the HPC software community.

© Springer International Publishing AG 2017
J.M. Kunkel et al. (Eds.): ISC High Performance 2017, LNCS 10266, pp. 394–412, 2017.
DOI: 10.1007/978-3-319-58667-0_21

In this paper, we introduce the Global Extensible Open Power Manager (GEOPM). GEOPM is an open source, plugin extensible runtime for power management. The primary goal of the project is to provide an open platform for community collaboration and research on co-designed energy management solutions to close the energy efficiency gap. We demonstrate a power rebalancing plugin for GEOPM targeting power-constrained systems which leverages feedback from the application to identify which nodes are on the critical path then adjusts processor power cap settings to accelerate the critical path and improve the application's time-to-solution. Subject to the power cap it is given, each processor attempts to maximize its performance while our software provides coordination of power budgets (and thus performance) across nodes. Through this marriage of software and hardware management of power and performance, we obtain up to 30% improvements in time-to-solution for CORAL procurement benchmarks on a power-constrained Knights Landing system.

In contributing this paper and the first plugin for GEOPM, we have taken a significant step toward closing the 2–3× energy efficiency gap. Much community collaboration will be required to close the remainder. For example, hardware vendors will need to provide improved or new software-tunable knobs in the future; GEOPM is influencing research along these lines at Intel. Additionally, the HPC software community will need to expose tunable knobs from various software layers to GEOPM (e.g. the application, runtime, system software, or operating system layers). Fully leveraging these knobs will require algorithmic advances in GEOPM and extensions enabling it to target different knobs than are supported today. These extensions will be developed in collaboration with the HPC community and will be added to GEOPM via plugins over time.

The GEOPM runtime framework is being developed for broad deployment on Xeon, Xeon Phi, and other HPC system architectures. The first deployment is expected on the Theta system, a Knights Landing Xeon Phi system at Argonne. The GEOPM software package is available under the BSD three clause open source software license in the GEOPM source code repository on GitHub (project page: http://geopm.github.io/geopm). The GEOPM runtime framework, test infrastructure, and power rebalancing plugin are all open source.

The remainder of the paper is organized as follows. Section 2 highlights GEOPM's primary contributions over prior works. Section 3 overviews GEOPM's design. Section 4 analyzes time-to-solution improvements obtained with the power rebalancing plugin for CORAL procurement and other benchmarks. Section 5 concludes and discusses future work.

2   Related Work

To our knowledge, GEOPM is the first open extensible runtime framework to be contributed to the community by a hardware vendor with the intent of collaborative research toward software-hardware co-designed energy management solutions in future HPC systems. This vision and early work was first publicized broadly to the community in a short workshop paper in PMBS'16 [1] and the

Emerging Technologies Showcase at SC'16. In this ISC paper, we have further developed the early work presented at PMBS for a full conference publication.

There are parallel software efforts to GEOPM contributed by a hardware vendor: OpenHPC [2] facilitates community collaboration on the HPC software stack by providing a framework for integrating, configuring, and testing open source components. OpenHPC has not been focused on fostering co-designed energy management solutions, but we note that we intend to submit the GEOPM package to the OpenHPC Technical Steering Committee for inclusion in the OpenHPC distribution when the production version 1.0 of GEOPM is released. There are parallel software-hardware co-design efforts to GEOPM such as Open-POWER [19]. While OpenPOWER enables the community to customize systems based on the IBM POWER architecture, we are not aware of activity within the OpenPOWER project to research software-hardware co-designed energy management solutions exploiting runtime feedback from applications. While GEOPM only currently provides plugins supporting x86 systems, users can add platform implementation plugins supporting POWER or other system architectures.

To our knowledge, GEOPM is the first open source job-level power management runtime for HPC systems to support extensible energy management control strategies through a plugin architecture, making it suitable for the differing energy management needs of a wide range of HPC installations around the world. The Power API Specification from Sandia [18] is a synergistic effort, but it is an orthogonal effort because it emphasizes power interfaces rather than runtime techniques for optimizing energy. The Power API project is defining community-standard interfaces for power monitoring and control at various granularities throughout the HPC stack. Runtimes like GEOPM and other components can collectively target these interfaces to achieve interoperability. We are collaborating with Sandia to explore changes targeted at future releases of the specification to increase support for GEOPM and its interfaces.

In this work, we develop a plugin for GEOPM for power rebalancing within a job. Prior works such as Conductor [4], Adagio [5], and Jitter [6] have demonstrated effective algorithms for reallocating power between nodes to compensate for application load imbalance – whether for the purpose of increasing application performance under a job power cap by accelerating the critical path or improving application energy efficiency by reducing performance in nodes off of the critical path. While these algorithms are effective at smaller scales (i.e. less than a few thousand nodes), their centralized designs are not intended for today's large-scale deployments or future Exascale deployments. The key difference is that the GEOPM power balancing plugin has a flexible tree-hierarchical design suitable for deployments ranging in scale from rack-scale to extreme-scale deployments. We note, however, that we have a collaboration underway with the authors of these prior works to compare approaches and meld together the best aspects of each approach in a future GEOPM plugin and paper.

There is a parallel work to GEOPM called the Argo project [26] which is developing a task-based programming model and runtime for Exascale HPC systems. Its design includes a hierarchical power manager. Unlike GEOPM, the

Argo power manager is not intended as a vehicle for the community and hardware vendors to collaborate on researching new energy management solutions. Furthermore, while the Argo project envisions this power manager performing automatic hierarchical power budgeting, that functionality is not complete to our knowledge. What has been demonstrated is hierarchical enforcement of power budgets that were adjusted manually at runtime. That said, the authors are interested in exploring if Argo's algorithms could be implemented as GEOPM plugins and brought to fruition in production deployments through GEOPM.

We note that there have also been orthogonal efforts [27] to develop hierarchical power management frameworks for enterprise data centers. They employ significantly different energy management strategies suitable for enterprise workloads and virtualized environments. There have been other related works that focused on saving power given a time bound. Some have used linear programming to optimize energy savings with nearly no runtime increase [21]. Others have achieved bigger power savings in exchange for small performance degradations [22–25].

Aside from prior works on saving energy while maintaining performance levels, hierarchical power capping, and rebalancing power across nodes to increase job performance under a power cap, there have also been prior works on power-aware scheduling algorithms for energy management at the system level [7–9]. These algorithms comprehend system-level power caps and assign a different power cap to each job based on its runtime and power characteristics with the goal of reducing job wait times or optimizing overall system throughput. GEOPM is synergistic with these works: the intent is for GEOPM to integrate with a power-aware scheduler in an extended energy management hierarchy. In particular, the scheduler can view GEOPM as a mechanism for optimizing the job's performance or energy efficiency within the scheduler-specified job power budget, and the scheduler can optimize system performance and efficiency by deciding the best allocation of the system budget among concurrent jobs. For maximum benefits, GEOPM supports dynamic adjustments to the job cap.

3   GEOPM Design Overview

This section provides an overview of the GEOPM design, beginning with discussion of how GEOPM integrates into the HPC system stack. We cover GEOPM's interfaces and responsibilities as well as its scalable, extensible design.

3.1   GEOPM Interfaces and Integration Architecture

Figure 1 illustrates how the GEOPM runtime fits into the HPC system stack. GEOPM is a job-level power manager. The GEOPM runtime interacts with the scheduling functions of the workload manager through the workload manager interface. This interface lets future power-aware schedulers assign an objective for the job and configure which energy management plugin GEOPM should use to manage the job. Supported objectives include but are not limited to managing

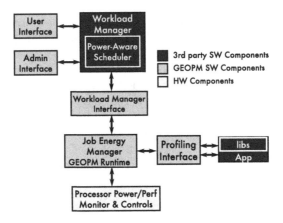

Fig. 1. GEOPM interfaces and HPC system stack integration

the job to stay within a power budget while optimizing job time-to-solution; in this case, the scheduler would use the interface to assign a job power budget as well. The workload manager interface allows GEOPM to report back how much power the job consumed and statistics about the job that GEOPM has collected. There is an option for the interface to be used at job start and finish (statically) or periodically while the job is running (dynamically). The GEOPM runtime runs in user space. Therefore, GEOPM does not control resources that are shared between users like network switches or the distributed file system; its scope is control of power and performance knobs in compute node resources.

There is also an interface to the application software or libraries shown at the middle right of the figure. The interface functions are listed in Table 1. This software profiling interface allows the programmer to mark up their code to hint to GEOPM about loops with global synchronization events in the application that could result in performance loss if some MPI ranks fall behind in the computation and reach synchronization points late (i.e. epochs). The interface also enables programmers to hint to GEOPM about phases (i.e. regions) in the application or library code between synchronization events as well as provide an application-level performance signal (i.e. progress) that GEOPM can use to adapt its decisions as the application transitions between phases. For

Table 1. Function list for GEOPM profiling interface

geopm_prof_epoch():	Synchronization loop iteration beacon
geopm_prof_region():	Get region ID from name
geopm_prof_enter():	Mark region entry
geopm_prof_exit():	Mark region exit
geopm_prof_progress():	Report region progress

example, GEOPM may use region information to monitor for memory-intensive or communication-intensive phases where processor frequency can be decreased to save power with little or no impact on runtime.

The GEOPM profiling interface is designed to be lightweight and minimally invasive, but future work will explore methods of automatically inferring phase and performance information to enable use cases where GEOPM can make per-phase decisions effectively without requiring programmers to mark up application or library code. See the GEOPM man pages in [10] for full details on the signatures and use of these functions. We also provide further documentation, tutorials, and example MPI applications in the GEOPM source code repository illustrating how to use them. See [20] for tutorial video walk-throughs on YouTube.

As depicted in Fig. 1, GEOPM provides interfaces to the user or administrator enabling them to configure GEOPM and request specific energy management plugins for a job. The interface is a JSON configuration file. The GEOPM software package provides a tool to generate configuration files from the command line called `geopmpolicy` and a C interface as well through the `geopm_policy_*()` APIs. The GEOPM configuration file is selected at runtime through the `GEOPM_POLICY` environment variable. On a system deploying the SLURM workload manager, SLURM's plugin infrastructure can be used to generate the file and set the environment variable. It can also be used to launch the GEOPM runtime and configure CPU affinity. Some other workload managers offer similar infrastructure. For those that do not, wrappers can be placed around MPI launch commands to configure and enable GEOPM.

3.2   GEOPM Scalable Tree-Hierarchical Design

The GEOPM runtime is designed for use on a wide range of system scales. This is accomplished through a flexible tree-hierarchical design. As illustrated in Fig. 2, the GEOPM runtime is implemented as a hierarchical feedback guided control system using a balanced tree. The energy management strategy employed is extensible through a plugin architecture. The depth and fan-out of the tree are automatically adjusted by the GEOPM runtime to accommodate different job sizes.

Controllers in the tree (and therefore energy management plugins) take a recursive approach to coordinating energy and performance policy decisions globally, across all nodes in the job. The root controller sets policy for its children, each of its children set policy for their children, and so on. Policies are defined hierarchically such that the parent constrains the space of policies that its children can select from and, in so doing, effects their decisions. Decisions at each level of the tree are based on feedback from each child. This feedback consists of a history of energy, performance, and other statistics collected over the last few control intervals. For scalability, the feedback is aggregated as it is communicated back from the leaves toward the root. Thus, decisions at the root are informed by feedback from the leaves, and decisions flowing down the tree effect decisions made at each leaf.

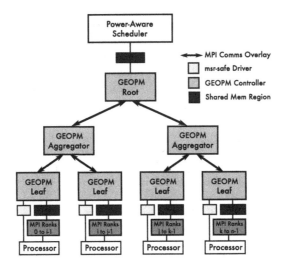

Fig. 2. GEOPM hierarchical design and communication mechanisms

To run the control tree hierarchy, the GEOPM runtime launches one user thread on each compute node. This thread runs for the duration of the job. On each compute node, this thread executes the responsibilities of the leaf controller. On some compute nodes, this thread also executes responsibilities of the aggregator controllers at higher levels in the tree. On one compute node in the job, the thread also executes responsibilities of the root controller of the tree.

The GEOPM thread can be launched in several ways, and the affinity of this thread should be controlled for best performance. On manycore systems with low single-thread performance and high-cost context switching, it may be a general performance benefit to leave a core unused by the application so that the operating system can execute threads without interrupting the application. In such systems, the GEOPM thread can be affinitized to this core and use it as well. In cases where GEOPM is run with computationally-intense plugins, results may be best if the GEOPM thread runs on the core that the application stays off of; developers and users should keep this in mind. For other application and system hardware combinations, it may benefit performance for the GEOPM thread to share a core with the application through context switching. See [10] for further information on GEOPM's launch and affinitization options.

Dynamic communication between levels of the GEOPM control tree hierarchy is currently achieved using MPI over the application's in-band network fabric. We use MPI's Cartesian topology functionality to map the leaf, aggregator, and root controllers to the GEOPM runtime threads on the compute nodes. When GEOPM is built against an MPI implementation with optimized Cartesian topology functionality, this minimizes communication distances over the network fabric for the controllers. We also use MPI's Cartesian topology to efficiently implement a balanced tree hierarchy supporting a wide range of job node counts. All communication uses one-sided operations through the `MPI_Put()` interface. In Sect. 4.4, we provide measurements of GEOPM's communication bandwidth requirements on the OmniPath network fabric in our test system. We demonstrate that bandwidth use is orders of magnitude less than 1% of the total available bandwidth. GEOPM can be extended to support out-of-band communication in the future.

Inter-process shared memory is used both for dynamic communication between the GEOPM root controller and power-aware scheduler and for communication between leaf controllers and application processes on the compute nodes. Communication between leaf controllers and processors is achieved via GEOPM `PlatformImp` plugins (discussed in Sect. 3.3). In the case of Intel systems, processors expose Model Specific Registers (MSRs) [17] for communication with software. GEOPM `PlatformImp` plugins for Intel systems perform MSR access from userspace via the msr-safe Linux driver developed by LLNL [11].

3.3 GEOPM Extensible Plugin Architecture

There are three types of plugins supported by GEOPM which enable user extension of the runtime. From lowest to highest level of abstraction these are: the `PlatformImp`, the `Platform`, and the `Decider`. The `PlatformImp` plugin is used to expose low-level hardware features to `Platform` plugins. The GEOPM package provides `PlatformImp` plugins for a range of Intel platforms exposing hardware features implemented with Model Specific Registers (MSRs). Support for other hardware platforms would be implemented with this type of plugin. The `Platform` plugin is used to express higher-level abstractions of the hardware features exposed by the `PlatformImp`, and it provides the bridge interface called by the controller to enforce a policy provided by a leaf `Decider`.

There are two types of `Decider`s: tree `Decider`s and leaf `Decider`s. The leaf `Decider` is responsible for managing power or other controls within a single compute node. The tree `Decider` is used for all levels of the control tree hierarchy above the leaf level. The lowest-level tree `Decider` is the parent of a leaf `Decider`. Collectively, the tree `Decider`s are responsible for managing power across nodes. The leaf and tree `Decider`s are each selected by name in the GEOPM configuration file provided by the end user, administrator, or workload manager.

All `Decider`s have six main responsibilities: collecting feedback information from their children in the GEOPM control tree hierarchy (or the software profiling interface and `Platform` in the case of leaf `Decider`s), aggregating this data into a reduced form, passing this reduced version up to their parent in the tree, receiving policy information from their parent above them in the tree, deciding how to set policy for their children (or how to set node power controls or other controls in the case of leaf `Decider`s) based on the policy given by their parent, and passing policy decisions down to their children (or to the `Platform` in the case of leaf `Decider`s).

The GEOPM policy defines a power budget, so each `Decider` is taking in a power budget from its parent and deciding how to divide that budget among its children (or how to divide that budget among the node hardware components that support control in the case of the leaf `Decider`). The leaf `Decider` may also manage controls beyond power limit controls to enable various additional optimizations. Each `Decider` plugin defines for itself the objective function it will try to maximize when making policy decisions for its children and implements an algorithm to maximize this objective function. Thus, by selecting a particular `Decider`: GEOPM users, administrators, or the workload manager are selecting a particular objective function and a particular energy management algorithm to try to maximize that objective function.

To help the `Decider` tree hierarchy achieve control stability, the GEOPM `Decider` interface includes functions that express convergence. Before introducing a new policy, the parent `Decider` waits for its children to signal that the existing policy has been enacted stably. Child `Decider`s wait until the aggregated feedback they would send to their parent would reflect the current policy before signaling convergence to their parent.

GEOPM is designed to support per-phase adaptation of node hardware controls and other node-level controls via the leaf `Decider`. To support this, the GEOPM framework and leaf `Decider`s must collect feedback and adjust controls at the cadence of application phase transitions. The current implementation of the GEOPM framework and governing leaf `Decider` provided with the GEOPM software package can sustain a 5 ms cadence with standard deviation of less than .5 ms when running on an Intel Knights Landing Xeon Phi platform. The control loop includes computations to feed input to the governing `Decider` and enact its decisions in the `Platform`. Those computations include sampling processor performance counters, reading from a log of application interface calls stored in shared memory, extrapolating application progress forward to when the processor counters were read, estimating power consumption over the last interval by applying linear least squares parameter fit over a moving window of energy counter readings, and writing RAPL MSRs to enact the governing `Decider`'s allocation. The control loop computation also includes the algorithm in the governing `Decider` that adaptively allocates power among the processor and external DRAM from the node power budget.

3.4   Example Power Balancing Plugin

We have developed an example plugin for GEOPM to demonstrate both its extensible architecture and a scalable hierarchical power management strategy to address the performance variation challenges expected in Exascale systems due to their need for power-capping. Power-capping exposes differences in the energy efficiency of like hardware components. These differences derive from manufacturing variation. Under power caps, even like hardware components from the same Stock Keeping Unit (SKU) will exhibit different performance which results in the nodes of the system taking different amounts of time to complete equal amounts of work [12, 13].

The GEOPM power balancing plugin mitigates this performance variation, minimizing its impact on application time-to-solution. The plugin targets iterative bulk-synchronous MPI applications running on power-capped systems and leverages application-awareness to first identify the nodes that are on the critical path due to their lower performance at a given power cap then accelerate them by diverting power away from nodes that are off of that path. This provides an overall improvement in application time-to-solution. The source code for this power balancing tree `Decider` plugin is hosted in the GEOPM repository [10].

The tree `Decider`s identify and accelerate the critical path hierarchically. The GEOPM controller framework provides the lowest-level tree `Decider` with samples of its children's runtime (not including time spent waiting for MPI synchronization) between application calls to the `geopm_prof_epoch()` function averaged over a moving window. The `geopm_prof_epoch()` call acts as a beacon, signaling each time the application reaches a new iteration of an outer loop containing an inter-node synchronization operation. The tree `Decider` takes in a power budget from its parent, compares the runtime reported by its children, then computes how to divide its power budget among its children such that they will reach the synchronization point at roughly the same time, avoiding wait time and associated performance loss. Each tree `Decider` reports the max of its children's runtime as aggregated runtime feedback to its parent.

4   Results

This section presents our analysis of the power balancing plugin for GEOPM. We describe our experimental setup, we demonstrate the improvements to application time-to-solution that the plugin provides, we analyze how the plugin obtains these improvements, and we report measurements of GEOPM's computational, communication, and memory requirements.

4.1   Experimental Setup

Our experiments use standard benchmark output as the final reference for time-to-solution and the other statistics we report. However, our analysis additionally leverages GEOPM's report and trace features. GEOPM may be configured with the environment variables `GEOPM_REPORT` and `GEOPM_TRACE` to generate two types of profiles after each application run: a summarizing report or a time series trace. The report file aggregates performance and energy metrics for the application both overall and for each individual region that the programmer has annotated in the application using the profiling interface described in Sect. 3.1. The trace file is a table of time series data containing samples of processor performance counters, information collected via application calls to the profiling interface, and control knob setting outputs recorded by GEOPM during the application run. This table contains exactly the same data provided to the leaf `Decider` plugin in the GEOPM control tree hierarchy.

In this paper, we performed our experiments on a cluster of 12 compute nodes. Each compute node has one Intel Xeon Phi Knights Landing processor (KNL-F B0 Beta SKU) and 256 GB of external DRAM. This processor SKU has 64 Turbo-enabled, 4-way hyperthreaded cores each with a 1.3 GHz sticker frequency. It has 16 GB of MCDRAM on-package memory, an integrated Omni-Path HFI used for communication over the network fabric, and a 230 W Thermal Design Power (TDP). The operating system is CentOS 7 Linux with the 'performance' frequency governor enabled. The C/C++ and Fortran software was compiled with the Intel tool-chain while using the MVAPICH2 MPI implementation. We used version 0.2.2 of the GEOPM software package [10].

In our experiments, we targeted the following workloads: Qbox, HACC, Nekbone, AMG, miniFE, CoMD, and FFT. Qbox is a quantum molecular dynamics code, HACC is a cosmology code for simulating the evolution of the universe, Nekbone is a thermal hydraulics code, AMG is an algebraic multi-grid solver for unstructured meshes, miniFE is a finite element code, CoMD is a proxy molecular dynamics simulation code, and FFT is a discrete 3-d Fast Fourier Transform kernel. Qbox, HACC, and Nekbone are Tier 1 scalable science workloads from the CORAL procurement benchmarks; AMG is a Tier 1 throughput benchmark; and miniFE is a Tier 2 throughput benchmark from the CORAL benchmarks [14]. CoMD is an ExMatEx benchmark for software-hardware co-design [15]. FFT is a key kernel from the NAS Parallel Benchmarks suite [16].

When configuring workloads, we applied standard conventions. We sized the problem to use the majority of the MCDRAM (on-package memory) in each node. With the system not power-capped – i.e. with the processors running at TDP – we swept over the different numbers of MPI ranks and OpenMP threads per rank using up all or almost all of the available hyperthreads in the processor; we then determined which configuration resulted in the best runtime for each workload and used it in all evaluations of our power balancing plugin. We found that all workloads performed best if they were affinitized to leave Linux CPU 0 unused by the application to avoid interference by operating system threads. We found that miniFE and CoMD performed best if using two hyperthreads per core, while all other workloads performed best if using one. Using the GEOPM profiling interface, we added mark up to these workloads to enable tuning them with the power balancing plugin. The modifications are available in [10].

To study how much application speedup our power-balancing plugin provides in power-constrained systems, we swept over a range of job power caps and compared the workload runtime achieved while using our power-balancing plugin versus a baseline. Our power-balancing plugin dynamically reallocates the job power budget among nodes to mitigate load imbalance while the baseline applies a static uniform division of the job power budget among nodes. In the baseline, all tree Deciders are inactive. However, both cases employ active leaf Deciders to enforce the node-level power budgets.

The leaves enforce the budget as follows: they dynamically measure the power consumed in the external DRAM via the processor RAPL feature, they subtract this power from the node budget (obtained from their parents in the GEOPM control tree hierarchy), and then they set the RAPL socket power limit equal to the remaining power so that the sum of socket and external DRAM power matches the node power budget. Node power budgets are defined in terms of the dynamic power controllable via the processor RAPL feature. The remainder of node power is not included but it is approximately static. Power consumed by the job in shared resources like the network fabric interface is not currently accounted for but may be in future work.

The workloads under study have well-balanced assignments of work across ranks yet they still exhibit load imbalance deriving from the effects of hardware manufacturing variation which have been discussed in Sect. 3.4. When interpreting the results in this paper, it is important to note that, while the analysis focuses on manufacturing variation, the GEOPM power balancing plugin can address load imbalance due to imbalanced work assignments across ranks as well. However, evaluating benefits of the plugin in that scenario is beyond the scope of this paper. We also note that we made no attempt to cherry-pick processors from extreme ends of the power efficiency distribution in the processor SKU. Therefore, we do not know if the processors in our cluster reflect the full potential for load imbalance. We will explore this in future work.

In our power cap sweep experiments, we set the max job power cap equal to the power at which each workload's time-to-solution reached its minimum (i.e. unconstrained performance), and we set the min job power cap to the value at which performance scaling hit an inflection point where the processor spent in excess of 8% of its time throttling inefficiently to reach the required power. Results at power caps below this inflection point may be meaningful in some research or production scenarios but they are omitted from this paper for brevity.

4.2   Runtime Improvements with Power Balancing Plugin

Figure 3 shows the mean runtime improvements obtained by our power balancing plugin over a range of job power caps. These experiments were repeated 5 times. The lighter colored bars are the results with our power balancing plugin, and lower values are better. Runtimes are normalized based on the rightmost darker colored bar (representing the baseline data) for each plot such that this bar always has a value of 1.0. The red whiskers that are above and below the top of the bars represent the max and min (respectively) of the observed runtimes. As the figure indicates, our power balancing plugin is able to provide substantial runtime improvements of up to 30% for Nekbone, miniFE, and CoMD. For the other workloads, the runtime improvements are up to 9–23%.

The amount of improvement varies depending on the power cap and the workload, but it tends to increase as the job power is increasingly constrained since the critical path can be operated at a higher and higher frequency relative to the other nodes. At the right side of each graph, job power is not very constrained and the nodes have enough power to run at closer to full frequency, so the critical path cannot be accelerated.

In all experiments, we note that we confirmed that the power balancing plugin obtains its runtime improvements without going over the job power budget. We also note that, in other clusters, the improvements may vary if the processors exhibit differing amounts of manufacturing variation than seen in our cluster.

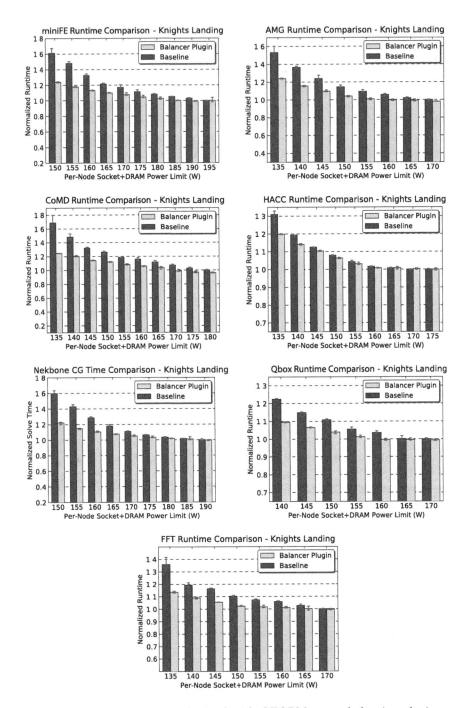

Fig. 3. Runtime improvements obtained with GEOPM power balancing plugin on a 12-node Knights Landing cluster. 5 runs averaged for each bar. (Color figure online)

4.3   Analysis of Runtime Improvements via Traces

Next, we trace the action of the power balancing plugin over the course of a run to show how the runtime improvements were obtained. In the left column of plots in Fig. 4, we show traces from a run of the HACC workload. In the right column, we show traces from a run of the Nekbone workload. For each, we highlight a run from one of the power caps studied in our sweeps. For brevity, we omit results collected for the other power caps and other benchmarks, but we note that we observed consistent trends in that data.

The top plot in the HACC traces shows the normalized runtime of each iteration of the HACC outer loop in the critical path node (i.e. the node with lowest power efficiency due to manufacturing variation) and compares the time taken when using the power balancing plugin versus the baseline. In the middle plot, we plot the power allocated to each node for each iteration of the outer loop when using the power balancing plugin. In the bottom plot, we plot the mean frequency that each node's processor runs at in each iteration of the outer loop when using the power balancing plugin. These traces were collected through GEOPM's tracing features.

As demonstrated in the top plot, the power balancing plugin is able to reduce the runtime of each iteration of the HACC outer loop which reduces the overall time-to-solution. The middle plot demonstrates how the power balancing plugin achieves this: it identifies the critical path nodes and allocates them a larger portion of the job power budget. In particular, Node 8 is allocated more power.

The power allocation is tuned using an objective function that penalizes variance in the time it takes the nodes to complete each iteration. From one iteration to the next, the amount of computation needs not be constant. In fact, the top plot demonstrates that the computation is not constant in HACC. Nonetheless, the power balancing plugin readily handles it. The bottom plot confirms that the variance-minimizing power allocation was the allocation that equalized frequency across processors in all nodes. This is expected when manufacturing variation is the cause of variation in iteration runtime across nodes.

The right column of Fig. 4 shows the corresponding traces for Nekbone, a more complicated example. The iteration loop time data in the top plot exhibits two phases. In the first phase, the runtime of the outer loop is slightly better than the baseline runtime when using the power balancing plugin, but in the second phase the power balancing plugin significantly improves the runtime. The two phases can be explained by observing that the Nekbone benchmark executes two conjugate gradient computations of different problem sizes. The second one is more sensitive to manufacturing variation because it is more compute-intensive. Thus, it offers more opportunity for acceleration.

In the middle and bottom plots, the traces confirm that the power balancing plugin is responding to differences in the outer loop runtime across nodes. In particular, Node 8 is allocated more power. This is expected based on additional experiments we performed to confirm that Node 8 has the processor with the lowest power efficiency (due to manufacturing variation) in our cluster: over a sweep of different power caps, we compared the average frequency each node's processor

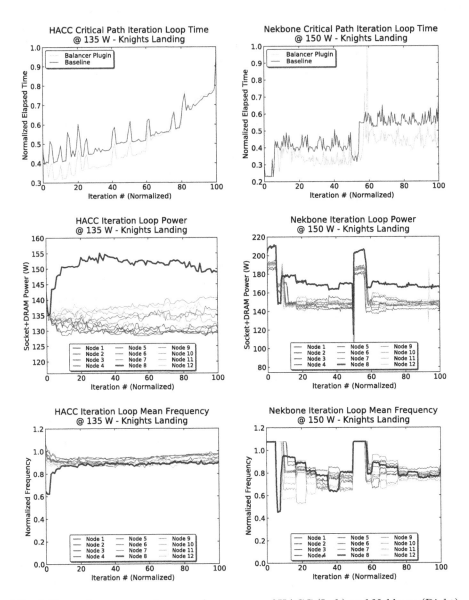

Fig. 4. Traces for an example run and power cap of HACC (Left) and Nekbone (Right). Top to bottom: time taken in the critical path node to complete each iteration, power allocated to each node in each iteration, and mean frequency in each node in each iteration

achieved when running a single-node compute-intensive synthetic workload and confirmed that the average frequency was consistently lowest on Node 8. We also note that the data demonstrates that our plugin adapts readily when Nekbone moves from the first conjugate gradient computation to the second. When the second begins, the plugin realizes that the previous power allocation is no longer ideal and it learns a new power allocation.

4.4   Overhead Measurements

Next we measure and report the memory usage and communication bandwidth costs associated with running the GEOPM framework and power balancing plugin as well as the overhead to the application's runtime associated with calling into GEOPM's profiling interface functions. GEOPM and its interfaces have been designed to minimize these costs.

To measure the memory working set, we queried the peak resident set size statistic (VmHWM) provided by Linux in /proc/<pid>/status/ for the GEOPM process on each node, at GEOPM shutdown time. To track communication bandwidth usage, we implemented accounting logic in the GEOPM code for tree communications to accumulate how many payload bytes are sent over the network. To track application overhead, we wrapped each GEOPM interface function with timers and implemented logic to accumulate the total time spent in all interface function calls. For each type of overhead, we obtain measurements on each node and report the maximum overhead across nodes.

We note that taking the maximum actually overestimates both the average network bandwidth usage per node and the overall application overhead. The node in which the GEOPM root controller lives uses more communication bandwidth than any other node, but it is the value we are reporting. Overhead on the critical path node will have greatest impact to overall application runtime, but we are reporting the maximum across any node; in our experiments, the overhead was typically lowest on the critical path node.

Table 2. Per-node memory usage, communication bandwidth, and application overhead

Workload	Memory working set	Communication BW (upper bound)	Application overhead (upper bound)
Qbox	40.8 MB	7.8 B/sec	2.32%
HACC	48.7 MB	36.2 B/sec	0.54%
Nekbone	37.1 MB	1121.3 B/sec	1.45%
AMG	34.9 MB	24.4 B/sec	0.97%
miniFE	34.8 MB	414.9 B/sec	2.38%
CoMD	34.7 MB	735.8 B/sec	2.88%
FFT	38.4 MB	338.6 B/sec	4.52%

Nonetheless, the costs are minimal as demonstrated in Table 2. They are easily outweighed by the large improvements in application time-to-solution presented earlier in this paper. We note, however, that we have not yet made a thorough effort to optimize the GEOPM code, so the overheads may be further reduced in the future.

5 Conclusion and Future Work

This paper introduced an open source, extensible, scalable runtime framework called GEOPM. GEOPM is being contributed to the community to accelerate collaboration and research toward software-hardware co-designed HPC energy management solutions. To demonstrate GEOPM's potential as a framework, this paper developed a power balancing plugin for GEOPM, and it presented results from our experiments with that plugin which demonstrated substantial improvements in time-to-solution for key CORAL system procurement and other benchmarks in power-capped systems.

In future work, we will expand upon our studies of the power balancing plugin to (a) determine bounds on how much benefit the plugin will provide in systems with processors spanning the full range of manufacturing variation possible in a given SKU, (b) evaluate benefits on additional benchmarks, and (c) demonstrate that the plugin's tree-hierarchical algorithm scales as well as expected in larger systems. In fact, the first scaling studies have already begun through a collaboration with Argonne National Laboratory. They are planned for the Theta system, a production system based on Intel Knights Landing hardware and Cray Aries Interconnect.

Lastly, the promising results presented in this paper motivate future work to spin up additional collaborations with the community to research new energy optimization strategies through GEOPM's plugin framework. It would be especially interesting to prototype plugins for GEOPM that optimize energy-to-solution or other objective functions beyond those demonstrated in this paper. It would also be interesting to explore optimizations that run in conjunction with power balancing optimizations to achieve speedups and energy efficiency improvements on top of the benefits of power balancing.

The authors are also seeking collaborations to (a) explore further integration of GEOPM with emerging power-aware scheduling functions in SLURM (or other workload managers) and (b) explore tuning power-performance knobs in software libraries/runtimes like MPI or OpenMP as well as knobs in the library or application layer of the HPC stack.

Acknowledgments. The authors would like to thank the following individuals for their input on this work: Vitali Morozov and Kalyan Kumaran of Argonne; Barry Rountree, Martin Schulz, and their teams from LLNL; James Laros, Ryan Grant, and their team from Sandia; and Richard Greco, Tryggve Fossum, David Lombard, Michael Patterson, and Alan Gara of Intel. Development of the GEOPM software package has been partially funded through contract B609815 with Argonne National Laboratory.

References

1. Eastep, J., Sylvester, S., Cantalupo, C., et al.: Global extensible open power manager: a vehicle for HPC community collaboration toward co-designed energy management solutions. In: Supercomputing PMBS (2016)
2. Schulz, K., Baird, C.R., Brayford, D., et al.: Cluster computing with OpenHPC. In: Supercomputing HPC Systems Professionals (2016)
3. Auweter, A., et al.: A case study of energy aware scheduling on SuperMUC. In: Kunkel, J.M., Ludwig, T., Meuer, H.W. (eds.) ISC 2014. LNCS, vol. 8488, pp. 394–409. Springer, Cham (2014). doi:10.1007/978-3-319-07518-1_25
4. Marathe, A., Bailey, P.E., Lowenthal, D.K., Rountree, B., Schulz, M., de Supinski, B.R.: A run-time system for power-constrained HPC applications. In: Kunkel, J.M., Ludwig, T. (eds.) ISC High Performance 2015. LNCS, vol. 9137, pp. 394–408. Springer, Cham (2015). doi:10.1007/978-3-319-20119-1_28
5. Rountree, B., Lowenthal, D.K., de Supinski, B., Schulz, M., Freeh, V.W.: Adagio: making DVS practical for complex HPC applications. In: ICS (2009)
6. Kappiah, N., Freeh, V.W., Lowenthal, D.K.: Just in time dynamic voltage scaling: exploiting inter-node slack to save energy in MPI programs. In: Supercomputing (2005)
7. Etinski, M., Corbalan, J., Labarta, J., Valero, M.: Optimizing job performance under a given power constraint in HPC centers. In: IGCC (2010)
8. Etinski, M., Corbalan, J., Labarta, J., Valero, M.: Linear programming based parallel job scheduling for power constrained systems. In: HPCS (2011)
9. Sarood, O., Langer, A., Gupta, A., Kale, L.: Maximizing throughput of overprovisioned HPC data centers under a strict power budget. In: Supercomputing (2014)
10. Global Extensible Open Power Manager Project. Intel Corporation (2016). http://geopm.github.io/geopm/
11. Shoga, K., Rountree, B., Schulz, M., Shafer, J.: Whitelisting MSRs with MSR-safe. In: Supercomputing Exascale Systems Programming Tools (2014)
12. Rountree, B., Ahn, D.H., de Supinski, B.R., et al.: Beyond DVFS: a first look at performance under a hardware-enforced power bound. In: HPPAC (2012)
13. Inadomi, Y., Patki, T., Inoue, K., et al.: Analyzing and mitigating the impact of manufacturing variability in power-constrained supercomputing. In: Supercomputing (2015)
14. CORAL Procurement Benchmarks. Livermore National Lab (2016). https://asc.llnl.gov/CORAL-benchmarks/CORALBenchmarksProcedure-v26.pdf
15. Mohd-Yusof, J.: Codesign molecular dynamics (CoMD) proxy app. In: ExMatEx All-Hands Meeting (2012)
16. Bailey, D., Barszcz, E., Barton, J., Browning, D., Carter, R., Dagum, L., Fatoohi, R., Frederickson, P., Lasinski, T., Schreiber, R., et al.: The NAS parallel benchmarks summary and preliminary results. In: Supercomputing (1991)
17. Intel: Intel-64 and IA-32 Architectures Software Developer's Manual, vols. 3A and 3B. System Programming Guide, Intel Corporation (2011)
18. Laros, J., DeBonis, D., Grant, R., et al.: High performance computing - power application programming interface specification, version 1.0. Sandia National Laboratories, Technical report SAND2014-17061 (2014)
19. Gschwind, M.: OpenPOWER: reengineering a server ecosystem for large-scale data centers. In: Hot Chips Symposium (HCS) (2014)
20. GEOPM Video Tutorials: Intel Corporation (2016). https://www.youtube.com/playlist?list=PLwm-z8c2AbIBU-T7HnMi_Pux7iO3gQQnz

21. Rountree, B., Lowenthal, D.K., Funk, S., et al.: Bounding energy consumption in large-scale MPI programs. In: Supercomputing (2007)
22. Cameron, K.W., Feng, X., Ge, R.: Performance-constrained distributed DVS scheduling for scientific applications on power-aware clusters. In: Supercomputing (2005)
23. Ge, R., Feng, X., Feng, W., Cameron, K.W.: CPU MISER: a performance-directed, run-time system for power-aware clusters. In: ICPP (2007)
24. Hsu, C.-H., Feng, W.-C.: A power-aware run-time system for high-performance computing. In: Supercomputing (2005)
25. Li, D., de Supinski, B., Schulz, M., Cameron, K., Nikolopoulos, D.: Hybrid MPI/OpenMP power-aware computing. In: IPDPS (2010)
26. Ellsworth, D., Patki, T., Perarnau, S., et al.: Systemwide power management with Argo. In: Parallel and Distributed Processing Symposium Workshops (2016)
27. Raghavendra, R., Ranganathan, P., Talwar, V., Wang, Z., Zhu, X.: No "power" struggles: coordinated multi-level power management for the data center. In: ASPLOS (2008)

Metrics for Energy-Aware Software Optimisation

Stephen I. Roberts$^{(\boxtimes)}$, Steven A. Wright, Suhaib A. Fahmy,
and Stephen A. Jarvis

University of Warwick, Coventry, UK
S.I.Roberts@warwick.ac.uk

Abstract. Energy consumption is rapidly becoming a limiting factor in scientific computing. As a result, hardware manufacturers increasingly prioritise energy efficiency in their processor designs. Performance engineers are also beginning to explore software optimisation and hardware/software co-design as a means to reduce energy consumption. Energy efficiency metrics developed by the hardware community are often re-purposed to guide these software optimisation efforts.

In this paper we argue that established metrics, and in particular those in the Energy Delay Product (Et^n) family, are unsuitable for energy-aware software optimisation. A good metric should provide meaningful values for a single experiment, allow fair comparison between experiments, and drive optimisation in a sensible direction. We show that Et^n metrics are unable to fulfil these basic requirements and present suitable alternatives for guiding energy-aware software optimisation. We finish with a practical demonstration of the utility of our proposed metrics.

1 Introduction

Advances in processor design have delivered improvements in CPU performance for decades. As physical limits are reached, however, refinements to the same basic technologies are beginning to show diminishing returns [6]. One side-effect of this is an unsustainable rise in system power consumption, which has been identified as a primary constraint for exascale systems [20].

Moore's law, which states that transistor density doubles every 18–24 months, led to exponential increases in processor performance during a period often referred to as the "free lunch" [23]. More recently, the breakdown of Dennard scaling has meant that performance improvements are increasingly reliant on microarchitectural changes rather than increases in processor clock speed.

Hardware manufacturers are increasingly prioritising energy efficiency in their processor designs [15]. Research suggests that software modifications will be required to fully exploit the resulting improvements in modern architectures [21]. This has spurred interest in the possibility of optimising software for increased energy efficiency.

A fundamental aspect of performance engineering is *performance assessment*. To comment on the performance of a high performance computing system or a particular software package, we must first define an assessment metric. Metrics provide a means to evaluate a code or system based on some property of

© Springer International Publishing AG 2017
J.M. Kunkel et al. (Eds.): ISC High Performance 2017, LNCS 10266, pp. 413–430, 2017.
DOI: 10.1007/978-3-319-58667-0_22

interest, allowing developers to perform high-level comparisons between different implementations and approaches. Some metrics also serve as fitness functions, combining various costs into a single *figure of merit* (FoM). Such metrics can be used to guide optimisation attempts and the search for better solutions [12].

New metrics which incorporate both energy and runtime costs will be required if developers are to identify and capitalise on new classes of energy-aware optimisations. Many early efforts have borrowed metrics developed by the hardware community, which has a long history of energy efficiency research. In particular, the Energy Delay Product (Et^n) family of metrics are frequently used for software optimisation.

In this paper we argue that Et^n and related metrics are not suitable for software optimisation. We discuss their shortcomings and provide examples of their failures in this domain. We then propose alternative metrics which address these shortcomings and compare their performance with Et^n. Finally, we demonstrate our metrics with an investigation of the energy efficiency of scientific codes. Specifically, this paper makes the following contributions:

– We present a set of criteria that we believe are necessary for effective software optimisation metrics. Additionally, we introduce fitness landscape diagrams to visualise the behaviour of these metrics;
– We evaluate the Et^n family of metrics against our criteria. Our analysis highlights weaknesses in metrics commonly used in the energy efficiency optimisation literature;
– We propose two new metrics to measure software energy efficiency. We evaluate our proposals against the same criteria and describe how they improve on established metrics;
– Finally, we validate our proposed metrics with a study into the efficiency of codes from the Mantevo application suite.

The remainder of this paper is structured as follows: Sect. 2 presents a survey of related work; Sect. 3 lays the foundations for this work, providing formal definitions and criteria which we use to compare and assess different metrics; Sect. 4 uses these criteria to assess the suitability of Et^n metrics for software optimisation; Sect. 5 introduces our proposed metrics and evaluates them against the same criteria; Sect. 6 demonstrates the metrics discussed in previous sections by studying the energy efficiency of various applications; and finally Sect. 7 concludes this paper and describes upcoming research.

2   Related Work

Although energy consumption is becoming a constraint for scientific computing, minimising runtime is still an important optimisation objective. Optimising software according to multiple properties simultaneously is known as *Multi-Objective Optimisation* (MOO). MOO requires a balance to be struck between the potentially conflicting requirements imposed by different objectives.

The simplest approach to dealing with multiple optimisation criteria is to handle each one in isolation. A solution is said to be *Pareto-Efficient* if it is not dominated by any other solution across all objectives. Pareto-Efficiency yields a partial ordering, with a set of maximal elements but no ordering between them. The set of maximal elements delineates the *Pareto Front*, as shown in Fig. 1.

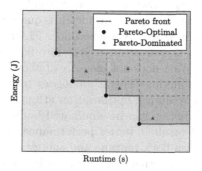

Fig. 1. Pareto-Efficiency

Pareto-Efficiency is useful when the relative importance of different requirements is unknown and the final choice of optimal solution can be deferred to the end user. For this reason it is often used by library developers who want their code to run efficiently in many different execution environments.

Balaprakash et al. use this approach to investigate the trade-offs between runtime and energy consumption for common kernels in scientific computing [2]. A similar technique has also been used to determine optimal checkpoint intervals for energy efficient fault tolerance [1].

A second MOO approach combines multiple objectives into a single scalar fitness function. This function then serves as a FoM metric for the overall utility of different solutions. Scalar fitness functions are in some sense fundamental to MOO; they can be used in isolation, but are also required by users choosing between solutions from a Pareto-efficient set.

Energy Delay Product was first proposed by Gonzalez et al. to measure the energy and runtime efficiency of microprocessors [9]. Martin et al. generalised this concept into the Et^n family of FoM metrics, with parameters E and t corresponding to energy and time [17]. They argue that Et^2 provides the best balance between the two optimisation objectives for microprocessor design. Srinivasan et al. reached the same conclusion, although for slightly different reasons [22].

Many authors have adopted these metrics originating from the hardware community and applied them to software optimisation problems. Vincent et al. describe a technique which minimises Et^1 using CPU throttling [8]. Bingham and Greenstreet use Et^n metrics to analyse runtime constraints imposed by a fixed energy budget for various algorithms [4]. Laros et al. use Et^n metrics to assess a number of production applications and state that Et^3 strikes the right balance between runtime and energy for high performance computing [16]. Et^1 has also been used extensively to quantify the efficiency of resource provisioning in a cloud computing environment [19, 24].

Bekas and Curioni further generalised Et^n metrics to the form $E \cdot f(t)$, a product between energy and an application dependent function of time [3].

Another metric related to energy efficiency is FLOPS Per Watt, which relates the number of Floating Point Operations Per Second (FLOPS) and the rate of power consumption. Despite its name, this metric is quoted in units of Operations per Joule (1 Joule is defined as 1 Watt-Second). FLOPS/Watt measures how effective an application is at converting energy into floating point results.

Unlike Et^n, FLOPS/Watt does not measure application cost and hence cannot be used as a fitness function. This is analogous to metrics like branch misprediction rate, which may inform optimisation attempts but are not measures of utility. Branch misprediction can be eliminated by disabling speculative execution, but this does not result in better performance. Similarly, optimising for FLOPS/Watt may increase both runtime and energy consumption.

Heuristic models offer another source of optimisation guidance. Choi et al. proposed the Energy Roofline model to identify the algorithmic conditions needed for trade-offs between runtime and energy [5]. Similarly, in previous work we developed the Power Optimised Software Envelope model to assess the scope a code has for power optimisations on any given platform [18].

Some of our objections to existing metrics have been raised before, most notably by Hsu et al. [14]. They point out that Et^n and related metrics are unfairly biased towards massive parallelism and argue that there is a need for the development of new metrics.

We believe our work is timely and interesting because it offers a rigorous assessment of energy-aware software optimisation metrics. We show the flaws in current approaches and propose novel metrics which can be used as fitness functions to guide energy-aware software optimisation. We believe this work will be useful to practitioners in this nascent area of performance engineering.

3   Foundations

In this section we provide formal definitions which underpin later discussions and outline the desirable properties an optimisation metric should exhibit. We begin by formalising the notion of a code as a repeatable sequence of instructions which, when executed by a processor, incurs energy and runtime costs.

Definition 1. *All processors consume non-zero amounts of time and energy to run programs. The cost of a code θ is the pair $(E_\theta, t_\theta) \in \mathbb{R}_+ \times \mathbb{R}_+$ corresponding to the energy and runtime costs incurred by running it on a given platform.*

Definition 2. *Codes can be composed by concatenating their instruction sequences. The composition of codes θ and λ yields the following cost:*

$$\theta \circ \lambda = (E_\theta + E_\lambda, t_\theta + t_\lambda)$$

The goal of energy-aware software optimisation is to minimise the runtime and energy costs of a given application. Energy-aware optimisation metrics are functions of energy and time which capture the utility of a code.

Definition 3. *An energy-aware optimisation metric is an element-wise monotonic function M which combines energy and runtime costs into a scalar FoM:*

$$M \colon (E, t) \in \mathbb{R}_+ \times \mathbb{R}_+ \to \mathbb{R}_+$$

Element-wise monotonicity means that for all fixed $E_0, t_0 \in \mathbb{R}_+$, the functions $M(E_0, t)$ and $M(E, t_0)$ are monotonic. In other words, increasing one cost without a corresponding reduction in the other leads to a worse FoM.

Software optimisation can be modelled as a hill-climbing problem. Starting from an initial code θ, performance engineers make incremental changes and measure their impact using a FoM metric. Changes which improve performance against this metric are kept while those which reduce it are discarded. Whether a given code change represents an optimisation depends on the metric chosen.

Definition 4. *For logically equivalent codes θ and λ, the transformation $\theta \to \lambda$ is an optimisation with respect to metric M iff $M(\lambda)$ strictly dominates $M(\theta)$.*

By Definition 3, all valid metrics identify code changes which reduce both energy and time costs as optimisations. Similarly, all code changes leading to strictly worse performance will be disregarded. Energy-aware optimisation metrics only differ in cases where energy-time trade-offs are possible.

Figure 2 shows how two valid metrics can disagree on whether the same code change $\theta \to \lambda$ is an optimisation. Lighter green areas correspond to optimisations and darker red areas to performance degradations. They are separated by a dashed *Isometric line* that connects all points with FoM values equal to $M(\theta)$. Both metrics agree on code changes in the solid shaded regions where costs change in tandem. Energy-time trade-offs are represented by cross-hatched quadrants. The MOO metric in Fig. 2a identifies $\theta \to \lambda$ as a valid energy-time trade-off, whereas Fig. 2b shows it is not an energy optimisation.

Energy-aware optimisation metrics ascribe a FoM to all (E, t) cost pairs. Returning to the hill-climbing analogy, we say that an optimisation metric defines a fitness landscape over the energy/time plane. Figure 3 shows how plots similar to Fig. 2 can be used to visualise the fitness landscape of a metric.

The isometric lines in Fig. 3 connect all points where the FoM is some multiple of a fixed value. Mathematically these lines represent level sets of our M function; intuitively they are contours in our fitness landscape. The closeness of these lines corresponds to the gradient of the fitness landscape.

Isotopic lines run perpendicular to isometric lines, and correspond to the path of fastest decent (steepest gradient) within the fitness landscape. Mathematically, these lines are orthogonal trajectories of a metric function M. Conceptually, they show the direction in which a metric drives optimisation.

Having formally defined what an energy-aware optimisation metric is and how it can be visualised, we now turn our attention to how it should behave.

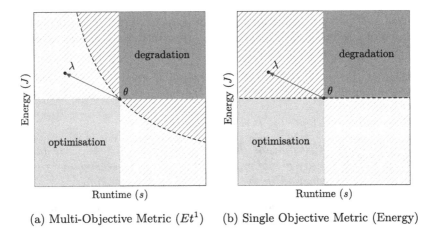

(a) Multi-Objective Metric (Et^1)   (b) Single Objective Metric (Energy)

Fig. 2. Metric optimisation regions (Color figure online)

The goal of an optimisation metric is to condense the utility of an application into a single, meaningful FoM. We have identified the following properties which an idealised optimisation metric should possess:

1. **Bounded:** A metric should bound regions of the optimisation space;
2. **Directed:** Drive optimisation efforts in a sensible direction;
3. **Additive:** Remain additive (linear) under code composition;
4. **Stable:** Provide a stable definition of optimisation under code composition;
5. **Tunable:** Be tunable to different application domains; and
6. **Intuitive:** Correspond to a tangible and intuitive property of the system.

We explore these properties in more detail in the next section.

4 Et^n Evaluation

In the previous section we listed several desirable criteria for energy-aware optimisation metrics. We now use these criteria to evaluate the suitability of Et^n metrics for guiding software optimisation.

4.1   Analysis of Et^n

Bounded: Our first criteria states that energy-aware optimisation metrics should bound regions of the optimisation space. By this we mean that a metric should place upper limits on how much energy or runtime can be consumed under a given FoM. This requirement is met if the isometric lines described by a metric intercept both the energy and runtime axes.

Figure 3 shows that Et^n isometric lines do not intercept either axis. In theory, codes can be modified to consume an arbitrarily large amount of either time or

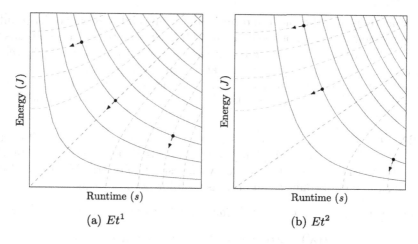

Fig. 3. Et^n metric fitness landscapes

energy while still improving their overall performance. We consider this to be a flaw and assert that such changes should not count as optimisations. Another benefit of bounded metrics is that they limit the space in which to search for optimisations; something which Et^n cannot do.

Directed: Our second criteria requires metrics to guide optimisation in sensible directions. Intuitively, we wish to speed up slow codes and reduce the power consumption of energy intensive ones. On the contrary, Et^n disproportionately rewards speeding up fast codes and saving energy in frugal ones. As energy consumption increases, Et^n gives higher priority to runtime optimisation and vice versa. This fault was encountered by Hsu et al. when they noted that Et^n metrics are unfairly biased towards massive parallelism in HPC systems [14].

Our first two criteria are linked. It is necessary (but not sufficient) for a metric to be bounded in order for it to guide optimisation in a sensible direction. The isometric lines of an unbounded metric never touch either axis, meaning the corresponding isotopic lines must intersect the axes at right angles. As the energy or time cost of a code approaches zero, the path of fastest decent therefore tends exclusively towards further reductions in this already close-to-zero cost.

Additive: Our third criteria states that FoM metrics should be additive under code composition. Performance engineers focus their attention on expensive procedures within a code. This involves profiling the code to identify areas causing poor performance, based on the assumption that the cost of a code is the sum of the costs of its constituent parts. While true for simple metrics like energy and time, this is not generally the case for compound metrics.

Definition 5. *A metric is additive iff for code segments θ and λ:*

$$M(\theta \circ \lambda) = M(\theta) + M(\lambda)$$

Metric functions must be linear in terms of both time and energy in order to fulfil this requirement. This is not the case for Et^n, where the cost of a code tends to be much greater than the costs of its constituent parts. Profilers cannot be relied upon to identify targets for Et^n optimisation. Furthermore, this additional *non-local* cost depends on total application runtime and energy consumption. An Et^n FoM is therefore meaningless outside the context of a single fixed application.

Stable: Our fourth criteria requires metrics to provide a stable definition for optimisation. If the same code change alters the cost of two applications by the same amount, and it is an optimisation with respect to metric M for one of the codes, then it should count as an optimisation for both of them.

Definition 6. *A metric is stable iff for equivalent code segments λ and λ':*

$$M(\lambda') < M(\lambda) \implies M(\theta \circ \lambda') < M(\theta \circ \lambda)$$

It is worth noting that linear metrics automatically fulfil this requirement. Linear metrics are inherently stable, however stable non-linear metrics also exist.

Et^n is an unstable metric as it does not provide a consistent definition of optimisation. Whether or not a code change counts as an optimisation under Et^n is *context sensitive*. Code changes can be counted as optimisations only when evaluated in the context of the full application. Targeted optimisation of particular subroutines is impossible, and all past optimisations must be re-evaluated every time a change is made to the application.

This failure of Et^n is best illustrated with an example. Suppose an application contains a procedure which consumes $10\,J$ over $10\,s$ to produce some result. This corresponds to an Et^1 FoM of $10 \times 10 = 100$. We then modify our procedure to produce the same result in $11\,J$ and $9\,s$. This is a valid optimisation because although it increases energy consumption it reduces Et^n to $11 \times 9 = 99$.

Once the procedure completes we are given the option to output results at a cost of $(5\,J, 10\,s)$. Our un-optimised application could execute its tasks and output the results with an EDP of $(10 + 5) \times (10 + 10) = 300$. The same sequence of actions in the 'optimised' application results in a higher (worse) EDP of $(11 + 5) \times (9 + 10) = 304$. Under Et^n, choosing to save the results of our procedure retroactively invalidates our optimisation.

Figure 4a shows how the same cost change applied to two codes with the same starting Et^n FoM may be considered either an optimisation or a performance degradation. Furthermore, Fig. 4b shows how any energy-time trade-off can be made to appear as an optimisation or a performance degradation depending on the context. Different ratios of E_θ and t_θ can shift the optimisation/degradation boundary to any point within the indeterminate quadrants.

Mini-applications are powerful tools in scientific computing [13]. They package relevant features of large production applications into smaller, more manageable codes. Performance engineers use them as test beds to search for optimisations which can be ported back to the original application. Sometimes optimisations which work at small scale will fail to improve the production application, signalling a discrepancy between the mini and production applications.

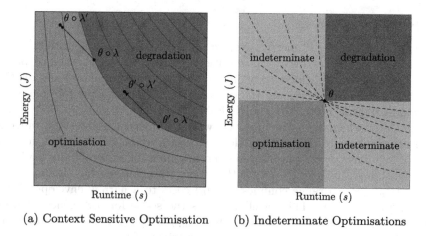

(a) Context Sensitive Optimisation   (b) Indeterminate Optimisations

Fig. 4. Et^n optimisation instability

Using Et^n metrics, however, optimisations to the mini-app may not count as optimisations to the production code even when they yield identical cost changes in both cases. This is further proof that Et^n metrics are incompatible with modern performance engineering techniques.

Tunable: Our penultimate criteria is that it should be possible to tune a metric to reflect the energy and time constraints of different domains. The Et^n metric meets this criteria via its n parameter. This parameter sets the 'exchange rate' at which small changes in runtime and energy can be traded against each other. This can be shown by equating the partial derivatives of Et^n as shown in Eq. 1:

$$\frac{\partial}{\partial E}\left(Et^n\right) = t^n \quad \text{and} \quad \frac{\partial}{\partial t}\left(Et^n\right) = nEt^{n-1}$$

$$t^n \cdot \partial E = nEt^{n-1} \cdot \partial t$$

$$\frac{\partial E}{E} = n\frac{\partial t}{t} \tag{1}$$

Intuitive: Our final and most subjective criteria is that a metric should be intuitive. In practice, this means it should correspond to some tangible property of a system, ideally with values measured in meaningful units. Et^n does not meet this requirement.

The costs of an extra Joule or second are not fixed under Et^n; in fact, the cost of increasing each factor depends on the current magnitude of the other. This implies that a Joule consumed by a long running process somehow costs more than a Joule consumed by a short-lived one. Furthermore, real systems impose maximum and minimum rates of power consumption on a code which we refer to as P_{max} and P_{min}. Given that $P_{min} \cdot t < E < P_{max} \cdot t$, the growth rate of Et^n is $\Theta(t^{n+1})$. The FoM cost of an additional second or Joule grows polynomially, hindering comparison between different scales.

4.2   Justification of Et^n

The continued use of Et^n metrics despite their flaws is a testament to the need for standardised energy-aware optimisation metrics. In the absence of better alternatives, software engineers rely on Et^n because of its popularity and relative ease of use. Et^n metrics remain the de-facto standard technique for combining energy and runtime costs into a single FoM.

One factor which hides the problems with Et^n metrics is the small range of power consumption exhibited by modern hardware running HPC workloads as a result of high base power consumption and marginal differences under load [10]. Figure 5a shows isometric lines for Et^1 and our proposed metrics. It shows how a small $[P_{min}, P_{max}]$ range confines (E_θ, t_θ) costs to a narrow envelope within the energy/time plane. This envelope limits the scope for divergence between different metrics. In the extreme case, when $P_{min} = P_{max}$, E_θ is a scalar multiple of t_θ and all energy-aware metrics become functions of time.

The scarcity of power-instrumented hardware means energy-aware optimisation is typically carried out at the level of individual nodes. Although single nodes exhibit narrow $[P_{min}, P_{max}]$ ranges, multi-node and system-level power draw is much less constrained. Figure 5b shows two performance envelopes, with the larger having P_{min} and P_{max} values three times those of the smaller one. This models the effect of running the same code on a single node and over three nodes in parallel. Similar discrepancies would occur when running code on alternative architectures with significantly differing power characteristics, such as GPUs and FPGAs, that are emerging as candidate platforms for improved efficiency [7]. Even at this small scale the discrepancies between Et^n and other metrics become readily apparent.

5   Proposed Metrics

In this section we propose two new FoM metrics for energy-aware software optimisation. These metrics have slightly different properties and the choice of which to use is left to the performance engineer. That said, they both significantly outperform Et^n metrics according to our assessment criteria.

Our first metric is a weighted sum of energy and runtime costs. Our second metric measures the cost of an application in terms of Euclidean distance from an 'optimal' point at the energy/time origin. The fitness landscapes for both metrics are shown in Fig. 6a and b respectively.

5.1   Proposed Metric 1: Energy Delay Summation (EDS)

Energy and compute time are limited resources which have costs associated with their consumption. The primary cost of energy consumption is the purchase price of electricity. Environmental impact and other concerns can also be included.

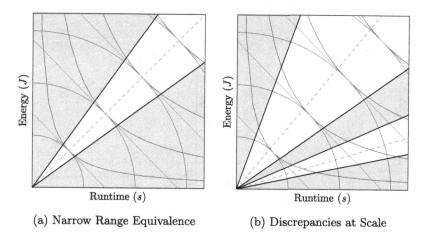

(a) Narrow Range Equivalence   (b) Discrepancies at Scale

Fig. 5. Power-limited isometric lines

Runtime also has a monetary cost – the purchase costs of the machine amortised over its limited lifespan. Energy and runtime costs are captured by the α and β parameters in Eq. 2.

$$M(\theta) = \alpha E_\theta + \beta t_\theta$$
$$= (\alpha, \beta) \cdot (E_\theta, t_\theta) \tag{2}$$

Bounded: Our first criteria requires metrics to bound regions of the energy/time space. The isometric lines in Fig. 6a intercept both axes, satisfying this criteria. An EDS FoM therefore places upper limits on energy and runtime costs. The runtime contribution to a metric is maximised when energy is minimised and vice versa, allowing us to deduce cost limits under a given FoM:

$$M(\theta) = \alpha \cdot E_{max} + \beta \cdot 0$$
$$\therefore E_{max} = \frac{M(\theta)}{\alpha}$$
$$M(\theta) = \alpha \cdot 0 + \beta \cdot t_{max}$$
$$\therefore t_{max} = \frac{M(\theta)}{\beta}$$

Performance engineers need not evaluate code changes with energy costs greater than E_{max}, or runtime costs greater than t_{max}. This is in stark contrast to the Et^n case, where any given energy or runtime cost could be considered an optimisation under the right circumstances.

Directed: Our second criteria requires metrics to guide optimisation in sensible directions. Fast, energy intensive codes are likely to require different optimisations to slow, energy efficient ones. As a linear function, EDS does not differentiate between these cases; the isotopic lines in Fig. 6a all run in parallel. Our

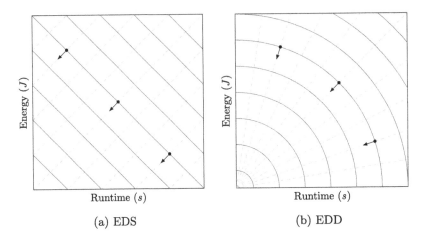

(a) EDS   (b) EDD

Fig. 6. Proposed metrics fitness landscapes

metric still outperforms Et^n in this regard however as it does not introduce perverse optimisation incentives.

Additive and Stable: Our third and fourth criteria require metrics to be linear functions of time and energy and to provide stable definitions of optimisation. The function $\alpha E + \beta t$ is linear in both parameters. Linear functions are automatically stable; meaning this metric fulfils both criteria, providing stable definitions for optimisation and allowing for meaningful code profiling.

Tunable: Our penultimate criteria is that metrics be tunable to different application domains. Different energy and runtime costs can be specified via the α and β parameters. Unlike the exponential formulation of Et^n, it is immediately apparent how different values will alter the balance between energy and runtime.

A single scalar parameter would be enough to express any ratio of energy and time components. One property of this metric is that with appropriate tuning factors it can be used as a proxy for the monetary cost of running a code. This use-case is why we include two tuning parameters within this metric, to allow us to provide notional value results.

Intuitive: Our final criteria requires metrics to correspond to some meaningful property of the system. Given appropriate coefficients this metric can report results in terms of monetary cost. Monetary cost has meaningful units, allows for fair comparisons to be made between different platforms and architectures, and is useful during procurement.

Equation 2 provides a dot product formulation of the EDS metric which suggests a second geometric interpretation. Dot products correspond to the projection of one vector onto another – in this case of (E_λ, t_λ) onto (α, β).

5.2   Proposed Metric 2: Energy Delay Distance (EDD)

Our first metric measured code performance in terms of separable energy and time costs. This definition fulfilled all but one of our criteria; as a linear function it was not able to direct the optimisation of codes according to their starting costs. Our second metric remedies this by defining the cost of a code as its distance from the most optimal point on our fitness landscape – the origin.

$$M(\theta) = \sqrt{E_\theta{}^2 + (\beta t_\theta)^2}$$

EDD can also be expressed as the magnitude of a weighted cost vector:

$$M(\theta) = \|(E_\theta,\ \beta \cdot t_\theta)\|$$

Bounded: The isometric lines in Fig. 6b follow semi-circular trajectories which intercept the axes. This satisfies our first criteria, meaning this metric also limits E_{max} and t_{max} for a given FoM. We can derive these limits as follows:

$$M(\theta) = \sqrt{E_{max}{}^2 + \beta \cdot 0}$$
$$\therefore E_{max} = M(\theta)$$
$$M(\theta) = \sqrt{0 + \beta \cdot t_{max}{}^2}$$
$$\therefore t_{max} = \frac{M(\theta)}{\beta}$$

Directed: The isometric lines for this metric form concentric ellipse segments centred about the origin. As a result, the corresponding isotopic lines converge on the origin. Figure 6b makes it clear that as a result this metric prioritises optimisations which minimise whichever cost is greater.

Additive: The formula for EDD is non-linear, meaning the overall FoM of a code is not equivalent to the sum of its parts. This is an unavoidable consequence of being a directed metric, and means that EDD is not well suited for accurate code profiling. Unlike Et^n, the discrepancy between the sum of component FoMs and the overall code FoM for EDD is bounded. As EDD is defined in terms of vector magnitude it obeys the triangle inequality. As energy and time costs are always positive, we have:

$$\sqrt{M(\theta)^2 + M(\lambda)^2} < M(\theta \circ \lambda) \leq M(\theta) + M(\lambda)$$

Stable: EDD does not meet our stability criteria. Figure 7 shows a case where $M(\lambda') < M(\lambda)$, yet $M(\theta \circ \lambda') > M(\theta \circ \lambda)$. The runtime axis is scaled so that isometric lines remain concentric for all values of β. That said, EDD instability is bounded by $M(\theta) + M(\lambda) - M(\theta \circ \lambda)$ as this metric obeys the following inequality:

$$M(\lambda') < M(\lambda) \implies M(\theta \circ \lambda') < M(\theta) + M(\lambda)$$

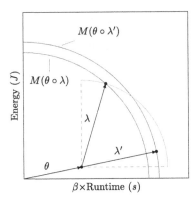

Fig. 7. EDD instability

Tunable: This metric is tunable via the β parameter. A single parameter is sufficient to achieve any ratio of energy to runtime contribution.

Intuitive: This metric has a direct geometric interpretation as the Euclidean distance to the origin. It does not treat energy and runtime as separate and distinct costs; in reality they are inseparable. In general, reducing the runtime of a code will also reduce its energy consumption. EDD defines the cost of a code in terms of how far away it is from being perfectly optimal.

6   Case Study

In this section we investigate the energy-efficiency characteristics of codes in the Mantevo [13] mini-application benchmark suite. Our results show that the issues with Et^n become more evident at larger scales.

We carried out our experiments on the Taurus system at TU Dresden, which is equipped with High Density Energy Efficiency Monitoring (HDEEM) instrumentation [11]. Taurus is a heterogeneous cluster with several classes of node. This work was carried out on the largest of these classes, with each node featuring two 12-core Intel Xeon E5-2680 v3 CPUs and 64 GB of memory.

All codes were compiled with ICC version 15.0.3. Application parameters were based on default values, with problem sizes tuned where necessary to ensure reasonable run times on single nodes. Results were averaged over 5 runs to minimise the impact of random variations in runtime and energy.

We use Et^3 in these experiments because Laros et al. found that this strikes the right balance between runtime and energy for high performance computing [16]. This implies that a 1% reduction in runtime is approximately three times more valuable than the same reduction in energy consumption.

In order to facilitate comparison we have based our EDS and EDD parameterisation on the same 3:1 ratio. Whereas the Et^n parameter operates in a relative fashion, however, EDS and EDD parameters are based on absolute costs of consumption. The power drawn by active Taurus nodes ranges between 207.68 W and 345.33 W [18], meaning the magnitude of energy costs will be around 300 times greater than that of runtime. In order to compensate for this effect we scale the runtime cost by a factor of 300 before applying the 3:1 ratio, resulting in the parameters $\alpha = 1$ and $\beta = 3 \times 300 = 900$.

In practice we would prefer to adopt a more fine-grained parameterisation which reflects real-world costs incurred by HPC systems. That said, exact cost figures are seldom made available in the public domain.

For our first test we measured the runtime and energy consumption of various codes running on a single node. The results for this test are presented in Table 1.

Table 1. Single node code costs

Code	Runtime (s)	Energy (J)	Et^3	EDS	EDD
TeaLeaf	323.8	99,810.3	3,388,489,410,000	391,230	100,280
PathFinder	337.1	71,943.9	2,755,945,330,000	375,334	72,646
CloverLeaf	214.3	57,861.2	569,447,289,000	250,731	58,214
CloverLeaf3D	153.1	43,755.9	157,022,581,000	181,546	43,991
MiniMD	125.5	31,162.1	61,596,822,000	144,112	31,387
CoMD	105.6	24,837.8	29,248,540,000	119,878	25,037
MiniFE	36.7	8,465.6	418,461,937	41,496	8,536
HPCCG	36.5	8,059.5	391,910,164	40,910	8,133

The first thing to note is that Et^n results rapidly become unwieldy even for relatively short runtimes and low node counts. The runtime of HPCCG is around 11.4% that of TeaLeaf, and it also exhibits a slightly lower rate of power draw. This translates to a four orders of magnitude difference in their Et^n values. Adding a single second to the runtime of TeaLeaf would further increase its FoM by 8613 times the total Et^n of HPCCG.

Another thing to note is that despite large variations in values, all metrics assign the same efficiency ordering to these codes. As previously mentioned, the limits of single-node power draw limit the scope for metrics to disagree.

For our second test we measured the runtime and energy consumption of MiniMD running at scale. The results for this test are presented in Table 2.

These results show how biased Et^n metrics are in favour of massive parallelism. The efficiency of MiniMD according to Et^n improves as the node count increases to 18. It is only at the point when adding nodes delivers little or no reduction in runtime that this trend reverses.

EDS identifies 4 nodes as the optimal node count. This configuration delivers roughly twice the runtime performance of a single node at the cost of doubling the energy consumption. Adding nodes beyond this point results in energy costs increasing faster than runtime performance improves.

EDD identifies 1 node as the optimal node count. This corresponds to the intuition that parallelism introduces overhead. As the parallel overhead grows, so too does inefficiency as measured by this metric.

Table 2. MiniMD Multi-node costs

Nodes	Runtime (s)	Energy (J)	Et^3	EDS	EDD
1	125.5	31,162.4	61,597,424,000	144,112	31,388
2	94.2	44,999.0	37,614,512,300	129,779	45,086
4	66.8	63,166.0	18,828,375,900	123,286	63,190
6	55.2	76,400.0	12,850,216,400	126,080	76,412
8	54.0	99,032.6	15,594,067,100	147,633	99,043
12	44.0	119,008.9	10,137,658,200	158,609	119,011
16	39.8	145,198.3	9,154,006,200	181,018	145,197
18	37.8	152,380.5	8,230,099,000	186,401	152,376
24	36.0	191,056.9	8,913,951,100	223,457	191,046
28	37.2	231,525.5	11,918,663,500	265,006	231,516
32	37.5	258,054.5	13,608,342,900	291,805	258,041
64	39.4	518,748.6	31,728,187,600	554,209	518,713
128	46.2	1,203,476.1	118,676,068,000	1,245,056	1,203,410

Et^3 gives the impression that below-linear speed-ups coupled with above-linear rises in energy consumption represent efficiency gains. Conversely, our EDS and EDD metrics conform to a more conventional understanding of energy efficiency. They identify optimal configurations which can be justified intiutively.

7   Conclusion

In this paper we argue that the Et^n family of metrics are not appropriate for energy-aware software engineering. We propose alternative metrics which can be used to measure the cost of applications and guide their optimisation. Finally, we compare the performance of our metrics against established techniques by studying codes taken from the Mantevo mini-application suite.

We began by showing how Et^n metrics are unable to provide meaningful values for individual experiments, cannot be compared between experiments and do not support optimisation efforts. Improving the Et^n FoM of a section of code can degrade overall performance. Et^n metrics drive optimisation efforts in counterproductive directions, encouraging developers to speed up already fast code and seek energy efficiency gains in energy efficient codes. Finally, these metrics provide no meaningful definition of an optimisation. In total, Et^n was able to fulfil only one of our seven criteria for software optimisation metrics.

We then proposed EDS and EDD, novel metrics which outperform Et^n against all of our assessment criteria. EDS is appropriate for measuring the cost of applications, while EDD is well suited to guiding application optimisation. Both our metrics fulfil the majority of our criteria, and EDS fulfils the maximum number possible.

Our paper finishes with a study into the energy-efficiency costs of several popular applications. This study shows how the flaws of Et^n have managed to remain hidden in small-scale optimisation studies. It also demonstrates that these flaws will prevent Et^n from being employed at scale. As a result, new metrics like EDS and EDD will be required to support performance engineers as interest in energy optimisation continues to grow.

7.1 Future Work

The properties of our metrics makes them particularly well suited to comparing codes running at different scales and on different architectures. We intend to use EDS and EDD to investigate the power optimisation characteristics of various codes running on accelerator-based technologies. Our ultimate aim is to demonstrate how the correct metric can facilitate the discovery of energy-aware software optimisations. In our ongoing work we focus our search towards GPU and FPGA platforms as promising candidates for energy optimisation.

Acknowledgements. The authors would like to thank Thomas Ilsche and the Center of Information Services and High Performance Computing (ZIH) at TU Dresden. This research is funded in part by research grants from AWE, ATOS and Allinea. Professor Stephen Jarvis is an AWE William Penney Fellow.

References

1. Balaprakash, P., Gomez, L.A.B., Bouguerra, M.-S., Wild, S.M., Cappello, F., Hovland, P.D.: Analysis of the tradeoffs between energy and run time for multilevel checkpointing. In: Jarvis, S.A., Wright, S.A., Hammond, S.D. (eds.) PMBS 2014. LNCS, vol. 8966, pp. 249–263. Springer, Cham (2015). doi:10.1007/978-3-319-17248-4_13
2. Balaprakash, P., Tiwari, A., Wild, S.M.: Multi objective optimization of HPC kernels for performance, power, and energy. In: International Workshop on Performance Modeling, Benchmarking and Simulation of High Performance Computer Systems, pp. 239–260 (2013)
3. Bekas, C., Curioni, A.: A new energy aware performance metric. Comput. Sci.-Res. Dev. **25**(3–4), 187–195 (2010)
4. Bingham, B.D., Greenstreet, M.R.: Computation with energy-time trade-offs: models, algorithms and lower bounds. In: IEEE International Symposium on Parallel and Distributed Processing with Applications, pp. 143–152 (2008)
5. Choi, J.W., Bedard, D., Fowler, R., Vuduc, R.: A Roofline model of energy. In: Proceedings of the IEEE International Symposium on Parallel & Distributed Processing (IPDPS), pp. 661–672, May 2013
6. Esmaeilzadeh, H., Blem, E., St. Amant, R., Sankaralingam, K., Burger, D.: Dark silicon and the end of multicore scaling. In: Proceedings of the International Symposium on Computer Architecture (ISCA), pp. 365–376. ACM, New York, NY, June 2011
7. Fahmy, S.A., Vipin, K., Shreejith, S.: Virtualized FPGA accelerators for efficient cloud computing. In: Proceedings of the IEEE International Conference on Cloud Computing Technology and Science, pp. 430–435 (2015)
8. Freeh, V.W., Lowenthal, D.K., Pan, F., Kappiah, N., Springer, R., Rountree, B.L., Femal, M.E.: Analyzing the energy-time trade-off in high-performance computing applications. IEEE Trans. Parallel Distrib. Syst. **18**(6), 835–848 (2007)
9. Gonzales, R., Horowitz, M.: Energy dissipation in general purpose processors. IEEE J. Solid State Circuits **31**, 1277–1284 (1996)
10. Hackenberg, D., Ilsche, T., Schöne, R., Molka, D., Schmidt, M., Nagel, W.E.: Power measurement techniques on standard compute nodes: a quantitative comparison. In: Proceedings of the IEEE International Symposium on Performance Analysis of Systems and Software (ISPASS), pp. 194–204, March 2013

11. Hackenberg, D., Ilsche, T., Schuchart, J., Schöne, R., Nagel, W.E., Simon, M., Georgiou, Y.: HDEEM: high definition energy efficiency monitoring. In: Energy Efficient Supercomputing Workshop (E2SC), pp. 1–10, November 2014

12. Harman, M., Clark, J.: Metrics are fitness functions too. In: Proceedings of the International Symposium on Software Metrics, pp. 58–69, September 2004

13. Heroux, M.A., Doerfler, D.W., Crozier, P.S., Willenbring, J.M., Edwards, H.C., Williams, A., Rajan, M., Keiter, E.R., Thornquist, H.K., Numrich, R.W.: Improving performance via mini-applications. SNL Technical report SAND2009-5574 (2009)

14. Hsu, C.H., Feng, W.C., Archuleta, J.S.: Towards efficient supercomputing: a quest for the right metric. In: Proceedings of the IEEE International Parallel and Distributed Processing Symposium (2005)

15. Kurd, N., Chowdhury, M., Burton, E., Thomas, T.P., Mozak, C., Boswell, B., Lal, M., Deval, A., Douglas, J., Elassal, M., Nalamalpu, A., Wilson, T.M., Merten, M., Chennupaty, S., Gomes, W., Kumar, R.: 5.9 Haswell: A Family of IA 22 nm Processors. In: IEEE International Solid-State Circuits Conference Digest of Technical Papers (ISSCC), pp. 112–113. IEEE, February 2014

16. Laros, J.H., Pedretti, K., Kelly, S.M., Shu, W., Ferreira, K., Vandyke, J., Vaughan, C.: Energy delay product. In: Laros, J.H., Pedretti, K., Kelly, S.M., Shu, W., Ferreira, K., Vandyke, J., Vaughan, C. (eds.) Energy-Efficient High Performance Computing: Measurement and Tuning, pp. 51–55. Springer, Heidelberg (2013)

17. Martin, A.J., Nyström, M., Pénzes, P.: ET^2: a metric for time and energy efficiency of computation. In: Graybill, R., Melhem, R. (eds.) Power Aware Computing, pp. 293–315. Springer, Heidelberg (2002)

18. Roberts, S., Wright, S., Lecomber, D., January, C., Byrd, J., Oró, X., Jarvis, S.: POSE: a mathematical and visual modelling tool to guide energy aware code optimisation. In: Proceedings of the 6th International Green and Sustainable Computing Conference (IGSC 2015), December 2015

19. Rodero, I., Viswanathan, H., Lee, E.K., Gamell, M., Pompili, D., Parashar, M.: Energy-efficient thermal-aware autonomic management of virtualized HPC cloud infrastructure. J. Grid Comput. **10**(3), 447–473 (2012)

20. Shalf, J., Dosanjh, S., Morrison, J.: Exascale computing technology challenges. In: Palma, J.M.L.M., Daydé, M., Marques, O., Lopes, J.C. (eds.) VECPAR 2010. LNCS, vol. 6449, pp. 1–25. Springer, Heidelberg (2011). doi:10.1007/978-3-642-19328-6_1

21. Shao, Y.S., Brooks, D.: Energy characterization and instruction-level energy model of Intel's Xeon Phi processor. In: Proceedings of the IEEE International Symposium on Low Power Electronics and Design (ISLPED), pp. 389–394, September 2013

22. Srinivasan, V., Brooks, D., Gschwind, M., Bose, P., Zyuban, V., Strenski, P.N., Emma, P.G.: Optimizing pipelines for power and performance. In: Proceedings of the International Symposium on Microarchitecture (MICRO), pp. 333–344 (2002)

23. Sutter, H.: The free lunch is over: a fundamental turn toward concurrency in software. Dr. Dobb's J. **30**(3), 202–210 (2005)

24. Yeo, S., Lee, H.: Using mathematical modeling in provisioning a heterogeneous cloud computing environment. Computer **44**(8), 55–62 (2011)

Author Index

Printed in the United States
by Baker & Taylor Publisher Services

Printed in the United States
by Baker & Taylor Publisher Services